The New York Times

BOOK OF
NEW
YORK

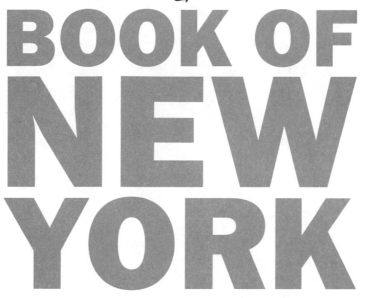

The New York Times

BOOK OF NEW YORK

**549 STORIES OF THE PEOPLE, THE EVENTS
AND THE LIFE OF THE CITY—PAST AND PRESENT**

Edited by
JAMES BARRON

Introduction by
ANNA QUINDLEN

Supervising Editor
MITCHEL LEVITAS

BLACK DOG
& LEVENTHAL
PUBLISHERS
NEW YORK

Published by:
Black Dog & Leventhal Publishers, Inc.
151 West 19th Street
New York, NY 10011

Distributed by:
Workman Publishing Company
225 Varick Street
New York, NY10014

Manufactured in USA
Cover design by Liz Driesbach
Interior design by Susi Oberhelman
ISBN-13: 978-1-57912-801-2
h g f e d c b a
Library of Congress Cataloging-in-
Publication Data available on request

A Note to Readers

In his Foreword to a selection of Joseph Mitchell's articles, mostly from *The New Yorker*, his colleague Calvin Trillin wrote that after Mitchell knew the city's "grim specifics" as a police reporter, and "even after he knew it as an acknowledged master of its neighborhoods, he never lost an out-of-towner's sense of wonderment."

That was our goal in choosing these articles, all but a handful by staff writers for The New York Times, from among the millions of articles about its own city that The Times has published over the years: to create a kaleidoscopic portrait of New York that residents, recent immigrants and visitors would find spontaneous and surprising, informative but not encyclopedic, and subjective but broadly inclusive. If we have come reasonably close to that goal, it is because Times reporters and editors have provided the skill and the judgment—day after day and year after year since the paper's founding in 1851—to make a collection like this possible.

That said, the pages here contain, for the most part, excerpts of the articles that appeared in The Times. Even in a book as thick as this one turned out to be, the available space was limited, and we had to give many of the stories a trim—but not, we believe, a buzz cut. We worked as carefully as possible to cut as few words as possible. We did very little rewriting or condensation—the words you will read here are largely the words that appeared in The Times on the dates indicated. We did take some liberties with deleting time elements like "yesterday" in passages where they seemed unnecessary in a book like this, published so long after the morning after the events described in the stories. We also rewrote some of the headlines to fit into the space available in the format of the book. But that is in keeping with what the copy editors who wrote the original headlines did in the first place: they were writing to fit the layout of a particular page. In all cases, we did our best to preserve the essence of what was originally published in The Times.

Chief among our partners in the effort are the writers and photographers whose work is gratefully represented here. Among the publisher's stalwarts, we are indebted to Lisa Tenaglia for indispensible, imaginative research into a mountain of newspaper clippings; Liz Van Doren for her editorial insight; Susie Tofte for her research—all under the guidance of J.P. Leventhal, the publisher. For The Times, we thank Alex Ward, editorial director of the book development program, for his continuing support; Phyllis Collazo, Ryan Murphy and Jeffrey Roth for their expertise in locating archival photos; and Tomi Murata for her managerial touch.

CONTENTS

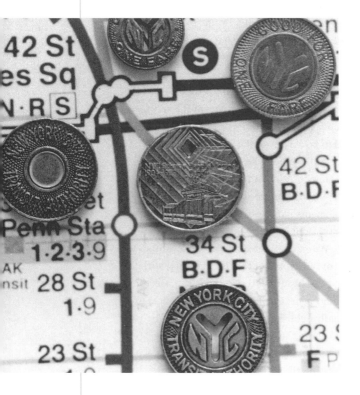

Introduction

By **ANNA QUINDLEN**

ONE SPRING AFTERNOON YEARS AGO I STOOD on a Manhattan corner peering at a street map, miming confusion. The experiment was part of a story; the point to count how many New Yorkers would stop to offer advice or assistance to what looked like a befuddled tourist. In an hour there were 21, unless you count the man in rags who bellowed "Gimme some change" and spit extravagantly at my feet when I ignored him.

> New York City is everything
> people say it is,
> and everything they persist
> in believing it is not.

New York City is everything people say it is, and everything they persist in believing it is not. It's passersby who look locked in a Lucite box of indifference, and those who will snap out of it in a second if you really seem to need help. It's a city of faceless glass-and-steel monoliths and a village of single-family houses and volunteer school safety patrols. It's places to eat where the tab defies belief, and corner falafel stands with a line down the street at lunchtime. It's tough and it's friendly and it's terrifying and it's homey. From the shores of Staten Island to the northernmost reaches of the Bronx, it's more or less everything, sometimes all on the same block.

And because of that it can be the easiest city in the world in which to be a reporter and writer. For three years I wrote a column for the New York Times called About New York, which is perhaps the best gig in daily journalism—two columns a week about anything you want, anywhere in the five boroughs. When, occasionally, the ideas evaporated, when there was no firehouse closing or hot dog-eating contest to investigate, I knew exactly what to do. I rode the subway to a random stop—Rockaway Boulevard, Parkchester—and began to walk. (Once, when I was expecting my first child, a patrol car followed me around a dicey area of Brooklyn, because, the cops said, it would be a real mess if a pregnant reporter was mugged on their patch.) Trust me: within a 15-minute walk of any subway stop in New York there is a beauty salon with a proprietor who has stories to tell, or a community garden with volunteers who can't wait to have someone notice their urban zucchini, or a playground with moms who have a bone to pick about the school system, or simply a bus stop with a sampling of New Yorkers. The benches along the boardwalk in Coney Island were my lodestone, filled with elderly men who knew the story of the city better than some historians; I had only to take a notebook and a pen from my bag, and the world, or at least a detailed and richly remembered part of it, was mine.

The pitfall for reporters is that there are as many clichés in the city as there are bodegas. Those elderly retirees, with their jaded view of the changing neighborhood and their mahjongg-playing wives, have long been staple of sitcoms and movies. Neon signs, crusty waiters, extravagant graffiti— it's all been done. Luckily the city itself provides a fresh perspective because of its never-ending metamorphosis. The bench sitters of my youth have been replaced in some areas by a new incarnation—black instead of white, Baptist instead of Jewish, former bus drivers instead of print shop

RIGHT: *Lower Manhattan from the Empire State Building's observation deck, 2002.*

owners. New Yorkers are always remaking themselves, and New York, too. The elegant and iconic main building of the New York Public Library, with the pair of stone lions guarding the entrance, looks as though it has always been there. But in fact it was built on what was once a reservoir, the park behind it a battle site in 1776 and a Potter's Field 50 years later. When I was a neophyte reporter that park was known mainly for drug deals and monster rats; today it is a beautifully manicured place to have a cup of coffee or a meal al fresco.

And yet even when New York changes there are some core principles that stay the same. New Yorkers are usually from somewhere else: Indiana, India. Washington Heights, once the destination of choice for displaced German Jewish families, is now the home to Dominicans looking for a new life. The funky downtown vibe of the Lower East Side has gotten an upwardly mobile gloss; there are limos idling in front of its restaurants now. Funky moved across the river, to the Williamsburg section of Brooklyn, although there are people living there who will tell you that it's already spoilt and the action is in Astoria, Queens. Live in New York City long enough, and someday you will pass an apartment building where you once rented a one-bedroom and discover it has become 24-karat cooperatives. Stay a little longer, and the area may become shabby, out of favor. Here is how old I am, and how fluid the city: I predate the very notion of a neighborhood called TriBeCa.

In a metaphysical feat, the more you know New York, the smaller it feels. Flying over it on the way to Kennedy or LaGuardia, the size of the sprawl is overwhelming, but at ground level it's intimate. A borough becomes a neighborhood, a neighborhood a block, and a block a single family in a single apartment. Real New Yorkers know that they live in the biggest little small town in

America, in which anonymity vies always with knowingness, and usually loses. Just because neighbors don't acknowledge one another by name or even eye contact doesn't mean they don't acknowledge the fights they hear through the walls, the routines of leaving for work and arriving home, even the contents and timing of the grocery deliveries. We're a laissez-faire tribe, perhaps because the city is so diverse. The street scene includes people in wheelchairs and people in drag, women in clown suits and women in Chanel suits. A subway car at rush hour often looks like a general assembly session at the United Nations.

> It's a city of strangers,
> as Stephen Sondheim wrote in
> one song; that's our wildlife.

The only thing that seems to disconcert New Yorkers is nature, perhaps because we've usurped it so with macadam. It's why a coyote that has wandered down into the Bronx, the occasional pet boa let loose in the plumbing, a pair of nesting hawks in Central park, all make for a surefire story. I've covered New York since I was 19, and the only day I was truly speechless was the morning several years ago when I came around a midtown corner just after dawn and saw three camels and a donkey standing in the street. They were participants in the Christmas pageant at Radio City Music Hall, out for some air.

It's a city of strangers, as Stephen Sondheim wrote in one song; that's our wildlife. And it's not the exotica that is really the backbone of the place, the naked cowboys, the sunglass-wearing celebs. New York

INTRODUCTION

belongs to the ordinary Joe, not the mayors or the millionaires. Its newspapers write plenty about politics and sports, but it's when the shortstops and the Senators can be seen as little guys—or cut down to size—that New Yorkers are happiest with them. Otherwise it's the working man and woman who make the town, the executive secretaries, the cab drivers, the track workers in the subway, the cops in the police car. New York likes rich people best when they get that way by winning the lottery, or are discovered to have money after years of living in a walk-up with cats and clipped coupons.

The stereotype is that we're hard and cold, and there's no question that loneliness is an omnipresent specter even though company is all around. New Yorkers have learned to mind their business, but they've also gotten good at knowing when their business extends further than the zone of privacy circumscribed by their shoulders and elbows. Witness those 21 who helped me with directions so many years ago, or those thousands who helped one another on September 11, 2001. The terrorist attack on the World Trade Center is known as our great tragedy, but it is also a day that illuminated what New York City truly is, not just because of the diversity of those who died and those who responded, but because of the empathy and connection that enshrouded its streets more indelibly than the dust of destruction. New Yorkers turned inwards to the small communities that make up this largest of American cities. We packed sandwiches and brought dog food for the firehouse in the neighborhood, stood outside and talked among ourselves as evening fell and the sky in lower Manhattan was lit with a hellish red-gold glow. One old man said he recognized the smell of the smoke, and it turned out afterwards that he was a survivor of a concentration camp. One young man trudged past our house every night smudged and slump-shouldered, and it turned out he was a firefighter digging in the ruins for his co-workers.

We were frightened, and we were heartsick, but we knew that the city would prevail because that is what it does. Once it was a wilderness of hills and streams, with the Dutch huddled at one end behind the wall that would become Wall Street. Someday it will be something else entirely. Those of us who write will try to pin it down with our pens, and sometimes we will tell it true and even make it fresh. But we will never get it all. There will always be new immigrants, new neighbor-hoods, new businesses, new restaurants, new street chic, new night terrors. Like the strata of the earth beneath the concrete, there will be new layers of New York over time, and newcomers who try to tell its story as, evanescent, its story changes.

Anna Quindlen is the best-selling author of five novels and seven works of nonfiction, most recently *Good Dog. Stay.* She joined The Times in 1977 as a metropolitan reporter and was subsequently a columnist (*About New York* and *Life in the Thirties*). She later moved to the Op-Ed page of The Times, where her column, *Public and Private,* won a Pulitzer Prize in 1992. Ms. Quindlen's commentary in Newsweek appears every other week. She lives in New York City.

The New York Times

BOOK OF
NEW
YORK

Eight Million Stories

PEOPLE

here are eight million stories in the naked city. In this chapter there are 48 of them.

The larger-than-life characters who strut across these pages are a singularly New York bunch: by turns charismatic, idiosyncratic and pragmatic. All the other things that non-New Yorkers say about New Yorkers are probably true, too: New Yorkers are contentious and cantankerous, aggressive and aggravating, tasteful or tasteless, thoughtful or thought-provoking or thoughtless. It's a big city. You don't have to look far to find someone who fits the description.

New Yorkers are accustomed to the city's bigness—the density, the relentlessness, the tabloid headlines, the extra zeroes in their paychecks and their bank accounts. New York has been the world's largest city since before most of them were born—New York stole the title from London in 1898, when five counties and a jumble of small municipalities on either side of the East River joined together.

The historian Kenneth T. Jackson maintains that there are ten ways that New Yorkers are different from people in every other city. Number One on his list is tempo. New Yorkers really do walk faster, work longer, eat later and, as he put it, "compete harder" than people in other cities. Certainly there are empirical measurements on the first three. You disagree about the fourth? Well, let's step outside and settle it. For his part the Tennessee-born Jackson, who still has something of a Southern drawl despite nearly forty years at Columbia University, even says that New Yorkers have been talking faster since at least the eighteenth century. Jackson quotes one colonial-era Bostonian who complained that New Yorkers "talk very loud, very fast and altogether. If they ask you a question, before you can utter three words of your answer, they will break out on you again and talk away."

So New York was the magnet for fast talkers and fast-money types, for movie stars and sports legends, for tycoons and heiresses and self-made everybodies. New York drew in the socialite philanthropist Brooke Astor and the rap star Biggie Smalls, the basketball star Kareem Abdul Jabbar and the artist Jean Michel Basquiat. It was home base for Phil Rizzuto, who needed no introduction at Yankee Stadium, and for Jacqueline Kennedy Onassis, who needed no introduction, period.

The people who make New York what it is are not all household names, though. There is the man who writes the weather forecasts for the National Weather Service, so when the radio announcer promises traffic and weather together every ten minutes, there is a forecast to read. Or there is the taxi driver who owned the last Checker cab—a big ride, like New York itself. That cab was more of a New York taxi than the rather conventional one that carried Audrey Hepburn up Fifth Avenue in the opening scene of "Breakfast at Tiffany's."

But if there are eight million stories in the naked city, consider three who made the line about the eight million stories famous: the man who wrote the gritty short story "The Naked City," the screenwriter who worked with him to turn it into a no-nonsense movie and the producer who read the famous closing line into a microphone off camera: "There are eight million people in the naked city. This has been one of them."

The short-story author was Malvin Wald, who set out to

▲ PAGE 21

portray "a hard-working police detective, like the ones I knew in Brooklyn." He found his inspiration, and the words "the naked city," in a book showing crime-scene coverage by the famous tabloid photographer known as Weegee. He wrote the screenplay with Albert Maltz, who was jailed in 1950 after being blacklisted as one of the "Hollywood Ten."

▼ PAGE 46

The producer was Mark Hellinger, a newspaper columnist-turned-movie maker for whom "the Mark Hellinger"—a Broadway theater—was named. Hellinger had been a hard-driving, hard-drinking reporter. Who pounded out staccato sentence fragments like this. Who lived in a world of shady characters. Who competed against Walter Winchell and Damon Runyon. And who went to Hollywood in the 1940s, but never forgot that he was a New Yorker. "Hellinger's personal romance with the City of New York," wrote Times movie critic Bosley Crowther when "The Naked City" was released in 1948, "was one of the most ecstatic love affairs of the modern day—at least, to his host of friends and readers who are skeptics regarding l'amour." Crowther said that Hellinger fell for Manhattan "in a blissfully uninhibited way." Crowther said "The Naked City" was "a virtual Hellinger column on film. It is a rambling, romantic picture-story based on a composite New York episode." And what other kind of New York episode is there but rambling and romantic?

Portrait of the New Yorker

By SIMEON STRUNSKY | January 31, 1932

Believe some of our national legislators, and New York City is populated by scheming international bankers. Believe some of our movies, and it is a city of sinful penthouses. And judging from sounds which go to the uttermost parts of the earth from radio broadcasting studios, New Yorkers must be a race of crooners, tuba players and night-club patrons. What, then, is the average New Yorker like?

FOR THE PURPOSE OF ARRIVING AT THE "average" New Yorker engaged in leading his average life, we might imagine seven million people run through the wrong end of a telescope so that they suffer a numerical shrinkage in the proportion of 7,000 to 1. This particular ratio is suggested because it will give us the convenient number 1,000 for the total population of our sample New York.

In this miniature New York, two policemen patrol the streets, direct traffic and arraign prisoners in court; they are two-thirds of our entire municipal police force, the other man being off duty. Our two policemen on their rounds are likely to stop for a moment to exchange news with the city fireman at work on the nickel trimmings of his engine. That fireman is our entire municipal firefighting force.

Around the corner from the firehouse is a schoolhouse—the only one in our town of 1,000 souls and more than enough to accommodate the second largest group in the city's population, the boys and girls of school age, now in due attendance. There are 185 of them all told. Elsewhere in our microcosm, this is what we see:

- 60 white-collar workers in office, factory and store;
- 60 men and women selling goods over the counter, of whom 25 are retailers on their own account and 35 are employees;
- 50 men and women sewing clothes, shirts, boots and shoes, hats and pocketbooks—everything that men, women and children wear or carry for need or decoration;
- 45 laborers;
- 30 ironworkers, masons, carpenters and plumbers building houses and office buildings;
- 25 chauffeurs;
- 15 machinists and engineers;
- 20 stenographers taking dictation;
- 10 waiters getting ready to serve lunch in the restaurants and hotels;
- 5 bakers providing the bread;
- 15 printers and publishers turning out the reading matter to be bought during the lunch period and later;
- 3 bankers and brokers exercising a firm control, according to report, over the lives and fortunes of the other 997 of us;
- 3 elevator runners in the business buildings and apartments;
- 1 foreman. ◼

Starting Salaries But Gotham Tastes

By CARA BUCKLEY | May 25, 2008

LAURA WERKHEISER KNEW SHE WOULD HAVE to make many sacrifices to live in Manhattan. Foremost among them was shopping for clothes.

Anticipating, rightly, that her Manhattan digs would be cramped and her budget stretched, Ms. Werkheiser, 26, shipped 18 boxes of her clothes to her parents' house in Omaha before moving here from San Francisco. When she feels she needs to freshen up her look, she has her mother ship her several outfits from what she dryly refers to as the "Nebraska boutique."

"If I shop," she said, "I can't have a social life and I can't eat."

Blimey! Locals to the Manners Born

By JAMES COLLARD | June 27, 1999

IT WAS ROBERT BURNS WHO NOTED WHAT A remarkable gift it would be to see ourselves as others see us. As a Londoner who has just spent over a year living in New York but who is now safely back in England, I'm in a good position to bestow a gift of this nature on New Yorkers. With due warning, then, that something well meant but vaguely unpleasant is coming, I now have to deliver a huge blow to the pride New Yorkers take in being rude and feisty, and that is to tell you that in comparison to Londoners, you come across as exceptionally polite and extremely well behaved.

Arriving in New York after 12 years of living in London, I was bowled over by the good will, pleasant manners and overall graciousness of Manhattanites. It was like finding oneself suddenly in the middle of a courtly but particularly good-natured Japanese tea ceremony, and I spent the first few weeks learning to replace my rude London ways with the cheerful, charming courtesies of New Yorkers: holding doors open, not cutting in line, saying "thank you" and generally trying not to behave like a savage at a cocktail party, throwing punches to get to the canapes.

I had to adjust rapidly to a world where people smile breezily on the street (although they laugh less), hold the elevator and say, "Have a nice day." And mean it.

Some of this can be ascribed to the fact that Manhattan, unlike London, has a culture of tipping waiters and bartenders; very little in life is as sure to put a smile on someone's face as the prospect of money.

But New Yorkers' good nature goes beyond that. This wasn't just an impression formed during a dewy-eyed honeymoon period in my new home. A succession of visitors from the old country agreed with me: New Yorkers are, well, nicer. ▪

Having one's mother mail rotating boxes of old clothing is just one of the myriad ways that young newcomers to the city of a certain income—that is, those who are neither investment bankers nor being floated by their parents—manage to live the kind of lives they want in New York. They are high on ambition, meager of budget and endlessly creative when it comes to making ends meet.

Some tactics have long been chronicled: sharing tiny apartments with strangers, for example. But there are smaller measures, no less ingenious, that round out the lifestyle: sneaking flasks of vodka into bars, flirting your way into clubs, subletting your walk-in closets, putting off haircuts.

Drinking and eating carry their own complications. Especially if you are, say, Noah Driscoll, a 25-year-old project manager for a Chelsea marketing company whose salary is comparable to what a rookie teacher might make.

"For a little while I only ate grapefruits for my lunch," said Mr. Driscoll, who pays $400 a month on his college loans, "because they have a lot of nutrients and they got me through the day."

He has since started packing two peanut-butter-and-jelly sandwiches for lunch. Dinner might be two baked potatoes. On a good night, he might spend up to $6.

"To live like a human being on the salary that I make is very difficult in this city," he said. "You've got to forget about, you know, what your mom made you growing up, and take what's out there." ▪

A Great-Great-Great-Great Day For Annie and Her Heirs

By **SAM ROBERTS** | September 16, 2006

FOUR GENERATIONS OF DESCENDANTS OF Annie Moore Schayer, the first immigrant to be processed on Ellis Island, gathered for the first time to celebrate her rediscovery—and their own—and to raise money for a headstone for her unmarked grave in Calvary Cemetery in Queens.

The first contributions, of $500 each, came from Brian G. Andersson, the city's commissioner of records, and Patricia Somerstein of Long Beach, N.Y., Annie's great-niece. They donated their share of a $1,000 reward they received from a professional genealogist who had been seeking clues to support the suspicion that a woman who died in Texas in 1923 and had been embraced by history as the Ellis Island Annie Moore was somebody else entirely. It turns out the Texan Annie Moore was not an immigrant at all.

In fact, the Annie Moore who was 15 in 1892 when she came to the United States from County Cork, Ireland, never moved west. She lived the rest of her life within a few square blocks on Manhattan's Lower East Side and died at 99 Cherry Street. One of her granddaughters lived in a public housing project in the neighborhood until her death in 2001.

Annie married the son of a German-born baker at St. James Church on James Street in 1895. Her husband was identified as an engineer and salesman at the Fulton Fish Market. They had at least 11 children, 5 of whom survived to adulthood.

Annie died of heart failure in 1924 at 47 and is buried with six of her children at the cemetery in Woodside, Queens, flanked by markers for a Maxwell and a Jimenez.

Of Annie's newly confirmed first-immigrant status, a great-great granddaughter, Maureen Peterson, 61, said: "We knew it was the truth, but we couldn't prove it." ∎

BELOW: *Visitors look at vintage photographs of immigrant families at the Ellis Island Museum.*

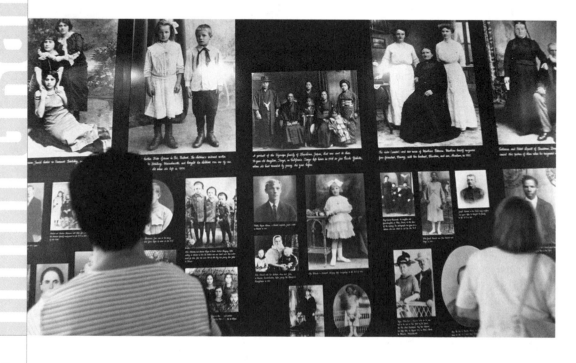

The Face Behind the Bagel

By **MIRTA OJITO** | September 18, 1997

Promised Land, Broken Dreams

August 12, 1906

YOU CAN RUN THE ENTIRE SCALE OF human emotion in the deportation division in the big federal building on Ellis Island. A little Russian boy, ill-shapen and pale from long suffering, was found packed in among a number of his fellow country-men in a large room on the upper floor of the immigration building. He could not have been more than 16 years old, and yet his pain-pinched features made him appear much older. He was eager to talk of his shattered hopes and to tell his story of bitter disappointment.

Less than two months ago this boy left the town of Kishinef in Russia. He could not make a living at home because he was a cripple and too weak to go into the fields. No one wanted to look on him, for his bent and twisted figure was unsightly to the superstitious peasants.

Then a letter written by an uncle arrived from America. This letter told of the great opportunities awaiting those who should hasten across the ocean. The hunchback boy's parents had saved a sum sufficient to send the little fellow to America. The uncle's address was written at the end of the letter, and with this the hunchbacked boy started on the long voyage.

When the big liner steamed slowly past the Statue of Liberty the boy stood on the forward deck. "Now they tell me I must return home," he said, "for they cannot find my uncle." ■

ON HIS WAY TO WORK AS A SUPERVISOR AT A downtown deli in the mid-1980's, Fahim Saleh, an Afghan refugee with an easy smile, would buy coffee from a chatty Greek vendor in a pushcart at Lexington Avenue and 43rd Street. Mr. Saleh had fled Afghanistan in 1980 and, while he liked his job at the deli, he wanted something to call his own. A business.

He dreamed of opening his own restaurant, but finances got in the way. Then Mr. Saleh learned that his new friend made a comfortable living selling coffee and bagels from his pushcart. Mr. Saleh liked the hours, 3 a.m. to 11 a.m., and the independence— working alone in a small space, no boss hovering over the coffee machine. He found a dilapidated pushcart for $600, spent another $500 fixing it up and, 10 years ago this month, parked it at Lexington Avenue and 41st Street. For four weeks, he barely covered expenses.

Since then, with the proceeds from the pushcart, Mr. Saleh has supported his growing family—his oldest child is 16 and his youngest is 4—and brought to the United States his five siblings, his parents and even his grandparents. Two brothers, Ali and Bashir, now own their own pushcarts.

In the mad rush from apartment to subway to the office, the coffee vendor's face is often the first face New Yorkers focus on every morning. Yet New Yorkers know very little about the person behind the counter, except that the steaming cup of coffee is delivered quickly.

Mr. Saleh says he was the first Afghan in New York City to own a coffee and bagels pushcart. "I tell all my friends that it's an easy business to get into," Mr. Saleh, who estimates he has introduced about 70 friends to the business, said in fluent English. "All you have to know is 'coffee doughnuts thank you have a nice day.' That's it. Something else: the coffee has to be good and you can't forget to smile." ■

Guardians of the Sleeping City

By **ANNA QUINDLEN** | December 28, 1978

THE LIGHTS BEGIN TO GO OUT ALL OVER THE city, in Brooklyn Heights, Forest Hills, Greenwich Village, Co-op City. The sidewalks grow still. Much of the city sleeps.

Thousands of people stir.

They are the night workers, those who go to work in the dark and travel home at dawn. They commute against the morning rush, sleep days, breakfast at dinner time, shower and shave in the evening. The Federal Labor Department estimates that there are 200,000 of them in Manhattan alone.

In Brooklyn, Rosa Lewis is surrounded by the darkness. She cleans the small office building in the downtown area with her shoulders set tight with fatigue and fear, convinced that somehow the ultimate felon she has constructed out of night noises will come up behind her when she is mopping and put her to sleep for good.

Mrs. Lewis picks up her bucket of cleanser, glass cleaner, smudged cloths and ammonia and trundles down the hall. "You know what I like," she says, cleaning another desk top. "I like taking the A train home in the morning when everyone else is coming to work. I just think: 'Fools! I'm done for the day.'"

· · · · ·

It is an average night in the emergency room at Beekman Downtown Hospital. A blind woman is reliving much of her life in loud, one-sided conversation punctuated with piercing screams, three Bowery derelicts have come in with one complaint or another to spend the night in a clean bed and a warm room, and a pretty girl in a torn silk dress and bare feet wanders in and out of the hospital lobby. She says that when the office Christmas party was over, a man pulled her into a car and raped her, not far from the hospital on Wall Street.

· · · · ·

By a counter that holds a tray of bloodied instruments and an artificial Christmas tree with a few strands of sad tinsel, Officer William Donohue of the First Precinct stands, holding his uniform jacket, the plaid flannel short he wears making him seem more a man, less a cop.

· · · · ·

The control tower at La Guardia Airport, a glass room that looks like the inside of a spaceship, makes every cliché about the lights of the city seem fresh. The airport at night is like an evacuated city—shiny, perfectly equipped, silent, deserted. So too are the night skies.

At 2 a.m., Gene Rodrigues and Chris Michaels, the two controllers on duty, stare at a sickly green radar-scope that shows almost no tiny airline blips for hours at a time. The calls they get are from ground crews who want to tow a plane from one place to another.

"Every controller here counts his planes," Mr. Rodrigues says. "It's not satisfying at night. I mean, would a writer rather write five words or five hundred?" ▪

The Lesson For Bus Drivers: Grin and Bear It

By **ARI L. GOLDMAN** | February 18, 1983

SOME PEOPLE WAITING FOR BUSES WILL swear the bus drivers aim for the slush puddles as they pull into a stop. Or that they like to close doors on old people trying to catch a bus. Or prefer to keep their bus's destination a secret from people seeking directions.

These situations—and what to do about them—were among the topics discussed around a table by 10 drivers at a two-day Bus Driver Sensitivity Training Course given by the Transit Authority.

Last of the Checker Cabs

By JODI WILGOREN | July 27, 1999

THE LAST DAY OF THE LAST CHECKER CAB IN New York should have been full of nostalgia and romance, the storied retirement of a much-loved machine integral to the city's lore and lure. Instead, it was filled with hassles.

There was the awkward moment when Mr. Johnson stopped abruptly at a Jamaican restaurant and his fare, a woman late for work, followed him inside to find out what he was doing (every cabdriver has his favorite pit stops).

Having decided that the cab had become too expensive to fix to meet the city's standards, Mr. Johnson spent the day juggling interviews so that each journalist had a solo ride-along, artfully avoiding questions about how much money he had made in the Checker or might make selling it.

There were lovely moments, too: the fares who shared poignant childhood memories. The drivers who leaned out of their windows to shout good luck and God bless. The comrade cabby who stopped at three successive stoplights for her own snapshots of history.

And two hours with Roberta Horton and James Donnelly, social workers who rode in Mr. Johnson's Checker to their wedding and who spent his last day celebrating their second anniversary in the back of the cab.

"The Checker is the ultimate urban luxury," Ms. Horton, 47, said as she held her beloved's hand during the drive up the East Side of Manhattan to the Conservatory Garden in the park. "It's a vehicle that belongs to New York."

Not anymore. The Taxi and Limousine Commission says his Checker needs a new chassis. Mr. Johnson says the car is fine, the commission's requirements too strict, and it's time to fold up his jump seats.

"I'm not looking for handouts," he said as he limped around, shaking hands and posing for pictures, "I'm finished." ◾

One driver, Richard Fisher of Staten Island, thought the authority had things backward. "Why don't we send the passengers to courtesy class instead of us?" he asked.

"But there is a courtesy class for passengers," the instructor, Donald Gaffney, said firmly, and the room quieted down. "And you know who the teachers are? You! You are the best public relations we have."

If there was a theme to the classroom instruction, it was that drivers should do their jobs safely, efficiently and politely, but, in the words of Mr. Gaffney, "never try to be a policeman."

The lesson was carried out on the second day of the course, when the class went out on the streets of Manhattan in a shiny, new General Motors bus. As it turned from a side street on to Riverside Drive—wham, wham, wham—three snowballs hit the windshield.

Nobody flinched. There was a time when a driver would stop his bus and give chase; but then there was a time when youngsters would run. The three snowball-throwers stood their ground on Riverside Drive and laughed.

The course was set up in response to complaints from the police, who said drivers were violating traffic regulations, and from the public, who said operators were violating common courtesy. One student, Mr. Fisher, said he thought the course was a good idea.

He said, "It sure beats driving a bus." ◾

CITY WORKERS

Homeless, but Far From Friendless

By **DAVID GONZALEZ** | April 20, 2004

WHEN ONE PERSON IS KIND TO MANY strangers, people make a big deal of it, heaping praise and talking about canonizing the do-gooder. But when many strangers are kind to one person—a homeless one who lugs his life in two bulging plastic bags on the subway—the upshot is a quick shrug of disbelief, and not the admiring kind.

Yet in his 53 years on earth, a chunk of it spent riding the rails, Tony Butler, the homeless man, brought around him a random clan who gave him food, money and friendship. The motormen and car cleaners who keep the subways running were a large part of that circle. But so, too, were riders who befriended him at the Broadway-Lafayette station, where he had taken it upon himself to announce system delays or route changes as a "volunteer transit associate."

They knew him as a subway philosopher and chess fiend in dark glasses. Some said he chose to be homeless, others said homelessness chose him. Whatever the case, their lives came together and stayed that way until he died last month from what doctors said was an overwhelming infection.

"He saw himself as a beacon of freedom," Steve Zeitlin said. "Someone once described street performers as instilling a homesickness for freedom in the lives of ordinary men. Tony prided himself on living in total freedom."

He may not have had a job, but he did keep to a schedule. Monday and Friday mornings he would rendezvous with Mr. Zeitlin, who gave him money and food. Other people had other days. He did not like to miss out on connecting with his friends.

And while he did not envy their schedules, he looked out for his subway worker friends, especially when bosses where on the prowl.

"He knew when the supervisors got on the train," said Anthony Smith, a train operator. "You wouldn't know, but he would. He'd warn you." ▪

The Ballad Of Sonny Payne

By **STEVEN KURUTZ** | May 16, 2004

WITH THE EXCEPTION OF THE MAYOR AND A stray actor or two, the subway trains are generally bereft of public figures. It's an anonymous journey. This is not the case on the F train, however, where every day a luminary rides alongside the commuters in the form of a small, sweet-natured old panhandler named Sonny Payne.

Sonny has worked the F train so long and with such success that along the Brooklyn stretch of the line, from Avenue X to the Jay Street/Borough Hall station, he is considered an esteemed part of the commuting. "He's like something out of 'Cheers,'" one passenger said. This makes him feel good.

He is either 65 or 67, depending on his mood when you ask him, and is most famous for his introductory speech, which he recites upon entering each car: "Pardon me, my name is Sonny Payne. I'm homeless and I'm hungry. If you don't have it, I can understand, because I don't have it. But if you have a little change, a piece of fruit, something to eat, I'd greatly appreciate it."

So catchy is the speech that it's some-

Sweeping Him Off His Street

By **COLEMAN COWAN** | March 18, 2007

AFTER 13 YEARS OF AVOIDING WHAT HE CALLS the "Giuliani sweeps"—when the streets were emptied of homeless by the police during freezing weather—Cadillac Man is finally coming in from the cold.

Cadillac Man plans to move into an apartment with the new woman in his life, a computer researcher from Astoria named Carol Vogel. Ms. Vogel, who at 32 is 25 years younger than Cadillac Man, met him a year and a half ago when she passed under the 33rd Street viaduct, his main haunt.

A tough man who grew up in Hell's Kitchen, he has chronicled his adventures on the streets of Astoria, Queens, in Esquire magazine and is the subject of a 2006 documentary.

Cadillac Man's writing grew out of another relationship, with a much younger homeless woman named Penny. They spent only a few months together, but after she left, Cadillac Man began to fill one spiral notebook after another describing his time with her and his life on the street. His gritty, spare prose caught the eye of Will Blythe, a former editor at Esquire who lives in the neighborhood. In May 2005, the magazine published a first-person account of Cadillac Man's life on the street. Sloan Harris, a literary agent at International Creative Management, noticed the article and brokered a deal for a book.

Ask him about his real name, and he replies tersely, "That's dead to me now." Ask him about his nickname, and he speaks of six Cadillacs that ran him down across the city—once sending him to the hospital—during a single month in 1994. These accidents occurred soon after Cadillac Man, who has been married twice and is the father of three, lost his job at a meat market in Hell's Kitchen and began a downward spiral of what he called "drinking and disappearing." ∎

BELOW: *Cadillac Man's book, "Land of the Lost Souls: My Life on the Streets," was released in 2009.*

times posted verbatim on the Web site Craigslist, and a less imaginative panhandler named Marty adopted it for his own use. Sonny doesn't feel slighted. "In a way," he said, "I take it as a backhanded compliment."

For Sonny, the jostling over spare nickels has long passed. He is above the fray. Through salient charm and learned observation, he has solved the mystery of what makes subway riders, already taxed, give to a beggar. He isn't even a beggar but an old friend, and in place of loose change he is often given bills. One evening not long ago he made $136. He took the money and booked a hotel room for two nights. "I treated myself," he said. "I really enjoyed it." ∎

Louis (Moondog) Hardin, 83, Musician, Dies

By **GLENN COLLINS** | September 12, 1999

THE GAUNT, BLIND MUSICIAN KNOWN AS Moondog, who was celebrated among New Yorkers as a mysterious street performer and among Europeans as an avant-garde composer, conducting orchestras before royalty, died Wednesday in a hospital in Munster, Germany. He was 83.

Day in and day out, the man who was originally named Louis T. Hardin was as taciturn and unchanging a landmark of the midtown Manhattan streetscape as the George M. Cohan statue in Duffy Square. From the late 1940's until the early 1970's, Mr. Hardin stood at attention like a sentinel on Avenue of the Americas around 54th Street.

No matter the weather, he invariably dressed in a homemade robe, sandals, a flowing cape and a horned Viking helmet, the tangible expression of what he referred to as his "Nordic philosophy." At his side he clutched a long spear of his own manufacture.

Most of the passers-by who dismissed him as "the Viking of Sixth Avenue," offering him contributions and buying copies of his music and poetry, were unaware that he had recorded his music on the CBS, Prestige, Epic, Angel and Mars labels.

One of his songs, "All Is Loneliness," became a hit when recorded by Janis Joplin. He wrote music for radio and television commercials, and one of his compositions was used on the soundtrack for the 1972 movie "Drive, He Said," with Jack Nicholson.

"He led an extraordinary life for a blind man who came to New York with no contacts and a month's rent, and who lived on the streets of New York for 30 years," said Dr. Robert Scotto, a professor of English at Baruch College of the City University of New York, who has just completed a biography of Mr. Hardin. "Without question, he was the most famous street person of his time." ■

BELOW: *Louis (Moondog) Hardin in 1965.*

His Stage, the Street

By **JAMES BARRON** | February 3, 2009

SOMEHOW, JOE ADES GOT PEOPLE'S ATTENTION as the crowds swirled by at the Union Square Greenmarket, on their way to eyeing and buying the produce. He was the white-haired man with the British accent, the expensive European suits and shirts—the man selling the $5 peeler. For carrots. Or potatoes.

"He made it look really fun," said Julie Worden, who dances with the Mark Morris Dance Company.

"The voice—you couldn't help but notice it," said Gordon Crandall, a mathematician who teaches at La Guardia Community College.

His was a particular kind of street theater in a city that delights in in-your-face characters who are, and are not, what they seem. For he was the sidewalk pitchman with the Upper East Side apartment. The sidewalk pitchman who was a regular at expensive East Side restaurants, where no one believed his answer to the "So what do you do?" question: "I sell potato peelers on the street."

My Days Underground

By **KIRK JOHNSON** | June 15, 1997

SHE WORE A BROWN CLOTH COAT AND LITTLE half-glasses, and she emerged from the side of the 14th Street platform with the light behind her, creating a halo effect around her hair, like an angel's. I never learned her name because she jumped onto an uptown No. 1 local train a minute later, but I will never forget her. She rescued a struggling musician in the grimmest moment of his first-ever afternoon playing for the passing throng of the New York transit system: she listened.

Every subway musician has a story like that. But how does it happen? How, in this least likely of places—the subway—where New Yorkers wrap their cloaks of anonymity and self-defense more tightly than almost anywhere else, does a subway musician break through? That's what I went underground with my guitar to find out.

For a musician, it is a world of soaring emotional highs and plummeting psychic lows, none of which—for better and for worse—lasts longer than the average wait for a train. Luke Ryan, a blues and rock performer who has been playing in the subway for 15 years, calls this effect the "constant audition." It's the only environment he knows, he said, where a performer wins hearts instantly, or fails completely, because there is no time for anything in between.

For most of my first afternoon on the subway stage, I was firmly in the failed category. I had played for perhaps half an hour without a single person's so much as acknowledging my existence until the woman in brown changed it all. She stepped out of the light, leaned in, listened, smiled, touched her forefinger and thumb together to signal, "O.K.," and threw a single quarter in the open guitar case. She brought hope.

I ultimately played and sang underground on two more occasions over a 10-day period at various times and stations around the city—morning rush hour on the Upper West Side 72nd Street downtown I.R.T. No. 1, 2 and 3 trains; afternoon into evening on Wall Street, uptown No. 4 and 5, as well as that afternoon on the 14th Street platform—and through it all I was always trying to recreate that first moment of victory.

I played the song she liked, "Maybelline," by Chuck Berry, just about to death. I did not make a lot of money: $61.39 for more than nine hours of physically exhausting work. Better than the minimum wage, though not by much. ■

Mr. Ades (pronounced AH-dess) died on Sunday at 75, said his daughter, Ruth Ades Laurent of Manhattan. She said he never talked about how many peelers he sold in a year, or how many carrots he had sliced up during sidewalk demonstrations. She said he stashed his inventory in what had been the maid's room of the apartment.

There were those at the Greenmarket who had heard the spiel, and heard the whispers. "Supposedly his wife is mega-mega-rich—we've done fashion shoots in that building," said Rose-Marie Swift, a makeup artist, as she shopped at the Greenmarket.

The facts? He was a widower. The apartment had been his wife's—his fourth wife's. He had followed Ms. Laurent from England to the United States, via Australia. "One of his marriages, I guess his third marriage, had broken up," she said. Making the rounds of state fairs, "he discovered the peeler—someone was selling the peeler and he saw it as a fantastic item to sell on the street. He loved the street more than anything," she said. ■

Jackie O; Friends Recall A Fighter for Her City

By **ROBERT D. MCFADDEN** | May 22, 1994

NEW YORK, WHICH CONFERS A MEASURE OF privacy on celebrities, counted Jacqueline Kennedy Onassis among its own for many years. Mrs. Onassis, who died Thursday at the age of 64, had spent much of her childhood here, and it was here she returned in 1964 after the assassination of President John F. Kennedy, here she went back to work in 1975 after the death of her second husband, Aristotle Onassis, and here she fought for her glittering, frustrating city.

All over town—at a Grand Central Terminal she helped to save, outside her Fifth Avenue apartment building, in Central Park where she jogged—people recalled her campaigns for treasured buildings, her work as a book editor, her affection for art, her quiet presence in church, and mostly her friendship.

"She had this tremendous enthusiasm— it was almost childlike at times—and when she talked about a book, you knew she was completely engaged," said Stephen Rubin, the president and publisher of Doubleday, where Mrs. Onassis had been an editor for the last 16 years.

One of her authors, Bill Moyers, for whom she had edited three books, recalled her yesterday in similar terms: "As a colleague, working closely on my books, she was as witty, warm and creative in private as she was grand and graceful in public."

Nancy Tuckerman, a lifelong friend and confidante who had been Mrs. Kennedy's White House social secretary, recalled roller-skating with Jackie Bouvier as children in New York in the 1930's, when they were fellow students at the Chapin School.

"She was always drawn back to New York," Ms. Tuckerman said. "She chose to bring up her children in the city. She got into publishing because she knew it would be an educational experience—she would learn something every moment."

Kent L. Barwick, president of the Municipal Art Society, recalled how Mrs.

Onassis was instrumental in persuading legislators in Albany to block the construction of an office tower beside St. Bartholomew's Church on Park Avenue. "Jackie got on the train to Albany, met with assemblymen and senators and the governor all day, gave testimony and at the end of the day, when the rest of us were exhausted, she stood for well over an hour while virtually every important legislator had a picture taken with her," Mr. Barwick remembered.

Like many New Yorkers, Mrs. Onassis got away occasionally—on weekends to her horse farm in New Jersey, in the summer to her estate on Martha's Vineyard, where she and her companion of recent years, Maurice Tempelsman, entertained President Clinton and his wife, Hillary, last summer.

But her friends said she was always glad to come home to New York. ∎

Eleanor Roosevelt Warmly Remembered In Her Hometown

By **DOUGLAS MARTIN** | October 5, 1996

ELEANOR ROOSEVELT WAS BORN AND DIED IN New York City, and spent big intervals of her life here. Today, she comes home—as a statue in Riverside Park.

History's longest-serving First Lady returns to a city where she was a rich if exceedingly uncomfortable debutante, a tireless worker for social causes, a newspaper columnist and a delegate to the United Nations. She comes to a place where she was so revered cab drivers would ask her to sit in the front seat so they could better converse.

The Boyhood Myth
That Helped Make Moynihan

By **DOUGLAS E. SCHOEN** | April 6, 2003

DANIEL PATRICK MOYNIHAN LIKED TO describe himself as a boy from Hell's Kitchen; until his death at the age of 76, it was one of his defining characteristics.

In fact, Moynihan and his family lived in the neighborhood for only a few years, and for most of that time he was away at college. But for subtle and complicated reasons, Hell's Kitchen became a powerful and enduring metaphor. The quintessential working-class Irish-American neighborhood sandwiched between Times Square and the bustling docks served as a reference point for Moynihan's young life. His youth was essentially that of a middle-class kid cast into downward mobility.

It was in 1928 that his father, Jack, took a job as an advertising copywriter in Manhattan, and moved his young wife and infant son from Tulsa, Okla., to New York. Jack was discontented with the lifestyle of what passed for a young post-Depression professional, and abandoned his family in 1937. What followed for Margaret Moynihan and her by-then three children was close to outright poverty.

In 1947, she opened a bar at 558 West 42nd Street, near 11th Avenue, that Moynihan would talk about for the rest of his life. The family lived in a railroad flat upstairs.

Moynihan, who had returned from a stint as a naval officer, felt duty-bound to keep both the bar and his family running smoothly, which he did. Moynihan took advantage of the G.I. Bill to finish college at Tufts University, near Boston. But the situation at home was volatile. Frequently Moynihan had to trek down in person, textbooks in hand and sleep-deprived, to put things right. He missed graduation week because he had to rush home to resolve a dispute that had erupted at the bar. ∎

It was here she fought Tammany Hall, the Catholic Church on aid to parochial schools, and the sweatshops on the Lower East Side. There are still people who remember seeing Mrs. Roosevelt run for a bus, ride a horse in Central Park or dance elegantly.

Lately, Mrs. Roosevelt has been in the news as a result of conversations the First Lady, Hillary Rodham Clinton, says she has with her as an exercise in dealing with First Lady pressures.

Mrs. Roosevelt could hardly walk down a New York street without people running up to thank her for some favor. Edna Gurewitsch, who with her husband shared a house with Mrs. Roosevelt during the last three years of her life, said Mrs. Roosevelt would usually just keep walking. At first, she thought she was hard of hearing but then realized it was something else.

"She really didn't care about thank you's at all," Mrs. Gurewitsch said. "She only cared about what had to be done now." ∎

Battle-Tested Sharpton Slips Into Familiar Role

By **ADAM NAGOURNEY** | February 13, 1999

ABOVE: *Al Sharpton at the National Action Network, his civil rights organization, in 2007.*

JUST BEFORE THE EVENING NEWS THE OTHER night, the parents of Amadou Diallo, the West African street vendor shot dead by plainclothes police officers last week, walked up to microphones to offer their first extended public remarks about the death of their son. The setting was a second-floor auditorium up a scuffed flight of steps in Harlem. And the host, wearing a crisp gray three-piece suit and clearly enjoying this latest bustle at his Harlem headquarters, was the Rev. Al Sharpton.

It was perhaps inevitable. In the 15 years since Mr. Sharpton took up the cause of one of the four black youths shot by Bernard Goetz, he has developed a network of supporters, an articulate public presence and a command of politics and media that few other figures in New York can rival. As was clear again yesterday, as Mr. Sharpton assumed a prominent role at Mr. Diallo's memorial service, that arsenal has established him as arguably more influential than any black leader in the city, including those who have been elected to public office.

Mr. Sharpton said in an interview that he has never imposed himself into any of the half-dozen racially charged police cases with which he has been identified. "I would not have contacted them," Mr. Sharpton said. I am not an ambulance chaser: I am the ambulance. People call me."

There was no need for Mr. Sharpton to chase anyone, indeed. Other Guinean immigrants called Mr. Sharpton after Mr. Diallo was shot last week, just as other Haitian immigrants called him after allegations that Abner Louima was assaulted in a Brooklyn police precinct in 1997.

The Diallo shooting has illuminated Mr. Sharpton's strengths in racially charged situations. Mr. Sharpton has been able to assemble large crowds, on short notice, for rallies. He has brought in a network of people, including fund-raisers and lawyers, to help the Diallo family.

"He has a genius for this," said Edward I. Koch, the former mayor whose relations with Mr. Sharpton have thawed somewhat since Mr. Koch left Gracie Mansion. "He has the respect of the black community. He can deliver a picket line of large numbers when he decides he wants to. He's very quotable. And he's very smart."

What is more, Mr. Sharpton has managed, with a few dissents, to present himself as a leader of a group of New Yorkers that is more politically, economically and ethnically diverse than ever: from old-line black Democratic leaders in Harlem, to the new groups of immigrants that are now jockeying for a place on New York's landscape, to prominent black business leaders who had once shunned him.

For his part, Mr. Sharpton said he had patterned his career after that of the Rev. Jesse L. Jackson Jr. And that, he said, accounted for his success in New York. "Let's face it: If Secretary of Transportation Rodney Slater walked down 125th Street, people wouldn't know him," Mr. Sharpton said, referring to the black Arkansan President Clinton appointed to his Cabinet. "But everybody would know Jesse Jackson. I do in New York what Jesse Jackson does in the nation." ■

public servants

Mr. Clinton, Your Harlem Neighbors Want to See You More Often

By **ALAN FEUER** | November 17, 2003

CONSIDER THIS AN OPEN LETTER FROM THE citizens of 125th Street to former President Bill Clinton. Its message is simple: Mr. Clinton, please come home.

Anthony Rembert, 39, says he misses Mr. Clinton in the neighborhood: "Come back to the area, please. We want you to be part of the community."

When Mr. Clinton moved into 55 West 125th Street in July 2001, it was hailed in certain parts of Harlem as the first installment of the Second Coming. A crowd of 2,000—chanting "We love Bill!"—gathered on the streets to greet Mr. Clinton, who appeared before the masses to a violin rendition of "We Shall Overcome."

The former president and Harlem seemed the perfect match. Both were in the early stages of a renaissance. Both loved soul food. Both had ties to the South. Speaking to his adoring audience that day more than two years ago, Mr. Clinton made a promise. "I want to make sure I'm a good neighbor in Harlem," he said.

In the past two years, however, Mr. Clinton, like many neighbors in New York, has been a passing, rather than a palpable, presence in the neighborhood. This year alone, he has traveled to Los Angeles to campaign for Gov. Gray Davis, to Kosovo to visit American soldiers serving with the United Nations peace-keeping force and to China to press its government to confront a growing AIDS crisis.

His absence has been noticed on 125th Street, where people say they have occasionally seen him, under Secret Service guard, ducking through the back door of his office—if, that is, they have seen him at all.

"Actually, I've only seen him once," said Thomas Hunn, 77, a retired waiter, who was leaning against a parking meter across the street from Mr. Clinton's office on a recent afternoon.

A spokesman for Mr. Clinton's office pointed out that while Mr. Clinton has certainly been on the move, he has still had time to visit Jimmy's Uptown (three times), the Sugar Hill Bistro, the Bayou restaurant, Londell's restaurant, the Studio Museum in Harlem, Dance Theater of Harlem, the Apollo Theater (three times), Sylvia's restaurant and Dee's Card Shop (for some Christmas shopping), to name more than a few.

When Mr. Clinton is not on the road, the spokesman said, he splits his time between his Harlem aerie and his home in Chappaqua, in Westchester County, where he is said to be working on his memoirs. "When he's in town, he comes by maybe once every couple of weeks," said Robert Collins, the chef at Lang's Little Store and Deli, one of Mr. Clinton's haunts in Chappaqua. "He's here a lot on weekends."

Over all, 125th Street still remains a thriving chapter of the Bill Clinton fan club, and there are those on the street who consider themselves lucky to actually have seen the man in recent weeks.

Sharon Alexander, 43, rode in the elevator with the former president last month as she was heading to work at the Department of Veterans Affairs.

Her message now is the same she had for him that day as they stood side by side: "I love you, Bill, but I need to see you more." ∎

BELOW: *Former President Bill Clinton meets with future President Barack Obama his Harlem office in 2008.*

Robert Moses, Master Builder

By **PAUL GOLDBERGER** | July 30, 1981

ROBERT MOSES, WHO PLAYED A LARGER ROLE in shaping the physical environment of New York State than any other figure in the 20th century, died yesterday in West Islip, N.Y. Mr. Moses, whose long list of public offices only begins to hint at his impact on both the city and state of New York, was 92 years old.

A spokesman for Good Samaritan Hospital said he had been taken there

BELOW: *Though Robert Moses remains controversial, Babylon, N.Y. paid homage to its native son with a statue on the lawn of its Village Hall.*

Tuesday afternoon from his summer home in Gilgo Beach. The cause of death was given as heart failure.

"Those who can, build," Mr. Moses once said. "Those who can't, criticize." Robert Moses was, in every sense of the word, New York's master builder. Neither an architect, a planner, a lawyer nor even, in the strictest sense, a politician, he changed the face of the state more than anyone who was. Before him, there was no Triborough Bridge, Jones Beach State Park, Verrazano-Narrows Bridge, West Side Highway or Long Island parkway system or Niagara and St. Lawrence power projects. He built all of these and more.

Before Mr. Moses, New York State had a modest amount of parkland; when he left his position as chief of the state park system, the state had 2,567,256 acres. He built 658 playgrounds in New York City, 416 miles of parkways and 13 bridges. For 44 years, from 1924 until 1968, Mr. Moses constructed public works in the city and state costing—in a recent estimate adjusting currency to 1968 value—$27 billion.

Mr. Moses built parks, highways, bridges, playgrounds, housing, tunnels, beaches, zoos, civic centers, exhibition halls and the 1964-65 New York World's Fair.

But he was more than just a builder. Although he disdained theories, he was a major theoretical influence on the shape of the American city, because the works he created in New York proved a model for the nation at large. His vision of a city of highways and towers—which in his later years came to be discredited by younger planners—influenced the planning of cities around the nation.

His guiding hand made New York, known as a city of mass transit, also the nation's first city for the automobile age. Under Mr. Moses, the metropolitan area came to have more highway miles than Los Angeles does; Moses projects anticipated such later

The Enduring Legacy of Jane Jacobs

By **DAVID W. DUNLAP** | April 27, 2006

THE IDEA THAT CITY PLANNING SHOULD BE informed by the city block—its people, texture, layering, scale and age—can be traced in good measure to Jane Jacobs's 1961 book, "The Death and Life of Great American Cities," written while she lived at 555 Hudson Street. It's little block between Perry and West 11th Streets peppered with old buildings.

She liked short blocks with a lot of diversity.

On Tuesday, she died at age 89 in Toronto, where she had moved in 1968. Along Hudson Street in Greenwich Village, diversity still reigned around the unremarkable three-story structure at No. 555 ("modest" seems too grandiose a word for it), now home to the Art of Cooking, a cookware and accessories store. Elsewhere on the block are the White Horse Tavern, three restaurants, a cafe, a news dealer and a combination card store, florist and T-shirt shop.

Farther downtown, Ms. Jacobs's hand can be seen in the redevelopment plan for the World Trade Center. A central tenet of that plan is to break down the super-block site into four smaller blocks

ABOVE: *Jane Jacobs at her home in Toronto on June 9, 2003.*

automobile-oriented efforts as the Los Angeles freeway system.

But where Los Angeles grew up around its highways, Mr. Moses thrust many of New York's great ribbons of concrete across an older and largely settled urban landscape, altering it drastically. He further changed the landscape with rows of red-brick apartment towers for low- and middle-income residents, asphalt playgrounds and huge sports stadiums. The Moses vision of New York was less one of neighborhoods and brownstones than one of soaring towers, open parks, highways and beaches—not the sidewalks of New York but the American dream of the open road. ∎

through the re-establishment of Greenwich and Fulton Streets.

It is no coincidence that this framework was developed while Alexander Garvin was vice president for planning at the Lower Manhattan Development Corporation. His roommate at Yale gave him a copy of "Death and Life" as a Christmas present in 1961. "It changed my life," Mr. Garvin said.

Another example of her influence, Mr. Garvin said, was the neighborhood preservation program that he oversaw as New York's deputy housing commissioner from 1974 to 1978. "We were trying to save old buildings," he recalled, "which was something I always had an inclination toward but until I read that you needed a mix of old and new buildings to have a healthy neighborhood, it wasn't part of my repertoire."

"She taught us how to look at blocks," said Ada Louise Huxtable, who was the architecture critic of The New York Times when Ms. Jacobs was battling Robert Moses and other powerful advocates of urban renewal and slum clearance.

"The intimate view of the city and its humanity really is indebted to her," Ms. Huxtable said. ∎

Being Brooke Astor

By **MARILYN BERGER** | May 20, 1984

BROOKE ASTOR, THE PHILANTHROPIST AND socialite, picked up the telephone and called Vartan Gregorian, president of New York Public Library. He was in the middle of a meeting in his office. He dropped everything and took the call. "Greg, it's Brooke," Mrs. Astor said in her rapid-fire, high-spirited staccato. "Are you sitting or standing?"

"I'm standing," Mr. Gregorian replied.

"Well, sit down," she said.

He did.

"I've just sent letters of resignation to all the major boards I am on and I'm going to dedicate myself to the New York Public Library."

"I was stunned," he says. "I said, 'You're fabulous, you're wonderful.' I got very excited and I said all kinds of nice things. Then I turned back to the meeting and said, 'You won't believe what has just happened.'"

He says he knew immediately that what had just happened meant that the library was entering nothing less than a new era. "It meant that New York philanthropists, New York society, would now rediscover the library. What Brooke's gesture did was to show that learning, books, education have glamour, that self-improvement has glamour, that hope has glamour."

The New York Public Library had, in recent years, been forced to curtail its activities. Many of its branches shut their doors on Saturdays. The institution, a not-for-profit corporation which gets some public funds, had been short of money. Schoolchildren seeking enlightenment are turned away in a manner that would have made Andrew Carnegie, the great library-giver, blush, not to mention John Jacob Astor, founder of the Astor fortune, the richest man in America when he died in 1848. Mr. Astor's personal collection of books (and $400,000) formed a cornerstone of the New York Public Library.

But the worst of the library's financial trouble may now be over. The institution has

ABOVE: *Brooke Astor, shown here in her Park Avenue apartment when she was 99, passed away in 2007.*

become, as Mr. Gregorian predicted, one of the city's most popular charitable causes, primarily because the Astor descendant-by-marriage, Mrs. Vincent Astor, whom almost everybody calls Brooke, has been devoting herself so publicly to library matters. This is in the tradition of Lila Acheson Wallace, Mrs. Russell Sage, Mary Lasker, Agnes Meyer, Alice Tully, Minnie Guggenheimer and others.

Few of these Ladies Bountiful, however, have had interests as varied as Brooke Astor's or enjoyed what might be called her leeway. She has been a widow for 25 years. She has a strong sense of responsibility for the money she inherited from Vincent Astor, who died after they had been married only five-and-a-half years. He left her $2 million outright, the income for her lifetime on about $60 million (the principal to be disposed of at her death according to her wishes), and he established her firmly in charge of a foundation with assests of another $60 million for "the alleviation of human misery." This is medium size, as foundations go (the Ford Foundation, the nation's wealthiest, has $3.4 billion in assets).

But the energy Brooke Astor devotes to the Vincent Astor Foundation has created astonishment and wide-eyed admiration. "You see," she says, "it's fun to give money away." ∎

As Mrs. Astor Slips, The Grandson Blames the Son

By **JAMES BARRON** and **ANEMONA HARTOCOLLIS** | July 27, 2006

ONCE, SHE AND HER PEARLS AND HER designer dresses were everywhere that was anywhere in New York society: this benefit, that party, this lunch, that dedication. At her 90th birthday party, she danced the first dance with the mayor. At her 100th, 100 well-connected friends toasted her with Champagne.

Then Brooke Russell Kuser Marshall Astor, doyenne of capital-S society by night, philanthropist by day, faded from view. Already, she had closed down her charity, having given away not quite $195 million. Her explanation was a single word: "Age."

No longer was she seen on the black-tie circuit, seated to the right of an attentive host. One neighbor has seen her only once in the last two years, asleep in a wheelchair outside her apartment building on Park Avenue.

Now Mrs. Astor, 104, is at the center of a bitter intergenerational dispute that has become public. In a lawsuit, one of her grandsons has accused her son of mistreating her and turning her final years into a grim shadow of the glittery decades that went before.

The grandson, Philip Marshall, accuses his father, Anthony Marshall—a Broadway producer and former C.I.A. employee who is 82—of failing to fill Mrs. Astor's prescriptions, stripping her apartment of artwork, confining the dogs she doted on to the pantry, reducing the number of staff members looking after her, and forcing her to sleep in chilly misery on a couch that smells of urine.

In court papers, Philip Marshall says that his father "has turned a blind eye to her, intentionally and repeatedly ignoring her health, safety, personal and household needs, while enriching himself with millions of dollars."

Philip Marshall asks that Anthony Marshall be removed as Mrs. Astor's legal guardian and replaced by Annette de la Renta, a friend of Mrs. Astor's who is married to the designer Oscar de la Renta, and JPMorgan Chase Bank.

The allegations shocked the circles in which Mrs. Astor once moved, simply because they involved Mrs. Astor, who always guarded her privacy, even though she was one of the most public figures in New York. Her name alone denoted power and old wealth. She is said to have thrown a would-be mugger off balance by saying, "Excuse me, we've not been introduced properly. I'm Mrs. Astor."

She became Mrs. Astor with her third husband. She had divorced the first, and the second had died. The third, Vincent Astor, was the son and heir of John Jacob Astor, who died on the Titanic, and whose fortune had begun in fur trading and real estate. Vincent Astor bequeathed Mrs. Astor $60 million for herself and an equal amount for a foundation "for the alleviation of human suffering."

But it is her suffering that Philip Marshall describes in court papers. There are allegations that her son vetoed purchases of a new outfit when she turned 104, of cosmetics, of hats and socks. There are allegations that he had curbed her physical therapy sessions and stopped her injections for anemia.

Vartan Gregorian, a former president of the New York Public Library who is now the president of the Carnegie Corporation of New York, said the last time he visited her, last year, was an unexpected emotional experience.

"When she was told it was I, she opened one eye," he said. "She kissed me. She said, 'I love you.' I said, 'I love you, too.' I kissed her hand, and broke down. I'd never seen her in that weak position. I'd always seen her triumphant. She was, will always be, the first lady of New York society." ■

On Rap Star's Final Ride, Homage Is Marred by a Scuffle

By **IAN FISHER** | March 19, 1997

CHRISTOPHER G. WALLACE, THE BROOKLYN tough who became the million-selling rap star known as Biggie Smalls and the Notorious B.I.G., was driven in a hearse yesterday for a final ride through the streets where he grew up. Several thousand people mourned both for him and for the violence that has shaken the rap world.

The procession itself was marred by a brief clash between the police and several dozen people, which erupted around the corner from Mr. Wallace's childhood home in Fort Greene. The incident began in a chaotic swirl of people flooding onto Fulton Street, when a group of teenagers jumped onto several parked cars and a Dumpster and began dancing shortly after Mr. Wallace's motorcade passed by.

After officers trying to remove people from atop the cars scuffled with several men, Vanessa Edwards, 28, stood with tears streaming down her face and wailed, "He wouldn't have wanted it like this!"

The police arrested 10 people, including a reporter who was covering the procession for The New York Times, and no one was seriously hurt. But tensions between the police and residents festered into the evening along Fulton Street, amid complaints that the police had used excessive force, including one officer who pounded a man on the head repeatedly with the butt end of a can of pepper spray.

The scuffles, though, stood in sharp contrast to the rest of the almost regal proceedings for Mr. Wallace, who at 24 was one of rap's biggest stars, making musical capital of the violence that surrounded him growing up. He was killed 10 days ago in a drive-by shooting in Los Angeles.

The mourners who turned up along the motorcade route in Brooklyn—from grade-schoolers to grandparents—said they regarded him not so much as a "gangsta" rapper but as a hero who had overcome his own early drug dealing to become rich and famous on the strength of his talent.

"He was kind of a role model to all of us," said Karla Boston, 11, who was standing with two of her sixth-grade classmates on St. James Place. "He found it to the big leagues. He found a way to get out of this neighborhood.

"I figured he tried hard and he's kind of giving us hope," she added. ∎

BELOW: *Actor Jamal Woolard, shown here in Fort Greene, played rapper Biggie Smalls in the movie "Notorious."*

A Bronze Plaque In Brooklyn Marks George Gershwin's Birthplace

By **JOHN S. WILSON** | September 23, 1963

A BRONZE PLAQUE MARKING THE TWO-STORY house in Brooklyn where George Gershwin was born will be unveiled at 11 a.m., Thursday, the 65th anniversary of the birth of the composer, who died on July 11, 1937. By proclamation of Abe Stark, borough president of Brooklyn, Thursday will be George Gershwin Day.

The plaque is a presentation of the American Society of Composers, Authors and

Memories of a Rock Star: My First Year in New York

By **LOU REED** | September 17, 2000

WHEN I MOVED INTO MY FIRST NEW YORK apartment, my uncle gave me a cot and a folding chair. I had been working as a copy editor for a divorce lawyer for two weeks to build up rent money. With $200 in my pocket, I quit and got the apartment ($45 a month) with a friend. It was one room with a bathtub. The bathroom was in the hall and unusable. We took electricity from the hall lighting fixture. There was no heat, but there was a window that overlooked the street three floors below.

Much of my income came from selling envelopes of sugar to girls I met at clubs, claiming it was heroin. This led to hours of feigned stonedness. What happened to the original drugs is another story.

I slept in a used Navy peacoat and did what laundry I had at a dealer's house on East Sixth Street, until a jealous lover shot my friend's leg off with a shotgun blast through the door. This caused some consternation in our crowd, and eventually eight of us banded together and moved en masse to a new apartment on Grand Street. There I slept on a small cut-up mattress that rested on the floor. It made me nervous because we had rats and I worried about being bit. At this point the Velvet Underground had sprung into being. The junkies who lived below us honored our first job by robbing the entire band of everything that was not with us at the gig.

The next apartment was on East 10th Street. This was a real apartment, $65 a month. I made the mistake of letting Ondine stay there once when I was out of town and returned to find the apartment flooded with water and a comatose body in the bathtub. Jimmy Smith had taken all my belongings. Rotten Rita had carved a poem on the front door, which hung off its hinges. The amphetamine elves had Magic Markered the walls, and the landlord had left the notice of eviction Scotch taped to the working stove. I still had my guitar and my peacoat and my B.A. in English. ▪

Publishers, of which Mr. Gershwin was a member. During the ceremonies the glee club of the nearby George Gershwin Junior High School will sing Gershwin songs.

The composer wrote the music for such shows as "Of Thee I Sing," "Girl Crazy" and "Strike Up the Band." His bigger works included "An American in Paris," "Rhapsody in Blue" and "Porgy and Bess."

George Gershwin lived in Brooklyn for only two or possibly three years before the family moved back to Manhattan.

The house, between Sutter and Belmont Avenues, was surrounded by trees when the Gershwins lived there. George Gershwin's brother, Ira, remembers eating grapes from a vine that grew in the fenced yard surrounding the house. He played in an open field on the Sutter Avenue side. The house had a front room, a dining room, a kitchen and possibly a maid's room on the ground floor. Upstairs there were three or four bedrooms, one of which was rented to a Mr. Taffelstein for $4 a week.

Today the house is hemmed in by other buildings. The only remnant of the open field where Ira Gershwin played is a space wider than any of the alleyways in the neighborhood, too wide for a driveway but not wide enough for a lot. In 65 years the semi-suburban atmosphere of the street has changed. Open space has given way to a solid row of buildings. Stores in the once predominantly Jewish neighborhood now display signs in English, Hebrew and Spanish. ▪

Miss Bankhead Returns, Purring

By **EUGENE ARCHER** | December 6, 1964

"HAND ME THE TELEPHONE, DARLING," SAID Tallulah Bankhead. It was only two feet away from her yoga perch, but before her startled visitor could oblige, the maid had darted around the pastel furnishing, and was brandishing the Princess. "Thanks," cooed the Buddha, accepting her alms. "Darling" she repeated, this time addressing the receiver, "I'm talking to the nicest gentleman from The New York Times, and I'm trying to be tactful as hell about the film."

Bankhead is definitely back. Back, this time, from a 10-week sojourn in England, where she played for Hammer Brothers in something called, to her chagrin, "Die! Die! My Darling!"

Curled up on her ladylike couch, rich brown hair streaming on either side of her big, bad eyes, the effect was decidedly kittenish, and her celebrated vocabulary rumbled forth in an alarming purr.

"I adore Huntley-Brinkley," she explained, turning on the sound full blast. "I hope it doesn't drive you mad. I don't know how I survived in England without the news. The British press, of course, were awfully nice to me, they always are, except when they say I'm a lousy actress, and sometimes I agree with them."

Her attention was momentarily arrested by an item on the news, involving a group of children in Eighth Street. Tallulah raised an eyebrow. "That's no place for children."

"I didn't choose this script, darling, it was forced on me, but my friends thought it was rather good. It isn't comedy though, nobody is writing good comedy these days except Iris Murdoch."

At the point, she had been talking nonstop for two hours. "You really must be disarming," she accused "because you made me miss Huntley-Brinkley. Oh, well. Come back again, and next time we'll play bridge." ∎

You Must Remember This: A Sign Is Not Just a Sign

By **MANNY FERNANDEZ** | June 25, 2006

YESTERDAY, ON HUMPHREY BOGART PLACE, there was only one fedora in sight. Yet the rain came down hard, the way it does in old movies, and people stood beneath their umbrellas looking for the ghost of Sam Spade.

They were not quite world-weary—this was the Upper West Side, after all—but they were at least a little wet.

The block of 103rd Street between Broadway and West End Avenue was named in honor of Bogart, the legendary actor who, 49 years after his death, remains an ageless

representative of another time, when the world had a bit more grace and a few decent gin joints. Bogart grew up on this block in the early 1900's, in a four-story brownstone at 245 West 103rd Street.

This city usually greets the naming of a street with a collective yawn. But the official unveiling of Humphrey Bogart Place was something else entirely, part block party, part film symposium, part history lesson. About 150 people gathered for the ceremony, and a hush of nervous excitement fell over the crowd when the chairman of the city's Housing Authority, Tino Hernandez, politely asked the people standing behind him to make room for the woman walking up the sidewalk.

She was the event's special guest, Bogart's widow, Lauren Bacall. She looked elegant in a black suit, elegant and dry, with their

ENTERTAINERS

Shards of a Life in 5F

By **MANNY FERNANDEZ** | October 2, 2005

RUSSELL AARONSON NEEDED A NEW BATH-room sink a few years ago. The old one in his Upper West Side studio apartment was a turn-of-the-century model, a cast-iron, white-enamel basin with two brass faucets that had outlived its usefulness. But he could never imagine simply throwing it out. After all, he explained, "It was James Dean's sink."

The lives—and even the bathroom fixtures—of Dean, a movie icon who died 50 years ago on Friday, and Mr. Aaronson, a Manhattan waiter, have been intimately and inextricably linked by a twist of fate, a stroke of good luck or the whims of that other force of nature, the New York real estate market.

The connection between the two men is Apartment 5F.

Mr. Aaronson resides in the same tiny studio at 19 West 68th Street where Dean lived in the early 1950's. It is a cramped unit on the top floor of a five-story brownstone walk-up off Central Park. There, in the corner, was where Dean slept, a matador's cape draped over a pair of bull horns on the wall above him.

There, nowadays, Mr. Aaronson's 7-year-old son sleeps, the cape and horns replaced by two framed photos of Dean and a wooden plaque from West Side Little League.

> It's not easy living in Dean's old apartment. Strangers frequently drop by and ask if they can take a look around.

It's not easy living in Dean's old apartment. Strangers frequently drop by and ask if they can take a look around. Mr. Aaronson said he had given tours to about 100 Dean fans over the years. Then there is the graffiti, the personal and often mysterious notes people scrawl in pen, pencil and lipstick on the white-painted wall downstairs across from the mail slots. "Jim Dean, thanks, you got me back on track," Clint wrote on July 24, 2004.

But Mr. Aaronson does not mind the visits or the graffiti. He has become a kind of curator of an unofficial Dean museum since he moved in 31 years ago. He has attended Dean tributes in Fairmount, Ind., the small farm town where the actor was raised, and even met Dean's first cousin, Marcus Winslow. And when it came time to figure out what to do with the old sink, he decided to put it in the trunk of a friend's car and drive it 750 miles to the Fairmount Historical Museum, where it is now on display.

"You might say," said Mr. Aaronson of the loyalty he feels to the former tenant, "it's a welcome obligation." ∎

son, Stephen Humphrey Bogart, by her side.

"It certainly was surprising," she told the crowd of the honor. "Bogie would never have believed it."

Bogart's parents—Belmont DeForest Bogart and Maud Humphrey—bought the brownstone in 1898, a year before Bogart was born. His father, a surgeon, used the first floor as his office and kept a pigeon coop on the roof. His mother, an illustrator, had a studio on the third floor. The brownstone is now owned by the Housing Authority and is part of a low-income housing development known as the Douglass Rehabs. Four families live in the building. There is a small garden in the back with a red-painted picnic table and a sign on a bulletin board that reminds tenants that exterminations are conducted on the fourth Saturday of the month. ∎

TriBeCa Yawns Hello to Film Studio

By **CONSTANCE L. HAYS** | May 6, 1990

TRUMPETED AS HOLLYWOOD ON THE HUDSON and organized by Robert De Niro, a former coffee warehouse in lower Manhattan opened this year as the TriBeCa Film Center, with production centers on seven floors and a stylish restaurant, the Tribeca Grill, on the ground floor. Yet for all the attention people in the neighborhood are paying to it, it might still be the warehouse.

"He's not the first celebrity in the neighborhood," said Dorothea Nicholas, a resident of the Independence Plaza apartment complex across the street.

Across TriBeCa, the area's supposed leap into the limelight is mostly met with an attitude of boredom, occasionally broken by a comment about the economic opportunities of such a change.

Mr. De Niro, the actor, "lives in the neighborhood and has for over 10 years," said Jane Rosenthal, executive vice president of TriBeCa Productions, the movie company that anchors the center. "It was really just a matter of being in the neighborhood."

At Greenwich Street Video, where Mr. De Niro has a membership and occasionally rents his movies, the management applauded the

film center. "It used to be a bombed-out warehouse," said Maria Hogan, who has worked at the store five years. When Mr. De Niro, who lives a block away on Hudson Street, wanted to rent his first videocassette, she added, he did not have to produce two forms of identification and a utility bill like the average customer.

Part of the local indifference to stardom may be that New Yorkers tend to recognize people more readily for their success in something other than show business, Ms. Kearney said. She added: "In New York, you're much more likely to hear someone say, 'Hey, there's Susan Sontag,' and in L.A. it's, 'There's Danny DeVito.' There's a lot more intellectual celebrity." ∎

"Wonder Years," By Way of Bed-Stuy

By **JOHN FREEMAN GILL** | December 4, 2005

BEDFORD-STUYVESANT IS USED TO HAVING its reputation defined by outsiders. For years this Brooklyn neighborhood had the rap of being so perilous a landscape that in 1980 a Long Island boy named Billy Joel sang, "I've been stranded in the combat zone/ I walked through Bedford-Stuy alone." By contrast, in the current overheated housing market, Bed-Stuy has been ballyhooed as the last frontier of affordable brownstones, a place overrun by real estate speculators panning for original wainscoting.

With the UPN television show "Everybody Hates Chris," the country is finally seeing a representation of Bed-Stuy shaped by one of its own: Chris Rock, the show's co-creator and narrator, on whose Decatur Street childhood the program is loosely based. The struggle to make ends meet

BELOW: *Robert DeNiro co-founded the TriBeCa Film Festival in 2002.*

ENTERTAINERS

Trying to Shake a Stereotype But Keep On Being Rosie Perez

By **PETER APPLEBOME** | February 14, 1999

ON A WATER-LOGGED DAY IN BROOKLYN, everything seems muted and muffled—the grays and browns of the buildings, the soggy drumbeat of the rain, the leaden thwock of the car wheels shooting out sprays of oily water as they rumble over manhole covers.

And then there is Rosie Perez, who, rain or shine, is about as muted and muffled as a stick of dynamite on a short fuse.

"All the time, all the time," she shot back when asked if she worries about being stereotyped as a feisty, foul-mouthed, working-class Latina, the Rosie Perez character she has played in most of her films. "Sometimes I really want to ask the studio

ABOVE: *Rosie Perez talks to students at LaGuardia High School on the Upper West Side.*

is played for laughs, so much so that at times the show has the misty tone of an asphalt-jungle "Wonder Years." Any sense of true jeopardy in the rose-tinted ghetto portrayed on screen is so slight that one episode hinges on little more than Chris's misadventures at the local Laundromat.

The reality was far more complex. During those years, street crime was as much a part of the scene as the neighborhood's 2,600 vacant and abandoned residential buildings, according to a study by the Bedford-Stuyvesant Restoration Corporation; in 1983, the rate of violent crime in Bed-Stuy was 80 percent higher than the citywide average, with nearly twice as many murders per capita as in the city as a whole.

"The image of people afraid to come out of their homes because of drugs and gang warfare was not the reality of how we were living every day," said Doug Jones, a 37-year-old real estate agent who grew up in a brownstone on McDonough Street, adding, "It was very apple pie, nondescript and even a little boring." ■

heads, 'Did you earn your college degree or did you pay for it? Are you stupid?'"

When she started acting, Ms. Perez was advised to take classes to lose her Brooklyn inflections and mannerisms. Instead, she has built an improbable acting career, which began with a chance encounter with the director Spike Lee, on being pretty much what she is: an intense, voluble, working-class Puerto Rican from Bushwick who is indelibly from her own unfashionable patch of turf.

She was born somewhere between 1964 and '66—she declines to be more precise—in the middle of a family of 11 children in Bushwick. Ms. Perez apparently spent part of the time living in group homes or with relatives and got into her share of trouble, but looks back on a place that for all its rough edges was definitely a neighborhood.

"I never thought of it as a tough neighborhood," she said. "I never thought I was poor until someone told me I was."

Casting director Sheila Jaffe said Ms. Perez at times may risk being perceived as too outspoken and aggressive for her own good.

But she thinks even if Ms. Perez does not conform to the Hollywood norm of user-friendly, blue-eyed blondes, she is smart enough and talented enough to make things work. ■

Seinfeld, Come Home?

By **JOHN TIERNEY** | March 5, 1995

A NEW HOPE GRIPPED NEW YORKERS EVER since an item appeared in Liz Smith's gossip column in January. "Jerry Seinfeld is looking to make a permanent move back to New York City," she revealed.

I can understand the excitement, because I, too, have longed for Jerry and the gang to come home. "Seinfeld" always struck me as a troubling paradox. Yes, it captures the travails of Manhattan better than any show ever on television, but it is written and filmed in Los Angeles. Yes, the characters Jerry and George seem to be quintessential New Yorkers, the kind who believe, as John Updike put it, "that people living anywhere else had to be, in some sense, kidding." But

BELOW: *Jerry Seinfeld on West 78th Street and Broadway, not far from his apartment which is on 81st Street and Central Park West.*

the characters' creators and real-life counterparts—Seinfeld and his friend Larry David, the show's executive producer—appear to be doing just fine in California.

After the rumors of their move started, I went out to Studio City to talk to Seinfeld and David, hoping to hear how anxious they are to return, how impossible it is to do good work without the city's daily stimulation. As they sat in their office, where they work at facing desks, Seinfeld explained that he had indeed suggested moving the whole show back to New York for several episodes or maybe even a whole season. The attempts to import the Upper West Side—weekly shipments of H & H bagels, a new $800,000 exterior set this season simulating the sidewalks of Columbus and Amsterdam Avenues—were no substitute for the real thing. But now it looked as if the move would be too complicated for the rest of the staff.

"People have really bought into this Hollywood life style," Seinfeld said. He insisted that he still considers himself a New Yorker and regards his 14 years in Los Angeles as an extended business trip. David, though, said he wasn't sure if he would ever move back—an ambivalence that deeply concerned me, particularly when he said that he hadn't been to New York for two years. How could the Brooklynite responsible for George's neurotic New York psyche be content . . . in Los Angeles?

"George is more or less based on you, isn't he?" I asked David. "I just can't see George out here. Of all the characters, he's the one who shouldn't be able to survive anywhere but New York."

"He definitely is a strong side of me," David said. "George is a good vehicle for a lot of the sick things you would think about doing. No, I couldn't really imagine him out here, either. Probably he'd yell at somebody in his car, and they would follow him home and kill him." ∎

Letterman Celebrates New York

By **BILL CARTER** | October 1, 2001

LATE IN THE SHOW ON HIS FIRST NIGHT BACK after the attacks on New York, following an emotional monologue about the anguish and rage of the country and of New York City, David Letterman broke for a commercial.

With the microphones off, Regis Philbin, a guest on Mr. Letterman's "Late Show" on CBS, leaned over to talk to him.

"He was in agony," Mr. Philbin said later about the show on Sept. 17. "He was so worried about that first segment and what he had said. He was really agonized over that, over whether he could possibly say anything that would matter at a time like this. I said: 'No, it was great. You spoke from the gut.' But I don't think he believed me."

Mr. Letterman, who even in the best of times is afflicted with a chronic self-effacement, said that he had come back on the air and spoken that way to the television audience simply because the mayor had urged New Yorkers to get back as soon as possible to their normal lives.

Jerry Seinfeld was in the midst of a concert tour with his new stand-up comedy act. "I canceled a bunch of dates," he said. "It was a very hard decision, when you could go back to doing comedy. Then I saw the things Letterman was doing. He handled it so well."

In dealing with the catastrophe Mr. Letterman had an advantage of sorts: he was in New York, while Jay Leno was 3,000 miles away in Burbank, Calif. So Mr. Letterman could tell a discreet New York joke and pull it off. He could take advantage of his association with the city, built up over eight years of lambasting New York with the particular kind of humor that natives could love only from one of their own. "Over the years and perhaps unintentionally, 'Late Show' has become a celebration of New York," said Rob Burnett, one of the show's executive producers.

New York has provided Mr. Letterman with targets like taxi drivers who don't believe in brakes and hot-dog vendors with antifreeze in their water, and a ready cast of characters for comedy in the streets, like shopkeepers and tourists.

No joke could touch directly on the tragedy in New York. Instead of selecting from-the-headlines topics for his popular Top 10 lists, as has been the custom, Mr. Letterman gravitated to off-the-wall topics, like "Top 10 Things That Almost Rhyme With Hat" (No. 7: "meat") and "Top 10 Signs Your Wife Is Having an Affair With the Jolly Green Giant (No. 3: "Your last two kids have been green"). None of this has been heavily planned, Ms. Brennan said. "We just come in in the morning," she said, "and sort of see how its going to go."

> "Over the years and perhaps unintentionally, 'Late Show' has become a celebration of New York."

Predictably, Mr. Letterman does not think it has been going especially well. "He hates the shows, as always," Mr. Burnett said. "The president and the mayor have said we need to get back to normal, so Dave is doing his best by hating the shows."

The audience apparently disagrees. Mr. Burnett cited an "unbelievable outpouring" of letters and e-mail, mostly about Mr. Letterman's effort to put words to the nation's reaction to the World Trade Center tragedy.

One example, from a captain in the Emergency Medical Service:

"I know this may sound very corny, but seeing you Monday night made me think that Dave is back and all will be O.K. in time." ■

Woody Allen's Vision: City As Star

By **LESLIE BENNETTS** | March 7, 1986

WOODY ALLEN'S NEW MOVIE, "HANNAH AND Her Sisters," opened on Feb. 7 to rave reviews. The film's cast includes includes Mia Farrow and Michael Caine, but as filmed by Mr. Allen with exquisite care, New York City itself is indisputably one of the movie's stars.

To Mr. Allen, who was born and raised in Brooklyn and is a longtime resident of Manhattan, the city seems a beautiful, glamorous place. He is the first to admit that his is a highly selective vision. "I have an affectionate view of it," he says. "I've just always loved it; I've only seen it as an extremely exciting, wonderful, romantic place, ever since I was taken here as a child. It's sort of automatic with me to use it; any time I make a picture in Manhattan, that's the way I see the city."

Not that Mr. Allen himself fails to see the ugliness. "I'm painfully aware of it," he says. "It depresses me and infuriates me all the time. I probably obsess over it—the constant disintegration of life style in the city."

Mr. Allen's New York is decidedly affluent. "It's clearly an upscale view of the city," says Ezra Swerdlow, the film's production supervisor. One of those people is Miss Farrow, whose own Upper West Side apartment was used as a major interior for the film.

But whatever the actual sites, all are infused with Mr. Allen's sense of the excitement of the city. In one scene, the character he plays emerges from a medical examination at Mount Sinai, burdened with the possibility that he may be seriously ill. As he walks down the street, he thinks aloud: "You're in the middle of New York City. This is your town! You're surrounded by people and traffic and restaurants. How can you just suddenly one day vanish?"

In Mr. Allen's New York, as it turns out, you most joyfully can't. ▪

Scene One: A Fire Escape

By **RICK LYMAN** | February 13, 1998

THE STOREFRONT DOOR GROANED OPEN AND A cloud of warm, fleshy air pushed into Elizabeth Street. "Mary, it's Marty," Martin Scorsese called to the 94-year-old woman sitting in a chair near the window in an otherwise empty butcher shop. The old meat cutter pushed herself out of her chair, squinted toward the door and squealed with delight. "Ah, Marty! It's Marty! You're back!"

Little Italy has changed considerably since an afternoon in 1950 when a terrified 8-year-old boy reluctantly transplanted from Corona, Queens, sat on his grandmother's fire escape and stared down for the first time at the urban cacophony of street kids, winos and wise guys. Many of the Italian-American families have moved out or died off; burgeoning Chinatown has pushed across Canal Street, and there is the usual gentrified

FILM

Spike Lee Tries to Do the Right Thing

By **MICHAEL T. KAUFMAN** | June 25, 1989

EVEN BEFORE "DO THE RIGHT THING," opens, Spike Lee, its producer, director, writer and star, has already got what he expected most from the film: hot debate, heavy discussion and even denunciation from some who think he did the wrong thing.

"Essentially what I hoped was that it would provoke everybody, white and black," said the iconoclastic, Brooklyn-born film maker of the movie, which describes how, on the hottest day of the year, the conflicting group allegiances of generally symbiotic neighbors in Brooklyn's Bedford-Stuyvesant escalate into a tragic killing of a black man by the police and the torching of a white-owned pizza parlor.

"For many white people, there is a view that black people have the vote and they can live next door to us and it's all done with and there's no more racism," Mr. Lee said during a series of interviews conducted by telephone as he shuttled from Los Angeles to Washington, to Atlanta and Houston, promoting the movie. "As far as I'm concerned, racism is the most pressing problem in the United States; and I wanted the film to bring the issue into the forefront where it belongs."

He said that the interviews he has given during the last month have taught him how to take the measure of his interrogators.

"I can tell exactly how white journalists feel about black people by the questions they ask. 'Hey, Spike,' they'll say, 'this Bedford-Stuyvesant looks too clean. Hey, Spike, where are the drugs? Where's the muggers? Hey, I don't see any teenage women throwing their babies out of windows.' Those were these people's perception of black people in general."

He added that magazine cover stories declaring that drugs were a pervasive problem extending through all sectors of American society. "But do those interviewers ask the people who made 'Rain Man' or 'Wall Street' why they did not include drugs in their pictures?" ■

ragout of boutiques and bistros amid the boarded-up storefronts.

But the old neighborhood is still there, if you know where to look and you have the eyes to see it: St. Patrick's School, where Marty struggled under the merciless ministrations of the Sisters of Mercy; the streets, where he made friends and insinuated himself into the life of the neighborhood; the tenements, where he slept, ate and watched endless hours of old movies on television.

Mr. Scorsese, 55, lives on the Upper East Side now. His production company is in a suite of midtown offices overlooking Park Avenue. But it was at his grandmother's apartment, on Elizabeth Street that Marty went out onto the fire escape and looked down with terror into the strange street below.

"The full force of coming back and looking out the window," he said. "It was so different, all this life, the noise, the kids running up and down the street, winos falling down. It was just a nightmare. I'll never forget that image." ■

The Streets of Queens Where Rizzuto Played

By ELLEN BARRY | August 16, 2007

WHEN PHIL RIZZUTO WAS A BOY IN GLEN-
dale, Queens, it was rare to get your hands
on an actual baseball. You played with
Spaldeens wrapped in string, or flapping
old cores patched with adhesive tape, and if
the ball rolled into the sewer the boys went
down after it.

Pearl Meyer Suss, who lived on
the same block as the Rizzuto family, became
closely acquainted with the balls because
they kept smashing through her front
windows, infuriating her mother. In those
days the neighborhood was largely German,
and a row of women appeared in front of
their houses every Friday to scrub their
front stoops by hand.

Phil did not stand out to her at the
time—all the neighborhood boys were
baseball-mad—but a few years later the
broken windows were something the Meyers
could brag about.

"We felt, 'Oh, boy, we really knew him,'"
Mrs. Suss, who is 83, said of the eventual Hall
of Fame shortstop for the Yankees.

Mr. Rizzuto, who died Monday, was
mourned with a special twinge in Glendale,
the Queens neighborhood where he joined in
sandlot games, the kind that used four rocks
as bases. Phil was no richer than any of the
other kids—his father, Fiore, drove a trolley
car on the Myrtle Avenue route—and he was
hardly a memorable physical specimen,
reaching 5 foot 6 as an adult. It was that
quality, his ordinariness, that Sal Calcaterra
has been remembering.

"He played with what he had, that's for
sure," said Mr. Calcaterra, 65, in the cool of
Tee Dee's Tavern around noon. Asked to recall
an anecdote about Mr. Rizzuto, Mr. Calcaterra
told a story about a friend of Mr. Rizzuto's,
known as Indian, who was bludgeoned to
death with a shuffleboard puck in a bar fight.
Then, then he returned to the subject of the
shortstop, who, he said, faced down rejection
with "the feeling of 'I'll show you.'" ∎

ABOVE: *The Scooter, Phil Rizzuto, at Yankee Stadium, 1995.*

Just Another Down-to-Earth Guy

By IRA BERKOW | February 8, 1995

THE BOYS AND GIRLS ASSEMBLED AND
seated restlessly in the folding chairs at the
St. Jude grammar school gymnasium on
204th Street in Manhattan heard their
principal make this announcement yesterday
afternoon: "We just got a call from our
special guest's limousine driver, and he is on
his way here."

"Ooh," came squeals from the kids. He
was coming from midtown, where he and six
others met the news media as the newest
inductees into the Naismith Memorial
Basketball Hall of Fame.

When Kareem Abdul-Jabbar, St. Jude
Class of '61, swept into the auditorium, natty
in blue blazer and charcoal sweater and
slacks and tie and shaved head, he was
greeted with cheers and applause. He shook
hands with the principal, Michael Deegan,
and, when he saw his former eighth-grade
teacher, now retired, the red-haired,

Between Home and Heaven, A Ball Field

By **SARA RIMER** | March 31, 1991

THE APPROACH OF SPRING IN WASHINGTON Heights, the Santo Domingo of New York: People fling open their windows, and into their tenement apartments comes the call of merengue, a dozen different variations blasting from speakers in bodegas and record stores and cars cruising Broadway. And they get ready for baseball.

Every morning at about 5, on their way to factory jobs in New Jersey, the neighborhood's Dominican immigrants see 18-year-old Manny Ramirez—the star of their own George Washington High School baseball team, their own major-league prospect—doing his roadwork on the steep incline of Fort George Hill.

Baseball, with all its fleeting promise, connects all kinds of people in Washington Heights—the commander of the local police precinct, the old man on the corner in the Yankees cap, the coach from Brooklyn, the teen-age girls who call out to Manny Ramirez in the hallways at school.

Last year, the 34th Precinct logged 109 of the city's more than 2,200 homicides, more than any other precinct except the 75th in the East New York section of Brooklyn. In his office, the deputy inspector, Nicholas Estavillo, points to a wall of snapshots of some of the 2,500 guns confiscated in the last five years. Then, smiling, he shows off a mahogany clock from the Dominican-run F. Alfonso Little League. This is a neighborhood, he says, with four separate Little Leagues.

bespectacled Sister Hannah, who came up to just past his elbow, he lowered his 7-foot-2-inch frame and kissed her on the cheek.

Abdul-Jabbar, who grew up close by, in the Dyckman Housing Projects, had come a long way, and not just yesterday afternoon.

"It was at St, Jude," Abdul-Jabbar told the 450 children in the audience, "where I learned values and respect for other people, and learned the importance of an education. I always loved sports—especially baseball when I was a boy, and only began to concentrate on basketball because I had grown too big for baseball. But I remember a priest in the parish here who said I would be too skinny for the N.B.A., and that I had to concentrate on my studies.

"Well, I proved him wrong about the N.B.A., and we laugh about it now. But he was right about school. You have to get a foundation of an education. I loved history, and I majored in history at U.C.L.A."

A girl asked him about his proudest accomplishment. "Well, there were many," he said, "but I am very proud that I got my college degree in four years, and made all-American at the same time." ∎

For fans and players here in Washington Heights, baseball is an escape from the harshness of New York. And it is something else. Dominicans may complain incessantly about the country they left—the disastrous economy, the devalued peso, the lights that are always going out. But they also talk incessantly of going home, where there are long hours working in the sugar-cane fields and factories, and there is baseball.

Javier Del Castillo, 22, is a shortstop from San Pedro de Macoris, a breeding ground for major league shortstops. Mr. Del Castillo is home from college, working at the post office. In free moments at work, he swings a cardboard mailing tube at wadded-up pieces of paper tossed into the air.

"What is there to do on a beautiful, tropical day in the Dominican Republic but play baseball?" he said. "Playing baseball is going to a new world—to paradise." ∎

Hopper's Vision of New York

By **ALFRED KAZIN** | September 7, 1980

IN THE DAYS WHEN MANHATTAN BRIDGE was still open to pedestrians, when you could stroll across the great central promenade of Brooklyn Bridge without being taken hostage, when nothing in this world was such a gift as the light over the East River bursting into a BMT car and breaking up the boredom, I would regularly make my way between Manhattan and Brooklyn with the feeling that these halves of my life were joined not by ceaseless daily travel but by images drawn from paintings of New York.

I did not know there was a New York to love more than a neighborhood, until I saw it in museums.

The trouble with growing up in a Brooklyn tenement was not so much that you were poor—there was nothing but other people's poverty to compare yours with—but that the struggle for existence made everything else seem trivial, unworthy. I had no genial New York images of my own until I discovered John Sloan in the old American Wing of the Metropolitan Museum of Art, Reginald Marsh in the Whitney Museum of American Art when it was on Eighth Street, forgotten prints of Columbia Heights in the Brooklyn Museum.

But there was one exception to the cozy, picturesque painters of New York: Edward Hopper. Unlike so many American paintings just before and after World War II, "representational" and "abstract" alike, his work was not slap-dash, hurried, theatrically self-conscious. The immensely tall, immensely quiet man I often saw walking in Greenwich Village and seemed tensely alone; he reminded me of Virginia Woolf's impression of Robinson Crusoe—"a man staring at a pot."

Hopper for me was like his unprecedented paintings of solitary people staring at the glass in New York bedrooms, coffee shops and offices. Perhaps he had taken the advice of the philosopher Wittgenstein: "Don't think! LOOK!" Yet you could not have guessed what the handsome man was looking at as he edged his way through Washington Square Park. His figures never looked through the glass they were facing. Their masked, identical, hawklike faces were concentrated in thought unavailable to anyone, perhaps, especially to themselves. ∎

The Return Of Andy Warhol

By **JOHN LEONARD** | November 10, 1968

"Since I was shot, everything is such a dream to me. I don't know what anything is about. Like I don't even know whether or not I'm really alive or—whether I died. It's sad. Like I can't say hello or goodbye to people. Life is like a dream." —ANDY WARHOL

On a Sunday afternoon last month, there was a very nice picnic in a courtyard at 5 Ninth Avenue at the foot of Little West 12th Street. The picnickers roasted a pig on a spit and chopped it up with an ax. They also made wine, removing their shoes to tromp on grapes, then conveying the sludge to a press. Children were present, enjoying themselves. And such stars of the Velvet Underground as Viva, Ultra Violet and Nico (with a black and silver saddle slung over her shoulder). And newspaper photographers, movie cameras, tape recorders, microphones. All thrilled under the Oriental lash of reciprocity: snapshots were snapped of people snapping snapshots; tongues and microphones were intertwined; there were various kinds of mirrors to record the various forms of eating.

At the calm eye of this eating stands Andy Warhol, former pop artist (he "retired" three years ago) and prolific film maker: a

ARTISTS

Jean-Michel Basquiat: Hazards Of Sudden Success and Fame

By **MICHAEL WINES** | August 27, 1988

IN A CITY THAT EXALTS SUCCESSFUL ARTISTS in the fashion of rock stars, Jean-Michel Basquiat seemed blessed. When he burst onto the art scene in 1981, his paintings of anguished figures were hailed by some critics as works of genius. Admirers besieged him at Manhattan's hottest night clubs.

Moon-Man, a sort of spectral janitor, silver-haired, deathly pale, oddly angelic behind his shades, inside his zipped-up black leather jacket, looking as though he had dropped from a star. He isn't doing anything; he hardly even moves. But he is the silent magnetic center around which the particles of the party revolve, reminding you of Ezra Pound's: "The fourth; the dimension of stillness;/ And the power over wild beasts." At the same time, he seems vulnerable.

Warhol, a child of the media, is unfailingly courteous to their janissaries. Every impertinence, every ghoulish probe, is patiently endured, for he needs us as much as we need him. "Well, really, I'm still too frightened to think about it." What he doesn't want to think about is the day last June when Valerie Solanas, a bit-player in one of his movies, entered the Factory—his studio—and shot him.

Warhol is the New Art. Even Norman Mailer in his recent incarnation as a movie maker admits indebtedness. Warhol exemplifies it in the division among per-former (for the media) and promoter (that superb entrepreneurial instinct which is responsible for the Electric Circus). The facade is personality, the function is games—play within the permutations permitted by the playthings, which are machines. And he is consistent, from silk-screen to stationary movie camera to tape-recorded novel. His art is an extended commercial for gadgets. ∎

Sales of his art grossed millions of dollars.

Mr. Basquiat was 27 years old when he was found dead in his apartment in the East Village two weeks ago from what friends say was an overdose of heroin.

Art experts have called his death a personal tragedy and a major loss to the art world.

Some say he resented being a black man whose fate twisted with the whims of an all-white jury of artistic powers. Others say he pined for fame but was crushed by its burdens. Some friends believe greedy art dealers and collectors exploited him. Some say wealth fed his longtime appetite for drugs.

"One knew from the start that he was going to live out his own time span," Henry Geldzahler, the former curator of 20th-century art at the Metropolitan Museum, said. "He lived very high, very fast, and he did a lot of great things."

Many of Mr. Basquiat's associates acknowledge that they were aware of his growing drug problems, and some say they had urged him to lessen or stop his use of drugs. But only one friend—Andy Warhol, Mr. Basquiat's idol—seemed to have had any influence. Friends say the artist dissuaded Mr. Basquiat from using heroin, and that Mr. Warhol's death last year removed one of the few reins on Mr. Basquiat's mercurial behavior and appetite for narcotics.

Mr. Basquiat's angry, primitive figures, boldly colored on canvases and on such everyday objects as doors and refrigerators, were judged by critics to show both an astonishing precocity and an innocence rare among contemporary artists. Basquiats have sold at auction recently for prices between $32,000 and $99,000, and they are "extremely sought after by both European and American collectors," said Susan Dunne, head of contemporary art sales at Christie's. ∎

Aura of Whitman's Brooklyn Lives On

By **THOMAS LASK** | May 16, 1971

BEYOND A NAME GIVEN TO A SQUARE OFF THE public path, there are no physical reminders of Walt Whitman in the Brooklyn Heights he loved so much. More's the pity, because Whitman would have loved and reveled in the informality of the Heights today, in the casualness of its people, their tolerance and public concerns.

He would have enjoyed seeing young mothers walking their baby carriages; husky workmen mixing cement for the high-price apartments off Cadman Plaza, high enough to cut off sight of any hills; strings of children shepherded by anxious teachers; older people catching a bit of sunlight; a man reading a paper on the morning stoop.

The silhouettes of the houses along Columbia Heights and Willow and Hicks Streets, among others, would appear familiar. Two houses, 40 and 38 Hicks Streets, between Middagh and Poplar, were there when the poet lived in the area, although 38 looks so shabby he would never know it. The siding, bare and in need of paint, is falling in; windows are barred or broken. And the place looks deserted except the street floor, where the Robert Fulton Civic League has its headquarters.

The poet's name lingers on in the Heights only in Whitman Close, an interior square of the Cadman Houses project on the site of the shop that published his "Leaves of Grass" in 1855. But of one thing Whitman can be certain: There are probably more copies of "Leaves of Grass" for a square foot of real estate in Brooklyn Heights than in any other part of town.

Although Walt Whitman was quite willing to take on the cosmos ("I am large, I contain multitudes"), he had a close relationship to Brooklyn. He came to it in 1823 when he was 4 years old and lived there more or less until middle age. It was Brooklyn that nurtured his optimism, that provided the feeling of kinship for the dynamic, invigorating humanity that he celebrated in his poems and for the different trades, pursuits and classes of people he encountered.

And it was in Brooklyn that his "Leaves of Grass," the unique volume that stands solitary in the annals of American letters, was conceived, printed and published.

It was no wonder that he memorialized the beauties of Brooklyn in his poetry ("Brooklyn of ample hills was mine") and that the poem cited by his biographer Gay Wilson Allen as the masterpiece of the first two editions of "Leaves of Grass" was called "Crossing Brooklyn Ferry." ∎

Putting Poetry Back Into Langston Hughes's House

By **JENNIFER KINGSON BLOOM** | April 9, 1995

WHEN ALBERT DAVIS BOUGHT THE FOUR-story brownstone at 20 East 127th Street in 1985, he knew that the writer Langston Hughes had lived there. But he was amazed to find, in the basement and attic, three of Mr. Hughes's typewriters, his piano and desk, dozens of original manuscripts and

WRITERS

"Howl" was Ginsberg's Country

By **FRANK BRUNI** | April 7, 1997

FOR ALL THE WORLDWIDE ATTENTION THAT Allen Ginsberg received, he was a creature and icon principally of downtown Manhattan, his world view forged in its crucible of political and sexual passions, his eccentricities nurtured by those of its peculiar demimonde, his individual myth entwined with that of the bohemian East Village in which he made his home.

"He embodied the East Village and the Lower East Side," Bill Morgan, a friend and Mr. Ginsberg's archivist, said. "It affected him, and he affected it. He was a lightning rod for the political activism and social issues that played out here."

Mr. Ginsberg died of liver cancer on Saturday in his apartment on East 13th Street near First Avenue at the age of 70. He had lived in this residence for about six months but had previously spent at least two decades in an apartment only a block away, on East 12th Street near First Avenue. Before that, he resided for many years on East 10th Street near Avenue C, friends and associates said.

These were his stamping grounds, the social laboratory he inhabited for the vast majority of his years since the late 50's, after

> "He embodied the East Village and the Lower East Side."

migrating south from Columbia University. Columbia, which he attended in the 40's, was where he met Jack Kerouac, Neal Cassady, William Burroughs and others at the forefront of the Beat Generation.

But the East Village and the Lower East Side were where he became a legend. In "Howl!" written in 1955-56, Mr. Ginsberg mined lower Manhattan for such images as people who "walked all night with their shoes full of blood on the snowbank docks waiting for a door in the East River to open to a room full of steam-heat and opium."

"The whole East Village ferment of the 60's began with what Allen did," Tom Savage, a Manhattan poet and longtime friend of Mr. Ginsberg, said. "The way downtown Manhattan evolved would never have happened without Allen Ginsberg." ▪

---

historic pictures, even an old tax return.

The cache inspired Mr. Davis, who had only a passing familiarity with Mr. Hughes's work, to turn the house into an informal museum. The piano, desk and a typewriter—a gray Royal manual—are displayed in a first-floor parlor. By appointment, visitors may tour the upstairs office where Mr. Hughes wrote poetry, plays, essays and nonfiction, and the bedroom where Mr. Davis's children found a copy of one of Mr. Hughes's musical plays, "Tambourines to Glory."

Mr. Davis, an engineer who serves on Community Board 11, said the artifacts

led him to create the shrine. "Here you have a landmark building, a famous African-American writer," he said. "What else could you do?"

Mr. Hughes lived in the house for 20 years until his death in 1967; it was a rooming house then and when Mr. Davis bought it. Mr. Davis, too, has several boarders, one of whom, David Mills, has also been inspired by the legacy of where he lives: in February, he began holding monthly poetry readings in the parlor. The first was on Feb. 5, four days after what would have been Mr. Hughes's 93rd birthday. It drew 200 people. ▪

Tom Wolfe as Novelist of New York

By **MERVYN ROTHSTEIN** | October 13, 1987

ABOVE: *Tom Wolfe in his Manhattan apartment in 1998.*

"IT'S OUTRAGEOUS THE WAY PEOPLE CONDUCT their lives in New York," Tom Wolfe said. "And yet I don't want to live anywhere else. I don't despair, because I find the comedy so rich. At the same time that people do vile things, they also create hilariously funny spectacles. The city dominates you if you're a player, but it never fails you if you're a viewer. It's always entertaining, and it's always funny, even in its grimmest moments."

Mr. Wolfe has been observing this city for a quarter century, and now he has written a book about it—a novel called "The Bonfire of the Vanities."

There is a Wall Street bond salesman who lives on Park Avenue, gets involved in a strange incident in the South Bronx with two black youths and winds up enmeshed in the city's criminal-justice system. There are Fifth Avenue socialites, crooks, cops, a Bronx district attorney, a Hasidic landlord, a politically connected black minister and a white mayor he hates—just about all of whom try to use the bond dealer's dilemma to their advantage. But the main character, Mr. Wolfe said, is New York.

"It struck me that nobody any longer seemed to be writing novels of the city, in the sense that Balzac and Zola wrote novels of Paris and Dickens and Thackeray wrote novels of London," Mr. Wolfe said, sitting in his East 60's town house and wearing his signature white vested suit. "And it was sort of strange to me that in this really bizarre period there are not novels of New York. And I think that although there is a central character, I always wanted in a way for the main character to be New York, and the way the city dominates its players and drives them to do reckless things."

Hence the title. "It wasn't a perfect analogy," he said. "In the real 'bonfire of the vanities' Savonarola sent his 'Red Guard' units into people's homes to drag out their vanities—which were anything from false eyelashes to paintings with nudes in them, including Botticellis. This bonfire is more the fire created by the vain people themselves, under the pressure of the city of New York. It may happen in other places, but it certainly happens here. People are always writing about the energy of New York. What they really mean is the status ambitions of people in New York. That's the motor in this town. That's what makes it exciting—and it's also what makes it awful many times."

One other thing likely to come out of the novel is gossip. The scene is New York, the situations are realistic, and readers are likely to wonder if they can match real people to the characters. They can't, Mr. Wolfe said—the characters are composites. "In some cases they're not even composites," he said. "They're made up. This isn't a roman a clef. If I had wanted to write about real people I'd write about them in nonfiction, as I've done before."

In the end, Mr. Wolfe said, what New York is really about is power. "Money alone won't do," he said. "The ultimate certification of your status is seeing people jump, and New York is a city set up to see people jump." ∎

WRITERS

I Write in Brooklyn. Get Over It.

By **COLSON WHITEHEAD** | March 2, 2008

I LIVE IN BROOKLYN. I MOVED HERE 14 years ago for the cheap rent. It was a little embarrassing because I was raised in Manhattan, and so I was a bit of a snob about the other boroughs. At the time there was a big buzz about the "Black Renaissance" of Fort Greene. It was one big house party thrown by Spike Lee and Branford Marsalis, Rosie Perez swinging from the chandelier. Who doesn't want to be part of a vibrant cultural scene? That didn't happen, but it was cheap, and I grew to love it.

> "What's it like to write in Brooklyn?" I expect it's like writing in Manhattan, but there aren't as many tourists, or like writing in Paris, but there aren't as many people speaking French.

It's changed a lot. As you may have heard, all the writers are in Brooklyn these days. It's the place to be. You're simply not a writer if you don't live here. Google "brooklyn writer" and you'll get, *Did you mean: the future of literature as we know it?* I have a hard time understanding all the hype. I dig it here and all, but it's just a place. It does not have magical properties.

In interviews, I get asked a lot, "What's it like to write in Brooklyn?" I expect it's like writing in Manhattan, but there aren't as many tourists, or like writing in Paris, but there aren't as many people speaking French. What do they expect me to say? "I built my desk out of wooden planks taken from the authentic rubble of Ebbets Field. Have I mentioned how I still haven't forgiven the Dodgers for moving to Los Angeles?"

Occasionally you hear the Brooklyn legends that feed the mystique. There was the famous case of the language poet from Red Hook who grew despondent when the Shift key on her MacBook broke. She couldn't write for weeks. She jumped into the enchanted, glowing waters of the Gowanus Canal. And she was cured! The metaphors came rushing back. With eccentric spacing between the letters, but still. Now you see people jumping off the Union Street Bridge all the time.

There are demons out there to keep you from working. They have switchblades, bicycle chains and adventuresome tailors. That's what it's like to write in Brooklyn.

I never did meet Spike Lee. He lives in Manhattan now. ■

BELOW: *Colson Whitehead received a MacArthur Fellowship, often referred to as a "genius grant," in 2002.*

I

t's endlessly chaotic. It's endlessly confusing. It's just plain endless: New York City's transportation system has 722 miles of subway tracks, 13,237 taxis, 12,507 bus stops, 11,871 traffic lights, 2,027 bridges, a dozen or so tunnels, a handful of public and private ferry operators, two major airports (with a third in New Jersey— more about that later), a couple of heliports and one tramway.

Its size and reach make the city's transportation system a unique aspect of the New York identity. Other cities have subways—the one in Seoul, South Korea, carries more people every day than New York's does—and the one in London is considerably older: British sandhogs

Take the A Train

TRANSPORTATION

▲ PAGE 58

were digging their tunnels while the Yankees and the Confederates were still fighting the Civil War.

More than in other places, though, the New York subway defines the city. Where else is it so much a part of a city's personality that lyrics like "Take the A train" or "The Bronx is up but the Battery's down, the people ride in a hole in the ground" instantly catch on? Where else could you make a movie like "The Taking of Pelham One Two Three," which starred a No. 6 train as itself? Where else would people put up with so many strange sights and smells—the unmistakable alcohol breath of the man in the three-piece suit next to you, the little dog peeking out from the green ski jacket of the man next to him, the woman next to him hurriedly applying her makeup?

That small sampling hints at something important about the

▲ PAGE 60

airports for a mayor who refused to disembark in Newark. When his flight landed there, he bellowed that the ticket said New York and this isn't New York. There was only one way to get Fiorello H. La Guardia off the plane: the pilot

◄ PAGE 62

subway: It's decidedly democratic. The billionaire mayor and the welfare mother, seen-it-all oldtimers and wide-eyed newcomers—they all get the same service, for the whole city is one big transit zone. From furthest Bronx to the Battery is about 19 miles. A single fare will take you as far as you want for as long as you want.

The subways have survived everything: breakdowns, fatal accidents, even the deterioration that came when hard times forced cash-strapped transit officials to skimp on maintenance. There's still no guarantee that you'll understand what the conductor says on the garble-prone public-address system. But the subways are cleaner nowadays, and safer than in the 1970's and 1980's. They are also less stylish than when the system opened in 1904. On opening day, the passen-gers dressed as if they were going to a ball. The women wore evening gowns, the men top hats.

The subways soon remade New York in the way that Lewis and Clark—and the westward-bound pioneers who followed them—had remade the United States in the preceding century. Old New York was packed into Lower Manhattan. Where the stately New York Public Library now rises above Fifth Avenue and

Forty-second Street was a reservoir for drinking water until the 1890s. That was the country in those days, far from the center of things, and people had no choice but to live in uncomfortable, unsafe tenements that were within walking distance of where the jobs were. The subways let the city spread out, to everyone's relief—and the construction industry's benefit.

There's more to transpor-tation in New York than the subways, of course. In the heyday of the railroads, Grand Central Terminal rolled out the red carpet and billed itself as the gateway to a continent. Now it is just another commuter station, the gateway to Pelham and Poughkeepsie—in the name of efficiency, Amtrak switched all its long-distance trains from Grand Central to Pennsylvania Station in 1991.

When airplanes came along, New York named one of its

▼ PAGE 94

returned to the cockpit and flew twenty-one miles to an airport within the city limits.

Take that flight now and you'll cruise over a jumble of taxis, buses, trucks, limousines and cars with gotta-get-there drivers pounding their dashboards. This is traffic so jammed that somebody invented a word to describe stop-and-go driving at its worst: gridlock. Crossing the city's bridges in bumper-to-bumper formation, most drivers never take a close look at the Verrazano-Narrows Bridge (the nation's longest suspension span) or the George Washington Bridge (whose two levels are nicknamed George and Martha). The cables can withstand a pull of several hundred million pounds, and at night they glimmer like necklaces.

On the sidewalks, pedestrians search out the shortest, fastest route from here to there. Reporters call it news when they can walk across town faster than the crosstown bus. In other cities, people call the ones who cross in the middle of the block—or when the light is red—jaywalkers. In New York, they call them New Yorkers.

The Disappearing Trolley Car
Still Rings a Bell in Their Hearts

By **MCCANDLISH PHILLIPS** | September 4, 1957

THERE IS A SORT OF TWILIGHT ZONE IN THE history of things when they are yet too young for cherished memory and too old for use. It is there that the trolley car dwells today, a thing of the too recent past.

A generation ago, 3,000 cars rasped and grated over Brooklyn. Now there is one line left, and that without passengers.

But if trolley cars are gone, trolley fans remain. Chief among them is Everett A. White, curator of the Trolley Museum of New York and a man who needs no lectures on the fragility of human institutions. Mr. White and 60 men of stern resolve have appointed themselves interim custodians of the trolley car.

There is something about the trolley that suggests the providential defiance of a principle of locomotion. The Toonerville Trolley may have been a caricature, but it drew abundantly on fact. Most old trolleys looked a bit improbable. Inside, where the motorman stood, there was a magnificent jumble of gears and gauges and handles and boxes and pipes and pedals and wheels. They may have been the work of mad genius, but they worked.

Mr. White and his friends have spent $2,400 to snatch four old cars from the death fingers of the scrap dealers. The museum sells about 60 $2-a-year passes that give the buyers the right to come down and work on the cars whenever they care to. Ten or fifteen years from now, he thinks, people will see trolley cars for the things of beauty they really were. ∎

BELOW: *Everett A. White at the controls one of the trolley cars at the Trolley Museum of New York.*

Midair Rescue Lifts Passengers From Stranded East River Tram

By **JENNIFER 8. LEE** | April 19, 2006

A four-minute trip on the Roosevelt Island Tramway turned into a harrowing ordeal that lasted hours as a series of power failures left about 70 people suspended hundreds of feet in the air, forcing a daring late-night rescue over the East River.

About 11 p.m., after the passengers on two tram cars, one headed in each direction, had been hanging for more than six hours, rescuers began moving the people in the Roosevelt Island-bound one. Passengers were

Aerial Tram To Roosevelt Island Opens With a Splash—on O'Dwyer

By **FRED FERRETTI** | May 18, 1976

AERIAL TRAMWAY SERVICE CONNECTING Manhattan with the city's newest urban community on Roosevelt Island was formally inaugurated with champagne and public expressions of hope for the city's future.

But, as usually happens with historic occurrences here, the ceremonies quickly became informal and a backdrop for a series of those awkward municipal embarrassments so dear to the hearts of New Yorkers.

The opening of the 3,100-foot connection between the East Side and the city's still-abuilding "New Town" in the East River was marked by Mayor Beame, who welcomed the first skyriders to "Roosevelt Avenue," and then smashed a bottle of New York State champagne against one of the two trams,

drenching City Council President Paul O'Dwyer, lapel to knee.

The mayor called it "a streetcar in the sky," and said it was one of the city's major achievements of the year—the others being Operation Sail and the July 4 planned festival, the continuing bicentennial observances and the Democratic National Convention.

Then it was time for the official christening. Mr. Beame swung the bottle, and it burst with a great splash gushing over Mr. O'Dwyer.

The City Council president, a politician with as much aplomb as anyone in the business, reached to his suit front, drew his finger across the wetness, put it into his mouth with a sipping sound, then said, "Finger Lakes District. Definitely. And dry." ▪

pulled from the side door and loaded into an orange wire gondola. By midnight, 22 of the approximately 50 people in the Roosevelt Island-bound tram had been rescued in two trips, including 12 children and an elderly woman who was using a walker.

Cheers erupted when the first group, with eight children and five adults, touched ground at the Roosevelt Island terminal about 11:30 p.m. The children exchanged high-fives with Mayor Michael R. Bloomberg. They were greeted with juice, cookies and, for several Hasidic Jews in the first group, matzo.

Rescuers were still debating whether to use a crane with a basket to rescue the remaining passengers. If not, they planned to use the gondola, which had crawled the 3,100-foot-long stretch of cable with self-generated diesel power.

"We want to get out of this with nobody injured," the mayor said, "and hopefully we learned something about how this will not happen again."

The ordeal began shortly before 5 p.m. when the power went out, leaving the two tram cars motionless on cables that rise as high as 250 feet above the East River between the East Side of Manhattan and Roosevelt Island.

Officials said the diesel generator that powers the system failed, and then the backup generator stopped working as well. Efforts to crank the cars manually also proved fruitless.

It was the second time the tram had stalled for hours in the past eight months, raising questions about the aging system, which went into service in 1976. "They have new cabs, new windows, new cables," said Judith A. Berdy, president of the Roosevelt Island Historical Society, "but it's old equipment." ▪

New Terminal the Heart Of City's Transit System

February 2, 1913

GRAND CENTRAL STATION AS THE MAIN entrance to New York City is naturally a most important point in the local rapid transit system. The present Interborough Subway was laid out to pass its doors, and the new Lexington Avenue Subway will come down its eastern side. These lines were designed to reach the Grand Central Station because of its existence, but to them must be added the very important Steinway Tunnel line, which will run across Times Square and was built from the end of 42nd Street.

So it will happen that, wonderful as is the new Grand Central Station, from the engineering point of view, the complex of subways just outside of it will be equally worthy of attention. The solid rock on which this part of Manhattan is built will in the next three or four years be absolutely honeycombed with rapid transit lines, and the ingenuity of the engineers will be taxed to the uttermost. ■

BELOW: *Plans to build a tower directly over Grand Central Terminal, shown here in the late 1970's, were stopped 1975.*

A Glittery Destination As Refurbished Grand Central Terminal Reopens

By **SUSAN SACHS** | October 2, 1998

ONCE THREATENED WITH DEMOLITION, gnawed by decades of urban grime, obscured by ungainly advertising signs, corroded by roof leaks and just plain unloved by the 500,000 people who sprint through its cavernous halls each day on the way to somewhere else, Grand Central Terminal celebrated its rebirth as a lustrous train station that ranks as a destination in its own right.

With sunlight pouring through steel-ribbed skylights and twin marble staircases curling to a platform on the east side of the main concourse, the 85-year-old structure is once again so imposing that it dwarfed those who came to praise it during a spirited rededication ceremony.

"The 'grand' has truly been put back into the Grand Central Terminal," declared E. Virgil Conway, chairman of the Metropolitan Transportation Authority, his voice so distorted by the echoing marble walls that it was indistinguishable from those simultaneously announcing track numbers for the next trains to Connecticut.

Grand Central's grandeur faded in the 1950s as rail travel declined. Its once pristine interior halls were rented out for billboards, and by 1968, developers were talking about surrounding the terminal with high-rise buildings and demolishing the main concourse. It was saved, after a 10-year court battle, with the help of preservationists who enlisted the high-profile help of Jacqueline Kennedy Onassis. ■

Cleansing "Triumphant Portal" Ceiling

By **JAMES BARRON** | February 3, 1996

THE KEEPERS OF GRAND CENTRAL TERMINAL are betting that what was good enough for the Sistine Chapel will be good enough for the 83-year-old train station. Like the Michelangelo fresco at the Vatican, the vaulted sky ceiling over the main concourse in Grand Central is about to get a soap-and-water scrubbing.

The cleansing of the star constellations and zodiac signs, which over the years have gone from glittering gold on bright blue to algae green under a thick coat of grime, is intended to restore the splendor of the Beaux-Arts terminal that opened in 1913 as "a triumphant portal to New York," in the proud but immodest characterization of its architect, Whitney Warren.

Grand Central quickly became a leak-stained, mildewed portal. In the 1940's, its owner, the New York Central Railroad,

replaced the original plaster ceiling, not by touching up the paint but by bolting and gluing on a whole new tableau made of 4-by-8-foot panels. A similar but less ornate constellation was then painted on.

Over the last few years some art historians have maintained that the 1940's panels should be removed and the more detailed 1913 ceiling restored. But the New York Central's successor, the Metro-North Commuter Railroad, ultimately decided to restore the 1940's ceiling.

"We spent an infinite amount of time investigating what would work," said Susan Fine, Metro-North's director of real estate and the executive in charge of the restoration. "What we needed to find was an extremely gentle way of getting the dirt off without contaminating, discoloring or burnishing the existing ceiling."

In other words, no abrasiveness, no bleach and no residue. She and the architect overseeing the restoration, James W. Rhodes, settled on a nontoxic product called Simple Green. ∎

ABOVE RIGHT AND BELOW: *The Main Concourse after the completion of a $197 million renovation project. The cleaned ceiling reveals the 2,500 stars that had been completely obscured by decades of grime.*

New Station Open for Business

November 27, 1910

THE PENNSYLVANIA STATION IN SEVENTH Avenue, between 32nd and 33rd Streets, opened to passengers between New York and points south, west, and southwest at 9:30 o'clock last night. A throng of some 2,000 persons was on hand when the big doors leading to the main station, from the Seventh Avenue side, swung open.

A little man ran through first and, running all the way, reached the first ticket booth to be opened and bought a ticket to Elizabeth, N.J. He has the distinction of being the first person to buy a ticket in the new station for a destination not on Long Island. (The Long Island service was inaugurated several weeks ago.)

As the crowd passed through the doors, into the vast concourse were heard exclamations of wonder, for none had any idea of the architectural beauty of the new structure. From end to end the station was ablaze with lights.

Baggage men were standing at attention waiting to check the first pieces of baggage while the station master, tall and military looking, hurried about to see that everything went as it should.

The first train to leave the new station this morning was a local for Perth Amboy, N.J. It was followed 28 minutes later by a through train for Philadelphia, Baltimore, Washington, Jacksonville, Atlanta, Birmingham, New Orleans and other cities in the southeast and southwest.

The opening of the station marked an end of the Pennsylvania's 23rd Street Ferry service to Jersey City. The last ferry west to Jersey City left New York soon after midnight. ▪

ABOVE: *Penn Station at rush hour in 1944. Its demolition in 1963 led to the creation of New York's Landmarks Preservation Commission.*

New Grandeur For Penn Station In Latest Plan

By **CHARLES V. BAGLI** | July 4, 2007

IT BEGAN AS A PROPOSAL TO RESTORE THE Beaux-Arts grandeur of the old Pennsylvania Station. It grew into a sweeping plan to transform the area around the station into a district of gleaming office towers. Now it is growing again.

In the next three weeks, two of the city's largest developers will unveil new plans for rebuilding the station, moving Madison Square

Rail Stations

Editorial: Farewell to Penn Station

October 30, 1963

UNTIL THE FIRST BLOW FELL NO ONE WAS convinced that Penn Station really would be demolished or that New York would permit this monumental act of vandalism against one of the largest and finest landmarks of its age of Roman elegance. Somehow someone would surely find a way to prevent it at the last minute—not-so-little Nell rescued by the hero—even while the promoters displayed the flashy renderings of the new sports arena and somewhat less than imperial commercial buildings to take its place.

It's not easy to knock down nine acres of travertine and granite, 84 Doric columns, a vaulted concourse of extravagant, weighty grandeur, classical splendor modeled after royal Roman baths, rich detail in solid stone, architectural quality in precious materials that set the stamp of excellence on a city. But it can be done. It can be done if the motivation is great enough, and it has been demonstrated that the profit motivation in this instance was great enough.

Monumental problems almost as big as the building itself stood in the way of preservation; but it is the shame of New York, of its financial and cultural communities, its politicians, philanthropists and planners, and of the public as well, that no serious effort was made. A rich and powerful city, noted for its resources of brains, imagination and money, could not rise to the occasion. The final indictment is of the values of our society.

Any city gets what it admires, will pay for, and, ultimately, deserves. Even when we had Penn Station, we couldn't afford to keep it clean. We want and deserve tin-can architecture in a tin-horn culture. And we will probably be judged not by the monuments we build but by those we have destroyed. ∎

Garden, replacing the Hotel Pennsylvania, and erecting a pair of skyscrapers, one of which would be taller than the Empire State Building, over the site of the existing station.

Though the new plan is broadly similar to a proposal offered a year ago, it is different in several important ways, starting with the cost: $14 billion, double that of the original plan, a real estate executive who has seen the plan said. It is also bigger than anticipated: the entire plan, involving buildings on six adjacent blocks, would create 10 million square feet of new office space off West 33rd Street, as much as in the old World Trade Center.

The developers, Stephen M. Ross and Steven Roth, have also burnished their vision for the station, which would be renamed after Senator Daniel Patrick Moynihan, who championed the original idea. Civic groups and the head of the City Planning Commission, Amanda M. Burden, had complained that last year's plan treated the underground station as an afterthought, without a grand public space worthy of the country's busiest transit hub.

The new plan would try to recapture the imposing aura of the original station inside the James A. Farley Post Office across the street, with a vast, street-level waiting room under a glass canopy that would spill sunlight onto the concourse two levels below. But it is far from a done deal. ∎

Our Subway Opens; 150,000 Try It
Mayor McClellan Runs the First Official Train

October 28, 1904

FOR THE FIRST TIME IN HIS LIFE, FATHER Knickerbocker went underground yesterday, he and his children, to the number of 150,000, amid the tooting of whistles and the firing of salutes, for the first ride in a subway car which for years had been scoffed at as an impossibility. New York's dream of rapid transit became a reality at exactly 2:35:30 o'clock yesterday afternoon, when the running of trains with passengers began.

With a silver controller Mayor McClellan started the first train, the official train which bore John B. McDonald, the contractor who dug the subway; William Barclay Parsons, chief engineer of the Rapid Transit Commission; and most of the other men who made the subway a reality.

The mayor liked his job as motorman so well that he stayed at the controller until the train reached Broadway and 103rd Street, when he yielded the place to the company's motor instructor.

OFFICIAL TRAIN ON TIME
The official train made its run exactly on time, arriving at 145th Street in exactly 25 minutes, and all along the way crowds of excited New Yorkers were collected around the little entrances talking about the unheard trains that they knew were dashing by below. All afternoon the crowds hung around the curious-looking little stations, waiting for heads and shoulders to appear and grow into bodies. Much as the subway has been talked about, New York was not prepared for this scene.

SEVERAL CASES OF "FIRSTS"
There are a few "firsts" to be noted in writing the history of this great change in New York transportation. The first man to give up his seat to a woman in New York's subway was F. B. Shipley of Philadelphia. The first man to ask for a transfer refused to give his name. It was on the return trip of the official train. He wanted to get off at Spring Street. It was 41 minutes after the start from 145th Street when, headed by Mr. Orr, the leaders of the subway emerged from the little station at City Hall Park and walked rapidly across the pavement. The mayor was smoking a cigar which looked guiltily short, as if he had lighted it on the train. ∎

LEFT: *The New York City Transit Authority was formed in 1953 and, shortly afterwards, subway tokens were introduced. A ride at the time cost 15 cents.*

In 35 Years, Subways Have Greatly Changed the City, And the Citizens As Well

By **ERNEST LA FRANCE** | November 26, 1939

FROM 8 O'CLOCK TO 9 IN THE MORNING, the briefest of intervals, the expresses thunder into the subway stations at Grand Central, Brooklyn Bridge and 14th Street with their freight shoe salesmen, private secretaries, beautiful shopgirls and plumbers. From 5 o'clock to 6 in the afternoon they collect the identical freight for distribution to remote cots far from the battlefronts of industry and commerce. The process, somewhat akin to the moving belt in mass production, has just passed its 35th birthday.

Today the city has more than a billion dollars invested in three subway systems totaling 273 miles (133 miles of them actually underground), and we take our cellar railroad calmly. The standard reaction to its coming, however, was bitter opposition from politicians, surface and elevated lines, and property owners fearful of the effect it would have on business.

On paper, the first link had existed since 1897, when William Barclay Parsons, chief engineer of the Rapid Transit Commission, submitted plans for a line rushing northward from City Hall to Van Cortlandt Park, with a spur from 96th Street through Harlem to Bronx Park, using part of the Bronx Third Avenue "El." Actual construction was blocked until March 24, 1900, a month after the city signed a $35 million contract with its builder, John B. McDonald, who had enlisted the financial aid of August Belmont—later the founder of the operating company, the I.R.T. With its extension to Atlantic Avenue, the route totaled 25.26 miles.

One lasting result of the subway was a beneficent decentralization from the crowded area within a four-mile radius of City Hall.

When the subway opened, Manhattan was crowding half the city's 4 million population into part of its 22.2 square miles and had reached a record density of 400,000 persons per square mile in part of the Lower East Side. The subway first poured new hordes into Manhattan's West Side. But as the I.R.T. and B.M.T. drove deeper into Brooklyn, Manhattan deflated. By 1930, when the two subway systems had completed their lines, it had only four-fifths of the population it had held in 1901. ∎

BELOW: *Crowds wait for the chance to ride the new subway in 1904.*

Subway Token, Currency of the City, Dies at 50

By RICHARD PÉREZ-PEÑA | March 15, 2003

THE NEW YORK CITY SUBWAY TOKEN, TOOL and talisman of city life since Vincent R. Impellitteri was mayor, is dead at age 50.

The causes of death were technology and economics.

Tokens will be sold for the last time on Saturday, April 12. After 12:01 a.m. on Sunday, May 4—the moment at which fares will rise, with the price of a single trip jumping to $2 from $1.50—any token plinked into a turnstile will be spit back out. Bus fareboxes will still accept the token—along with 50 cents cash, thank you—through the end of the year.

The death of the token has been a planned, gradual demise, conceived in the 1980's and set in motion in 1994, when the first electronic turnstile was installed and the first MetroCard sold. Handling all those tokens—emptying them from turnstiles, delivering bags of them to token booths, counting them out to riders—is cumbersome and expensive, and transit officials have long looked forward to the day when most of their business with riders would involve exchanges of electrons, not metal and paper.

The token can look forward to an afterlife as a nostalgia fetish, a cherished little piece of a bygone New York, like Brooklyn Dodgers gear, Automats and Checker cabs. But for now, there is little lament for the token's passing.

"We're not in mourning," said Gene Russianoff, staff lawyer for the Straphangers Campaign, the riders' advocacy group. "The MetroCard is a better deal for riders. I have such powerful associations with the token from most of my life, so yeah, there's some emotional attachment, but it's no more than nostalgia."

The token is survived by the turnstile and the farebox, as well as Fun Pass and other members of the MetroCard family. The transit agency will not say what will become of the remains, 60 million of them, except that it has no plans for disposing of them. ■

With F Trains On the C Line, The G Runs on . . .

By RALPH BLUMENTHAL | July 18, 2008

HOW MANY ENGLISH MAJORS DOES IT TAKE to figure out the meaning of a subway "Service Changes" poster?

Let's see, between 12:01 a.m. Saturday, and 5 a.m. Monday, F trains were replacing the C in Brooklyn. G trains were replacing the F between Hoyt and Schermerhorn Streets and Stillwell Avenue. The poster explained that F trains were running between 179th and Jay Streets, then on the C line between Hoyt and Schermerhorn Streets and Euclid Avenue.

Travelers like me going from Manhattan to Brooklyn were to transfer at Hoyt-Schermerhorn for the G, making all F station stops to Stillwell Avenue. (Or was it and transfer at Hoyt-Schermerhorn for the F, making all C station stops to Euclid Avenue?)

I got off my southbound F just as the G rumbled in on the next track. I jumped aboard. But instead of seeing my regular F stops (Bergen Street, Carroll Street, etc.) I was in unfamiliar territory. I finally got off at Classon Avenue, thoroughly disoriented.

A young woman saw my confusion and offered a quick diagnosis. "F train problem, huh?" she said, calling the train by an unprintable nickname. She explained that at

Surviving in the Land Down Under

By **RANDY KENNEDY** | August 29, 2004

THE INTREPID TRAVEL WRITER AND NOVELIST Paul Theroux once spent a week in 1981 riding the New York City subway and conveyed the advice of a friend about how to ride more safely: "You have to look as if you're the one with the meat cleaver."

Fortunately, that advice can be ignored these days. The graffiti is gone, crime is down, service is (mostly) reliable and almost no one carries a cleaver anymore, except maybe a sous-chef on his way to work at a restaurant where you will not be able to get a reservation. The guidelines for a better subway experience no longer speak to the fear of being mugged; they speak to the much more pervasive fear of being annoyed (and they also try to help you avoid annoying others).

Here are some things to remember:

AVOID EYE CONTACT AT ALL COSTS— This does not mean you or your fellow riders are unfriendly. When you are locked underground in a lurching metal room with a crowd of strangers in a big city, it is simply much easier if everyone pretends that everyone else is not there. You will be amazed at how assured you will feel.

> "You have to look as if you're the one with the meat cleaver."

SEAT YOURSELF STRATEGICALLY—All seats are not created equal. If you see one at the end of the row, near a door, take it immediately. It means that only one person can sit next to you. And this means that you will never be sandwiched between the woman eating kung pao chicken with her fingers, and the snoring guy with the blaring headphones who is trying to bed down on your shoulder.

KNOW WHERE YOU ARE GOING—Despite all the improvements in the subway, many on-board announcements are still unintelligible and a map is hard to read on a moving train, especially with someone's head blocking it. Do not be afraid if you hear the conductor announce something that sounds like "Tetanus. This is canned duck. We make all loco. Reefer. Loco! Loco!" Veteran riders might act as if they understand, but they don't, either. If you are unsure, stick with the loco (translation: local) train, which makes all stops.

POSITIONING—Figure out the quintessential New Yorker trick: prewalking. While you are waiting for your train, walk to the place on the platform that gets you into the car that lets you out at the best place at your destination to make a quick exit (that is, right in front of the best staircase up to a Madison Square Garden entrance). ■

Hoyt-Schermerhorn I should have crossed over instead of staying on the same platform, and taken the train in the opposite direction. But the M.T.A. poster made no clear mention of crossing over.

That night, returning to Manhattan, I took the G (replacing the F) to Hoyt-Schermerhorn. As I arrived, the A was pulling in across the platform, so I jumped on. Wrong move. I soon found myself hurtling through Brooklyn in the wrong direction.

On Sunday, I foolishly tried my luck on the West Side. Posters at the 81st Street station said the express A train was running on the local C track, so I waited. Nothing came. A musician on the platform told me the way to go downtown was to take an uptown A train to 125th Street and cross over. I got out and took the M11 bus. ■

Subway Graffiti Called Epidemic

By **FRANK J. PRIAL** | February 11, 1972

ABOVE: *Most subway cars in the 1970's and 1980's were covered in graffiti.*

SUBWAY GRAFFITI ARE FAST REACHING WHAT an IRT conductor has called "the epidemic stage" here. In fact, Frank T. Berry, general superintendent of rapid transit for the Transit Authority, says that it costs the authority more than $500,000 a year to remove the scrawls made by vandals and that "every station porter so spends an hour a day on it."

Once confined principally to car and station advertising placards—because they were most easily marked by ballpoint pens— the onslaught of ink and paint has spread to steel and tile walls, to route maps in cars, to station ceilings and to trackside walls reachable only through subway car windows or by standing between the cars of a stopped train.

Transit officials link the current wave of graffiti to the felt-tipped pen, often called the Magic Marker, although that is merely one of many brands in the field. And officials at the Magic Marker Corporation note that cans that spray paint may be replacing felt-tipped pens for graffiti writers.

The police are hampered, officials say, by a lack of laws governing this kind of vandalism. At present, youthful offenders—and almost every graffiti offender is a teenager—

are given youth referral cards. This means that the police send someone around to talk to the young scrawler's parents.

Under existing law an adult convicted of defacing Transit Authority property is subject to a $25 fine or 10 days in jail or both.

Philadelphia, which some of its officials call the graffiti capital of the nation, and which spends $200,000 a year trying to curb it, is trying several different approaches.

One is the Graffiti Alternative Workshop, where known graffiti offenders are allowed to vent their creative urges by painting fences around construction projects. At present, a number of young markers and sprayers are participating in a contest to create a design for city bases.

The winning design will be painted on a bus. ∎

Graffiti Wars in the Subway: It's Round 2

By **CLYDE HABERMAN** | December 19, 1995

MARILYN SULLIVAN DOESN'T LIKE THE layers of scratched gibberish that make it difficult for her to see out the windows of the No. 6 subway train. No, that's putting it too mildly. She really hates the scrawlings, etched into the glass by vandals who, when you can read the junk at all, assign themselves names like ICE and DIMS and SHAWTS.

"It's disgusting," said Ms. Sullivan, who rides the Lexington Avenue line to her job as a nanny on the Upper East Side. "You're already depressed being on the subway, and this just makes you feel more frightened."

It does indeed seem futile at times. Get control of the graffiti blight, as subway bosses finally did in the late 1980's, and next thing

Underground Artist Admits To Graffiti in 3 Boroughs

By **ANEMONA HARTOCOLLIS** | October 5, 2007

THE LEGENDARY 1980'S GRAFFITI CREATOR Mr. Alan Ket, whose real name is Alain Maridueña, was in a Manhattan courtroom making the second stop in what his lawyer, Ron Kuby, termed the "triborough tour": traveling from courthouse to courthouse to dispose of charges that he had vandalized subway cars in Manhattan, Brooklyn and Queens from 2004 to 2006.

In the plea deal, Mr. Maridueña, 36, agreed to plead guilty to one felony count of criminal mischief in each of the three boroughs and to pay more than $12,000 in fines and restitution. In exchange, prosecutors agreed that he would not have to serve any prison time.

Mr. Kuby noted that his client was a recognized artist who has worked as a consultant to companies like Atari, Moët &

Chandon and MTV and to the fashion designer Marc Ecko. So in his view, a mural makes sense.

"You wouldn't turn down a Picasso simply because Picasso doodled on some other person's guitar or on some donkey cart in Madrid," said Mr. Kuby, who is better known for defending left-wing causes and civil rights cases than for his art criticism.

Mr. Maridueña was arrested in March and accused of vandalizing subway cars in the three boroughs. He was charged with criminal mischief, a felony, and possession of graffiti tools, a misdemeanor. In a novel twist, the police had not caught Mr. Maridueña in the act of painting graffiti. Rather, they executed a search warrant at his home in Manhattan, seized his computer and graffiti-related items, and matched photographs in the computer to photographs of graffiti-painted subway cars with Mr. Maridueña's tag, KET, on them, his lawyer said.

After his arrest, Mr. Maridueña said that he had moved beyond painting graffiti after the birth of his daughter, who is now 13, and that the KET tag had been written by copycat artists.

"Never in my wildest dreams did I think a grown man could be charged with possession of a marker in my own home," he said. ■

you know, young Visigoths take aim at train windows, boring into the glass with shards of ceramic or broken spark plugs or sandpaper.

Here's how bad it can get, said Vincent Ricciardelli, supervisor at the subway's Jerome Car Maintenance Shop, near Mosholu Parkway in the Bronx. One time, his crew sent out a spanking-clean train on the No. 6 line, a notoriously vandal-prone route. The train made a single run from Pelham Bay Park and came back with 182 scratches.

They conducted an experiment on another vandal-prone line, the No. 4. Regular windows were coated with thin sheets of a polyester, Mylar. The Mylar is far from scratch-proof. But in the experiment it kept the regular windows from harm—a "sacrificial barrier," in transit talk.

Best of all, each sheet can be replaced for one-third the cost of installing a new window. And that, if you will, can save a lot of scratch. ■

BELOW: *Graffiti artists Alan (tag name ZENO), left, and Anton (tag name KET) painting graffiti on a #6 train at Buhre Avenue stop in the Bronx in 1991.*

Man Tells Police He Shot Youths in Subway Train

By **SUZANNE DALEY** | January 1, 1985

ABOVE: *Bernard Goetz was acquitted of attempted murder and convicted of criminal possession of a weapon in the third degree. He served eight months in jail.*

A MANHATTAN MAN SURRENDERED TO THE Concord, N.H., police yesterday, saying he was the gunman who wounded four teenagers on a subway car 10 days ago, police officials said.

They said the man, Bernhard Hugo Goetz, 37 years old, of 55 West 14th Street, had already been identified as a suspect in the shooting, which took place after the teenagers approached him and asked for money.

The police said Mr. Goetz, a slim man with blond hair, matched a police composite drawing of the suspect, who escaped into the subway tunnel after the shooting.

HUNDREDS EXPRESSED SUPPORT

A special telephone line that police set up to receive tips to lead them to a suspect instead attracted hundreds of callers who expressed support for the gunman's actions. Some people offered to help pay legal expenses and others suggested that he run for mayor.

In response, Mayor Koch condemned the gunman's act, declaring that "vigilantism will not be tolerated in the city."

Neighbors said Mr. Goetz had been active in community affairs and concerned about crime in his neighborhood. He had organized several petition drives to improve police protection on his block, between Fifth Avenue and the Avenue of the Americas, including a recent one after a doorman in the building had been beaten up.

"But it didn't really help," said a neighbor, Scott Sedita, who said he had known Mr. Goetz for about four years. "And I think that made him upset."

The police in New York had been looking for Mr. Goetz since Dec. 26, when an anonymous caller told them that Mr. Goetz fit the description of the gunman and was known to have a gun, Chief of Detectives, Richard Nicastro said.

According to the police, the shooting occurred about 1:30 P.M. on a southbound No. 2 train just north of Chambers Street. The man, neatly dressed and wearing wire-rimmed glasses, had been approached by the teenagers, who asked for the time and then for a match.

'$5 FOR EACH OF YOU'

The police said the teenagers—one of them sitting next to the man, and the others clustered around—then asked for $5.

"Yes," the teenagers have said he responded, "I have $5 for each of you." He then stood and fired at each of the teenagers, hitting all of them in the upper body.

The police said that the four teenagers all had arrest records and that three of them were carrying long screwdrivers in their jackets. They lived near each other in the Bronx and apparently were friends. ∎

SUBWAYS

Goetz: A Private Man In A Public Debate

By **ROBERT D. MCFADDEN** | January 6, 1985

THE EMERGING PICTURE OF BERNHARD HUGO Goetz is a kaleidoscope of clashing opinions reflecting the debate over vigilantism and public safety that has arisen since he shot four youths who harassed him on a Manhattan subway train. It is also a picture of a lonely 37-year-old man who has sustained two major traumas in his life—criminal charges against his father, and a 1981 mugging that shattered his faith in the administration of justice.

"As far as Bernie was concerned," said a neighbor in his apartment building, "it was equivalent to a woman being raped."

Bernhard Hugo Goetz was born at Kew Gardens Hospital in Queens on Nov. 7, 1947, the youngest of four children of Bernhard Willard and Gertrude Goetz. The elder Mr. Goetz owned a 300-acre dairy farm near Clinton, N.Y., and for some years he ran a bookbinding company in Queens during the week and the farm on weekends. In 1949, when Bernhard was 2, the family moved to the farm.

In 1960, the elder Mr. Goetz was accused of molesting two 15-year-old boys at the Clinton farm. A jury found him guilty of 8 of 18 counts. He appealed, and three years later the state's highest court ordered a new trial. At that point, Mr. Goetz agreed to plead guilty to a single charge of disorderly conduct.

Ludwig Goetz, speaking for the family, denied that the father had done anything wrong, and said that the boys had lied and tried to blackmail him.

The aftermath of the 1981 mugging, in a subway station on Canal Street, appeared to bother Mr. Goetz most.

The apprehended suspect, 16-year-old Fred Clarke of Brooklyn, was taken to Criminal Court. "He was kept for 2 hours and 35 minutes," Mr. Goetz later recalled. "Now, I was there in the Criminal Court Building for 6 hours and 5 minutes, along with the police officer who made the arrest." Mr. Clarke eventually pleaded guilty to a misdemeanor, was sentenced to six months in jail and served four months.

Citing the mugging and his frequent need to carry large sums of cash, Mr. Goetz applied for a pistol permit later in 1981, but was turned down. The police believe that he went to Florida, where it was not difficult to buy the chrome-plated, .38-caliber revolver used in the subway shootings. ∎

Seeking to Delay Seizure of Assets, Goetz Will File For Bankruptcy

By **FRANK BRUNI** | April 29, 1996

ENRAGED BY LAST WEEK'S JURY AWARD OF $43 million against him and terrified that he might lose all his possessions, down to the pet guinea pig and chinchilla he considers his closest companions, Bernhard H. Goetz will file for bankruptcy, according to his lawyer, Darnay Hoffman.

Ronald L. Kuby, the lawyer representing Darrell Cabey, said he was not concerned about Mr. Goetz's maneuver. "Good!" Mr. Kuby said yesterday. "I specifically asked the jury to bankrupt Mr. Goetz."

Mr. Goetz is unable to pay even a fraction of the $43 million. And according to Mr. Hoffman, he is concerned that his creditors, having seen the astronomical prices fetched in the recent auction of Jacqueline Kennedy Onassis' belongings, would demand a similar sale of his possessions, including his pets.

"Now, he doesn't consider himself a Jackie O.," Mr. Hoffman said. "But there's no question that something that was owned by Bernie Goetz could bring in a lot." ∎

Scores Killed or Maimed In Brighton Tunnel Wreck

November 2, 1918

A Brighton Beach train of the Brooklyn Rapid Transit Company, made up of five wooden cars of the oldest type in use, which was speeding with a rush-hour crowd to make up lost time on its way from Park Row to Coney Island, jumped the track shortly before 7 o'clock last evening on a sharp curve approaching the tunnel at Malbone Street, in Brooklyn, and plunged into a concrete partition between the north and south bound tracks.

Nearly every man, woman, and child in the first car was killed, and most of those in the second were killed or badly injured. At 11 o'clock 85 bodies had been taken from the wreckage, and the police announced that no more bodies were in the tunnel. The police estimated that at least 100 had been injured.

District Attorney Lewis announced at midnight that the train was being run by a train dispatcher. This man had been pressed into service in the rush hour because of the strike of motormen, which began in the early morning. At 2 o'clock this morning, as a result of the wreck, the motormen called off the strike, leaving the adjustment of their grievances to the Public Service Commission. The D.A. ordered all the officials of the B.R.T. who could have been responsible and members of the train crew put under arrest. He said the B.R.T. officials had withheld the name of the man who operated the train.

Just before 1 o'clock this morning, the missing motorman, Anthony Lewis, who is 20 years old, was arrested at his home, 160 33rd Street, Brooklyn, by Detectives McCord and Conroy, and brought to the Snyder Avenue station to be questioned by the district attorney, Mayor Hylan and the police commissioner.

> At 11 o'clock 85 bodies had been taken from the wreckage, and the police announced that no more bodies were in the tunnel. The police estimated that at least 100 had been injured.

Afterward, it was stated that his story indicated criminal negligence in hiring him to run the train. Mayor Hylan said:

"This man confessed that he had never run a train over that Brighton Beach line before. He also admitted that, when running around that curve, he was making a speed of thirty miles an hour."

A post on the curve warns motormen not to go faster than six miles an hour. ▪

ABOVE: *It's estimated that 100 people were killed in the wreck.*

SUBWAYS

Trapped Riders Saved In Team Effort

By **JAMES C. MCKINLEY JR.** | August 29, 1991

OFF-DUTY JUST AFTER MIDNIGHT, OFFICER John Debenedetto of the Transit Police was standing with a colleague on a Union Square subway platform waiting for a No. 4 train to take him home. Headlights appeared in the southbound express tunnel.

Then the train's wheels screamed. As the two officers watched, it derailed a hundred yards north of the station, smashing and twisting into a mash of crushed metal.

Stunned, the officers sprinted toward the wreck. Within 15 minutes, they were joined by more than 700 other police officers, firefighters and paramedics, plunged into four hours of terrifying rescue work in a tunnel choked to the ceiling with subway cars that had been shredded like aluminum cans.

"The explosion was as loud as anything you can think," the 25-year-old officer said an hour later. "Half the train is cut in half, like a laser sliced it."

In the next few hours, rescuers pulled dozens of people from the wreckage and used motor-driven wrecking tools, saws and crowbars to free eight people pinned inside. "There's metal sticking out, bodies, body parts," said Capt. Bill Olsen of the Emergency Medical Service. "The train is teetering at points. It's a very dangerous scene."

The rescuers spoke less of individual heroism than of dogged teamwork. At 3:45 A.M., as Mayor David N. Dinkins and Transit Authority officials were talking to reporters, a group of 20 men and women finally freed the last trapped man, an off-duty conductor, Steven Darden, 33. Mr. Darden had been buried in tons of debris in the third car, with only his left arm free, the police said. An officer spotted the fingers wiggling.

Several Emergency Service Unit officers and firefighters said they worked for three hours trying to keep Mr. Darden alive. "He was pinned by some steel wreckage from the waist down," Officer Andrew Nugent of Emergency Truck 1 said. "If the wrong move

were made, we would have impaled him."

The officers used saws to cut away portions of the doors above Mr. Darden and then dug out the debris under him while the paramedics ran intravenous tubes into his arms to pump blood and plasma into him. The whole time Officers Robert Bierman and Joseph Grogan talked to him, about his girlfriend, about his pain, about living.

After most of the other debris was cleared, Officer Donald Costliegh, who was underneath the wreckage looking up at Mr. Darden, jammed a hydraulic jack under the remaining metal sheet pinning him and pumped it off. They pulled him out at about 3:45 A.M. Mr. Darden was taken to St. Vincent's Hospital. He suffered open fractures to his left forearm and a collapsed lung, said Dr. Jesse Blumenthal, the director of the hospital's trauma unit. ∎

BELOW: *The derailment at Union Square killed five people. The motorman, Robert Ray, who was drunk and going more than 40 mph, was eventually convicted of manslaughter.*

Girl Pushed in Front of Oncoming Subway; Hand Severed

By LAURIE JOHNSTON | June 8, 1979

A 17-YEAR-OLD FLUTIST AND SOPRANO suffered a severed right hand yesterday when, witnesses said, a youth pushed her in front of an oncoming IND subway train at the West 50th Street station.

The girl, Renee Katz, a senior at the High School of Music and Art, was attacked about 8:15 a.m., while she was on her way to the school at 135th Street and Convent Avenue in Manhattan.

Miss Katz, who lives in Flushing, Queens, remained conscious while she was pinned between the train's second car and the platform overhang until she was taken by ambulance to Bellevue Hospital. Her severed hand, found by the police between the tracks after the train was removed from the station, was sent to the hospital packed in ice from a nearby bar.

An operation to reattach it, begun about 10:30 A.M. by a 12-member Bellevue surgical team, was expected to continue until early today. In yesterday's incident, Justo Barreiro, motorman of the train, said he saw the slightly built young woman, with her shoulder-length hair and wearing jeans, pushed from the platform by a black youth "between 15 and 17 years old" wearing orange pants and a brown shirt. The assailant, Mr. Barreiro said, fled immediately to the street.

"She was screaming for her mother and about how 'I've got to go to college,'" Mr. Barreiro said. "Everybody in the train could hear the screams but there was really nobody on the platform to chase the kid who pushed her."

Once a Victim, She Is Seeking New Spotlight

By CLYDE HABERMAN | November 21, 1997

EVEN IF YOU KNEW NOTHING ABOUT HER, you could tell right away that something really bad had once happened to Renee Katz. When she smiled hello, she stretched out her left arm to shake hands.

Nothing personal, the smile said. But no way was she going to entrust her fragile right hand, which had been through so much, to the grip of a stranger.

If you are a longtime New Yorker, odds are fair that the name has jostled old memories and set you to wondering, "Renee Katz, wasn't she the one ...?'"

And the answer is, yes, she was. She was the one who lived every subway rider's nightmare one day in 1979.

How many times has she been called upon to relive that morning? More than she'd care to count, she said the other day. All it takes is for somebody to land on the subway tracks, and, sure as God made the rush hour, the question will be asked: Whatever happened to Renee Katz?

What happened is that she got on with her life, and that includes music. At 36, she is trying to make a career as a cabaret singer. Playing the flute or the piano is out of the question. But she can hold a mike in that well-bandaged right hand, and can deliver a ballad as sweetly as a breeze caressing the leaves. She has just recorded her first CD.

She cannot escape the fact that her personal disaster was a turning point for many New Yorkers, permanently altering how they behave in the subways. The subways are safer now than in 1979, but they are still not safe enough for Ms. Katz. "I'll use them in the daytime, with lots of people around," she said. "But I don't take them more than I have to."

Why Our Hero Leapt Onto the Tracks and We Might Not

By **CARA BUCKLEY** | January 7, 2007

MAYBE SOME PEOPLE ARE MORE HARD-wired for heroism than others. Like, for example, Wesley Autrey, the man behind a stunning rescue last week in a Manhattan subway station.

People wondered, because they had asked themselves, "Could I have done what he did?" and very often the answer was no. Mr. Autrey, 50, a construction worker and Navy veteran, leapt in front of a train to rescue a stranger who had suffered a seizure and fallen onto the tracks. He covered the stranger's body with his own as the train passed overhead. Both men lived.

Mr. Autrey, who left two young daughters on the platform when he jumped, later chalked up his actions to a simple compulsion to help another in distress.

But is there something in Mr. Autrey that the rest of us lack? Probably not, experts say. When Mr. Autrey saw the stranger, Cameron Hollopeter, 20, tumble onto the tracks, his brain reacted just as anyone else's would. His thalamus, which absorbs sensory information, registered the fall, and sent the information to other parts of the brain for processing, said Gregory L. Fricchione, an associate professor of psychiatry at Harvard Medical School.

Mr. Autrey's amygdala, the part of the brain that mediates fear responses, was activated and sent sensory information to the motor cortex, which sent it down for emotional processing. His anterior cingulate, a sort of brain within the brain that helps people make choices, kicked in, hel ping trigger his decision about how to act, Dr. Fricchione said.

That Mr. Autrey served in the Navy most likely played a role, too—he had been trained to act quickly in adverse situations. Acts like jumping in front of trains to rescue strangers are easier for people who are prepared, said Michael McCullough, a psychology professor at the University of Miami.

Considering that people tend to act more altruistically toward those who fall within their perceived group, Dr. Post said, it was notable that differences in race—Mr. Autrey is black, Mr. Hollopeter is white—didn't enter the picture.

"Not only is he going beyond the narrow interest that we all seem to have toward our children, but he is reaching out toward a shared common humanity. And he's doing it across a racial line," Dr. Post said. "And I think that's really impressive." ■

BELOW: *Wesley Autrey became known as the "subway hero," and his story captivated the country.*

Vast Bus System Planned For New York

By **R. L. DUFFUS** | March 14, 1926

NEW YORK CITY'S GREAT-GREAT-grandfathers journeyed up and down their island by means of stagecoaches. Then came horse cars, steam railways, elevated railways, electric surface lines and subways. Now the stagecoach is about to return on a large scale, through it will be propelled by gasoline-burning rather than hay-burning horsepower, and will be called by the newfangled name of motorbus.

At present, according to the figures recently given out by Frederick T. Wood, president of the Fifth Avenue Coach Company, only 6 percent of the passengers in New York City's transportation systems are carried in buses, whereas 39 percent are carried on surface lines. But it is not impossible that a few more years may see these percentages reversed.

"Surface tracks in the city," Mr. Wood has said, "cost $550,000 a mile. Buses now accommodate 67 passengers and when one bus breaks down, there is no tie-up in the system as when a trolley car is out of order. There is no powerhouse trouble, and in the event of a parade of torn-up street the bus can detour."

> ## Surface tracks in the city cost $550,000 a mile.

The plans call for a little less than 300 miles of bus routes—287.6, to be exact—in the four boroughs of Manhattan, the Bronx, Brooklyn and Queens. In Manhattan, the buses will not go south of the City Hall, principally for the reason that no more traffic could be squeezed into that area without the aid of a bootjack. The traveler will be able to go as far north as Inwood on the west side, or as far as 126th Street and First Avenue on the east side. ∎

Tracking the Slowest Buses
October 25, 2006

THE STRAPHANGERS CAMPAIGN AND TRANS-portation Alternatives, two transit advocacy groups, yesterday announced the fifth annual Pokey Awards, which are intended to single out the city's slowest buses.

The award is based on data collected by volunteers who time their rides on bus lines in each borough. To calculate the speed of the bus, the total time from the beginning to the end of the route is divided by the number of miles covered.

The groups also gave an award for the least reliable routes, expressed as a percentage of the buses on the route that arrive in bunches or with major gaps in service, or that start significantly behind schedule.

SLOWEST BUS ROUTES, all in Manhattan. (Average m.p.h. in parentheses)
M14A—14th Street from West Village to Lower East Side (3.9)
M34—34th Street crosstown (4.2)
M23—23rd Street crosstown (4.3)
M27—49th and 50th Streets crosstown (4.4)
M14D—14th Street, Chelsea to the Lower East Side (4.4)

LEAST RELIABLE
M1—Fifth and Madison Avenues, East Village to Harlem (27.6)
M3—Fifth and Madison Avenues/St. Nicholas Avenue, East Village to Upper Manhattan (25.0)
B15—(Brooklyn) Marcus Garvey Blvd./New Lots Avenue, Bedford-Stuyvesant to J.F.K. (24.7)
M7—Columbus/Amsterdam/Lenox/Sixth/Seventh Avenues, Union Square to Harlem (24.6)
Bx41—(Bronx) Webster Avenue/White Plains Road, Wakefield to the Hub (24.2) ∎

Trying to Get Buses To Crawl a Little Faster

By **SEWELL CHAN** | March 30, 2005

AFTER WATCHING NEW YORK CITY BUS speeds struggle to the point where some Manhattan buses crawl at 4 miles per hour—only slightly faster than the average human walks—transportation planners now think that if they can make buses move even 10 percent faster, they can revolutionize travel in the five boroughs.

That's right, just 10 percent.

New York City Transit, whose buses run on some of the most congested streets in the world, says it would be delighted to achieve even half of those speed gains. Thus, 10 m.p.h. could become 11 m.p.h. The agency has teamed up with the city and state Transportation Departments on a $2.9 million study of bus rapid transit, as the improvements are broadly known in the transit world.

"Anything would be an improvement because most people can walk faster than the buses run," said Beverly L. Dolinsky, executive director of the Permanent Citizens Advisory Committee to the Metropolitan Transportation Authority, the transit agency's parent.

The study, begun last July, started with 100 of the city's busiest streets. Planners selected 36 bus corridors and presented them for comment at public workshops across the city in December and January. Next month, they will narrow the list to 15 corridors; they intend to begin a demonstration project on 5 routes by 2007.

Keith J. Hom, the chief of operations planning for the transit agency, views the city's roads as a contested battlefield, with pedestrians, cyclists, automobiles, taxicabs and trucks vying with mass transit for control of every spot, from the center lane right to the curb. Progress, they say, can be measured only in small increments.

Perhaps the best-known feature of bus rapid transit is what planners call "intelligent transportation systems." A device will transmit a bus's position and speed, through centralized computers, to a traffic light as the bus approaches. The traffic light will then remain green for, say, 10 seconds longer than usual, or change from red to green 10 seconds sooner than usual, to allow the bus to pass. ■

BELOW: *The Straphangers Campaign presents an annual "Pokey Award" to the slowest bus in the city. In 2003, the award went to the M23.*

Double-Decker Bus Makes Trial Run, Delighting Riders And Avoiding Branches

By **MARTIN ESPINOZA** | September 28, 2008

ABOVE: *The MTA double-decker bus arrives next to a 1939 model. The new bus combines the efficiency of high-capacity with a low-floor entry and exit.*

BECAUSE OF A HEIGHT ISSUE—WHICH WOULD seem to be a built-in obstacle—the Metropolitan Transportation Authority has had to put off its plans to test its double-decker bus on two routes, including one that traverses Fifth Avenue.

The reason? Tree branches on Riverside Drive and Fifth Avenue are in the way.

Instead, the authority is currently limiting the trial to one route, the X17J from Staten Island to Manhattan.

Even on a good day, it can take about an hour and 45 minutes to complete its journey, from Huguenot Avenue on Staten Island to East 57th Street in Midtown, during peak commuting hours.

Gabriella Pettinato got out of bed determined to track down that bus. As her husband drove, she watched for the 13-foot-tall, 45-foot-long behemoth.

She spotted it near the Staten Island Mall.

"We drove two stops ahead of it to make sure I made this bus," said Mrs. Pettinato, an accountant, sitting on the upper level of the coach as it approached the Goethals Bridge. "Anything different is exciting."

Most of the passengers who first boarded the bus headed straight for the upper level, lowering their heads as they walked up the narrow stairs. While the height clearance on the first level is 5 feet 11 inches, the upper level's clearance is only 5 feet 7 inches.

> The Metropolitan Transportation Authority has had to put off its plans to test its double-decker bus on two routes. The reason? Tree branches on Riverside Drive and Fifth Avenue are in the way.

Yara Lantigua, a planner for a New York media company, had no trouble making her way to the front seat on the upper level.

Ms. Lantigua said she got up a little earlier to make sure she caught the bus, which started its run from Huguenot Avenue and Woodrow Road at 7:16 a.m. A wide smile revealed her excitement as the bus rolled along the Staten Island Expressway.

"I like sitting in front," Ms. Lantigua said, putting on her sunglasses. "I like to know what is happening." ■

Buses

On These Commuter Buses, Passengers Hold All Calls, or Else

By **MIKE RICHARD** | September 4, 2008

THE NEW JERSEY COMMUTER BUS HEADING to New York City one day last week rolled to a stop on the side of the highway. The morning holdup was caused by a passenger who was talking on her cellphone.

"I've got all day, ma'am," the driver announced into his microphone, with the bus idling, about half an hour from the Lincoln Tunnel. "I'll wait till you're done."

> "Cell phone use restricted to emergency use only."

Nearly 50 passengers heard the warning, which the driver said was aimed at "the woman seated behind me in the third row by the window." The woman, embarrassed by the sudden attention, hurried to wrap up her phone conversation.

Once the bus started rolling again toward the Port Authority Bus Terminal, she said to a passenger next to her, rather sheepishly: "I had to cancel an order. Sorry . . . but what's the big deal?"

One of the few upsides to commuting from the suburbs—aside from being able to afford a bigger home—is the ability to take care of personal business, or business business, on the way to work. But Lakeland Bus Lines has signs on its buses that warn: "Cell phone use restricted to emergency use only."

Leo Homeijer, vice president of operations for Lakeland, based in Dover, N.J., said the cell phone rule was put into effect about 10 years ago because of complaints from drivers and passengers. He said that of all the grievances his company heard, inconsiderate cell phone use topped the list.

"Eighty percent of the time, cell phones don't bother people," he said. "But let's face it, people who talk on their cell phones are basically talking loudly. Some people and drivers handle it differently. Do I wish that my drivers could be more diplomatic about it sometimes? Probably."

One day recently, a woman being particularly loud on her phone was asked by a bus driver—this driver used the word "please"—to stop. The woman shot back, "No, I think I'm going to make one more call—to your boss at Lakeland!" The driver, exasperated by the brief exchange but doing his best to remain calm, responded, "Feel free."

Courtney Carroll, a spokeswoman for New Jersey Transit—which transports the greatest number of commuters in the state on its bus and train lines—said that while cell phones were not banned on its carriers, common courtesy was stressed. And a Long Island Rail Road passenger was arrested on assault and harassment charges after an argument with other passengers who annoyed him with their phone chatter. The passenger, John Clifford, was acquitted. ∎

BELOW: *NJ Transit has a daily ridership of nearly a million and most of those commuters are traveling into Manhattan.*

Quill Dies of Heart Attack; T.W.U. President Was 60

By **MURRAY SCHUMACH** | January 29, 1966

MICHAEL J. QUILL, PRESIDENT OF THE Transport Workers union, died of a heart attack 28 days after he had led his union into a transit strike that paralyzed the city for 12 days.

With the 60-year-old union leader when he died in his apartment on the 37th floor of a luxury apartment house was his wife, Shirley, who had been with him in many of his stormiest labor controversies.

After a priest administered the last rites in the apartment at 15 West 72nd Street, and while more than a dozen policemen stood in awkward silence, Mrs. Quill suddenly cried: "No! It can't be. It can't be."

Mr. Quill, one of the most colorful of modern labor figures, had been involved in a series of events that made him a national figure this month. Three weeks ago, when the transit strike was in its fourth day, he collapsed in the Civil Jail of congestive heart failure. He had been ordered to jail for refusing to obey a court order to call off the strike.

He emerged from the hospital only last Monday and held a news conference the next day in which he displayed all of the native Irish wit, lilting that marked his public appearances.

One of the first to express sorrow was Mayor Lindsay, with whom, during the complex transit negotiations, he had clashed. The mayor issued the following statement:

"Michael Quill's death marks the end of an era. He was a man who was very much a part of New York. My sympathy goes to his wife and family."

Mr. Quill was dead before any doctors could get to him, though they came quickly. Dr. Hyman Zuckerman, Mr. Quill's personal physician, said later that Mr. Quill was in bed and napping when his wife checked on him shortly after 5 p.m. ■

2005: Biking And Car-Pooling Together

By **JENNIFER STEINHAUER** | December 21, 2005

SHIVERING, INTREPID AND OCCASIONALLY befuddled, New Yorkers faced down the first citywide transit strike in a quarter-century, walking, biking and car-pooling through their city as transit workers and the state agency that employs them remained locked in intransigence.

As people competed for the quickest or most creative way to get to work, and businesses struggled in one of the most important retail weeks of the year, the conflict between the Metropolitan Transportation

TRANSIT STRIKES

1980: City Faces First Day of Strike With Aplomb

By **CLYDE HABERMAN** | April 2, 1980

ON THE DAY NEW YORK WAS SUPPOSED TO come to a halt, it didn't.

It crawled in some spots, to be sure. It fretted mightily in others, but then it always does that. It even grew downright surly on occasion.

But Day One of the Transit Strike reinforced a semi-truth that tends to make New Yorkers feel better about themselves— that no matter what the adversity, they can handle it wit aplomb.

For the most part, they did so in a spirit of buoyancy and adventure. If there was a prevailing wisdom it was that good cheer was possible because (1) many people stayed home on the first day of Passover, (2) public schools were closed, (3) it was an incandescent day, or (4) all of the above. Of course, that produced an inescapable corollary: Things are likely to get only worse.

"Today, it's ha ha ha," said Officer John Maronna, on patrol outside City Hall. "It's only a matter of time, and it's going to change."

People had to get to work, and they did. Brigades of foot soldiers in the latest urban war came over the Brooklyn Bridge—happy warriors, even though crowding on the footpath produced several brushes between pedestrians and bicyclists who did not have horns, bells or whistles.

But people like John Donovan, a mail supervisor who works on Canal Street, wondered why he normally spends a dollar a day for the privilege of riding bumpily in a hole in the ground. "I was just thinking of why I don't do this more often," he said. stepping off the bridge and onto Park Row, "All these health spas that they have—why, you can't beat walking." ▪

Authority and its largest union moved into the courts. The initial decisions went against the union, with a State Supreme Court justice in Brooklyn calling the strike illegal, ordering union members back to work and imposing a $1 million fine against the union for each day it is on strike.

Mayor Michael R. Bloomberg decried the strike as "thuggish" and "selfish" and declared that negotiations—in which the city does not participate—should not resume until the 33,700 subway and bus workers return to their jobs.

Mass confusion reigned on many major arteries, where police halted vehicles with fewer than four occupants. North of 96th Street on the Upper West Side, cars were backed up for miles as drivers begged strangers to hop into their cars. Other commuters had less fortuitous journeys.

Rashi Kesarwani, 23, began her journey from Prospect Heights as well, but trudged for almost two miles along a desolate strip with few drivers to the Long Island Rail Road Station on Atlantic Avenue to get a train. When she arrived in Jamaica, Queens, she waited for 90 minutes in a line that wound through 10 blocks.

"I could not feel my toes or my fingers by the time we entered the train station," said Ms. Kesarwani, whose commute ended three and a half hours after it began, with a 12-block walk to her job in Rockefeller Center.

Mayor Bloomberg made his way, somewhat crankily and looking tired, across the Brooklyn Bridge, recalling Mayor Edward I. Koch's triumphant march in 1980, when he joined New Yorkers flowing into Manhattan during the city's last transit strike. ▪

Taxis a Traffic Plague

February 24, 1924

NEW YORK, FROM ALL INDICATIONS, IS suffering with a plague—a whirring, rattling, noisy plague, not of locusts, but of taxicabs. Nightly, at the hours when the theaters are discharging their audiences and the amusement district for a score of blocks is crowded by a mass of pleasure-seekers and homegoers, there appears a legion of taxicabs, thronging in from north and south and east and west to complete with another for fares. Almost the entire 18,000 taxicabs of the city, it would seem, are bent on pressing into the jam of Broadway.

This is but one of the many angles of the taxi problem with which New York is confronted. Twenty-seven thousand men, almost a full army division, are engaged in driving it night and day. It appears prolifically in the newspapers and traffic court records in cases of accident, and when a crime wave is afloat not infrequently in the commission of serious misdeeds.

> Twenty-seven thousand men . . . are engaged in driving [taxis] night and day.

"There are too many taxicabs in the city," is the declaration of Deputy Police Commissioner John A. Harriss, in charge of traffic. "There are not 30 days of bad weather in the year that call for the number of taxis now running about the streets. The city would be better off it they were reduced to 12,000. That is what we want—just about 12,000 taxicabs." ▪

Tips and Taxicabs

October 9, 1907

TO THE EDITOR OF THE NEW YORK TIMES:

In reply to the letter of Oct. 4 regarding the question of tipping the driver of the taxicab, I should like to make the following remarks:

It is not the intention of the New York Taxicab Company to force the public to tip the drivers. They are not paid wages, but receive a percentage of their takings; each man is thus put in a position of being a partner in the enterprise, and it is to his interest to work as hard as he can and give the best of satisfaction, as his takings depend on these two items.

It would be absurd for us to ask the American public to refrain from tipping; this has been tried in many enterprises and has never succeeded; the American public are always apt to express their satisfaction at good treatment at the hands of any employees, and it is more or less as a token of appreciation that this custom has become prevalent.

At the same time, our drivers are under strict orders to give the best attention and care to all passengers, whether they expect to receive gratuities or not, and I shall take it as a favor if the public will complain to me if they do not receive such treatment.

It is very customary in France for drivers to try and bargain with a passenger as to what tip they will receive before they will accept him as a fare. This will not be permitted on any account in the New York Taxicab Company, and a report of such an offense, if sustained, is sufficient cause for the instant dismissal of any driver. ▪

NEW YORK TAXICAB CO.,
H. N. Allen, President.
New York, Oct. 8, 1907

Cabdrivers Sweat It Out Bidding on Medallions

By **WINTER MILLER** | November 2, 2007

"DROPPED, DROPPED, STILL GOOD, DROPPED, dropped." Gary Kanterman was talking to himself as he ran his pen down his list of taxi drivers.

Mr. Kanterman, 41, a taxi broker, was assessing the bids of his 35 clients—most of whom were out driving fares—at an auction yesterday of 63 medallions by the Taxi and Limousine Commission.

About 13,000 cabs honk and swerve through the streets of New York City, yet even with recent strikes over the cost and purview of new technology mandated in the cars, owning a medallion remains a shot at independence and equity for many drivers.

"This is one of the best investments— better than Merrill Lynch," said a driver, Mahmoud Sadakah, 42. "This is a guaranteed investment, because it will never go down."

The auction by the commission was the first of two offering a total of 150 medallions. Most are for the opportunity to drive wheelchair-accessible taxis.

The trick of this sealed bid auction was how much over the commission's minimum bid of $189,000 to go. To compare, the market value of an independent medallion sold in October was $426,000. Medallions are perceived as low-risk investments because resale prices have continued to rise and there is a fairly stable cap on the number of new cars allowed on the streets.

In the second row, Mohammad Islam, 32, was leaning forward in his chair, eagerly watching the bids land. "I put $341,000," he said, explaining that he had borrowed $20,000 from relatives and 90 percent from the broker, who also agreed to finance the cost of a new car.

As the 155th bid hit the screen, brokers jumped to their feet to compare notes about who got what. The highest bid was $384,999, and two of Mr. Kanterman's clients made the cut with matching bids of $277,777.

"I got a deal. I'm happy," said Vladimir Nisanov, 34.

But he did not look happy. He was already tabulating his worries: What if the car he buys breaks down? What if medallion prices fall? ■

BELOW: *There are over 13,000 licensed, yellow cabs currently operating in New York City.*

All Licensed Cabs Must Be Yellow by Jan. 1

December 17, 1969

MAYOR LINDSAY REMINDED THE CITY'S taxicab operators yesterday that all city licensed cabs must be painted yellow by the first of next year to make it easier for customers to distinguish between licensed and unlicensed, or "gypsy," cabs.

At the same time, he pointed out that a local law that becomes effective Jan. 1 requires all gypsy cabs, known legally as "private livery vehicles," be painted "some color other than yellow."

"Since the service provided and the rates charged by licensed taxicabs and private liveries may vary considerably," the Mayor said, "the public must be provided with an easy means of rapid identification to distinguish between the licensed taxicabs and the non-licensed private liveries. The new coloring law will serve that purpose."

Mayor Lindsay's statement repeated the city law requiring cabs with the Police Department medallion to respond to hails by the public and to take passengers to any location within the city for the amount shown on the meter.

> All city cabs must be painted yellow to distinguish between licensed and unlicensed cabs.

He also pointed out that nonmedallion cabs are prohibited by law from cruising and responding to hails. He said gypsy cabs could only be retained in advance, "normally by telephone."

Calvin Williams, who operates the Black Pearl Car Service, a Brooklyn gypsy cab system, questioned the legality of the new law but said his company would not challenge it if the city would allow gypsy cabs to be painted part yellow in combination with other colors .

It's Fall in New York, and Cabs Are in Bloom

By JENNIFER 8. LEE | November 6, 2007

MANY NEW YORKERS HAVE BEEN DELIGHTED this fall by the florid colors coursing through the city streets. Like real flowers, the petals and pistils painted by some 23,000 schoolchildren flourish in the sunshine. That is thanks to the work done at night by Garden of Transit workers, who coax drivers into allowing the flowers to be applied to their cabs.

Garden in Transit—a project of the community art organization Portraits of Hope, founded by Bernard Massey and his brother, Ed—persuaded the Taxi and Limousine Commission to approve the privately financed $5 million public art program a year ago to mark the centennial of the metered taxi in New York.

Their goal is to decorate 50 percent of New York's cab fleet, but they are lucky if one out of seven drivers says yes. When they do get a yes, the workers swoop in and apply the adhesive sheets in just a few minutes.

"It's almost like a Nascar pit stop," Ed Massey said. "They are out of there in three and a half minutes."

But workers also have to dispel the rumors heard by the drivers: That the flower project has something to do with the taxi commission's mandate that global positioning devices be installed in every cab. Or that it is a protest against the war in Iraq. Or a huge, rolling advertisement for a new Austin Powers movie. Or a celebration of Mayor Michael R. Bloomberg's birthday (it is on Valentine's Day). Or even that Upper East Side residents just want to look down from their apartments and see something pretty. ▪

taxis

Taxi TV, Brisk as the Traffic You're Stuck In

By **ALESSANDRA STANLEY** | December 15, 2007

WHERE ONCE THERE WAS ONLY PEELING vinyl, printed fare rates and the cabdriver's ceaseless cell phone chatter, there is now a television screen.

Suddenly, brash ads for banks and credit card companies ("Your morning mocha could be on us"), an almost endless supply of health tips and features about family-run bagel factories and cookie drives to cure cancer, and even, in some cases, movie times and restaurant reviews, are all part of the Manhattan cab ride experience.

But is there anything on Taxi TV worth watching? Stay tuned.

As it turns out, there is a ferocious network battle for backseat viewers. Of the four companies that have contracts with the city, there are only two major providers who together control most of the taxi programming, and they offer starkly opposite philosophies. VeriFone Transportation Systems, which has an alliance with WABC-TV, calls its system Taxi-TV, and favors aggressively interactive content: Alongside ads and news briefs, its touch-screen monitors offer gallery listings, restaurant reviews and ads disguised as quizzes. ("What is Donald Trump's rank in the Forbes 400?" asks Forbes magazine.) Its monitor even comes with a dimmer to soften the screen's brightness after dark.

Creative Mobile Technology Inc., which is in league with Clear Channel and NBC Universal, and which offers NY 10, the Taxi Entertainment Network, believes that less is more: Its screens are designed to encourage passenger passivity; the main choice is whether to turn the crawl under the screen from sports to entertainment news.

Taxi-TV, via WABC and VeriFone, offers more consumer information, but is also more demanding, and sometimes more enervating. The screen does not always instantly respond to touch ("Please be patient while data is loading"), and trying to scroll through the Zagat Guide's restaurant listings while the cab maneuvers potholes and stop-and-go traffic is a little like trying to thread a needle on horseback.

The programming provided by Clear Channel and NBC is more prosaic and tightly bound to corporate sponsorship, including its own. NBC provides promotional clips from "The Tonight Show With Jay Leno" and "Saturday Night Live" and many, many ads for "The NBC Nightly News With Brian Williams" and the next season of "The Apprentice."

At the moment, the cab tube has novelty, but that can wear off pretty quickly after one too many loops of Chase credit card ads or movie reviews from NBC's "Reel Talk." But the technology allows for more and better programming, and viewers do have a voice in what they watch while traveling. All taxi television sets are equipped with an off button, and that is the captive cab rider's last resort. ∎

BELOW: *Taxi-TV screens, like this one in Ahmed Zaheer's cab, include a live GPS map and can be used to pay for rides with a credit card.*

New York's Cabbies Show How Multicolored Racism Can Be

By **THOMAS J. LUECK** | November 7, 1999

IT MAY BE THE MOST BLATANT FORM OF RACISM in New York City: a cab driver refusing to pick up someone who is black.

Former Mayor David N. Dinkins says it has even happened to him. And now the actor Danny Glover has gone public over what he described as a string of such slights.

"I was so angry," Mr. Glover told a news conference, recounting how several empty cabs had refused to stop for him, his college-age daughter and her roommate. Later, when one finally did, the driver refused the "Lethal Weapon" star access to the front seat even though he has a bad hip and is entitled under taxi industry rules to stretch out in front.

A simple case of traditional American racism? Perhaps. But in New York such incidents often have the distinct flavor of the melting pot: In this case the driver was nonwhite, too—apparently from southern Asia, Mr. Glover said.

And so the actor's experience may illustrate not just continuing American racism, but one way it is subtly changing with demographics: As recent immigrants from Asia, the Middle East and Africa come to dominate the taxi industry, they are bringing with them new strains of bigotry. Most often, according to people in the taxi industry, racism is perpetuated by cabbies whose attitudes have roots not only in colonial rule and the strict social stratification of their native lands, but also in the more recent distorted images of the global media.

Randolph Scott-McLaughlin, a lawyer who accompanied Mr. Glover at the press conference and a 20-year veteran of civil rights litigation, said drivers like the one who antagonized Mr. Glover "have adopted the same patterns of racial profiling that emerged when most drivers were Irish, Italian-Americans, or from somewhere else in Europe."

Acts of racial discrimination by cabbies are illegal, punishable by a fine or the revocation of the offender's taxi-driver license.

But Mr. Scott-McLaughlin, who himself is black, said Mr. Glover did not intend to pursue a formal complaint with the Taxi and Limousine Commission because he had no interest in punishing a single driver. Instead, the actor spoke out last week to focus fresh attention on racism in the taxi industry.

"No one is educating these people that we are not dangerous criminals," said Mr. Scott-McLaughlin. ∎

An A.P.B. For Yo-Yo Ma's Lost Cello

By **KATHERINE E. FINKELSTEIN**
October 17, 1999

YO-YO MA, THE WORLD'S MOST FAMOUS living cellist, could not have planned a more dramatic or nail-biting performance. And an array of New Yorkers, including a phalanx of police officers and city officials and a cabdriver in Queens, could not have composed a more gracious finale: the safe return of his $2.5 million cello.

It was 1 p.m. when Mr. Ma, still exhausted from playing at Carnegie Hall some 16 hours before, got into a yellow cab at 86th Street and Central Park West, putting his 18th-century cello in the trunk.

Eighteen minutes later, when he got out at the Peninsula Hotel on 55th Street, he forgot the cello, made in 1733 by Domenico Montagnana, one of the greatest luthiers of his age.

THE NEW YORK TIMES BOOK OF NEW YORK

Yellow Taxis Battle to Keep Livery Cabs Off Their Turf

By **RANDY KENNEDY** | May 10, 2001

A FORMER NEW YORK CITY POLICE DETEC-tive stood on the corner of 67th Street and Central Park West the other morning trying to hail a taxi. What made this unusual was that he was not going anywhere.

Instead, the former detective was working as a foot soldier in a war being waged on the streets of Manhattan, one whose battle lines became apparent the minute he raised his hand: the cabs that raced to his side were not yellow. They were livery cabs, from sleek corporate sedans to battered gypsies, and they arrived in a virtual procession, rushing over and stopping illegally to haggle over a price.

Turf wars are nothing new between the medallion and livery cab industries—the complex two-class taxi system that has evolved in New York since the 1930's. Medallion taxis were always supposed to be restricted to picking up street hails. Liveries were to be restricted to pre-arranged calls—though they have always picked up street hails on the sly, usually in neighbor-hoods where yellow cabs have no interest in going. But over the last two years liveries have increasingly invaded the yellow cab's traditional stronghold, south of 96th Street in

> Liveries have increasingly invaded the yellow cab's stronghold.

Manhattan, cruising around business areas, hotels and restaurants and illegally taking hails.

The reasons they say this is happening now more than ever include a dearth of yellow cabs, especially during the day; more people in Manhattan trying to hail them; and what yellow cab owners see as a lack of enforcement by the taxi commission against liveries.

But both yellow taxi fleet owners and livery owners say that they think the problem will persist because the agency has only about 200 taxi officers to cover all five boroughs and those officers usually must concentrate on more pressing public safety problems. And the Police Department, though able to respond to illegal pickups, almost never does.

The other day on Central Park West, it was not easy to find anyone who really cared one way or the other so long as he could find a cab. And if a yellow one wasn't around, he did not hesitate long to hop into a livery. ∎

What followed—an all-points search for the rare instrument—was more Hollywood than Haydn.

All the thunderstruck musician had was the receipt for his ride, which had the taxi's medallion number on it, which he gave to hotel security officers.

They alerted the Midtown North precinct on West 54th Street, which put out a bulletin to patrol cars around the city to hunt for the taxi.

Around 3:30 p.m., the 108th Precinct in Long Island City, Queens, sent a patrol car to

the taxi's home base, the Maria Cab Company at 44-07 Vernon Boulevard. The taxi driver, Dishashi Lukumwena, was scheduled to get off work at 4 p.m.

When he pulled in, he opened his trunk as worried police officers and curious taxi drivers stood by. There, in its oversize blue plastic case, was the cello.

Back at the hotel when cello and cellist were reunited, Mr. Ma was asked why someone so famous was taking a regular yellow cab.

"I'm like a regular person," he said. "I like to hear Jackie Mason tell me what to do." ∎

Brooklyn Bridge At 100, Embodies the Spirit of an Age

By **PAUL GOLDBERGER** | May 24, 1983

ABOVE: *Contruction of the Brooklyn Bridge, 1878*

FEW THINGS IN NEW YORK LAST FOR 100 years, and fewer still mean as much at the end of a century in this city as they did at the beginning. But the Brooklyn Bridge seems only to grow in importance. It no longer seems as daring an act of engineering as it did in the 19th century, or as overwhelming a presence on the skyline, but on its 100th birthday today it remains as potent, and as beloved, an icon as New York City has. It has always been something apart from other bridges. It was, of course, the first great bridge, the first roadway anywhere in the world to leap across so much water. But now that bigger suspension bridges are commonplace, the Brooklyn Bridge still holds sway over our imaginations.

It stands for many things—for movement, for thrust, for the triumph of man over nature and, ultimately, for a city that prized these qualities over all other things. It is important to remember that the Brooklyn Bridge was completed at the beginning of New York's great and heroic age. The 1880's were the beginning of the modern New York of skyscrapers and mass immigration, of explosive growth and intense creativity, and the bridge is the embodiment of that ages spirit.

The bridge did not make modern New York happen, of course, but the fact that the bridge itself happened—that New York City could build a monument that was so brilliant a synthesis of art and technology—served as a convenient symbol of the city's new power as a world capital. At the end of the 19th century, New York was a city that felt itself rapidly becoming the center of the world, and the bridge that joined it to its neighbor, Brooklyn—then a separate city—seemed to epitomize its potential.

It was not merely that the bridge crossed the East River and suddenly made ferries obsolete. A lesser structure might have done the same. The bridge was so much more than a roadway; it was, by itself, the tallest and grandest manmade thing in the city. The bridges Gothic towers of granite were New York's first skyscrapers, for in 1883 they stood high above everything else on the skyline; its roadway provided a spectacular panorama of the city that could be obtained nowhere else. To see the city and the river from the Brooklyn Bridge was like flying.

But the genius of John Roebling's design goes beyond even this. The bridge is an object of startling beauty. As suspension bridges go, it was not even approached until the George Washington Bridge half a century later and the Golden Gate Bridge a few years after that. It is not quite as graceful as these newer bridges; one could not say of the Brooklyn Bridge, as Le Corbusier said of the George Washington, here, finally, steel architecture begins to laugh. The Brooklyn Bridge is more somber, more blunt and hard; those towers of stone do not laugh, and neither do the steel cables in their exquisite, lyrical webbed pattern. ∎

BRIDGES

Honors for Bridges Many Take for Granted

By GLENN COLLINS | September 16, 2008

THOUGH MORE MARINE TRAFFIC CROSSES under it than under any other city drawbridge, most drivers who traverse the humble Pelham Bay Bridge in the Bronx barely take notice. This buff-and-blue span in Pelham Bay Park—a heavily traveled approach to City Island—is certainly not a bridge to nowhere. But it is only a bit player in the transportation firmament of bridges with star names like Brooklyn and George Washington.

Yet the centennial of this workhorse is about to be greeted with a brass marching band. There will be a color guard, a parade of Clydesdales followed by a horse and carriage, a canoe flotilla and a procession of dignitaries expected to include the Bronx borough president, Adolfo Carrión Jr., and the city parks commissioner, Adrian Benepe. There will be speeches. And the clamshell drawbridge will be ceremonially opened as a fireboat spouts in red, white and blue.

But why?

"Our bridges get no respect," said M. Barry Schneider, founder of the New York City Bridge Centennial Commission, which has given itself the mission of celebrating the 100th anniversary of six city bridges from 2008 to 2010. Before this year the commission had little more than a logo (a jaunty suspension bridge in blue and gray), but now has two centennial celebrations under its belt: the University Heights Bridge (January) and the Borden Avenue Bridge (March).

That will be followed by the big bash for the Pelham Bay Bridge (2008) and, later, honors for the Queensboro Bridge (2009), the Manhattan Bridge (also 2009) and the Madison Avenue Bridge (2010).

The revelry has not been inspired by any official arm of the city government, but rather, by a nonprofit group that has won enthusiastic cooperation from the borough presidents' offices, the mayor's office, the city's parks department and its Department of Transportation. Mr. Schneider created the commission with his wife, Judith, in 2006. "I picked the name 'commission' so we could all be commissioners," he said with a laugh.

His agenda, however, is entirely serious. "We take our infrastructure for granted," said the 73-year-old Mr. Schneider, a retired advertising executive who is a current member and former president of Community Board 8. "And if we don't take care, we'll wind up with bridges that fall down." ∎

BELOW: *The Manhattan Bridge celebrated its centennial in 2009.*

His View From the Bridge

By **JAKE MOONEY** | December 30, 2007

Because Ben Cipriano is a wisecracking kind of guy, maybe it's best to begin his story in the form of a joke: How many electricians does it take to screw in all the light bulbs on the Brooklyn Bridge? The answer is six. Not much of a punch line, but it has the advantage of being factually correct. Their names are Jerry, Tommy, Richie, Mike and Bobby, plus Mr. Cipriano, the boss, who has been climbing bridge cables for more than 20 years and does not plan to stop any time soon.

Mr. Cipriano is 58, and he got a job with the city's Department of Transportation in 1985 after serving in Vietnam, driving a taxi and working as a laborer on construction sites, where he couldn't help noticing that electricians never seemed to have to carry around heavy tools and trash barrels. He learned the trade and started working in a private shop, then saw an ad for a job working on the city's bridges.

They were low bridges at first, on Third Avenue over the Harlem River or Hamilton Avenue over the Gowanus Canal, where the view was somewhat less inspiring.

After two years, he hit the big time: the four East River bridges—the Brooklyn, the Manhattan, the Williamsburg and the Queensboro—where his crew maintained power supplies, controls, clocks and, yes, light bulbs. Some time later he was put in charge of them. He doesn't have to climb bridge cables anymore, but he often does anyway. For one thing, it beats sitting in the office. For another, the view is unparalleled.

We check in with Mr. Cipriano just now because of the mayor's announcement this month that a host of city landmarks, including the Brooklyn Bridge, will soon be outfitted with new, energy-efficient bulbs. The bulbs—light-emitting diodes, actually—should last much longer than the existing bulbs, which themselves last for years. One wonders what this means for the future of bridge-top bulb-changing.

Do not worry, though, about Ben Cipriano. There is plenty of other work up there, and no one is sure how the new lights will respond to the extreme weather conditions. He will be watching closely, as he already does, whenever he drives past when the lights are on, or sees one of his bridges while watching television with his family.

"Maybe I should get a hobby," he said. But getting the lights right is important to him, and the problem with the current lights, 100-watt mercury vapor bulbs, is that they turn green as they start to burn out. "Even if you have a couple of them out—160 bulbs are up there—people are going to notice," Mr. Cipriano said. "They don't look so hot if you have some bright ones and some green ones and so on and so forth."

> Up on top of the bridge,
> Mr. Cipriano still marvels at it all.

He doesn't remember his first glimpse of the Brooklyn Bridge, but he remembers pulling into New York Harbor, on a ship called the Volcania, as an 8-year-old immigrant from Sicily. He was right up in the front of the boat with his little brother, who was pushing a little to get them to the dock quicker.

Up on top of the bridge, Mr. Cipriano still marvels at it all, this time from a place with an unobstructed 360-degree view. "People would pay to go up there," he said, "and we're getting paid to go up there."

He has, in his pocket, a little camera: 35-millimeter before, digital now. He has spent enough time looking at New York to know what he likes. "No clouds is no good," he said. "Overcast is no good, obviously. But if you have clouds in the background with the buildings, it's just a great picture. ∎

BRIDGES

R.F.K. Bridge May Meet Fate Of Avenue of the Americas

By **JAMES BARRON** | June 6, 2008

WHAT'S IN A NAME, ANYWAY? WOULD THAT which we call the Triborough Bridge by any other name—oh, let's skip the Shakespeare and get to the point. Would anybody call the Triborough anything but the Triborough?

The short answer seems to be, no.

"It connects three boroughs," said Susan Breslaoukhov, the manager of a French Connection clothing store in Rockefeller Center. "That's self-explanatory. I expect people will keep calling it Triborough for a long time."

The what-will-they-call-it question came up after the State Assembly voted to rename the Triborough the Robert F. Kennedy Bridge, for the former attorney general who was elected to the United States Senate from New York in 1964. He died 40 years ago Friday, after being shot in Los Angeles, just after he won the California Democratic primary.

But some said the renaming could be confusing for commuters. "It's been that way for a million years," said Morton Mozzar, an automobile-service consultant in Queens. "If they had renamed it right afterwards, O.K., like they did with J.F.K. Airport." (The airport was called Idlewild but was renamed after President John F. Kennedy's assassination in 1963. It only seems as if the Triborough has been around for a million years. Next month it will have been open for 72 years.)

Some New Yorkers pointed to name changes that did not take. Consider the Marine Parkway-Gil Hodges Memorial Bridge, as it has been known for 30 years in honor of the former Brooklyn Dodgers first baseman and Mets manager.

Or what about renaming the Miller Highway the Joe DiMaggio? Mayor Rudolph W. Giuliani and Gov. George E. Pataki agreed to that in 1999, soon after DiMaggio's death.

The Miller Highway? Nobody called it that in the first place (except, perhaps, relatives of Julius Miller, the Manhattan borough president when the first section was opened in 1930). It ran from West 72nd Street to Battery Place and was not to be confused with the Henry Hudson Parkway, which runs north from 72nd.

"And what about the Thruway?" asked Mimi Marenberg of Airmont, N.Y. "Its name is the Thomas E. Dewey Thruway, but who calls it that? No one. We spend money on big signs, renaming these things, but all it does is generate money for the sign people."

And Avenue of the Americas, that avenue's official name for decades?

"I call it Sixth Avenue," said Ms. Breslaoukhov, the clothing-store manager, whose shop is at 1270 Avenue of the you-know-what. "If I say 'Avenue of the Americas,' people get confused and say, 'What?'" ■

BELOW: *Robert F. Kennedy Jr. spoke during the ceremony which renamed the TriBorough Bridge after his father, former NY Senator Robert F. Kennedy.*

First Week of Operation Reveals The Holland Tunnel, Marvel of Engineering

By **WALDO WALKER** | November 20, 1927

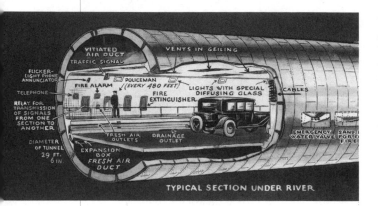

ABOVE: *An early plan of the Holland tunnel, which took seven years to construct. Today, the annual average daily traffic is close to 100,000.*

IN THE WEEK SINCE THE HOLLAND TUNNEL was opened to vehicular traffic it has more than justified all the claims made for its engineering perfection. Just as the tubes were bored out from either shore so unerringly that the two ends met to a friction of an inch in midriver, so everything planned by the engineers for the finished tunnel worked out.

The first week of operation accordingly answered the momentous questions that arose during the tunnel's construction. Would the $48,400,000 the tunnel cost provide the expected traffic relief for miles up and down the river and for miles inland? How would the public take to the new utility, and, if as heartily as anticipated, how would the twin tubes themselves behave under pressure? Would the ventilation system eliminate the deadly carbon monoxide gas discharged from the automobiles?

At the very outset the Holland Tunnel withstood a traffic shock that it probably will not have to sustain again in a long time. The opening day developed what is called the greatest single traffic rush ever seen along the Hudson River. Exactly 51,748 public cars streamed through the tubes during the first 24 hours.

Thereafter the number of "sightseers" decreased and the tunnel traffic was reduced to a volume large enough to pay expenses and leave something over to put in the bank. The estimated "maximum daily traffic" was put at 46,000 cars, but after the sensational opening day the weekday average dropped to around 18,000 cars. However, traffic experts say this falling off really means nothing as an index of the tunnel's future. They predict it will prove only temporary, and that there will be steady gains as motorists discover the new travel route. ∎

On the Job, Way Under Water

By **GRETCHEN KURTZ** | April 13, 2003

ON PAPER, JOANNE WILLIAMS HAS THE OFFICE everyone dreams of—not far from the water, with lots of windows and no chatty co-workers dropping by. But her location is one of the last places that most people want to find themselves these days: inside the Lincoln Tunnel. Not that Ms. Williams, 49, officially a tunnel and bridge agent with the Port Authority of New York and New Jersey, is complaining.

"They told us in training that this is a dangerous job," she said. "If you're not prepared, then don't do it."

E-Z Pass to Start At Hudson River Tunnels

By **DAVID M. HALBFINGER** | October 27, 1997

JUST AFTER MIDNIGHT TONIGHT, AN ELEC-tronic cordon around New York City will be complete when the E-Z Pass system is switched on at the toll plazas of the Holland and Lincoln Tunnels. For the first time, commuters will be able to drive to and from the city by any route without having to dig for dollar bills, scrounge for coins or hold up traffic asking for a receipt.

Lest anyone hope, however, that radio reports of "15-minute delays at the inbound Holland Tunnel" or "25-minute delays at the Lincoln Tunnel helix" will quickly fade into memory, officials with the Port Authority of New York and New Jersey warned that the E-Z Pass system is unlikely to ease morning rush-hour traffic at the two tunnels any time soon.

Two of the 13 lanes at the Lincoln Tunnel will be dedicated for E-Z Pass users, as will at least one of the nine lanes at the Holland Tunnel, although all lanes at both tunnels will be able to read the E-Z Pass transponders. E-Z Pass users—including infrequent travelers—will save 10 percent off the $4 toll, the same discount regular commuters now enjoy.

"I got mine," shouted John Canizaro of Lodi, N.J., waving his audiocassette-size transponder as he rolled through a toll lane.

But Ellen Seidman, an editor at Glamour magazine who lives in Hoboken, N.J., said she had heard stories of criminals breaking into cars and stealing the E-Z Pass transponders. "It's another thing to worry about," she said. "I've left the lights on in my car a few times. I don't want to have to think about this, too." ▪

> E-Z Pass system is unlikely to ease morning rush-hour traffic.

The job seemed only mildly dan-gerous when she signed up 17 years ago. Ms. Williams's biggest worry back then was what it would be like working 97 feet under water. But since the terror attacks of Sept. 11, 2001, and subsequent threats to both the Lincoln and the Holland Tunnels, things have changed. Their primary role—to keep traffic moving—has remained the same since the job was created in 1973. To keep traffic moving is not an easy task considering that nearly 21 million vehicles, about 60,000 on an average weekday, passed through the tunnel's three tubes to New York City last year.

Agents monitor traffic 24 hours a day, seven days a week. The agents typically sit in a slightly crouched position inside tiny electric-powered catwalk cars, parked inside booths of about 4 by 8 feet that are placed strategically where most accidents occur in the tunnel. When traffic stops, the agent on duty leaves the booth in the catwalk car and rides to the scene. Once there, the agents do everything in their power to solve the problem. If the vehicle has a flat, they fix it. If it is stalled, they jump-start it or call for a tow. If the driver or a passenger needs first aid, they administer it. The agents are given three months of classroom and on-the-job training in everything from firefighting to cardiopulmonary resuscitation.

"The best part of the job is the immediate satisfaction," tunnel agent Bob Murphy said. "When you show up, people want you there." ▪

How to Beat a Writer Across Town

By **CLYDE HABERMAN** | November 1, 2002

FOR A PERSONAL CHALLENGE, NOTHING compares to the New York City Marathon. Take it from someone who has completed the 26.2-mile course several times. Grinding along the streets of the five boroughs requires reservoirs of endurance, discipline, patience, resourcefulness and good cheer.

I really should try running it one of these days.

The preference here is to drive the marathon route, a ritual that was performed on Wednesday morning for the fourth time in the last eight autumns. As ever, the reason for schlepping through town in a rented car was to see if the mysteries of New York traffic had changed. (If you are now thinking that this exercise was nothing but a newspaper gimmick, I have only one thing to say to you: you're right.)

It took me 2 hours and 44 minutes on Wednesday to get from the starting point, the Verrazano-Narrows Bridge, to the finish line at Tavern on the Green in Central Park. Records kept by New York Road Runners show that 195 men and women ran last year's marathon in less time.

At 8 a.m., crossing downtown Brooklyn was a singular chore. Nor was there joy in getting onto and across the Queensboro Bridge headed toward Manhattan. It took 26 minutes, from 8:46 to 9:12.

The good news, if you can call it that, is that Wednesday's drive took 12 fewer minutes than the 2:56 recorded the last time out, two years ago. That's an improvement of nearly 7 percent. So it must mean that New York traffic is getting better, right?

Yeah, right (a rare example of two positives making a negative).

The sorry state of New York traffic is on many minds these days. One reason is a new experiment in mid-Manhattan, where traffic is often as congealed as a day-old lamb chop. Turns onto north-south avenues have been banned at certain times on 10 crosstown streets, the hope being that this will pick up the pace in Midtown, where vehicles were clocked last spring at an average speed of 4.8 miles per hour. Even Congress moves faster than that. ◾

BELOW: *Traffic congestion is typical along Park Avenue. More than half the people driving to and from work in Manhattan are not from the suburbs.*

$8 Traffic Fee For Manhattan Fails In Albany

By **NICHOLAS CONFESSORE** | April 8, 2008

ALBANY—Mayor Michael R. Bloomberg's far-reaching plan to ease traffic in Manhattan died here on Monday when Democratic members of the State Assembly held a final, closed-door meeting and found overwhelming opposition.

The plan would have charged drivers $8 to enter a congestion zone in Manhattan south of 60th Street during peak hours. It was strongly opposed by a broad array of

Who's Driving May Be Surprising

By **WILLIAM NEUMAN** | January 12, 2007

IT'S A COMMON ENOUGH THOUGHT AMONG city drivers inching through traffic: Everyone around me came from the suburbs, making my life miserable. But it's wrong, because more than half the drivers who crowd into Manhattan each workday come from the five boroughs.

That is only one fact about traffic in New York City that may surprise some people. For example, 35 percent of government workers drive to work, many because they have free parking. Also, one in five drivers entering the busiest parts of Manhattan are only passing through, on their way somewhere else.

"There's a lot of myths, and when you look at the data, the myths go pop, pop, pop, one by one," said Bruce Schaller, a transportation consultant who has studied regional traffic patterns.

One of the most prevalent beliefs to crumble beneath the data might be called the suburban myth, the notion that suburbanites make up a majority of the commuters who drive to work in Manhattan.

Census data show that more city residents than suburbanites drive to work in Manhattan every day, according to Mr. Schaller. When plotted on a map, the data make a striking picture, showing that some of the densest concentrations of auto commuters are from the outer fringes of Queens and Brooklyn, where access to subways is limited.

That applies to Dennis Alicea, of Bayside, Queens. Mr. Alicea, a banker for JPMorgan Chase, drives from Bayside to Manhattan. To commute on public transportation, Mr. Alicea, 38, would have to take a bus from his home to the Long Island Rail Road station at Bayside, ride a train to Pennsylvania Station, then take a subway.

"You have to go into a stuffy, over-crowded train with people with attitudes," he said. "I prefer driving for the peace of mind. It's much easier." ∎

politicians from Queens, Brooklyn and suburban communities, who viewed the proposed congestion fee as a regressive measure that overwhelmingly benefited affluent Manhattanites.

The plan's collapse was a severe blow to Mr. Bloomberg's environmental agenda and political legacy. The mayor introduced his plan a year ago as the signature proposal of a 127-item program for sustainable city growth that helped raise his national profile.

Without the approval from Albany, the city now stands to lose about $354 million worth of federal money that would have financed the system for collecting the fee and helped to pay for new bus routes and other traffic measures. New York had hoped to use the revenues from congestion pricing to finance billions of dollars in subway expansion and other improvements by the Metropolitan Transportation Authority, money that must now come from somewhere else.

Assemblyman Mark S. Weprin, a Queens Democrat, estimated that opinion among Assembly Democrats at the meeting ran four to one against the plan. But no formal vote was taken.

"It takes a special type of cowardice for elected officials to refuse to stand up and vote their conscience on an issue that has been debated, and amended significantly to resolve many outstanding issues, for more than a year," Mr. Bloomberg said. "Every New Yorker has a right to know if the person they send to Albany was for or against better transit and cleaner air." ∎

A Pedestrian's Lot Is Not A Happy One

By **ELIZABETH ONATIVIA** | July 7, 1929

THE DAY OF THE HERO WITH THE LONG careless stride is over. Pedestrianism in city streets today involves executive ability, planning and foresight, specialized knowledge and concentration. It's pure paradox that walking is often quicker than motoring. And it's paradoxical that it should be equally complicated.

It's hard on the pedestrian, for he has to keep turning and craning; and stopping and starting. Assuming that he has the right of way, and that no driver wants the satisfaction of running over him, he still has some justification for retaining his timidity. In the first four months of this year, according to recent figures, because motorists refused to grant the right of way, 54 persons were killed and 5,152 injured in New York State.

The crafty New Yorker, therefore, walking for so-called exercise, to save money, to save time, plots his journey like a trip to Europe. He goes crab-like from east to west, say, crossing with the lights. He may even go crab-like down the main lanes, two blocks to this side to avoid the debris and boardwalks of construction work, two blocks to the other, to avoid the detour around the excavation. He develops all sorts of unconscious tricks and fancies. His mind is always on the job. If it isn't, the blast of a horn, or the gentle push of a fender, will recall it.

In some places, the arcades and underground, passages afford relief, but these take practice. For instance, the new passage from the station to 46th Street, under the New York Central Building, its delightful, after you have round the entrance, but even then you may end up in the more intimate quarters of the Railway Express. The pedestrian who is an adept at these passages exhibits his knowledge as proudly as if he were driving a car. ∎

Think You Own The Sidewalk? Etiquette by New York Pedestrians Showing Strain

By **MARC SANTORA** | July 16, 2002

ON THE SIDEWALKS OF NEW YORK THERE ARE jaywalkers, baby walkers, dog walkers, night walkers, cell phone talker-walkers, slow walkers, fast walkers, group walkers, drunken walkers, walkers with walkers and, of course, tourist walkers.

Unfortunately, all of these walkers are walking into one another.

"There was a time that any real New Yorker had a built-in sonar in terms of walking down the sidewalk, even a crowded one, and never bumping into someone," said John Kalish, a television producer in Manhattan. "Now—forget it."

Sometimes it is impossible to be a graceful walker. Still, strollers say that many problems could be avoided if basic rules were followed.

First, walking rules are like driving rules.

"Stay to the right is the golden, No. 1 rule," said Chris Avila, 29, who has lived in the city for nine years.

Second, don't be a sudden stopper.

"People who stop short really get me," said Carla Melman, 26, a lifelong New Yorker. She said it was the equivalent of a car wreck on the Long Island Expressway on a Hamptons weekend.

'Walk' Signals Set an Example For a City Losing Weight

By **DAVID W. DUNLAP** | August 13, 2005

IS IT JUST COINCIDENCE THAT IN THE SUMMER that New York City went to war against trans fats, a new generation of "Walk/Don't Walk" icons began appearing around Columbus Circle with a noticeably skinnier walking man and an almost emaciated red hand?

Your typical walking man—a familiar silhouette around town in the five years since the first new light-emitting diode pedestrian signal was installed at 35th Street and Queens Boulevard—is a pretty robust, smooth-shouldered, round-headed fellow who steps off confidently into traffic, as bubbly as a Keith Haring figure.

This new guy, by contrast, seems a bit rickety. There isn't a curve to his body. His head—is this too cruel to say?—is pentagonal. His arms and legs are mere sticks. Indeed, he looks as though he's stooped over with a bad back. (Maybe from waiting so long for the light to change.)

About that upraised hand. The one that New Yorkers have grown accustomed to is as smooth and solid as a porcelain glove mold. The new hand is so skeletally thin it might be the crypt keeper's.

But they say you can never be too thin. After all, the skinny man is formed of 45 light-emitting diodes, where the older version tips the scales at 60. The new hand has 64 diodes, the old one 120. So maybe this was an energy conservation step.

Well, it turns out that the Department of Transportation is not quite sure what those skinny men are doing around Columbus Circle, though it may be the case that the noncon-forming signals were installed mistakenly. They are not, in any event, tied into the antifat campaign the city announced this week.

"We're happy to do our part to encourage a healthy New York," Iris Weinshall, the transportation commissioner, said in a statement. "However, the pedestrian signals will be inspected to ensure that they are the D.O.T. standard figure and hand."

And that may be the end of "Walk/Don't Walk" lite. ∎

Third, when walking with friends, don't crowd every lane of the sidewalk.

Ms. Avila said she reserves a special sidewalk in hell for "mall walkers," which she defined as groups who insist on walking three or four abreast. "They make me so mad," she said. "When you are around a group of mall walkers, you just have to find a way around them."

Fourth, keep it moving.

The average fast walker does not have to get stuck behind a pack of mall walkers to grow sour. A single person moving can be enough. There is even a word for this slowpoke: meanderthal, defined by an Internet dictionary of slang as "an annoying individual moving slowly and aimlessly in front of another individual who is in a bit of a hurry." ∎

BELOW: *Given New Yorkers' tendency to ignore traffic lights, it seems unlikely that they'll pay attention to a 45-diode weakling.*

For the Hard Core, Two Wheels Beat Four

By **J. DAVID GOODMAN** | July 27, 2008

IT WAS 7:30 A.M. ON A HUMID MONDAY, AND David Muller, a doctor and a suburban bike commuter, was sweating his way to work. As he rode along the George Washington Bridge and into Manhattan, Dr. Muller, 44, seemed indifferent to the low roar of rush-hour traffic. He was halfway from Teaneck, N.J.—where he lives—to Mount Sinai Medical Center—where he works—and was happy to be on his bicycle.

"It's free, it's good for the environment, good for your health," he said about 5 miles into his 12-mile ride. "And it's a little danger-ous, so you get a little thrill at the beginning and the end of each day." He also gets satisfac-tion from beating cars across the bridge.

Five minutes later, another commuter pedaled along. Henry Minnerop, a partner in a Manhattan law firm and "70-plus" years old, said he drives each day—year round — to Englewood Cliffs, N.J., and then bikes about 12 miles into Midtown. "There's a gym in my office," he said. "I shower and come out looking like a lawyer." ◼

BELOW: *New Yorker's have been biking to work for decades, and its popularity is growing. Figures suggest there currently are over 25,000 bike commuters in the city.*

Police and a Cyclists' Group, And Four Years Of Clashes

By **JAMES BARRON** | August 4, 2008

THE NEW YORK CITY POLICE DEPARTMENT, with its 35,000 officers, has in recent years been on the front lines of the citywide decline in serious crime. It has protected visiting dignitaries like Pope Benedict XVI at events that drew thousands of people, and it has posted officers in foreign capitals to gather information on terrorism and trends that could threaten New York.

But the Police Department continues to be flummoxed by bicyclists riding together once a month.

The rides are known as Critical Mass. The police say that the cyclists who take part in them break the law—running red lights and blocking side streets to allow riders to pass while shouting disparaging comments at officers. Over the past four years, the cyclists say, the police have arrested about 600 riders and issued more than 1,000 summonses during Critical Mass rides.

A cyclist arrested in the latest rally was accused of riding straight into an officer in Times Square. When a video surfaced showing the officer going out of his way to shove the rider off his bike, it seemed to surprise officials.

"From what you could see on the video, it looked to me to be totally over the top," Mayor Michael R. Bloomberg said. Police Commissioner Raymond W. Kelly told a

Not So Merrily, They Roll Along: Pedicabs Vie for Midtown Riders

By **SEWELL CHAN** and **NICHOLAS CONFESSORE** | January 2, 2005

television reporter, "I can't explain why it happened. I have no understanding as to why that would happen."

The antagonism between the police and Critical Mass riders has festered for years. The police, unable to convince the courts that the cyclists need permits that would force them to adhere to some restrictions, have adopted what the riders consider belligerent tactics. For their part, the riders have avoided negotiations with the city—and oversight—by refusing to name anyone as their leader.

"It's just a bike ride, but the cops are treating it like a war," said Bill DiPaola, the director of Time's Up, an environmental group that says it promotes the rides but is not involved in organizing them.

The mood changed, cyclists say, in August 2004, when the city was preparing for the Republican National Convention. About 5,000 cyclists took part in that month's ride. Some shouted "No more Bush!" as they neared Madison Square Garden, where the convention was to be held. The police arrested more than 100 people, mostly on charges of disorderly conduct.

Since then, the relationship between the bicyclists and the police has been "antagonistic," said a former commander of a Manhattan precinct often traversed by Critical Mass riders. "We look at them as just a bunch of radical bikers," he said.

Cyclists say labels like "radical" or "anarchist" are unfair. "Since the police decided to treat it as a criminal act, the entire tone of the rides has changed," said Eric Goldhagen, a longtime rider who works as a technology consultant. "Instead of being fun, it's now something that I don't enjoy, but feel I have to do." ∎

AT FIRST, THE GIANT TRICYCLES DID NOT seem quite so threatening.

Pedicabs were more of a novelty than a legitimate mode of transport when a group of environmentalists and artists in Manhattan began pedaling them—and peddling rides on them—nine years ago.

But in the past two years, according to unofficial estimates, the number of pedicabs has nearly doubled, spurred by an influx of entrepreneurs and popularized when they were featured on Donald J. Trump's reality television show, "The Apprentice."

Long popular in Southeast Asia, pedicabs are now combatants in a quiet war on the streets of Midtown, with tourist dollars as the primary spoils.

Drivers of horse-drawn carriages and taxicabs are demanding a crackdown on the unlicensed three-wheelers. Along Central Park South, hackney drivers accuse pedicab operators of stealing their customers in what has long been their domain. Cabdrivers say their exclusive license to pick up passengers who hail them on the streets is slowly being undermined.

"These guys have just gone out into the streets, and nobody's questioned them," said Cornelius P. Byrne, who inherited his father's stable and hackney carriages in 1964. "It's kind of crazy. Nobody is asking if it's right, or legal."

Their growing presence at heavily trafficked intersections has rivals complaining, loudly. Mohammed Diarra, a cabdriver for five years, estimates that he has lost 10 percent of his business, concentrated in the Midtown theater and business district, since the pedicabs began to explode in popularity.

"Business has definitely dropped off," he said. "If I had a choice, I'd get rid of them. The traffic isn't safe, and they pick up our passengers. We pay a lot of money to pick people up in Manhattan." Three months ago, Mr. Diarra said, the weekly rental fee he pays for his medallion rose to $780, from $650. ∎

Thirty-Three Ferries In New York District

By JOHN T. VOGEL | March 30, 1930

THE MOTORING MANHATTANITE, POISED LIKE a satyr for the green fields of spring, has a choice of 22 green routes to the countryside. Sunlit waves lapping the island are cut by more than a score of shifting ferry lanes. Even a Venetian has fewer boats to choose from.

The domain of the Doges has its bridges, and so has Manhattan with the new Holland Tunnel added, but ferries still serve the convenience and contribute to the pleasure of many motorists. The Port of New York Authority lists 33 ferries in the metropolitan district. Two-thirds of the lines have terminals in Manhattan.

An excursion trip in itself, the municipal line from Whitehall Street to St. George, S.I., is the longest ferry trip within the city limits. Motorists have found this a pleasant prelude to Jersey coast resort trips, the route going from St. George by way of Bay Street and Hylan Boulevard along the east shore of Staten Island. A confusing hairpin turn at the Outerbridge Crossing plaza has been eliminated, the motorist continuing in a more direct line across the bridge to Perth Amboy, N. J. ▪

BELOW: *The Staten Island Ferry Terminal at St. George in 1953.*

Investigation Begins Into Ferry Crash That Killed 10

By JANNY SCOTT | October 16, 2003

A STATEN ISLAND FERRY MOVING AT A RAPID clip in gusting winds crashed into a pier at the St. George ferry terminal, killing 10 people and injuring dozens of others as the concrete and wood pier sliced through its side, mowing down tourists and commuters.

The exact cause of the 3:20 p.m. accident was not clear. Law enforcement officials said the ferry's pilot fled the scene to his home in the Westerleigh neighborhood of Staten Island, barricaded himself in a bathroom, slit his wrists and shot himself twice in the chest with a powerful pellet gun.

The pilot, identified by city officials as Assistant Capt. Richard J. Smith, survived and was in critical condition at a local hospital, where detectives were waiting to interview him. Mr. Smith was in charge of the boat when it neared the Staten Island terminal at a high speed, and his captain noticed that the ferry was off course, according to one police official. The captain tried to get control of the boat, the official said, but it slammed into a concrete maintenance pier about 400 feet from the nearest ferry slip.

Investigators were trying to determine last night whether Mr. Smith had been drinking or taking drugs, had fallen asleep or was perhaps incapacitated as a result

FERRIES

Fifty Years, Five Cents: The Staten Island Ferry Has a Birthday

By **McCANDLISH PHILLIPS** | October 23, 1955

THE STATEN ISLAND-MANHATTAN FERRY, whose charge it is to connect the North American continent to Staten Island, is going to take a satisfied look at its 50-year history this week and congratulate itself on having come so far and done so well.

The 50th anniversary of the city-owned service will be celebrated with (a) wisps of white smoke, or (b) billows of black smoke or (c) a light, almost invisible haze, depending upon the art with which the stokers below decks compound the oil and the air that are the elements of their fuel formula.

A reporter recently undertaking his maiden voyage on the ferry was led to the Kolff, a vessel 269.5 feet long and 69 feet wide built in 1951 at a cost of $7 million. Its passenger capacity, 2,954, is about as great as that of the Queen Mary, and the Kolff usually makes the five-and-a-half-mile run between the Battery and Staten Island in 22 minutes at an average speed of about 14 knots. Tide, traffic and weather affect the time of the trip and a dense fog will occasionally extend it to 50 minutes. Forty-four passenger vehicles can fit into the Kolff's three-lane, street-level craw.

The Staten Island Ferry (everybody speaks of it as if there were but one, though in fact there are 10) is essentially a seaworthy streetcar. Passengers sit on trolley-like benches, facing one another in long rows and encountering difficulty in finding something sensible to do with their eyes.

One of the best ways not to demonstrate that you are in the nautical know is to go about referring to Staten Island ferries as ships. They are not ships; they are boats. You may call them vessels if you wish, but to speak of them as ships is to betray a schooling that has been largely acquired ashore. (In the Navy, any boat that is large enough to carry another boat on it or in it is called a ship. And if you go around calling it a boat, you are likely to find yourself furnishing regular assistance to the boys in the galley. The ways of the sea are mysterious.) ∎

of a medical condition, a law enforcement official said.

Passengers compared what ensued to a scene from "Titanic." They said there was an ominous grinding sound followed by a bang, like an explosion. Then the pier, like an iceberg, sheared into the side of the main deck, tearing it open. With no announcements or instructions by the boat's crew, passengers began fleeing in confusion and panic.

"The beams are coming directly at you, and the side of the boat is disappearing," said Robert Carroll, a lawyer for the state court system, who was on board. "They're ripping up steel, glass, chairs. People were falling. At one point I was in a pile, and I just got up and kept running. It kept coming and coming. If you didn't keep running, you were dead." ∎

BELOW: *The ferry, shown here transporting morning commuters to Manhattan terminal, services 65,000 riders a day.*

325,000 See Mayor Dedicate Airport to World Service

October 16, 1939

ABOVE : *Mayor LaGuardia presides over ground-breaking ceremonies for the new airport. It was voted "greatest airport in the world" in 1960 by the worldwide aviation community.*

Already approved by most of the major airlines, which have rented hangar space, and unqualifiedly accepted by the pilots as the safest in the United States, the field awaits only official acceptance by the Civil Aeronautical Authority to begin operation as a transcontinental and transatlantic terminus.

If any proof was needed of its worthiness of designation as the world's greatest airport, the 150 planes that landed and took off yesterday with only one minor mishap must have supplied it. Army and navy pilots who saw it for the first time said it was as fine a field as ever they had used.

> Conceived in 1935, it was begun in September 1937 and rushed to completion by the Works Projects Administration in a little over two years at a cost of $40 million to $45 million.

THE WORLD'S POTENTIALLY GREATEST AIR terminal, the newly completed municipal airport at North Beach, built on the accumulated refuse of the city, was dedicated yesterday by Mayor La Guardia before 325,000 persons under the most auspicious circumstances of wind and weather.

Conceived in 1935, when the Post Office Department declined to accept Floyd Bennett Airport in Brooklyn as the air terminus for the city, it was begun in September 1937 and rushed to completion by the Works Projects Administration in a little over two years at a cost of $40 million to $45 million. It thus became W.P.A.'s biggest project.

There was not a cloud in the sky and a northwest breeze of only 18 miles an hour was blowing as the airplanes and the vanguard of the crowd began to arrive at 9 a.m. Two thousand policemen, under the personal direction of Commissioner Lewis Valentine and Chief Inspector Louis F. Costuma, were on hand to keep them moving and out of harm's way. The mayor, who was so happy that he said he could even find it in his heart to forgive all those who had criticized the undertaking, arrived before noon so he would not miss any of the fun. ∎

To Pilots, Shea Is Less Ballpark Than Landmark

By **MICHAEL S. SCHMIDT** | September 26, 2008

FOR 44 YEARS, THE PROCESSION OF PLANES from nearby La Guardia Airport has contributed to an unusual ballpark soundtrack at Shea Stadium, the roar of jet engines a thousand feet above the crack of the bats and the cries of the hot dog vendors.

With the stadium about to shut its gates for the final time, the spectators who can claim perhaps the most peculiar relationship with the ballpark may be airline pilots who, with a bird's-eye peek at the field through cockpit windows, have participated in that uncommon convergence of baseball and aviation.

"You are so low and close you can see it and almost smell it," said Glen Millen, who estimates that he has flown into and out of La Guardia 1,800 times since he began flying for American Airlines in 1986.

La Guardia is one of the few airports in the country where pilots use land markers instead of instruments to guide their landings. Shea Stadium, which from the sky looks like a blue circle with a green center, is a primary runway guidepost. For one of the more common landing routes, pilots are instructed to follow the Long Island Expressway until they arrive at the eastern side of the stadium, at which point they bank the plane left around the outfield wall and head straight for Runway 31.

"We make a sweeping turn around Shea Stadium to land, and you bank the airplane and out of the corner of your eye you can see the scoreboard and the players," said Joe Romanko, a pilot with American Airlines since 1990. "It's more dramatic at night because you track the lights on the stadium from way out."

> La Guardia is one of the few airports in the country where pilots use land markers instead of instruments to guide their landings.

In 1964, the Mets' first season at Shea, a pilot got an even closer look. He mistook the lights on top of the stadium for the runway and nearly hit it as the team took batting practice before a game against the St. Louis Cardinals. ∎

Mayor La Guardia Won't Land In Newark

November 25, 1934

NEWARK, WHICH TRIED TO TAKE AWAY NEW York's Stock Exchange and now is making faces at the metropolis across the river because New York is taking traffic from its airport, was shunned by Mayor La Guardia on his return from Chicago by airplane last night.

Unlike other passengers, the mayor remained in the TWA plane on its arrival at the Newark Municipal Airport. While several of the others went by automobile to Manhattan, the mayor traveled in the plane to New York's municipal airport at Floyd Bennett Field. Mr. La Guardia, who had attended the conference of mayors in Chicago, was greeted at the flying field by his wife, who was accompanied by his secretary, Lester Stone.

On alighting, the mayor confirmed reports that he had refused to be deposited at Newark. "My ticket says New York," he said, "and that's where they brought me." ∎

Idlewild Is Rededicated As John F. Kennedy Airport

By **PHILIP BENJAMIN** | December 25, 1963

SHORTLY AFTER NOON YESTERDAY, THE PILOT of a transcontinental airliner flicked a switch and announced to his passengers, "Ladies and gentlemen, we will be arriving shortly at Kennedy International Airport." A half hour earlier New York International Airport at Idlewild, Queens, had been formally renamed John F. Kennedy International Airport.

Just before that, in a ceremony at the International Arrivals Building, Senator Edward M. Kennedy of Massachusetts, brother of the president, unveiled three letters—J.F.K.—that will form part of a sign 242 feet long and 8 feet high.

"The name is already assured of remembrance in the chronicles of these times and of all times," Mayor Wagner told the assemblage. "Thus we do not pretend to add to the name's luster by adopting it for even this great crossroads of the world's skyway." ■

BELOW: *The JetBlue Flight Center officially opened on October 22, 2008.*

Airline Terminal For the Post-9/11 Era

By **DAVID W. DUNLAP** | March 11, 2008

FROM THE MOMENT THE FIRST PASSENGERS arrive at JetBlue Airways' new, $750 million terminal at Kennedy International Airport, they will face an unmistakably post-9/11 world.

Most airline terminals have been jury-rigged since 2001 to accommodate all the extra security workers and equipment. But JetBlue's new Terminal 5 is among the first in the United States designed from the ground up after the terrorist attacks.

The 340-foot-wide security checkpoint will dominate the departures hall the way ticket counters once did, with 20 security lanes. Travelers will find a lot of benches where they can pull themselves back together after running the security gantlet. There will be subtler touches, too: a resilient rubber Tuflex floor (instead of cold, hard terrazzo) for the areas where one has to go shoeless.

"We want the security process to be thoroughly rigorous but minimally intrusive," said William R. DeCota, director of aviation at the Port Authority of New York and New Jersey, which runs Kennedy. "The design of that terminal was intended to make sure that no one will have to worry that their wait time is going to be greater than 10 minutes."

The new terminal has been overshadowed by that abandoned embodiment of the "Come Fly With Me" era of jet-setting, the Trans World Airlines Flight Center, designed by Eero Saarinen and also known as Terminal 5. JetBlue passengers will be able to pass through it on their way to the new Terminal 5. ■

Century After Wright Brothers, A Computer-run Train to J.F.K.

By **MICHAEL LUO** and **STACY ALBIN** | December 18, 2003

A HUNDRED YEARS TO THE DAY AFTER THE Wright brothers first flew, nearly 60 years after Robert Moses dismissed an early version of the idea, 40 years after Idlewild Airport became Kennedy, and 34 years after man landed on the moon, New York City got its long-awaited train-to-the-plane link yesterday.

Sort of.

Before a phalanx of cameras, Mayor Michael R. Bloomberg and Gov. George E. Pataki stepped off the AirTrain into the gleaming new terminal in Jamaica, a few hours before it opened to the public. But the carefully choreographed moment was marred when the new train's stainless steel doors closed too quickly on Mr. Bloomberg, causing him to stagger. He was caught by Mr. Pataki.

Righting himself, Mr. Bloomberg pronounced: "The ride was great."

Last night, the train experienced other problems, when an electrical malfunction halted service for about 20 minutes. The hiccups were in many ways symbolic of this project, which has been studied more than a dozen times over the decades. Transit advocates and politicians have long sought a "one-seat ride" directly from Manhattan to Kennedy Airport.

The AirTrain is a sleek, computer-operated train that connects the airport to local trains and subways at airy terminals in Jamaica and Howard Beach. But commuters coming from Manhattan, especially those taking the subway, must still endure a long ride and transfer. Proponents predict that the service will be popular nevertheless, because it will spare travelers from an unpredictable taxi ride that can take as long as two hours in bad traffic and costs $35 plus tolls and tip.

According to the Port Authority, taking the Long Island Railroad from Penn Station to Jamaica, Queens, and then the Airtrain to the Airport should take 35 minutes, at a total cost of $11.75. But on the subway, the same trip takes an hour or more and costs a total of $7. The AirTrain alone is $5.

Transit advocates point out that Cleveland got its rapid transit to the airport 30 years ago. Washington, Chicago, Paris and London all have model systems. In London, the trip from the center of the city takes 15 minutes. Meanwhile, Kennedy, which has more international passengers than any other airport in the country, has evolved into one of the nation's least accessible, with chronic congestion on the two main routes to it, the Van Wyck Expressway and the Belt Parkway.

Yesterday, a crowd of about 100 people, mostly just the curious, gathered at the Jamaica Terminal at 2 p.m. to be the first passengers. The trains were free until midnight.

Many standing in taxi lines said they did not know about the new service. But when told that the service was free for the day, Lawrence W. Safer, visiting from Los Angeles, stepped out of a taxi line to try what he was told was a New York first.

"It looks pretty cool on the outside," he said. ▪

BELOW: *Construction of the AirTrain system began in 1998, but was delayed by the derailment of a test train on September 27, 2002, which killed 23-year-old operator Kelvin DeBourgh, Jr.*

"Architects said nothing would be higher; engineers said nothing could be higher; city planners said nothing should be higher; and owners said nothing higher would pay."

That sounds like the recipe for a New York skyscraper—equal parts bravado, genius and limit-pushing. The architect Harvey Wiley Corbett had all three (and a client with plenty of money). The building he was talking about, one that he had designed, was the city's tallest. In 1890.

Years later E.B. White said New York had to expand toward the sky "because of the absence of any other direction in which to grow," and even before the Great

The Cityscape

ARCHITECTURE & PARKS

Depression, the race was on for bragging rights: my tall new building is taller than your tall new building. Everything on the skyline at the beginning of the twentieth century was dwarfed by the 792-foot-tall Woolworth Building, a five-and-dime-store millionaire's dream that opened in 1913. The architecture critic Paul Goldberger said its tall and relatively thin shape added to the sense that one's imagination could soar—if not get carried away: in the lobby are bas-reliefs of F. W. Woolworth himself, contentedly counting his nickels and dimes.

Nowhere did the imagination soar higher than at the corner of 42nd Street and Lexington Avenue, where the Chrysler Building's stain-

▲ PAGE 106

less steel top crowned a romantic fantasy too delicate for King Kong. Better to look down on it from the observation deck at the sleeker, plainer Empire State Building, which came along in 1931.

The Empire State Building is taller than the original blueprints said it would be. It grew by some 200 feet after the financier John J. Raskob looked at a scale model of the flat-topped original and said, "It needs a hat." The one that was grafted on was designed as an airport in the sky. Passengers in gas-filled dirigibles were to de-blimp on the 102nd floor, but updrafts from Manhattan's street-level canyons made landings all but impossible. Only two airships ever managed to tie up there. Both lifted off again without discharging any passengers.

No buildings went that high for another forty years. Rockefeller Center, a city-within-the-city, spread out over block after block of Midtown Manhattan. It was praised by some as the most ambitious construction project since the Pyramids and panned by Lewis Mumford in The New Yorker as "mediocrity—seen through a magnifying glass." The GE Building (originally the RCA Building) was tall, but not that tall. Neither were the MetLife Building (originally the Pan Am Building) or the General Motors Building on Fifth Avenue, to name two newcomers from the 1960's.

But New York's architecture is not just about tall, taller and tallest, it's about variety. On any avenue brownstones sit proudly next to massive high-rises that co-exist with flashy hotels. But some buildings are more distinctive than others: the triangular Flatiron Building, for example, looks like an ocean liner cruising up Fifth Avenue. It was so captivatng that the photographer Alfred Stieglitz said the Flatiron Building was to the United States as the Parthenon was to ancient Greece.

New York has official landmarks, designated by a city commission established in the 1960's after the old Pennsylvania Station was demolished—a Gilded Age marvel, preservationists said, even if it had grown shabby since World War II. Now New York has more than 400 buildings with landmark status and more than 25 neighborhoods that have been named "historic districts," with restrictions on changes inside and out. New Yorkers worried not only about losing their old buildings, they worried about how their new buildings would change the skyline. The Time Warner Center was scaled down after preservationists including Jacqueline Kennedy Onassis complained that its shadow would darken Central Park.

Central Park is 870 acres of grass and ball fields and curving paths and unobtrusive stone bridges, a giant green rectangular carpet in the middle of Manhattan

that was laid out before there were neighborhoods to surround it. And it's just one park—the city has more than 1,700 in all, from "vest-pocket" parks sandwiched between midtown office buildings to parks that cover thousands of acres. The architects behind Central Park also designed Prospect Park and Fort Greene Park in Brooklyn and Morningside Park in Manhattan. The century-old New York Public Library backs up to Bryant Park, where you can lounge through your lunch hour on a warm day.

In the 1970's, the quarter-mile-high towers of the World Trade Center soared over Lower Manhattan. Some critics groused that they were unbearably plain-looking. The architectural guidebook writer Francis Morrone said the best thing about them was was the view from the top, "the only high vantage points in New York from which the World Trade Center itself is not visible." But the twin towers captivated tourists and stunt men, who provided the romance and drama the architects had left out. The mountain climber George Willig clawed his way up one tower; the tightrope walker Philippe Petit danced from one to the other.

And then, on a bright morning in September 2001, they were gone. They collapsed less than two hours after terrorists took aim with hijacked airliners. From the emptiness at ground zero, the Woolworth Building a few blocks away once again looked tall.

▼ PAGE 126

A Baker's Dozen of Masterpieces

By **PAUL GOLDBERGER** | July 31, 1987

THE FIRST TEMPTATION FOR THE ARCHITEC-
ture buff in New York City is to track down
the latest things, be they good or bad: the office
towers and apartment blocks of Battery Park
City, for example, or the glitzy office buildings
of the East 50's. But as the new buildings
often physically overwhelm the old, a fixation
on the most au courant architecture can
overshadow the classic structures of the city,
those works of architecture that, though they
be neither the biggest nor the newest, remain
the greatest, the works that transform our
vision of what architecture and the city can be.

A baker's dozen of such structures
follows. It is a particular irony that the two
greatest works of architecture in New York
are not buildings at all—Central Park and the
Brooklyn Bridge. The park came first, an
esthetic, engineering and social achievement
of monumental proportions.

And if the bridge is not so completely a
symbol of New York as the Eiffel Tower is of
Paris, it deserves to be. The Gothic towers,
once the tallest thing on the skyline, are true
gateways, harking back to 19th-century New
York; the soaring roadway carries the city
into the present, and beckons it onward still.

Here are the others of this baker's dozen
of great New York structures:

HAUGHWOUT BUILDING, 488 Broadway,
at Broome Street.

DAKOTA, Central Park West and 72nd Street.

UNIVERSITY CLUB, One West 54th Street,
at Fifth Avenue.

WOOLWORTH BUILDING, 233 Broadway,
between Park Place and Barclay Street.

GRAND CENTRAL TERMINAL, 42nd Street
at Park Avenue.

CHRYSLER BUILDING, 405 Lexington
Avenue, at 42nd Street.

ROCKEFELLER CENTER, Fifth and Avenue
of the Americas, from West 48th to West 51st
Streets.

SEAGRAM BUILDING, 375 Park Avenue,
between 52nd and 53rd Streets.

GUGGENHEIM MUSEUM, 1071 Fifth
Avenue, at 89th Street.

FORD FOUNDATION, 320 East 43rd Street,
between First and Second Avenues.

BATTERY PARK CITY, Battery Place,
Chambers Street and outward from West
Street. ▪

BELOW: *The Woolworth building, built in 1913, is one of
the oldest skyscrapers in the city.*

arCHITECTURE

Hey, New York, Tear Down These Walls

By **NICOLAI OUROUSSOFF** | September 28, 2008

EVEN THE MOST MAJESTIC CITIES ARE pockmarked with horrors. There are countless dreadful buildings in New York; only a few (thankfully) have a traumatic effect on the city. So here's what I propose. Why not refocus our energies on knocking down the structures that not only fail to bring us joy, but actually bring us down?

I toyed with mentioning the AT&T Building (now the Sony Building) on my list of buildings that should be removed. I've disliked it since 1984, when it appeared (in miniature) cradled in the arms of its architect, Philip Johnson, on the cover of Time magazine. Its farcical Chippendale top was an instant hit, and a generation of architects grew up believing that any tower, no matter how cheap and badly designed, could be defended if you added a pretty fillip to the roof. Yet Johnson's building also represents a turning point in architectural history. And I eventually came to the conclusion that destroying it would be cultural censorship.

So my list will not include affronts that are merely aesthetic. Tearing down the following buildings would make room for the spirit to breathe again and open up new imaginative possibilities:

MADISON SQUARE GARDEN AND PENNSYLVANIA STATION—The demolition of McKim, Mead & White's monumental Pennsylvania Station in 1964 remains one of the greatest crimes in American architectural history. What replaced it is one of the city's most dehumanizing spaces.

TRUMP PLACE—You may find his Trump Tower on Fifth Avenue gaudy, but doesn't its cockiness makes you grin? So how to explain Trump Place, a cheap, miserable residential complex on the Upper West Side that is as glamorous as a toll plaza.

JACOB K. JAVITS CONVENTION CENTER—The black glass exterior gives it the air of a gigantic mausoleum.

ANNENBERG BUILDING, MOUNT SINAI MEDICAL CENTER—This towering structure, clad in rusted Cor-Ten steel, looks like either a military fortress or the headquarters of a sinister spy agency. But what's more disturbing is the tower's savage effect on its surroundings.

> There are countless dreadful buildings in New York; only a few (thankfully) have a traumatic effect on the city.

375 PEARL STREET—The New York Telephone Company (now Verizon) tower at 375 Pearl Street is a unique kind of horror. Seen from the Brooklyn Bridge, it blots out one of the world's greatest urban vistas, and each time I cross the East River, I want to throw my cell phone at it.

ASTOR PLACE—Gwathmey Siegel's luxury residential tower makes obvious reference to one of the masterpieces of early Modernism, Mies van der Rohe's unbuilt 1922 Glass Skyscraper project. His vision was slender and refined. Gwathmey's tower is squat and clumsy.

2 COLUMBUS CIRCLE—Edward Durell Stone's building, which opened as the Gallery of Modern Art in 1964, incited one of the most bitter preservation battles in recent memory. But the cowardly New York City Landmarks Preservation Commission never rendered a verdict. If the city had chosen to preserve it, a historical landmark would still be intact. If the building had been torn down, a talented architect might have had the opportunity to create a new masterpiece. Instead we get the kind of wishy-washy design solution that is apt to please no one. ∎

New Peaks in Tall Manhattan's Range

By H. I. BROCK | February 9, 1930

THE TOWER OF BABEL IS STILL A-BUILDING in spite of the confusion of tongues and the diffusion of scientific information to the effect that the original aspiration of tower builders—setting up a scaling ladder to high heaven—is an unrealizable dream. But at the moment our skyline has two screeching high notes, each an office building.

The Chrysler Building, stabbing up out of the tall thicket of new architecture that hedges about the Grand Central Station, is almost matched by the Bank of the Manhattan Company's bid for first skyscraping honors, shooting out of the heart of the downtown acropolis of finance and giving that group a higher ascent than the Woolworth tower.

The Chrysler Building outdoes even the Eiffel Tower and thus robs Paris of world primacy in man-made structures upward bound. The Bank of the Manhattan Company's entry, which falls short by 105 feet (according to the official figures), must still yield place to France's entry, but overtops everything else of the sort in the world—except the Chrysler Building. That veteran local recordholder, the Woolworth tower, is left all of 133 feet below.

Thus the old and the new combine to make and remake New York in its latest image, which is a city humped like a camel. The city's two humps are below Central Park and these two buildings are the sharp points on the humps. Very sharp points they are. You can see both of them with great effect from the Jersey side of the Hudson on a clear day. Or—again on a clear day—you can see both humps from the Queensboro Bridge. And a grand sweep it is—the camel being viewed off the port quarter aft, as it were. If you wish to carry out the simile and remember that you are speaking of a ship of the desert the two tallest towers may do duty as horns of the saddle. ∎

Which Is The Mightiest Of the High?

By DAVID W. DUNLAP | September 1, 2005

HAPPY 75TH BIRTHDAY, CHRYSLER BUILDING. New Yorkers in the know think you're the best.

One hundred architects, brokers, builders, critics, developers, engineers, historians, lawyers, officials, owners, planners and scholars were asked this summer by the Skyscraper Museum in Lower Manhattan to choose their 10 favorites among 25 existing towers, from the Park Row Building (1899) to the Time Warner Center (2004).

Ninety of them named William Van Alen's Chrysler Building of 1930, which, despite or perhaps because of its ebullient eccentricity, may come as close as any to expressing New York's cloud-piercing ambitions.

The surprising runner-up was Ludwig Mies van der Rohe's Seagram Building of 1958, which is the antithesis of Chrysler: cool, tranquil, rectangular and restrained. What they have in common is that both express the spirit of their times, Chrysler playing a jazz-age flapper to Seagram's man in the gray flannel suit.

"These are irreconcilable choices if you try to evaluate them by one single system," said Carol Willis, the director of the Skyscraper Museum. Rather, she said, the voting showed that people judge some skyscrapers emotionally, others rationally.

Ms. Willis's own favorite, the Empire State Building, tied with Lever House, behind the Flatiron and Woolworth Buildings. The most recently built of the Top 10 was Eero Saarinen's CBS Building of 1964. ∎

CHRYSLER BUILDING

How It Sparkled in the Skyline

By **ELAINE LOUIE** | May 26, 2005

EVEN IF THEY WALK PAST IT EVERY DAY, MOST people know the Chrysler Building as a symbol on the skyline, a cocktail shaker of style. But for these artists and critics, it's a personal landmark. Here's how it affected them.

SARAH JESSICA PARKER, Actress
When my husband and I were courting, we used to walk everywhere, from Battery Park to the Chrysler Building, and we went into the lobby, quite late at night, many, many times— summer nights and cold nights. The Empire State Building symbolized what I think we wanted in coming to New York: to be New Yorkers and to thrive in the city. The Chrysler Building was this magnificent piece of art.

ROBERT A. M. STERN, Architect
Dean of the Yale School of Architecture; an author of a book series that began with "New York 1900" and will include "New York 2000," to be published next year.
The Chrysler Building caught the exuberance and the spirit of the 1920's in a way that no other building in the world has. Chrysler built it, and he had the showrooms in it, he embellished the outside with symbols that were explicit with his hubcaps, his radiator hood ornaments. When Chrysler moved out, Texaco moved in. But they couldn't change the name of the building to Texaco. It's Chrysler inside and out.

RON CHERNOW, Author
Wrote "Alexander Hamilton" (Penguin Press, 2004) and "Titan: The Life of John D. Rockefeller Sr." (Random House, 1998).
What's fascinating and consistent about the Empire State Building, the Rockefeller Center and the Chrysler Building is that they were conceived during the giddiest part of the 1920's boom and were completed during the bust, and they embody the dizzying hopes of the 1920's and reflect the dismal reality of the 1930's, the Depression and the collapse of the Manhattan real estate market.

CARL SPIELVOGEL
Chairman, Carl Spielvogel Enterprises, a global investment manager; former chairman, Backer Spielvogel Bates Worldwide, which rented Floors 12 to 24 from 1983 to 1995.
There was never a day when I walked into the building that I didn't have what I call a rush. There was a great feeling getting into an elevator. They're patterned wood and metal.

DOROTHY TWINING GLOBUS
Curator of exhibitions, Museum of Arts and Design.
This was 1969. My father had an office in the Chrysler Building. He was undercover with the C.I.A. I came up from Swarthmore one day to meet him for dinner. I was supposed to meet him at the Chrysler Building. I knew it was on 42nd Street, but I couldn't find it, because I only knew it from the skyline. I'd never seen the bottom. ∎

The Empire State Building Wins
The Race to the Top

May 2, 1931

COMPLETION OF THE EMPIRE STATE BUILDing marks the attainment of a new record in building height which is likely to stand for many years, in the opinion of leading builders and real estate men.

Opening of the new structure, which rises 1,250 feet above Fifth Avenue, has brought to an end, for the time being at least, a friendly contest for skyscraper honors, which during the last two years has resulted in a frequent revision of height records.

For 17 years the Woolworth Building, with its 60 stories towering 792 feet above lower Broadway, held the distinction of being the tallest Manhattan structure.

But early last year, almost simultaneously, the giant steel skeletons of the Chrysler Building and of the Bank of the Manhattan Company at 40 Wall Street were lifted skyward. From original plans it had appeared that the bank edifice would look down upon every other building, but a revision in the Chrysler design providing for a needle spire which reached up to 1,046 feet gave the palm for a while to the automotive manufacturer's project.

The record was not destined to hold for long, however. Even then the framework of the Empire State Building was being pushed upward with a new height as its goal, 1,050 feet. The bare margin of four feet was stretched to 204 feet when ex-Governor Alfred E. Smith announced that a 200-foot dirigible-mooring mast would cap his structure. Thus, within less than two years, the Woolworth Building record has been surpassed three times. ■

That Inseparable Trio: Girl, Ape, Skyscraper

By CARYN JAMES | August 15, 2004

OF ALL THE TRIBUTES TO FAY WRAY, WHO died last week at 96, the sweetest did not come from a person but from a building. The Empire State Building turned off its lights in her honor for one night, and its Web site mourned her under the romantic headline, "King Kong's Beauty Dies." This wasn't grandstanding, but the recognition of a deep and genuine tie between Wray and the building that helped make her famous.

In the 1933 film, it may have been the ape who was called "the eighth wonder of the world," but at the time the Empire State Building seemed equally wondrous. It was only two years old and still the tallest building in the world when Kong climbed its

Romance on the Observation Deck

By **EMILY VASQUEZ** | July 13, 2006

MIDNIGHT AT THE EMPIRE STATE BUILDING. Gone are the long lines, the strollers and the tour bus crowds. Instead, at 1,050 feet, with rain clouds colored pink, romance abounds.

With the lights of Wall Street glimmering in the distance, Kevin Livingston, 28, of Queens, takes advantage of the setting.

He turns to Charlotte Harrison, 27, who is also from Queens and who has been dating him for three weeks. "Will you be my girlfriend?" he asks. Then he declares that even New York City's lights have nothing on her.

On the east deck another couple, more serious, are locked in a tight embrace.

Yes, she has just whispered. Yes, of course she will be his wife.

The couple, Aisha, 25, and Imran, 32, who would give only their first names, met on Naseeb.com, a Muslim social networking site. Six months' worth of e-mail messages later—Aisha from Montreal, Imran from London—they made plans to meet for the first time in New York.

Now, atop the Empire State Building, they share their first kiss, and Imran whispers the proposal.

When many of the city's most popular attractions—the Statue of Liberty, the Bronx Zoo—have been closed for hours, the Empire State still beckons. Three nights a week, it does not close until 2 a.m. The platform becomes a lovers' lane for couples in search of a late-night view. Their idea, of course, is nothing new—from "An Affair to Remember" to "Sleepless in Seattle," the platform has been a classic stage.

How many proposals could the observation deck have seen in its 75 years?

Mira Akerman, 34, who flew to New York from Sweden for her wedding, has come to the top for a postnuptial kiss with new husband, Martin Nilsson, 33. Running out on the deck, still in her white wedding dress, she explains, "It's such a New York thing to do." ▪

side and Wray was forever typecast as the screaming blonde in the gorilla's hand. And that ape carrying off the woman he loved didn't take her just anywhere. The film was enacting the conflict between Kong's primitive passions and the high-tech future that the skyscraper symbolized.

When Kong reaches the top of the Empire State Building, he towers over any structure on Earth, but in the end he is no match for the men with guns who shoot at him from biplanes. Civilization wins, yet there is something noble about Kong's passion. He has carried his love to such heights that the Empire State Building is almost a third player in a peculiar but touching ménage à trois.

Wray herself seemed to recognize as much. As she said in her autobiography, "On the Other Hand," published when she was 81, "Each time I arrive in New York and see the skyline and the exquisite beauty of the Empire State Building, my heart beats a little faster." ▪

BELOW: *Iraqi war veteran Sgt. David Aloonso, kisses his new bride Natalie Malloy, right, on the observation deck of the Empire State Building.*

The City That Was, And the City That Is Now

By **PAUL GOLDBERGER** | August 18, 1991

THERE HAS BEEN NOTHING LIKE MCKIM, Mead & White before or since. Charles McKim, William Mead and Stanford White reigned over New York at the turn of the century. They designed Pennsylvania Station, the original Madison Square Garden, the Villard mansions, the Pulitzer mansion, the Morgan Library, the University Club, the Century Club, the Metropolitan Club, the main post office, the Washington Square arch, the Brooklyn Museum, the campus and most of the buildings of Columbia University, and on and on and on.

All their work in New York—which was but a fraction of their total output— was characterized by a sure sense of urban presence. These were buildings in the city and of the city; even the most private of their private houses uplifted the public realm through an elegant facade, handsome detailing and a respect for the street. And the firm's truly public buildings, like Pennsylvania Station, the Morgan Library and the Municipal Building behind City Hall, did more than just acknowledge the public realm; they truly ennobled it. These buildings were the output of an imperial city in its ascendance.

Few of McKim, Mead & White's buildings followed any historical model exactly. These architects looked to history not for something to copy, but for inspiration; they were consistently inventive within the historic framework in which they operated. If they did not believe, as their near contemporaries Frank Lloyd Wright and Louis Sullivan did, that the past was a drag on their creative energies, neither did they have any sense of being enclosed or trapped by it. Historical architecture was able to do for McKim, Mead & White precisely what Frank Lloyd Wright argued it could never do for anyone, which was spark creativity. Both

McKim and White loved the city they were making, and believed deeply in the notion that every building contributed something to the larger idea of the city, to the idea of a public realm that everyone, including those who never had any reason to enter a particular building, could benefit from. They believed that architecture could be not only ennobling but sensuous as well. ■

Subdued Tower Of Light

By **NICOLAI OUROUSSOFF** | March 22, 2007

IN THE YEAR SINCE THE CONCRETE FRAME OF Frank Gehry's first New York building began to rise along the West Side Highway in Chelsea, architecture fans have been quarrelling over its design. Are the curvaceous glass forms of the IAC headquarters building, evoking the crisp pleats of a skirt, a bold departure from Manhattan's hard-edged corporate towers? Or are they proof that Mr. Gehry's radical days are behind him?

Well, both. Mr. Gehry is adding a much-needed touch of lightness to the Manhattan skyline just as the city finally emerges from a period of mourning after the 9/11 attacks. The IAC building, serving as world headquarters for Barry Diller's media and Internet empire, joins a growing list of new projects that reflect how mainstream developers in the city are significantly raising the creative stakes after decades of settling for bland, soul-sapping office buildings.

Yet the building, which is not quite complete, also feels oddly tame. For those who have followed Mr. Gehry's creative career, these easy, fluid forms are a marked

Suddenly, a Landmark Startles Again

By **CHRISTOPHER GRAY** | July 21, 1991

PERHAPS IT WILL NEVER LOOK AS DRAMATIC as it did in 1902 and 1903, when its surprising triangular form shot up at the foot of Madison Square. But the Flatiron Building is still as startling an architectural sight as one can find.

In 1901, a syndicate including Chicago's George A. Fuller Construction Company filed plans for a 20-story building on the triangular plot bounded by 22nd and 23rd Streets, Broadway and Fifth Avenue. The building was never the city's tallest, but its location in what was then the main shopping district made it one of the most famous. Making full use of the small, oddly shaped lot, it rose straight up, directly and bluntly, from its wedge-shaped site—no setbacks, turrets, towers or domes.

But what was to a professional journal simply a "conventional skyscraper" attracted crowds, "sometimes 100 or more," said The New York Tribune in 1902. They looked up "with their heads bent back until a general breakage of necks seems imminent."

Stories of the wind effects of the building are apparently true. In February of 1903, a gust magnified by the great triangle blew John McTaggart, a 14-year-old messenger, out into Fifth Avenue where he was killed by a passing automobile.

In 1929, the Fuller Company moved out, and the Flatiron Building gradually became a gritty symbol of an aging section of town. But now the building's owner, Jules Olsheim, is cleaning accumulated years of grime off the facade, a $1 million project that is turning heads as the massive, familiar wedge suddenly seems to float out of a dingy shroud. ▪

departure from the complex, fragmented structures of his youth. Rather than mining rich new creative territory, Mr. Gehry, now 78, seems to be holding back. The results—almost pristine by Mr. Gehry's standards—suggest the casual confidence of an aging virtuoso rather than the brash innovation of a rowdy outsider.

Mr. Gehry's structure looks best when approached from a distance. Glimpsed between Chelsea's weathered brick buildings, its strangely chiseled forms reflect the surrounding sky, so that its surfaces can seem to be dissolving. As you circle to the north, however, its forms become more symmetrical and sharp-edged, evoking rows of overlapping sails or knifelike pleats. Viewed from the south, the forms appear more blocky.

This constantly changing character imbues the building's exterior with an enigmatic beauty. And it reflects Mr. Gehry's subtle understanding of context. Rather than parodying the architectural style of the surrounding buildings, he plays against them, drawing them into a bigger urban composition. The sail-like curves of the west facade seem to be braced against the roar of the passing cars. The blockier forms in back lock the composition into the lower brick buildings that extend to the east. ▪

BELOW: *The Flatiron building at night.*

A New City Is Emerging Downtown

By **ADA LOUISE HUXTABLE** | March 29, 1970

LOWER MANHATTAN, THE SOUTHERN TIP OF the island behind all the famous skyline views of those clustered Wall Street spires, is not so much in a state of renewal as in a state of explosion. The rising towers of the 110-story Trade Center will only be the top of the iceberg. What is going on from the Battery to Brooklyn Bridge is the remaking of a city. It usually takes bomb damage or bulldozer public renewal to produce clearance and rebuilding on a comparable scale.

An expatriate New Yorker with Lower Manhattan memories of small buildings redolent of coffee and spices and the graces of the Greek Revival would be lost. The handsome, five-story, red-brick rows that survived the 1830's and 1840's virtually intact along the East River are almost all gone. So are slips and streets with historic names.

There are a few 19th-century survivals and landmarks—India House, Fraunces Tavern, Sweet's restaurant in the Fulton Street row are slated for lonely preservation as the South Street Seaport.

BELOW: *Lower Manhattan in the late 1960's.*

What has been lost is New York's past, and that part of the story casts no glory on the city or its developers. What is being gained is a kind of planning and architectural quality all but unknown to 20th-century New York. The best will be spectacular. We are witnessing the coming of New York's Second Skyscraper Age. ■

From the Rubble, Ideas for Rebirth

By **DEBORAH SOLOMON** | September 30, 2001

INEVITABLY, WE TALK OF REBUILDING THE World Trade Center, envisioning a moment beyond the ash-coated present. Such thoughts console. Building is not just a matter of office space and revenue. It is also a basic human impulse, a means for imagining an ordered universe.

Still, many feel that the void created by the fallen towers needs to be preserved, preferably in the form of a park. Empty space can have its own eloquence, be a place of memories, of unrushed reflection.

What should rise on the site where the twin towers stood? Following are suggestions from some esteemed architects and artists.

LOUISE BOURGEOIS, Sculptor
That we will have to make a memorial is obvious. The memorial should be a list of the victims' names; names beautifully hand-carved into stone. I have a lot of carvers. We will do that with a chisel and a hammer.

RICHARD MEIER, Architect
The site should not be a park. We already have a great new park along the west side. A park is not an appropriate symbol of what

Stuntman Walks a Tightrope Between Trade Center Towers

By **GRACE LICHTENSTEIN** | August 8, 1974

COMBINING THE CUNNING OF A SECOND-story man with the nerve of an Evel Knievel, a French high-wire artist sneaked past guards at the World Trade Center, ran a cable between the tops of its twin towers and tightrope-walked across it.

Hundreds of spectators created a traffic jam shortly after 7:15 a.m. in the streets 1,350 feet below as they watched the black-clad figure outlined against the gray morning sky tiptoeing back and forth across the meticulously rigged 131-foot cable.

Finally, after perhaps 45 minutes of knee bends and other stunts, Philippe Petit turned himself over to waiting policemen. (He was released from custody a few hours later at the direction of Richard H. Kuh, the Manhattan district attorney, who made a deal to drop the charges in exchange for a free aerial performance in a city park "for the children of the city.")

No date or place has been announced yet.

"If I see three oranges, I have to juggle. And if I see two towers, I have to walk," Mr. Petit, a professional stuntman, explained afterward in heavily accented English, punctuating his sentences with a Gallic "bon!"

The day was an extraordinary climax to months of scheming by Mr. Petit, 24, and several accomplices. They masqueraded as construction workers wearing hard hats when they began taking their cable, rope, guy lines and other equipment to the uppermost floors of the still-unfinished North Tower three nights ago. With a five foot crossbow, they shot an arrow carrying a hemp cord across to the south tower. They passed heavier lines until they were able to lay a galvanized steel cable across the gap.

Mr. Petit said he had hesitated about taking the initial steps because there was a stiff breeze.

He was finally brought in by a policeman who shouted, "Get off there or I'll come out and we'll both go down." As he was led away, street-level spectators booed the police while construction workers tried to shake Mr. Petit's handcuffed hand. ∎

---

happened here. We need office space, we need new buildings that are an even greater symbol of New York than what was there before.

JAMES TURRELL, Sculptor
People want a memorial now because they're feeling emotional, but emotion passes, all emotion passes, and then the memorial has no meaning. We should not feel bad about building on top of the ashes. All cultures are built on top of earlier cultures. The new buildings should be higher than the old ones, and there should be three of them.

DAVID M. CHILDS, Skidmore, Owings and Merrill, architects
We need to go back in and make downtown absolutely breathtaking. There should be some great piece of sculpture that reminds us of the tragedy, spaces of landscape where one could sit and contemplate, and some kind of cultural center, maybe a jazz museum.

ROBERT ROSENBLUM, Professor of art history at New York University
It sounds like a Richard Serra opportunity. But I think it should be a ghost monument. It should be a tall building that is reminiscent of the original building and that is totally useless. A phantom building. I'm thinking of a Jenny Holzer, with phantom lights and something that is immaterial, translucent, gossamer. Or else we could just have a pile of rubble. ∎

A Familiar Haunt, But in a New Light

By **RITA REIF** | April 4, 1999

THE GLOOMY WINTER AND THE BRIGHT spring have provided the proof. The glorious fullness of light that the architects John M. Carrere and Thomas Hastings envisioned 90 years ago for the New York Public Library's main reading room has returned.

The room—the length of a football field, the height of a cathedral nave—was darkened during the blackout days of World War II when its 15 soaring windows were painted over. Over time, entire tiers of bulbs in the chandeliers short-circuited and lighting fixtures on the book stands and reference shelves burned out, never to be repaired or replaced. Now, after a $15 million renovation, the room is filled with light, even on the darkest days. The windows gleam with exquisite clarity, each pane replaced with energy-efficient glass that prevents ultra-violet damage to the books and the painted or stained-wood surfaces throughout the room. Lighting fixtures—new or, in some cases, refurbished—have made the titles on the spines of the books easy to read again.

"Architecture is all about light," said the architect Lewis Davis, who masterminded the restoration, paraphrasing his mentor, Louis Kahn.

Light even influenced the choice of new finishes on the American white oak furniture throughout the room. The sun had bleached some surfaces in the north and south sections, so they were refinished in a paler tone than their original nut brown.

As for the lights, 60 baluster-shaped lamps with bronze bases and brass shades were made by the Excalibur Bronze Sculpture Foundry of Brooklyn to go along with 100 originals that survived. Excalibur also made the cone-shaped white-glass hanging lamps in the book delivery and retrieval area. These replaced those with green-glass shades, which people who studied in this room decades ago remember.

Jerry W. Henderson, who fields questions at the information desks in the room and has worked at the library for 39 years, said visitors still asked, "What ever happened to those emerald green lamps?" He said he didn't miss them: "They were part of the darkness that's gone now." ∎

LEFT: *Mayor Fiorello LaGuardia named the library lions Patience and Fortitude, for qualities he felt New Yorkers would need to survive the Great Depression.*
ABOVE: *The Rose reading room.*

NY PUBLIC LIBRARY

The Glow at the City's Heart

By **PAUL GOLDBERGER** | December 24, 1976

THE PRESENCE OF WHAT MUST BE THE world's most famous Christmas tree would alone make Rockefeller Center the city's symbolic heart at Christmas; the nearness of St. Patrick's Cathedral and the great stores of Fifth Avenue confirms it. Tourists swarm about the center, attracted by the tree and the free show of ice skaters gliding across the sunken plaza. But the thick crowds at this time of year contain a fair share of New Yorkers as well, who come remembering Christmases past at Rockefeller Center and see in the great Christmas tree and decorated plaza a sense of continuity in a changing city.

Rockefeller Center is at its best at Christmas. In the clear, crisp December air the towers stand out sharply against the sky with an air of nobility unmatched by postwar skyscrapers. The tree is only the beginning of the holiday decorations—the best part of the center's display is doubtless the angels sculpted of white metal wire that line the promenade from Fifth Avenue to the central plaza; they appear to be raising their

trumpets not only the Christmas tree but also in celebration of the height and drama of 30 Rockefeller Plaza, which rises grandly at Rockefeller Center's midpoint.

> The plaza is constant theater, its ice skaters the cast of a pageant, and all we as visitors need to do to understand the plaza is allow ourselves to be pulled toward it and to look down into it.

Rockefeller Center's design strikes a brilliant balance between the traditional and formal values of 19th-century Beaux-Arts design and the machine-age romanticism of 30's modernism. On the promenade at Fifth Avenue, the center's traditional aspects hold sway. The Maison Francaise is to the left, the British Empire building to the right, low, symmetrical structures defining a comfortable pedestrian street between them. The sense is of a clear order leading to a central focus, the sunken plaza and, behind it, the 70-story tower of 30 Rockefeller Plaza.

Walk down the promenade toward the central plaza: its power as a magnet is considerable. The plaza is constant theater, its ice skaters the cast of a pageant, and all we as visitors need to do to understand the plaza is allow ourselves to be pulled toward it and to look down into it. Paul Manship's Prometheus at the edge of the plaza enhances the central focus of the complex. Inside the GE Building—originally the RCA Building—is a lobby that is a grand setting for a 30's movie about corporate power. ∎

BELOW: *The 71st annual lighting of the tree at Rockefeller Center in 2003.*

"Cesspool of the World"

By **THOMAS F. BRADY** | February 21, 1969

"TIMES SQUARE HAS BEEN A RUNNING SORE as long as I've known it—anyway for 15 years," Chief Inspector Sanford D. Garelik says.

A plainclothes inspector calls it "the cesspool of the world," adding, "The dregs of the whole country drain into our sump."

In December, the last month for which complete statistics are available, the arrests made in the Times Square area for robbery, felonious assault, larceny, narcotics, disorderly conduct and prostitution and other sex offenses amounted to 25.6 percent of the city's total, slightly more than double the proportion from December 1966.

Ten years ago a New York Times report on conditions in 42nd Street between Seventh and Eighth Avenues said, "It is frequently asserted that it is the 'worst' block in town, that it has been so for many years, and that it is certainly not getting better."

One minor problem has been solved in the decade: An arcade entrance to the IRT subway at Times Square was closed to eliminate a nest of delinquency. But a similar arcade remains on Eighth Avenue just north of 42nd Street.

The Transit Authority police, responsible for patrolling the Eighth Avenue arcade, arrested three young men there early this month, charging one with felonious assault. The city police patrol the sidewalk, but the stairway appears to be a no-man's land. In the daytime many of the patrons are teenage boys who show little sign of aggressiveness. At night, the habitues are tougher and also drearier.

Above ground are bookstores that sell magazines of nude women and men in the most specific detail. The police say the judicial definition of pornography has been narrowed to the point where nudity is now beyond their reach.

The police also feel that judicial preoccupation with the protection of individual liberty has reduced conviction rates to a relatively low level, and consequently the doubtful characters they arrest are often released almost at once. A 1967 law that reduced the maximum penalty for prostitution to 15 days in jail has, however, increased the guilty pleas. The record for last year, according to police statistics, showed a conviction or guilty-plea rate of more than 60 percent in prostitution arrests. The penalties are considered so light that they are hardly worth fighting. ■

BELOW: *Once besieged by adult entertainment, Times Square has become family-friendly.*

Manifestoes for the Next New York: Bring Back New Yorkers—and Sex

By **FRANK RICH** | November 11, 2001

LABOR DAY BROUGHT THE ROMANCE IT always does to Broadway: the whiff of a new season. In the Times Square that Disney helped build in the late 1990's, you could squint your eyes and imagine that the crossroads of the world was as vital as ever. The blazing lights, after all, seemed even brighter than those of "42nd Street" lore, and foot traffic had become so dense that Broadway sidewalks had just been widened to accommodate it.

So the shock was real when the attack on the World Trade Center claimed Times Square's economy and optimism as collateral damage. As tourists fled, four Broadway shows folded, and fear supplanted "The Producers" as the street's No. 1 topic of conversation. It wasn't idle talk when Rudolph W. Giuliani and even Colin Powell, another native New Yorker, urged Americans to partake of an activity as seemingly frivolous as seeing a play. Broadway's survival was at stake. Though a modest bounce followed, decimated advance sales suggest it will be short-lived.

Many of the gains of the area's redevelopment, led by the decline in crime, are undiminished, but the cataclysm of Sept. 11 revealed starkly what's missing when the office workers go home each night: New Yorkers. It's the paradox of the Times Square comeback in the late 1990's that the neighborhood that epitomizes New York to the world is no longer on the map of many of its own residents. According to one good barometer—the League of American Theaters and Producers' surveys of Broadway ticket buyers—the overwhelming majority of Broadway's customers were metropolitan-area residents through the 1980's. Now far fewer than half are, with less than a fifth of Broadway audiences coming from the city itself. The confirmation of these statistics could be found in the post-Sept. 11 ruins. It was the spectacles pitched at out-of-towners—typified by "Les Misérables" and "The Phantom of the Opera"—that were hardest hit. To be truly disaster-proof, Times Square, we now know, needs the New Yorkers to come back and love it too.

But the theater isn't the whole Times Square story. The beauty of the district has always been its rude amalgam of high and low, class and crass. The street's late-20th-century decline was in a symbolic way sealed when, in the period from 1966 to 1972, it lost its last old-time freak show (Ripley's Believe It or Not "Odditorium") and its last old-style showgirl cabaret (Lou Walters's Latin Quarter) as well as its last high-culture institution (the Metropolitan Opera House). That crazy-quilt hodgepodge is missing in the new Times Square, where the nontheater entertainments and services tend to be neither high nor low, but part of the bland middle of national chains.

Sex must also be in the mix. It has always been part of the neighborhood's DNA. Even before The New York Times moved into Longacre Square in 1904, prompting its name change, the West 40's were overrun by "parlor houses." In 1913, the New Amsterdam's roof theater—right above the stage where "The Lion King" prowls now—featured Ziegfeld's "Midnight Frolic," where a trick of lighting on a "see-through runway" displayed the pulchritude of chorus girls. A decade later the Shubert Theater housed "Artists and Models," a revue featuring female frontal nudity. Fiorello La Guardia stamped out the "incorporated filth" of burlesque in the 1930's, and his successor in spirit, Rudolph W. Giuliani, tried to do the same with porn. But there must be a way to get sensible adult sexuality back into Times Square entertainment. It wouldn't mean importing prostitution, 10-cents-a-dance halls or wretched XXX emporiums, but perhaps at least a touch of Vegas (which also tried to stamp out sex revues in favor of family entertainment in the 1990's but this year reversed course). ■

Unveiling Was Rained Out

October 29, 1866

IT IS REALLY A PUBLIC MISFORTUNE, ALMOST A national misfortune, that the weather should have interfered to prevent the ceremonies with which the Statue of Liberty was presented and accepted from being brilliantly successful. Unhappily the unpropitious weather robbed the pageant of much of its effect. To be effective as a symbol a pageant must first of all be effective as a spectacle. That was not possible when the statue was draped in a drizzling mist that made it invisible from the Battery, and when it refused to be "unveiled" even when the bunting that covered the face had been withdrawn.

The failure of the spectacle to make its due impression is the more to be regretted because the conditions of the celebration were otherwise so favorable. The nature of the ceremony made a naval parade not only admissible but necessary, and the facilities our beautiful bay confers upon us for naval parades are such as no other great city enjoys. Even the Venetians, the most famous of all pageant makers, in the procession of the Bucentoro had no advantages over us for this purpose, except in the architectural setting of their display. Even in this respect the recent and huge structures at the lower end of Manhattan Island, at a distance from which the details are lost and the outlines and masses are alone visible, make New York a fit background for the most sumptuous aquatic spectacle.

The parade in honor and welcome of the arrival of the statue showed what capabilities the harbor had for such a purpose, and the program prepared for the final ceremony gave promise of a display more extensive and more impressive.

It is not too much to say that the monument thus finally exposed gives to the harbor what it has heretofore lacked in a single dominant feature. ∎

ABOVE: *From base to torch, the statue is 151 feet high.*

Reopened Ellis Island Proves Sellout Attraction For Tourists

By **MURRAY SCHUMACH** | May 30, 1976

ELLIS ISLAND, WHICH CLOSED IN 1954 AFTER a 62-year run as the greatest immigration center in history, was reopened yesterday to the public to become an instant smash hit as a tourist attraction.

About three hours after the ticket window at the Battery had opened, the ticket manager, Robert Moakler, was standing in front of the closed window, announcing:

"No more to Ellis Island today. Completely sold out."

The line for tickets had begun forming at 6 a.m., three hours before the first ticket was sold. In the first capacity boatload of 130 tourists to the island were several who had come as immigrants, many whose parents had gone through the immigrant crush, and

Ellis Island:
Whose Gateway is it Anyway?

By JAMES BARRON | May 17, 1994

THE AREA CODE ON THE TELEPHONES ON
Ellis Island is 212, not 201. But the electricity
that lights the Great Hall and the water
that tourists drink come from New Jersey.

Mail to Ellis Island is routed through
New York, but Federal Express and
United Parcel Service deliveries go through
New Jersey. The National Park Service
office on the island subscribes to three
newspapers: one from New York and two
from New Jersey.

The footbridge to New Jersey built for
workers refurbishing the historic buildings
on the island was fabricated at a foundry in
New Jersey, not New York. But the island
itself is a New York City landmark.

The dispute over which state owns Ellis
Island, New York or New Jersey, has long had
that kind of on-the-one-hand-this, on-the-
other-hand-that uncertainty. The United States
Supreme Court, which agreed yesterday to
hear New Jersey's claim to ownership, could
end the back-and-forth barbs.

Maybe, maybe not.

"It's a matter of common sense," said
Rita Manno, a spokeswoman for Gov.
Christine Todd Whitman of New Jersey.
"Territory-wise, it belongs to New Jersey."

Across the Hudson River, no one
was conceding a single square inch of the
27.5-acre island.

"Of course it belongs to New York," said
Speaker Peter F. Vallone of the City Council.
"Who are they kidding? When my grandfather
came here in 1900, he wasn't going to New
Jersey, he was going to New York."

quite a few who felt they should visit a place
so important to American history.

A nun, Sister Janet O'Neill, who had
come in 1922 from Ireland and had had very
little trouble being cleared, said, "I felt I just
had to go through the place again."

For those who arrived early enough to
buy tickets, pleasure did not come from the
usual tourist appeals. The visitors were
limited almost entirely on the guided tour to
the massive building where immigrants had
been processed from 1900 to 1954, when the
island acquired the nickname "Isle of Tears."

They trudged through dusty corridors
with peeling walls. They peered into the
rubble of what were once waiting rooms.
They murmured indignantly as the guides
from the National Park Service told them
how pipes and motors had been stripped for
the copper by vandals. They were so curious
about everything that, repeatedly, on the
first tour the guides—most of them in their
20's—appealed to the visitors not to linger
because a schedule had to be maintained so
that the boat would be free to bring other
tourists from Liberty Island. ▪

New Jersey has staked its claim on a
compact between the two states that was
drafted in 1833 and approved by Congress the
following year. The compact put the boundary
between the two states in the middle of the
Hudson River. It gave New York the rights to the
three acres of Ellis Island that existed at the
time. Now New York is concerned about losing
its standing as the gateway for the tourists who
visit what used to be the gateway to America.

New York? New Jersey? No one lives
on Ellis Island. The Park Service employees
who work there live in both states, and
the superintendent, M. Ann Belkov, says
their conversations betray neither Noo Yawk
nor New Joizey accents. She herself is
"strictly Southern," she said, having worked
in Louisiana and Tennessee before being
assigned to Ellis Island in 1990.

"It doesn' t make a difference to us,"
Ms. Belkov said. "We belong to the people of
the United States." With the emphasis, she
said, on united. ▪

ARCHITECTURE & PARKS   119

The Palaces Mansions Are Almost Gone

By **VIRGINIA POPE** | August 10, 1930

NEW YORK'S MANSIONS ARE VANISHING. There is scarcely a porte-cochere left in the city. For one reason or another, chiefly the high cost of land, the palaces that symbolized great fortunes a generation ago are falling under the wrecker's hammer.

At the northeast corner of Fifth Avenue and 66th Street stands the Henry O. Havemeyer house, a well-known landmark, soon to be torn down. With it will go its neighbors to the north, the homes of Mr. and Mrs. J. Watson Webb and Mr. and Mrs. Horace Havemeyer.

Each vanishing mansion carries with it an example of architecture that may be termed historic, so distinctive was it of its time. For instance, Stanford White, when he designed the Joseph Pulitzer home on East 73rd Street—now yielding to a skyscraper—broke away from the "château tradition" and created a beautiful house in the style of the Italian Renaissance. Its facade, with balustrades and high arched windows, was representative of the dignity of New York's mansion era.

When the late history of social New York is written, it will probably mention the postwar years as the era of the "cooperative migration"; it will tell how New Yorkers left the ground to live in the air, taking with them all the comforts and none of the inconveniences of their former mode of living. One tenant may wish to transplant the paneling from his old home, the family mansion, to his sky-dwelling. Presto—rooms are designed to receive it. Another owning Gobelin tapestries, which require immense wall space, will demand that windows be blocked out. The cooperative has taken over the functions of the mansion in a simplified form. ∎

A Full Block Of Elegant Houses

By **CHRISTOPHER GRAY** | July 27, 2008

AFTER THE COLLAPSE OF LAWRENCE Salander's Salander-O'Reilly Galleries amid accusations of fraud, the magnificent town house that Salander-O'Reilly rented at 22 East 71st Street is on the market.

The architecture of that whole block—indeed the entire city block back to 70th Street—is unusual: All but two structures were built as private houses. That peculiar situation goes back a century, when what was soon called the Frick block was sold off for development all at once.

Henry C. Frick, a steel-industry pioneer, was the first to buy, taking the entire Fifth Avenue frontage, but he could not get possession until 1911, and completed his limestone mansion there, now the Frick Collection, in 1914.

Private-house construction swept the lots behind the Frick mansion site from 1909 through 1913. John C. Moore, president of

BELOW: Morris-Jumel Mansion, one of the few remaining mansions in New York, was built between 1765 and 1770.

The Mansion-Museums Of Old New York

By **CAROL VOGEL** | March 8, 1985

WHEN WE THINK OF PRIVATE RESIDENCES that have become museums, the Cooper-Hewitt and the Frick Collection generally come to mind. But there also exist a handful of lesser known museums that have been preserved as period houses and are worth an expedition. These buildings are some of the last vestiges of old New York not yet swallowed up by the city's ferocious urbanization. And half the fun of visiting them is the chance to explore the different neighborhoods of Manhattan.

Tiffany & Company, had Charles I. Berg design the sober Renaissance-style house at 15 East 70th. Dave Hennen Morris retained Thornton Chard to design his house at 19 East 70th, with its unusual recessed loggia; it is now the entrance to the Knoedler & Company art gallery.

On the 71st Street side, William W. Cook had the bank specialists York & Sawyer design a little jewel box for his use at 14 East 71st Street. Mr. Cook was a prominent lawyer whose book "Cook on Corporations" was a standard reference work. The architects gave him a striking limestone house with a two-story-high central bay and inset balcony at the top floor, with impressive bronze entry gates.

After the Frick house, the largest house on the block is the one that Salander-O'Reilly had rented for $1.8 million a year. It was built in 1923 by a wool merchant, Julius Forstmann. He had the veteran mansion architect Charles P. H. Gilbert design a 45-foot-wide limestone structure. It went into institutional use in the 1940's; the current owner is asking $75 million. ▪

The Morris-Jumel mansion at 160th Street and Edgecombe Avenue is a grand Georgian structure that was built in 1765 as a summer residence by Col. Roger Morris, who fought for the British in colonial days. The house served briefly as George Washington's headquarters and was headquarters for the British for most of the period between 1776 and 1783. The house was converted into a tavern for a short time. Stephen Jumel, a French wine merchant, later bought the house where he lived with his wife Eliza Bowen. After Jumel's death in 1832, Mme. Jumel married Aaron Burr in the front parlor.

The Dyckman house, on Broadway between 204th and 207th Streets, is the last Dutch Colonial farmhouse left on Manhattan. This relic is now a museum. While the property once consisted of 300 acres, the building now stands on a sliver of land surrounded by postwar high-rises, gas stations and an array of seedy shops.

The land chosen for what is now the Abigail Adams Smith Museum, 421 East 61st Street, was the countryside a century ago. This stone structure was the coach house and stable on a 23-acre estate built by Col. William S. Smith, husband of Abigail Adams, daughter of John Adams. The fireplaces in every room remain from the days when the building was an inn.

Two other house museums are in Victorian brownstones. One is the Theodore Roosevelt Birthplace, 28 East 20th Street. This building was reconstructed on its original site by the architect Theodate Pope Riddle to resemble the brownstone where Theodore Roosevelt spent his first 14 years. And the Old Merchant's House, built in 1832 at 29 East Fourth Street, is the only 19th-century house in Manhattan to survive with its original furniture and family memorabilia. Seadbury Treadwell, a hardware merchant, bought it in 1835; his youngest daughter, Gertrude Treadwell, lived there until 1933. ▪

Landmark Status For Sugar Hill

By **NINA SIEGAL** | June 15, 2000

THOUGH THEIR DAYS WERE EMBITTERED BY segregation and prejudice, African-Americans in Jazz Age New York always suspected that life was sweeter on Sugar Hill.

As they gazed up the hill from "the valley," as central Harlem was sometimes called, Harlemites saw a hub of elite black society. The names of those who lived there read like a Who's Who of black history: Ralph Ellison, Thurgood Marshall, Joe Louis, W. E. B. Du Bois, James Baldwin, Adam Clayton Powell Sr., Zora Neale Hurston, Duke Ellington and Paul Robeson, to name a few.

Now the New York City Landmarks Preservation Commission is designating a section of the neighborhood as an official historic landmark, the Hamilton Heights/ Sugar Hill Historic District.

Landmark designation is always a subject of debates, and talking about race in any context is touchy. Landmarks officials seem to be particularly wary of combining the two.

Once the commission finally began carving out the new district in an area almost consecrated in black lore, the debates became more complicated: Should a historic district be created based on its architectural merits or on its cultural history?

This question is not unique to New York. In other cities where "heritage tourism" is encouraged in historic areas like Bronzeville in Chicago's South Side and Beale Street in Memphis, preservationists have also encountered difficulty in convincing officials to define these areas as "black historic districts."

Most of the historic row houses on the hill were designed for rich white families at the beginning of the 20th century. It was not until the end of the 1920's—late in the Harlem Renaissance—that blacks were allowed to buy and rent the palatial homes.

"Whatever the commission calls it, there's no question that we're into a celebration of revolutionary terrain," said Carolyn Kent, a chairwoman of the landmarks committee for Community Board 9 in West Harlem, "because this is the central launching pad for black leadership in postwar America." ■

BELOW: *Two apartment buildings on Sugar Hill, Harlem.*

Mothering Brooklyn

By **SUSAN DOMINUS** | December 31, 2006

IT REQUIRES A FEAT OF MEMORY TO PICTURE gentrified Brooklyn as it was a mere 40 years ago: Manhattan's poor, troubled relation. Consider, then, the near-hallucinatory vision it took at the time to imagine the Brooklyn of today. In the mid-'60s, when many of Brooklyn's brownstones had been carved into decrepit rooming houses, when cabs in Manhattan wouldn't cross the Manhattan Bridge, an interior designer named Evelyn Ortner not only had that vision but also believed that by sheer force of will, she and her husband could conjure it into existence.

Ortner wanted to live someplace beautiful and culturally alive, surrounded by people who felt the same way. After moving to the neighborhood of Park Slope when she was 39, she saw potential

Clean and Spare, or True to History?

By **JOYCE WADLER** | February 22, 2007

SOON AFTER RENOVATING THEIR BROWNSTONE in Fort Greene, Brooklyn, in blow-out modern style two years ago—with a concrete floor, a back wall of glass and not one scrap of period trim—Kirsa Phillips and Doug Cardoni opened it up to a local house tour. Later, Ms. Phillips went to brownstoner.com, a blog devoted to historic Brooklyn brownstones, to find out what her visitors had really thought.

The reviews were mixed.

"A lot of people were interested in the floor," Ms. Phillips says, but "then there were comments like, 'These people should keep their mitts off Brooklyn brownstones!'"

Several blocks away, in Clinton Hill, is another Brooklyn town house—one that has been returned to its original grandeur since its owners bought it 21 years ago. The gleaming walnut floors date to the turn of the last century and the old library wallpaper has been cleaned of grime with the care usually reserved for an old painting. The owners are Jim Barnes and Sharon Barnes. They have done much of the restoration themselves, with Ms. Barnes standing on scaffolding to clean the plasterwork with dental tools.

There was a time when renovation always equaled restoration when it came to a Brooklyn brownstone, and tossing out original pocket doors was the architectural equivalent of shooting Bambi. But more people are choosing to go modern, and finding ways to do it within the landmark regulations of the borough's historic neighborhoods.

Not that they always set out to buck convention. Ms. Phillips and Mr. Cardoni, both 35, originally hoped to find a traditional brownstone when they discovered Fort Greene in 2000. But when they decided to make some changes, they hired Edwin Zawadzki and Mason Wickham, husband-and-wife architects whose firm, In Situ Design, leans heavily toward modern design.

"It became pretty clear that the way Doug and Kirsa lived—and their attitude in general—was much more modern than we had suspected," Ms. Wickham says. "They were clearing out walls faster than we could draw them and gravitating heavily toward our most extreme ideas. They weren't afraid of big spaces or big gestures."

It was not an inexpensive renovation. The couple had budgeted $200,000; they estimate that they spent over $400,000. The rest of the brownstone, including the entrance hall with its green painted stairway, has yet to be touched. At the moment, Ms. Phillips says, she doesn't have the energy for another big renovation. ∎

everywhere. "She was proud of Brooklyn when no one else was," says Alan Fishman, chairman of the board of the Brooklyn Academy of Music.

While other middle-class residents fled urban blight in the 1960's, Ortner set about transforming her community, one family at a time. She wooed young couples she met outside the borough, inviting them back to her exquisitely maintained Victorian brownstone for dinner with her husband and an assortment of other guests—all Brooklynites. After cocktails or dinner with the Ortners, dozens of young couples opted for life in the outer boroughs.

Ortner's agenda was always Brooklyn. And with that devotion came a tireless diligence to rummage through papers at the Department of Buildings until she had catalogued the history and architecture of some 1,800 buildings in the neighborhood, procuring landmark status for Park Slope. It was a shrewd tactical move and with it she secured what every mother wants for her child: protection in perpetuity. ∎

Brooklyn's Best and Brightest

By **PAUL GOLDBERGER** | November 14, 1986

WHILE IT IS HOUSES THAT REALLY MAKE Brooklyn—row after row of town houses, in every style the 19th century dreamed of, stretching on in a way that seems implausible to a Manhattanite—Brooklyn also possesses some splendid public architecture, some of it unique in the City of New York. What follows is a look at 10 places, all of which are Brooklyn's own—buildings, or places, that offer some kind of architectural experience that neither Manhattan nor any other borough can equal.

AN ESPLANADE WITH A VIEW

The Esplanade, the promenade behind Columbia Heights that overlooks New York Harbor, has arguably the greatest view in all New York; it is all of lower Manhattan, looking far more spectacular from here than it ever can from Manhattan itself. It is as if Brooklyn Heights were all one great building and the Esplanade were its veranda.

FIRST-RATE FIREHOUSE

There are firehouses all over New York, and many of them are first-rate works of architecture, but none is quite like the old City of Brooklyn fire headquarters in downtown Brooklyn at 365 Jay Street, finished in 1892. It is strong and sensual, and too derivative to be called truly original. But it is no less wonderful for that: this noble building seems to reach out and give us a bear hug, reminding us that public architecture can be both monumental and friendly.

BEAUX-ARTS BANK

Not far away, at the intersection of Fulton Street and DeKalb Avenue, stands another essay in civic grandeur, the Dime Savings Bank. No other grandiose bank teaches us so fine a lesson in urban design. The block it occupies is three-sided. It is not easy to build a triangular classical temple, but the architects did it, with such ease that one would have assumed it was done this way in Rome. And there are few interiors in New York as monumental yet as welcoming and uninhibiting.

THE DARK WONDER OF WAREHOUSES

After the Brooklyn Bridge itself, the most important work of architecture in the neighborhood is the Empire Stores, the blocks of somber brick warehouses on Water Street between Dock and Main Streets, built in 1870 and 1885 by Thomas Stone. Here is brooding monumentality. To ponder them is less to think about architecture than it is to have an experience similar to looking at the dark paintings of Mark Rothko.

MODEL HOUSING

The apartments in the Tower Buildings—a complex in Cobble Hill built around a central rear open space—represented a spectacular advance. They predated public housing by two generations: this was a case of a private philanthropist deciding to build not for maximum profit, but for the public good.

A GREAT LAYOUT

Carroll Gardens in the Red Hook area of South Brooklyn in 1846 is a set of brownstone streets as they ought to be—in neat, even rows, placed way back from the street behind gracious, well-planted front yards. The idea was that it was possible to merge urban density with landscaped streets, and this Carroll Gardens does better, surely, than any other place in New York.

SUMPTUOUS BROWNSTONES

So far as row houses are concerned, the block of South Portland Street, between Lafayette and DeKalb Avenues in the heart of Fort Greene, is nearly as special. The layout is not innovative this time, but the houses are far better—truly grand-scale Italianate

BROOKLYN

brownstones, larger and more sumptuous not only than most of their Brooklyn neighbors, but than most of their Manhattan counterparts as well.

A LANDMARK CEMETERY

Green-Wood Cemetery is itself one of New York City's most impressive public open spaces, and in Brooklyn only Prospect Park is arguably better. But even Prospect Park, which the designers Frederick Law Olmsted and Calvin Vaux believed superior to their own Central Park in Manhattan, does not have an entrance like Richard Upjohn's Gothic gateway at Green-Wood. Upjohn is perhaps more famous for Trinity Church at the head of Wall Street in lower Manhattan. But he gave Green-Wood a monumental arch, a garden gate, and a means of passage to a very separate world, all in one. ∎

"Moonstruck House" Is Sold for $4 Million

By **J. COURTNEY SULLIVAN** | August 31, 2008

THE LOCALS KNOW THE FOUR-STORY Federal-style brownstone at Cranberry and Willow Streets in Brooklyn Heights as the "'Moonstruck' house" because it was the setting for the 1987 movie starring Cher and Nicolas Cage.

Neighborhood history buffs know the 1829 home for quite another reason: It was owned for nearly 50 years by Edwards Rullman, who was instrumental in persuading the city to declare Brooklyn Heights the first historic district in New York more than four decades ago.

Mr. Rullman and his wife have just sold the house for nearly $4 million. The reason was a familiar one: their children had long moved away and the house felt too big for just the two of them.

"We got 100 times what we paid for it back in 1961," said Mr. Rullman, a retired architect whose wife, Francesca, is a former opera singer. They now live on Cape Cod.

When the Rullmans bought the house, the neighborhood was gritty: it had fallen into disrepair in the 1940's and '50s, and the construction of the Brooklyn-Queens Expressway had eliminated a number of architectural treasures, including the literary group house whose residents included W. H. Auden and Carson McCullers.

As early as 1958, some families began meeting to discuss ways to preserve their neighborhood. They called themselves the Historic Preservation Committee of the Brooklyn Heights Association. Mr. Rullman became chairman of the committee's Design Advisory Council, which offered free advice to homeowners on proper preservation methods.

Finally, in November 1965, the Landmarks Preservation Commission granted the Brooklyn Heights Historic District protected status. Other neighborhoods like Greenwich Village followed.

That same year, Mr. Rullman quit his job at a Manhattan architectural firm to open a small shop devoted to restoration in Brooklyn Heights. All told, he restored more than 50 local buildings, including St. Ann's School.

Mr. Rullman said that moving to Cape Cod made sense for him and his wife, except for one problem. "After two weeks away," he said, "I already miss Brooklyn Heights." ∎

Map and Description of the Plan for the Central Park

May 1, 1858

WE HAVE ALREADY MENTIONED THE FACT that the Commissioners of the Central Park have awarded the first prize, of $2,000, to the plan which was numbered 33, and which proved to be the joint work of Messrs. F. L. Olmsted and C. Vaux. The Plan was accompanied by the following description, which, for the sake of convenience, we have slightly abridged:

The ground allotted to the park is very distinctly divided into two tolerably equal portions, which, for convenience sake, may be called the upper and lower parks.

THE UPPER PARK

The horizon lines of the upper park are bold and sweeping, and the slopes have great breadth in almost every aspect. As this character is the highest ideal of a park under any circumstances, and as it is in decided contrast to the confined formal lines of the city, it is desirable to interfere with it as little as possible. Formal planting and architectural effects, unless on a very grand scale, must be avoided.

THE LOWER PARK

The lower park is far more heterogeneous in its character, and will require more varied treatment. The most important feature in its landscape is the long rocky and wooded hillside lying south of the Reservoir. Inasmuch as beyond this point there do not appear to be any leading natural characteristics of similar consequence in the scenery, it will be important to draw as much attention as possible to this hillside, to afford facilities for rest and leisurely contemplation upon the rising ground opposite, and to render the lateral boundaries of the Park in its vicinity as inconspicuous as possible.

THE TRANSVERSE ROADS

Our instructions call for four transverse roads. Each of these will be the single line of communication between one side of the town and the other, for a distance equal to that between Chambers Street and Canal Street. They will be crowded thoroughfares, having nothing in common with the park proper. They must be constantly open to all the legitimate traffic of the city, to coal carts and butchers' carts, dust carts and dung carts; engine companies will use them, those on one side the park rushing their machines across it, with frantic zeal at every alarm from the other; ladies and invalids will need special police escort for crossing them, as they do in lower Broadway. ∎

Enjoying Nature's Magic Act

By **DOUGLAS MARTIN** | July 19, 2002

ONE NOON IN LATE SPRING I WENT TO THE Lake in Central Park and rented a boat. I glided leisurely on the water. Mallards swam in pairs. Often little fish would jump. My oars made tiny whirlpools. The woods around me seemed 10,000 shades of green; wisps of clouds floated on a perfectly blue sky. Almost hidden in the rushes, I saw a pair of swans: the female purposefully gathered twigs for a nest, even as the male behind her appeared to be trying to mate.

Was this the ultimate in multitasking? Was their relationship in trouble? Did I have an overactive imagination? Perplexing, for sure. Fascinating.

I rowed near a cormorant, its ebony feathers glistening in the dancing sunlight. It began to follow me! As I rowed here, there and everywhere, the beautiful bird followed

A Garden for All as a Private Eden

By **HERBERT MUSCHAMP** | May 23, 2003

CENTRAL PARK LOOKS GREENER THIS SPRING than it has in recent memory. Is this my imagination or the result of scientifically verifiable causes, like rain? I prefer to think that nature is making a bigger effort than usual this year to celebrate a very special occasion: the 150th anniversary of Central Park's birth.

Where else on earth has nature's floral bounty been appreciated by so many? Where else, this side of Eden, has animal, vegetable and mineral variety been more densely combined to such voluptuous effect?

Nowhere that I know of. This is worth a rousing cheer. Though perhaps a contemplative moment is more in keeping with the spirit of our great urban oasis. How about a round of applause for contemplative moments, then? Let's meditate until we're blue in the face, our lungs give out and our hands are raw from clapping. We've got all eternity to hold our peace.

I suspect that when good New Yorkers die, they go to Central Park. We, the living, go there to rehearse. Or perhaps to become more worthy of life in paradise. Frederick Law Olmsted, who designed the park along with Calvert Vaux in 1857, would not have quarreled with this hopeful interpretation.

The idea had been under discussion for some years. Public support reached a high point in 1853, when New York City staged its version of the Crystal Palace, the great imperial fair held in London two years earlier. In July of that year, the State Legislature approved the project, setting aside more than 750 acres as the site. ▪

me like a dog. It periodically dived underwater, surfaced and continued to follow. Somewhere near the blossoming lily pads, it left without saying why.

When I returned the boat, I told the man who helped me land that I had just had one of the finest experiences in the city.

To the west are the great apartment houses of Central Park West: the San Remo, the Dakota, the Century. To the south the jagged skyscrapers sprout like scraggly weeds. On the road visible from the Lake is a whole panoply of purposeful motion: runners, skaters, bikers, horse-drawn carriages. The noise of distant sirens can be heard.

But the 22-acre body of water somehow feels like nothing so much as a lake in the Adirondacks. With its man-made coves and peninsulas and the towering natural cliffs and rock formations, there is an illusion of much greater size and complexity. This is the genius of Central Park: as trails twist and turn, over bridges and under arches, through hills and valleys, one feels enmeshed in the mystery and expanse of nature. ▪

BELOW: *The Bow Bridge over the Lake in Central Park.*

A Day in the Life of Central Park

By **BRUCE WEBER** | July 2, 1995

ABOVE: *The Great Lawn in Central Park on a spring day in 2007.*

ON THE FIRST SATURDAY OF CITY SUMMER—a week early by the calendar, but tell that to the unseasonably warm weather—Central Park, as public as an ocean, became, in effect, the city's rumpus room. There was a groggy wakening, a flurry of morning activity, a lassitude at noon, a kaleidoscopic frenzy in the late afternoon, a gradual relaxation into evening and, in the end, a descent into an eerie night.

5:40 a.m. To enter the park at this hour is to be wary of disturbing things. Daylight has not yet woken the homeless. Inside the entrance at 96th Street and Central Park West, a man wearing a baseball cap is curled in a fetal position on the grass beneath a rocky crag. Squirrels leap over him.

6:15 a.m On East Drive, just north of the 79th Street Transverse, bicycle racers are queueing up to register for the weekly competitive sprint, sponsored by the Century Racing Club, around the park's 6.2-mile inner circumference. "It's a good road course, a clear road most of the time," says Jim Boyd, the club's president. "And it's not the roller rink it can become."

9 a.m. The Rubies, one of four all-girl teams in the Catholic Youth Organization's Manhattan Youth Baseball League, arrive in the park's North Meadow for their game against the Diamonds. The players, ages 8 to 10, gather around their coach, Tom Hock, who reminds them to drink plenty of liquids because it's such a hot day.

Then, with cries of "Remember, we're the Rubies!" they take the field, hoping to improve on their 4-2-2 record. "We'll never lose again!" declares Danielle Bolling, 9, the team's best hitter. Alas, she is wrong. The Diamonds prevail, 10-0.

10 a.m. The first model yacht race of the day gets under way on the Conservatory Water, better known as the boat pond, on the east side of the park at 74th Street. Eleven men, members of the 75-year-old Central Park Model Yacht Club, stand on the edge, holding transmitters that control their boats, which are painted a variety of exquisite colors and range in value from $200 to $3,500.

"I can tell you that compared to a real boat, it's much easier to throw this one in the water," says Michael Gianturco, whose 17-year-old son, Alexander, is racing "Viper."

NOON There's a waiting line at Claremont Stables on West 89th Street, where it costs $33 an hour to rent a horse for a clip-clop along the park's 4.5 miles of bridle paths. "I stopped therapy so I could go riding in the park," says Cecelia Marcus, a lawyer in full riding regalia.

12:30 p.m. George C. Wolfe, producer of the New York Shakespeare Festival, takes the stage at the Delacorte Theater to begin rehearsal of the Festival's first summer production, "The Tempest," which he is directing. Today is the first time the actors are in costume, on a near 90-degree afternoon.

5:15 p.m. On a ramp leading down to the Wollman Skating Rink, Yolanda Cortez, just back from an extended stay in Italy, is walking with several relatives when she is run over by an in-line skater; her ankle is

Coyote Leads a Crowd
On a Central Park Marathon

By **JAMES BARRON** | March 23, 2006

A COYOTE'S OVERNIGHT ROMP IN CENTRAL Park ended with a tranquilizer dart and a nap, but only after a messy breakfast (hold the feathers), a dip in a chilly pond and a sprint past a skating rink-turned-movie set.

There was also a final chase that had all the elements of a Road Runner cartoon, with the added spectacle of television news helicopters hovering overhead, trailing the coyote and the out-of-breath posse of police officers, park officials and reporters trailing it.

The coyote's pursuers joked that it even tried to turn itself in. It was hunting for a place to sleep it off after being hit by a single tranquilizer dart, and that place was a Fire Department dispatching station next to the Central Park station house overlooking the 79th Street transverse.

The coyote—named Hal by his captors, who said he was about a year old—woke up in a cage on the bed of a pickup truck carrying him out of the park. This was a couple of hours after Mayor Michael R. Bloomberg had delivered some one-liners at Hal's expense. "Are New Yorkers in danger?" the mayor asked at a breakfast at the New York Public Library. "This is New York, and I would suggest that the coyote may have more problems than the rest of us."

Where Hal came from remained a mystery. The parks commissioner Adrian Benepe said that he had probably been driven out of Westchester County and meandered down the West Side to 72nd Street, where Riverside Park ends. And then, Mr. Benepe said, he turned left.

That was news in the neighborhood. "I see a lot of things pass this way," said Ralph Mascolo, a doorman on West 72nd Street near Central Park West, "but never a coyote." ∎

broken. As the Emergency Medical Service ambulance arrives, Ms. Cortez smiles at the man who hit her, Damon Johnson, a 28-year-old stockbroker who lives in Brooklyn. She flashes him a peace sign.

8:45 p.m. In a hansom cab on the east side of the park, Jason Oshins, a 30-year-old lawyer, gets down on one knee and proposes to Alice Hurwit, a 28-year-old television producer.

"Will you do me the honor of being my wife?" he says.

She sobs and kisses him.

MIDNIGHT The park is empty enough that individual sounds are carried clearly on the cool night wind. "The Tempest" is still in rehearsals at the Delacorte, dramatic bellows issuing out over the Great Lawn. In the guardhouse on the south end of the Jacqueline Kennedy Onassis Reservoir, the security guard is passing time watching television.

What will he do for the rest of the night? Not much, he says, though he looks forward to dawn. "I watch the sun come up," he says. "Now that's peaceful." ∎

BELOW: *Otis, another coyote that was captured in Central Park in 1999, now resides at the Queens Zoo.*

Squares, Beatniks, Children, Dogs Et al. Coexist From 2 to 6 P.M.

By **GAY TALESE** | April 9, 1962

YESTERDAY MARKED THE BEGINNING OF A long season of Sunday afternoon song around the circular, gray pool in Washington Square Park, and it was a scene of peaceful coexistence between the hipsters and squares. Nobody brought bongos—which are outlawed in the park—but people softly sang sad ballads together, or listened to the competitive strumming of guitars, or made casual conversation, or just wandered through the crowds.

A quintet sang "Down By the River Side," and 20 yards away a crowd watched a lasso being twirled by a Manhattan cowboy who calls himself Texas Weinstein. Behind him, a slinky girl sat reading Proust, her expression hidden behind sunglasses; next to her was a monkey on a chain who seemed interested in the poetry that William Brown, the Brooklyn bard, was delivering to his followers on the other side of the pool.

"... he was choked-up tight ... in his white-on-white," said the poet, "and he wore a cocabrown ... that was down a candy-striped tie ... and he looked real fly ... and he had on a gold-dust crown ... and it was the 15th frame of a nine-ball game, and as Bud stood watching the play, with a casual shrug, he looked up and dug ... a strange cat coming his way ...."

The young people at his knees seemed visibly moved by the lines and, when the bard had finished, some put money into his hand. "Splendid," said the poet. "My money has turned green ... on the New York scene."

With the temperature in the middle 60's, they sang on and on, undisturbed by the children on tricycles scooting under their guitars, or the teenagers who hurled pink high-bouncers past them, or the dogs that were giving their all to "fetch" for their masters.

This mellow afternoon in Greenwich Village went on from 2 to 6 p.m., at which time the police declared the self-expression hours at an end. And so everybody took their guitars and songs, their poetry and perambulators, their high-bouncers and dogs, and went peacefully home. ∎

The Battle Over Washington Square

By **GRAHAM BOWLEY** | November 23, 2008

CATHRYN SWAN TOOK OUT A TAPE MEASURE and leaned into the bushes to indicate the height—four feet—of an imaginary iron perimeter fence, one proposed by the city's parks department as part of its $16-million-plus redesign of Washington Square Park.

Marching off past chess players, guitar strummers, baby strollers, magazine readers and people watchers—the usual Greenwich Village crowd—she headed to a spot where benches and trees would soon vanish. She posted a flier. "Stop Mayor Bloomberg from destroying Washington Square Park," it read. "Who is behind the destruction of our magical park?"

We all want to write our desires on New York. But in a metropolis of eight million overlapping voices, that is rarely possible. Public spaces like parks are a particular battleground, equally prized as green oases and places for personal expression.

And other than Central Park, perhaps none are more valued than the 181-year-old Washington Square Park, a seemingly round-the-clock distillation of the frenetic spirit of New York.

Ah, the Heat, the Crowd, Bryant Park and the Booze

By **CARA BUCKLEY** | July 16, 2008

WITH BARS ON EVERY CORNER, AND—THANKS to buses, subways or cabs—no need to drive after the drinking is done, New York City can be like a giant—and boozy—college campus. This is never more true than in the summer.

Even going to the movies involves drinking. Michael Treanor and Brianna Jacobson, both 23, were sitting with their friend Christopher Jarrod Thomas, also 23, in the middle of Bryant Park. It was a recent Monday evening, and a free film, "The Man Who Came to Dinner," was about to be shown. They were polishing off two bottles of Yellow Tail shiraz, without cups. And, to their surprise, no one was stopping them.

"I'm a little shocked," said Mr. Treanor between swigs, his eyes widening. "In California, this is way not allowed."

New York City is somewhat of a drinker's paradise year round, but a certain extra layer of permissiveness seems to infuse the city in the summertime, along with a wellspring of opportunities to get sloshed, slightly or mightily.

The Bryant Park scene is replicated to an extent around the sweating city, be it at the Great Lawn in Central Park, Cunningham Park in Queens, or Van Cortlandt Park in the Bronx. Whenever there are free events, the throngs follow, alcohol stealthily—or not so stealthily—in tow.

The official line from the city's parks department is that alcohol cannot be brought into city parks, though in the summer of 2003, Mayor Bloomberg suggested that drinking wine at concerts in Central Park was O.K. At Bryant Park on July 7, a security guard said he turned a blind eye to booze on movie nights, "so long as it is covered, like in a bag."

It's enough to make Elizabeth Brady— "Boozeabeth" to her friends—shrug.

"I think it's normal for people our age, out of college, to learn how to function with a hangover," Ms. Brady, 24, said at a "Williamsburg block party" at McCarren Park Pool in Brooklyn. "It's like when people have a baby, and they say they haven't slept in weeks. C'est la vie." ■

In 2004, responding to what it said were numerous calls for repairs and improvements, the parks department announced a plan to renovate the space, a proposal quickly met with bitter opposition from residents who complained that their park was being violated. In 2007, after candlelight vigils, demonstrations and rancorous fights at community board meetings and in the courts, the city won and workers moved in.

Many people who use the square have since accepted the changes as improvements. But a core group remains unconvinced and bitterly angry. For them, the battle for Washington Square is not over. Their frustration speaks to the question of who controls the public spaces that many city residents treat as personal fiefs.

The parks department saw an opportunity to replace the swaths of asphalt and clunky seating and lighting dating to 1970 and transform it.

"From the beginning," said Adrian Benepe, the parks commissioner, "the idea was to try to restore some of its historical character and to try to make it a greener park."

But Ms. Swan hopes that she may yet persuade parks department officials to save some of the trees or the alcove seating that she says was such a facilitator of conversation.

"The biggest question people ask is, 'Why?'" Ms. Swan said. "Why are they doing this?" ■

The Renewal of Union Square Park

By **DEIRDRE CARMODY** | August 3, 1986

THE FLOWERS ARE BLOOMING IN UNION Square Park.

Only a few years ago, no grass could be found there. Lights were ripped out, benches were broken and the area had been so taken over by drug dealers that passers-by walked through at their peril.

Now, there are deep-pink roses and a profusion of snapdragons around the statue of George Washington. Dozens of orange flowers surround the base of the flagpole, brilliant against the lush green of the well-tended lawns.

This now-cheerful park just north of 14th Street between Broadway and Park Avenue South marks one of the city's real success stories, according to virtually everyone who knows anything about it, from neighborhood regulars to former critics to city officials.

"It can only be termed a great triumph," said Joseph Rose, chairman of Community Board 5, which just a few years back was one of the most outspoken critics of the park and the city's neglect of it.

Walking through the 153-year-old, 3.6-acre park last week, one could see people lying on the grass looking up at the sky, while mothers took care of toddlers in the new play area and office workers drank coffee at little white tables under blue-and-white umbrellas. Two park attendants were picking up litter. Several members of the City Volunteers Corps were sweeping the sidewalk near the entrances. Even the drinking fountains worked.

Keeping a promise by city officials to keep the drug dealers away, two police officers are stationed inside the park and others flank the park on Fifth Avenue and Park Avenue South. Community leaders like to tell the story of the surprise visit paid to the park by Police Commissioner Benjamin Ward shortly after it reopened in May 1985 following the first phase of its $3.6 million renovation. There were still a few shadowy figures lurking around. The Commissioner noted with a smile that he knew them all but could not acknowledge it publicly. They were all undercover police officers. ∎

A Date With Serenity At the Cloisters

By **ANDREW L. YARROW** | June 13, 1986

PERCHED HIGH ABOVE THE HUDSON IN THE forested hillsides of craggy upper Manhattan, the tower of what appears to be a medieval monastery etches its brown granite profile against the sky. This imposing building is the Cloisters, a branch of the Metropolitan Museum of Art, and it is like an intricate puzzle whose pieces form a tableau of medieval culture. Tapestries such as the renowned "Hunt of the Unicorn" and "Nine Heroes" series, Gothic stained glass, frescoes, sculptures, enamels, illuminated manuscripts, bejeweled reliquaries and panel paintings such as the Merode Altarpiece are among its treasures.

The Cloisters and its collections have their origins in the remarkable obsession of George Grey Barnard, sculptor and medieval-art collector extraordinaire. For the first quarter of the 20th century, Barnard prowled

The Guardian of Gramercy Park

By ERIC KONIGSBERG | June 19, 2008

ARLENE HARRISON CALLS HERSELF THE mayor of Gramercy Park, and she does not just mean that she knows almost everybody who walks through the lush, private two-acre expanse in the East 20's well enough to say hello. Ms. Harrison's influence over that particular piece of prime Manhattan green space and its neighbors—some 900 units in 39 buildings border the park—is felt in the "Keep off the grass" signs and the holly bushes she had installed recently "to block out the streets and the sidewalk."

Since Ms. Harrison started the Gramercy Park Block Association in 1994, after her son was attacked and beaten up in front of their apartment building at 34 Gramercy Park, she has effectively remade the area in her own image.

She has added to a list of regulations (no dogs, no feeding of birds, no groups larger than six people, no Frisbees or soccer balls or "hard balls" of any kind) that, in turn, have served to dictate how the park is—and is not—used. Most recently, she helped pave the way for Zeckendorf Realty to redevelop a 17-story Salvation Army boarding house on the south side of the park, and for the company's plan to convert the 300 rooms into 14 floor-through apartments plus a penthouse duplex. The company would not confirm the transaction.

"It will change the neighborhood for the better," she said. "It will be less use on the park."

Indeed, while a key to Gramercy Park—or, more precisely, an address that entitles one to such a key—is among the most coveted items of New York real estate, under Ms. Harrison's stewardship, the park has become perhaps the least-used patch of open space in the city. Most days, in nice weather, one would be hard-pressed to find more than a handful of people in the park at once, and few linger.

"Honestly, we don't use it that much," said Gale Rundquist, a real estate broker who has lived on the park for five years. Still, she said, access "adds a lot to a listing; it's panache."

Over the years, Ms. Harrison and her supporters have feuded with O. Aldon James Jr., president of the National Arts Club (which is on the park and thus is entitled to keys), and his supporters. The rift has essentially come down to access (he is for more, imagining the space as a delightful one for arts club functions).

"There used to be concerts and dance recitals in the park, but Arlene Harrison is afraid of who'll show up," Mr. James said in an interview last week. "It would be much truer to the spirit of the place if more people from the community could use it." ▪

the French and Italian countryside, going from abandoned churches and monasteries to farmhouses and even pigsties in search of medieval art objects. He acquired some 700 pieces, including major parts of four cloisters, and transported them to New York, where he opened a museum in 1914 near what is now 190th Street.

Barnard's enthusiasm for medieval art was nearly matched by that of John D. Rockefeller Jr., who envisioned a new city park on the heights of upper Manhattan with a great museum devoted to the Middle Ages. Between 1917 and 1927, Rockefeller bought several Washington Heights estates, underwrote the Metropolitan Museum's purchase of Barnard's collection and hired the landscape architect Frederick Law Olmsted Jr. to fashion the treacherously hilly site into Fort Tryon Park. The new Cloisters—designed by the architect Charles Collens under the curatorial guidance of James J. Rorimer of the Metropolitan—opened in 1938, barely three weeks after Barnard's death and three years after the park was dedicated. ▪

The Rescue of Prospect Park

By **DOUGLAS MARTIN** | May 27, 1990

ARMIES OF PICNICKERS, MANY LUGGING elaborate barbecuing gear, will descend on Prospect Park in Brooklyn this Memorial Day weekend. Others will come just to sit or sleep or sip in the Long Meadow, six times the size of the Sheep Meadow in Central Park and said to be the longest continuous open space in any American urban park. "Coming to the park is like taking a bath," said a 60-year-old man who has been a regular for half a century. "I leave with a refreshed mind."

This essay will stroll through the optimistic origins and triumphant rise of this 526-acre patch of green, pause to consider its decades-long decline, then let out a bit of a hoot over its resurgence.

In the 1860's, the value of Brooklyn's manufactured goods and its population had both burgeoned. But just across the East River, Manhattan was growing faster and richer. Brooklyn was in danger of becoming a dumping ground for Gotham's most obnoxious industries, bone-boiling for one. And as the cost of Manhattan living surged, more poor people arrived on the busy ferries. By building a park arguably superior even to the newly completed Central Park, Brooklyn's city fathers hoped to lure affluent residents and increase the tax base.

BELOW: *The Soldiers' and Sailors' Arch at Grand Army Plaza forms the main entrance to Prospect Park.*

Enter the kings of park design. Frederick Law Olmsted, a social philosopher, and Calvert Vaux, an architect, first collaborated on Central Park, begun in 1859. Prospect Park, begun in 1866, was their next achievement, the one Olmsted always deemed greatest. These two visionaries working together, and then Olmsted working alone, would leave their mark on magnificent parks from Buffalo to Chicago to Montreal to Seattle to the Capitol.

From the beginning, Prospect Park fulfilled its joyful purpose. Sepia photographs show Sunday-only gentry and a flock of sheep crowded on the Long Meadow. There was a wind-powered carousel on the lake, a penful of deer in the woods. Traditions coalesced: fishing contests, ice carnivals, Maypole dancing. In the 1930's, parks commissioner and master planner Robert Moses brought more pedestrian but utilitarian things—a zoo, bandshell and skating rink with all the charm of a freeway Howard Johnson's.

After the Korean War, the world and Prospect Park changed. Soldiers bought houses in the suburbs; poor blacks forced from their homes by urban renewal landed in the houses of those who left. By the 1960's, the Dodgers and neighboring Ebbets Field were history and Brooklyn was a sadder place.

By the mid-1970's, the fiscal crisis had dealt more brutal blows. Maintenance grew dreadful; buildings were boarded up. A poll showed 44 percent of New Yorkers thought no one should ever venture into the park.

But as money came back to the city, people came back to the park. A park administrator was appointed in 1980; a torrent of volunteers has also descended. The Prospect Park Alliance, formed in 1987 by prominent private citizens deeply committed to the park. Though much poorer than the Central Park Conservancy, the alliance represents a watchdog, a high-powered independent advocate in case City Hall, in the words of the park administrator, Tupper Thomas, "drops the ball." ■

Coney Island is Alive!
Step Right Up and See for Yourself!

By **ALAN FEUER** | April 4, 2009

CONEY ISLAND WAS LOOKING PRETTY GOOD for being dead. A new gear had been put on the Wonder Wheel. The sun licked at the windows of the Freak Bar. There was the smell of fresh-laid paint. Last September, when the Astroland amusement park was shut down in a battle with its landlord, erroneous reports went out around the world that all of Coney Island was a corpse. Overnight, it seemed, obituaries were composed.

But the rumors of demise had been exaggerated greatly. All of Coney Island, from Nathan's Famous Hot Dogs to the world-renowned Cyclone, had not dropped off the Boardwalk into the sea.

"They're all surprised when I tell them we're still open," said a frustrated Dennis Vourderis, whose family has run the Wonder Wheel for more than 40 years. "Unfortunately, the press did a great job announcing Astroland had closed, so now people think that Coney Island is closed."

The blame for the confusion has fallen partly on an inattentive public and partly on the media, which flocked to Coney Island last fall to cover the removal of Astroland's iconic six-ton rocket as if it were a visit from the pope.

"The thing is, we ain't closed," said Jimmy Carchiolo, an old salt with a pigskin voice who has run a dart game behind the Wonder Wheel for 43 years.

Ever since the first carousel was installed on Surf Avenue in 1876, Coney Island has been a jumble of competing institutions, an amusement park cooperative of sorts. Today, there is the Cyclone, Nathan's, the Wonder Wheel, KeySpan Park, the New York Aquarium, the Coney Island Circus Sideshow and the Coney Island Museum.

The separate parts exist together, squabbling and sharing like a family, and giving off a tribal fractured energy, a mirror of New York's.

"People think amusement parks are Disney World, where you pay one price and enter at the gate," said Aaron Beebe, the director of the museum. "But Coney Island isn't like that. It isn't homogenized. It has lots of moving parts."

But the mood is such that 2009 is already known as the Second Annual Last Summer. Joseph J. Sitt, a developer who owns most of the land in Coney Island, has proposed to bring in shopping malls and large Las Vegas-style hotels.

"It always feels like New York is on the edge of losing its soul," he said, "and Coney Island represents that." ▪

BELOW: *Luna Park in Coney Island, 1912.*

The Forest Premeditated

By **EDWARD ROTHSTEIN** | June 16, 2008

SPEND SOME TIME AT THE NEW YORK Botanical Garden and the entire idea of a garden, let alone a "botanical garden," starts to become even more strange. Is the garden a small part of nature, a set of organisms and plants replicating in miniature the vitality of their larger host? Yes, sure, but it is we, not nature, who create the garden, who give it its character within its man-made borders, and then labor to order it according to rules we establish. A garden is as much about the human world as the natural one.

This garden in the Bronx, for example, began in 1891, when the New York State Legislature carved out 250 acres of the city's undeveloped land for "the collection and culture of plants, flowers, shrubs and trees."

The inspiration came from Nathaniel Lord Britton and his new bride, Elizabeth Knight Britton, who, on their honeymoon in 1888, were smitten not with the untamed wild of Europe's forests and mountains, but with the stupendous systematic achievements of the Royal Botanic Gardens, Kew, in London. They returned home, campaigning for a counterpart in New York; the project was supported by Carnegie, Morgan, Rockefeller, Vanderbilt—the same men who in the space of 50 years helped create the great cultural institutions of New York.

That's what the garden literally is: a cultural institution. Or better, an institution that is about cultivation. All gardens are a form of culture on display, but a botanical garden incorporates scientific culture as well. And the garden has the fourth-largest herbarium in the world, a collection of 7.3 million dried and catalogued plants. There are branches dating from the late 18th century, cut by venturesome botanists sailing with Capt. James Cook and samples found by John C. Frémont's expedition in the Oregon Territory and California in 1842-45.

These plant fragments, decorously mounted on flat sheets, are stored in fireproof

> That's what the garden literally is: a cultural institution.

cabinets in a specially constructed storage space. They are gradually being digitally scanned and made available online (sciweb.nybg.org/Science2/vii2.asp). The herbarium is the garden's antipode: natural habitats replaced by filtered air, living branches by dried twigs, bright colors by faded leaves and printed DNA analyses. But each part feeds the other. ∎

Pool, and Pride, In the Bronx

By **SARA RIMER** | August 11, 1985

TO THE PEOPLE WHO GREW UP IN THE neighborhood, who saw it flourish and then nearly die, the Crotona Park Pool sometimes seems like an enormous mirage, its Caribbean-blue waters shimmering amid the empty lots and tightly packed brick apartment buildings of the South Bronx.

"Every day my mother would say, 'Go to the pool! Go to the pool! Get out of the house!'" said Teresa Gonzalez, 25, from her lifeguard's chair. "But then the neighborhood went down and turned into what was known as 'The South Bronx.' All the abandoned buildings. The park was neglected. The pool got infamous. When I was a teenager, going to Crotona Pool was taking your chances."

Vandals cut the fence, ripped out the brass pipes and littered the walkways with broken glass. In 1980 the pool was closed,

The Bucolic Pleasures of Vanny

By **ANDREW L. YARROW** | July 31, 1987

ASK EVEN THE MOST CITY-SMART NEW Yorker to free-associate about the Bronx, and you're not likely to hear of forests and wetlands, horse trails and farmhouses. But all that and more can be found in one of New York's greatest natural and recreational treasures: Van Cortlandt Park, known to those who use it as "Vanny."

"If you want to see what much of New York looked like before it was developed, this is it," said Paul Berizzi, the administrator of Van Cortlandt and Pelham Bay Parks. "What occurs naturally here is what Olmsted and Vaux went to great pains to create in Central and Prospect Parks."

becoming a walled fortress to the neighborhood's children, for whom other city pools were too distant or too crowded or too small.

Crotona Park Pool reopened last year after a $6 million renovation by the Parks and Recreation Department. It is just as grand now as when Robert Moses, who loved pools and had been a champion freestyle swimmer at Yale University, opened it and nine others in 1936.

"Look at it!" Miss Gonzalez said in wonderment. "It's beautiful!"

The pool lies at the edge of the 147-acre Crotona Park, which has new picnic benches, rebuilt playgrounds and a newly dredged and beautified fishing and boating lake. Across from the pool, on Fulton Avenue, new windows gleam along a row of apartment buildings. A block away is the new Bathgate Industrial Park.

And Julius Hardaway, the Parks Department's 53-year-old chief of operations for the Bronx, can park his shiny green truck outside the pool and not lock the doors. "There's hope everywhere now," he said. ▪

A trip to Van Cortlandt Park might well begin where the subway ends. The IRT No. 1 train conveniently deposits end-of-the-line riders near the park's visitors' center at Broadway and 242nd Street. Just south of the nearby cluster of ball fields known as the Parade Ground and a heavily used recreational area equipped with tennis courts, a 160-foot swimming pool and a small football stadium, stands the three-story Van Cortlandt Mansion.

The Georgian-style fieldstone farmhouse takes its name from the family that owned this large tract from 1699 until it was acquired by the city for parkland in 1888. The house, built in 1748, is noteworthy not only as the oldest intact building in the Bronx and one of the oldest in the city, but also as a museum of Dutch, English and early American period furnishings. A 17th-century Dutch kas, or storage chest, is in a ground-floor parlor, great poster beds stand in second-floor bedrooms, and an early American dollhouse is in the nursery on the third floor.

> "If you want to see what much of New York looked like before it was developed, this is it."

On Vault Hill, where the Van Cortlandt family burial plot is located, dense, hilly forests extend as far as the eye can see. "Because of its size, Van Cortlandt has the kind of scenery you just don't find in other New York parks," said Mr. Berizzi. Only the sound of cars on the Mosholu and Henry Hudson Parkways and Major Deegan Expressway reminds one that this not the rolling hills of rural New England. ▪

A Rusty Relic from 1964

By **JAKE MOONEY** | June 24, 2007

The city is studying the possibilities for restoring and reusing the site, Parks Commissioner Adrian Benepe said—but he added pointedly that the pavilion was originally intended to be a temporary structure. The city recently spent $70 million on a new pool and skating rink in Flushing Meadows-Corona Park, he said.

"The question, given all the other demands for Flushing Meadows Park, is, is this the best use of that money?" Mr. Benepe said. "I honestly don't know the answer." ■

YOU MIGHT NOT THINK A RUSTY 1964 STRUC-ture in Flushing Meadows-Corona Park has much in common with venerable edifices like the Church of the Holy Nativity in Bethlehem, or Monte Albán, a 2,500-year-old Zapotec ruin on a mountaintop outside Oaxaca, Mexico. This month, though, the New York State Pavilion, a crumbling relic of the 1964 World's Fair that sits in the park, was named along with the other far-flung sites to the World Monuments Fund's list of 100 endangered sites, which is released every two years.

The pavilion, designed by Philip Johnson and familiar to drivers on the Grand Central Parkway for its three towers and open-air Tent of Tomorrow, made the list because it is in danger of collapse from rotting founda-tions, the group said.

"It's hard to see things that were built in your lifetime as important as something that's been around for 200 years," said Michelle Berenfeld, who oversees the endangered list. But she added, referring to the pavilion: "It's been there for 43 years. It's part of our cultural landscape now."

ABOVE: *The Unisphere, on the left, and New York State Pavilion, on the right, were part of the 1964 World's Fair.*

A Thoroughfare For Wildlife

By **DOUGLAS MARTIN** | May 16, 1994

CARLTON BEIL SAYS HE HAS NEVER HEARD A mockingbird imitate a wood duck, though generations of Staten Islanders are sure for some reason that he has. But he has heard a wood frog in mating season. It sounds like a duck with a sore throat.

Mr. Beil, 86, talks of turtles and American chestnut trees and finding his first rare fossil. Children gaze at him with awe as he lights a fire the Indian way. He is a naturalist, a teacher, a student.

"Carlton is kind of a repository of the natural history of Staten Island," said Thomas A. Paulo, the borough's parks commissioner.

The accomplishment Mr. Beil most treasures is his part in preserving a 2,500-acre slice of forests, swamps and meadows called the Greenbelt, where great blue herons nest, raccoons roam and 16 species of dragonfly flit about. The Greenbelt straddles the very middle of the island. It is bordered on the west by the Fresh Kills landfill, on the

Queens Sculpture Garden Is Made A Permanent Park

By **DOUGLAS MARTIN** | December 6, 1998

NEW YORK CITY HAS SIDED WITH ARTISTS and their allies over developers and will make Socrates Sculpture Park in Long Island City, Queens, a permanent park.

The park's future had been unclear until now. Developers had long been eager to build on the four-and-a-half-acre site, a former marine terminal with stunning views of Manhattan, Oz-like across the East River. Though the site has been a park for 14 years, its status was only temporary. Mayor Rudolph W. Giuliani took the final step and declared the site a permanent park last week.

"It is a spectacular setting for major works of sculpture," said Parks Commissioner Henry J. Stern.

The city's decision to preserve the park came in the face of a private proposal by a physician, Angelo Joseph Acquista, to spend $100 million to build luxury apartments and a marina. Many in the community had supported the plan as a way to bring life to a pretty dreary area. "They don't even have a delicatessen in that neighborhood," said George Delis, the district manager of Community Board 1 who pushed strongly for Dr. Acquista's idea.

But officials decided a stunning cultural attraction was the better bet. "I have a lot of other land on the East River to develop," said Claire Shulman, Queens borough president. "The truth of the matter is that they cleaned that whole area up and made it beautiful. It's like an oasis on the New York City waterfront." ∎

east by Moravian Cemetery, on the north by Todt Hill and on the south and southeast by historic Richmondtown.

The emerald swath snakes through precisely the place the city planner Robert Moses figured on building a freeway, between the Outerbridge Crossing, which connects New Jersey to Staten Island, and the Verrazano-Narrows Bridge. Only because hundreds of what Moses called "daisy sniffers" resisted—led at one point on a hike through the snowy woods by a new mayor, John V. Lindsay—was technology's march stopped in its tracks.

"It's the city's first great post-Moses park," said Parks Commissioner Henry J. Stern, who persuaded Mayor Edward I. Koch in 1984 to acquire the land.

Another important symbol is that the Parks Department is erecting rustic signs along the Greenbelt's perimeter, giving it a collective identity its parts and parcels have lacked. As this goes forward—along with other elements of a $40 million, 20-year development plan announced last year   Mr. Paulo said, "Young people will see the Greenbelt as an entity rather than the symbol of some kind of argument over a road." ∎

BELOW: *Opening day of the exhibition, 'Ozymandias' at Socrates Sculpture Park in Astoria, Queens, in 1999.*

Lions (and Tigers and Bears) In Winter

By **BRUCE WEBER** | January 3, 1997

FOR SOME TIME NOW, BECAUSE I HAVE A friend who travels frequently, I have lived in close proximity to animals—hers. They are a dog and a cat, Lucille and Maggie— granted, not exactly critters you find in the wild, but there is a zoolike quality that my apartment has taken on. I've been witness to (and occasionally a victim of) a lot of stalking, a participant in a lot of nonverbal communication, a monitor of mood swings.

All this prepared me nicely for a couple of days at the International Wildlife Conservation Park, a k a the Bronx Zoo, which I hadn't visited in decades. The cold-weather season is a particularly good time for adults to visit, I discovered, largely because the great herds of tiny cotton-candy eaters (a populous species of the genus children) are thinned out.

The zoo is open 365 days a year (where are the animals going to go?), but in spring and summer, it has up to 40,000 visitors on Wednesdays, when admission is free; last Wednesday, Christmas, there were 357. The local residents feel considerably less overwhelmed, and thus the possibility of encountering them closely is high. You can get near enough for long enough that, like pets, they reveal themselves.

Timmy, for example, the patriarch of the zoo's gorilla clan, doesn't care for hoopla; he tends to seek privacy when there's a crowd. Unlike a number of his showoffy relatives, "he's very, very shy," a keeper in the gorilla house told me.

But there he was sitting in full view when I wandered in, his regal belly protruding, sheltering one of his granddaughters with a protective arm. He was true to form, though, when I was followed by a chattering family of Scandinavian tourists: he stood slowly and lumbered off.

Pat Thomas, the assistant curator of mammals, said the relatively small monkey house can be maddeningly busy and shrill in high season. "It's not a good educational experience," he said. "You spend more time jockeying for position than watching the animals."

But on the day after Christmas, I was alone there. And I feel as though I left an impression, at least on the white-faced capuchins, many of which paused in their regular antics to regard me. One waited patiently until I tentatively reached out my hand and touched the glass. A gesture of friendship, I thought. But with a yawp that sounded like "Aha!," he reacted as though I'd fallen into a trap he'd set, leaping immediately to his feet and pounding on the glass with both hands.

"You fool!" he said. Or so I thought. ∎

ABOVE: *At the Bronx Zoo, visitors can view the tigers in their habitant through a glass panel.*

ZOOS

Stay-at-Home SWB, 8, Into Fitness, Seeks Thrills

By **JOHN KIFNER** | July 2, 1994

So the polar bear in the Central Park Zoo has a therapist. Big deal.

Anybody who is anybody in Manhattan has a therapist, to say nothing of a personal trainer and a nutritionist. What is this bear's problem?

He swims too much.

What?

Right. The polar bear, whose name is Gus, keeps on swimming in a tight little figure 8, gracefully pushing off his artificial rock pile with a huge hind paw, languorously backstroking, then turning a neat diving flip by the underwater window. Over and over and over, as if he were doing laps in the Yale Club pool.

"He's not meeting our criteria for quality of life," said the bear's therapist, Tim Desmond. "We're trying to perfect his life style."

Naturally, Mr. Desmond is from California.

Everybody is very concerned about Gus at the zoo, which, by the way, is officially not a zoo anymore but the Central Park Wildlife Center. Once it was like Rikers Island, locking up lions, elephants and yaks like miscreants. But it was redesigned and reopened in 1988 as a state-of-the-art showcase for a few carefully chosen species in near-natural environments.

There had been, along the way, some unfortunate incidents, including one in which a prior polar bear ate a visitor, resulting in his (the bear's) banishment to the Bronx. So there is genuine worry that a star attraction like Gus is not just having a bad fur day but is, well, you know, a little loony.

The problem, said Mr. Desmond, who is being paid $25,000 for treating Gus—which is not so bad considering he weighs about 700 pounds, four or five times the size of most neurotics—is that he really doesn't have enough to do. In zoo talk, the result is called "stereotypical behavior," in which an animal fills the void by doing exactly the same thing over and over again without any real reason. Hey, people who work in offices, sound familiar?

Gus's media-age status was certified the other morning when a group of elementary-school-age children were told by their teacher, "This was the bear that was on television." They went wild. Meanwhile, a photographer from People magazine, with an assistant taking Polaroids to check the lighting, was shooting a portrait of the bear.

Zoo people were solemnly spreading crunchy Skippy peanut butter over all kinds of plastic objects that they would toss into the environment to give the bear something to do. This is the main element of the therapy. Gus was backstroking, kicking off and flipping over. And he was smiling. ∎

BELOW: *Gus resting on a very hot day in the Central Park Zoo in 2006.*

P eople who complain about New York can't complain that it's short on museums, concert halls, theaters and art galleries. It has more of them than any other major American city—so many that it is difficult not to think about the artists, writers and musicians who have built the city into their work, from Edward Hopper to William Rauschenberg, from titans of Tin Pan Alley like George Gershwin to stars of hip-hop like Jay-Z.

New York has the studios for the artists and the stages for the performers. It still has everything from Carnegie Hall, where Tchaikovsky conducted on opening night, to Radio City Music

Lullabies Of Broadway

ARTS & LEISURE

▲ PAGE 172

Hall, where the Rockettes go high-kicking across a stage that is not that much wider. And it has Lincoln Center, where the Metropolitan Opera and the New York Philharmonic and the New York City Ballet and other resident companies put on more than 5,000 performances a year. It was at Lincoln Center that Pavarotti and Domingo navigated the high C's and Leontyne Price and Marilyn Horne and Renee Fleming gave some of their finest performances. It was there, too, that another well-known soprano, Beverly Sills, took on a leadership role when her singing days were over, first as general director of the New York City Opera. Later, as chairwoman of Lincoln Center itself, she laid the groundwork for an ambitious, multibillion dollar renovation that has turned Lincoln Center into the second-largest

▲ PAGE 152

construction zone in Manhattan, after the World Trade Center site.

New York established itself as a theater capital even before the Civil War; the Philharmonic traces its origins to 1842. Later, other nineteenth-century stars like Edwin Booth brought Shakespeare to New York audiences well aware that his brother had assassinated President Abraham Lincoln.

As the city spread north from Lower Manhattan, it set aside land for an art museum—a green rectangle at the edge of the then-new Central Park. The Metropolitan Museum's collection contains far more than paintings and statues. The oldest items at the Met are a set of flints from the Lower Paleolithic period (300,000 to 75,000 B.C.). The Met also has the world's oldest piano, a relative youngster from the early eighteenth century.

But the Met has added modernistic architecture that transcended its nineteenth-century formality, starting with a modern temple for an ancient one. In the 1970's, the Met built a steel-and-glass addition to house the fifteenth-century B.C. Egyptian Temple of Dendur. Some museum-goers still find the juxtaposition of ancient and modern startling. The architecture critic Paul Goldberger said the addition slams into the museum's

original Beaux-Arts facade "with all the subtlety of a train collision."

There was a time in the 1950's when people registered a similar complaint about Frank Lloyd Wright's Guggenheim Museum—a bright, white sphere—was, they fumed, incompatible with the townhouses and massive Fifth Avenue apartment buildings that face Central Park. Here, though, the critics disagreed. Goldberger called the spiraling ramp inside the Guggenheim "one of the triumphant creations of the 20th century."

That word triumphant also comes to mind across town, on the other side of Central Park, where the heroic statue of Theodore Roosevelt on horseback dominates the entrance to the American Museum of Natural History. It has a collection of 32 million specimens. They're not all on display, of course. But there are intriguing rare gems, rebuilt mammoths and a fierce-looking Tyrannosaurus Rex. And if you don't want a glimpse of the creatures that roamed the earth in prehistoric times, you can look to the sky from the jewel-like heavenly ball of the Hayden Planetarium—the largest suspended-glass curtain wall in the United States.

Broadway builds fantasies with greasepaint and dialogue and

melody that draw big audiences every year, and big money. But Broadway's glitzy surface masks deep troubles: fewer shows, smaller audiences, fewer jobs. About half as many new productions go on the boards as did a generation ago. Some critics worry that pop and rock have drowned out whatever it was that made Rodgers and Hammerstein musicals so enduring. "Rent," a modern-day version of "La Bohème," definitely wasn't Rodgers and Hammerstein.

But the shows that succeed can go on and on: Andrew Lloyd Webber's "The Phantom of the Opera" has run for more than 9,000 performances, which is 7,800 more than the original-cast run of Irving Berlin's "Annie Get Your Gun" (with a book by Herbert and Dorothy Fields). But "Annie Get Your Gun" is notable for the five-verse Ethel Merman showstopper that summed up why Broadway is magical, night after night: "There's no business like show business."

▼ PAGE 168

The Opening of the Metropolitan Museum of Art

March 30, 1880

TODAY, THE METROPOLITAN MUSEUM OF ART will be opened with quite imposing formalities. Some 3,500 invitations have been sent out, and, doubtless, this, one of the leading events in the art history of New York, will be appropriately celebrated. On the 1st of April the museum will be open to the general public, and as in the former locality, on 14th Street, admission will be free on Wednesday, Thursday, Friday, and Saturday from 10:30 a.m. to 6 p.m. while on Monday and Tuesday an entrance fee of 50 cents will be charged—free, of course, to members and holders of tickets. What with the facilities the elevated railroads give, this museum in Central Park, on Fifth Avenue and 82nd Street, is today most readily approachable.

Yesterday a private view was held, which was largely attended. The building itself, as far as the outside goes, is unpretentious, being built of brick with stone cappings, and is constructed more to give full admittance to light than with much idea of symmetrical proportion. Inside, its decoration is somber. The floors are of tessellated stone, the staircases are wide, not too steep, and the ventilation and light are excellent.

In the central hall are placed the loan collections, with the laces and embroideries; at the east end is a collection of Greek vases, while the Kensington reproductions are at the west end. Mr. Pruyn of Albany has loaned his carved Chinese Ivories; Mr. Drexel has sent his Egyptians antiquities; Mr. Prime shows his old volumes, as does Mr. How his many examples of fine binding. Here are collection of miniatures, Limoges emamels, old arms, Sevres, Dresden, and majolics. There are Oriental and Japanese stuffs, with silver *repoussé* in fine, an endless variety of strange, beautiful, or curious objects. In the north and south aisles in the east hall and the east entrance hall are the Cypriote antiquities—the vases, terra-cottas, bronzes, busts, statues of the Cesnola collection.

These, including a great number, which could not be shown in 14th Street, have all been arranged with excellent judgment and good taste. Falling down from the gallery above are suspended a number of tapestries, old French, Spanish, and Flemish ones, which are singularly effective. An excellent color has been used throughout for the lining of the cases, and, as the light seems to be evenly diffused from above, there is no reason to suppose that much fading of the material will take place. ▪

A Panoramic Backdrop For Meaning And Mischief

By KEN JOHNSON | April 22, 2008

WITH ITS BREATHTAKING, PANORAMIC VIEWS of Central Park and the Manhattan skyline, the Cantor Roof Garden at the Metropolitan Museum of Art may strike you as an excellent place to mount a seasonal outdoor sculpture show, which it does every year. In truth, it is an inhospitable site for sculpture, as demonstrated by the 2008 display: three wonderful, previously unexhibited works by the celebrated Pop artist Jeff Koons. Each of these sculptures is a greatly enlarged, glossily lacquered, stainless-steel representation of something small: a toy dog made of twisted-together balloons; a chocolate valentine heart wrapped in red foil, standing en pointe; and a silhouette of Piglet from a "Winnie the Pooh" coloring book, randomly colored as if by a small child.

Private Lessons
In the Halls of Old Masters

By **DAN BARRY** | December 20, 2003

IN THAT HUSHED HOUR BEFORE THE DOORS open to Fifth Avenue, a young man named Fabian Berenbaum enjoys private consultations with Rembrandt and Rubens, El Greco and van Dyck. They whisper across the centuries. Notice, they say. Learn.

On some mornings the great masters demonstrate the varied uses of light and shadow. Other mornings they suggest ways to convey emotion through the smallest details: purity of soul in a child's eye, perhaps, or world-weariness in the arch of an old man's brow. Their ability to grant a kind of everlasting life to those long dead—with paint, brush and canvas—can leave Mr. Berenbaum breathless.

These lessons end when the wooden floor says so. It creaks faintly under the weight of the day's first visitors to the European Paintings galleries.

The Metropolitan Museum of Art employs hundreds of guards and supervisors to provide assistance to visitors and to protect its priceless collections. You may take photographs, but please, no flash. You may bring your face within inches of a Manet, but do not touch, do not brandish a pen, and please—please!—never use your umbrella as a pointer while making some profound observation about artistic technique.

If you do, you may hear from Fabian Berenbaum.

> They whisper across
> the centuries.
> Notice, they say. Learn.

They are mischievously meaningful works. But placed on the architecturally nondescript patio, where there are also shaded areas for patrons of the Roof Garden Cafe, the sculptures too easily turn into benign, decorative accessories.

The biggest problem is scale. Seen in an indoor gallery, the elephantine, shiny metallic "Balloon Dog (Yellow)," which rises to 10 feet at its highest point, would have a weirdly imposing, slightly menacing presence. On the roof it appears dwarfed by the vast sky and by the open expanses of space to the south and west of the museum.

The intimacy of Mr. Koons's sculpture is also diminished. Perfectionist attention to detail is one of his work's most compelling aspects: note the exactingly formed knot that serves as the balloon dog's nose, or the folds, pleats and stretch marks in the heart's wrapper. The distracting outdoor environment, though, discourages careful, contemplative looking.

Their setting aside, Mr. Koons's sculptures remain intellectually and sensuously exciting objects—"Balloon Dog" is a masterpiece—and they are worth visiting under any circumstances. ∎

Mr. Berenbaum, 29, has worked as a guard at the museum for four years, and has stood in silence, eyes wide, in just about every section of the building. But years ago he requested that his primary assignment be in European Paintings, among the work of artists born before 1865.

He had his reasons. He is also an artist, with a master's degree in fine arts.

When his shift ends, Mr. Berenbaum boards the 4 train to the 7, and gets out in Sunnyside, Queens. He walks up two flights to his small apartment, where he has converted his bedroom into a studio that is furnished with two easels. This is where he paints, often until well past midnight.

He does not listen to music. He has no television. There are just those whispers. ∎

Where MoMA Has Lost Its Edge

By **NICOLAI OUROUSSOFF** | February 4, 2005

PHILIP JOHNSON DIED LAST WEEK WITHOUT having seen Yoshio Taniguchi's completed expansion of the Museum of Modern Art. He was too frail to travel to the museum's opening event and had stopped offering ideas to the Modern's curators.

But his presence still haunts the museum. Whatever you thought of Johnson's aesthetic agenda or impish charm, he never lacked a strong point of view. And it is hard to imagine that Johnson, the founding director of the Modern's department of architecture and design, would have been impressed by the reinstallation of the department's main galleries more than 60 years after he organized its inaugural show in the museum's old Fifth Avenue home.

Under his guidance, the department's early exhibitions on architecture and industrial design not only marked significant shifts in architectural thought, but also made the museum the nation's most powerful platform for changing the way Americans viewed design. That role continued through the 1960's and the museum's publication of Robert Venturi's "Complexity and Contradiction in Architecture," the first sign that cracks were appearing in the Modernist narrative.

The new installation, by comparison, is unlikely to burn a hole in our memories. Nor is it likely to shake up our view of the world. Tucked away on the third floor of Mr. Taniguchi's elegant monument to classical Modernism, it is a surprisingly lifeless mix of design objects, often-superb drawings and architectural models. The bulk of the installation feels haphazard and lackluster; when it strives for a little originality, it stumbles.

Johnson's best shows always managed to convey a sense of urgency. The Modern has lost that sense of purpose. Surely curators know that "good taste" is not enough to give coherence to an all-important installation, let alone to turn an audience on. The museum needs to find a bolder mission than defining who or what constitutes the mainstream. ▪

Museum Acquires Its First Van Gogh

September 30, 1941

THE MUSEUM OF MODERN ART HAS JUST acquired one of the most important paintings to come into its collection—"The Starry Night," by Vincent van Gogh.

Although the museum probably has done more than any other museum in this country to make the work of van Gogh known to Americans, it has not owned a canvas by the artist until the present one was acquired through the Lillie P. Bliss bequest.

The museum's large exhibition of van Gogh's work held from Nov. 5, 1935, to Jan. 5, 1936, was one of the few art exhibitions ever held in this city that attracted long lines of standees awaiting admittance.

The newly acquired work was not in that exhibition at the outset. It was then in the collection of Miss G. P. van Stolk of Rotterdam, and although lent to the show, did not arrive here in time. When the exhibition returned to New York after its tour for a final two-week period, the canvas was added.

Alfred Barr Jr., director of the Museum of Modern Art, called it "one of the most important paintings ever acquired by the museum." It was painted in San Rémy, France, in 1889. ▪

MoMA

146   THE NEW YORK TIMES BOOK OF NEW YORK

A Tour With Mr. Wright

By **ALINE B. SAARINEN** | September 22, 1957

Guggenheim To Restore Its Most Valuable Asset: Itself

By **CAROL VOGEL** | June 10, 2004

AFTER 45 YEARS THE SOLOMON R. Guggenheim Museum, the soaring spiral that has become one of Manhattan's greatest tourist attractions, will undergo a major facelift. And while it has good bones, like many Frank Lloyd Wright buildings the Upper East Side landmark is plagued with cracks, leaks and corroding surfaces.

Calling it "the most important piece of art in the collection," Peter B. Lewis, a Cleveland-based philanthropist who has been chairman of the museum's board and a trustee since 1993, has pledged to match trustee gifts three to one for the project.

The building on Fifth Avenue at 89th Street will remain open during the restoration, which is expected to take two years. In addition to removing nine coats of paint, right down to the building's structure, to fix its cracking surface, the project also includes repairing the sidewalk, with its metallic rings set into concrete. ▪

NEW YORK'S MOST EXTRAORDINARY AND controversial building is beginning to reveal itself above the contractor's protective wood fences. Mothers dragging children and baby carriages pause to gaze at the concrete snail slowly growing against a background of conventional, boxlike apartment houses. Young students, with crew cuts, blue shirts and khaki pants, aim the Cyclops-eye of a camera upward toward the astonishing structure. Then they turn eagerly, hoping to get a glimpse of Frank Lloyd Wright, the world's best-known living architect, who, in this slowly rising Solomon R. Guggenheim Museum, is making his first imprint on the New York cityscape.

There, Mr. Wright conducted this reporter on a tour of the museum-in-process, talking all the while of what it all meant, what architecture is or should be, of the arts, of all manner of things. He walks with a springy step that belies his 88 years, his figure tall and spare. His vertically lined, handsome face seemed weathered rather than wrinkled.

"This is the only organic building in New York," he announced, "the only 20th-century architecture; the only permanent building. This is all one thing, each part is the consequence of the other, the way things are in nature."

But what of the curving walls? Didn't some artists object to these? Yes, they did but they didn't realize that the circumference is so great that one will not be aware of the curve and that there are many vertical sections. Also there is a "grand gallery"—rectilinear and 25 feet high—off the entrance floor for the permanently exhibited older paintings. And what of the fact that the walls slant outward at a slight angle? That angle, Mr. Wright explains, will not be perceptible. Then why have it? Because—patiently explaining—the painter has his canvas at just such an angle when he paints and because, so placed, the pictures will be in a natural perpendicular relation to the spectator's line of vision. ▪

Hailing a Past and a Future

By **ROBERTA SMITH** | December 14, 2001

WITH THE UNVEILING OF ITS LONG-AWAITED new building on West 53rd Street, the American Folk Art Museum has assumed a new identity. Known until this year as the Museum of American Folk Art, it has rearranged its name to reflect its growing interest in 20th-century folk art from abroad.

The new eight-story structure, designed by Tod Williams Billie Tsien Architects, gives the museum a presence in the city's cultural scene that had long eluded it. Now its reconfigured name will evoke not only an exemplary collecting and curatorial record, but also a destination of distinction.

The fresh start is inaugurated with two displays of recent acquisitions that symbolize a redefinition for the institution as surely as the new building does, while also summing up the evolution of folk art itself. Three of the museum's four gallery floors are devoted to a dense installation of Ralph Esmerian's gift of traditional American folk art. It could be said to represent where the museum is from.

The remaining floor houses the work of the great 20th-century outsider artist Henry Darger, including 7 of his bound manuscripts and 27 large two-sided watercolors. It represents where the museum is going.

Ralph Esmerian's primary focus is traditional folk art: objects usually made from the late 17th to early 20th centuries in the eastern half of the country by European immigrants (or their descendants). They built on European folk models: painted chairs, tables and chests, for example, or the lavishly decorated religious texts and birth and wedding certificates, called frakturs, that are another of the Esmerian gift's strong suits.

A further achievement of the new American Folk Art Museum is its role in setting a record. Its opening on Tuesday followed by exactly 25 days that of the Neue Galerie New York, a museum for German and Austrian art on Fifth Avenue, giving the city two outstanding new museums in less than a month, and the Asia Society's expansion makes almost three. Top that. ∎

Talent Call: Hot New Artists Wanted

By **CAROL VOGEL** | February 3, 2005

"This is why artists are living here," Alanna Heiss exclaimed as a panoramic view of the Manhattan skyline appeared through the taxi window. Ms. Heiss, director of the P.S. 1 Contemporary Art Center in Queens, and Klaus Biesenbach, a curator at P.S. 1 and its big-sister affiliate, the Museum of Modern Art, were heading over the Brooklyn Bridge into Manhattan. It had been a long afternoon in Brooklyn visiting artists' studios. Now Ms. Heiss and Mr. Biesenbach were on their way to Columbia University to call on a 27-year-old art student whose work Mr. Biesenbach had spotted at a fair in Miami.

This is more or less how they have spent the last 10 months—stopping by studios, inviting artists to P.S. 1 and poring over thousands of submissions from painters, sculpto rs and conceptual artists as well as photographers and film and video artists. From 2,400 submissions, 175 will be chosen for a giant survey show of the city's contemporary art scene.

For Brooklyn's Dowager, Hard Sell and Hip-Hop

By **CELESTINE BOHLEN** | January 2, 2001

"GOLD INSIDE," SHOUTS A SIGN OUTSIDE THE Brooklyn Museum of Art. A close reading of the small type reveals that what lies inside are not gold chains or nuggets, but "Gold of the Nomads," the remains of the Scythian civilization from the first millennium B.C.

It's not your usual museum advertisement, but the Brooklyn Museum is trying hard not to be a usual museum. It has been just a year since "Sensation," an exhibition of works by cutting-edge British artists that lived up to its name by kicking up a ruckus that reached City Hall and boomeranged to the museum and its director, Arnold L. Lehman.

When Mr. Lehman, a Brooklyn native, arrived three years ago after 22 years as a museum director in Miami and Baltimore, the great Beaux-Arts museum was the borough's dowager empress: rich and awe-inspiring but with a reputation for sleeping between shows.

Then Mr. Lehman led the museum into the "Sensation" maelstrom. It began before the show even opened, with an aggressive promotional campaign that warned of artworks so upsetting they could cause vomiting. Outraged by an image of the Virgin Mary festooned in elephant dung, Mayor Rudolph W. Giuliani threatened to cut the museum's subsidy.

The Brooklyn museum's board took the city to court and won. But the victory turned out to be Pyrrhic for Mr. Lehman. He was shown to have allowed Charles Saatchi, the owner of the artworks in the show, not only to be the exhibition's anonymous sponsor but in some matters virtually its curator too. This arrangement seemed to cross a vaguely drawn line between sponsorship and self-promotion.

Mr. Lehman makes no apologies for his populist approach, saying that if the choice arose, he would have no trouble favoring a broader audience over deeper scholarly research, while bearing in mind that the mission of the museum is always about art.

"My only direction to our curators was that they had to clearly define which audiences were being served," he said. "The only audience that I would not support was us, the internal audience." ■

For the curators, their studio forays are an exercise in discovery—a chance to break away from the routine of organizing exhibitions by proven names. For the artists, they are a nail-biting exercise, not unlike a callback audition for an Off Broadway production.

Seth Price's studio in Williamsburg was a stop on the curators' tour through Brooklyn. Among his creations are black CD's with digital images of a recent beheading in Iraq that he downloaded off the Internet. "I purposely inverted the image—that was the art gesture," Mr. Price said.

But the curators had other works in mind. On one wall was a series of wall reliefs that each show one breast. Fashioned from vacuum-formed plastic like that used in commercial packaging, each had a different color or pattern: one clear, another gold, still another a blue pattern whose surface resembled flocked Victorian wallpaper. "The breast is a familiar image, dating back to Classical statuary," Mr. Price explained. "It has been so emptied out by art history, it's a depleted form."

"We should give him a wall to do his pieces and videos," Ms. Heiss said under her breath.

And, later, P.S. 1 officials confirmed that he had made the cut. ■

Sassy Sculpture Casts Whimsical Cityscape in Bronze

By **IAN FISHER** | May 11, 1996

"DID YOU CATCH THE ONE ON THE END— the rat?" Marie Ricca, a 40-year-old receptionist, asked as she whipped past the sculpture at lunchtime.

The rat in question was balanced perhaps 12 feet off the sidewalk, dressed cutely as a police officer with a billy club in a busy subway scene of 40 bronze figures. Like the other pint-size statues, the rat looked like a harmless cartoon character, except he was chasing another figure, a hapless white-collar worker, off the edge of a steel construction beam.

Small children bugged their eyes and giggled at "Life Underground," a fanciful work of public art expanded this week at Doris C. Freedman Plaza, at Fifth Avenue and 60th Street. But this artwork, which will eventually be installed in the subway station at 14th Street and Eighth Avenue, is more devious than it at first looks: An alligator in a suit pokes from a sewer to devour a man with a moneybag for a head. A second moneybag-head looks on without helping. A frowning telephone sucks up another man. And two knee-high figures work calmly to saw the whole thing down.

"I think it's a lot of fun and also whimsical," said Salli Lovelarkin, an art gallery director from Cincinnati who was one of many who gawked at and pondered the work yesterday. "But he gets a little dark, too. He's got some people being squashed over there."

"He" is the artist, Tom Otterness, who, inspired by 19th-century political cartoons that skewered corruption in New York, said he wanted to show, among other things, the struggle between rich and poor—and do it with a sense of humor. He said the sculpture reflects something any subway rider can appreciate: "The impossibility of understanding life in New York is the subject." ∎

Bovine Crimes Strike an Unlikely Cow Town

By **ELISSA GOOTMAN** | August 24, 2000

IT HAS BEEN ALMOST THREE MONTHS SINCE 500 life-size fiberglass cows arrived on city streets. Some people welcome the herd, with their imaginative designs by local artists. Others consider the whole cow parade just a hokey import from Chicago.

Now there has been some old-fashioned rustling.

"Cow Hands," one of the fiberglass creatures, was unfastened from its concrete base at West Houston Street and La Guardia Place. The police arrived as "Cow Hands" was about to be loaded into a blue Jeep Cherokee.

The officers found Patrick Kraft, 24, of East Windsor, N.J., and Michael Macisco, 23, of Stratford, Conn., clearing their Jeep, apparently to make room for the cow. Detective Andrew McDermott said the two men soon confessed to plotting a prank, claiming that they were probably going to station "Cow Hands" in front of a friend's Manhattan home.

Before long, "Cow Hands" was standing silently in the Sixth Precinct station house, on West 10th Street, where she was to be kept for 48 hours as evidence. Snapping a Polaroid picture for the station house scrapbook, Officer Jon Goldin shook his head, saying that when he first saw the cow at the station house, he figured that it was a prop in a publicity stunt.

"Well, that's life in a big city," he said. ∎

PUBLIC ART

A Billowy Gift to the City

By **MICHAEL KIMMELMAN** | February 13, 2005

IT IS A LONG, BILLOWY SAFFRON RIBBON meandering through Central Park—not a neat bow, but something that's very much a gift package to New York City: "The Gates," by Christo and his wife, Jeanne-Claude.

In the winter light, the bright fabric seemed to warm the fields, flickering like a flame against the barren trees.

"The Gates" is a work of pure joy, a vast populist spectacle of good will and simple eloquence, the first great public art event of the 21st century. It remains on view for just 16 days. Time is fleeting.

An army of paid helpers gradually released the panels of colored fabric from atop the 16-foot-tall gates, all 7,500 of them. The shifting light couldn't have been better to show off the effects of the cloth. Sometimes the fabric looked deep orange; at other times it was shiny, like gold leaf, or silvery or almost tan. In the breeze, the skirted gates also appeared to shimmy like dancers in a conga line, the cloth buckling and swaying.

Fans mobbed their car. Like all projects by this duo, "The Gates" is as much a public happening as it is a vast environmental sculpture and a feat of engineering. It has required more than 1 million square feet of vinyl and 5,300 tons of steel, arrayed along 23 miles of footpaths throughout the park at a cost (borne exclusively by the artists) of $20 million.

From outside the park, the gates looked like endless rows of inert orange dominoes overwhelming Frederick Law Olmsted's and Calvert Vaux's masterpiece. But as the artists have insisted, the gates aren't made to be seen from above or from outside. The gates need to be experienced on the ground, at eye level, where, as you move through the park, they crisscross and double up, rising over hills, blocking your view of everything except sky, then passing underfoot, through an underpass, or suddenly appearing through a copse of trees, their fabric fluttering in the corner of your eye. They have transformed the paths into boulevards decked out as if with flags for a holiday. Everyone is suddenly a dignitary on parade. ■

BELOW: *Experiencing "The Gates" at eye level: photographing them, walking beneath them.*

The Dinosaurs Are Moving

By **W. H. BALLOU** | December 28, 1924

THAT LONG-EXTINCT SHARK THAT CAME UP from the chalk beds of South Carolina is about to emerge from storage and unfold his 100 feet of length and tell the world how an army of Jonahs would make just one filling meal. He will be followed by a procession of gigantic extinct creatures that have long been hidden in boxes at the American Museum of Natural History, facing Central Park at West 77th Street.

The new southeast wing and Hall of Ocean Life will be followed by the School Service Building, for which the city has appropriated $733,800. It will be devoted to the relations of the museum to the schools of the city. The first floor will constitute the main exhibition hall. The building will also provide classrooms for visiting classes of children, laboratories and offices of the educational staff and nature study collections. Many offices of curators and assistants will be on the fifth floor and its mezzanine.

Two skeletons, a perfect matched pair of the largest carnivorous dinosaur extant,

Tyrannosaurus rex, will stand in the reptile exhibit, with heads towering 20 feet above the floor. From tip of snout to end of tail they are 47 feet long.

Nearby will be Allosaurus, another mighty carnivore, the reptile balanced on heavy hind limbs and long, heavy tail. The hind legs are nine feet in length. His chief prey, as shown by the fossil remains found with his, was the equally huge herbivorous dinosaur Brontosaurus. "We may imagine," states the label, "Allosaurus lying in wait, watching its prey until near approach stimulates him into semi-instinctive activity. Then a sudden swift rush, a fierce snap of the huge jaws and a savage attack with teeth and claws until the victim is torn in pieces and swallowed."

Not less in size and power was the American gigantic dinosaur Deinodon, carnivorous and terrible in action. His limbs show climbing powers, and he would be credited with ability to scale skyscrapers in quest of prey—if alive today and running loose on Broadway. ■

To Visit a Museum, Perchance to Dream

By **DAVID K. RANDALL** | March 27, 2007

SEEING YOUR FIRST TIGER CAN BE SUR-prising, worrying, fascinating and ultimately tiring. Especially if you are a toddler on your first visit to the animal dioramas at the American Museum of Natural History.

Young museum visitors typically start with its tigers and gorillas, and then head to the Milstein Hall of Ocean Life, a

cavernous two-tiered room capped by a 94-foot-long model of a blue whale hanging from the ceiling.

Unlike much of the museum, the Milstein Hall is dark and serene, meant to simulate being underwater. It also appears to be a prime spot for a family nap.

On a recent weekday afternoon, a collection of parents and their strollers were parked in front of a screen underneath the blue whale's head that plays a film of underwa-ter scenes and ocean sunsets. The strollers were full of sleeping children, the benches filled with adults in the head-to-the-sternum pose of subway sleepers. Whale songs played

Outer Space vs. Parking Space

By **GLENN COLLINS** | January 25, 2000

THE AMERICAN MUSEUM OF NATURAL History's sleek new $210 million planetarium is almost finished, and the museum is bracing for an onslaught. The first of as many as a million extra visitors over the next year are about to descend on the museum and its new Rose Center for Earth and Space.

Even if the planetarium had not been a New York City icon for 65 years, this debut would be no ordinary opening. Expressing everything from jubilation to intense concern, city officials and neighborhood naysayers have at last found themselves in agreement about something: the impact of the new building will be off the charts. Even other museums say so. "We think the Rose Center is a perfect addition to the neighborhood," said Harold Holzer, a spokesman for the Metropolitan Museum of Art.

That opinion is not shared by all. The courts rebuffed community law suits trying to block the new building's construction. But the museum still faces opposition from neighbors, some of whom are opposed to the look of the new planetarium.

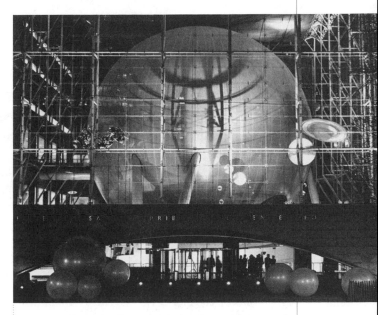

ABOVE: *The Hayden Planetarium, in the sphere at the American Museum of Natural History, is the largest virtual reality simulator in the world.*

over the speakers, and the blue panels on the ceiling moved like a passing wave.

Politeness prevented this reporter from waking anyone to ask what made the spot relaxing, and several people who appeared to have only recently awakened were not in the mood to be interviewed. "It's dark, it's comfortable, there's the ocean sounds," said one man, who declined to give his name. As he spoke, he wiped his eyes. A security guard in the room, who did not give his name, saying he was not allowed to speak to reporters, called the room "the most peaceful place" he had ever worked. ▪

"They could have put the new Zeiss projector in the original landmarked Hayden Planetarium and preserved it," said Samuel H. Leff, president of the Community Alliance for Responsible Museum Development, one of two groups that sued the museum and lost. "They wanted to put something in there that was very flashy, so they'd have something like the Pyramide at the Louvre and get a lot of attention," he said, referring to I. M. Pei's acclaimed addition to the Louvre.

Mr. Leff claimed that many in the neighborhood oppose what he called "the traffic disaster" caused by automobile and bus visitors "and the additional congestion and pollution in an already densely populated neighborhood." Although dozens of school buses could park in the old street-surface lot on the planetarium grounds, there is room for only 10 of them in the Rose Center's new 370-space garage. ▪

Recalling the Heyday of the Great White Way

By **ALLEN CHURCHILL** | January 24, 1982

TALK OF THE DEMOLITION OF TWO OR MORE established Broadway theaters to make way for a glossy supra-hotel brings particular pangs to the nostalgia-conscious. As an author who has researched and written two books about what used to be called the Great White Way, I can easily shut my eyes and visualize today's theater district back in 1900, when no theaters at all stood above 42nd Street.

The area was then no more than a neighborhood, largely filled by cheap boarding houses for aspiring actors and vaudeville acts between bookings—"at liberty," it was called. One who passed hot summers on these boarding house stoops was Will Rogers, before he was tapped for glory in the "Ziegfeld Follies."

In 1900, New York's legitimate theaters ran up Broadway like a string of pearls from 34th to 42nd Street, capped on the right by the hallowed Empire and on the left by the now-forgotten Casino. But there was more. A sharp left on 42nd Street (this corner was

called "the crossroads of the world") brought playgoers to a street of theaters that included the New Amsterdam, Lyric, Apollo and Republic, in the last of which "Abie's Irish Rose" ran in the 1920's.

Electric bulbs were called Mazdas in those days, and soon Times Square as far north as 50th Street was alight with an estimated million Mazdas. Inevitably, it was christened Mazda Lane, or Alley, and finally the Great White Way. The nation allegedly hummed a song I have never heard rendered—"There's a Broken Heart for Every Light on Broadway." But Diamond Jim Brady may have said it best. Stepping from a midnight supper into this blazing brilliance, he exclaimed, "Street of the midnight sun!"

Until 1916, the theater's galaxy stopped at 45th Street, but in that year another Brady—William A.—built his Playhouse on 48th. It opened with "Bought and Paid For," by George Broadhurst, about a millionaire in love with a telephone hello-girl. Bold Mr. Brady was concerned about his production, but really worried about whether people would travel so far north for a play. Of course they did. ∎

ABOVE: *A few playbills from the thousands of shows that have played on Broadway.*

"South Pacific"

By **BROOKS ATKINSON** | April 17, 1949

IF NEW YORK SEEMS PLEASANTLY RELAXED and languid again, it is doubtless because "South Pacific" has opened successfully and has settled down to the quiet luxury of a long run. There is nothing more for any New Yorker to worry about now. To judge by the gossip when "South Pacific" was on the road, Richard Rodgers and Oscar Hammerstein II and Joshua Logan were not the only people uneasy about the reception their new musical drama would have on Broadway.

On the day of the opening, business practically stopped all over town, as on the day before Christmas. Everyone was obsessed with one idea. The teller at the bank murmured wistfully over the top of a pile of bills, "I hope 'South Pacific' is as good as they say it's going to be."

Although the expectations had been fabulous, "South Pacific" mercifully fulfilled them. Mr. Rodgers and Mr. Hammerstein fulfilled them. Like "Oklahoma" and "Carousel," "South Pacific" has a genuine theme and develops it with skill and continuity. Rogers and Hammerstein respect their craft and the theater and they have composed another top-shelf drama of music. Having survived the drama of the opening of "South Pacific," New York can now go back to work with no further anxiety. ■

A Season's Indelible Moments

By **ROBERT SIMONSON** | June 1, 2008

THE DEFINING MOMENT OF LINCOLN CENTER Theater's lavishly praised revival of "Rodgers & Hammerstein's South Pacific" arguably comes before the show has actually begun, when not a single actor is onstage. This nonprofit theater has made much of its decision to employ a full complement of orchestra musicians at a time when pits are being pared down to the core. At the beginning of the overture, just as the violins introduce the lushly melodic lines of "Bali Ha'i," the stage floor above the musicians' heads begins to recede, drawing back to reveal every one of the pit's 30 members.

At least one person on the Lincoln Center Theater staff jokingly calls this gasp-producing moment in the director Bartlett Sher's production the "802 reveal," referring to the musicians' union local, to which all the players belong. Mr. Sher knew he had found a showstopper with this "now you don't see them, now you do" sleight of hand. If it's possible for theater audiences to swoon in these cynical times, they do so here. ■

BELOW: *The cast of "South Pacific" on the stage at the Vivian Beaumont Theater in 2008.*

15 Record Years of "A Chorus Line"

By JOHN P. MACKENZIE | March 4, 1990

ON THE DAY THEY ANNOUNCED THAT "A Chorus Line" would finally close, you could walk over to the Shubert Theater and ask whether any good seats were available for tomorrow night. The answer would be "You never can tell . . . Sixth row center all right?" Those seats would be fine.

The performers, too, carried on as though nothing were amiss. On stage at least, there was no unprofessional melancholy. It was basically the same production it had been for all 15 record years. And for one who luckily had forgotten which of the 19 gypsies won the eight places in the chorus line, the show evoked the same suspense, the same sense of caring: what

would happen to each of those desperate, talented dancers?

Isn't that what made this musical great? The audience's thrill was the thrill familiar to other notable musicals. What put "A Chorus Line" in that class, indeed at the head of it, was the insidious way it made audiences care. We took instruction from those who so committed their talent and emotions. Can I afford to put my whole self on the line? Don't I need some reserve as a buffer against betrayal or failure?

The character Diana Morales, of course, has the only right answer: Tell it straight. Give it your all; then don't forget, don't regret.

Just thinking about that show will always have me on the edge of my seat. ∎

Rock Opera à la "Bohème" and "Hair"

By BEN BRANTLEY | February 14, 1996

THE SUBJECT OF THE WORK IS DEATH AT AN early age. And in one of the dark dramatic coincidences theater occasionally springs on us, its 35-year-old author died only weeks before its opening. Yet no one who attends Jonathan Larson's "Rent," the exhilarating, landmark rock opera at the New York Theater Workshop, is likely to mistake it for a wake.

Indeed, this vigorous tale of a marginal band of artists in Manhattan's East Village, a contemporary answer to "La Bohème," rushes forward on an electric current of emotion that is anything but morbid. Sparked by a young, intensely vibrant cast directed by Michael Greif and sustained by a glittering, inventive score, the work finds a transfixing brightness in characters living in the shadow of AIDS.

"Rent" inevitably invites reflections on the incalculable loss of its composer, who died of an aortic aneurysm, but it also shimmers

with hope for the future of the American musical. While Mr. Larson plays wittily with references to Puccini's masterpiece, the excitement around "Rent" more directly recalls the impact made by a dark-horse musical Off Broadway in 1967: "Hair." Like that meandering, genial portrait of draft-dodging hippies, this production gives a pulsing, unexpectedly catchy voice to a generation's confusion, anger and anarchic, pleasure-seeking vitality.

The denizens of Mr. Larson's bohemian landscape are directly descended from their Puccini prototypes but given a hip, topical spin. Obviously, poverty is less picturesque in Mr. Larson's world than in Puccini's. This show's equivalent of the Latin Quarter café scene, with its jolly parade of children and vendors, is an angry Christmas Eve vignette set among bag people on St. Mark's Place. And this Mimi has cold hands because she needs a fix. ∎

The Subway Hums Bernstein

By **JIM DWYER** | February 21, 2009

YES, OF COURSE, SUZETTE MCLAURIN SAYS, she knows the musical "West Side Story," and yes, she has been a conductor on the No. 2 train for quite a while—nearly eight years.

So along the way, has she heard the electronic whine from the trains that sounds just like the beginning of "Somewhere," a ballad from the show?

This is not the kind of question Ms. McLaurin ordinarily fields during the 30 seconds or so that her train stops in the Times Square station. She leans slightly through the window.

"When the train is moving?" she asks.

Just when the train is starting, as if the cars were screeching, "There's a place."

"I never noticed it," Ms. McLaurin says.

Once heard, it is unmistakable: an echo of "Somewhere" that rises from the ceaseless tide of shrieks and moans in the subways.

The sound is a fluke. Newer trains, most of them are on the 2, 4 and 5 lines, run on alternating current, but the third rail delivers direct current; inverters chop it into frequencies that can be used by the alternating current motors, said Jeff Hakner, a professor of electrical engineering at Cooper Union. The frequencies excite the steel, he said, which—in the case of the R142 subway cars—responds by singing "Somewhere." Inverters on other trains run at different frequencies and thus are not gifted with such a recognizable song.

"Everyone sort of noticed it, and then this corroboration process started where people said to each other, 'Did you hear it?' " said Jamie Bernstein, a writer and broadcaster whose father, Leonard Bernstein, composed "West Side Story." The music was composed before the words, which were written by Stephen Sondheim, Ms. Bernstein said. "For a while, there was a dummy lyric to the tune," she said, singing it: "There goes whatshisname."

As her No. 2 train was leaving Times Square a few days ago, Ms. McLaurin scanned the platform. The train sang out, a breeze lifting a curtain. Her face lit up. ▪

"West Side Story"

By **BROOKS ATKINSON** | September 27, 1957

ALTHOUGH THE MATERIAL IS HORRIFYING, the workmanship is admirable.

Gang warfare is the material of "West Side Story," which opened at the Winter Garden last evening, and very little of the hideousness has been left out. But the author, composer and ballet designer are creative artists. Pooling imagination and virtuosity, they have written a profoundly moving show that is as ugly as the city jungles and also as pathetic, tender and forgiving.

The story is a powerful one, partly, no doubt, because Arthur Laurents has deliberately given it the shape of "Romeo and Juliet." In the design of "West Side Story" he has powerful allies. Leonard Bernstein has composed another one of his nervous, flaring scores that capture the shrill beat of life in the streets. And Jerome Robbins, who has directed the production, is also its choreographer.

Since the characters are kids of the streets, their speech is curt and jeering. Mr. Laurents has provided the raw material of a tragedy that occurs because none of the young people involved understands what is happening to them. And his contribution is the essential one.

As Tony, Larry Kert is perfectly cast, plain in speech and manner; and as Maria, Carol Lawrence, maidenly soft and glowing, is perfectly cast also. Their balcony scene on the fire escape of a dreary tenement is tender and affecting. From that moment on, "West Side Story" is an incandescent piece of work. ▪

Eugene O'Neill Returns After Twelve Years

By **S. J. WOOLF** | September 15, 1946

AFTER A LAPSE OF TWELVE YEARS A NEW play by Eugene O'Neill will soon be seen on Broadway. And after an even longer absence the man whom many Americans consider the most distinguished dramatist this country ever produced has come back to New York from California as a permanent resident. Even the locale of the new play suggests that the production is in every sense a home-coming. The setting of "The Iceman Cometh" is New York—specifically, the lower West Side of 1912—the play has been the subject of intense curiosity along Broadway for several seasons.

Now that the author has settled into a Manhattan penthouse and has been regularly attending rehearsals, word of its theme and contents has got around quite generally. It ignores the coming not only of automatic refrigeration but of the atomic age as well, but its subject is as much a matter of pity and terror in 1946 as in 1912. His iceman, O'Neill explains, is death, and his use of the archaic verb "cometh" is a deliberate reference to biblical language and universality.

Even among his prized possessions O'Neill seems a curiously detached person. He is tall and thin with a repressed manner that is almost shy. Greenwich Village, where his plays first attracted attention, has left no apparent impress on him. He dresses immaculately, his hair is neatly brushed, and when he smokes, as he does almost continuously, he is careful to have an ashtray by his side.

Whatever reception "The Iceman Cometh" may receive, it is undoubtedly the work of a man who takes both the theatre and life seriously. The setting may be a bar, but it will not be the most unlikely place in which O'Neill has staged a tragic drama. In the past he has found drama of stature in the jungle, the New England village, the Midwestern farm and the forecastle. And the emotions of his characters invariable transcended the specific time and place. ▪

Honoring Eugene O'Neill

By **JOHN CORRY** | November 28, 1973

THEY HUNG A PLAQUE FOR EUGENE O'Neill on Broadway yesterday, and they hung it exactly one block from where they were supposed to do it. They did it in rain and drizzle, and while they did, people stopped and stared.

"And who the hell is Eugene O'Neill?" one man finally said.

"There, that's him over there," another man answered. He was pointing at Brooks Atkinson.

Mr. Atkinson, The Times's drama critic, retired in 1958. O'Neill, the great playwright, died 20 years ago yesterday. The plaque, however, was supposed to mark where he was born, which was the old Barrett House on 43rd Street. Somehow it got hung in front of a bank on 44th Street, although this may not have mattered much at all.

O'Neill was a chaotic man, with a great sense of the impermanence of things. "Born in a hotel room, and God damn it, died in a hotel room," he said on his death bed in Boston. Still, before him, there was no true American theater, but when he died there was. He has practically made it himself.

So, yesterday in what may have been the least formal ceremony in New York's history, some people came to honor O'Neill.

The people who were passing by, meanwhile, were plainly baffled.

"What's going on?" one of them said.

"I think they're opening a new bank," someone answered him. ▪

"A Streetcar Named Desire"

By **BROOKS ATKINSON** | December 4, 1947

TENNESSEE WILLIAMS HAS BROUGHT US A superb drama, "A Streetcar Named Desire," which was acted at the Ethel Barrymore last evening. And Jessica Tandy gives a superb performance as rueful heroine whose misery Mr. Williams is tenderly recording. This must be one of the most perfect marriages of acting and playwriting. For the acting and playwriting are perfectly blended in a limpid performance, and it is impossible to tell where Miss Tandy begins to give form and warmth to the mood Mr. Williams has created.

Like "The Glass Menagerie," the new play is a quietly woven study of intangibles. But to this observer it shows deeper insight and represents a great step forward toward clarity. And it reveals Mr. Williams as a genuinely poetic playwright whose knowledge of people is honest and thorough and whose sympathy is profoundly human.

Miss Tandy is a trim, agile actress with a lovely voice and quick intelligence. Her performance is almost incredibly true. The rest of the acting, is also very high quality indeed. Marlon Brando, as the quick-tempered scornful, violent mechanic; Karl Malden as a stupid but wondering suitor; Kim Hunter as the patient though troubled sister—all act not only with color and style but with insight.

By the usual Broadway standards, "A Streetcar Named Desire" is too long; not all those words are essential. But Mr. Williams is entitled to his own independence. For he has not forgotten that human beings are the basic subject of art. Out of poetic imagination and ordinary compassion he has spun a poignant and luminous story. ∎

Those Foul Words

By **CAMPBELL ROBERTSON** | February 23, 2008

WAS BIG DADDY ALWAYS SUCH A POTTY mouth?

While the current production of Tennessee Williams's "Cat on a Hot Tin Roof" has garnered attention for its all-black cast, it is the saltiness of Big Daddy, played with unrestrained ribaldry by James Earl Jones, and particularly his liberal use of a certain four-letter word, that has raised the eyebrows of some theatergoers.

Williams wrote "Cat on a Hot Tin Roof" in 1954, but he made changes for the 1955 Broadway production in accordance with the wishes of the director, Elia Kazan.

The language in the first three lives of "Cat" is strong, but only as strong as would be allowed in the 1950's. Hence the presence of cute but weird modifiers like "rutting" and "ducking." Williams had reservations about the Broadway "Cat," saying, in a 1973 interview, "I was never happy about it."

In 1973 Williams revisited the play for a production at Stage West, a regional theater in Springfield, Mass. He produced a revision that combined elements of the 1955 Broadway version and his original version, restoring his preferred, ambiguous conclusion. He also, at this point, added the swearing.

Maybe the shock comes from watching the actor known from "On Golden Pond" and "Star Wars" get so down and dirty. When the play was written, you couldn't utter certain words onstage, Mr. Jones said, adding, "I love saying"—well, you know—"onstage." ∎

Arthur Miller, Moral Voice Of American Stage, Dies at 89

By **MARILYN BERGER** | February 11, 2005

ARTHUR MILLER, ONE OF THE GREAT American playwrights, whose work exposed the flaws in the fabric of the American dream, died Thursday night at his home in Roxbury, Conn. He was 89.

"Death of a Salesman," which opened on Broadway in 1949, established Mr. Miller as a giant of the American theater when he was only 33. It won the triple crown of theatrical artistry that year: the Pulitzer Prize, the New York Drama Critics' Circle Award and the Tony.

But the play's enormous success also overshadowed Mr. Miller's long career: "The Crucible," a 1953 play about the Salem witch trials inspired by his virulent hatred of McCarthyism, and "A View From the Bridge," a 1955 drama of obsession and betrayal, ultimately took their place as popular classics of the international stage, but Mr. Miller's later plays never equaled his early successes. Although he wrote a total of 17 plays, "The Price," produced on Broadway during the 1967-68 season, was his last solid critical and commercial hit.

His reputation rests on a handful of his best-known plays, the dramas of guilt and betrayal and redemption that continue to be revived frequently at theaters all over the world. These dramas of social conscience were drawn from life and informed by the Great Depression, the event that he believed had a more profound impact on the nation than any other in American history, except, possibly, the Civil War. "In play after play," the drama critic Mel Gussow wrote in The New York Times, "he holds man responsible for his and for his neighbor's actions."

The Broadway producer Robert Whitehead, who worked frequently with Mr. Miller, said in reminiscing about their work together that he found a "rabbinical righteousness" in the playwright. "In his work, there is almost a conscious need to be a light unto the world," he said, adding, "He spent his life seeking answers to what he saw around him as a world of injustice."

Broadway theaters dimmed their marquee lights last night at curtain time in his memory. ∎

It's Free Theater In The Park, But New Yorkers Still Pay a Price

By **MANNY FERNANDEZ** | August 20, 2006

FRIDAY NIGHT'S PERFORMANCE OF BERTOLT Brecht's "Mother Courage and Her Children" began about 8 p.m. at the Delacorte Theater in Central Park. David Suker showed up about 8:45 p.m. He was not late. He was early.

Mr. Suker, 38, was the first person in line for tickets to the next night's performance. He had a long wait ahead of him—some 16 hours before the theater would hand out the free tickets—but he had his blue air mattress and its battery-powered pump, a bottle of seltzer, a sleeping bag, a lantern and his Army training.

Why did he wait so long? The political nature of the play—a 17th-century drama

Visions of Heaven—and of Hell; "Angels in America"

By **DAVID RICHARDS** | May 16, 1993

NOT UNTIL THE VERY END OF "MILLENNIUM Approaches," Part 1 of Tony Kushner's "Angels in America," do we see an actual angel—crashing through a bedroom ceiling, as it happens, and sending chunks of plaster raining down on a young man dying of AIDS.

Her majestic wings are spread wide and high. The billows of her blindingly white gown could have been styled by Bernini. From the impassive expression on her face, however, there's no knowing if she's come on a mission of vengeance or mercy, retribution or deliverance.

For that, we will have to wait until the fall, when "Millennium Approaches" will be joined at the Walter Kerr Theater by "Perestroika," Part 2 of the vision. If nothing

else, Mr. Kushner has written the greatest cliff-hanger in Broadway history.

The winner of this year's Pulitzer Prize for drama, "Angels" has ridden into New York on a tidal wave of publicity that began building 16 months ago when the play was staged by the Royal National Theater in London. No work of art is ever well served by ballyhoo. In this instance, by encouraging monumental expectations, the hype may be pointing us in exactly the wrong direction. If you want the most out of Mr. Kushner's unfettered dramaturgy, it helps to think smaller, not bigger. The characters have great feverish declarations to make, but it is their confessional side that usually ends up being the most moving.

When that Angel finally does appear in a shaft of opalescent plaster dust, she has this to announce: "Greetings, prophet; the great work begins: the messenger has arrived." She is addressing a character who is spent and confused, just as she is addressing a checkmated nation. But I had the odd impression that she was talking to Mr. Kushner himself, whose great work also lies ahead.

Having described the illness in "Millennium Approaches," does he now have it in him to envision the cure? And if there is none, will the compassion of his art provide the solace we all crave? ■

starring Meryl Streep as a resourceful mother who profits from a war that ultimately claims her children—appealed to him. But really, he said, he did it for a woman. They had a date planned for last night, and he figured what better way to impress her than with two tickets to one of the most popular shows in the city.

The Shakespeare in the Park play, presented by the Public Theater, has created a kind of theatergoers' endurance test, with people like Mr. Suker camping out overnight, hoping to get a ticket for one of the theater's 1,872 seats.

The lines have become the Delacorte's unofficial second stage, as lively, improvised and quietly dramatic as the play itself. And time is indeed money in New York City: people were selling tickets to last night's show on craigslist.com for $45 each and up to $150 for a pair. One ticket holder wrote, "$100 for my time on line or best reasonable offer." ■

LEFT: *Aurther Miller.* BELOW: *A scene from "Romeo and Juliet" performed in the Public Theater's 2007 Shakespeare in the Park season.*

"Fantasticks" Will Trip The Lights No More

By **JAMES BARRON** | January 14, 2002

THERE WERE NAYSAYERS WHO SAID THAT after creaking along for nearly 42 years, it had become "The Anachronisticks." There were those who found it so uplifting they called it "The Optimisticks."

And then there were all the actors who said they had once been in the cast of "The Fantasticks," at the tiny Sullivan Street Playhouse in Greenwich Village. Some probably would call them "The Egotisticks."

"The Fantasticks," the Methuselah of musicals, closed last night after its 17,162nd performance. Now theatergoers can only try to remember. And to stop spelling words that end in "istic" with a K.

The chief producer, Lore Noto, once dreamed of catching up to "The Mousetrap," the Agatha Christie murder mystery that has been playing in London since 1952. Mr. Noto had to settle for claiming that "The Fantasticks" was "the world's longest-running musical" and "the longest-running live theater performance at a single location." ("The Mousetrap" has played in more than one theater.)

"I thought this thing would never end," said Liz Bruzzese, who was in the cast in the 1980's. "It's like the Empire State Building—you always think you'll go see it someday."

But less-than-sellout crowds and a real estate deal finally doomed "The Fantasticks." "The new owners of the playhouse did their best to accommodate our productions," Mr. Noto said on the show's Web site, thefantasticks.com, "but dwindling grosses combined with escalating costs decided the issue for us." On closing night, a ticket cost $40, or 10.66 times the $3.75 price on opening night, May 3, 1960.

"The Fantasticks" was a career-starter or career-builder for scores of actors. Its alumni include F. Murray Abraham, who said he made $70 a week when he was in the show; Jerry Orbach, who went on to Broadway and to "Law and Order" on television; and Eileen Fulton, who managed to appear on "As the World Turns" and in "Who's Afraid of Virginia Woolf?" at the same time. ∎

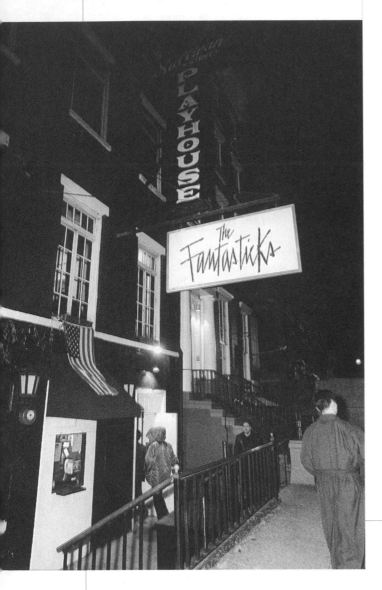

LEFT: *Exterior of the Sullivan Street Theater in 2002. A revival of the show opened on August 23, 2006, at the Snapple Theater Center.*

Big Finales, All Together Now: A Month of Broadway Closings

By **CHARLES ISHERWOOD** | January 3, 2009

FOR THOSE SUSCEPTIBLE TO THE ROMANTIC allure of attending the last performance of a Broadway show, January will be one for the history books. The annual post-holiday doldrums in the theater district are proving particularly doleful in 2009, as more than a dozen plays and musicals—almost half of the current lineup, incredible though it may seem—get ready to close by the end of the month.

Harvey Fierstein, who has returned to the cast of "Hairspray," will saunter forth from a giant, glitter-bedecked aerosol can and rasp his last girlish rasp. Patti LuPone will tear into the worn soul of Mama Rose for the last time. And the questing kids from "Spring Awakening" will sing their last moody hymn to the wondrous ache of self-discovery.

It is haunting to think that that there could be more shows closing on one Sunday than there will be running on all of Broadway by the time the Tonys roll around in June. It's also undeniable that the undertow of sadness at these closings will be unusually strong this year.

So, as you watch the lights dim, look at the real human being through the mask of the fictional characters a little more vividly. The chorus kid with the megawatt smile, the all-but-legendary musical diva with a devoted following, the up-and-coming young leading man—when the curtain falls they will all be actors anxiously awaiting their next engagement, at a scarily perilous time for everybody. So keep clapping, please, and a "Bravo!" or two would surely be appreciated. ▪

When "Off" Meets "Off Off"

By **CHARLES ISHERWOOD** | May 4, 2008

CASUAL THEATERGOERS MAY HAVE LITTLE OR no idea of the difference between Off Broadway and Off Off Broadway. So here's a quick primer.

If you are paying $65 or $75 for a full-price ticket, you are seeing an Off Broadway show. If you are fanning yourself with your program and wondering about fire-code violations, it's definitely a double-Off experience.

Actor you recognize from television: Off. Actor you recognize because he's your son's second-grade teacher and he invited you (well, actually implored you) to see the show: Off Off.

Engulfed by the sound of uncrinkling candy wrappers: Off. Surrounded by tattoos and Obama buttons: Off Off.

There often seems to be little overlap—in either aesthetics or audiences—between these large categories of New York theater. The major Off Broadway companies have thousands of subscribers in the general vicinity of middle age, reasonably ample resources and a site to call their own. They specialize in straightforward narrative theater. The world of Off Off Broadway is a welter of scrappy companies fighting for attention, producing when and where they can, and forsaking linear storytelling and text-based work in favor of productions that mix mediums more freely. And the cultural and financial divide between these two classes of theater often seems to outstrip the gap between Broadway and Off Broadway. ▪

The New Opera House—
"Faust," Witnessed by 3,000 People

October 23, 1883

A VERY GREAT AUDIENCE ASSEMBLED LAST evening in the new Metropolitan Opera house on the occasion of its formal public opening. The lines of carriages were so long that the three entrances were unequal to the task of receiving their occupants promptly, and at 8:23 o'clock, when Signor Vianesi lifted his baron, people were still pouring in from every side. An outburst of applause greeted the signor's appearance, whereat he halted, wheeled about, and gravely bowed to every corner of the vast auditorium before repeating his signal for the opening overture. The curtain rose on the first act of "Faust" at 8:30 o'clock, and Signor Campanini was warmly greeted. At this time the house was well filled. The exceedingly comfortable seats in the parquet were all occupied, the rows of boxes were tenanted, the balcony was nearly filled, and the family circle was not full by a good deal.

The artists were all warmly received: Medames Nilsson and Scalchi and Signor Campanini particularly. The artists received numerous floral baskets and bouquets, and Signori Campanini and Del Puente were given wreaths of laurel and oak leaves respectively. ■

Never Misses a Cue. Never Sings, Either.

By JAMES BARRON | December 1, 2002

WHEN THE TRUMPETS STRUCK UP THE FIRST bars of the triumphal march, he had to know that his cue was just moments away. This performance was not, after all, his debut in "Aida" at the Metropolitan Opera. It was the seventh time since the season opened that he had appeared in Verdi's famous love triangle. So, standing backstage as choristers in white-and-gold costumes and stagehands in sweatshirts and jeans swirled by, he waited.

His big moment is in Scene 2, one of the most famous triumphal scenes in opera. Night after night, he is perhaps the most recognizable figure in the throng celebrating Radames's victory. He is also the only one in "Aida" who has never missed a cue and never forgotten the words. (All right, he doesn't have any.)

He is Casco, the white horse who leads the triumphal procession in "Aida." Loaded with shiny props, Casco clomps across the stage just before the king complicates everything by giving Amneris's hand in marriage to Radames.

Casco is in his late teens or maybe 20, the equivalent in human years of someone approaching retirement age. And while not as temperamental as some tenors, he can throw a teeth-baring, floor-stomping tantrum when he feels like it. But only backstage.

"Once he's onstage," said Maeve Deady, a riding-academy instructor who uses Casco for lessons when he is not at the Met, "he's an angel."

There is no star on his dressing-room door because his dressing room does not have a door—it is the south tunnel, a long driveway under the Metropolitan Opera House near a door leading to the Met's tight backstage corridors—and he does not get the red-carpet treatment, either. The Met puts brown paper over the red carpet that runs past the singers' dressing rooms on the way to the stage. A horse is a horse, of course. ■

The Met Gives Gala Hug to Itself

By **DONAL HENAHAN** | October 24, 1983

THE METROPOLITAN OPERA'S GALA IN honor of its 100th birthday reminded me of the old song about a fellow determined to get his arms around a very large lady. He hugs a bit, makes a chalk mark, hugs some more, chalks some more and goes on working away in sections, a-huggin' and a-chalkin', until the embrace is accomplished. Over 11 hours, with time out for dinner, the company did a magnificent job of hugging itself. There were many thrilling moments, though not until almost the 11th hour, literally, did sentiment take over the proceedings.

> At the rear of the stage,
> as an honorary audience,
> sat 25 of the Met's former stars,
> looking rather like a
> jury at a vocal audition.

When the curtain rose after the evening's final intermission, an authentically gala touch was added and the night went up in a grand crescendo from there on. At the rear of the stage, as an honorary audience, sat 25 of the Met's former stars, looking rather like a jury at a vocal audition. The names alone were exciting enough—Ramon Vinay, Helen Jepson, Rïse Stevens, Dorothy Kirsten, Zinka Milanov, Jarmila Novotna, Eleanor Steber, Cesare Valletti, Bidu Sayao and Ferruccio Tagliavini, to mention a few. Of course, one could name at least as many great artists from the Met's past who chose not to be on hand for one reason or another. But it was worth the whole evening to study those faces as two young Met artists, Leona Mitchell and Giuliano Ciannella, sang the bridal-night duet from "Madama Butterfly" and to wonder what was going on in these experienced heads as young Timothy Jenkins sang the hero's prayer from "Rienzi."

The plain, unsentimental approach was completely swept away at last by Marilyn Horne and Birgit Nilsson. After Miss Horne's sumptuous delivery of Dalila's "Mon coeur s'ouvre a ta voix" from "Samson et Dalila," she walked over and embraced Rïse Stevens. No explanation was necessary: it was Miss Horne's tribute to the woman who owned that Saint-Saëns role for so many years. Did the audience love it? Is the ocean damp?

And then came Miss Nilsson to sing Isolde's Narrative and Curse from "Tristan und Isolde" with chandelier-shaking top notes that would do any Wagnerian soprano proud, let alone a 65-year-old. One fan, determined to give her a bouquet, struggled briefly with an usher in the aisle, then lofted the flowers onstage. ▪

BELOW: *Patrons file in to watch "Madama Butterfly" at the Metropolitan Opera in September 2006.*

Pavarotti Dies a Final Time in Last Performance at Met

By **ALLAN KOZINN** | March 14, 2004

LUCIANO PAVAROTTI OFFERED HIS FAREWELL to the opera stage with a performance of Puccinis "Tosca" at the Metropolitan Opera, and when the curtain fell on the third act, the packed house gave him a 15-minute standing ovation, including several minutes of insistent rhythmic clapping when it appeared that he would not return to the stage.

There was, surprisingly, neither the tossing of bouquets or the rain of program-book confetti that often occurs on such occasions. But after the third of 10 curtain calls, a large red and white banner on the second tier was unfurled and spotlighted. It read, "We Love You Luciano," with a heart-shaped "o" in "Love." The banner was from the Met.

The performance was the 68-year old tenor's 379th at the Met since his debut in 1968. Of those, 357 were in full-fledged opera productions; the rest were in galas (which often include operatic scenes and arias), special concerts and recitals. Of his operatic appearances, 61 were of the doomed painter Mario Cavaradossi, the hero of "Tosca."

Buoyed by the energy of the occasion, Mr. Pavarotti sang better and with a touch more subtlety last night than he had earlier in the week, and if his voice never approached the kind of power it had in his prime, there was no mistaking that distinctive timbre and his way with a musical phrase.

Now and then, he raced ahead of James Levine, who conducted, and at intermission one heard murmurs from operagoers about dropped notes. Still, when he was at his best, one heard the magic that made him the most famous tenor of his time, with only Placido Domingo able to challenge him for that distinction. One of those moments was the third act showpiece, "E lucevan le stelle" ("The Stars Shone"), which drew an extended ovation. ▪

BELOW: *Luciano Pavarotti received a standing ovation that lasted 15 minutes after his final appearance at the Met.*

An Appreciation: Beverly Sills

By **VERLYN KLINKENBORG** | July 4, 2007

WHENEVER I THINK OF BEVERLY SILLS, WHO died Monday at 78, I find myself imagining a baseball player—New York-born, raised on the sandlots, rising through the big leagues, M.V.P., Cy Young award—who then went on to become the commissioner. I don't think Ms. Sills ever played much baseball, but I stand by the analogy.

Laszlo Halasz,
First Director of City Opera

By **ALLAN KOZINN** | October 31, 2001

LASZLO HALASZ, THE FIRST MUSIC DIREC-tor of the New York City Opera, died on Friday at his home in Port Washington, N.Y. He was 96.

During a tumultuous eight-year tenure, which began in 1943, Mr. Halasz established several crucial elements of the New York City Opera's artistic personality. He believed that tickets should be inexpensive and insisted on offering at least one production in English every season. Unable to compete with the Metropolitan Opera for big stars, he made his company an important platform for young singers, particularly Americans. But perhaps his most important contribution was his insistence that the company's repertory include not only the standard works, but new ones as well. This put him at odds with the board, but Mr. Halasz prevailed and the company came to be known as one of the country's most adventurous houses.

Mr. Halasz was born in Debrecen, Hungary on June 6, 1905. He enrolled at the Liszt Academy in Budapest and in 1928 he joined the Royal Hungarian State Opera as an assistant conductor. He became music director of the Sakharoff Ballet in 1932 and in 1939 was appointed artistic and music director of the St. Louis Grand Opera.

When the New York City Opera was formed in the fall of 1943 under the imprimatur of Mayor Fiorello H. LaGuardia as a way to bring opera to the masses, Mr. Halasz was appointed its music director. The company's first season included productions of Puccini's "Tosca," and Bizet's "Carmen." Tickets were priced between 75 cents and $2.

In 1946, Mr. Halasz conducted the City Opera's first world premiere, William Grant Still's "Troubled Island," with a libretto by Langston Hughes. But the board was uneasy with Mr. Halasz's ventures into modern opera, and it opposed him when he scheduled the world premiere of "The Dybbuk," by David Tamkin. Mr. Halasz resigned.

After he left the City Opera, Mr. Halasz began a second career as a record producer and conducted opera at houses in Frankfurt, Barcelona, Budapest, London and South America. ∎

She had that kind of popular hometown importance to her sport, which was opera. For many years, her singing career seemed to illustrate the tensions between the American League of opera—that is, the New York City Opera, where she got her start—and the National League—the Metropolitan Opera. And when she stopped singing, she took over the whole shebang and made Lincoln Center her enterprise.

The force of Ms. Sills's personality, the extraordinary quality of her voice, the powerful dramatic presence she created on a stage and the ease with which she occupied her many public roles made her seem somehow inevitable. But there is nothing inevitable about someone who excelled at the highest level of her art and was able, at the same time, to make audiences unfamiliar with opera feel as though they had access to it through her. She represented her art as though she had been elected to the task, and she took the job of representing it seriously.

It will be hard to imagine Lincoln Center without her. A decade ago, she was even then threatening to step back into her private life. But it was an idle threat. There was never any emerita in her. ∎

Baryshnikov and "King Rudolf"

By **CLIVE BARNES** | August 18, 1974

IN DANCE THINGS HAVE BEEN PRETTY COOL for a hot August. At Lincoln Center, where American Ballet Theater and the National Ballet of Canada were playing across the plaza from one another, we saw some pretty remarkable dancing. The other Friday night, for remarkable example, we had Rudolf Nureyev and Erik Bruhn dancing in "La Sylphide" at the Metropolitan Opera House, while Mikhail Baryshnikov was dancing he "Don Quixote pas de deux" at the New York State Theater, for the first time in New York.

Bruhn, Nureyev and Baryshnikov, all three great dancers and all, in their diverse ways, supreme examples of the great Franco-Danish-Russian tradition that Christian Johansson brought to St. Petersburg around the end of the last century.

It is interesting that after some years of eclipse men are at least the equal of women in dance today, and in some respects even rather bigger stars. Russia seems a little short on the distaff side at present, apart, of course, from Ekaterina Maximova, Natalia Bessmertnova and Maya Bessmertnova, Maya Plisatskaya, who admittedly are pretty big "aparts"—the men seem to be emerging as the really big box-office stars.

Mr. Baryshnikov is a phenomenon, and we have seen nothing like the best of him yet. He is the last product of that greatest Soviet teachers, Alexander Pushkin. I will always recall seeing the very young Mr. Baryshnikov in Pushkin's class in Leningrad 1967; he was dancing next to the reigning Kirov stars, Valery Panov and Yuri Soloviev. He and Mr. Panov laughed a lot, and were fiercely competitive in class, with that good-natured camaraderie that Russian dancers so often possess.

Now they have both followed that other great Kirov dancer, the one that an audience banner on the last night of the Canadian season proclaimed, as "King Rudolf," into the West. ∎

The Child In Balanchine Still Jumps for Joy

By **JENNIFER DUNNING** | November 26, 2007

WHY HAS GEORGE BALANCHINE'S PRODUC-tion of "The Nutcracker" remained the gold-standard version of this holiday classic?

The New York City Ballet began its annual run of the piece the other night at the New York State Theater and worked its usual magic, despite generally run-of-the-mill performing. Part of the charm comes from the timelessly old-fashioned costumes by Karinska and sets by Rouben Ter-Arutunian: like candy but not too sweet and blessedly unchanged in spirit over the 53 years since the premiere. And there are a few choice choreographic set pieces and effects in the second act, which essentially departs from the narrative to spool out a series of traditional divertissements, most of them alluding to holiday treats.

But no one goes to "The Nutcracker" to see the choreography, though casting can exercise a special pull. I think the greatest attraction is the way Balanchine approached the work. True, the production was seen as a validating popular spectacle for a company better known for challenging common notions about the art of ballet. But there is something here of the impressionable child he might have been when, as a ballet student, he performed the child prince in "The Nutcracker" in St. Petersburg.

At Last, Shimmering Acoustics In Alice Tully Hall

By **ANTHONY TOMMASINI** | February 23, 2009

FINALLY, AFTER WHAT FEELS LIKE ENDLESS years of planning, fund-raising and sometimes contentious debates among the constituent institutions of Lincoln Center over the scope of the renovation and redevelopment of the 16-acre campus, the first tangible results of the formidable project were shown off.

Alice Tully Hall, closed for nearly two years, opened its grand, airy and people-friendly new lobby to the public and presented a large roster of fine musicians, ranging from living masters to eager students. In an inspired choice, the first music heard by an actual audience in the extensively renovated auditorium, now called the Starr Theater, was not some brassy fanfare or festive overture, but three mournful, elegiac Sephardic Romances from the 15th century. These timeless pieces by anonymous composers were offered, as the program stated, as a "Sephardic Invocation." Sometimes serious music befits a joyous occasion.

And Balanchine treated his "Nutcracker" as seriously as any new bit of brilliant experimentation. He did not condescend to his child performers, giving them dances that, though based on their level of accomplishment, are every bit as authoritative as anything he gave the grown-ups to do.

The evening's most exciting performing came from Ashley Bouder, the most daringly quicksilver of Dewdrops, and from Robert La Fosse, whose delicately nuanced Drosselmeier has come to look eerily like Balanchine himself. Nicholas Smith as the child prince performed the mime scenes, so lovingly unstinted on by the choreographer, with refreshing boldness and clarity in a lead children's cast completed by Margot Pitts as Marie and Jonathan Alexander as her brother Fritz. ■

The music was immediately revealing of the question that really matters as Alice Tully Hall returns: what are the new acoustics like? The astonishing early music performer Jordi Savall played a gently melancholic melody on the vièle, an early string instrument. And the quiet sounds—ancient and earthy—carried beautifully in the hall. When the soprano Montserrat Figueras, another luminary in the early music movement, joined in, along with the period instrument ensemble Hespèrion XXI, concerns about whether the acoustics in the hall could be markedly improved were largely allayed. Ms. Figueras's tender, pale tones, as she shaped the yearning phrases of the romance, shimmered.

I, for one, never thought the acoustics of Tully Hall were really poor. The sound was clear and honest, just a little dull and distant. And even as some halls feel smaller and more cozy than they are, Alice Tully Hall, at 1,087 seats, somehow always felt larger than it actually was. Both the auditorium and the sound of performances in it lacked intimacy.

The most remarkable and it seems to me indisputable achievement of the renovation, which is the work of Diller Scofidio & Renfro in collaboration with FXFowle Architects and of the acoustical consultant firm Jaffe Holden, is that the Starr Theater, though not any smaller, now feels intimate and warm. The interiors have been covered with rich, russet African veneer wood. The stage area can now be extended farther into the house. And those purposeless low-wall dividers between different sections of seats have been eliminated.

I was especially impressed when, after the Sephardic Romances, the pianist Leon Fleisher played a rhapsodic and affecting performance of Bach's Chromatic Fantasy and Fugue. I had never found the hall ideal for piano recitals before. But Mr. Fleisher's tone, especially in softer passages, had a presence and body that seemed to be evidence of the new acoustical bloom. ■

The Thrill and Kicks Of Being a Rockette

By **LYNNE AMES** | December 21, 1997

RADIO CITY

ROCKEFELLER CENTER WITH ITS TOWERING tree and Radio City Music Hall with its resident Rockettes are arguably the most famous contemporary Christmas spots in America. And here in the epicenter, the ground zero of all this holiday spirit—in fact, almost exactly in the middle of the kick line—is a lifetime Westchester resident, 29-year-old Laureen Repp-Russell.

"It's thrilling, really it is, to be on the stage and to look out at all of the seats, at the beautiful musical, and know that you are part of history," she said in an interview. "Sometimes, even after all these years, it's a little overwhelming."

If she felt overwhelmed on this recent afternoon, she did not show it. At 5-foot-9, 120 pounds, with chiseled features, bright blue eyes and an even brighter smile, she is friendly and poised. Chatting with a visitor and wearing blue jeans and no makeup, she could have been any young woman with good looks and a nice personality.

Then, in a matter of minutes, came the transformation: she disappeared into a

dressing room and emerged pure Rockette from head to toe. Her eyes were framed in flattering blue eyeshadow and dark mascara; her lips glistened red. She was wearing a green velvet costume adorned with glittering, silvery rhinestones and a bright red bow. On her legs were flesh-toned tights studded with hand-painted silver sparkle. (It takes 2½ months to make these stockings for all 36 Rockettes.) Onstage, she became virtually indistinguishable from the other Rockettes—which is exactly the way everyone wants it to be.

"We are a team, we work as a team," she said. "We sometimes refer to ourselves as sisters."

The Rockette team had its genesis in 1925 in St. Louis as the "Missouri Rockets." Later, they were taken to the Roxy Theater in Manhattan and nicknamed the Roxyettes by the showman S. L. (Roxy) Rothafel. On Dec. 27, 1932, Radio City's opening night, they first performed as the Rockettes—and, according to publicity material, were an "instant sensation.

Ms. Repp-Russell said her favorite numbers are "The Parade of the Wooden Soldiers" and "Christmas in New York," in which the orchestra rises onto the stage.

She also gets—well, a kick—out of the perennially popular kick line. Each dancer is instructed to kick to eye level, adding to the amazingly effective illusion that all are the same height. (Actual height ranges from 5 feet 5½ to 5 feet 9½ inches, with the tallest woman at the center and the shortest ones at the end.)

People everywhere recognize the Rockettes and want to speak to them and get their autographs.

"You can feel their excitement when we're on stage. You can feel their appreciation. It's hard work, but I like to think, this is our Christmas gift to them." ∎

ABOVE: *Hundreds of young, aspiring dancers audition for a spot on the Radio City Rockette dance line.*

The Last Act Is Charity, by Accident

By **DAN BARRY** | January 1, 2005

SANTA SHARED A HIGH-FIVE WITH A STAGE-hand as he waddled past. One of the elves, maybe Tinker, maybe Inkwell, sighed a weary "whew" from close to the backstage floor. Rockettes rushed to exchange their revealing costumes for robes long enough to control any involuntary high kick during the "Living Nativity" scene.

With the finale drawing to a close, Joseph grasped the hand of Mary, Christmas music swelled, and Radio City Music Hall glittered with camera flashes.

An entertainingly holy moment, a thoroughly New York moment: done. The second of the day's five performances of the "Radio City Christmas Spectacular" had ended, and now it was time to shepherd 5,900 people out of the landmark theater to make room for the 5,900 people waiting for the next show, beginning in less than an hour.

Politely pushy ushers nudged the former out of fantasyland and into the midafternoon Midtown glare.

In the half-hour or so before the next show, cleaning crews vacuumed the errant popcorn, picked up discarded programs and collected any forgotten valuables. A red-jacketed usher hustled to a desk in the lobby and handed over a Radio City gift bag stuffed with the 1 o'clock show's leftovers.

Some hats, some gloves. A pair of sunglasses, a pair of prescription eyeglasses, a pair of cheap silvery earrings still in their case. A boy. A girl.

The last two did not actually arrive by way of gift bag. They seemed surprisingly calm, given that they had misplaced their adult chaperons. One reason for their poise was perhaps reflected in the boy's response when he was asked where he lived.

"The Bronx," he said, as if to say, You wanna make something of it?

Word of two lost "sheep"—Radio City code for children—was radioed to the security office, near a side entrance on West 51st Street. This is where Stage Door Johnnies drop off flowers for Rockettes who have beguiled them, and where security officers collect and record lost things found.

After 30 days, anything unclaimed goes. Cellphones are destroyed, although there is talk of donating them to shelters for battered women. The rest of the stash is forwarded to the Salvation Army or some other charity. Gifts, you might say, from visitors to this great metropolis.

But not everything lost remains lost. Claimed in the late afternoon of the penultimate day of 2004: two young sheep. ▪

BELOW: *Crowds of mostly tourists leave the Christmas Show at Radio City Music Hall in 2005.*

Making History Began On Opening Day In 1891

By **TIM PAGE** | December 16, 1986

FROM THE SPRING EVENING IT FIRST OPENED its doors as the Music Hall through its near demise by a wrecker's ball, Carnegie Hall has been at the center of some of the most dramatic moments in the musical world.

On May 5, 1891, it was the setting of the first American performance of Berlioz's "Te Deum," featuring the New York Symphony Society and the Oratorio Society Chorus, under the direction of Walter Damrosch. And Tchaikovsky made his American debut, conducting several short pieces. More than a negligible chunk of musical history already—and all on opening night!

In 1917, the 16-year-old violinist Jascha Heifetz made his American debut at Carnegie Hall and was immediately hailed as a phenomenon. Vladimir Horowitz played his first concert at Carnegie Hall in 1928 and for years Mr. Horowitz would play only at Carnegie Hall.

Carnegie Hall was the site of the first New York performance of Mahler's Symphony No. 8, in 1912, and of Schoenberg's "Gurre-Lieder," in 1932. Until the completion of Lincoln Center, Carnegie Hall was long the home of the New York Philharmonic.

Popular music is also prominent in Carnegie Hall's history. The hall was the site also of Benny Goodman's "Sing Sing Sing" concert in 1938. The Beatles made their initial New York concert appearance at Carnegie Hall on Feb. 12, 1964.

Some day, members of the audience who attended last night's gala may tell their children about the night the hall reopened after a six-month renovation. Think of it—Isaac Stern, Benita Valente, Marilyn Horne, Yo-Yo Ma, Frank Sinatra, Zubin Mehta with the New York Philharmonic, a world premiere by Leonard Bernstein and a surprise performance by Vladimir Horowitz, all in one evening. Just one more night of history at Carnegie Hall. ■

Isaac Stern, Crusading Virtuoso

September 28, 1960

ISAAC STERN WAS A LOGICAL CHOICE FOR soloist with the New York Philharmonic at the first concert last night in the newly saved and refurbished Carnegie Hall, and not just because he sparked the successful fight to save the 70-year-old hall. By upbringing, training and predilection, Mr. Stern can be classified as an American violinist.

Like many other famous violinists, he was born in Russia, but he arrived in San Francisco at the age of 10 months. Not only is he one of the few first-rank musicians of his generation who was trained entirely in this country, but also nearly all of his studies were in California. He describes his style of playing as "American," and he has proved to be a successful musical ambassador for this country. He was touring Russia at the time of the U-2 incident

A Requiem for Tenants of Carnegie

By **JIM DWYER** | August 1, 2007

THE PROCESS SERVER PLAYED HIS KNUCKLES on the door, fortissimo.

Door to door, knuckle to metal, the rap-rap-rap ringing through the space beyond, not a flicker of hesitancy. And in the eviction papers delivered by the process server, the language was just as decisive, with one exception.

The landlord "prays for a final judgment of eviction, awarding to the petitioner possession of the premises described as follows: all rooms and areas, Studio 1110, in the building known as 881 Seventh Avenue, a.k.a. 154 West 57th Street, New York, New York." The building has yet another alias, which was not mentioned: Carnegie Hall.

For more than a century, artists and performers and musicians have nested, unnoticed but in plain sight, directly above Carnegie Hall in tower studios built by the industrialist Andrew Carnegie. Some artists actually lived there; others used the space to write scores or choreograph dances or practice for concerts. Now, the last 50 of these tenants are being evicted, a process that began two weeks ago. The trustees of Carnegie Hall say they need the space for educational programs, rehearsals and backstage areas.

Mr. Bergman, a screenwriter and filmmaker, has worked in the studios for 25 years.

"I don't have to be in that building," he said. "But I love that building. When I moved in 25 years ago, I was next door to a ballet studio; it was like a Degas painting. Wynn Handman was teaching actors—he's still there, they served his papers on his 80th birthday.

"Brando, who I later worked with, had lived on my floor," Mr. Bergman continued. "Marilyn Monroe took acting lessons there, Lucille Ball took voice. It's a great feeling of an artistic community. If you're a writer, it's great. You can't get that in a building of lawyers."

The music hall was built by Andrew Carnegie in 1890, and the towers, including studios with double-height ceilings, were added a few years later. The property was sold by his family in 1925.

Carnegie Hall now has spaces and subdivisions called Zankel, Weil, Kaplan, Rohatyn, Shorin. Just as teenagers sneak into train yards to spray-paint their tags on subway cars, the fabulously rich are queued to put their names on great works. Philanthropy is both an expression of love for humanity, and the graffiti of wealth.

881 Seventh Avenue a.k.a. 154 West 57th Street a.k.a. Carnegie Hall is in the market for yet another alias. ▪

and the Summit Conference breakdown last spring, but the Soviet public cheered him just the same.

Although he made his debut with the San Francisco Symphony Orchestra under Pierre Monteux at the age of 11, he did not explode onto a startled musical world in the way that prodigies are supposed to do. Even as a seasoned 17-year-old, his New York debut did not take the town by storm. Mr. Stern matured slowly and the critics and public grew with him. Now, at 40, he has worked his way into recognition as one of the handful of violin greats.

Mr. Stern is short, stocky, full of energy. On a Russian trip a number of years back, he burned the ear of Premier Nikita Khrushchev at a garden party on the subject of cultural exchange. That was before it had become Soviet policy to encourage artistic swaps, and Mr. Stern wanted to see more of it.

And, at a moment when few thought there was any hope, Mr. Stern headed the Citizens Committee for Carnegie Hall and turned the tide in a last-ditch battle with the city. He has now been elected president of the new Carnegie Hall Corporation. ▪

A Musician's Musician

By **BERNARD HOLLAND** | October 16, 1990

IGOR STRAVINSKY CALLED HIM "A DEPART-
ment store of music," but Leonard Bernstein
had one permanent place of business. It was
the New York Philharmonic.

The Philharmonic launched his career
in a now famous substitution for Bruno
Walter in 1943. Mr. Bernstein was its music
director from 1958 to 1969 and its laureate
conductor thereafter. And for the musicians
in the orchestra, working with Bernstein
was a singular experience.

"Bernstein came from a different era,"
said Newton Mansfield, a violinist in the
orchestra for 30 years. "Conductors today work
for reliability and competence. They prepare in
rehearsal for exactly what's going to happen in
the concert. Bernstein would talk about a piece
in rehearsal, but if you asked him if that was
what he'd do in performance, he said, 'I don't
know.' He might get a little faster than
planned. The audience might get him excited.
It was the unexpected that drew us all in."

Bernstein's spontaneity forced the
orchestra to go along with the mood, not
just with the movement of the hand. "Today
too many conductors are worried about a
section coming in at just the right time or
that ensemble is exactly together," said
Mr. Mansfield. "With Bernstein you always
stood a chance of a sloppy entrance but
nothing stopped the movement of the line.
He treated phrases as if they were a play with
a plot. He wanted you to know what the
phrase meant, where it was going, the peaks
and valleys, where you would end up. He
didn't have much technique, but personality
overrode the need for it."

Did players resent the theatricality of
Mr. Bernstein's stage presence, his tendency
toward loquaciousness and overt displays of
affection? "Every once in a while," said Mr.
Mansfield. "In the long run, however, we
knew where our interests lay. We had a
relationship with Bernstein like that with no
other conductor I have ever known."

Despite the theatrics, musicians
recognized him as a professional. Orchestra
players pride themselves on being able to spot
phonies on the podium in a matter of a few
minutes. They remember Mr. Bernstein as
someone who came to rehearsal with his
homework done. "He studied all the editions,
and he had specific reasons for the way he
phrased music," said Leonard Davis, who is in
his fifth decade as a violist in the orchestra.
"We re-recorded the Mahler Second with
him. He found little details down deep that
few of us in the orchestra had noticed. We
were surprised they were there."

"And really, he had the modesty of all
truly talented people," said Mr. Davis. "He did
all his work in private. No one ever knew how
long it took him to learn a piece or compose
something." Mr. Bernstein told a concert
audience several summers ago that he would
have given 10 years of his life to have written
the introduction to "Stars and Stripes Forever."

Sharry Sylar, an oboist said, "In my years
at the orchestra, we yearned for his
conducting. I was in that concert at the Berlin
wall"—on Christmas Day 1989, when he
conducted Beethoven's Ninth Symphony,
with its "Ode to Joy" finale—"and in the last
movement, when the chorus sang the word
'Freiheit' instead of 'Freude,' I shall always
remember how his face lit up." ■

Views Back (and Forward) On an Outdoor Stage

By **ANTHONY TOMMASINI** | July 17, 2008

WHEN THE CONDUCTOR ALAN GILBERT WAS A boy, some of his first inspiring experiences with classical music came from attending the New York Philharmonic's concerts in the city's parks. At the time he was tagging along with his parents, both violinists in the orchestra, he explained to the crowd that turned out for Tuesday night's Philharmonic concert in Central Park.

"I love the New York Philharmonic, I love New York, I love Central Park, and I love the Philharmonic's concerts in the parks," Mr. Gilbert told the audience.

Then, after mentioning that his mother, Yoko Takebe, was still playing with the orchestra, he turned to her and said, "Hi, Mom!" which brought applause from all corners of the Great Lawn, where 63,000 people, according to official estimate, had turned out to hear some music and enjoy the perfect weather.

Mr. Gilbert is poised to become the Philharmonic's music director in the fall of 2009. That he was so eager to conduct this summer's final park concert, only his second (the first was on Monday night at Prospect Park in Brooklyn), seemed an encouraging indicator of his desire to connect with New York audiences.

The concert was terrific. For the first half the enormously popular young pianist Lang Lang was the soloist in Tchaikovsky's Piano Concerto. Onstage was a concert grand of a rich red color. Chinese Red?

It is one of only two red Steinways in the world, Mr. Lang said, speaking in English from notes he had jotted down. It is being auctioned to raise money to aid the victims of the May 12 earthquake in China, "my home country," he said.

He then sat down and gave an exciting and brilliant account of the Tchaikovsky concerto. When he first gained attention in America some years ago, Mr. Lang was an unquestionable virtuoso, with white-hot energy, awesome technique, intuitive instincts and exuberant personality. But his playing could be undisciplined and indulgent, and he took a lot of criticism for his excesses.

After intermission Mr. Gilbert conducted an intelligent and lively performance of Beethoven's Fourth Symphony and ended the program with a rhapsodic account of Sibelius's "Finlandia."

Then came the encore, selected as in earlier concerts this summer by audience members who chose between two options— the "Toreador's Song" (arranged for orchestra) from "Carmen" and Rossini's "William Tell" Overture—by sending text messages to an announced address. Rossini won, and the performance was rousing. And most people stayed around for the postconcert fireworks display, which looked especially splendid on this balmy and enjoyable night. ▪

BELOW: *Concertgoers enjoy the Philharmonic on a hot summer evening at Central Park.*

The Twilight of a Zany Street

By **GILBERT MILLSTEIN** | January 1, 1950

HAVING SURVIVED 32 SPEAKEASIES, TWO varieties of jazz, burlesque and a general casting away of inhibition, West 52nd Street is now decaying noisily in the face of imminent demolition and respectability.

It has lived dangerously for the past 25 years or so, lit up in five colors of neon tubing. Ultimately the wreckers will haul it away, piece by piece, like a musical comedy heading for Cain's after a long run. The first phthisic intimation of this came when Rockefeller Center put up the Esso Building a few years ago and a damp granite chill fell over the street.

Until the early 20's the old five-story brownstones housed Rhinelanders, Iselins, Wagstaffs and Bernard M. Baruch. They were followed by some of the most outstanding speakeasies in America, including Leon & Eddie's and Jack & Charlie's "21." In a newspaper interview on his return from Europe in 1932 George Jean Nathan, the drama critic, declared: "Jack and Charlie of my favorite speakeasy would make the best president and vice president. The speakeasy makes money and the customers and owners are happy. In what other business is that true?"

Today 52nd Street is scarred with all the dubious accretions of a quarter-century. These include bebop, or bop, a style of music whose adherents say a thing is "cool" when they mean it is hot; and burlesque, a form of entertainment theoretically banished from New York in 1942 by the late Fiorello H. La Guardia.

Four of the clubs on the block are devoted to the strippers, who call themselves "exotic dancers" and exponents of "bacchanals" these days. They still take off most of their clothes, however, and their owners get into trouble with the authorities. Several weeks ago, three of the four were under suspension by the State Liquor Authority for indecent performances. The proprietor of one place, the Nocturne, pasted a large sign above the small suspension notice announcing that the place was being redecorated and would reopen on Nov. 14. That was also the day his suspension was lifted.

There is an inclination to forget that "21" was once nothing more than a pleasant speakeasy that went to extraordinary lengths to foil the prohibition people. Nobody ever got anything on Jack & Charlie's.

The place devised an extraordinary system which included four push-buttons in the vestibule. There were four so that the doorman would be sure to reach one no matter how muscular the agents became. When the alarm rang, all the drinks in the place were picked up and placed on the bar. Another button was pushed, and the whole bar tipped back into a wall. Everything went down a chute into the sewers.

On the day that repeal took effect, "21's" customers poured en masse into the street in the late afternoon to assist the help in carting indoors the first legal shipment of liquor. But all that has passed, like Judge Crater and the Stutz Bearcat. Very likely there will never be another street like it, because the same things won't happen in the same way to people. ▪

ABOVE: *Jazz cafes and nightclubs lined the famed "Swing Street" (West 52nd Street) in 1948.*

JAZZ CLUBS

Celebrating Coltrane And a Shrine to Jazz

By **PETER WATROUS** | September 23, 1997

THERE ARE MUSICAL SHRINES THAT ARE BIG and lofty and well-heeled, and then there is the Village Vanguard, which is small and in a basement and which affects a down-at-heels look. The Carnegie Hall of jazz, the Vanguard, in Greenwich Village, is jazz's heart and soul. It is now paying tribute to the saxophonist John Coltrane, who died in 1967, and whose towering reputation is in part based on the recordings he made there.

> The Carnegie Hall of jazz, the Vanguard, in Greenwich Village, is jazz's heart and soul.

To that end, Impulse Records is releasing a four-CD set today called "Coltrane: The Complete 1961 Village Vanguard Recordings," which collects the tapes of a recording session Coltrane led at the Vanguard in early November of 1961. The original album, "Live at the Village Vanguard" (Impulse), is part of every progressive jazz musician's collection; its influence on jazz is incalculable.

It was no accident that Coltrane chose to record there. By the time he and his band walked down the stairs leading into the pie-shaped room at 178 Seventh Avenue South, at 11th Street, the Vanguard already had a reputation for consistently inciting some of the best performances in jazz.

In part that was because of its history: great jazz musicians regularly played there, and they, in various ways, were always inspiring the musicians on the bandstand.

In part it was the ownership; the club, run by Max Gordon, who died in 1989, was considered a good place to work and a place that valued music above commerce. And its small size made performances there especially communicative: audiences were sucked into the ebb and flow of a good performance.

But something else prodded the musicians, too, something more competitive. And it still does.

"The Vanguard is where musicians come and listen," said Eric Reed, a young and gifted pianist who has performed there on his own and as part of the Wynton Marsalis group. "Whenever I play there, I'm always aware that my peers are in the audience, or that an older musician might come in to check me out," he said. "That fires me up. I'd better be playing my best."

And Coltrane and his group were at their best those nights in 1961. "We always were experimenting with something, expanding perimeters, looking for new horizons," recalled the pianist McCoy Tyner, who was part of Coltrane's legendary quartet at the time. "That was the nature of the band, but when we played the Vanguard, it was an especially fresh period in the band's history. We had been spurred on by meeting Ravi Shankar, and we were planning to do an album with him that never happened. But the whole band was really on fire." ▪

BELOW: *Inside the Village Vanguard in the 1960's.*

One Last Night of Rock

By **BEN SISARIO** | October 16, 2006

ABOVE: *Crowds gather outside of CBGB's for its last night of rock.*

SHE HAD PLAYED THERE MANY TIMES OVER the last three decades, but last night, before making her last appearance there, Patti Smith made sure to snap a picture of CBGB.

"I'm sentimental," she said as she stood on the Bowery and pointed an antique Polaroid toward the club's ragged, soiled awning.

Last night was the last concert at CBGB, the famously crumbling rock club that has been in continuous, loud operation since December 1973, serving as the casual headquarters and dank incubator for some of New York's most revered groups—Ms. Smith's, the Ramones, Blondie, Talking Heads, Television, Sonic Youth—as well as thousands more whose blares left less of a mark on history but whose graffiti and concert fliers might still remain on its walls.

After a protracted real estate battle with its landlord, a nonprofit organization that aids the homeless, CBGB agreed late last year to leave its home at 313 and 315 Bowery. And Ms. Smith's words outside the club encapsulated the feelings shared by fans around the city and around the world: CBGB is both the scrappy symbol of rock's promise and a temple that no one wanted to see go.

"It's the cultural rape of New York City that this place is being pushed out," said John Nikolai, a black-clad 36-year-old photographer from Staten Island whose tie read, in big white letters, "I quit."

But Lenny Kaye, Ms. Smith's guitarist and a longtime rock critic and historian, echoed what she said from the stage during a set that was sprinkled with New York rock classics like the Velvet Underground's "Pale Blue Eyes": "CBGB is a state of mind."

"When I go into a rock club in Helsinki or London or Des Moines, it feels like CBGB to me there," Mr. Kaye said. "The message from this tiny little Bowery bar has gone around the world. It has authenticated the rock experience wherever it has landed." ▪

It's Been Quite A Party, but the Days Grow Short

By **BEN SISARIO** | August 1, 2008

FOR THREE YEARS ROCK 'N' ROLL HAS HAD A great summer romance at McCarren Park Pool in Brooklyn.

Instant I-was-there concerts in the big, empty pool basin by M.I.A., Blonde Redhead and TV on the Radio. Packed free shows on blazing Sunday afternoons. The thrift-store couture, the human mural of tattoos,

Honoring Hip-Hop's Cool Side

By JENNIFER BLEYER | March 20, 2005

FOR HIP-HOP STARS IN NEW YORK, MARCH got off to a flashy start. An eruption of gunfire outside Hot 97, the popular radio station, was attributed to tensions between 50 Cent and the rapper the Game. That same week, the rapper Lil' Kim went on trial in Federal District Court in Manhattan on charges related to a shooting, also outside Hot 97, in 2001. (She was convicted of lying to a grand jury that was investigating the shooting.)

But hip-hop has another face. In Bedford-Stuyvesant, Brooklyn, a 20-foot-high depiction of the rapper and actor Mos Def was unfurled outside the Restoration Plaza shopping center. It was as if he was casting a protective gaze over Fulton Street.

"People here know and love and respect Mos—he's very pro-Bed-Stuy, and Bed-Stuy is very pro-Mos Def," said Brian Tate, a marketing consultant who devised the idea of celebrating noted Bedford-Stuyvesant figures.

For others, the crucial question wasn't whether a rapper should loom large over Fulton Street but whether Mos Def was the rapper most deserving of such an honor.

"Me, I'd rather see Jay-Z up there," said Michael Matthews, one of a group of teenagers who were on their way home from Boys and Girls High School. "He comes from Marcy Houses."

His friend Joseph Coye added: "I think Biggie should be up there. Biggie's from St. James Place."

> "But we got a lot of stars coming out of Brooklyn."

Elijah Lamey had another idea. "What about Fabolous?" he asked, pointing east. "He's from Brevoort projects."

"Mos Def deserves to be up there," Joseph Coye said approvingly. "But we got a lot of stars coming out of Brooklyn."

His friend Michael chimed in: "And we're next." ▪

piercings, sunburns and hair dye. Every other midriff drenched from a Pete Rose dive down the Slip 'N Slide.

Like every sweet summer fling, though, this one is destined to end. According to a city plan, McCarren, on the border between Williamsburg and Greenpoint, will soon quit its current state—a combination performance space, hula hoop and dodge-ball playground, alt-fashion catwalk and reclaimed ruin— and revert to its original purpose as a public swimming pool.

Built by Robert Moses in 1936 with money from the Works Progress Administration, the 50,000-square-foot pool fell into decrepit condition and was closed in 1984, its steep brick archway a gravestone to the fun once had there. Now, after two decades of political stalemate, Mayor Michael R. Bloomberg has pledged $50 million to its renovation. The plan is to go before the New York City Landmarks Preservation Commission this month; if approved, shovels could be in the ground by spring, and the new pool could open in 2011. The last scheduled concert is Sonic Youth on Aug. 30.

"It was a good run," said Emmy Tiderington, a 27-year-old Williamsburger with a tattoo snaking down her right shoulder. "Nothing lasts," she added. ▪

An 'In' Crowd and Outside Mob Show Up for Studio 54's Birthday

By LESLIE BENNETTS | April 28, 1978

OUTSIDE IT WAS CHAOS: PUSHING, SHOVING mobs squashed against the barricades at the front and back entrances, shouting and pleading to be let in by the harried sentries at the door.

Inside, however, the scene was something else entirely. "It's like the end of the Roman Empire," marveled one wide-eyed young women. "It's like being inside a Fellini film," remarked a curly-haired man. "It's the best floor show in town," giggled Truman Capote. "It's show business," purred Bianca Jagger.

It was, in fact, the first anniversary of Studio 54, and the birthday party marked what seemed, in the short and racy life span of the disco, a ripe old age indeed. One year old this week, Studio 54 is still drawing the kind of night people "everyone said wouldn't last more than a couple of months," recalled Steve Rubell, the owner, with a grin.

Lasted they have, and the beat goes on. The fierce music throbs like a pulse in the brain, strobe lights flicker over hundreds of seething bodies, the air is musky with the fragrance of marijuana, and the spectacle is so riveting a lot of people never get around to dancing at all.

Up in the balcony, Mr. Capote, in black leather, simply stood and watched, looking blissful. "I've been to an awful lot of nightclubs, and this is the best I've ever seen," he said happily, waving a tiny hand at the cavorting multitudes below. "It's very democratic. Boys with boys, girls with girls, girls with boys, blacks and whites, capitalists and Marxists, Chinese and everything else—all one big mix!"

That it was, and rather an exotic mix, too: close to 3,000 people of assorted (and sometimes indeterminate) gender, looking a bit like the effluence of a time warp machine gone berserk. They were gorgeously rouged half-naked boys dressed as slaves; there were emperors with capes of gold and silver lamé;

there were courtesans and vamps, denims and furs, leathers and feathers, sequin-spangled faces and wild hair shot through with glitter.

"I think Studio 54 brought a glamour back to New York that we haven't seen since the 60's," mused Liza Minnelli. "It's made New York get dressed up again."

It certainly made Miss Minnelli dress up: she arrived on Halston's arm in rippling red silks, swathed to the neck in red furs. After rounding up Bianca Jagger and Andy Warhol, the four of them made their way to a piano that had materialized on the dance floor.

There Miss Minnelli sang to Mr. Rubell, "Now that it's your birthday . . . I can't give you anything but love, baby!" ∎

Owners of Studio 54 Sentenced To 3½ Years For Tax Evasion

By ARNOLD H. LUBASCH | January 19, 1980

STEVEN RUBELL AND IAN SCHRAGER, TWO owners of Studio 54, were sentenced to three and half years in prison and fined $20,000 each on charges that they had evaded more than $400,000 in income taxes on cash that was "systematically skimmed" from their discothèque.

While imposing the sentences in Federal District Court in Manhattan, Judge Richard Owen criticized the two men for "tremendous arrogance." He noted that they had achieved an "incredible overnight success" with Studio 54.

Mr. Rubell and Mr. Schrager pleaded guilty on Nov. 2 to charges of personal

In Club Land, 'Neighbors' Doesn't Mean Nearby

By **PAUL BERGER** | March 26, 2006

A STEADY LINE OF CARS, MAINLY YELLOW taxis and white limousines, crawled eastward through the night past the floodlit entrances to two of Manhattan's best-known nightspots, the strip club Scores and the nightclub Crobar. It was 2:30 a.m. on a Saturday in West Chelsea, and the party was in full swing.

This is the heart of New York club land, a hodgepodge of former warehouses and factories that by day is busy with gallery hoppers and by night becomes an adult playground. In five years, nightlife capacity has increased to 10,000 people from 1,000, and the area bounded by 10th and 11th Avenues and 24th and 29th Streets is home to a score of clubs and bars.

and corporate tax evasion. In return, the government agreed to drop additional charges, including conspiracy to obstruct justice. The defendants also arranged to pay the taxes they owed.

Judge Owen said at the sentencing that Mr. Rubell and Mr. Schrager had indicated a willingness to talk to Arthur H. Christy, the special prosecutor who is investigating their allegation that cocaine was once used at Studio 54 by Hamilton Jordan, the White House chief of staff. The judge appeared to leave open the possibility that he might reduce their sentences later if they cooperated in the investigation.

Mr. Jordan has denied the allegation.

Mr. Rubell arrived at Studio 54 little more than 12 hours after the sentencing, around 2 o'clock this morning. Regulars swarmed around, offering their sympathy. He told his friends he had been treated unjustly, but, hugging one, he said: "I'll survive." ∎

The nightlife, while helping reinvigorate an area once troubled by prostitution and crime, has brought its own problem: noise. Starting two years ago, Crobar on West 28th Street, the large nightclub, with a capacity of 3,000, has tried to make friends in the community by opening its doors and bar to neighbors once a month. But its definition of "neighbor" is broad.

Last Friday Crobar, a former metal factory, was doing a brisk trade at the unusually early hour of 11 p.m., with free entry for anyone who had replied to a "Get to Know Your Neighbor" party invitation. Although the front bar was crowded with people trying to make themselves heard above the music, West Chelsea neighbors proved elusive.

Max Erickson, a record label owner who lives on the Upper West Side, said he had been invited by Baird Jones, a gossip writer who used to organize parties at Studio 54. Also present was Robert Capria, a video editor who lives in Bushwick, Brooklyn, who said he had come to meet well-connected filmmakers but had been disappointed to find the bar filled mainly with what he called "the bridge and tunnel crowd."

There appeared to be no sign of the 800 or so people who live in residential pockets in the neighborhood, or of occupants of the 1,100 public housing apartments nearby. Tim Bauman, Crobar's strategic marketing director, said the club viewed its community as wide: "It's not residential here; it's commercial mixed-use properties."

A few hours later, with the club still in full swing, people started making their way outside onto West 28th Street. As cars headed east past the Chelsea and Elliott Houses, the public housing developments that are home to 1,100 families, impatient drivers started to honk. "Yes, they honk their horn," one cabbie said. "But it's O.K. Nobody lives around here." ∎

10 Parties That Shook the Century

By **PENELOPE GREEN** | December 26, 1999

WHEN IT COMES TO MEMORABLE PARTIES, success is in direct proportion to the outrage produced. Nothing succeeds like wretched excess. With this guideline in mind, your correspondent combed through the shelf of cocktail-party literature (the journals of Edmund Wilson, the columns of Liz Smith) and compiled a party canon. Here are 10 of the most famous, and infamous, celebrations in the last 100 years. Cheers!

The Cult of the Magazine, Part I: Fund-Raiser for The Masses, Webster Hall, 1913.
The Masses was a radical socialist magazine, the flower of the new bohemia that had taken root in Greenwich Village. Its desperate editor, Max Eastman, organized a fund-raiser at Webster Hall. (Yes, the same Webster Hall on East 11th Street where drag go-go dancers later shimmied.) Admission was $1 with costume, $2 for plain clothes. Drunkenness ensued, followed by nudity as the costumes inevitably came off.

Thanks to the ball, The Masses was able to continue publishing into the early days of World War I, known chiefly for its antiwar, front-line reports by John Reed.

Downtown, Uptown: Opening Party for the Dark Tower, 1928.
At the peak of the Harlem Renaissance and Prohibition, a hair-straightening heiress named A'Lelia Walker Robinson opened her mansion, known as the Dark Tower, as a literary salon and dining club. Rothschilds, rebels and writers like Langston Hughes and Countee Cullen drank her exquisite Champagne but ignored her reportedly banal conversation.

A Block Party and an Angry Mayor: V-E Day, May 7, 1945.
"Unofficial" news of Germany's surrender set New Yorkers to dancing in the streets around Times Square. But then the disapproving

voice of Mayor Fiorello H. La Guardia boomed over a public-address system, telling the revelers "to go home or return to their jobs." The crowds dispersed.

The Blockbuster: Party for "Around the World in 80 Days," Madison Square Garden, Oct. 17, 1957.
Marilyn Monroe rode in on an elephant. Elizabeth Taylor played host to what was probably the first over-the-top party for a blockbuster movie. It was given by her husband of the time, Michael Todd, the P. T. Barnum of Hollywood, and arguably ushered in the modern Hollywood era.

PARTIES

In the Mix: Truman Capote's Black and White Ball, the Plaza, Nov. 28, 1966.
It was probably the purest example of the "Towering Inferno'" theory of party-giving: cram as many bold-face names into as large a space as will hold them. The novelist John Knowles was quoted as saying: "I felt as if we were in Versailles in 1788."

Radical Chic: Fund-Raiser for the Black Panthers at the Park Avenue Apartment of Leonard Bernstein and Felicia Montealegre, Jan. 14, 1970.
"I dig absolutely," Leonard Bernstein said in response to a Panther field marshal's call for Marxist revolution.

But he didn't dig, not really. How could he know that the little fund-raiser he'd organized for the Black Panthers in his duplex would unleash such a torrent of scalding ink, most famously "Radical Chic," the social satire by Tom Wolfe first published in New York magazine that included a long and delightfully wicked riff on the hors d'oeuvres.

The Last Days of Disco: Bianca Jagger's Birthday, Studio 54, May 1978.
The male model Sterling St. Jacques, naked and drenched in silver glitter, led a white horse onto the dance floor. Astride was another model, a glittery Godiva. Then Bianca—that's what everyone learned to call her—changed places with Godiva, and that picture, said Bob Colacello, then editor of Interview magazine, made the front pages of tabloids all over the world.

Wretched Excess, Parts I and II: The Birthday Parties of Saul Steinberg in Quogue, L.I., and Malcolm S. Forbes in Tangier, Morocco, August 1989.
Lordy, what a to-do for a couple of oldish rich guys: there were tableaux vivants of the Flemish paintings collected by Mr. Steinberg in Quogue and a cavalry charge in Tangier. Mr. Forbes, celebrating his 70th birthday, wore a kilt and staged a kiss with Elizabeth Taylor.

And the costs! Mr. Steinberg, a financier, spent $1 million, and Mr. Forbes, the patriarch of Forbes magazine, spent $2 million.

Rapper's Delight: Puffy Combs's 29th Birthday, Cipriani Wall Street, Nov. 4, 1998.
It was the night that Puffy Combs, an indifferent rapper but a gifted music executive and entrepreneur, simultaneously arrived and peaked. Guests like Muhammad Ali, Donna Karan and Sarah Ferguson had to wait in the cold behind police barricades, while Martha Stewart and Naomi Campbell snuck in through a back door. Mr. Combs himself was four hours late. The price tag was $600,000, which included go-go girls with spangled pasties, in cages.

The Cult of the Magazine, Part II: Debut Party for Talk, Liberty Island, Aug. 2, 1999.
Eight hundred celebrities—from Madonna to Al Sharpton—and 2,000 Japanese lanterns twinkled gamely at Tina Brown's last party of the decade as the fog rolled in, a dank curtain ringing down on a show that had gone on just a little too long. "It was just picnic food, and Queen Latifah screaming at us," said Michael Musto, who has covered parties for The Village Voice since 1985. "But over all, I gave it a thumbs up. I mean, everybody was there." ▪

LEFT: *Truman Capote with Katharine Graham, publisher of The Washington Post, at the 1966 Black and White Ball he gave in her honor.* BELOW: *Sean "Puff Daddy" Combs arriving at his 29th birthday party at Cipriani's in 1998.*

The Natives Don't Go There

By **MICHAEL COOPER** | January 1, 1997

THE NEW YEAR'S EVE COUNTDOWN IN TIMES Square is another example of the cultural divide between New York City and the rest of the country. While millions watch the ball drop on television each year and hundreds of thousands make the pilgrimage to Broadway to see it in person, all the revelry and whooping and hollering tends to send many native New Yorkers running for cover.

"Being from New York, it's not that appealing," said Greg Colbert, 24, a stockbroker trainee who fled Midtown before the hordes arrived, the streets were closed, the beer started to flow, the noisemakers began to bleat and the ball dropped. "I don't want to spend New Year's Eve packed like a bunch of sardines in the freezing cold."

But as 1996 gave way to 1997, visitors still found New Year's in Times Square irresistible, as close as one could ever come to the center of the action. "We're from Alaska! Are We On TV Yet?" asked the sign held up by Gabe Layman, 18, who had timed a trip to look at colleges in the east so he could ring in the New Year in Times Square.

The celebration's popularity among out-of-towners is a testament to the power of television. Just as tourists are drawn to Rockefeller Center these days less for the ice skaters and the statue of Prometheus and more for the chance to watch the "Today" show being broadcast live, many revelers from elsewhere went to Times Square with hopes of being part of a party that they have seen, on television, back home.

"This is something I've always dreamed of being a part of," said Glenda Jones, 38, who moved to New York from Columbus, Ga., last year, "and now I'm in it, in it."

This time around, the crowds were illuminated by the lights of the neighborhood's new arrivals: the Disney Store, the Virgin Megastore, the All Star Cafe. And if there seemed to be less flesh around, with the once-ubiquitous underwear advertisements disappearing nearly as fast as the pornographic stores and theaters, visitors could at least take in a giant billboard of a nude Howard Stern (obscured partly by the Chrysler Building). ■

1907 Comes In Noisily; Moon Scatters Fog

January 1, 1907

WITH THOUSANDS OF PEOPLE THE LENGTH OF the Broadway in the Tenderloin provided not only with horns, ticklers, cowbells but with umbrellas as well, the New Year was ushered in in a fog, the presence of which had been vaguely noticeable during the early evening, but which had increased to almost a London thickness in the upper air. Five minutes before the midnight whistles sounded the hour, the fog was quite thick, and the searchlights could not penetrate it for more than half a mile.

new year's eve

Four-Mile Party, Sweaty Guests

By **LYNDA RICHARDSON** | December 16, 2005

CHAMPAGNE IN A FABULOUS PARTY SPACE or a bottle of Bud in a rock club? In a city that is party central on New Year's Eve, there can be something artificial, even pathetic, about an evening of obligatory revelry. How about taking a different path, the one in Central Park where the annual midnight run is held? Feel virtuous. Feel healthy. Sweat a bit. What better way to spend the night and to end up with something truly worth gloating about later?

I did. The run, four miles, is big fun. At least this is what I recall, though the exact details are more than a bit hazy. Blame it on that nonalcoholic champagne at the midrace mark. It was cold but I was snug in Polartec fleece, joined by a friend, a veteran of the New York and Boston marathons, who good-naturedly slowed his pace.

We registered at the New York Road Runners building at 9 East 89th Street. The run goes off at the stroke of midnight with fireworks. But there's also a prerace masquerade parade and D.J. music that gives you dancing feet.

I didn't stumble into the New Year.

We ran alongside runners dressed in tuxedos, and others in wackier costumes from comic books. I liked Father Time and Baby New Year, and I didn't feel like mugger bait. The park is well lighted and patrolled, and it was filled with 3,000 to 5,000 of us running revelers—or reveling runners, depending on your take on things. The crowds cheered us on, and there was the exuberant feeling of crossing the finish line. I didn't stumble into the New Year. I sprinted. ▪

Almost at the moment the midnight hour struck and the whistles began to blow their greeting to the new year, the clouds parted, and a brilliant moon, almost full, shone directly over the Times tower. It was a transformation so sudden and unexpected that almost everyone in the streets looked up at what was apparently a happy augury for the new year. The gloom faded away, the fog and haze lifted, and the Times flashlight shot its beams across the sky to the east and the Jersey hills on the west.

In Times Square, when the Times tower searchlight shot out a glowing "1907" and told of the passing of the old year, the tumult of horns, cowbells and noise machines which had died down in anticipation burst forth again, and joined a steady chorus of screams of whistles from the east and west where factories are.

All of the hotels and big restaurants along Broadway in Times Square and its vicinity did a tremendous trade. Despite the weather conditions, the crowds which had engaged seats in the better-class dining rooms and restaurants were not deterred from occupying them, in order to usher in the new year with festal merriment. At nearly all of the hotels, large-sized men were posted in front of the doors to see that no one who had not already engaged a table was permitted to enter. In one case, where there was a little bit of a squabble, the decision of a municipal judge was quoted showing that it was quite legal for restaurant men to reserve tables if they wished. ▪

new year's eve

Live From New York, It's Cold People Waiting in Line

By **BEN SISARIO** | February 16, 2007

ABOVE: *Louis Klein waits for "Saturday Night Live" tickets, which he has done every week since the show began in the 1970's.*

THE HOUR AND A HALF I SPENT ON WIND-whipped 49th Street in, hunched in the predawn freeze with 100 other people, turned out to be a weak, amateur effort. That kind of commitment may be enough—barely—to get into a taping of one of the daily comedy shows on cable. For those of us in the shadow of 30 Rockefeller Plaza that morning, however, it would take a much more punishing, more frigid, more sleepless dedication to get what we wanted: a low-numbered standby ticket to "Saturday Night Live."

Studio-audience tickets are free, but free almost always comes with qualifiers, of course. The price for those free seats is time. In deep winter there is another cost: the price of long johns. And something to protect ears from bitterly unfunny gusts.

Each year thousands of organized, forward-planning people arrange for tickets months in advance. The rest of us have standby lines. That, at least, was what I was counting on with "Saturday Night Live." Its procedure is somewhat cruel. Numbered tickets are handed out on Saturday at 7 a.m.,

and suppliants return that night to await the possibility of getting get in. Standby does not guarantee it.

I set my alarm for 5 a.m. and headed for Rockefeller Center. My confidence sank when arrived and I saw the masses huddled beneath the "NBC Studios" marquee on West 49th Street. At 6:57 a perky woman from NBC came out and explained the deal: We had a choice of standby tickets to either the dress rehearsal or the live broadcast. One ticket per frozen nose.

I chose the live show, got a nicely printed blue card bearing No. 41 and headed home to thaw.

That night we queued up according to number—inside, thankfully—and waited for orders from the young women who mind this line. Around 11:15 one explained with a smile that we could still be let in until just before the broadcast began. It was 11:26 before I learned that I would not be so lucky.

So I tried again the following week. This time, I decided to go at 3 a.m. I was 17th in line. At 7 a familiar face came out holding two stacks of tickets. I took No. 8 for the live show, a big improvement over 41 but still no sure thing.

Fast forward to 10:55 p.m. The first 12 of us were screened by security and then lined up, tantalizingly, in front of the elevator bank. By 11:15 I was starting to lose hope when a woman with a clipboard leaned around the corner and told the guard, "Let 'em up."

It wasn't the funniest episode I had ever seen, but I contributed my quota of laughter and applause.

As I left 30 Rock, the barriers were up on the sidewalk again and new lines were forming, this time to spot celebrities on their way out. I was tempted to join them. But I decided instead that it was time to head for what was clearly the best seat in the house: my couch. ■

comedy

The Serious Business Of Comedy Clubs

By **STEPHEN HOLDEN** | June 12, 1992

"THERE ARE TOO MANY COMEDIANS," RITA Rudner declared recently. "Pretty soon the government is going to pay you not to be a comedian the same way they pay you not to grow wheat." Ms. Rudner, who is one of the country's four or five most successful young female comics, was commenting on the glut of performers in a field that until Eddie Murphy's ascent to superstardom and the proliferation of comedy on cable television was difficult to break into.

Then in the early 1980's, comedy became "the rock of the 80's," as Caroline Hirsch, the owner of Caroline's—New York's most prestigious comedy club—called it a decade ago, and the stampede began.

"Nowadays, when children tell their parents they want to be lawyers, their parents say, first learn how to be a comedian so you'll have something to fall back on," Ms. Rudner said.

Her comedians-are-a-glut-on-the-market observations join a long list of jokes about the profession's overcrowdedness that some trace back nearly a decade to Randy Credico's quip: "Every time a steel mill closes in Pittsburgh, another comic joins the work force." But there is a painful side to the jokes about the superabundance of stand-up comedy. Although the comedy boom hasn't exactly gone bust, the bubble has burst. Around the country as well as in New York City, comedy clubs are struggling for survival.

"Although there are still more than 400 full-time comedy clubs around the country, people are selling cut-rate tickets, papering the house, anything they can do to stay in business," said Campbell McLaren, a television producer of comedy specials who has been affiliated with several New York comedy clubs. "People are telling me they have to work twice as hard to stay even."

Although female comedians are flourishing, she sees the slump in the club business and cable television's demand for comedy as helping to lower the standards of professional humor.

"When I was starting out, people had to work very hard to get a shot on television," said Ms. Rudner, who took up stand-up comedy after working as a professional dancer for 10 years. "Now because of all the cable channels, people only have to get five minutes together, and all of a sudden they're on TV, and they think they've made it. Then they don't have another five minutes, and then they're gone." ▪

BELOW: *The Comic Strip Live, which bills itself as the oldest stand-up comedy showcase club in the world, is located at Second Avenue between 81st and 82nd Streets.*

Starring New York, City of Grit and Glamour

By **CARYN JAMES** | May 25, 2007

To walk through Grand Central Terminal is to step onto a real-life movie set. Cary Grant passes through it while escaping his would-be killers in "North by Northwest." Jim Carrey grabs Kate Winslet's hand and dashes across it in "Eternal Sunshine of the Spotless Mind," watching people vanish as his memory is erased. And it is the site of a pivotal moment in "The Fisher King," when Robin Williams, as a pure-hearted, emotionally unbalanced man, spots the quite plain woman of his dreams heading for her train. Suddenly everyone in the room breaks into a waltz, and this grimy, everyday place becomes a scene of glittering romance.

James Sanders's 2001 book "Celluloid Skyline: New York and the Movies" shrewdly observes that two New Yorks—the real city and the screen fantasy—feed each other in a never-ending circle. Film has made New York a communal experience, familiar even to people who have never been here.

But what is a New York film? It's not one that simply happens to be set here; whether it's shot here doesn't matter either (though that helps). In a genuine New York movie the characters and their stories can't be separated from the life of the city. There is a dynamic between character and place like the one that makes Mr. Williams in "The Fisher King" insist that no threat of criminals will chase him out of Central Park because "This park is mine just as much as it is theirs."

Mr. Sanders is right to point out how reality fuels the movies' fantasy of New York, which in turn helps shape real New Yorkers' perceptions of the city. Push that idea further, and you see that those fantasies are almost always close to the soul of the city, to what New York is or wants to be. Fred Astaire and Ginger Rogers danced through a city of dazzling, black-and-white Deco elegance. The changing, freewheeling 60's saw the tawdry street hustlers of "Midnight Cowboy," as well as the glamorous Holly Golightly (a more refined hustler) in "Breakfast at Tiffany's."

Today the bracing, multiethnic realism of Spike Lee make him the pre-eminent New York filmmaker. He doesn't romanticize the city as Woody Allen did in his classic comedies from the 70's, "Annie Hall" and "Manhattan," but obviously loves New York every bit as much. Mr. Lee, like Martin Scorsese in 70's masterworks like "Taxi Driver," depicts it without sugarcoating. ■

ABOVE: *Tiffany's on 57th Street and 5th Avenue was immortalized in "Breakfast at Tiffany's."* BELOW: *Dennis Farina on the set of "Law and Order." The series has been filmed in New York since 1990.*

From Mean Streets to Clean Streets

By **JOHN CLARK** | April 30, 2006

OVER THE LAST SEVERAL YEARS, NEW YORK has become a kind of permanent film set, a glorified back lot, replete with enormous trailers, groaning craft-services tables, blazing lights and barking production assistants. A partial list of coming films that were shot or are scheduled to shoot in the city includes "Che" (Benicio Del Toro), "American Gangster" (Russell Crowe), "Michael Clayton" (George Clooney) and "The Nanny Diaries" (Scarlett Johansson).

It's a far cry from the lean days when the director Sidney Lumet shot Times Square through a car windshield for "Stage Struck" (1958) and filmed street dancers for the shattering finale to "Fail Safe" (1964). "I grabbed those shots at the end of 'Fail Safe' from streets around the studio, on 10th Avenue and 54th, where the Puerto Ricans sat on the steps in the summertime," he said in a recent interview in his small theater-district office. "We didn't have any money."

Now, of course, entire blocks would be shut down to film those exteriors. The city has changed along with the budgets and scale of today's studio films. Times Square, once home to drug dealers, prostitutes and beleaguered theaters, has morphed into a Mickey Mouse mall. The West 50's, formerly part of the notorious Hell's Kitchen, have sprouted condos, fancy restaurants and the Comedy Central studio.

Even as more and more movies and television shows are being shot in New York, the city that turns up on the screen is far more likely to be the teeming, terrifying, exhilarating, unforgiving New York of the popular imagination. Kevin Lima's coming film "Enchanted," for example, is about a peasant girl who is banished from her fairy-tale world to a New York that is both gritty and romanticized. As Mr. Lumet put it, "If a director comes in from California and doesn't know the city

at all, he picks the Empire State Building and all the postcard shots—and that, of course, isn't the city." To many filmmakers, the postcard is all that's left.

To a large extent, the driving force behind the flood of productions is less creative than pedestrian: New York offers competitive logistics and cost efficiencies. There has been a big expansion of studio space, thanks to facilities like Silvercup Studios in Queens and Steiner Studios in Brooklyn, and the state and city offer tax rebates of 15 percent to filmmakers who shoot at least 75 percent of their movies in New York City.

> Times Square, once home to drug dealers, prostitutes and beleaguered theaters, has morphed into a Mickey Mouse mall.

James Sanders, editor of "Scenes From the City: Filmmaking in New York, 1966-2006," foresees a new crop of filmmakers who will chart new territory in movies about the crosscurrents emanating from ethnic neighborhoods in Brooklyn, Queens and the Bronx. "We are going to see the story of a Pakistani kid meeting the Hindu kid," he said. In fact, he added, because the very nature of the city forces people into close contact with one another, New York still transcends the malls, the box stores and the coming of Trader Joe's. "There is no rival for the life of the street," Mr. Sanders said. "You run into lovers, ex-lovers. There are so many ways for different kinds of people to meet each other. That has never changed." ■

The Business Of New York

BUSINESS

▼ PAGE 192

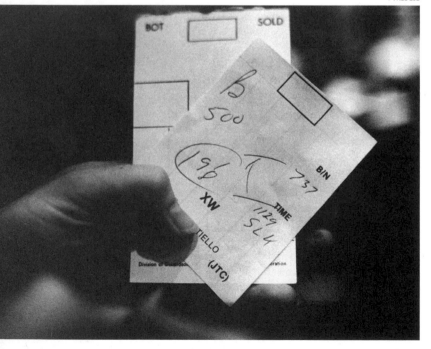

"Who knows what to expect of a financier who just saw the Dow drop 777 points?" Eduardo Porter wrote in The Times after a random walk on Wall Street on September 29, 2008, the day of the single largest point loss in history. Outside the New York Stock Exchange, he saw some long faces, but mostly the same crowded, noisy scene you'd see there at the end of any trading day. Brokers and investment bankers headed home, jabbering to each other, jabbering into their cellphones. "The sense of everyday bedlam did impress upon me just how many conversations can be going on at the same time. And they are all going on here."

New York has been at the center of the nation's financial conversation for so long that you could almost forget that the hoopla on Wall Street—the order-barking traders, the big-money deals, the bonus-happy investment bankers—started under a buttonwood tree. Five stocks changed hands on May 17, 1792, opening day at the forerunner of the New York Stock Exchange. The trading floor was an eighteenth-century sidewalk.

So New York became the money city—and a moneyed city. Big profits came from manufacturing: Manhattan was full of factories, even on Park Avenue (but only until about 1910, when the factories were exiled by new city zoning rules). New York still had more than a million manufacturing jobs at the end of World War II, from dress makers in the garment district to steel fabricators in Queens. It had stores to sell the products consumers wanted—the nineteenth-century dry goods emporiums became the big department stores of the twentieth. And it had the financiers who all but invented the modern economy that paid for expansion after

▲ PAGE 214

expansion—Cornelius Vanderbilt, J.P. Morgan, Andrew Carnegie, John D. Rockefeller.

But why? Why was New York accepted as the capital of capitalism—and of retailing, advertising, publishing, culture and, perhaps most of all, of expensive real estate? Why didn't Boston or Philadelphia or Chicago become the nation's economic powerhouse?

One reason is that New York's all-consuming energy draws aggressive stockbrokers, gutsy entrepreneurs and canny real estate developers willing to double up their bets. That has given New York rags-to-riches characters like Harry B. Helmsley, who went from a $12-a-week office boy to consummate real estate deal maker and part-owner of the Empire State Building. Donald J. Trump's father built apartment complexes in Queens and Brooklyn. Trump himself moved to Manhattan and resurrected a hotel on East 42nd Street in the 1970s, when the city's own fortunes were sinking. Soon he was putting his name on buildings all over town, and bragging about perfecting the art of the deal.

People like Helmsley and Trump prospered as the city was changing around them. Manufacturing jobs were disappearing because factories were relocating to places where doing business was cheaper—the South, for example, where unions were far less powerful if they existed at all, or overseas. New York went from a city with 1.1 million manufacturing and industrial jobs after World War II to a service-oriented city with fewer than 200,000 "blue collar" jobs now. And that made the city more vulnerable than ever to the ups and downs of Wall Street.

New York makes its money on other streets besides Wall Street, of course, like West 47th Street, still the Main Street of America's diamond district. In the popular imagination, the big advertising agencies are on Madison Avenue (although few of them are actually located there anymore). They dreamed up characters and slogans that stuck in people's minds: the Excedrin headache, for example, and "I want my MTV."

New York is also home to television networks that broadcast primetime hits and book publishers that fill the best-seller lists, and to trend-making fashion designers and retailers. In New York's stores are the clothes worn by the models who glide along the catwalks at the fashion shows in Bryant Park—clothes made by apparel-industry workers in the

garment district nearby, in a neighborhood choked with men pushing racks filled with dresses and suits through the streets.

A few blocks away are stores that are choked with shoppers—Macy's claims that its Herald Square store is the world's largest, with 2.15 million square feet, or about as much space as 35 football fields. There are shop-till-you-drop New Yorkers who remember visiting the tree at Rockefeller Center as a prelude to Christmas shopping at Saks. They remember Union Square as the home of S. Klein, the discount department store mentioned on sitcoms from "I Love Lucy" to "All in the Family." They also know the big B's of stores (Henri Bendel, Bergdorf Goodman and, a few blocks away, Bloomingdale's), and they also know Burberry's, Baccarat and Bulgari. These are world-class shoppers like the late playwright Wendy Wasserstein, who once said she never mentioned shopping when she was asked about her hobbies or interests. But shopping must have been in her DNA: "There is no department store, specialty shop or even supermarket," she said, "that doesn't whisper to me, 'We're open. Please come in.'"

▼ PAGE 207

Stock Prices Slump $14 Million In Nationwide Stampede to Unload

October 29, 1929

THE SECOND HURRICANE OF LIQUIDATION within four days hit the stock market yesterday. It came suddenly, and violently, after holders of stocks had been lulled into a sense of security by the rallies of Friday and Saturday. It was a countrywide collapse of open-market security values in which the declines established and the actual losses taken in dollars and cents were probably the most disastrous and far-reaching in the history of the Stock Exchange.

That the storm has now blown itself out, that there will be organized support to put an end to a reaction which has ripped billions of dollars from market values, appeared certain last night from statements by leading bankers.

It was calculated last night that the total shrinkage in American securities on all exchanges yesterday had aggregated some $14 million, with a decline of about $10 million in New York Stock Exchange securities. It was not so much the little trader or speculator who was struck by yesterday's cyclone; it was the rich men of the country, the institutions which have purchased common stocks, the investment trusts and investors of all kinds.

Shares of the best-known American industrial and railroad corporations smashed through their old lows of Thursday, and most of them to the lowest level for many years, as wave after wave of liquidation swept the market during its day of utter confusion and rout. General Electric lost 47½, United States Industrial Alcohol, 39½; Standard Gas, 40½; Westinghouse Electric, 34¼; Western Union, 39½, and Worthington Pump, 29.

One of the difficulties that beset the market was the popular misconception that the banking pool, organized by J. P. Morgan & Co., the First National Bank, the National City Bank, the Guaranty Trust Company, the Equitable Trust Company and the Chase National Bank would throw funds into the market to save it. What the bankers had set out to do, with their consortium, was merely to supply bids where no bids existed and to plug up the "air hole" which the market had developed on Thursday. They had no idea of putting the market up, or saving anyone's profits. Rather the general plan was to provide a degree of stabilization on which further liquidation could take place, if it proved necessary. ◼

The Market Plunge: Board Sale of Stock Funds Helped To Spur Drop

By **KURT EICHENWALD** | October 20, 1987

YESTERDAY'S HISTORIC PLUNGE IN THE STOCK market was fed in large part by huge sales of shares in stock-oriented mutual funds. Several of the largest mutual fund management companies said the number of phone calls from investors was about double the normal volume.

Trading activity by the investors was extremely heavy as shareholders switched out of stock funds and into other funds, primarily money market funds that invest in short-term fixed-income securities. Funds oriented toward medium- and long-term bonds and gold also attracted investors frightened by the falling market.

But activity was so hectic that it was difficult to gauge the numbers of investors who were calling and how many were switching their investments.

New York's Resilience Put to the Test

By **PATRICK MCGEEHAN** | September 21, 2008

AFTER THE RECESSION OF 2002, MAYOR Michael R. Bloomberg said that New York City's economy had diversified enough through the fostering of tourism, manufacturing and other businesses that the city had "reduced our dependency on the fortunes and failures of Wall Street."

Now, with the financial sector in turmoil after the failure of two of its biggest investment banks, the forced sale of another and the loss of thousands of its best-paying jobs, the mayor and his city face a true test of that claim. When the current mess is over, many economists and analysts predict, Wall Street will emerge a smaller and less lucrative place than it was before.

By some measures, the city entered this crisis more reliant than ever on Wall Street, with its big profits and bonuses, raising difficult new questions about how quickly the city will recover.

Last year, financial sector workers collected more than a third—35.9 percent—of all the income earned in the city, even though they held just one of every eight jobs in New York, according to the federal Bureau of Labor Statistics. That share is double the industry's portion of the city's wages and salaries from 30 years ago, and it has continued to grow even as the number of financial jobs in the city has declined, to about 470,000.

Last week, the state Labor Department projected that about 40,000 of those jobs would be eliminated in the next year—in addition to the more than 10,000 that are already gone—sharply reducing the amount of money being pumped into the local economy and the amount of taxes the city and state will collect. (City officials are more hopeful, predicting the job loss to be about half of the state projection.)

"For the Manhattan and New York City economy, it's like pulling a big plug out," said Rosemary Scanlon, an associate professor at the New York University Schack Institute for Real Estate.

She said it could take two or more years for the metropolitan area to recover from the various blows it has sustained in the last few weeks. That would be a relative blink compared to what transpired after the stock market crash of 1929. ▪

"At this point, we don't know what's happening," Tracey K. Gordon, a spokesman for Fidelity Investments, said during yesterday's early trading. "Things are happening too fast."

'A GENUINE PANIC'

Thomas V. Williams, senior vice president and managing director of mutual funds at Kemper Financial Services, said: "We've just seen a genuine panic. In equity funds, up till about a week ago, we were running positive cash flow. That has now turned to negative cash flow, with the vast majority of that in exchanges."

Most investors were switching funds within a family of funds rather than redeeming their shares and seeking a refund of their money. Such a move to a money market fund is usually available at no cost, and gives investors the option of moving back into the stock market with as much ease as they left.

Managers of mutual funds said that the number of investors switching funds compared with the number asking that their shares be sold was at least 10 to 1.

But the managers said they had prepared for the volume of yesterday's telephone calls after last week's market drop. ▪

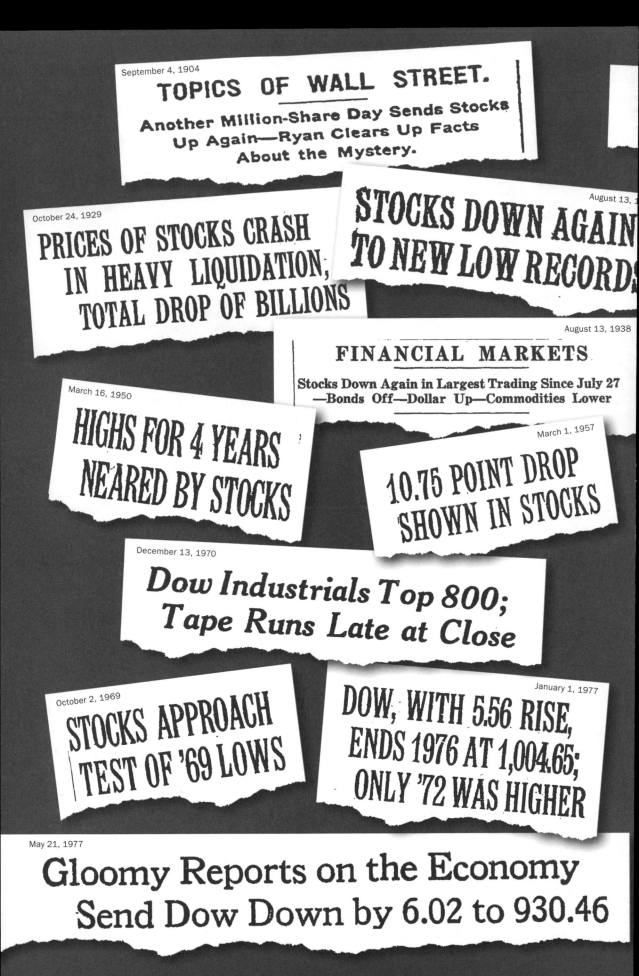

September 4, 1904

TOPICS OF WALL STREET.

Another Million-Share Day Sends Stocks Up Again—Ryan Clears Up Facts About the Mystery.

August 13,

STOCKS DOWN AGAIN TO NEW LOW RECORDS

October 24, 1929

PRICES OF STOCKS CRASH IN HEAVY LIQUIDATION; TOTAL DROP OF BILLIONS

August 13, 1938

FINANCIAL MARKETS

Stocks Down Again in Largest Trading Since July 27 —Bonds Off—Dollar Up—Commodities Lower

March 16, 1950

HIGHS FOR 4 YEARS NEARED BY STOCKS

March 1, 1957

10.75 POINT DROP SHOWN IN STOCKS

December 13, 1970

Dow Industrials Top 800; Tape Runs Late at Close

October 2, 1969

STOCKS APPROACH TEST OF '69 LOWS

January 1, 1977

DOW, WITH 5.56 RISE, ENDS 1976 AT 1,004.65; ONLY '72 WAS HIGHER

May 21, 1977

Gloomy Reports on the Economy Send Dow Down by 6.02 to 930.46

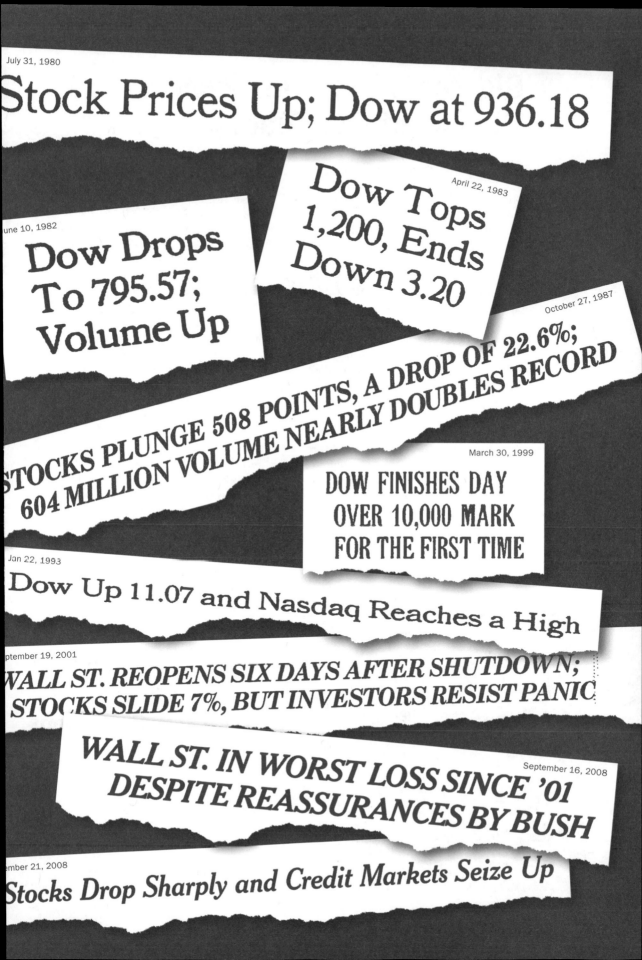

July 31, 1980

Stock Prices Up; Dow at 936.18

April 22, 1983

Dow Tops 1,200, Ends Down 3.20

une 10, 1982

Dow Drops To 795.57; Volume Up

October 27, 1987

STOCKS PLUNGE 508 POINTS, A DROP OF 22.6%; 604 MILLION VOLUME NEARLY DOUBLES RECORD

March 30, 1999

DOW FINISHES DAY OVER 10,000 MARK FOR THE FIRST TIME

Jan 22, 1993

Dow Up 11.07 and Nasdaq Reaches a High

ptember 19, 2001

WALL ST. REOPENS SIX DAYS AFTER SHUTDOWN; STOCKS SLIDE 7%, BUT INVESTORS RESIST PANIC

September 16, 2008

WALL ST. IN WORST LOSS SINCE '01 DESPITE REASSURANCES BY BUSH

mber 21, 2008

Stocks Drop Sharply and Credit Markets Seize Up

Big Board Deal May Mean The End of Floor Trading

By **JENNY ANDERSON** | April 21, 2005

THE NEW YORK STOCK EXCHANGE, WHOSE shouting traders and frenzied activity have become a global symbol of capitalism, announced yesterday that it would acquire a leading electronic trading system in a deal that allows the exchange to become a public company but casts doubts on its 213-year-old system of auction trading.

The exchange will merge operations with Archipelago, one of the biggest electronic trading operators, to form the NYSE Group. The deal will give the holders of the exchange's 1,366 seats $400 million in cash and 70 percent of the shares of the combined publicly traded company.

More important, it will enable the New York Stock Exchange to expand its ability to handle trades electronically, staving off challenges from its traditional rival Nasdaq and global competitors like Euronext and Deutsche Börse.

The merger is the most significant acknowledgement yet that the Big Board's traditional market, driven by human traders, may not be able to survive in an era increasingly dominated by instantaneous trades.

On the storied trading floor of the New York Stock Exchange, hundreds of men and women in blue and green jackets spend their days monitoring screens, handling multiple calls and yelling at each other in an effort to get the best prices for buyers and sellers of stock.

Defenders of the system say their judgment is critical; critics say the system is overrun with conflicts and rife with a history of misdeeds. After a three-year investigation, seven firms on the floor paid more than $240 million in fines for trading violations. Last week, 15 traders were indicted on related charges.

Many members of the exchange have resisted moving to greater automation, fearing for their jobs and their wealth, which for many is tied up in the price of a seat. Seat prices have fluctuated as sentiment about the exchange's future has wavered. In August 1999, a seat sold for $2.7 million, falling in January 2005 to $975,000. The most recent sale was back up to $1.6 million. ∎

The Bronze Bull Is For Sale, but There Are a Few Conditions

By **DAVID W. DUNLAP** | December 21, 2004

THE SNORTING, PAVEMENT-PAWING, 11-FOOT-tall, 7,000-pound, bronze "Charging Bull" is being offered for sale by its sculptor and owner, Arturo Di Modica. The buyer must keep it in place and donate it to New York City.

The minimum bid is $5 million.

"It's become one of the most visited, most

Stock Exchange's Former Chief Wins Court Battle to Keep Pay

By **JENNY ANDERSON** | July 2, 2008

FOR NEARLY FIVE YEARS, RICHARD A. GRASSO was vilified for the riches he reaped while running the New York Stock Exchange.

But on Tuesday, an appeals court ruled that Mr. Grasso could keep the $139.5 million he was paid.

Mr. Grasso, who symbolized for many the exuberance and excess of the now-faded bull market, won the final round in his long legal battle over the compensation he amassed during his eight years as head of the Big Board, when the New York State Court of Appeals threw out the remaining claims against him.

The 3-to-1 ruling brings to an end one of the ugliest fights in modern Wall Street history and hands a remarkable victory to Mr. Grasso against his antagonist, former attorney general —and now former governor—Eliot Spitzer, who pressed the case against Mr. Grasso.

A tireless cheerleader for the exchange, Mr. Grasso was lionized for his work in reopening it in the aftermath of 9/11.

But two years later he was forced out amid a furor over his pay, even though he maintained that the stock exchange's directors, who included many Wall Street executives, approved his compensation. Mr. Grasso, who spent 35 years at the exchange, working his way up from a clerk to the chairman's office, always insisted the fight was not about the money, but about his personal honor. He never showed any inclination to settle the case, despite pressure from Mr. Spitzer.

In Tuesday's decision, the Appellate Division of New York State Supreme Court overturned a lower court's ruling that Mr. Grasso hand over more than $100 million of his compensation.

The decision means the case was not decided on whether Mr. Grasso's pay had been unreasonable but rather was thrown out because the exchange had merged with Archipelago Holdings in 2006, becoming a public company. The appeals court concluded that the attorney general had no standing to sue Mr. Grasso since the exchange had been converted from a nonprofit entity to a for-profit corporation, negating the attorney general's ability to sue on behalf of the public rather than for private shareholders. ▪

photographed and perhaps most loved and recognized statues in the city of New York," said Adrian Benepe, the city parks commissioner. "I would say it's right up there with the Statue of Liberty."

Mr. Benepe said the city did not have the money to acquire it but would welcome it as a donation. The donor would be recognized on a plaque designed by Mr. Di Modica, a 63-year-old artist who divides his time between Sicily and a studio in Lower Manhattan. Mr. Di Modica would use most of the proceeds to finance other sculptures he is planning for New York. He would also recoup more than $300,000 that he spent on "The Charging Bull" and donate some money to charity.

"The Charging Bull" made its startling debut outside the New York Stock Exchange on Dec. 15, 1989. Mr. Di Modica installed it overnight, without permits, as a tribute to America's rebound from the 1987 stock market crash. It was quickly hauled away. Six days later, it was relocated in Bowling Green by Henry J. Stern, who was then the parks commissioner.

Since then, passers-by have rubbed to a bright gleam its nose, horns and a part of its anatomy that, as Mr. Benepe put it gingerly, "separates the bull from the steer." ▪

J. P. Morgan's Life One of Triumphs

April 1, 1913

J. PIERPONT MORGAN HAD BEEN THE LEADING figure in American finance for almost as many years as the present generation could remember and had often been described as the biggest single factor in the banking business of the entire world. Combination, concentration, and development were his aims, and the story of his life is indissolubly intertwined with the periods of expansion in this country in the world of railroads, industrial organization and banking power.

The pinnacle of his power was reached in the panic of 1907, when he was more than 70 years old, and to some extent had withdrawn from participation in active affairs. By general consent he was put at the head of the forces that were gathered together to save the country from financial disaster.

Unlike many of the men of great wealth in this country, Mr. Morgan, who was born in Hartford on April 17, 1837, did not have the incentive of poverty to spur him on. He was not born poor. On the contrary, he was heir to a fortune estimated at from $5 million to $10 million. It was one of the notable fortunes of the country in the 50s, and when John Pierpont Morgan went into business here in the early 60s there was open to him a career entirely honorable and very comfortable that would have carried him to an inconsequential old age and an unhistoric grave.

He did not choose this career, but rather chose to work as few men have worked in the last half century. At the opening of the new century Mr. Morgan was easily the largest financial figure on this side of the water, if not in the world.

His United States Steel enterprise was perhaps as notable an example of J. P. Morgan's persistent optimism as anything in his whole life. It was capitalized on the expectation that the conditions of the most prosperous year in the history of the country up to that time would continue indefinitely. When the depression of 1903 came along, and the Steel

> Mr. Morgan did not
> have the incentive of poverty
> to spur him on.

stocks dropped off until the common, dividend-less, was down to 8¾, a banker went to Mr. Morgan to ask him what he thought about it.

"I am not concerned with the stock market conditions of the Steel stocks," was the gruff reply, "but I can tell you that the possibilities of the steel business are just as great as they ever were." ■

At the Touch of A Finger, Edwin Shaw Shut the Door Nightly on Wall Street's Billions

By **MEYER BERGER** | July 2, 1958

NINE YEARS AGO, J. P. MORGAN & CO., INC., needed a new head of security; someone to guard the great vaults and supervise the inward and outward flow of billions of dollars in negotiable paper—someone who would be keenly aware of the job's responsibilities but not so awed by it that he could not keep the traffic moving smoothly and flawlessly.

Edwin Shaw drew the assignment. He had worked on coupons. He had been a signer of the corporation's most confidential messages and documents and no secret had passed from his lips. Yet the boy from Bay Ridge was no scrooge.

Chase Is Reported On Verge Of Deal To Obtain Morgan

By **PATRICK MCGEEHAN** and **ANDREW ROSS SORKIN** | September 13, 2000

THE CHASE MANHATTAN CORPORATION, THE third-biggest banking company in the United States, is expected to announce today that it has agreed to acquire J. P. Morgan & Company, one of the most storied banks, for $30.9 billion in stock, executives close to the talks said.

Chase has been striving to transform itself into a global financial powerhouse, and acquiring Morgan could sharply accelerate the process. Since the early 1980's, Morgan has changed from a commercial bank with a blue-chip list of clients into a firm focused on investment banking.

Buying Morgan could catapult Chase into the big leagues of investment banking, the business of raising money for large corporations and advising them on mergers and acquisitions. It would also continue the consolidation among the nation's largest banks, leaving only a handful of huge institutions at the top of the industry.

Together, Chase and Morgan would have more than $650 billion in assets, ranking second to Citigroup's $800 billion.

Most of Chase's banking customers would probably not notice much immediate change as a result of the combination. Most of the overlap between the two companies would be in investment banking functions, like underwriting stocks and bonds and trading currencies.

"The resulting organization would clearly be powerful because both firms are both bank and investment bank," said Robert Albertson, president of Pilot Financial, an investment firm in New York. "The old Chase and the old Morgan a decade ago would have been oil and water, but now they're made of the same liquid. They've grown closer rather than further apart." The new firm will be called J. P. Morgan Chase. ∎

Last Monday was Edwin Shaw's last day on the job. At 9 a.m. he came in with a vice president of the bank and stood by as the 53-ton steel vault door swung open. The vice president withdrew. Mr. Shaw nodded to his seven vault assistants and they moved through the opening.

At noon, Ed Shaw was summoned to the old partners' dining room. Junius S. Morgan was there, and Henry C. Alexander, chairman; H. P. Davison, president; and others. They dined and they reminisced.

When it was over, they shook hands with Ed Shaw. They gave him a handsome silver cigarette case with his initials engraved in it and with the years of his long service marked. Then he went down to the great vault, and the floodgate of memories opened.

Funny the things that come to mind— that day a few years ago when one $15 coupon could not be found. It never turned up, somehow. That was the only loss from the vault in his period of stewardship. Not bad when you handle billions every day. ∎

BELOW: *JP Morgan Chase Bank acquired failing investment bank Bear Stearns in 2008 for $236 million.*

First Woman to Join the Big Board Finds "Grand" Reception

By **VARTANIG G. VARTAN** | January 1, 1968

"MURIEL SIEBERT IS PLEASED TO ANNOUNCE her admission," the announcement card says, "as a member of the New York Stock Exchange."

This discreet wording is apt to rank as one of the great understatements on Wall Street for the simple reason that "Mickie" Siebert at the age of 38 has become the first woman in history to own a seat on the Big Board. For 175 august years, the nation's leading stock exchange had been the private preserve of men.

"It was last Thursday," she said. "The board of governors approved my membership. I went to the exchange and handed over a check covering the balance of the $445,000 seat purchase, plus the $7,515 initiation fee. I walked outside and bought three bottles of French champagne for the people in my office. I still couldn't believe it was me. I was walking on cloud nine."

A few of the more conservative members in the financial community had hinted to the personable Ms. Siebert that perhaps she ought to let a man buy the seat.

"But the people at the exchange were grand," she exclaimed.

The reaction of one brokerage-house partner was typical. "I couldn't care less if a woman bought a seat," he said. "God bless America. I think it's great."

She arrived on Wall Street in 1954 and went to work for Bache & Co. as a research trainee at $65 a week. In 1958, when she was an analyst at Shields & Co., she received her first commission order from an investment company, as a reward for a research idea.

That opened her eyes to the wider and more profitable vistas of selling and led, in time, to partnerships at two other firms. Last week, she said good-bye to a partnership at Brimberg & Co., another member firm of the Big Board, after three years.

Ms. Siebert starts out this week on her own with offices at 120 Broadway. "There will be just myself and a secretary," she said. "I hope to hire a trader." ▪

BELOW: *Muriel Siebert founded her own firm, Muriel Siebert & Co., Inc., in 1967.*

No Longer the 1980's

By **MICHAEL S. SCHMIDT** | November 3, 2006

WHEN KAREN L. FINERMAN GRADUATED from the Wharton School at the University of Pennsylvania in 1987, she and many of her classmates—both men and women—headed directly to Wall Street.

When she returned to campus for her 15-year reunion, she said she was amazed at how few of her women classmates were still working on the street.

Ms. Finerman, who runs her own hedge fund, Metropolitan Capital, started her career working as a trader, which, she said, seemed the most intellectually challenging. Now, she says, it allows her to balance work with family. (She has two sets of twins.) "The hours for trading are pretty set and they are not long."

Gender Bias on Wall Street?
The Numbers Tell the Story

By **PATRICK MCGEEHAN** | July 14, 2004

DURING SEVERAL YEARS OF DRAWN-OUT litigation over how they treat the women they employ, Wall Street firms have adamantly disputed all contentions that they discriminate—until the time has come to do the math.

In a sex discrimination lawsuit that Morgan Stanley has just settled, as in those that Merrill Lynch and Smith Barney settled in the late 1990's, executives decided not to go public with their track records of hiring, paying and promoting women. In each case, labor lawyers said, the numbers painted a picture that would have been hard to defend.

They show that a few years into the 21st century, Wall Street is still dominated by the white men who fill the bulk of the most powerful and highest-paying jobs in the industry. Data from the Equal Employment Opportunity Commission show that men made up more than two-thirds of the officials and managers in the securities industry in 2002, even higher than the ratio in other industries.

Supported by figures like those, Elizabeth Grossman, who was the commission's lead trial lawyer in the Morgan Stanley case, was comfortable predicting that more complaints of sexual and racial discrimination on Wall Street will surface now that Morgan Stanley has agreed to pay $54 million to settle the commission's suit.

That case stemmed from a 1998 complaint by a bond saleswoman, Allison K. Schieffelin, who contended that she was denied a promotion because of her sex. The firm countered that Ms. Schieffelin, who will receive at least $12 million of the payout, was disappointed about her inability to rise higher and was later fired for being insubordinate.

"That settlement sends a big statement that maybe she was a troublemaker, but her claim must have had merit or they wouldn't have paid so much," said Hydie Sumner, a broker who knows how hard big firms will fight to avoid paying out discrimination claims.

While women traders may still be a rare sight at Wall Street trading desks and in trading pits on exchange floors, dozens of them gathered at a party at Le Cirque in Manhattan given by Trader Monthly, whose current issue features women traders. Industry estimates say that about one in 10 traders is a woman.

"I have never thought of it as a men's industry," said Lisa M. Utasi, who started as a retail broker at E. F. Hutton two decades ago and is now an equities trader at ClearBridge Advisers specializing in mutual funds. "I have never been inhibited by being a woman." And, as trading has become more electronic, it has put men and women on a more level playing field, because everyone has access to the same quotes in real time, she said. ∎

> The numbers painted
> a picture that would have
> been hard to defend.

Ms. Sumner, who worked for Merrill Lynch in San Antonio until 1997, received an award of $2.2 million from a panel of arbitrators this spring after she complained about harassment and discrimination. In ruling, the arbitrators decided that the statistical evidence proved that there had been a pattern and practice of discrimination against women in Merrill's brokerage operation—the first such finding against a Wall Street firm. ∎

Milken Gets 10 Years For Wall Street Crimes

By **KURT EICHENWALD** | November 22, 1990

MICHAEL R. MILKEN, THE ONCE-POWERFUL financier who came to symbolize a decade of excess, was sentenced to 10 years in prison for violating federal securities laws and committing other crimes.

> "What I did violated not just the law but all of my principles and values."

The sentence, handed down by Federal District Judge Kimba M. Wood in Manhattan, was the longest received by any executive caught up in the Wall Street scandals that began to unfold in 1986, and many legal experts and people on Wall Street expressed surprise at its severity.

After Mr. Milken serves his term he faces a three-year period of probation. Mr. Milken, who paid $600 million in fines and restitution when he pleaded guilty to the violations, will also be required to perform 1,800 hours of community service during each of three years of probation, or a total of 5,400 hours.

Judge Wood said the former financier had to be sentenced to a long jail term to send a message to the financial community. "When a man of your power in the financial world, at the head of the most important department of one of the most important investment banking houses in this country, repeatedly conspires to violate, and violates, securities and tax laws in order to achieve more power and wealth for himself and his wealthy clients, and commits financial crimes that are particularly hard to detect, a significant prison term is required," she said.

As head of the "junk bond" operations of Drexel Burnham Lambert Inc., which collapsed earlier this year, Mr. Milken financed some of the largest corporate takeovers in the 1980's. He pioneered the use of high-yield, high-risk junk bonds as instruments for corporate warfare, successfully convincing investors that the bonds' high returns more than compensated for the risk that the issuers would default.

The sentence came at the end of a highly emotional hearing, in which Mr. Milken frequently broke into tears as he listened to one of his lawyers plead for leniency. He made only one comment during the proceeding, tearfully telling Judge Wood: "What I did violated not just the law but all of my principles and values. I deeply regret it, and will for the rest of my life. I am truly sorry." ■

Richard Whitney, 86, Dies; Leader In Stopping '29 Panic Was Jailed in '38 as Embezzler

By **ALBIN KREBS** | December 6, 1974

RICHARD WHITNEY, THE ONE-TIME PRESIDENT of the New York Stock Exchange who was credited with halting the Wall Street panic of 1929 but later went to prison for embezzlement, died yesterday at the home of a daughter in Far Hills, N.J. He was 86 years old.

A descendant of the Pilgrim Fathers and son of a Boston bank president, Mr. Whitney bought a seat on the New York Stock Exchange at the age of 23, and soon became principal broker for J. P. Morgan & Co. Cast as

scandals

Victims Seek a Glimpse Of the Schemer

By **SUSAN DOMINUS** | March 13, 2009

DEBRA SCHWARTZ, 67, MAY BE THE ONE woman in New York City who feels compassion for Bernard L. Madoff. "I just pity him," she said Thursday morning, while waiting in the line outside the courthouse where he later pleaded guilty to bilking investors. "I feel bad for this man who lost all sense of reality."

By 7 a.m., a bustling line was indeed crowding Worth Street outside the courthouse, but it consisted mostly of bleary-eyed journalists hoping to identify, from a telltale cashmere scarf or well-preserved camel hair coat, a Madoff investor who might talk.

Ms. Schwartz, one of the very few Madoff investors who showed up early—she said she lost two-thirds of her retirement savings—was happy to oblige. Though she felt pity for Mr.

the public hero in the halt of the stock panic of 1929, he then served four terms as president of the stock exchange.

But Mr. Whitney, unknown to all his admirers, was a miserably poor manager of his own financial affairs, and as he fell deeper and deeper into debt, he descended into thievery to cover himself.

In 1938, exposed as the embezzler of funds entrusted to him by the stock exchange and the New York Yacht Club, of which he was treasurer, as well as for misappropriating funds from his father-in-law's estate, the one-time hero of Wall Street was sent to Sing Sing Prison.

Mr. Whitney's downfall was one of the most sensational scandals ever to hit Wall Street. It hastened the adoption of drastic reforms governing stock market dealings, long pressed by the Securities and Exchange Commission and resisted by an old-guard clique on the Street whose powerful leader had been Mr. Whitney himself. ∎

Madoff, she clarified, she did not want leniency. "I would love for him to have nothing," she said. "In jail, he'll have food, clothing and shelter, and there will be people who are affected who are going to be out on the street."

Ms. Schwartz had arranged to meet at the courthouse a new friend, Bennett Goldworth. Mr. Goldworth, a formerly retired real estate broker with a master's degree in business, said he had lost $2 million in savings, everything he had. Ahead of them in line was Helen Chaitman, a commercial litigator in her 60s who was hoping to retire in 10 years, but now, having lost all her savings with Mr. Madoff, said she was "looking forward to retiring at 95."

Revelation about Mr. Madoff's scheme did not bring down the financial markets, but they did deepen the sense of crisis, financial and moral, citywide. It was not just that billions of dollars vaporized overnight—it was also that a crime so vast could go undetected. It came to symbolize an era of runaway wealth, a time when the golden coffers were so dazzling they apparently all but blinded the regulators supposed to be keeping guard.

When Bernard Madoff takes up residence behind bars New Yorkers will surely allow themselves another sigh of relief, one step closer to not only law, but also order. ∎

BELOW: *Bernard Madoff pleaded guilty in federal court to all the charges against him on March 12, 2009.*

Dividing Harry Helmsley's Empire

By **DAVID W. DUNLAP** | November 26, 2000

IF HARRY B. HELMSLEY'S BUILDINGS WERE his children, as he liked to say, dozens have found more munificent foster parents in the four years since his death.

The sale of about half the Helmsley properties and leaseholds nationwide has yielded some $2.5 billion. It has also yielded something else: an enormous capital investment in properties that some purchasers say were indifferently managed, if not downright neglected, in the later years of stewardship by Mr. Helmsley and his colleagues Irving Schneider and Alvin Schwartz.

"I'm cheap," Mr. Helmsley allowed in 1982, explaining that he had changed the name of the New York Central Building at 230 Park Avenue to New York General so that he would have to replace only two letters in the facade. (He later rechristened it the Helmsley Building.)

When he died in January 1997 at the age of 87, Mr. Helmsley owned or held at least a minority interest in an astonishing lot: about 35 office, loft and showroom buildings in Manhattan, four in Newark and six in Chicago; more than 25 apartment buildings, including the seven-tower Park West Village on the Upper West Side and the 3,500-unit Parkmerced complex in San Francisco; and 13 Harley hotels in seven states.

And, of course, there is Dunnellen Hall in Greenwich, Conn., the house at the heart of the 1988 tax-fraud case that ended with Mr. Helmsley declared mentally unfit to stand trial and Mrs. Helmsley convicted and sentenced to a four-year prison term.

Larry A. Silverstein, president of Silverstein Properties, is investing more than $60 million in the renovation of one former Helmsley building, at 140 Broadway. By the time Mr. Silverstein bought it in 1998, he said, it "required everything." Building systems needed modernization, asbestos had to be removed and the porous plaza had to be sealed because it was leaking into a tenant's basement space.

"The fact that he retained this huge volume of real estate until his death is nothing short of remarkable," Mr. Silverstein said. "The fact that it is being sold by his estate to be transformed yet again is something that's typical of New York." ∎

Leona Helmsley, Dogs' Best Friend, Left Them Up to $8 Billion

By **STEPHANIE STROM** | July 2, 2008

SURE, THE HOTELIER AND REAL ESTATE magnate Leona Helmsley left $12 million in her will to her dog, Trouble. But that, it turns out, is nothing much compared with what other dogs may receive from the charitable trust of Mrs. Helmsley, who died last August.

Her instructions, specified in a two-page "mission statement," are that the entire trust, valued at $5 billion to $8 billion and amounting to virtually all her estate, be used for the care and welfare of dogs, according to two people who have seen the document and who described it on condition of anonymity.

It is by no means clear that all the money will go to dogs. Another provision of the mission statement says Mrs. Helmsley's trustees may use their discretion in distributing the money, and some lawyers say the statement may not mean much anyway, given that its directions were not

Long, Long Legal Battle for Tall, Tall Building

By **CHARLES V. BAGLI** | December 12, 2001

THREE POWERFUL REAL ESTATE FIGURES— Irving Schneider, Peter L. Malkin and Leona Helmsley—are battling once again for control of the Empire State Building. The squabbling adds to the uncertainty surrounding the status of the 102-story skyscraper and other tall buildings after the 9/11 attack on the World Trade Center.

The skirmish comes as Mr. Malkin is trying to buy the property outright from a Japanese group led by Donald J. Trump for about $60 million.

Naturally, it is all about money. And for now, Mrs. Helmsley, who controls the formidable estate of her husband, Harry B. Helmsley, is siding with Mr. Schneider.

"You've got a real battle going on involving millions and millions of dollars," said Alvin Lane, an investor in the Empire State Building.

Mr. Schneider, whose company manages the landmark skyscraper, filed a lawsuit in State Supreme Court recently against Mr. Malkin, alleging a host of misdeeds in his role as a partner and supervisor of the investment group that owns the master lease for the building. Mr. Schneider, who owns one of 3,330 shares in the group, is seeking to oust Mr. Malkin.

> "You've got a real battle going on involving millions and millions of dollars."

incorporated into Mrs. Helmsley's will or the trust documents.

The two people who described the statement said Mrs. Helmsley signed it in 2003 to establish goals for the multibillion-dollar trust that would disburse assets after her death.

The first goal was to help indigent people, the second to provide for the care and welfare of dogs. A year later, they said, she deleted the first goal.

Mrs. Helmsley, the widow of the real estate developer Harry B. Helmsley, was best known for her sharp tongue and impatience with humanity. She became a household name after she was featured in glossy advertisements for the Helmsley hotels. "It's the only palace in the world where the queen stands guard," advertisements for the Helmsley Palace proclaimed.

But for many Americans, she later became a symbol of unbridled arrogance and belief in entitlement, particularly after she was convicted in 1989 of $1.2 million in federal income tax evasion and was sent to prison. She was the subject of a 1990 television film, "Leona Helmsley: The Queen of Mean," with Suzanne Pleshette in the title role, and at least three books. ▪

The building was bought in the 1990's by a company led by a Japanese businessman, Hideki Yokoi. His daughter then cut a deal with Mr. Trump, in which he would get half of any increased value in the building. The only problem was that under the terms of its lease, the Japanese are entitled to only $2 million a year in rent.

So Mr. Trump secretly backed a small tenants' group that sued, alleging that Mr. Malkin and Mrs. Helmsley had turned the landmark building into a "high-rise slum." But Mr. Trump's five-year legal offensive ultimately failed.

Thomas Dewey, a lawyer for Mr. Malkin, dismissed Mr. Schneider's charges as nonsense. For her part, Mrs. Helmsley said Mr. Malkin "is up to no good." ▪

Blue-Collar Builders Expand Empire To Glitzier Shores

By **CHARLES V. BAGLI** | October 9, 2007

SAMUEL J. LEFRAK, THE VOLUBLE PATRIARCH of New York's most prolific real estate family, often declared, "We serve the mass, not the class," during the five decades he presided over an empire of apartments in sturdy brick buildings from Queens to Manhattan, office towers on both sides of the Hudson River, and oil wells in Louisiana.

Mr. LeFrak died in 2003, and now the family is striking out in a dramatically new direction to serve the class, not the mass. Mr. LeFrak's son, Richard, 62, has reached beyond the New York area to buy office buildings in the Golden Triangle area of Beverly Hills, Calif., and a development site on Hollywood Boulevard for a luxury high-rise apartment building. The LeFrak Organization is also actively hunting for a big development site in London.

> "The capacity to make something from nothing— that's the sex."

Known for boxy, unremarkable buildings, the LeFraks are now using brand-name architects like Arquitectonica to design stylish towers. They also sold 2,000 of their older working-class apartments in Brooklyn and Queens earlier this year for $250 million, and more are headed for the auction block.

"We have a huge amount of assets in this city," Richard LeFrak said during an interview in his blond-wood offices, where the walls are lined with images of the family's buildings and paintings of Sam LeFrak. "It's the best market in the country. But we need diversification. I think L.A. has a lot of pluses."

A genial, straightforward and even-keeled tycoon, he displays none of the noisy flamboyance of his father, but all of the family's work ethic and aversion to high-risk financing. There is little or no debt on the family's holdings: 22 million square feet of residential property, the equivalent of about 25,000 apartments, and 12 million square feet of office space.

Like his father and his sons, Mr. LeFrak said his most satisfaction comes from developing complexes like Newport from the ground up. "The capacity to make something from nothing—that's the sex," Mr. LeFrak said. "The other stuff is kissing." ■

EDITORIAL: Up, and Down, With Donald Trump

June 9, 1990

WHAT'S THE RIGHT WORD, ARROGANCE or audacity?

Is Donald Trump a tarnished golden boy, on his way from riches to rags in a real live morality play? Or is he still the daring risk-taker, maker of magic deals who has simply run into short-term cash problems from which he'll come out stronger than ever?

To many Americans, Donald Trump is both. They are pleased to imagine that, with a little more luck, they could be holding off their creditors, Trump-like, while preparing the next coup. And at 3 a.m., staring at a late-notice mortgage payment reminder, it gives them solace to remember that the famous Donald Trump is also in trouble.

The Donald, people call him now, not many years after he charged out from the shadow of his father, a prosperous Brooklyn builder, with a scheme to revise Manhattan's dormant East 42nd Street. It ended up costing

Real estate

Donald Trump Builds Image As He Buys Buildings

By **JUDY KLEMESRUD** | November 1, 1976

HE IS TALL, LEAN AND BLOND, WITH DAZZLING white teeth, and he looks ever so much like Robert Redford. He rides around town in a chauffeured silver Cadillac, with his initials, DJT, on the plates. He dates slinky fashion models, belongs to the most elegant clubs and, at only 30 years of age, estimates that he is worth "more than $200 million."

Flair. It's one of Donald J. Trump's favorite words, and both he, his friends and his enemies use it when describing his way of

millions more than he could possibly have found alone, but he shrewdly made a tax-abatement, tax-exemption deal with the New York City government, courted the owners of the Hyatt Hotel chain into partnership, acquired the charmless Commodore Hotel at 42nd and Lexington and turned the neighborhood around.

Now he is the owner of three gambling casinos, a shuttle airline, glittering towers, plazas, palaces, and hotels, all of which together were said to be worth $1.5 billion, net of debts, only a few weeks ago.

The Donald has given nonadmirers plenty of reasons for the malicious glee with which they hear of his problems. Good at his business, at every opportunity he tells the world how good. He feels compelled to paint the name TRUMP on every acquisition. He flaunts his possessions: the biggest yacht, the biggest house, the grandest helicopter, and not long ago pronounced his intention of building the tallest building in the world.

Arrogance? For sure, and yet in a world lacking individual heroes, even some of the Donald's critics must confess to a sneaking respect for his insistence on being himself, however outrageous. ■

life as well as his business style as New York's No. 1 real estate promoter.

"If a man has flair," the energetic, outspoken Mr. Trump said the other day, "and is smart and somewhat conservative and has a taste for what people want, he's bound to be successful in New York."

Mr. Trump, who is president of the Brooklyn-based Trump Organization, which owns and manages 22,000 apartments, currently has three imaginative Manhattan realestate projects in the works: a large Manhattan convention center over the Penn Central Transportation Company's 34th Street yards; a 1,500-room Hyatt Regency hotel near Grand Central Terminal; and construction of 14,500 federally subsidized apartments on the Penn Central's 60th Street yards, to which Mr. Trump has acquired the development rights. The site is bounded by West 59th and West 72nd Streets, West End Avenue and the Hudson River.

"What makes Donald Trump so significant right now," said one Manhattan real estate expert, "is that there is nobody else who is a private promoter on a major scale, trying to convince entrepreneurs to develop major pieces of property." ■

BELOW: *Donald Trump, shown here in 1976, is now one of the highest paid personalities on television.*

Finally, the Debut of Wall Street West

By **WINSTON WILLIAMS** | August 25, 1985

BEFORE MAMMOTH REJUVENATION PROJECTS like Manhattan's Battery Park City ignited building booms and changed cityscapes in the nation's downtown areas, it seemed that a deadly cancer was spreading unchecked through urban America.

Only a few years ago, major metropolises were facing financial ruin. Aging industrial slums and dilapidated residential neighborhoods had a choke hold on inner cities, discouraging development. And much of corporate America, complaining about crime and the poorly educated urban labor force, fled to the lush greenery and superior schools of the suburbs.

Manhattan's downtown financial district was as battered by these forces as most others. But now, major corporations like Merrill Lynch, American Express and Dow Jones will soon begin moving into Battery Park City, the bold renewal project that is adding a new dimension to Wall Street.

Conceived in the late 1960's by Gov. Nelson A. Rockefeller and a pet project of his three successors, it is a complex of residential and commercial buildings built on 92 acres of landfill skirting the Hudson River. When it is completed in the next decade, its price tag is likely to be between $3 billion and $4 billion.

> Its commercial space, the World Financial Center, will house 30,000 office workers.

Its commercial space, the World Financial Center, will house 30,000 office workers. Fueled by sharp growth in the financial services industry, the World Financial Center's four glass and granite-sheathed skyscrapers are already 90 percent spoken for.

But its sponsor, Olympia & York, the world's largest privately held real estate developer, had to buy some older downtown buildings to entice tenants to move. ■

Today Is Moving Day for Goldman, Sachs & Co.

April 1, 1957

THIS IS MOVING DAY FOR GOLDMAN, SACHS & Co., the big investment banking concern. It's shifting from 30 Pine Street, home since 1869, to ultra-modern quarters at 20 Broad Street.

The most striking innovation in the new offices is a 16-telephone turret trading desk, designed especially by the New York Telephone Company. It is said to be the first of its kind and size installed anywhere. Unlike the flat keyboards of conventional trading desks, the new phone turrets are vertical to give considerable working space for each trader. Each turret handles 120 direct circuits independently of the firm's main switchboard. In all, they provide 1,920 private lines. Traders can also dial into a circuit on any trading turret for greater flexibility in transacting business.

Goldman, Sachs managed or co-managed underwritings last year with a value of $1.1 billion. Most prominent was the largest corporate issue to date, the first public financing of the Ford Motor Company, $657 million of common stock. The firm was one of the managing underwriters. ■

Can Google Come Out to Play?

By **DEBORAH SCHOENEMAN** | December 31, 2006

THE GAME ROOM AT GOOGLE'S NEW OFFICES in Chelsea was being put to good use. Two engineers were taking a break from coding at the pool table. A programmer in a purple Phish T-shirt was practicing juggling. "Sweet Child O' Mine" by Guns 'N' Roses blasted from the flat-screen television, where two 22-year-olds played Guitar Hero, a video game that lets players strum scaled-down guitars—karaoke without the singing.

Only one guitarist, Aaron Karp, worked for Google. "It's very convenient that he works in such a cool place and invites me over," said Mr. Karp's roommate, Alex Hurst, who works in the breaking news division of CNN. "We don't have this, or Razor scooters, at CNN. It makes me want to work here."

Google started moving its 500-plus employees in New York from a cramped Times Square office to a former Port Authority building on Eighth Avenue last summer. The new office is the company's largest engineering center outside its headquarters in Mountain View, Calif.

From lava lamps to abacuses to cork coffee tables, the offices may as well be a Montessori school conceived to cater to the needs of future science-project winners. The Condé Nast and Hearst corporations have their famous cafeterias designed by, respectively, Frank Gehry and Norman Foster; but Google has free food, and plenty of it, including a sushi bar and espresso stations. There are private phone booths for personal calls and showers and lockers for anyone running or biking to work.

The campus-like workspace is antithetical to the office culture of most New York businesses. It is a vision of a workplace utopia as conceived by rich, young, single engineers in Silicon Valley, transplanted to Manhattan. The New York tradition of leaving the office to network over lunch or an evening cocktail party has no place at Google, where employees are encouraged to socialize among themselves. ■

BELOW: *Google employees blow off steam by playing "Guitar Hero" in the company game room.*

141 Men and Girls Die In Waist Factory Fire

March 26, 1911

THREE STORIES OF A 10-FLOOR BUILDING AT the corner of Greene Street and Washington Place were burned yesterday, and while the fire was going on 141 young men and women—at least 125 of them mere girls—were burned to death or killed by jumping to the pavement below.

Nothing like it has been seen in New York since the burning of the General Slocum. The fire was practically all over in half an hour. It was confined to three floors—the eighth, ninth, and tenth of the building.

The victims were employed at making shirtwaists by the Triangle Waist Company, the principal owners of which are Isaac Harris and Max Blanck. Most of them could barely speak English. Many of them came from Brooklyn. Almost all were the main support of their hard-working families.

There is just one fire escape in the building. That one is an interior fire escape. The building was fireproof, and the owners had put their trust in that.

The girls rushed to the windows and looked down at Greene Street, 100 feet below them. Then one poor, little creature jumped. There was a plate-glass protection over part of the sidewalk, but she crashed through it. Then they all began to drop. The crowd yelled "Don't jump!" but it was jump or be burned—the proof of which is found in the fact that 50 burned bodies were taken from the ninth floor alone.

Messrs. Harris and Blanck were in the building, but they escaped. They carried with them Mr. Blanck's children and a governess, and they fled over the roofs. Their employees did not know the way, because they had been in the habit of using the two freight elevators, and one of these elevators was not in service when the fire broke out. ■

BELOW: *Crowds around the site of the Triangle Shirt Waist fire in 1911. The factory was inside what is now the Brown Building of Science, which is located in Greenwich Village.*

Labor Marking 75th Anniversary Of Triangle Shirtwaist Fire

By **WILLIAM SERRIN** | March 25, 1986

IT LASTED 18 MINUTES.

"I was just fixing my hair and putting on my coat," said Pauline Cuoio Pepe, 94, a sewing machine operator who is one of three remaining known survivors of the fire at the Triangle Shirtwaist Company. When she saw the flames, she ran.

"There were about 100 people right next to the door," she said, "but it was closed."

Doors were locked, said Mrs. Pepe, who resides in Broadlawn Nursing Home in Amityville, L.I. "We saw people throwing themselves out the window, but I said, 'I wouldn't do it,'" she recalled in an interview with Justice, the newspaper of the International Ladies Garment Workers Union. "We went down the steps."

The tragedy brought workplace health and safety laws. It generated reform that led two decades later in passage of New Deal legislation. It shaped views of a generation, among them Alfred E. Smith, later governor of New York; Frances Perkins, who would become secretary of labor in the Roosevelt Administration; and Senator Robert F. Wagner, an architect of the National Labor Relations Act of 1935, still the foundation of union rights.

The fire brought the idea "that government has a responsibility, that there are things the boss and the union can't do," said Leon Stein, the author of "The Triangle Fire," a definitive account.

Triangle, owned by Isaac Harris and Max Blanck, was the nation's largest manufacturer of the shirtwaist-style blouse, a popular, closely fitted garment with long sleeves and buttons to the neck.

They were acquitted of manslaughter, and the company, which ultimately faded out of existence, received $64,925 more in insurance benefits than claims for which they could prove loss; Mr. Stein said it was a profit of $445 for each of the 146 victims. A few, small settlements were made with workers' families. ■

New York, Cradle of Labor History

By **STEVEN GREENHOUSE** | August 30, 1996

NEW YORK MAY BE NOTORIOUS FOR BULL-dozing over its history, but somehow the wrecking ball has spared many sites that served as crucibles for labor. Not far from Manhattan in-spots like the Union Square Cafe and CBGB's, not far from the Bowery and Orchard Street, many of the nation's epic labor battles took place.

Probably the best place to start a tour is the site of the Triangle Shirtwaist Factory, east of Washington Square at the northwest corner of Washington Place and Greene Street. New York University now uses the stately building for biology and chemistry studies. The only hint of the place's history comes from two plaques, one from the International Ladies' Garment Workers Union reading: "Out of their martyrdom came new concepts of social responsibility and labor legislation."

Head next to the JEFFERSON MARKET COURTHOUSE, now a public library, at the Avenue of the Americas and West 10th Street.

BELOW: *Jefferson Market Courthouse was made a National Historic Landmark in 1977 and now is used as a branch of the New York Public Library.*

Here the police dragged hundreds of female strikers arrested during the Uprising of the 20,000. The workers went on strike to protest low wages, the requirement that they pay for their needles and thread, and favoritism toward compliant workers. Mrs. August Belmont once sat up all night in this courthouse and put up her palatial Madison Avenue mansion as collateral to get several strikers out of jail pending trial.

Nearby are two picturesque cul-de-sacs, PATCHIN PLACE (off West 10th Street, between Greenwich Avenue and the Avenue of the Americas) and MILLIGAN PLACE (on the Avenue of the Americas between West 10th and 11th Streets). Here, rooming houses were built around 1850 for the Basque waiters at the Brevoort Hotel on Fifth Avenue. Patchin Place's tenants included E. E. Cummings, Theodore Dreiser and John Reed, the Harvard dropout turned radical who chronicled the Russian Revolution in the book "Ten Days That Shook the World."

Next is UNION SQUARE, which contrary to popular belief is not named after labor unions. Even so, New York's first Labor Day Parade was held here in 1882, when 25,000 people under a Knights of Labor banner marched for an eight-hour day and a ban on child labor. In 1930, 35,000 demonstrators protested the Depression and clashed with the police here, leaving 100 people injured.

Union Square has been the home of the Amalgamated Clothing and Textile Workers Union and the Amalgamated Bank, the nation's first labor-owned bank, the Communist Party and its newspaper, The Daily Worker.

Next, walk to 208-210 East 13th Street, an orange-brick tenement where Emma Goldman, the anarchist and advocate of free love, lived from 1903 to 1913. Her lover Alexander Berkman tried to assassinate Henry Clay Frick, the steel magnate, during the 1892 Homestead steel strike near Pittsburgh.

Head to WEBSTER HALL, at 119 East 11th Street, where Woody Guthrie sang on

David Dubinsky, 90, Dies; Led Garment Union

September 18, 1982

DAVID DUBINSKY, FORMER PRESIDENT OF THE International Ladies Garment Workers Union and an influential labor leader for more than three decades, died yesterday at St. Vincent's Hospital in Manhattan after a long illness. He was 90 years old and lived in Manhattan.

With extraordinary flair and boundless energy, Mr. Dubinsky was the major force in converting a union that was on the verge of bankruptcy in 1932 into a dynamic organization that had $500 million in assets in behalf of unions in the 1930's and where earlier the Socialist magazine The Masses held fund-raising balls. Walk next to TOMPKINS SQUARE PARK, at 10th Street and Avenue A. In the recession of 1874, 6,000 protesters from the Workingmen's Party gathered to hear New York's mayor, William F. Havemeyer, speak about helping the unemployed. When he failed to appear and the police declared the rally illegal, the protesters clashed with the police, injuring hundreds of officers. Samuel Gompers cowered in a doorway nearby, and it is said that the riot turned him away from radical unionism.

Then walk along St. Marks Place to COOPER UNION, founded in 1859 by Peter Cooper, the philanthropist who made the first rolled steel railroad tracks and helped Samuel Morse lay the first Atlantic telegraph cable. Cooper created this school to provide free art and technology education to working people. In 1860, Abraham Lincoln gave a major address in the school's Great Hall. In 1909, Gompers led an emotional meeting of shirtwaist workers that authorized the Uprising of the 20,000. "There comes a time," he said, "when not to strike is but to rivet the chains of slavery upon our wrists." ■

1966, when he became its honorary president.

The influence of Mr. Dubinsky, a short man with gray crew-cut hair, extended well beyond his union. He played a major role in the formation of the Committee for Industrial Organization, forerunner of the Congress of Industrial Organizations, in the mid-1930's; he was the first head of an American Federation of Labor union to demand action against organized racketeering in unions; he pushed labor toward greater social responsibility, and he was for many years one of the forces behind the Liberal Party in New York.

Mr. Dubinsky, whose personality was once described as ranging from "that of global statesman to that of a dead-end kid," was sometimes captious, sometimes overbearing, but always able to bring high drama into every report and talk.

He never lost his Yiddish accent, his tendency to wave his arms at the slightest provocation or his loud voice, which started as a shout and went up from there.

Under his leadership, the I.L.G.W.U. accumulated a long list of firsts. Among them were the publication of financial statements long before it was legally required, the establishment of research and engineering departments to improve the efficiency of the garment trade and the creation of educational and cultural programs for thousands of members.

Perhaps Mr. Dubinsky's most notable achievement was in bringing a standard 35-hour week to a sweatshop industry that was in a constant state of chaos. The union was less successful, however, in establishing high wage levels in New York and other garment centers in the Northeast.

Prof. Joel Seidman of the University of Chicago said that under Mr. Dubinsky "the union itself changed from a radical organization with a Socialist goal into one of more moderate tendencies, advocating reform within the context of private enterprise." ■

100,000 Men and Women Fill The Apparel Needs of the World

By **DANIEL LANG** | November 5, 1939

BUSINESS RECOVERY WHICH HAS COME WITH the autumn will find few more enthusiastic celebrants than those employers and workers concerned with New York's half-billion dollar dress business, the largest industry in the city.

New York's—and the nation's—apparel capital occupies an area of six or seven blocks. If the visitor enters one of the garment center's factories, he will come upon the buzz of high-speed sewing machines, designers creating new fashions, finishers sewing on buttons and belts and pressers ironing out the still-wrinkled dresses.

Somewhat over 100,000 metropolitan inhabitants make their living answering the apparel needs of this worldwide market. At least another 20,000 are engaged in such neighboring trades as the manufacture of buttons, belts, artificial flowers and buckles.

Yet wholesale dressmaking is by no means a very old industry. Immigrants who found refuge here went into the needle trades. Like the pioneers of an earlier day, they were confronted with great obstacles. Theirs was the wilderness of sweatshop and firetrap.

On a fateful day 28 years ago the conditions under which they worked were dramatized in a frightful fire. Sheer chance picked out a place called the Triangle Shirt and Waist Company. The Triangle fire did not take long—just 15 tragic minutes. But that was long enough. One hundred forty-six young bodies lay charred in Washington Place.

Today conditions are very different. Impressive fireproof, day-light factories stand in Triangle's stead. The union runs a health center. The day's working hours have dwindled to seven, the week's days to five. In non-slack seasons, every worker makes at least $31.50 each week.

Before dress manufacturing could emerge from its wallowing sweatshop stage, it had to solve the vexing problem of seemingly endless strikes and lockouts. So successful has the garment industry's method of settling

ABOVE: *Seamstresses and tailors fashion coats to fill numerous orders at Originala Inc, a former maker of women's clothing in Manhattan.*

capital-labor difficulties proved, that it has been imitated far beyond the borders of Manhattan. Within those borders fully a quarter-million manufacturers and employees in some half-dozen industries have achieved peaceful relations along lines modeled after the arbitration set-up of the dress business. ∎

Buttonholes to Go

By **N.R. KLEINFIELD** | January 17, 1993

WHEN YOU'RE IN MELVIN REICH'S BEAT-UP shop and just sort of gazing at the people lined up, you see a lot of clothing that seems to have nothing in common but actually does. The other afternoon there was an indigo dress, an ocher pair of pants, a woman's bright-orange coat that you had to wonder who would wear, a lime shirt and a tiny lavender sweater that was probably for someone no more than about 3. Try to get into any of these items and it would

Beene Gives His Regards To Seventh Avenue

By **BERNADINE MORRIS** | January 8, 1991

GEOFFREY BEENE SAID FAREWELL TO Seventh Avenue last week after laboring in the turbulent center of the garment district for more than 30 years. About 8 a.m. the day after New Year's, after a vacation in Hawaii, he stopped in to say goodbye to the people who will continue working in his old showroom at 550 Seventh Avenue. Then he headed uptown to his new salon at 37 West 57th Street.

Sleekly sophisticated with lacquered black furniture, silver walls and black and white marble floors, it will be the kickoff site for his new approach to global fashion. This is where he will create his new collections, deal with his growing group of private customers, make plans for projected boutiques in Paris and Vienna and handle the overflow from his tiny shop, his first experience in retailing, which opened a year ago at 783 Fifth Avenue, in the Sherry-Netherland Hotel.

"Seventh Avenue was good to me," said the designer, who opened his own company there in 1963.

In recent years he has been widely acclaimed as this country's most adventurous designer, second to none in inventing new ways to cut cloth. Among his ground rules: clothes must be comfortable; fabrics must be lightweight; there are no retro designs and no place for astonishment for its own sake.

> "Seventh Avenue was good to me," said the designer.

"What I am always trying to do is to idealize a woman's form, never to vulgarize it or to expose it," he said. "Designing is an architectural problem. You are faced with a piece of crepe or wool, the flattest thing in the world, and you have to mold it into the shape you want. Clothing is nothing until it hits the body. The body gives it shape."

The serenity of his new salon with its Art Deco overtones will be conducive to his work, he believes. "If I get stuck, I have the continuing theater that is New York for inspiration right outside my window," he said. ∎

be awkward. They were without buttonholes. That alone was why they were here.

"Buttonholes are what we do," Mr. Reich said crisply. "I am specialized, like the doctors. The one who takes care of the throat does not take care of the eyes. I take care of the buttonholes."

He is a spry 68, and by now he knows that his is ultimately dark and desperate work only for the ardent-hearted, for there is not much hope for arcane specialists anymore when clothing can be made cheaper on foreign soil or by nonunion low-wage labor. Emissaries from Bill Blass, Geoffrey Beene, Ralph Lauren,

Oscar de la Renta and Albert Nippon still regularly troop to Mr. Reich's unprepossessing quarters for some of their buttonholes. There used to be 2,000 or more buttonholes a day, while now a very active day means 1,000.

Fashion is about a lot of things, and it is always easier to focus on the big and ignore the little, but what is a garment without the small touches? For instance, no fine blouse is fine, no suit absolutely perfect, without a good buttonhole.

Mrs. Reich elaborates: "You think it's nothing. Just a buttonhole. But it's something. It's not nothing." ∎

Syndicate Plans New Diamond Center

July 10, 1958

PLANS FOR A DIAMOND CENTER AT 49 TO 55 West 47th Street, between Fifth Avenue and the Avenue of the Americas (Sixth Avenue), were announced yesterday by Philip Gelfand, an attorney. He represents a syndicate that has taken a 99-year lease on the property.

Mr. Gelfand said the four brownstone houses occupying a plot 80 by 100 feet would be demolished soon. Preliminary plans being considered by the syndicate include one for a two-story building.

Forty-seventh Street is expanding rapidly as a jewelry and diamond district, according to the attorney. He cited as an example of rising land values there the recent sale of a plot 20 by 100 feet for more than $200,000. ∎

Diamonds Are Forever (Until Nightfall)

By **STEVEN KURUTZ** | January 29, 2006

IF YOU WORK IN THE DIAMOND DISTRICT, where spectacular robberies seem to occur every couple of months, it is necessary to take certain security measures. According to Jack Grant, who is better known as Jack of Diamonds and has been selling jewels on West 47th Street since the 1970's, you need a good safe, security cameras, a gun and, if one judges by Mr. Grant's eternally arched eyebrow, a general mistrust of everyone.

It also helps to have well-developed spatial skills and a tolerance of routine, because to foil thieves, storeowners pack up their wares every night, leaving their display windows looking empty and forlorn. If you wander through the diamond district between 6 p.m. and 9 a.m., you might think that the entire operation had up and folded. That is, until the morning, when dealers unpack the jewels and lay them out again.

"First thing you do is look to see if everything is still there," said Mr. Grant, standing behind a glass counter on a recent morning and inspecting the contents of a brass-colored floor safe. Everything was: rings in trays stacked atop one another like egg cartons; loose stones wrapped in paraffin paper and tucked inside white envelopes; gold necklaces stretched across display boards, a small fortune of jewelry given the flea-market treatment. Thousands of these items are laid out each morning in the space of 20 minutes.

"In a store in Westchester, they might display their items nicely," Mr. Grant said. "Here, you just schlep it out" to the display windows. Mr. Grant, 61, has schlepped out his merchandise about 7,000 times in his lifetime. At one point, in the early 80's, he sold gold finery to R & B stars ("I had the Commodores") and the occasional Times Square pimp.

At 4:30, Mr. Grant and his three part-time employees began packing up. In his younger days, he might have stayed open a little longer to catch a late customer. Now he likes to leave by 5. He and his assistants made quick work of the jewelry, stacking the trays inside the safe as if they were packing a miniature U-Haul for an important move.

By 5, the store was dark and the front window empty, except for an oversized playing card—a Jack of Diamonds—and a sign that read, "We buy diamond and gold jewelry." ∎

William Goldberg, 77, Dies; A Trader in Rare Diamonds

By **DOUGLAS MARTIN** | October 26, 2003

By **DOUGLAS MARTIN** | October 26, 2003

WILLIAM GOLDBERG, A LEADER OF MANHATtan's diamond district known both for dealing in some of the biggest diamonds sold in modern times and for trying to lift his industry's historic veil of secrecy, died Monday at his apartment in Manhattan. He was 77.

The cause was pancreatic cancer, Barry Berg, his son-in-law, said.

Modern Jeweler magazine in 1990 said Mr. Goldberg was the first gem dealer to find fame while remaining part of 47th Street, as the diamond-littered block-long stretch on the West Side is internationally known. A buzzing, cluttered bazaar of wholesalers, retailers and everybody in between, it lies between Fifth and Sixth Avenues.

The magazine said that industry giants like Harry Winston and Lazare Kaplan either bypassed the street or rose above it. Mr. Goldberg not only stayed but also served three terms as president of the Diamond Dealers Club, where billions of dollars worth of diamonds are exchanged every year on the strength of a handshake and the Yiddish expression "mazel und brucha," meaning luck and a blessing.

"He wields the greatest influence ever of any United States diamond dealer," the magazine said.

Mr. Goldberg's voice was heard on matters from security on 47th Street to "conflict diamonds" in Africa, but his greatest fame came from quietly buying and selling some of the world's biggest and best gems—and then, of course, talking vociferously about the deals to anybody who would listen.

In the 1970's, there was the Queen of Holland diamond, part of a necklace once owned by an Indian maharajah. Mr. Goldberg found it in a Swiss bank vault and bought it, in an episode he described as "right out of the movies" in an interview with Newsday in 1991.

Then there was the 353.9-carat rough diamond he picked off a conveyor belt at a South African diamond mine. It was cut into

ABOVE: *Diamond dealer William Goldberg in his shop at 20 West 47th Sreet in 1978.*

three flawless diamonds, including a 137-carat pear-shaped gem known as the Premier Rose, which sold in 1989 for $10 million, a price many believe was the most ever paid for a diamond, then or possibly ever.

Mr. Goldberg was celebrated for the colors of his diamonds as well as for their size. The rarest are red, and he sold the largest flawless red diamond known, the 5.11-carat Red Shield. His famous Pumpkin gem was a vivid orange and had a finished weight of 5.54 carats.

Laurence Graff, one of the world's largest diamond dealers, said in an interview that Mr. Goldberg was unusual because he would shave off more of the stone to improve the gem's appearance, even though a lighter stone fetched a lower price.

"He loved every stone he handled," Mr. Graff said. ▪

Publishing on Fifth Avenue
What E. P. Dutton Contributed to American Literary Enterprise

By **ALLEN SINCLAIR WILL** | December 23, 1923

MIDDLE FIFTH AVENUE HAS BECOME THE literary Rialto of America, the grand arena of successes and failures in authorship and publishing, and the dean of a group of daring leaders of the book industry who made it such passed away only recently. Edward Payson Dutton, who died Sept. 6 at the age of nearly 93 years, was a link between a half-forgotten day when Boston held up her queenly head as the mistress of letters on this side of the Atlantic, and these new times when the writer's door of fame is planted firmly in the rocky soil of Manhattan Island.

Much more than half of the total publishing in the United States and fully 95 percent of the strictly literary publishing is now done in New York City, the largest proportion in this small district. When Mr. Dutton, coming from Boston, set out to realize his ambitions here, this district had none of the character of a great literary mart which it possesses today.

As early as 1874 E. P. Dutton & Co. had printed 700 books. Soon afterward came Mr. Dutton's first success with a "best seller." It was characteristic of the kind of books that he preferred to publish that this was Canon (afterward Dean) Farrar's "Life of Christ." Other publishers had turned it down on the ground that there were too many works of the same kind on the market. One of them told Mr. Dutton later that it made him heartsick to contemplate his own mistake of judgment. ■

A Vision for Books That Exults In Happenstance

By **DINITIA SMITH** | January 13, 2001

IT IS SOMETIMES SAID OF JASON EPSTEIN, the longtime editorial director of Random House now in retirement, that he has had four great ideas in his life.

One: At 22 he invented the high-quality paperback in the form of Anchor Books. Two: In 1963, during the New York newspaper strike, he had the idea for The New York Review of Books. Three: In 1982 he created the Library of America with its definitive editions of American classics, conceived earlier with Edmund Wilson at the Princeton Club while Wilson drank a half-dozen martinis. Four: In 1986 Mr. Epstein invented the Reader's Catalog to market books directly to readers, a precursor of Amazon.com.

And now, perhaps, Mr. Epstein has a fifth: that the World Wide Web, contrary to gloomy predictions, may be the best thing to happen to literature and book publishing since Gutenberg. While publishers tear their hair out over slender profit margins and worry that the Internet will be the end of books as people know them, Mr. Epstein says he believes that the Web will save the book business, enable books to be published more cheaply, and bring bigger royalties for corporations and authors.

For most of his time in publishing, Mr. Epstein has been part of the intellectual elite that defined the city's cultural horizons. Looking ahead, he posits a utopian universe in which books will be ordered from the Internet and printed on demand by A.T.M.-like

PUBLISHING

German Media Giant Will Buy Random House for $1.4 Billion

By **DOREEN CARVAJAL** | March 24, 1998

BERTELSMANN A.G., THE GERMAN MEDIA conglomerate, struck an estimated $1.4 billion agreement to buy the shiny crown jewel of American publishing, Random House, in a deal that will solidify Bertelsmann's claim that it is the world's largest English-language publisher of trade books.

By merging its Bantam Doubleday Dell division with Advance Publications' Random House, Bertelsmann will increase to 10 percent from nearly 6 percent its share of the $21 billion book market in the United States, which ranges from Bibles to mass-market paperbacks.

Half of the top 20 American publishing houses, with a 28 percent share of the total market in the United States, are now in foreign hands.

The announcement by Bertelsmann executives in Germany surprised executives in the gossipy world of New York publishing. "It's as if the New York Yankees were sold," said Paul Aiken, the executive director of the Authors Guild, which represents more than 7,200 published authors. "Our fear is that with this sort of situation they're going to look for efficiencies and some ways to cut costs."

> Half of the top 20 American publishing houses . . .
> are now in foreign hands.

The deal further heightens the power of Bertelsmann, which ranks as the world's third-largest media conglomerate, behind Walt Disney and Time Warner. It already owns the RCA and Arista record labels, and magazines like McCall's and Family Circle. In addition, the company recently announced plans to create an online venture to sell books that would challenge the two Internet leaders, Amazon.com and Barnes & Noble.

The secret negotiations for Random House—and its highly desirable backlist of classics by authors from James Joyce to Dr. Seuss—started in mid-November when Bertelsmann's chief executive-elect, Thomas Middlehoff, approached S. I. Newhouse Jr., the chairman of Advance Publications, during a celebration of his 70th birthday.

For months, Bertelsmann executives had made public their goals to buy an American company to expand into the United States. Mr. Middlehoff, a rising star who will become chief executive in October, had moved temporarily to the United States several months ago to learn more about the American side of Bertelsmann's publishing operations and to improve his English.

"I came here to study English and instead I bought a company," joked Mr. Middlehoff, 44. ■

machines, doing away with middlemen and resulting in lower costs for readers.

"There will be no shelf space problem," he said. "The publisher doesn't buy paper, order a printing, ship books to retail stores. He doesn't need a sales force." In this view Barnes & Noble and Amazon.com, unprofitable because their businesses still require middlemen, will become brokers of books.

With the innovations Mr. Epstein foresees on the Web, publishing will become a cottage industry once again. In his vision books will not disappear and neither will bookstores, which will become local shrines, still redolent with the smell of paper and glue.

"I've never been wrong about the future of the business," Mr. Epstein said. "It sounds boastful. But it's not boastful to tell the truth." ■

Editorial:
Mr. Pulitzer and The World

May 10, 1908

THE TRANSFORMATION WHICH MR. JOSEPH Pulitzer has wrought in The New York World since it passed into his ownership and control 25 years ago today justifies the ceremonies of rejoicing and commemoration with which our neighbor marks its anniversary. From a newspaper of small circulation and little influence there has been developed by his energy and under his directing mind a great property, one of the chief newspapers of the world, an effective force for right and sound things in public affairs, a salutary influence in the community, a journal that, in the broad lines of its policy and its effort, stands for what right-minded men ought to think and desire, for what good citizens do think and desire. To a multitude of good causes The World has lent and is continually lending its great influence.

> To a multitude of good causes The World has lent and is continually lending its great influence.

Mr. Pulitzer has exhibited a veritable creative genius in newspaper making. In a degree quite unusual in journalism, The World is his personal work; it is what he has sought to make it, what he has with great ability, unsparing labor, and infinite painstaking actually made it. The Times heartily joins in the congratulations he receives today. ∎

The New York Times Introduces A Web Site

By **PETER H. LEWIS** | January 22, 1996

THE NEW YORK TIMES BEGINS PUBLISHING daily on the World Wide Web today, offering readers around the world immediate access to most of the daily newspaper's contents.

The New York Times on the Web, as the electronic publication is known, contains most of the news and feature articles from the current day's printed newspaper, classified advertising, reporting that does not appear in the newspaper, and interactive features including the newspaper's crossword puzzle.

The electronic newspaper (address: http:/www.nytimes.com) is part of a strategy to extend the readership of The Times and to create opportunities for the company in the electronic media industry, said Martin Nisenholtz, president of The New York Times Electronic Media Company.

The company, formed in 1995 to develop products for the rapidly growing field of digital publishing, is a wholly owned subsidiary of The New York Times Company, and also produces The Times service on America Online Inc.

"Our site is designed to take full advantage of the evolving capabilities offered by the Internet," said Arthur Sulzberger Jr., publisher of The Times. "We see our role on the Web as being similar to our traditional print role—to act as a thoughtful, unbiased filter and to provide our customers

newspapers

In 1900, Readers in New York Had A Choice of 15 Newspapers

By **PHILIP H. DOUGHERTY** | August 16, 1966

IN 1900 THE READING PUBLIC IN NEW YORK had a choice of 15 daily newspapers of general circulation. The list has now dropped to four.

Yesterday The Herald Tribune joined the newspapers relegated to history by mergers and failures—papers such as The Globe, The Commercial Advertiser, The Press, The Sun, The American and The Mirror. During the 66 years there were papers that came and went—The Daily Graphic, 1924–32; The Daily Mirror, 1924–63; PM, 1940–48; The Star, 1948–49; and The Daily Compass, 1949–52. One that came and prospered was The Daily News, founded in 1919.

Twelve of the 15 dailies that were on the newsstands at the turn of the century were represented in last spring's merger of The Herald Tribune, Hearst's Journal-American and Scripps Howard's World-Telegram and The Sun. The other papers on the stands were a five-year-old paper called The Daily News that was to perish in 1905; The Post, founded in 1801 and now the city's oldest paper; and The New York Times, founded in 1851.

"The most sensational merger in an era of mergers"—that is what Frank Luther Mott in his book "American Journalism" called the 1931 consolidation of Roy W. Howard's Telegram with Joseph Pulitzer's World and Evening World. Mr. Pulitzer had died 20 years earlier.

The merger of The Journal and The American in 1937 was an all-Hearst consolidation.

Things were quiet on the merger front until 1950 when The World Telegram took over The Sun, the newspaper that had been made great by Charles A. Dana.

The next newspaper death, and the last until yesterday, was that of Hearst's morning tabloid, The Mirror, which was bought by The Daily News. The Mirror had had the city's second-largest circulation after The News. That was in 1963 following the winter of the 114-day newspaper strike. ◾

with information they need and can trust."

With its entry on the Web, The Times is hoping to become a primary information provider in the computer age and to cut costs for newsprint, delivery and labor. Companies that have established Web-based information sites include television networks, computer companies, online information services, magazines and even individuals creating electronic newspapers of their own.

"The New York Times name will get people to look at the product once or maybe twice, and the fact that The New York Times has the kind of reach and credibility it does may persuade people to look three or four times," said John F. Kelsey III, president of the Kelsey Group, a consulting firm. "The market is booming for newspapers on the World Wide Web." ◾

BELOW: *New York's top five newspapers have a combined circulation of 5 million copies daily.*

In Defense of Madison Avenue

By **JAMES KELLY** | December 23, 1956

LIKE HOLLYWOOD, WALL STREET AND Broadway, Madison Avenue is known by the companies it keeps. Like them also, Madison Avenue has been dreamed about, written about, lied about—and become a label. It is, last of all, a narrow thoroughfare running from 23rd Street to the Harlem River on the east side of Manhattan and peopled during the daylight hours by messenger boys, chic office girls, and level-eyed executives with undented hats and shiny shoes. First of all, it is the accepted capital of a community of 45,000 advertising people (about 25,000 of them in New York City alone) who have been entrusted by hardheaded big and little businessmen with the spending of an estimated $10 billion in 1956. By popular consent, it is the voice, image and brandmark of our own free enterprise. Or by not-so-popular consent.

Madison Avenue these days is under sharp indictment. Advertising is America's pagan religion, the Account Executive for Indictments says, and it forces a fantastically false way of life through expert use of its own Golden Rule: "We have something to sell and we can make you buy it." Tantalized and tempted by dreamworld pictures dangled before them, the victims of Madison Avenue have an itchy urge to buy now and pay later. They mortgage their futures in installment buying.

It is shocking (the indictment goes) that nobody seems to care whether an advertising campaign is good or bad for the country. It is all a numbers game, with virtuoso agency men playing the public like a piano. Headlines with a benefit twist, short copy and shorter ideas designed to fit the reader's attention span, illustrations that people can identify themselves with—the tired old one-two-three pitch for the mass audience.

And here's that bright new medium, television, operating in exactly the same way. On behalf of a television client, an agency will prepare hard-sell commercials and frame them in an elaborate show supplied full-blown by one of the super-specialist television package companies. And success or failure depends upon how many people saw the show (reported by hocus-pocus ratings), not upon how many enjoyed it. The same success or failure applies to politics as well as products. Madison Avenue sells ideologies and candidates just as it sells soap, in quantity and by advertised brands. All right. ∎

Madison Avenue Likes What It Sees In the Mirror

By **STUART ELLIOTT** | June 23, 2008

A TELEVISION SERIES ABOUT AN ADVERTISING agency in the 1960s may be generating almost as much buzz on Madison Avenue as the three-martini lunch once did.

The series, "Mad Men," is inspiring commercials; designer fashions; window displays in department stores; merchandise like cigarette lighters, CDs and calendars; and a mock issue of the trade publication Advertising Age.

The series was even the subject of an $8,000 question on a recent episode of "Who Wants to Be a Millionaire," asking which business "Mad Men" is about. When a contestant asked the audience for help, 86 percent answered correctly.

The impact of the show is indicative of the constant interplay between advertising and popular culture, which is intensified because of its setting. "Mad Men" tells stories inside a fictitious New York agency, Sterling Cooper, that are about not only how the industry was

advertising

Selling New York as the Place to Be

By **PHILIP H. DOUGHERTY** | June 28, 1977

THE MOST AMBITIOUS AND EXTENSIVE ADVER-tising program ever undertaken to make New York State a tourist mecca broke last night on TV in 20 markets in and around the state.

"I love New York," shouts a woman from West Virginia and men from New Hampshire, Massachusetts and Brooklyn, filmed in a variety of beautiful locations by Mike Zingale, director-cameraman. The background music, as a camera zooms around the Finger Lakes, Niagara Falls, Fire Island, Lake Placid,

Whiteface Mountain and other scenic spots, is a new song, "I Love New York," by Steve Karmen.

The State Commerce Department, working with an unprecedented $4.3 million budget, is mounting a five-week media blitz to establish the state in vacationers' minds as the place to be. Wells, Rich, Greene is the agency.

The TV commercials, a 30-second spot for use in prime time and a 60-second version for fringe, went into production about six weeks ago, when an agency team went to check out locations scouted by the production company, Lou Puopolo Inc.

The creative work is based on the results of a consumer study conducted by Consumer Behavior. Among many other things, it showed that New York had the lowest awareness as a vacation spot of any state. The marketing game plan calls for the state and the city to be promoted separately. The advertising for the Big Apple starts in September, using the same song, "I Love New York." ∎

five decades ago but also meatier subjects like the price of success and how far America has—or has not—come on issues like gender, race and religion.

"It's a mirror on ourselves from another time," said John Nuzzi, senior vice president and group director for entertainment at the Los Angeles office of Initiative, part of the Interpublic Group of Companies.

Lionsgate, which produces "Mad Men," is sponsoring a make-believe issue of Advertising Age, a 16-page ad section in the actual June 23 issue. The idea was the brainchild of Initiative, the Lionsgate media agency.

The ad supplement is designed to resemble how Advertising Age looked in 1960, when the first season of "Mad Men" is set. One highlight is an imaginary interview with the main character, a conflicted creative director named Don Draper. (The executive producer, Matthew Weiner, provides the answers.)

Interspersed with the faux articles in the ad section, which cover plotlines from "Mad Men" as if they actually happened, there are articles carrying headlines like "How TV Alters U.S. Elections" (after the Kennedy-Nixon presidential race) and "Auto Sales Hitting 6.6 Million" (compared with 16.15 million last year). ∎

BELOW: *Looking down onto Madison Avenue from the offices of advertising agency Young & Rubicam.*

Melancholy Pervades Wanamaker Staff in the Final Days

By **MEYER BERGER** | December 17, 1954

THE DIGNIFIED RETAIL ESTABLISHMENT founded by Alexander Turney Stewart, first of the city's great merchant princes, will close its doors forever at 4 o'clock tomorrow afternoon. The store has been an institution at Broadway and Ninth Street—as Stewart's from 1862 to 1904 and since as John Wanamaker's.

What is left of the department store's stock will go to S. Klein's or to some other shop that disposes of remainders. Several such establishments have put in bids.

Unfortunately, though, there probably will be nowhere near the same lively bidding for the services of a good part of 200 older men and women who have served Wanamaker's for a quarter century or more.

The New York State Employment Service put 13 of its hands at desks on the store's 12th floor a week ago and registered 800 Wanamaker employees who are still fairly young and have good job prospects. Many of the older folk did not go near the desks. They stayed at their counters, shocked and hurt.

And there seemed to be something unthinking and pitiless in the rush of buyers eager to snatch bargains at 30 percent off. They emptied the bins and showcases and denuded most of the counters.

You couldn't find out what will become of the old store with its pale-green columns, softly lighted white ceilings, lovely old murals, its long-empty and long-silent auditorium where the carriage trade came to pipe organ concerts long ago. Only here and there did the despair show. One bit of evidence was the scrawl on one office wall: "Sic Transit Gloria." ∎

A Bittersweet Finale for Gimbels

By **ELIZABETH KOLBERT** | September 28, 1986

EVERYONE, IT IS SAID, LOVES A SALE. So when a store slashes its prices 40, 60 and, in some cases, 80 percent, one could expect to see a lot of euphoric faces rummaging through the racks.

But when the store is Gimbels at Herald Square, a New York shopping institution for 76 years, and the sale is in honor of its last day of business, even an inveterate bargain hunter might feel glum.

"It's like seeing someone get buried," said Irving Zand of Brooklyn, who was testing a chair of uncertain stability down in the basement. Mr. Zand's wife, Helen, described him lovingly as "a real shopper."

"It was an ugly death," Mr. Zand said, casting a sad eye over the desolate scene of empty shelves, unhappy sales clerks and rickety furniture. "Gimbels was a good store. It was a nice store."

The two Manhattan stores—the flagship, on 33rd Street at the Avenue of the Americas, and the other at 86th Street and Lexington Avenue—have been sold to a group of developers for "considerably in excess of $150 million," in the words of one of the purchasers. The developers—a partnership among Silverstein Properties Inc., the Zeckendorf Company of New York and Melvin Simon Associates of Indianapolis—said they planned to maintain a retail center on the street level of the 33rd

Macy's in Its 100th Year Is Still as Breezy as Ever

By **NAN ROBERTSON** | January 6, 1958

MACY'S IS A CENTURY OLD THIS YEAR, BUT she doesn't look a day over 16.

Sophistication laid a fine veneer on the store as it grew and grew and grew. But underneath, there remained the same bumptious, breezy and slightly breathless personality that keeps Macy's young. Nowhere is this more evident than in the store's advertisements, which have become bigger and certainly better over the years, but hardly less full of hope and confidence.

Rowland Macy opened his "fancy dry goods" shop on 14th Street and Sixth Avenue on Oct. 27, 1858. The first day's sales totaled $11. On the second day, they soared to $51.70.

Less than a month later, while other, older stores murmured discreetly about their "modest prices," Macy's plunged into public view—yelling at the top of its lusty infant lungs.

One of the first ads read: "CHEAP RIBBONS!!! You want them, of course. Go to Macy's. He is now opening 10,000 yards for 12½ cents a yard that are worth 31 cents." He also offered linen cambric handkerchiefs for $1.50 a dozen and "linen bosoms" at 12½ cents apiece.

On Christmas Day 1858, Macy's ad fore-shadowed Madison Avenue's use of constant repetition and the "positive sell." Flannel was the subject, starting at 35 cents a yard.

"Thirty-five cents—for fine, all-wool Flannel," it said. Then: "40 cents—for a little finer Flannel; 45 cents—for still finer Flannel; 50 cents—for much finer Flannel; 55 cents—for a superior Flannel; 60 cents—for much the best Flannel."

The women came in droves.

By 1908 Macy's had moved uptown to 34th Street, where it now stands. The store's slogan—"R. H. Macy & Co.'s Attraction Are Their Low Prices"—was considerably less brisk than the later "It's Smart to Be Thrifty." But it carried the same message. As Macy's explained: "We have never varied a hair's breadth from the original idea that had for its motive—lower prices." ■

Street store and convert the rest of the building to office space.

"It's heartbreaking," said Rose Berlast, 71, who was trying unsuccessfully to negotiate a further reduction in the price of a $350 chest of drawers, which, she pointed out, had deep gashes in the veneer.

"Just look at it," she said.

"Lady, I've been looking at it for three months now," the clerk replied.

It was hard for most shoppers to work up much enthusiasm for the merchandise that was left in the store. "It's all picked over," said one assistant sales manager who had started out at the store 40 years ago as a stock boy.

"Who would ever think that Gimbels would close down?" he asked ruefully. "They always said, 'Gimbels would outlive you,' but look, I've outlived the store." ■

BELOW: *Macy's store in Herald Square was designated a National Historic Landmark in 1978.*

The Blooming of Bloomie's

By **STEPHANIE STROM** | November 28, 1993

ABOVE: *Bloomingdale's in Soho on Broadway.*

FROM 1950 TO 1991, MARVIN TRAUB WORKED at a circus called Bloomingdale's, one of the world's best known and most flamboyant department store chains, and for the last 13 of those years he presided over the entire enterprise. His career and the evolution of the store into one of the icons of modern American business lore are one and the same.

His book, "Like No Other Store . . . : The Bloomingdale's Legend and the Revolution in American Marketing," chronicles changing postwar appetites, preferences, life styles and mores as much as it gives a history of Bloomingdale's and Marvin Traub.

He sketches his rise, after the Army and Harvard Business School (in the famed class of 1949), from the bargain basement in Bloomie's flagship store on Lexington Avenue and 59th Street to the executive suite. He also outlines the changing role of the department store in American society as it went from being a place to buy staples, rather like a Wal-Mart or Kmart today, to catering to sophisticated shoppers who pay premium prices for unusual, high-quality merchandise.

But Mr. Traub and his co-writer, Tom Teicholz, also attempt to rebut the two

principal complaints about Mr. Traub's regime at Bloomingdale's, voiced after he was forced out in 1991. He ably dispels the notion that while he was a good merchant, he knew nothing about marketing Bloomingdale's as a brand name. He repeatedly underscores the methods he and his executives used to give the store an identity—those eye-catching shopping bags and those provocative direct-mail pieces, like a 1976 catalogue called "Sighs and Whispers" that featured scantily clad models in bordello-like settings. The catalogue, he says, is now a collector's item.

Mr. Traub is less successful at refuting the criticism that Bloomingdale's did not exist for him beyond 59th Street. He mentions the branch stores only in passing, and the 11 pages he devotes to describing Bloomingdale's expansion beyond 59th Street give the subject short shrift, particularly if the strategy was as unusual for the time as he claims. ■

At Lord & Taylor, A Star-Spangled Banner Yet Waves

By **JAMES BARRON** | May 26, 2008

THE DOZEN OR SO PEOPLE IN THE FOLDING chairs did not quite know what to do when 10 a.m. finally rolled around and the sound system stopped playing soft, up-tempo jazz and started playing "The Star-Spangled Banner."

"We should stand, right?" a woman in a black dress asked no one in particular.

So she did, in time for the rockets' red glare.

That is how the day, every day, begins at Lord & Taylor. Every morning at 10 a.m., before it allows customers to set foot inside its flagship

Retail

Bloomingdale's, Is That Really You?

By **RUTH LA FERLA** | April 20, 2004

MENTION BLOOMINGDALE'S TO JODI Sweetbaum and the name uncorks a stream of nostalgia. "Bloomingdale's," rhapsodized Ms. Sweetbaum, the business manager for a New York advertising agency, "it was very coveted when I was in my teens. It was where you went for real fashion, for the new, most fashion-forward clothes. They had everything."

In those days, the 1970's and 80's, the department store at Lexington Avenue and 59th Street, in Manhattan, was a shrine to consumption scarcely rivaled in New York. Style-struck shoppers experienced the thrill of snapping up the latest bougainvillea-tinted lipstick from Yves Saint Laurent, dagger-heeled shoes from Charles Jourdan or fashions from standard-bearers of the avant-garde like Kenzo and Norma Kamali. Once a fashion-crazed passerby smashed a window to swipe an armload of Claude Montana suits.

Fast-forward a couple of decades to a store still thriving but much altered. A jewel in the coronet of the Federated Department Stores, with 32 branches generating about $2 billion in annual sales, Bloomingdale's outshines most department-store rivals. But it has also ceded fashion excitement and leadership to smaller, more narrowly focused stores, sliding, some say, into complacency.

Hoping to change that, to get its groove back, the chain is dropping anchor in SoHo. Built at a cost estimated at $30 million to $35 million, the six-level Bloomingdale's SoHo is meant to capitalize on the flood of young, fashion-focused shoppers, who prowl SoHo on weekends.

"Getting into that location raises the bar on being cool, and it gives Bloomingdale's the opportunity to go all out on the grooviness scale," said Candace Corlett, a principal in WSL Strategic Retail, a New York consulting firm. "This can't be my mom's Bloomingdale's. ▪

store on Fifth Avenue, Lord & Taylor plays the national anthem—an orchestral recording that sounds like the Philadelphia Orchestra from the 1950s.

The morning routine at Lord & Taylor is probably the longest-running ritual that can be traced to the 444-day Iran hostage crisis that began in 1979. Joseph E. Brooks, the retailing legend who was the chairman of Lord & Taylor at the time, ordered "The Star-Spangled Banner" played daily "because," he said at the time, "with all its problems, this is still the greatest country in the world."

Mr. Brooks handed in his resignation in 1986, days after new owners bought the company. But Lord & Taylor continues to play "The Star-Spangled Banner," even as it focuses on what a spokeswoman called "rebranding and re-imaging" and on bringing

in new designers and new merchandise.

Other stores treat the beginning of the day as a different kind of collective experience, more like a scrimmage in which managers give sales clerks last-minute pep talks. That is something of a throwback to the days when retail titans like Marshall Field himself "would walk around and summon the troops to battle," said Nancy F. Koehn, a retail historian and professor at Harvard Business School.

Bloomingdale's plays "New York, New York," something it started a couple of years ago. "The sensibility—if you can make it here, you can make it anywhere—for us, the sensibility's right," said David K. Ender, a spokesman for the store. "Also, a large portion of people standing around waiting to come in at 10 o'clock are tourists, and that song has a resonance to them." ▪

Selma Koch, 95, Famed Brassiere Maven

By **DOUGLAS MARTIN** | June 14, 2003

SELMA KOCH, A MANHATTAN STORE OWNER who earned a national reputation by helping women find the right bra size, mostly through a discerning glance and never with a tape measure, died Thursday at Mount Sinai Medical Center. She was 95 and a 34B.

Her grandson Danny said he guessed that her only regret would be not dying in the family's store, the Town Shop on Broadway at 82nd Street, something she had often said she hoped to do.

But she certainly lived there almost as much as in her Manhattan apartment, in the end helping the great-grandchildren of her original customers. She kept the original customers, too.

"Sometimes a lady will come in with either a walker or a wheelchair or a nurse," she said in an interview with The Associated Press last year. "She can barely move and she'll say to me, 'You know, you sold me my trousseau.'"

Selma Rose Lichtenstein was born in Manhattan on June 29, 1907. Her first job was in advertising, and a client was the Town Shop. The owner's son Henry Koch flirted with her, but she thought he was married. Then a friend referred to him as "the most eligible bachelor around."

"So I went back," Mrs. Koch told The A.P. "With more charm."

Their first date was the opening night of "Showboat" in 1927, and they were married the next year. Mrs. Koch soon went to work in the family store, learning to fit bras from her husband's sister.

In the final years of her life Mrs. Koch never stopped wondering why people kept asking her questions. "What's the big deal?" the small woman asked in her raspy, staccato voice. "I'm just selling bras." ∎

ABOVE: *Selma Koch fitted four generations for bras at the Town Shop.*

Rents Soar. Stores Close. Life Goes on, A Little Poorer.

By **DAN BARRY** | April 2, 2005

THE FATHER AND SON KEEP THE LETTER IN A lockbox behind the counter of their hardware store on the Upper East Side, out of sight but never out of mind.

"Gentlemen," it begins. As of May 1, your rent for the narrow storefront at 1396 Madison Avenue will double to $6,600 a month. Should you not acknowledge your acceptance of the above, we will assume that you will be vacating the premises by and not later than April 29.

The father and son did not write back. How could any letter convey the despair caused by a nonnegotiable doubling of the rent? How could it capture the decades of sweat equity invested by the father, a Holocaust survivor, or the pride that a son took in carrying on the family business, M and E Madison Hardware?

They're Her Colors.
We Just Wear Them.

By **AMANDA PRISCHAK** | June 22, 2008

ESSIE WEINGARTEN IS AN ANIMATED TALKER, but as she spoke one recent afternoon in her glass-enclosed office in Astoria, a listener might well have been distracted by her nails. They were perfectly manicured, and she was sporting a base of Mademoiselle, a pastel pink, with a top layer of the best-selling Ballet Slippers, an even paler pink.

Ms. Weingarten's 27-year-old company, Essie Cosmetics, is a beige, windowless building, but behind its nondescript exterior is a cornucopia of color. Essie Cosmetics is famous for its more than 200 cheekily named nail polishes. Some have adorned the fingertips of A-listers like Madonna and Jennifer Lopez.

As Manhattan gradually morphs into a precious outdoor mall for the affluent, let us remember what it loses in the process: character; neighborhood distinctions; places like this hardware store, where good customers have credit accounts and the kids all call the father Pops.

That father sits at his counter, eating a cheese sandwich from home. His name is Manny Schwarz; the "t" in the family name got misplaced somehow when he arrived here by boat in 1950. He is small, unshaven, nearly 80. He says he did all right for a while, selling "bobby pins and whatnot, thread and needles." After Eric Schwarz graduated from college, he nudged his father into changing the product to hardware. Their world became one of flathead screws and saws, caulking guns and hammers.

Now Eric Schwarz looks out onto Madison Avenue and talks about all the other small stores that will surely be displaying similar signs. In the background, his father is getting angry again. Then the egg timer went off. And an old man watched from his little store as his son went out to feed the meters. ▪

Ms. Weingarten names her products herself, and the names are as attention-getting as the colors. The new Neon collection, for example, includes Short Shorts, a "shockingly flamingo pink," and Bermuda Shorts, a "high-voltage violet." Another shade, Aruba Blue, was born during a Caribbean vacation.

Ms. Weingarten launched Essie after noticing, during a stint in the late 60's and early 70's as an assistant buyer at Henri Bendel, that the best polish colors went to department stores. "Salons only had pearly white, platinum, red, mauve and some boring pink," Ms. Weingarten said, explaining how Essie added everything from inky blacks to pale pinks.

She has taken heat for some of the saucier names she has coined. Prune Face went off the market in response to incensed customers in California, and After Sex was rechristened After Six in more conservative markets.

"Of course, in New York," Ms. Weingarten said, "we had no reason to change the original name." ▪

BELOW: *Essie Weingarten, founder and president of Essie Nail Polish based in Astoria, Queens.*

City Hall
And Beyond

Who really governs New York? For generations, the city's power structure was controlled by old-time political bosses. They filled patronage jobs with supporters and brokered city contracts for business associates. They were just following in the footsteps of the nineteenth-century Tammany retainers who believed in what one loyalist famously called "honest graft." No one explained this better than the ward boss of Hell's Kitchen, George Washington Plunkitt, who declared, "I seen my opportunities, and I took 'em."

It took another larger-than-life character to topple the last Tammany leader: Edward I.

GOVERNMENT &
POLITICS

◀ PAGE 262

Koch ended the long reign of Tammany's Carmine De Sapio as the Democratic leader in Greenwich Village in 1961. Koch—a combative, opinionated dynamo who could happily outtalk anybody—was elected mayor sixteen years later, only to be undermined by an old-fashioned patronage scandal involving officials he himself had appointed. (Koch claimed he was unaware that corruption reached into his administration, and was never implicated in the parking-ticket and taxi-meter scandals that contributed to his downfall).

How innocent New York's first mayors seem by comparison. They were British appointees, so they could not get the job by buying votes. The city's first mayor was Cambridge-educated Thomas Willett, a seventeenth-century sea captain who had made his reputation as magistrate of the Plymouth Colony in Massachusetts. He served one year and was appointed again two years later.

After the Revolutionary War, New Yorkers elected a parade of Clintons, Livingstons and Schuylers. But these bluebloods also had competition from a new political organization, Tammany Hall, whose founding principle called for asserting the rights of the middle class.

From that egalitarian beginning Tammany became synonymous with big-money municipal corruption. When William Magear Tweed became Tammany's chief just after the Civil War, its stranglehold on city government was already apparent. The New York Times soon rocked Tammany with its first major exposé. Simply by printing ledgerlike lists of expenditures, The Times confirmed the worst of the public's suspicions: Tammany was on the take in a big way. The "Tweed Courthouse" cost between $11 million and $12 million—more than $230 million in today's dollars. Construction dragged on for twenty years. The longer it took, the more the Tammany bosses took. Tweed's own trial was held there in 1873, and the courthouse still wasn't finished.

Neither was Tammany. It unquestionably controlled Democratic politics in the city until 1932, when Mayor James J. Walker resigned in yet another corruption scandal. Summoned to appear before then-Governor Franklin D. Roosevelt, Walker, a ladies' man and fancy dresser whom the tabloids had nicknamed "Gentleman Jimmy," simply quit.

That left Tammany foundering. Walker's successors more closely

reflected the ethnicity and awareness of New York in the twentieth century: Irish, Italian, Jewish, black. City Hall had its white knights. In the 1930's, crime-busting, graft-hating Fiorello H. La Guardia was elected after Walker had resettled himself in Europe, beyond the reach of prosecutors. La Guardia, the son of Italian immigrants was probably New York's most successful and colorful mayor since Peter Stuyvesant. In the 1960's a dashing East Side congressman, John V. Lindsay, could have been the most successful mayor since La Guardia (and also the first Republican). But Lindsay was no match for the racial unrest, antiwar protests and municipal strikes that began days after he took office.

Organization man Abraham D. Beame, a Democrat, followed Lindsay and presided over a fiscal crisis that all but forced the city to declare bankruptcy in 1975. Koch defeated Beame in the Democratic primary in 1977 and went on to serve three terms before he, in turn, lost the Democratic primary to David N. Dinkins in 1989. Dinkins, the city's first black mayor, defeated the Republican nominee, Rudolph W. Giuliani, the United States Attorney in Manhattan, just as population shifts made

▲ PAGE 258

non-Hispanic whites a minority in the city. Racial tensions erupted in Crown Heights, Brooklyn, and quickly engulfed Dinkins' administration. The 1993 election was a rematch between Dinkins and Giuliani, but this time Giuliani won. In his eight years in City Hall, crime declined and the city prospered under pro-business policies that spurred real estate development, particularly in Manhattan.

Giuliani tried to delay his exit after the 9/11 attacks. But not even "America's mayor," as Giuliani was nicknamed, could undo a law that blocked mayors from running for more than two terms. That took a million-dollar campaign by his successor, Michael R. Bloomberg, a billionaire businessman and Democrat-turned-Republican who had been in search of a mission beyond making money. He found it at City Hall, where Bloomberg achieved two milestones that had eluded his immediate predecessors. He won control of the public school system, and he undid the term-limits law. He couldn't have been more different from his Tammany predecessors, but they certainly would have been impressed by how much he spent—from his personal fortune—to achieve his political goals.

▼ PAGE 252

City Hall Cornerstone Was Laid 125 Years Ago—Winning Design Cost $350

May 20, 1928

WHEN THE CORNERSTONE OF NEW YORK'S City Hall was laid on May 26, 1803, 125 years ago, there were but 17 states in the Union and Jefferson was president. The population of the entire country was about 5.5 million, considerably less than that of the city today. Lewis and Clark were preparing to penetrate the wilderness of the Rockies. Travel was still by horse, boat and wagon; the invention of the steamboat was yet four years in the future.

The Council selected the plans submitted for a marble structure in Italian Renaissance style by the architectural firm of Mangin & McComb and instructed the controller to pay $350 for the successful design. For more than a decade the work was under way, hindered from time to time by dilatory resolutions of overcautious councilmen.

Delays were also caused by epidemics among workmen and by dislocation of city finances due to corruption or mismanagement. On Dec. 1, 1807, work had been completed up to the second floor at an expenditure of $207,000.

With the exception of the roof, temporarily shingled while awaiting copper from England, the outside work was finished in 1810. The interior was so far completed as to furnish a room for the City Council, but it was not until August 1811, that the city fathers moved into their new quarters. The total cost of the structure had been almost $500,000.

Not the least interesting part of the City Hall is the cupola. The original plan, admired for its classic chasteness, provided for a single clock in the front window. Public sentiment had a good deal to do with the change from one to four dials.

These changes detracted from the simplicity of the cupola, and there began to be requests that the original be restored. An opportunity to do that came in 1858, when the cupola was destroyed by sparks from fireworks used in the celebration of the laying of the Atlantic cable; but instead a duplicate of the burned cupola was erected and the beautiful conception of the architect neglected. Another fire in 1917 offered a second opportunity. This time the world of art as well as the public successfully insisted on a return to the classic prototype. ■

The Secret Treasure Of City Hall; Significant Art Collection Goes Mostly Unnoticed

By **DAVID M. HERSZENHORN** | August 10, 1999

ARCHEOLOGISTS KEEPING A STEP AHEAD OF the bulldozers churning the earth during renovations to City Hall Park have found all sorts of historic artifacts. But far more valuable treasures are secreted away inside City Hall itself: the city's little known but extensive collection of 19th-century portraits and other artwork, which is rarely seen by the public that owns it all.

There are portraits of revered Americans—presidents, governors and, of course, the city's mayors—but the crown jewel in the collection is a portrait of a Frenchman, Marie Joseph Paul Yves Roche Gilbert du Motier—the Marquis de Lafayette—who was beloved by Americans for fighting valiantly in the Revolutionary War. The Common Council, predecessor to the City Council,

Old Building, New Finances; Lean Times Don't Stop Renovation at City Hall

By **ANDREA KANNAPELL** | December 30, 1994

SOME 180 YEARS AGO, NEW YORK'S NEW City Hall, with its gracious French Renaissance facade and elegant Georgian interior, was considered one of the most handsome buildings in the country.

Today, after 56 mayoral administrations, several technological revolutions and multiple fiscal crises, City Hall is a mixture of the grand, the pedestrian and the crumbling. Gawky metal coatracks line graceful corridors. A grandfather clock insists it is 2:35, 24 hours a day. The rotunda's white marble is chipped and discolored.

The Giuliani administration would like to see City Hall returned to splendor, and then kept that way with a self-perpetuating maintenance budget. It has set about devising, for the first time, a long-term renovation and maintenance plan for the building.

But in these days of private-sector financing, city officials have found themselves looking at some admittedly novel ways to foot the bill.

> Today, City Hall is a mixture of the grand, the pedestrian and the crumbling.

commissioned the portrait in 1824 and paid Samuel F. B. Morse somewhere between $700 and $1,000 to paint it.

Most days, it sits unseen in the dark, empty chamber. Even when there are Council meetings, few eyes turn away from the politics long enough to notice the painting.

"To be really honest with you, the tours that we give are really dealing with the government," said Katharine Hicks, one of the sergeants at arms who leads the tours.

When it comes to where paintings are placed, as with everything else at City Hall, the mayor is ultimately in charge, which can make for some interesting arrangements. Mayor Rudolph W. Giuliani, for instance, has the portrait of Mayor Fiorello H. La Guardia, his hero and a fellow Republican, hanging in his office, over his desk.

Last year, the Giuliani administration sparked a small controversy when it renovated the Blue Room, where the Mayor holds his news conferences, and removed the portraits of his immediate predecessors, David N. Dinkins and Edward I. Koch. The two former mayors may compete with Mr. Giuliani for attention on the airwaves, but not in City Hall: their portraits now hang in a hallway near a bathroom. ∎

John S. Dyson, the deputy mayor for finance and economic development, has already altered one longstanding city policy to raise money, allowing the building to be used for filming in exchange for a fee. Castle Rock Entertainment paid what Mr. Dyson called a "small honorarium"—reportedly $50,000—to get its cameras inside recently to shoot a new movie, "City Hall," starring Al Pacino.

Officials are also considering renting out, for receptions, two stately City Hall chambers—the Committee of the Whole and the Governor's Room. "I could imagine somebody might pay $5,000 to welcome somebody," Mr. Dyson said.

Other ideas include installing vending machines in the lobby and putting carts out front to sell food and drink. Or paid tours of City Hall on weekends. "We could show the mayor's office," Mr. Dyson said. "He's usually out at a parade or something at those times." ∎

Drab Setting, But Joyous Work: Making 2 Into 1

By **FERNANDA SANTOS** | October 5, 2008

ABOVE: *Martha Batalha, 35, and Juan Suarez, 30, tied the knot at the Municipal Building on October 4, 2008.*

RUMMAGING BACK THROUGH THE THOUSANDS of weddings he has performed at the Manhattan Marriage Bureau, Walter Curtis can find a wealth of vivid memories: The bride who showed up in a princess costume one Halloween. The 126 couples who came before him over the course of a single Valentine's Day. The former Balkans freedom fighter who, when instructed to kiss the bride, turned and planted a smooch on Mr. Curtis's cheek.

He has a harder time finding anything colorful to say about the setting: a warren of offices on the second floor of the Municipal Building, where city employees like him have been giving true love a brief, secular send-off since 1916.

"I love my job," said Mr. Curtis, who is in charge of the marriage records room, as he rested his large frame on a creaky chair in the bureau's conference room. "But I don't think I'll miss anything about this place."

The bureau will soon move to new quarters—a grand hall lined in marble and lighted by chandeliers—in a city office building nearby. The move is an idea that Mayor Michael R. Bloomberg has nursed for almost as long as he has been in office.

City officials see in the revamped marriage bureau an opportunity to market the city as a wedding destination, offering it as a more tasteful alternative to Las Vegas, where a bride can be led down the aisle by an Elvis impersonator or married in a drive-through chapel.

There will be none of that in New York. But, for the first time, the city will offer conveniences like a dressing room where brides can touch up their makeup. And couples will not have to endure the metal detectors or X-ray machines that greet visitors to the Municipal Building.

Fancier quarters will probably lead to higher prices. A ceremony now costs $25, and though the first deputy city clerk, Michael McSweeney, said it was unlikely the fee would go up by the time the new bureau opens, he did not rule out an increase soon after that. ∎

No, 311 Is Not Her Telephone Number

By **JAMES BARRON** | July 16, 2003

IN THE UNIVERSE OF CALLERS, MISS UNIVERSE sounded less querulous than some who have dialed New York City's 311 number. But her question? Asked, with help from a cue card, and answered, with help from a computer. In two languages.

Miss Universe—Amelia Vega, from the Dominican Republic—was promoting 311. To demonstrate that the call takers can field questions in Spanish, Ms. Vega walked through the 311 center on Maiden Lane in

CITY HALL

Trouble Big or Small? New York Has a Number to Call: 311

By **JENNIFER STEINHAUER** | April 23, 2003

THE TELEPHONE OPERATORS AT THE CITY'S 311 center had the alternate-side-of-the-street parking rules down pat. They knew what to do with a complaint about a broken traffic light. Marriage license issue? Loud car alarm? Recycling laws? Check! Check! Check!

But then there was the chicken. A woman in the Bronx had one living in her hallway, and she was not happy about it. It seems she and her landlord had divergent views on rent and heat, a dispute that culminated in the landlord placing a rather menacing bit of fowl at her front door.

The operator typed into the computer: "Chicken on stoop." The results were quickly forthcoming. What the lady had was an agricultural problem, and she was referred to the Department of Health.

Of the changes undertaken by Mayor Michael R. Bloomberg since he took office, few are as ambitious as his insistence on overhauling the way city residents receive information from their government.

Appalled to learn during the campaign that there was no central clearinghouse where residents could call—there were over 40 call centers and help lines connected to dozens of different agencies—Mr. Bloomberg decided after he was elected that he would set up a single line to give answers and take complaints.

City Council members have complained frequently and bitterly about the $25 million start-up costs for 311, but Mr. Bloomberg is undaunted.

Just yesterday, when confronted with a newspaper article detailing the city's many potholes, Mr. Bloomberg shot back. "If you see a pothole, what do you do? 311. It's very easy. That's the whole idea of it. Call 311. They'll give you a number so that you can call back the next day and see when the pothole is going to get fixed. It works, and I'm tired of people complaining about it." ∎

Lower Manhattan and picked up a phone, and someone held up the cue card.

Aides to the city's information technology commissioner, Gino P. Menchini, explained that she believed that her English was not up to par, so she had thought up the question ahead of time to make sure she got the wording exactly right. They had printed it on a cue card—a piece of paper, actually, but the type was very large. The question was, "What time does the Highbridge pool in Washington Heights close tonight?"

A citizen service representative came on the line. First Ms. Vega asked her question about the hours at the pool—in Highbridge Park at West 173rd Street in Washington Heights, an area she said she knew well—in Spanish. The call taker replied in Spanish.

Then she hung up, dialed 311 again, reached a different call taker and asked the question again, this time in English.

"O.K., I have here it's open till 7," the service representative told her.

Ms. Vega smiled as she hung up. Mr. Menchini was asked if he had been trying to impress her as he showed her around the 311 center's newsroomlike quarters.

"I'm not sure middle-aged, balding, chubby men on Civil Service salaries impress her," Mr. Menchini said. "What could I possibly say? There are some times you don't even bother to try. She's Miss Universe, for crying out loud." ∎

City Thrilled 50 Years Ago By Exposure of Boss Tweed

August 26, 1923

IT IS HALF A CENTURY SINCE A PAUNCHY MAN, bearded and slightly bald, stood in the registration office of the penitentiary on Blackwell's Island, and, in answer to the questions of the recording clerk, gave his name as William Marcy Tweed and his occupation as statesman.

The conviction of Boss Tweed, late in 1873, and his sentence to 12 years' imprisonment and a fine of $12,000, was a pivotal point in the story of the greatest graft case America has ever known. Today the name of Tweed is a symbol and his figure is legendary: he stands as an archtype, a political bogeyman—and occasionally, here and there, a Colonel Bogey of corruption.

The crisis came two years before, and it came through The New York Times. On July 22, 1871, the readers of The Times found upon the front page what was for that day a great news display. It was little more than an itemized list of accounts, set three columns wide, and the heading read: "The Secret Accounts." The aggregate figure of the items listed on that day alone was $5,663,646.83. The story was a direct transcript from the city's books, showing up unprecedented corruption. For 14 months The Times had attacked the Tweed ring, meeting much opposition and gaining little support except from the cartoons of Th. Nast. The revelation of the secret accounts—copied from books which had been literally withheld from scrutiny—turned the tide.

"Well," said Boss Tweed, "what are you going to do about it?"

But he died in jail after years of dodging and turning against 20 indictments, of escapes and captures, of criminal and civil suits.

One historian of the subject has estimated that, with fraudulent issues of bonds, the tax dodging that was connived at, the extortion and the downright thefts, the Tweed ring, first and last, cost the City of New York $200 million. The ring's direct graft was at least $30 million in 30 months and the grand total of plunder is estimated at $50 million to $100 million.

At that period George Jones was the publisher of The Times. Early in the summer of 1871 a friend of his, a lawyer, asked him to a conference. In the lawyer's office was Richard B. Connolly, "Slippery Dick," one of the four who made up the ring. Connolly offered Jones $5 million if The Times would drop the fight.

"I don't think the devil will ever bid higher for me than that," said Jones.

Connolly leaned forward. "Think what you could do with $5 million," he said. "Why, you could go to Europe and live like a prince."

Then Jones became explicit in his refusal of the bribe.

And there was Nast. He was a young man. His cartoons in Harper's Weekly had made a name for him, yet there was his earlier ambition to be a painter. A lawyer friend told him there were some admirers who wanted to send him to Europe—to study art. A day or two later a banker repeated the suggestion.

$500,000 "TO STUDY ART"

"You could get $100,000 for the trip," said the banker.

"Could I get $200,000?" asked Nast.

"Yes."

"500,000?"

"You can."

"Well, I don't think I'll do it," said the cartoonist. "I'm going to put those fellows behind the bars."

The exposure in The Times stripped the ring bare, yet in the end Tweed came to fear Nast's cartoons more than the printed details.

"My constituents," he said, "can't read, but they can see the pictures."

ARREST AND FLIGHT

Eventually, after one hung jury, he was convicted, in 1873, of grand larceny and forgery. After 19 months he was released on a

The Secret Accounts—Proofs of Undoubted Frauds Brought to Light

July 22, 1871

THE FOLLOWING ACCOUNTS, COPIED WITH scrupulous fidelity from Controller Connolly's books, require little explanation. They purport to show the amount paid during 1869 and 1870, for repairs and furniture for the New Courthouse. It will be seen that the warrants are drawn in different names, but they were all indorsed to "Ingersoll & Co."—otherwise, J. H. Ingersoll, the agent of the ring. Each warrant was signed by Controller Connolly and Mayor Hall. What amount of money was actually paid to the persons in whose favor the warrants were nominally drawn, we have no means of knowing. On the face of these accounts, however, it is clear that the bulk of the money somehow or other got back to the Ring, or each warrant would not have been endorsed over to its agent.

The dates given for the work done are obviously fraudulent. For example: On July 2, 1869, a warrant was drawn for furniture supplied for County Courts and offices, from Oct. 18 to Nov. 23, 1868, for $49,560.64. On July 16—14 days afterward—another warrant was drawn for $94,038.13 for furniture supplied to the same offices from Nov. 7 to Dec. 31. That is to say, the bill was fully paid by the first of these two warrants down to Nov. 23. And yet a fortnight afterward another warrant was drawn paying the bill over again from Nov. 7. It is obvious that the fictitious dates were not remembered by the city authorities when these warrants were drawn. Many similar cases will be observed in the figures given below.

1869	INGERSOLL & CO.	1869
July 2.—Paid for Furniture in County Courts and Offices from Oct. 18 to Nov. 23, 1868		$42,550.64
July 16.—Paid for Furniture in County Office from Nov. 7 to Dec. 31, 1868		94,038.13
Aug. 4.— Paid for Furniture in County Offices July 19, 1868		53,206.75
Sept. 7.—Paid for Furniture in County Offices Aug. 30, 1868		60,334.71
Sept. 8.—Paid for Furniture in County Courts and Offices, Sept, 23,1868		49,901.47

1870	INGERSOLL & CO	1870
Aug. 9.—Paid for Cabinetwork in Armories and Drill-rooms, April 16, 1870		77,949.58
Mar. 28.—Paid for Repairs in Armories and Drill-rooms, Aug. 28, 1869		49,742.45
Mar. 31.—Paid for Repairs in Armories and Drill-rooms, Oct. 20, 1869		38,818.84
April 16.—Paid for Fitting up Armories and Drill-rooms, Oct. 2, 1869		22,612.10
Grand Total		$5,663,646.83

technicality, but was unable to raise bail on civil suits designed to secure a return of the loot, such suits having been made possible by a special act of the Legislature. Yet with all the suits against the ringsters less than $1 million was recovered.

While he was nominally a prisoner in the Ludlow Street Jail, Tweed did much as he wished. In 1875 he fled to Florida, thence to Cuba and on to Spain.

One by one the ring's chiefs slunk away. A few underlings were prosecuted; some received pardons. Mayor Hall hung on to his office till the end of his term. Hall was tried twice; in the first trial a juror died; of the second jury, five stood for acquittal. He went to England under another name and came back at last to practice law as he could and to write for the comic papers. ■

It will be seen that on one day furniture is supposed to have been supplied to the amount of $129,469.48—at least a warrant for that sum was signed by Hall and Connolly in favor of C. D. Bollar & Co., and indorsed by Ingersoll & Co. ■

The Rise and Fall
Of Society of Tammany

By **MCCANDLISH PHILLIPS** | March 3, 1962

TAMMANY HALL, A POLITICAL INSTITUTION virtually as old as the Federal Government, appears to be dead. Yesterday, Edward N. Costikyan, one of the earliest supporters of Mayor Wagner's campaign to overthrow Tammany, was elected New York County Democratic leader.

If Tammany Hall is dead, its Tammany's legacy is a bottomless mine of gaudy celebrations, malaprop toasts, genuine and sham reforms, fist fights and factions, patriotism and plunder, stuffed shirts and stuffed ballot boxes.

Two weeks after the establishment of the national government in 1789, William Mooney, an upholsterer who kept a small shop at 23 Nassau Street, founded the Society of Tammany or Columbian Order, a patriotic, social, charitable and marching fraternity.

To distinguish Tammany from all things European, Mooney required members to parade at times in aboriginal dress, with bucktails and tomahawks, escorting squaws with papooses. Meeting halls came to be called wigwams. The legendary Tammany was a sort of Indian Paul Bunyan, skilled at turning aside floodwaters single-handedly, repelling evil spirits, quelling natural disasters and curing plagues.

As early as 1796, it was a potent, partisan force. Aaron Burr worked behind the scenes as the society's first major political leader, and Tammany soon took full control of the city.

FROM MANY, MORE

Poll frauds were a staple of the 19th century, and Tammany did not despise their potential. Wards containing fewer than 1,000 legal Democratic voters yielded 2,000 Democratic votes at times.

In 1854, it was shown how a group of Alderman called the "Forty Thieves" had

BELOW: *The Tammany Hall building, in 1924.*

Still DeSapio's Tiger

August 26, 1951

TAMMANY HALL IS NO LONGER THE POLITICAL power it was half a century ago, when it ran practically all New York politics, but the Tiger still has some teeth.

Tammany is, formally, the executive committee of Manhattan's Democratic organization. The basis of its strength is the ability to get its followers elected or appointed to political jobs. Tammany usually controls Manhattan Democratic nominations. When the Democrats have been in power, it has generally had the privilege of picking men for a lot of appointive jobs—high city officials made almost every other official act a basis for extortion. City jobs were marketed for the best fees.

The city at one point was caught buying 4,000 glass ballot boxes at $15 each from a brother of the mayor, who had got them for $5 each.

All of this, however, was made to look insignificant when Boss William Marcy Tweed took over in 1867. In one day's work, on May 5, 1870, the Board of Audit, composed of Tweed and four Tammany subordinates who became known as the infamous Tweed Ring and controlled municipal spending, appropriated $6,312,500, of which about a tenth was legitimately expended.

A new county bookkeeper, Matthew J. O'Rourke, found frauds in many ledgers and presented the evidence to The New York Times. The story ran day after day. The figures were startling.

Tammany Sachem George Washington Plunkitt gave the world the imperishable distinction between "honest graft" and "dishonest graft": If a man's inside position gave him information that helped him to invest his money in a place where fiscal lightning was guaranteed soon to strike—that was honest graft. Dishonest graft was the kind got by taking money from hoodlums for resisting the temptation to arrest them.

Tammany's capacity to rally large numbers of voters to the Democratic cause made it an important factor in state and national elections. By helping such men as Robert F. Wagner Sr., James J. Walker and Alfred E. Smith up the Democratic ladder, Boss Murphy, who died in 1924, bequeathed to his successor a much-talked-of image of a new Tammany Hall.

But investigations directed by Samuel Seabury from 1930 to 1932 piled scandal upon scandal and forced the resignation of the charming, ever tardy, vacation-loving Tammany Mayor Walker. The revelations showed unsavory liaisons between magistrates and criminals. Something like $10 million appropriated for relief was used mainly for party purposes.

In 1953, Carmine G. DeSapio, leader of Tammany, and Edward J. Flynn, boss of the Bronx, helped Manhattan Borough President Robert F. Wagner to Gracie Mansion, an act that may have been suicidal for both the Manhattan and Bronx regular Democratic organizations.

The next year, Mr. De Sapio promoted the election of W. Averell Harriman as governor. The Society of Tammany had been so diminished that it lost its headquarters, and Governor Harriman persuaded it to abandon regular meetings because he did not want the name to haunt him in the pursuit of a presidential nomination. ▪

named by the mayor, laborers and technicians employed by the Borough President's office, law secretaries to elected city judges and, finally, federal judgeships, commissioners and other United States positions in the area.

Since he was elected as an independent last year, Mayor Vincent Impellitteri has been trying to shake up the leadership of Tammany. It has been largely a personal feud—based on the fact that Tammany's leader, Carmine DeSapio, was instrumental in denying Mr. Impellitteri the Democratic nomination. The mayor has called on Tammany members to fire Mr. DeSapio. To put pressure on them he has cut Tammany off from all patronage dispensed

by the mayor's office and channeled jobs through a special political adviser of his own, Frank Sampson.

Nevertheless, Mr. DeSapio is still running the Hall. Most of the Tammany members do not like Mr. Impellitteri and do not trust him—they fear reprisals if an Impellitteri man gets the leadership. They also consider Mr. DeSapio a good leader, the strongest Tammany has had for a long time.

Second, despite being shut off from the mayor's patronage, Mr. DeSapio still has a lot of jobs to give out. Most federal patronage in the area is cleared through him, and so are the jobs from the local judges, the borough president and other elected officials who are not beholden to Mr. Impellitteri. ▪

Mayors Who Have Held New York's Spotlight

By **CATHERINE MACKENZIE** | January 1, 1933

NEW YORK WILL INAUGURATE A NEW mayor—John P. O'Brien—next Tuesday to serve out the unexpired term of James J. Walker, and Acting Mayor McKee will return to his post as president of the Board of Aldermen.

Numerically the roll of mayors goes back to 1665 and to Captain Thomas Willett, who was the first mayor after the English took the city from the Dutch and when the offices of Schout, Burgomaster and Schepen were changed to Mayor, Alderman and Sheriff. But James Duane, who took office after the Revolution, is commonly called the first mayor.

Next came Richard Varick, whose administration is remembered for George Washington's oath of office, administered by Chancellor Livingston out on the gallery of the old Federal Hall, and for the organization of the Tammany Society, its charitable, social and fraternal purpose overlaying an intent to combat the aristocrats, who were getting control of the government.

In those days New York's mayor was appointed by the governor of the state. The saying went that, like Gaul, New York was divided into three parts—the Clintons, the Livingstons and the Schuylers. The Clintons had power, the Livingstons had numbers and the Schuylers had Alexander Hamilton.

In the 19th century, the administration at City Hall moved with the times. Municipal suffrage, formerly held only by property owners, was extended to all adult males, enormously increasing the power of Tammany. Its strength was now coming from the immigrant, particularly the Irish vote.

And then along came that glittering figure as mayor—Abraham Oakey Hall. He had been a Republican, but as the result of a deal he became district attorney under Tammany. Thomas Nast lampooned him as Mayor Haul, but he was acquitted, and the town went wild with delight.

New York has never wanted reform—for very long. A reform administration came in with John Purroy Mitchel in 1914. Three years later, up for re-election, Mitchel, popular and young, stood on the steps of City Hall while Theodore Roosevelt led the crowd that cheered him as "the best mayor we ever had." The Citizens Union said that the defeat of Mayor Mitchel by John F. Hylan was inconceivable, but Hylan defeated him nevertheless. ▪

Walker's Statement Explaining His Decision to Resign As Mayor

September 2, 1932

The following statement was issued last night by Mayor Walker on his resignation:

A LETTER FROM MY COUNSEL, MR. JOHN J. Curtin, received today has caused me to make a momentous decision. That is, whether or not I shall refuse to go again to Albany to further subject myself to an un-American, unfair proceeding conducted by Governor Roosevelt against me.

Three weeks ago I went to Albany with my counsel confident that we would be accorded a fair hearing, conducted in accordance with rules established under our principles of government.

Day after day during the course of the proceedings it became more and more apparent that I was being subjected to an extraordinary inquisition. I was not accorded even the elementary rights guaranteed to any defendant in a court of law. Instead of an impartial hearing, the proceeding before the governor developed

mayors

Mayor Walker Questioned About Receiving 'Gifts' From Friends

By **ARTHUR KROCK** | May 29, 1932

THE NATION STRETCHED ITS EARS TO HEAR what replies Mayor James J. Walker made to Samuel Seabury before the Hofstadter Committee's investigation in New York City this week. It heard confessions, evasions, contradictions of other witnesses, jests, threats, and, at the end, a lecture to the committee from His Honor.

It learned of "many kindnesses" extended to the mayor by lavish friends to the amount of more than $300,000. Paul Block,

the advertising agent and publisher, put Mr. Walker into a joint stock account into which no capital was required of the mayor.

The publisher testified that he opened this account, from which Mr. Walker drew profits of more than $250,000, after his 10-year-old son had asked how the mayor could get along on just his $25,000 salary.

The mayor denied that he had exchanged any city favors for these "kindnesses." The mayor also absolutely denied any firm connection with a missing committee witness, Russell T. Sherwood. He admitted that Sherwood had performed many voluntary fiscal services for Mrs. Walker and one or two for himself.

As for a $10,000 letter of credit, purchased for Mr. Walker by an employee of the Equitable Bus Company (which was then seeking favors from the city and received them) the mayor knew nothing about it. He did not know why the same Equitable employee had made good a Walker overdraft of $3,000 on the letter of credit while abroad.

When the drama ended, Tammany expressed itself as pleased. Its practical view was that "nothing had been proved on Jimmy."

into a travesty, a mock trial, a proceeding in comparison to which even the practice of a drumhead court-martial seems liberal.

Upon my counsel's insistence the conduct of this proceeding was submitted to the Supreme Court in order that the validity of the objections of my counsel might be impartially adjudicated. The court decided on Monday of this week that the governor proceeded in excess of jurisdiction and without warrant of law.

The governor has announced that he will persist in his illegal course. Under these circumstances the question which I am faced with is: Shall I permit myself to be lynched to satisfy prejudice or political ambition?

I feel, if I further submit, that I would demean myself as well as the citizens of New York, who have twice honored me by electing me mayor by overwhelming majorities, because the verdict, whether for or against me, would not be on the merits but dictated by political expediency.

I am not trying to avoid responsibilities. I am incurring it by submitting my case to the people who made me mayor, the people of the City of New York. To this decision I have been urged by the most loyal and distinguished Democrats in the country.

BELOW: *Mayor Walker resigned from office on September 1, 1932.*

La Guardia Is Dead; City Pays Homage To 3-Time Mayor

September 21, 1947

FIORELLO H. LA GUARDIA DIED IN HIS SLEEP at 7:22 a.m. yesterday. He was 64 years old. At the bedside were his wife, the former Marie Fisher, who had been his secretary while he was in Congress; their adopted children, Jean, 18 years old, and Eric, 15; and Mrs. La Guardia's sister, Miss Helen Fisher.

The former mayor's losing fight began last June when he underwent surgery at Mount Sinai Hospital. The operation confirmed fears that the ailment that had troubled him on and off for many years was cancer of the pancreas. It had reached the incurable stage, and his days were numbered.

A city of which he was as much a part as any of its public buildings awoke to find the little firebrand dead. Its people had laughed with him and at him, they had been entertained by his antics and they had been sobered by his warnings, and they found it difficult to believe that the voice he had raised in their behalf in the legislative halls of city and nation, on street corners and over the radio, was stilled forever.

Mayor O'Dwyer, his successor, expressed this feeling. Although Mr. La Guardia's death was expected, the mayor said, his passing brought with it "a shock of awful finality."

"In his death the people of the city, the state and nation have lost a great, patriotic American citizen," the mayor said.

FIRE DEPARTMENT TRIBUTE SOUNDS

The Fire Department's 5-5-5-5 signal, repeated four times, was heard in fire houses throughout the city at 8:06 a.m. It is sounded as a mark of respect on the death of a fireman killed in line of duty or on the passing of a high official. At 8:15 the announcement of Mr. La Guardia's death went out over the police teletype system. Custodians of all city buildings were directed to lower flags to half staff. During the morning the facade of City

BELOW: *A peaceful after-the-election scene at City Hall. Mayor La Guardia with New York County's new district attorney, Thomas E. Dewey, at City Hall on Wednesday, November 3, 1937.*

mayors

Hall, nerve center of Mr. La Guardia's multifarious activities for the 12 years he was mayor, was draped in black.

Expressions of sorrow were voiced by President Truman in a message sent to Mrs. La Guardia. Diplomats attending the United Nations General Assembly paid tribute, Assembly President Oswaldo Aranha saying that the world had lost "a champion of democracy."

SET MODERN CITY RECORD

Fiorello H. La Guardia was the first man elected mayor of New York for three consecutive terms in modern times. He was the first reform mayor ever re-elected in the domain which Tammany Hall had ruled almost continuously for many years until the fiery little man with the black hat and the angry tongue crashed in to put the old-line politicians to rout. He was probably New York's most colorful mayor since Peter Stuyvesant.

Dynamic and aggressive, he appeared to be everywhere at once, rushing to fires at times and at other times flying all over the country by airplane. A fighter by nature, he was always ready to take on all comers, big or little, from Hitler to the man in the street.

In the first World War he was the pilot of a bombing plane on the Italian front, and he kept on dropping bombs all his life—on "reactionaries," prohibitionists and Ku Klux Klanners in Congress during the 1920's, and on Tammany Hall during his long mayoralty.

He was a New Dealer even before the New Deal came into being and was associated with some of the most progressive legislation in Congress, including the Labor Anti-Injunction Act in the pre-Roosevelt days, and later the TVA Act.

His life was full of contradictions. Although nominally a Republican during most of his pre-Mayoralty Congressional career, he was generally in revolt against his party leadership. Elected Mayor for the first time the year after Franklin D. Roosevelt's first election as president, Mr. La Guardia proved much more of a New Dealer than most old-school Democratic politicians. Although he professed disdain and contempt for "politicians," calling them "clubhouse loafers" and "tin-horn gamblers,"

ABOVE: *A statue of Mayor Fiorello H. La Guardia, designed for the south mall of Washington Square park by the Greenwich Village sculptor John Bennett 40 years after La Guardia's death.*

the mayor was himself one of the shrewdest politicians in the country.

Partly because of his good relations with the New Deal, Mr. La Guardia was able to get large amounts of federal money for public works, and his administration left New York with many improvements in the way of parks and playgrounds, health clinics, public markets, bridges, housing clinics, public markets, bridges, housing developments and other projects, including the La Guardia Airport and the Flushing Meadow Park, on the site of the 1939–40 New York World's Fair.

On Dec. 31, 1945, Mr. La Guardia moved out of City Hall after having served 12 years as mayor. In that time he had drastically altered the city in many ways. Its physical plant, its governmental structure and its political and social patterns had all been changed tremendously. A new city charter had been adopted in 1938; appointees of Mr. La Guardia filled the board of magistrates and virtually every other long-term appointive office; and the power of Tammany Hall had been reduced to a shadow. ∎

The Eight Years of the Lindsay Era
He Began With a Major Problem and Learned to Live With Many

By **JOHN DARNTON** | December 16, 1973

THE EIGHT YEARS OF JOHN V. LINDSAY fall into three periods, each a chapter to be read against his ambitions for higher political office.

There was his first term, beginning in the glow of lofty ideals and anticipatory excitement. He was the young, dashing Republican congressman from the silk-stocking district, the patrician with his shirt sleeves rolled up who, as image-makers liked to put it, was rising up from Washington on a white steed to battle the urban dragon.

But while the Lindsay image was projected nationally, the reality back home was less than promising: a series of unprecedented municipal strikes, including a devastating transit strike commencing on his inauguration day, scandals, crises and confrontations led more and more people to the conviction that, simply put, their government no longer functioned.

Finally, in mid-1972, Mr. Lindsay emerged a more mature, pragmatic mayor, who was concentrating intently on the business of running the city.

Though it took six years of on-the-job training, and lessons that were humbling to him and painful for the city, he has become by all accounts, even his enemies', a good administrator. More important, he no longer interjects himself as an advocate in community controversies but instead reserves the role of behind-the-scenes mediator.

His handling recently of the tensions over busing black children from a Brownsville housing project to a school in predominantly white Canarsie, in which he worked in the background to open the schools, stands in contrast to his role in earlier disputes, which some regarded as provocation.

Areas where the mayor's achievements have been considerable include: the establishment of a strong consumer-affairs department;

stiff antipollution laws that have measurably cleaned the air; establishment of the Offtrack Betting Corporation; enactment of the commuter income tax and revenue-sharing through vigorous lobbying; a creative use of special zoning districts to guide development and a construction program that went from $200 million in 1965 to $1 billion in 1972.

> Though it took six years of on-the-job training, and lessons that were humbling to him and painful for the city, he has become by all accounts, even his enemies', a good administrator.

But critics, perhaps unfairly, point to urban ills that worsened during the Lindsay years: 250,000 jobs lost over the past three years; the transit fare up to 35 cents; welfare rolls that have lately declined somewhat but climbed overall during his tenure from 500,000 to 1.1 million.

The prisons had riots, the courts had logjams, the Giants left town and school decentralization was termed a failure by one of its chief architects. And the larger historical forces—a changing population, rising costs and an eroding tax base—continued unabated.

In a jocular mood, when asked his single greatest accomplishment, Mr. Lindsay is apt to respond with a single word: "survival." It is hard to tell whether he is referring to his own political fortunes or to the city that has been so intricately bound to them. ∎

mayors

Mailer and Breslin Enter Race

By **RICHARD REEVES** | May 2, 1969

NORMAN MAILER OFFICIALLY OPENED A "serious campaign" for the Democratic nomination for Mayor yesterday with a 14-microphone news conference featuring jokes by Jimmy Breslin—his running mate for City Council President—a staff of solemn young writers, promises of a dozen position papers, and a three-word slogan, one word of which will be blipped out on television.

Mr. Mailer, who wants New York City to become the country's 51st state, is the first winner of a National Book Award to run for office. Mr. Breslin, a former newspaper columnist, is continuing a short tradition begun four years ago by William F. Buckley, an editor and columnist who received 340,000 votes as the Conservative party candidate for mayor.

The writer-candidates promised that if elected they would make New York "famous around the world again for the charm, ferocity, elegance, strength, calm and racy character of our separate neighborhoods."

The Mailer-Breslin candidacy was announced at the Overseas Press Club, 54 West 40th Street.

Their campaign literature had four major points: 'Make New York City the 51st State!...Power to the Neighborhoods!... Achieve local control of Education, Housing, Sanitation, Parks and Police!...Kiss Off the Boredom of the Democratic Machine!"

The campaign began in two acts. The first, Mr. Mailer, was dead serious.

"We believe poor people must be given money and tools to solve their own problems their way," he declared. "Our election in mayoralty election would be a miracle...Mayor Lindsay is a good example of how a man can do his best and fail...Robert Mayor is a grand seeing-eye dog—the greatest political disaster in the city's history. Government cannot solve huge social problems...I'm not entering this to write a book. I promise you that."

Mr. Breslin came to the news conference 50 minutes late because of "a traffic jam in Queens." He listened to a few whispered words from campaign aides and then began:

"Are we kidding? Have you seen the guys we're running against? Do you call Mario Procaccino a serious candidate?"

Then Mr. Mailer, who is 5 feet 7 and refused to stand on the box that television people offer to short men, reappeared behind the cluster of microphones that partly hid his face.

"We have a simple slogan," he said. "No more ———! I present you gentleman with the problem of communicating our slogan to the public. On television it will come out 'No more blip-blip!'"

A helpful writer suggested that the reporters point out that the blipped word "is an impolite way of saying baloney. ∎

BELOW: *Mailer and Breslin campaigning in New York's Garment District in June of 1969. Their bid was unsuccessful as Mayor Lindsay was reelected that year.*

So How Are We Doing? Ask Mayor Koch

By **ANNA QUINDLEN** | December 26, 1981

ABOVE: *Edward Koch, shown here at a press conference, served as mayor of New York from 1978 to 1989.*

BOUNCING DOWN THE WEST SIDE OF Manhattan in the back of the blue sedan was a typical New Yorker, Edward Irving Koch.

He was, as usual, a public-opinion pollster's dream, having a plethora of opinions and no qualms about making them public. If he only had less faith in Gov. Hugh L. Carey and Sen. Alfonse M. D'Amato, and had a friend who had been mugged in the last year or two, he would have been in the mainstream of his constituency, at least as that constituency was reflected in a recent poll by The New York Times.

Unlike the 1,146 others who answered the poll questions, the mayor was surveyed in the back seat of his official car, rather than on the telephone, and was permitted to expound on his answers. Some of those answers came as no surprise: They have been the subject of campaign speeches, luncheon talks and town-meeting rejoinders.

The mayor favors—or "FA-voors," as he put it—capital punishment, and supports gun control. He likes Ronald Reagan except for his budget cuts, and approves heartily of himself. Like 78 percent of those surveyed, he says he is proud to live in New York. Like 32 percent, he says he thinks things are going "fairly well."

What one thing would he miss most if he were to leave New York? Not Broadway shows or family and friends, said Mr. Koch. "The energy and vitality," he said, "because you can always come and visit your relatives, but you can't take the energy with you." And what would he miss least? "That's a tough one. That small group of people who are discourteous and antisocial. The single major illustration of that would be the grafitti."

When he was asked to describe the average New Yorker in one word, the mayor grinned and uttered a mildly offensive anatomical adjective synonymous with chutzpah. He then came up with "self-confident…and occasionally brassy…but very nice."

In the Bronx, the mayor left his car to read from a prepared speech at the opening of the Bathgate Industrial Park. About 100 people looked on. When five of them were asked for one word to describe the mayor, they responded with: "terrific," "the best," "chutzpah," "insensitive" and "bald."

Back in the car, the mayor's most surprising comment came in response to the question "Do you or does any other member of your household work for the City of New York?" "No," said the Mayor. A press aide poked him in the shoulder with a tape recorder.

"Oh, I'm sorry, me," said Mr. Koch. "I work eight hours for pay and eight hours for love." ∎

David N. Dinkins:
A Groundbreaker Bound by Tradition

By **CELESTINE BOHLEN** | November 8, 1989

DAVID N. DINKINS COMES TO THE OFFICE OF mayor after three decades of loyal, quiet service to the Democratic Party, making him a man who is a groundbreaker and very much bound by tradition.

In a race against two high-profile opponents—first Mayor Edward I. Koch in the Democratic primary, and then the Republican-Liberal nominee, Rudolph W. Giuliani—Mr. Dinkins was the candidate of moderation, a middle-of-the-road choice for a city that seemed eager to lower its own decibel level. His strategy was to soothe, not excite, and it worked.

Mr. Dinkins's victory will make him the first black mayor in the city's history. New York is one of the last of America's big cities to elect a black mayor, and to recognize politically the mass migration of blacks from the rural South to the urban North after World War II. But Mr. Dinkins's appeal went well beyond his base, in large part because he was able to project himself as a candidate not of one group, but of the mainstream.

Because of the symbolism of Mr. Dinkins's candidacy, his campaign sometimes had the feel of a crusade, while his example as a role model for the city's minorities gave him special star quality. From the start, his campaign theme was an appeal to the city's diversity—what he calls a gorgeous mosaic.

His repeated fumbling on questions about his personal finances revealed a carelessness that clashed with his otherwise meticulous attention to detail. He chafes when his campaign style is called flat or dull, suggesting he is being compared unfairly to the Rev. Jesse Jackson, who became an issue in the campaign.

At Mr. Dinkins's primary night victory party, Mr. Jackson gave a speech that grabbed the limelight and more importantly, television coverage. Since then, Mr. Jackson has not returned to New York to campaign for Mr. Dinkins.

A tennis player since college, Mr. Dinkins has developed such a passion for the game that, asked about his interests besides tennis and politics, he answered half-seriously, "What else is there?" He plays on weekends and on vacations, at swank midtown tennis clubs and Southampton beach clubs. Some of his closest political friendships have been made on the court.

From his early days when he hung posters at Harlem subway stops, to his last appointed post, as the $71,000-a-year city clerk, where his most visible duty was signing marriage certificates, Mr. Dinkins paid his dues up the ladder of the Democratic Party hierarchy.

An appointment as deputy mayor under Mayor Abraham D. Beame was withdrawn after Mr. Dinkins revealed he had not filed income taxes four years in a row. He subsequently paid back taxes, plus penalties, and soon after became city clerk.

His elected career was less smooth. After he served one term in the New York Assembly from 1965 to 1967, his district's lines were redrawn and he chose not to run again. He lost two races for Manhattan borough president before winning in 1985. ◾

BELOW: *David N. Dinkins was the first African-American elected Mayor of New York. He served from 1990 to 1993.*

A Reborn City, Stamped 'Giuliani'

By JIM DWYER | December 31, 2001

VIEWED FROM THE BALCONY OF HISTORY, Rudolph W. Giuliani's mayoralty will mark an era when the nation and the world saw New York anew, and New Yorkers saw their hometown fresh, vibrant and renewed. Those at the ground floor of daily life in the city have made it clear in opinion polls that while they approve of much of Mr. Giuliani's work, they are ready, and indeed would prefer, to view him from the distance afforded by history.

> Giuliani's mayoralty will mark an era when the nation and the world saw New York anew.

Perhaps he had just worn people out the way politicians do. Over the last two years, as he attacked the character of an unarmed man who had been shot by the police, or announced a marital separation at a news conference before informing his wife, or disclosed that he suffered from impotence as a result of cancer treatments, few have run through so many exhausting lives as Mr. Giuliani. That list does not include the glittering dresses, wigs and pumps he occasionally donned for skits.

His provocative behavior seemed to bear little resemblance to well-considered strategy and quite a bit to impulses that were not particularly attractive when rendered in headlines. In the fine print, they read downright ugly.

Yet most of this dizzying series of incarnations may well end up forgotten behind the astounding revival of New York during his time. His pledge to fight crime was executed to stunning ends by his first set of police managers. Every crime was weighed on the same scale. A mugging in Bushwick was just as bad as one in Carnegie Hill. There were no excuses for criminals or, perhaps more important, for police commanders.

When he took what were, by New York terms, novel or extreme stands, he said he was acting tactically, to stir movement in an intellectually stagnant political culture dominated by the Democratic Party. For example, this approach, he said, was behind his proposals to finance scholarships at private schools to give poor children an exit from failing public schools.

The results were mixed. Reforms were won in the management of the school districts, and in the principals' contract, which traded raises for an end to lifetime job security that was virtually guaranteed without regard to performance. His key demand—direct mayoral control of the schools—never got very far. The notion of turning over the schools to this particular mayor won few advocates in Albany, where the final decision rested. ▪

For Giuliani, Ground Zero as Linchpin And Thorn

By RUSS BUETTNER | August 17, 2007

AS RUDOLPH W. GIULIANI CAMPAIGNS FOR the Republican presidential nomination, highlighting his stewardship of New York City after the Sept. 11 attacks, he is widely hailed for bringing order to a traumatized city.

But he has also raised the hackles of rescue and recovery workers by likening his experience to theirs. In one appearance he

A Man Who Became More Than a Mayor

By **DAN BARRY** | December 31, 2001

SO BLURRED HAS THE MAN BECOME WITH the office that it may take a while to remember who owns what. The large portrait of Fiorello H. La Guardia behind his desk stays; it belongs to the city. But that small portrait of Theodore Roosevelt? His.

"It's a great job. It's a great job," he said. And then the present tense became the past. "This was an absolutely great job." There was the palpable sense that eight years—of tumult and change, of political wars won and lost, of loud baseball celebrations and quiet personal crises—had passed in, well, a New York minute.

Four months ago he was a lame duck. He was remaining conspicuously silent while his divorce lawyer said nasty things about his estranged wife. He was openly dating another woman, to the chagrin of old friends. He was sleeping in a spare bedroom at a friend's apartment, and no longer living in Gracie Mansion, the mayor's official residence.

All in all, there was the whiff of irrelevance about him. Then, on Sept. 11, a mayor whose signal achievement had been to reduce crime in his city witnessed the worst crime ever committed on American soil: a terrorist attack on the World Trade Center that killed almost 3,000 people.

For weeks afterward, Mr. Giuliani was more than just a mayor. Day after day, his calm explanation of complicated, awful news helped to reassure a traumatized city that it would pull through, and that someone was in charge. The man who had seemed so finished just a few weeks earlier was now being greeted with cheers wherever he went: Rudy! Rudy! Rudy!

Now, preparing to step aside, Mr. Giuliani could not resist delivering one more summa-tion of the city's 8 million people in that familiar, father-knows-best tone of his. "They really don't know how badly they were attacked," he said, adding: "Two of our largest buildings get destroyed, thousands of people dead, more than that injured. And here they are, back on track with their lives—enthusiastic, exceedingly patriotic, more united, defiant."

"And I just reflected that," the departing mayor said. "People ask me how I do it. I just reflect the way they are." ∎

declared that he had been in the ruins "as often, if not more" than the cleanup workers who logged hundreds of hours in the smoldering pile.

A complete record of Mr. Giuliani's exposure to the site is not available for the chaotic six days after the attack, when he was a frequent visitor. But an exhaustively detailed account from his mayoral archive does exist for the period of Sept. 17 to Dec. 16, 2001. It shows he was there for a total of 29 hours in those three months, often for short periods or to visit locations adjacent to the rubble. In that same period, many rescue and recovery workers put in daily 12-hour shifts.

BELOW: *Former mayor Giuliani shown here in his office towards the end of his term.*

Rich as Mayor Is, New Yorkers Feel He Cares

By **SAM ROBERTS** | August 7, 2008

SEVEN YEARS AGO, MICHAEL R. BLOOMBERG brashly introduced himself to New Yorkers as a billionaire candidate for mayor. Since then, he has periodically upbraided them for expecting government to solve every problem. At times, he seemed to suggest that constituents bedeviled by adversity just get over it. Meanwhile, he graduated from a mere garden-variety billionaire to possibly the richest person in New York.

But a funny thing has happened: A growing number of Mr. Bloomberg's constituents, regardless of their own income, say he cares about people like them. The gain is most pronounced among New Yorkers earning under $75,000 a year.

Early in his first term, only about 1 in 20 New Yorkers making less than $30,000 said he empathized a lot with their needs and problems. Now, according to a comparison of New York Times polls, about 1 in 4 do—nearly the same proportion as among people who make more than $75,000.

Put another way, five years ago 44 percent of those in the lower income group said the mayor cared "not at all" about their needs. Now, only 12 percent say so.

And this is a man who has been known to appear out of touch, insensitive and more likely to imply "suck it up" than "I feel your pain." He girded for a transit strike in 2002 by buying a $600 24-speed mountain bike (he later donated it for Christmas to a 16-year-old diabetic from Brooklyn). Two summers ago, he did the unthinkable and congratulated Con Edison for its expertise in sparing customers beyond western Queens from a devastating blackout.

Despite all that, Mr. Bloomberg has managed to project himself as just one of the guys, and whatever the underlying reason, his cultivated "Mayor Mike" persona seems to be sticking. So what if he is worth a lot more today than when he became mayor?

"His money is his," she said Hilary Marmon, 73, a former teacher who lives in Queens on an income she said is less than $30,000. "He doesn't have to give it to me." ■

BELOW: *Bloomberg is running for a third term in 2009.*

Streetscapes: A Residence With A View, Even Without The Mayor

By **CHRISTOPHER GRAY** | May 26, 2002

PERHAPS IT IS NOT SURPRISING THAT MAYOR Michael R. Bloomberg has decided not to live in Gracie Mansion at 89th Street and East End Avenue, preferring his limestone town house on East 79th Street off Fifth Avenue. For many years, the bank of the East River, with Gracie Mansion, was considered a peculiar backwater.

The mansion was built in the 1790s by Archibald Gracie, a Scottish trader who lived far downtown; presumably this was his family's country house. Gracie was a leading figure in Federal-era New York. He was a friend of Alexander Hamilton and a founder of The New York Post.

Bloomberg's Gift to the People: Moi

By **CLYDE HABERMAN** | October 7, 2008

AN E-MAIL PEN PAL OF MINE IN ALASKA (no, not Gov. Sarah Palin, someone else) wrote the other day mentioning Marshal Philippe Pétain. This was in the context of Mayor Michael R. Bloomberg's backroom campaign to keep himself in office beyond the limit of two terms that New York voters have quite clearly said are plenty.

For those unfamiliar with the name, Pétain led the wartime Vichy regime in France, which collaborated with Nazi Germany. In no way is this meant to compare Mr. Bloomberg to him. But a Pétain quotation from 1940 leapt to mind for my Alaskan pal. As he assumed leadership of the government under Nazi occupation, Pétain said loftily, "I make a gift of myself to France to lessen her misfortune."

Which is essentially what the multibillionaire businessman turned $1-a-year politician is saying: "I make a gift of myself to New York to lessen its misfortune."

> "I make a gift of myself to New York to lessen its misfortune."

These are tough times, and it is a present that many in the city would happily accept. But there's this pesky thing standing in the way. It is called the expressed will of the people. Twice in the 1990s, New York voters approved referendums limiting the mayor and other officeholders to two terms.

There is no reason that Mr. Bloomberg could not have gone back to the voters to ask if they'd had a change of heart and would bend the system to give him a third term. Instead, he worked behind the scenes to have the City Council change the rules all on its own.

A term-limits referendum could have easily been arranged for next month, with a high voter turnout assured thanks to the presidential election. But Mr. Bloomberg teased New Yorkers about his political intentions for so many months that time ran out on that option.

O.K., some officials said, why not hold a special election on term limits early next year? "A couple of hundred thousand people voting is better than 51 council members," said Betsy Gotbaum, the public advocate.

Those several hundred thousand won't get the chance if Mr. Bloomberg gets his way. He seems to have a preferred French quotation of his own, a variation on a line attributed to Louis XV: "Après moi, moi."

Originally it faced southeast toward what is now Queens, but in 1804 Gracie built an addition to the northwest and made the main entrance face the mesmerizing waters of Hell Gate, where currents, and often ships, collided. Gracie suffered financial troubles and sold the house in 1823. Eventually it became a part of East End Park, now Carl Schurz Park.

According to Mary Black, author of "New York City's Gracie Mansion: A History of the Mayor's House," it was Robert Moses, the longtime parks commissioner, who had the idea for Gracie Mansion as an official residence for the mayor, an idea resisted by Fiorello H. La Guardia. But La Guardia gave in, moving from his modest apartment at 109th Street and Fifth Avenue in 1942.

The house retains some unusual elements from earlier tenants—Mr. Giuliani's daughter, Caroline, etched her name on a windowpane in the library in 2001, as did Mayor John V. Lindsay's daughter, Margie, in 1965. ■

GOVERNMENT & POLITICS   **251**

Spitzer Unpopular on the Street He Made Into His Beat

By JONATHAN P. HICKS | March 20, 2003

FRESH FROM A STRING OF APPEARANCES ON magazine covers and a statewide race in which he was re-elected state attorney general with a commanding two-thirds of the vote, Eliot Spitzer is widely considered to be a politician with a future.

His favorability ratings are high, according to the polls. But a poll of people on Wall Street would probably show different results. Reeling from a contracting economy and a loss of faith in the stock markets, many in the securities industry say he pursued his investigations for his own political gains. And they are angry.

Some said their feelings were evident this week, for example, when Mayor Michael R. Bloomberg, Gov. George E. Pataki and Rudolph W. Giuliani, the former mayor, were among the political notables invited to the gala 70th birthday party for Sanford I. Weill, the chairman of Citigroup—and Mr. Spitzer was not.

Whatever the reason, he has certainly left bitter feelings in his wake. "Look I've seen this movie before," said Michael Holland, a former Salomon Brothers partner and a fund manager at Holland & Company. "Spitzer has obviously over-reached. I view all of this as very Rudy Giuliani-like. Both of these guys made their mark the same way, and it turned out that a lot of it was overreaching and overzealousness. Eliot Spitzer is a good politician—he saw his opportunity and he took advantage of it."

In response, Mr. Spitzer said that his investigations were necessary to clean up practices among Wall Street firms. But will the anger hurt him should he decide to run for governor?

"Maybe we'll find out," Mr. Spitzer said. ▪

From White Knight To Client 9

By MICHAEL POWELL and MIKE MCINTIRE | March 11, 2008

HE STANDS CLOSE TO RUIN'S PRECIPICE, THIS tireless crusader and once-charmed politician reduced to a notation on a federal affidavit: Client 9.

The ascent and descent of Eliot Spitzer's career have been dizzying. He was the brainy kid who graduated from Princeton and Harvard Law School and became an avenging state attorney general, hunting down Wall Street malefactors with moralistic fervor. Everywhere he found "betrayals of the public trust" that were "shocking" and "criminal."

Then he ran for governor in 2006. Reformers chortled at the thought of this young bull with a national reputation stomping about the calcified halls of Albany.

Mr. Spitzer cast himself, self-consciously, as the alpha male, with a belief in the clarifying power of confrontation. Long predawn runs, fierce basketball games: He did nothing at half-speed. "Listen, I'm a steamroller," he told a State Assembly leader in his first days as governor, adding an unprintable adjective into the mix for emphasis.

Soon enough, his enemies and even admirers and friends came to affix another adjective to his name: reckless. The tawdry nature of his current troubles—to be caught on tape arranging a hotel-room liaison with a high-priced call girl, according to law enforcement officials—shocked even his harshest critics.

Spitzer Resigns in Sex Scandal

By **DAVID KOCIENIEWSKI** and **DANNY HAKIM** | March 13, 2008

GOV. ELIOT SPITZER, WHOSE RISE TO POLITical power as a fierce enforcer of ethics in public life was undone by revelations of his own involvement with prostitutes, resigned, becoming the first New York governor to leave office amid scandal in nearly a century. Lt. Gov. David A. Paterson, a state legislator for 22 years and the heir to a Harlem political dynasty, will be sworn in as New York's 55th governor, making him the state's first black chief executive.

Mr. Spitzer announced he was stepping down at a grim appearance at his Midtown Manhattan office, less than 48 hours after it emerged that he had been intercepted on a federal wiretap confirming plans to meet a call girl from a high-priced prostitution service in Washington, leaving the public stunned and angered and bringing business in the State Capitol to a halt.

With his wife, Silda Wall Spitzer, at his side, Mr. Spitzer, a Democrat, said he would leave political life to concentrate on healing himself and his family.

Mr. Spitzer, 48, spoke in a somber but steady voice, softening his usual barking tone. He took no questions. His wife, in a dark suit and a brightly colored scarf, looked off to the side, occasionally glancing up to reveal deep circles beneath her eyes.

For the last three days, Mr. Spitzer has been consumed with crisis, trying to salvage his marriage and his career and avoid federal charges stemming from the case. Mr. Spitzer did not address the pending criminal investigation, and it remained unclear what legal issues, if any, he will face.

Mr. Paterson issued a brief statement offering condolences to the Spitzers and promising to quickly turn his attention to governing.

"It is now time for Albany to get back to work as the people of this state expect from us," Mr. Paterson said. ▪

He was not the first politician to burn with a moral fervor; but he sometimes failed to recognize that his own footsteps could fall in ethically dodgy territory. In 1994, he denied—and later acknowledged—secretly borrowing millions of dollars from his father to finance an unsuccessful run in the Democratic primary for state attorney general. Mr. Spitzer the prosecutor might have pursued this sort of behavior as possibly illegal. The Republicans complained, yet he sidestepped questions and won election four years later.

As attorney general, Mr. Spitzer cast himself as Wall Street's new sheriff and took off at full gallop. His office extracted vast civil settlements from defendants eager to avoid criminal indictment. But his style wed toughness to what looked to some like bullying.

John C. Whitehead, the former chairman of Goldman Sachs, wrote in The Wall Street Journal of taking a phone call from Mr. Spitzer. The attorney general, Mr. Whitehead said, had launched into a tirade, threatening him with "war" over his public criticism of a case.

"I was astounded," Mr. Whitehead wrote. "No one had ever talked to me like that before. It was a little scary."

Few on Wall Street expressed much sorrow at Mr. Spitzer's predicament this week. In particular, friends of Richard A. Grasso, the former chairman of the New York Stock Exchange and a favorite Spitzer piñata, recalled that Spitzer aides had circulated allegations, never substantiated, that Mr. Grasso had had an improper relationship with his secretary. ▪

In a Volatile City, a Stern Line On Race and Politics

By MICHAEL POWELL | July 22, 2007

THOSE WERE GRIM DAYS FOR RACE RELA-tions in New York City, the early 1990's. There were nearly 2,000 murders each year, blacks and whites died in high-profile racial killings, and a riot held the Bedford-Stuyvesant neighborhood in Brooklyn in thrall for three dangerous nights.

On Jan. 9, 1994, another match landed in this tinderbox: a caller reported a burglary at a Harlem mosque. The police ran in, and Nation of Islam guards threw punches and broke an officer's nose.

The mosque's minister, accompanied by the Rev. Al Sharpton, drove downtown to register their outrage with the police commissioner, a street theater ritual grudgingly tolerated by past mayors.

Except the new mayor—Rudolph W. Giuliani, fresh off his November victory over the city's first black mayor, David N. Dinkins—decreed that no one would meet with Mr. Sharpton. No more antics, no more provocations.

"I've taken a golden opportunity to act like a sensible mayor rather than a mayor who will be moved in any direction," he said. "I'm an observer of the last 10 years of this city, and I hope to God we don't continue in that direction."

His 1993 mayoral campaign slogan, often repeated, of "one city, one standard," emphasized his view that no ethnic or racial group should expect special treatment.

In the years to come, Mr. Giuliani would rebuff not just the histrionic Mr. Sharpton but nearly every high-ranking black official in the city, even those of moderate politics: congress-men, a state comptroller, influential ministers.

"He just drew a line and said, 'Anyone who represents the black community, all of the elected officials, are irresponsible and I won't meet with you,'" said former State Comptroller H. Carl McCall, a black Democrat who had a long record of building alliances with whites. "If you're the leader of the city, you really can't justify that."

In Harlem, Delight Over a Favorite Son's Rise to Governor

By JONATHAN P. HICKS | March 13, 2008

AMONG PEOPLE IN CENTRAL HARLEM, where Barack Obama posters seem to be taped to nearly every store window and where many residents say they feel disconnected from political power, there is a palpable mixture of pride and fascination that one of their own is to become governor of New York.

The No. 1 topic was the unexpected ascension of David A. Paterson, who repre-sented the neighborhood in the State Senate for two decades before becoming lieutenant governor little more than a year ago.

"I can hardly believe it," said Aisha Diallo, a co-owner of La Perle Noire Café and Bakery, a block from Lenox Terrace, the complex of buildings where Mr. Paterson lives. "It's like something out of my wildest dreams. I have met him a few times in here and he's a good person. I think it's a good thing for this community and for the people of New York."

Theo Caviness, a graphic designer who lives near the cafe, said he was thrilled to see a Harlem resident as governor. But, he said, "I wish he would have just won the position rather than to have him get it this way. "

Race Relations

ABOVE: *Governor Paterson, seen here with mayor Bloomberg, was born in Brooklyn and attended Columbia University.*

A record plunge in homicides earned the mayor a large measure of good will. Black New Yorkers appreciated safer neighborhoods and applauded that thousands more of their young men remained alive. But even as crime dropped by 60 percent, officers with the street crime unit stopped and frisked 16 black males for every one who was arrested, according to a report by the state attorney general.

Then came three terrible episodes that raised a pointed question for black New Yorkers: Was crime reduction worth any cost?

One hot night in August 1997, police officers grabbed Abner Louima, a black security guard, during a tussle in Flatbush. Mr. Louima exited a precinct house bleeding after officers jammed a broken broomstick into his rectum and his mouth.

Mr. Giuliani was eloquent in his disgust. "These charges are shocking to any decent human being," he said.

He created a task force to examine police-community relations, and invited adversaries to join. But when the task force released a report the next March, Mr. Giuliani belittled its findings as "making very little sense."

Two police shootings of unarmed black men followed, one death upon another. In February 1999, the police fired 41 bullets at Amadou Diallo, an African immigrant. They said they thought he was reaching for a gun; he was trying to pull out his wallet. A year later, an undercover officer sidled up to Patrick Dorismond, an off-duty security guard, and asked to buy marijuana. Mr. Dorismond took offense; punches flew. Another undercover officer shot him.

Mayor Giuliani released the dead man's juvenile arrest record. Mr. Dorismond, he said, was no "altar boy." In fact, he had been.

There were marches and a civil disobedience campaign—Mr. Dinkins and Representative Charles B. Rangel were arrested. Mr. Powers, the mayor's friend, said Mr. Giuliani fell victim to racial provocateurs and an amnesiac city. "A lot of the people in the minority community forgot all the good he did in lowering crime," he said. "Rudy got demonized." ■

Protesters' Encounters With Delegates on the Town Turn Ugly

By **RANDAL C. ARCHIBOLD** | August 31, 2004

OUTSIDE A HOTEL IN TIMES SQUARE, DELE-gates to the Republican National Convention were swarmed by protesters dressed in black and swearing at them. Blocks away, delegates engaged in shoving matches with protesters seeking to spoil their night at the theater. And outside "The Lion King" on 42nd Street, a delegate was punched by a protester who ran by.

Although the organized protests have been largely peaceful, there has been a starkly different tone to smaller incidents in Midtown and elsewhere: angry encounters and planned harassment of convention delegates as they go out on the town.

Sometimes the delegates answer back in toe-to-toe, finger-pointing shouting matches. Other times the police, who are guarding delegate gatherings, have dispersed protesters, who move on to other locations to taunt other delegates.

The harassment of delegates came as organized protests continued to draw thousands of people. The Still We Rise march by advocates for social issues was peaceful, and a Poor People's March, a column several blocks long, proceeded from the United Nations to the Madison Square Garden yesterday after the police decided to let it go ahead without a permit.

When marchers approached the Garden, a police detective was knocked off his scooter. He was then repeatedly kicked and punched in the head by at least one male demonstrator, the police said.

The detective, William Sample, was listed in serious condition at St. Vincent's Manhattan Hospital, where Mayor Michael R. Bloomberg and Police Commissioner Raymond W. Kelly both visited him, the police said. There was no immediate word of an arrest in the assault, but as of 9 p.m., the police said there had been 11 protest-related arrests.

The heavy police presence at the Garden apparently inspired the coordinated plan by anarchists and other radicals to strike out at the delegates at their hotels, breakfasts, parties, and on the streets.

The police are bracing for another round of unsanctioned demonstrations today, which protesters have designated a day of "nonviolent civil disobedience and direct action." Among the parties expected to be a target is the Tennessee delegation's gathering at Sotheby's. A group calling itself the Man in Black Bloc plans to protest it, saying it is angered that the convention intends to honor the late country singer Johnny Cash. ▪

War Protesters Say They Were Bound for Rally, But Ended Up In Human Traffic Jam

By **SHAILA K. DEWAN** | February 17, 2003

TENS OF THOUSANDS OF PEOPLE GATHERED peacefully on Saturday, filling 23 blocks of official, fully permitted, rally-ready blocks on First Avenue beginning near the United Nations headquarters to protest a war against Iraq.

But tens of thousands more never made it, thronging Second and Third Avenues in what some described as baffling attempt to reach the protest.

The pedestrian traffic jam led to accusations that the police were unprepared,

POLITICAL PROTESTS

City Police Spied Broadly Before G.O.P. Convention

By JIM DWYER | March 25, 2007

FOR AT LEAST A YEAR BEFORE THE 2004 Republican National Convention, teams of undercover New York City police officers traveled to cities across the country, Canada and Europe to conduct covert observations of people who planned to protest at the convention, according to police records and interviews.

From Albuquerque to Montreal, San Francisco to Miami, undercover New York police officers attended meetings of political groups, posing as sympathizers or fellow activists, the records show. They made friends, shared meals, swapped e-mail messages and

aggressive or even threatening, plunging through crowds on horseback or suddenly sealing off sidewalks. Organizers of the rally seized on those reports, saying that officers mistreated people that they took into custody and unnecessarily militarized the event.

The Police Department, on the other hand, gave itself high marks, saying that the huge event had resulted in only 257 arrests on mostly minor charges, no major injuries and no formal complaints of police misconduct. The police estimated the crowd at 100,000, but organizers of the protest said it was more like 500,000.

Organizers stopped short of accusing the city of discouraging antiwar demonstrators as a favor to President Bush, though they admitted that the thought had crossed their minds. Mostly, they criticized what they saw as an oppressive approach to crowd control, noting that the police had even refused to allow portable toilets on the demonstration site, citing security concerns. ■

then filed daily reports with the department's Intelligence Division. Other investigators mined Internet sites and chat rooms.

From these operations, run by the department's "R.N.C. Intelligence Squad," the police identified a handful of groups and individuals who expressed interest in creating havoc during the convention, as well as some who used Web sites to urge or predict violence.

But potential troublemakers were hardly the only ones to end up in the files. In hundreds of reports stamped "N.Y.P.D. Secret," the Intelligence Division chronicled the views and plans of people who had no apparent intention of breaking the law, the records show.

These included members of street theater companies, church groups and antiwar organizations, as well as environmentalists and people opposed to the death penalty, globalization and other government policies. Three New York City elected officials were cited in the reports.

Paul J. Browne, the chief spokesman for the Police Department, confirmed that the operation had been wide-ranging, and said it had been an essential part of the preparations for the huge crowds that came to the city during the convention.

But Christopher Dunn, the associate legal director of the New York Civil Liberties Union, which represents seven of the 1,806 people arrested during the convention, said the Police Department stepped beyond the law in its covert surveillance program.

"The police have no authority to spy on lawful political activity, and this wide-ranging N.Y.P.D. program was wrong and illegal," Mr. Dunn said. "In the coming weeks, the city will be required to disclose to us many more details about its preconvention surveillance of groups and activists, and many will be shocked by the breadth of the Police Department's political surveillance operation."

The Police Department said those complaints were overblown. ■

New York's Voting Machines: If We Find 'Em, We'll Fix 'Em

By **JAMES BARRON** | September 13, 1989

IT TAKES 22,000 PEOPLE TO RUN AN ELECTION in New York City, which is like bringing in the entire populations of Garden City, L.I., or Emporia, Kan., and having them make sure that everyone who goes into the voting booths comes out. New York City did not do that. But it did bring in John Miers of De Ridder, La.

Mr. Miers repairs voting machines. While New Yorkers voted in the primary, there he was, riding around in the back seat of a taxi that the Board of Elections had hired for the whole day. At the wheel, to carry him to his assigned precincts in northern Manhattan, was Constantin Jacob, who is from Brooklyn and who knows as much about finding the assigned precincts as Mr. Miers.

Mr. Miers, who is 23 years old, arrived in July to set up the machines for the primary. He has been living in a room at the Ramada Inn at 790 Eighth Avenue, near 49th Street. What he has seen of the city has not measured up to downtown De Ridder.

"Central Park didn't impress me," he said. "Dirty. Bums everywhere. But I did get my wife a gold chain for $15. I saw this guy coming out of a jewelry store. He threw a credit card in a garbage can and started putting stuff in his pockets. Then he said, 'Hey, man, want to buy a chain?' It still had the price tag, $249.95. He said $40. I said $15. I really enjoyed that."

Someone called in a reported of a broken machine in the 46th election district polling place, at 3782 10th Avenue. Mr. Miers piled into the taxi. Mr. Jacob got lost. Before long, they were on West 57th Street, miles south of the assigned precincts. A turn and they were on the only 10th Avenue Mr. Jacob knew. The 700 block went by, then the 800 block. Tenth Avenue became Amsterdam Avenue.

After an hour and 18 minutes on the road, Mr. Miers finally arrived. He aimed his flashlight deep inside the problem machine and tugged a cable. Two minutes was all it took. And then he was back in the cab. ∎

BELOW: *John Costello, a Board of Elections technician, checking a unit at the board's warehouse at 85 10th Avenue on October 27, 1992. He was making sure names on the ballot were co-ordinated with keys on the machine.*

Politics of Voting Machines: 6-Year Fight for $300 Million

By **DEAN BAQUET** with **MARTIN GOTTLIEB** | October 20, 1990

SID DAVIDOFF WAS NO POLITICAL NOVICE. But when he saw New York State Assembly bill A-10238 in 1984, he says, he could not believe his well-traveled eyes.

The bill would have knocked his California employer out of the running for the biggest plum in the American voting machine business, the New York City contract, and presented it on a platter to a politically influential archrival, the R. F. Shoup Company, which had been doing business with the city for almost 30 years.

With the addition of 131 words to the state election law, the bill would have required square buttons on any machine sold in New York. None but the Shouptronic had square buttons. It also required a special electronic device to keep track of absentee ballots. Only the Shoup machine had one of those.

Mr. Davidoff, a consummate lobbyist with extensive political connections, was able to help kill the bill. But in doing so, he stepped squarely into a multimillion-dollar, six-year political scramble that underscores how the patronage of New York's election system—a system that political leaders have used to generate contributions and limit insurgents' access to the ballot—has also made politicking a near-requirement for potential contractors.

The battle reached something of a resolution three weeks ago. Shoup, based in Bryn Mawr, Pa., won the $50 million contract to supply 7,000 computerized machines to the city's Board of Elections. It sold New York City its mechanical machines in 1962 and steadfastly kept the contract to maintain them even when underbid.

The new battle lines began to form nearly a decade ago, when the two companies that had supplied most of New York's mechanical voting machines—Shoup and the Automatic Voting Machine Corporation—decided to discontinue their old machines and develop computerized ones that are lighter

and give official vote tallies within hours. Their decision meant that, with a diminishing reservoir of replacement parts, New York's machines were destined for extinction.

For the Shoup company, selling a new machine to New York City must have seemed like a sure thing. But New York City politics was changing, and the Board of Elections was one of the first institutions to feel it. The 1984 primary featured the first major black Presidential candidate, the Rev. Jesse Jackson, and it had been a disaster for the board, with machine breakdowns and other complaints in black neighborhoods.

Mayor Edward I. Koch, responding to the pressure, set up an outside agency of longtime government reformers to take over important responsibilities from the board, most importantly, buying new voting machines. For many in the Koch administration, the choice—not Shoup, but Sequoia Pacific—came none too soon.

The story should have ended there. But a series of bizarre mishaps delayed a contract for at least another year.

First, Shoup executives admitted having received an advance copy of the highly secret S.R.I. report, and city officials accused them of using it to enhance its bid. Shoup said the report arrived at its offices in a plain envelope; how Shoup got it is unknown.

Then a Sequoia Pacific lobbyist accused Anthony Sadowski, a member of the Board of Elections, of trying to shake him down, an allegation that started a criminal investigation. Mr. Sadowski, a longtime Queens politician who made headlines when he showed up at a 14-hour lunch with a mobster, a police official and District Attorney John J. Santucci of Queens, has denied the allegation.

Soon the board started considering alternatives to Sequoia Pacific. Some members wanted to start the process all over, arguing that Sequoia Pacific had met only 63 percent of their requirements. ∎

Garbage Barge Prods Officials

By **PHILIP S. GUTIS** | May 2, 1987

As it floats aimlessly around the Gulf of Mexico, the garbage barge to nowhere from Islip, L.I., has drawn anger from politicians, chuckles from Johnny Carson and chagrin from the very red-faced community from which it came.

But as the embarrassment continues to multiply, so does concern about the crisis over solid waste disposal—not only in the New York region but nationwide.

"The barge certainly has high symbolic value," Gerald M. Boyd, the executive director of New York's Legislative Commission on Solid Waste, said in an interview. "It does create a very strong image of the notion that the garbage has to go somewhere. And if people continue to say we don't want it here, the question is now better framed: Where should it go?"

But the barge's journey has also raised a larger question: Can environmental and elected officials capitalize enough on the barge's plight to turn its sorry odyssey into action?

The barge is now in its 41st day in search of a resting place for its cargo, with Lowell L. Harrelson, the contractor in charge of the barge, still frantically searching for a state or country willing to take his outcast garbage. Mr. Harrelson, who has failed to dispose of the garbage in North Carolina, Louisiana, Alabama, Mexico and Belize, said the barge was 150 miles due west of Tampa, Fla.

What the barge has done, to some extent, is prod elected officials into taking action. In a speech to solid waste management officials today in Washington, Senator Quentin N. Burdick, the North Dakota Democrat who is chairman of the Environment Committee's Subcommittee on Toxic Waste and Hazardous Substances, said he would focus his attention on making landfills or incinerators more palatable.

"I am determined," he added, "not to let the garbage barge—the so-called Flying Dutchman—now being towed around the Gulf of Mexico waiting for a storm, become a permanent symbol of our inability to deal with a growing crisis in handling municipal solid waste." ▪

ABOVE: *The so-called "Flying Dutchman" was still looking for a place to unload when it arrived in New York Harbor on May 18, 1987.*

Fresh Kills Landfill Comes to End of Its Run

By **KIRK JOHNSON** | March 18, 2001

SOMETIME OVER THE NEXT WEEK OR SO, THE last barge will bring its load to the Fresh Kills landfill in Staten Island, and then, in a stunning anticlimax, the future will arrive and that will be that. The last of the New York landfills, a place that has defined the nation's trash disposal dilemma for millions of Americans, will end its run.

Few will mourn the passing of Fresh Kills. Its name is etched on too many 10-worst lists, its stench too great a symbol of all that Staten Islanders endured.

But the deepening silence in southern Staten Island, environmentalists, waste experts and politicians say, is also, in a strange way, revealing Fresh Kills as though for the first time. The distractions during its life—its immense scale, its hectic activity and especially the chronic controversies of its creation and its impact on the environment—have been muffled. The marks that it left on the New York psyche, and the imprint that millions of New Yorkers left upon it with the things they discarded, are only now emerging.

Fresh Kills (1948–2001) was a baby boomer's landfill. It opened just as the miracle plastics developed during World War II were reshaping what people used and threw away, and as the consumer culture of convenience was about to unfold. Staten Island, meanwhile, was largely rural and politically powerless—connected to Manhattan only by a ferry line—a reasonable place for things that were thrown away, or so decision makers said.

The landfill's life spanned what waste experts call the Age of Disposability in the 1970's and 1980's, when the use-and-toss lifestyle of butane lighters and plastic foam hamburger boxes reached its pinnacle. Environmentalists say that sometime in the late 1980's or early 1990's, the pendulum began to shift back. The health care industry began turning back to the idea of resterilizing hospital equipment and using it again. The auto mobile industry, under pressure to cut costs, changed the way it packaged parts and began recycling. McDonald's went back to paper wrappers.

The overall amount of trash per person in the nation and in New York City has continued to climb, according to Sanitation Department figures, but some experts say they are cautiously optimistic that a corner has been turned. Business attitudes have changed. People are aware of limits and environmental costs in a way that the planners of 1948 were not.

"It's like turning an ocean liner," said Eric A. Goldstein, a lawyer at the Natural Resources Defense Council, a nonprofit conservation group. "The orders have come down, but it takes a long time to know whether you're really turning." ∎

BELOW: *In Staten Island, bulldozer compactors were left idle after the Fresh Kills landfill closed.*

Parking By Meter Goes Operational

By **JOSEPH C. INGRAHAM** | September 20, 1951

SLOT-MACHINE PARKING WENT INTO operation here yesterday, 16 years after the first parking meters in the country were installed in Oklahoma City.

Acting Mayor Joseph T. Sharkey dropped a borrowed dime in one of 25 meters installed on West 125th Street between Seventh and Lenox Avenues, and for the first time New York started collecting a fee from motorists for use of the streets.

Mr. Sharkey, filling in for Mayor Impelliterri, on vacation abroad, made a short speech in which he declared that if the city's test of meters was a success, "as I have every reason to believe it will be," the administration intends to install 25,000 to 30,000 meters throughout the city in the next few years.

> For the first time New York started collecting a fee from motorists for use of the streets.

As soon as the dignitaries had left for a luncheon at Frank's Chop House, 315 West 125th Street, to mark the historic occasion, motorists moved into white-lined stalls that delineate the metered parking places. Two motorcycle policemen on new three-wheeled low-gear vehicles also moved into the area and by 6 p.m., the end of the paid parking day, had served summonses on three overtime parkers. ◾

New Meter Eases Parking, Once You Get Used to It

By **THOMAS J. LUECK** | June 19, 1999

FOR THE INTREPID DRIVER TRYING TO PARK legally on Manhattan streets, here's a new test. What is a Muni Meter? (A clue: it's from Europe.) And how do you use it? (Another clue: it takes quarters, and be sure to take the receipt.)

Such is the puzzle posed by the New York City Department of Transportation in an experiment, now in its 10th month, at 12 spots in the city where more than 600 battered, comfortably familiar parking meters have been replaced by 41 newfangled parking gizmos. Under blue signs reading "P-Muni Meter" atop eight-foot poles, they have spawned a minor revolution in parking habits.

City officials have now deemed their experiment a success and are planning to install more of the machines this fall. Sometime soon, they say, the Muni Meter may be on a curb near you.

First-time users may find the biggest surprise is that the Muni Meter, unlike the parking meter, will probably not be located next to their parking space. As an example, the block along West 72nd Street between Columbus Avenue and Broadway provides a model of Muni Meter logistics since six of the new devices have replaced 60 parking meters. Drivers are required to walk as far as five standard parking spaces to reach a Muni Meter box and insert their coins.

Receipt in hand, the driver is required to return to his or her car. Then, as a final step, the receipt must be displayed on the car's dashboard in clear view of any passing traffic control officer, providing precise information on how long it can be parked legally.

No Need to Repark.
Which God to Thank?

By **JENNIFER 8. LEE** | October 4, 2008

THERE ARE 43 HOLIDAYS THIS YEAR (SOME overlapping) on which alternate-side parking rules are suspended in New York City—10 days this month alone.

Some are national—Independence Day, for instance. But most are religious. There are so many that this week, for the first time in anyone's memory, four religious-holiday parking days happened in a row: two days for Rosh Hashana, on Tuesday and Wednesday, and three days for Id al-Fitr, ending on Friday.

This proliferation of religious parking holidays is a result of a flare-up 40 years ago between Mayor John V. Lindsay and just about everyone else.

Before cars, there were horses, and horse parking was not much of a sanitation issue in the city (though other horse-related matters were). But when cars arrived, the Sanitation Department complained in an article in The New York Times that parked cars made "the cleaning of the streets a nightmarish procedure—backbreaking, dangerous and unsuccessful." Streets back then were cluttered with "sodden leaves, yellowing newspapers and decaying rubbish," the article said. So alternate-side parking regulations started in 1951.

They were suspended by the mayor for many holidays by administrative discretion (much like snow days now). There were so many exceptions that in 1968, Mayor Lindsay announced that the only religious holiday (in addition to national holidays) for which the city would suspend the parking regulations was Christmas.

An immediate uproar prompted Mr. Lindsay, who had run with much Jewish support, to announce the next day that he would add Yom Kippur and Rosh Hashana. Two days later, he reconsidered again, and his office announced that it would ask the Sanitation Department to issue a report looking at which holidays would qualify. Finally, in 1970, Mayor Lindsay signed a law that suspended parking regulations on holidays, taking the issue out of administrative discretion.

The initial list included Christmas, Yom Kippur, Rosh Hashana, Good Friday, the first two and last two days of Sukkot, Shavuot, the first two and last two days of Passover, and all state and national holidays. Since then, the City Council has used the diversity of New York City to pile on the number of religious parking holidays. Everyone likes parking holidays except the Sanitation Department, which has to reassign workers to other tasks.

Of the days when alternate-side parking rules are suspended, 14 are Jewish holidays. But there is still a mother lode out there. Some Muslims have suggested that the rules should be suspended for the entire holy period of Ramadan: 30 days. ▪

If that sounds simple, the current Muni Meter experiment is being mounted against a legacy of frayed nerves and municipal backtracking.

"We have a culture of feeding parking meters that is hard to uproot," said United States Representative Anthony D. Weiner of Brooklyn, who, as a member of the New York City Council in 1994, was instrumental in persuading the Department of Transportation to abandon its first experiment with Muni Meters, along a Kings Highway commercial strip in Brooklyn.

"People just couldn't figure out how to use them," he said.

On West 72nd Street, parking habits have changed, but not without problems. "At first, people didn't know where to put their money, and some of them thought parking was suddenly free," said Ed Schwartz, the manager of Tip Top Shoes, a store on the same block as the Muni Meters. The result, he said, has been a torrent of parking tickets. ▪

Dodge City, in More Ways Than One

By **DAVID GONZALEZ** | January 14, 1998

ABOVE: *"There's city pride associated with jaywalking,"
said Justin Harrington, a senior partner at an advertising
agency that studied pedestrian attitudes in New York.*

IF YOU LISTENED CLOSELY TO THE SOUNDS OF
the city yesterday, you could hear a giddy
addition to the streetside symphony of
bleating horns, cursing cabbies and rumbling
trucks. Laughter—knee-slapping, get-real
guffaws, in fact. The cause of this metro
mirth? Mayor Rudolph W. Giuliani's
suggestion to crack down on the legions of
curb-jumping Capones who have the criminal
nerve to cross the street wherever they can.

"How can he do that?" said Carlos
Llopiz, after breaking the current and rarely
enforced jaywalking law on the Grand
Concourse and 161st Street in the Bronx.
"Can't be. It's dangerous to wait for the light.
So many people are huddled together waiting
for it to change. When it does, everybody is
tripping over each other. I'm for crossing
when there aren't too many cars out there."

Precisely when and how the mayor was
going to step up enforcement of the law was
unclear, but an informal poll of New Yorkers
suggested that the mayor himself was a bit out
there when it came to his latest quality-of-life
idea. Most New Yorkers, it seems, accept some
measure of low-level lawlessness as the price
for big-city life. And in a city where cabbies
honk and hurtle down streets oblivious to
people or impatiently nudge into crosswalks
while turning, jaywalking is a chance to share
in the defiant joy of Ratso Rizzo's cri de coeur
from "Midnight Cowboy": I'm walking here!

At the corner of Flatbush and De Kalb
Avenues in Brooklyn, a boombox blasted
out beats for a fitting soundtrack. "Move ya
body! Move ya body!" And move they did,
against the light.

"How can you tell New Yorkers they can't
jaywalk?" said Seedy Sanyand, who sold music
tapes near the corner where he has seen a few
people hit by cars. "This is a moving city.
That's why it's a better place. It's crazy. It's
beautiful. It's dangerous."

And complicated. Standing near Mr.
Sanyand's display of tapes, Tammy Robinson
dismissed the jaywalker menace. "There are
more important things the mayor should be
worried about," she insisted. "Let me tell you
something. I'm homeless. They say I can't stay
in a shelter because I used to live with my
grandmother. She's 83 and wanted me out. The
city says I have to stay with her. Now I'm going
from home to home and people are taking
advantage of me. Jaywalking? That's absurd."

Sometimes pedestrians don't look where
they are going. That's why Nelson Melendez
rigged his car to play a computerized voice
whenever it was in reverse. "Attention," the
voice said as he pulled into a space on West
44th Street. "This car is backing up."

"People jaywalk a lot," said Mr. Melendez,
a hotel doorman. "It's pretty dangerous. Not
only do we have to look out for ourselves. We
got to look out for them, too."

He excused himself and crossed the
street. In mid-block and against the light.

Scoop It Up or Pay

By **J. DAVID GOODMAN** | June 5, 2008

IT WAS JUST AFTER DAWN WHEN THEO OTIBU began prowling Ditmas Park in Brooklyn in his unmarked Sanitation Department car. He scanned the sidewalk for an elusive prey, the dog owner who does not scoop.

He spotted a woman in a long black coat leading a small white dog. Mr. Otibu, who has been a police officer in Ghana and a United Nations monitor in Bosnia, could see the telltale signs of negligent intent: the irritated expression, the hurried pace, the absence of a plastic bag in the pocket. "You can look at some people right away and say, 'This person is not going to pick up after their dog,'" he had said earlier.

The woman and her dog made their way down the street, and Mr. Otibu trailed them. But after five long minutes of hushed stakeout, the dog did not go. Mr. Otibu drove on.

Dressed in plain clothes and driving white hybrid Toyotas, Mr. Otibu and the 14 other agents in the Sanitation Department's Canine Task Force fan out across the five boroughs every day to enforce the city's "pooper scooper" law, which went into effect 30 years ago and became the model for other large cities.

The city's 311 complaint line received about 3,000 complaints about dog waste last year. The most summonses have been issued in the Bronx, with 335 in the first 11 months of this fiscal year, compared with 215 in Brooklyn, 157 in Queens, 109 in Manhattan and 53 in Staten Island.

"The more people you put out there, the more summonses you get," said Sanitation Commissioner John J. Doherty. "We put more people on it. But still it's not always easy to catch someone."

By 9 o'clock, prime dog-walking time was waning and Mr. Otibu still had not found any violators. He was anxious. As he made a second trip around the corner of Bushwick Avenue and Seigel Street, he spotted a man in gray sweatpants with two dogs, one of which

was crouching, off-leash. "I have him for the off-leash, but now I'm going to wait to see if he picks up."

He did not. It was the moment Mr. Otibu had been waiting for. "I'm going to write him a ticket," he said, getting out of the car.

The man showed Mr. Otibu his identification and a Patrolmen's Benevolent Association card. He said that he was a police officer, but that he had forgotten his badge in his apartment. As he went with his dogs to retrieve it, Mr. Otibu wrote a $200 ticket for not having a dog on leash. When the man returned, he still did not have his badge. He took his ticket.

"I'm not sure he's a real cop," Mr. Otibu said. "But that's not my problem." ■

BELOW: *View from a sanitation agent's car as he cruises looking for violators in Brooklyn in 2008.*

Parking Court: Everything But "The Devil Made Me Do It"

By **AMY WALDMAN** | April 26, 1998

LOOKING SORROWFULLY AT THE JUDGE, THE young woman explained that her dog had been injured, and she had thought it more important to pay his veterinary bills than her seven parking summonses. Besides, she said, shifting in her suede jacket and leather pants, she was a struggling actress.

"Economic hardship is not a basis to reduce or dismiss a summons," said the judge at the hearing, which took place in Brooklyn. "But I will take into account the injury of the dog." He reduced her penalties; she smiled.

With millions of parking summonses issued in New York City each year, some 5,000 people a day walk into one of the Parking Violations Bureau's five "Help Centers"— one in each borough—and have a hearing on the spot. The traffic agent who wrote the ticket will not be there: it is just you and a judge waiting to be moved, or unmoved, by your word, your persuasiveness and any evidence you can muster.

Some people bring photographs or draw maps. A few drag in witnesses. They make their cases to administrative law judges—attorneys paid on a per diem basis—who in the Brooklyn center, at least, are crammed three to a room. Whether "Help Center" seems an accurate label or Orwellian euphemism depends, of course, on the verdict.

> "Economic hardship is not a basis to reduce or dismiss a summons," said the judge at the hearing, which took place in Brooklyn. "But I will take into account the injury of the dog."

The Parking Violations Bureau adjudicated disputes concerning 2.6 million summonses last year. Guilty verdicts were handed down in 21 percent of the cases, not guilty in 35 percent, guilty with a reduced fine in 37 percent. The remainder were adjourned for later proceedings.

The rulings can often seem arbitrary. In one room, a man and a woman made virtually identical claims: by their watches, they had moved their cars just before "no parking" regulations had gone into effect. His judge believed the officer's time; hers did not. ∎

LEFT: *As the demand for parking spots grows, the city's regulations are becoming increasingly complex.*

Excuses From Jury Pool?
He's Heard Them All

By **ANEMONA HARTOCOLLIS** | April 13, 2006

IF YOU HAVE BEEN CALLED TO SERVE ON A jury in Manhattan, you may remember Norman Goodman, if only by name. His name appears on every state summons that goes out to a prospective juror in Manhattan, which, even in these times of low crime, number about 6,000 a week.

It is a name that fills otherwise imperturbable citizens with fear, loathing and often a need to come up with excuses probably last used in fifth grade.

One woman sent in a small plastic bag, filled with gray powder, on behalf of her husband, the subject of the summons. "Some of his ashes from the crematorium" the woman scribbled next to the bag.

Woody Allen sent a note, in cramped printing, protesting that he had been so traumatized by his experience in court during a child-custody dispute with Mia Farrow that returning to sit on a jury was out of the question.

Given the subliminal perfection of the name Norman Goodman (a reminder that serving on a jury makes one a "good man," get it?), it might seem entirely possible that Mr. Goodman does not exist, that he is a fictional creation of some bureaucrat in the office of the Manhattan State Supreme Court. He could be one of those apocryphal creations intended to humanize otherwise faceless products, as Uncle Ben is to rice or Betty Crocker to cake mix.

So on a recent day, Mr. Goodman agreed to entertain a visitor in his spacious office—decorated with photographs of celebrity jurors, like Julianne Moore, and an award for "Your Turn," the film about the importance of jury duty—in the Greek-columned courthouse at 60 Centre Street, to prove that he does, in fact, exist.

As county clerk, clerk of the State Supreme Court and commissioner of jurors for Manhattan, he supervises about 180 employees who do everything from filing cases to collecting the $210 fee for the index number needed to start a civil action. But his true talent is for sniffing out malingering jurors and prodding and cajoling Manhattan's many prima donnas, from Hollywood stars to titans of Wall Street, to do their civic duty.

Manhattan jury pools are rich in celebrities, and Mr. Goodman can summon a deputy, Vincent Homenick, to provide a comprehensive list of those who have been called: Kevin Bacon, Roberta Flack, Henry Kissinger, Walt Frazier, Harvey Keitel, and so on, scores of them.

Mr. Goodman, a strong believer in equal treatment, insisted that Mr. Allen show up, bad memories and all. Mr. Allen arrived wearing what Mr. Goodman describes as "army fatigues and a Fidel Castro cap," surrounded by his lawyer, his agent and a bodyguard. Mr. Goodman escorted him to the jury room, where Mr. Allen insisted on standing, rather than sitting like everybody else. The rest of the jurors gawked at him.

"We eventually offered him the opportunity to get out of there," Mr. Goodman said. "Frankly, we were glad to get rid of him." ■

BELOW: *Norman Goodman is the county clerk responsible for every jury trying cases in Manhattan state courts.*

Mean Streets

CRIME

New York's first reported murder was a stabbing in 1638.

These were the facts of the case: A newcomer from Rotterdam named Jan Gysbertsen got into a knife fight and killed one Gerrit Jansen. The Dutch council that ran the fledgling city believed in capital punishment—and did not believe a defendant was innocent until proven guilty. The council wasted no time issuing a declaration: "Accused, whenever apprehended, is to be punished by the sword until he is dead."

But like too many perps who have followed in his tracks over the years—and anyone who has watched more than few minutes of "Law & Order" knows that the word "perp" is police slang for "perpetrator"—Gysbertsen got away.

So crime has been a part of New York experience from the beginning, and New York remains fascinated by crime even as it is repulsed by it.

In the early 1970's there was the "Looking for Mr. Goodbar" murder that provided the framework for Judith Rossner's novel. The victim was a 28-year-old schoolteacher, her killer a man she had picked up in an Upper West Side singles bar.

A few years later, the "Son of Sam" murders terrified a city where self-confidence was already in short supply after a financial crisis had pushed it to the edge of bankruptcy. One of the steps that Mayor Abraham D. Beame had taken to avoid insolvency was to cut the police force. That left New Yorkers feeling all the more desperate in the summer of 1977 with the "Son of Sam" killings. A psychopathic gunman shot and killed six people and wounded seven others, mostly young women making out with their boyfriends in parked cars in Queens and Brooklyn. The police solved the

▲ PAGE 290

case with old-fashioned detective work that was rooted in the notion that there is no such thing as a perfect crime: They sifted through hundred of parking tickets issued in the neighborhoods where the shootings had taken place, hoping for a clue. They found one. The loner they arrested, David R. Berkowitz, had been ticketed for parking beside a fire hydrant on the evening of one of the murders.

By the 1980s, New York had become a battlefield in a drug-fueled crime wave marked by drive-by shootings and deadly turf fights. As the murder rate climbed past 1,000 a year, many New Yorkers said they were fed up with a criminal justice system they believed was protecting criminals, not convicting them. Some considered taking matters into their own hands. One did.

Bernard H. Goetz, an electrical engineer, carried the psychological scars of an earlier mugging—and an unlicensed pistol. He pulled it out when four young men asked him for $5 on the subway. He fired, they were trying to rob him. Then Goetz walked over to one of them, Darrell Cabey, who was lying on the floor of the subway car, bleeding. "You don't look so bad. Here's another," Goetz said as he fired

again. Cabey, 19, was paralyzed from the waist down; the others were less seriously wounded.

The case polarized the city, in part because Goetz was white and the four young men were black. The Goetz case also reinforced many New Yorkers' sense that the police had lost control. In 1990, there were 2,262 homicides, making New York the murder capital of the nation.

Things soon changed. The crime rate dropped by double-digit percentages and kept going down: 2007 ended with 496 murders, the fewest since 1963. Officials credited a police offensive against minor crimes like loitering or subway-fare beating, which they said deterred more serious crime. They also credited CompStat, a computerized system for tracking crime statistics that was created under Mayor Rudolph W. Giuliani's first police commissioner, William J. Bratton. Police officials used CompStat to hold police command-ers accountable when the numbers in their precincts went up.

Despite the improvements, minorities did not feel safer. A disturbing string of incidents left unarmed, innocent black or Hispanic New Yorkers dead or injured at the hands of the police.

In 1999, officers were accused of brutality in the killing of Amadou Diallo, who had reached into his pocket, apparently for identifica-tion papers, when officers on a manhunt ordered him to put his hands up. They fired 19 shots.

No history of crime in New York would be complete without a mention of Mafia shootings that shocked the city even as they satisfied its appetite for grisly details. Consider the case of the two men who walked into a hotel barber shop and fired 10 shots at a customer getting a haircut.

The man in the chair wasn't just any customer: he was Albert Anastasia, like John Gotti a kingpin of organized crime.Anastasia had been the cold-blooded mastermind plotting the contract killings of the ruthless gangland syndicate Murder Incorporated. The police blamed Murder Incorporated for more than 60 deaths.

There were witnesses in the barber shop, just as there had been when Gerrit Jansen was killed three centuries before, but Anastasia's killers were never caught, either. Officially, that case remains open, just like Jansen's.

▼ PAGE 283

New York Numb

By **S. J. ROZAN** | March 12, 2006

CERTAIN CRIMES SEAR THEMSELVES INTO the collective imagination.

In 1987, when a Greenwich Village lawyer named Joel Steinberg was arrested for killing his illegally adopted 6-year-old daughter, Lisa, New Yorkers recoiled, as though no adult had ever before beaten a child to death.

In 1986, when Jennifer Levin, 18, was strangled in Central Park by Robert Chambers Jr. after a night of partying at an Upper East Side preppy hangout, people were appalled, as though underage drinking and casual sex were news.

> The most resonant crimes
> are the ones in which
> the victim is most innocent.

In 1990, when Brian Watkins, a clean-cut, 22-year-old tourist from Utah, was knifed to death defending his parents from muggers on the platform of a Midtown subway station, New Yorkers were horrified, as though seeing before them the realization of their deepest fears.

And although 96 homicides were recorded in New York in the first nine weeks of 2006, none have riveted the attention of the press and the public as powerfully as the rape and killing of Imette St. Guillen, the 24-year-old John Jay College graduate student whose body was discovered two weeks ago in a deserted patch of land in East New York, Brooklyn.

The most resonant crimes are the ones in which the victim is most innocent, or perceived as innocent. Everyone is, in his own eyes, innocent. It is terrifying to think that coming home late from work, or unwinding with a quiet drink, or smooching in a parked car—

things everyone does—could get you killed.

The death of Nixzmary Brown, the 7-year-old from Bedford-Stuyvesant, Brooklyn, who was beaten to death in her home earlier this year, held the public's attention for a time, because it was shockingly brutal enough to overcome her disadvantages in the climb to iconic status: she was from the wrong ethnic group and from the wrong class.

The poor and minorities are disproportionately both crime's perpetrators and its victims. People are saddened when this happens, but not surprised. The furor over Nixzmary's death focused largely on how the system failed her, and though she may be memorialized by changes to the law, her name is unlikely to bring a shudder of recognition a decade from now.

The horror of Lisa Steinberg's death, on the other hand, stemmed from the identities of the couple raising her, upper-middle-class professionals. The middle class and the rich were appalled: This can happen here? Equally appalled were the poor, those struggling to make it into the middle class, as a refuge from the dangers and ills of poverty: If a lawyer and an editor living in a Greenwich Village brownstone can do this to a child, where is safety?

After children, young women get the most credit for innocence. The Central Park jogger. Roseann Quinn, a 28-year-old schoolteacher whose horrific murder in 1973, by a man she had met in an Upper West Side singles bar, was the model for the tale "Looking for Mr. Goodbar." And now, Imette St. Guillen.

Almost none of these victims are men, except where they're auxiliary to young women. This was the case with the victims of Son of Sam, whose target was young couples stealing a private romantic moment. This culture has a harder time assigning innocence and its associated vulnerability to men. Men are expected to be able to take care of themselves, and if they can't, that in itself puts them at fault. Two recent victims of crimes that lingered powerfully in the public mind, though, were

The Night That 38 Stood By

March 12, 1984

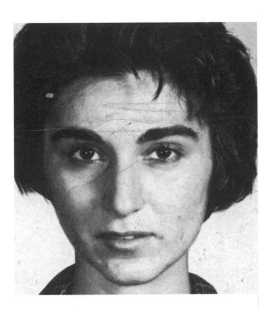

IT FLASHES THROUGH MARGARET Swinchoski's mind, each time she walks past the Kew Gardens, Queens, train station: This was where Kitty Genovese met her killer. Even in the small town in Vermont where Miss Swinchoski grew up, Catherine Genovese's case became a shocking symbol of apathy.

Now Miss Swinchoski lives in the same quiet, middle-class neighborhood where Miss Genovese was slain 20 years ago as she tried to make her way from her car, parked in the train station lot, to her apartment on Austin Street. For more than half an hour that night, Miss Genovese's killer stalked and stabbed her, again and again, as 38 of her neighbors silently turned away from her cries.

"I walk here during the day but not at night," said Miss Swinchoski, a 25-year-old flutist, "because of what happened then and because of what might happen now."

The killer, Winston Moseley, had followed Miss Genovese into the parking lot at 3:20 a.m. on March 13, 1964. Mr. Moseley, a 29-year-old machine operator, was convicted after he confessed that he had been cruising around, planning "to rape and to rob and to kill a girl." He is serving a life sentence in Green Haven state prison, and was recently denied parole.

Most of the witnesses have moved away, or died. One who remembers is an 83-year-old woman who lived next door to Miss Genovese. She was awakened at 3:30 a.m. that night when a friend called to say he had seen the attack but was intoxicated and did not want to deal with the police. She put on a coat over her nightgown and went down the street to find a door ajar and Miss Genovese crumpled behind it.

The woman said she wished people would forget. "We weren't apathetic," she said. "There are good people here. There's so much else bad in the world. Poor Kitty." ■

both male and black: Michael Griffith, chased to his death on a highway in Howard Beach, Queens, in 1986; and Amadou Diallo, shot 19 times at his own front door in 1999 in the Bronx. These cases achieved iconic status because both victims, though men, were overwhelmingly innocent, and because in each case a larger fear came into play.

Mr. Griffith was the stranger, a man whose car broke down in a hostile, insular neighborhood and who was killed for that: for being from out of town. Who, on a dark rural highway, has not had that worry? And to see that it can happen here? That is terrifying.

Mr. Diallo's death embodies the deepest of fears. Unarmed, mistaken for someone else, reaching for his papers to correct that error, he was killed by police officers, the final bulwark against the forces of chaos. If the protectors become the perpetrators—not deliberately, through wickedness, but casually, by mistake—what hope does order have? ■

".44-Caliber Killer" Wounds Two In Car Parked on Queens Street

By **EMANUEL PERLMUTTER** | June 27, 1977

THE PSYCHOPATHIC KILLER WHO CALLS himself "Son of Sam" struck again early yesterday when he shot at a young couple, wounding them as they sat in a car parked on a street in Bayside, Queens.

Detectives said the four bullets that wounded the couple—Judy Placido, 17 years old of the Bronx, and Salvatore Lupo, 20, of Maspeth, Queens—had been fired from the same .44-caliber "bulldog" revolver that had already been used to kill four young women and a young man and to wound three women and a man in six other car and street attacks since July 1976.

Yesterday's victims were shot about 3:20 a.m. as they sat in a car on 211th Street south of 45th Road, under a large oak tree and beside a white picket fence at a frame house. The shooting took place three blocks from the 111th Precinct stationhouse.

Yesterday's attack followed the pattern of other assaults on car occupants by the ".44-caliber killer," the police said. He approached the vehicle from behind and fired through the closed window. Neither victim saw him either before or after the shootings, according to the police.

Most of the women victims had shoulder-length dark hair. This, the police said, has caused anxiety among women in Queens and the Bronx, where all seven of the shootings have taken place. Miss Placido, too, has shoulder-length hair. ∎

Where the "Son of Sam" Struck, Women Walk in Fear

June 30, 1977

"MOST OF MY FRIENDS ARE WEARING THEIR hair up," Debby Pannullo said, as she slowed her car for a red light on Northern Boulevard in Queens. "My boyfriend wanted me to dye mine, it's so scary. If I have to go out, I try not to come home late."

In Bayside, brunettes—and even a few blondes and redheads—are piling their hair on top of their heads or staying in after dark these days.

It was in Bayside that the elusive "Son of Sam" killer struck for the seventh time since July 29, 1976, wounding a couple as they sat parked in a parked car four days ago.

No sooner had Barbara French returned from vacation Monday night than three friends called her about the shooting. "They wanted me to promise I'd put my hair up," she said. Barbara de Muccio puts hers up as soon as it gets dark now and, like Miss Pannullo, she admits to being "very frightened."

"Three women have had their hair cut to here because of the shootings," said Andy Petrides, proprietor of a beauty salon on Northern Boulevard, pointing to a spot an inch below the hairline of the customer whose hair he was setting. "Even in the past four or five weeks people have come in and said, 'Cut my hair, I'm afraid.' I've heard of a couple of women who have dyed their hair, and one woman I know went out and bought a wig." ∎

> "People have come in and said, 'Cut my hair, I'm afraid.'"

Recalling the Year of "Son of Sam"

By **COLIN MOYNIHAN** and **SEWELL CHAN** | August 7, 2007

THIRTY YEARS AGO NEW YORKERS WERE HELD in horrified thrall as a serial killer armed with a .44-caliber revolver and calling himself Son of Sam prowled the nighttime streets for just over a year. He killed six people and injured seven, mostly in Queens and the Bronx, before being captured.

The killer, whose name was David Berkowitz, created his own pseudonym in apocalyptic, taunting letters that he sent to the police and the press.

Yesterday, dozens of people revisited the facts and emotions surrounding those events during a symposium at the John Jay School of Criminal Justice, where three panels of speakers reminisced about the case and analyzed the killer and his impact.

Participants included criminologists, journalists, Police Commissioner Raymond W. Kelly (a young lieutenant when the killings took place) and Edward I. Koch, who attributed his election as mayor in 1977 to the hysteria and paralysis partly created by the string of murders, which had begun in the summer of 1976.

"The reason I believe I ultimately won was because of the fear in the city—and what should be done about it," Mr. Koch said. "The fear was palpable."

Some of the accounts yesterday elaborated on well-known stories, including a description by former Detective Bill Clark of the thorough police work and odd twists of fate that solved the case. Detectives traced a parking ticket issued on the night of what turned out to be his final murder to a car registered to a 24-year-old postal worker living in Yonkers: David R. Berkowitz. He confessed to the crimes and is serving several life sentences.

Other scraps of information that emerged from the three panel discussions were far from familiar. Louis B. Schlesinger, a professor of forensic psychology at John Jay, said that Mr. Berkowitz had set nearly 1,500 fires in his life, a little-noted fact.

Part of what separated Son of Sam from many other serial killers was the way he communicated with the public through letters sent to detectives and reporters.

One of the recipients of those communiqués, Jimmy Breslin, then a columnist for The Daily News, described the energy and cadence of Mr. Berkowitz's literary style, saying his early letters were full of "the fear, the blood and the cracks in the sidewalk of the city."

Some attending the symposium said they remembered those dangerous days.

Joan Boyd, 49, a journalist from Belfast, Northern Ireland, said she was living in Sunnyside, Queens, when the murders were taking place. She said that one night in the summer of 1977, she went out for a walk and realized it was the first anniversary of Mr. Berkowitz's first killing. It was also a night on which, he had suggested in a letter to Mr. Breslin, he might strike again.

The normally bustling neighborhood was eerily silent.

"There was not one single person on the street," Ms. Boyd said. "I was terrified." ∎

BELOW: *Berkowitz, convicted of the "Son of Sam" shootings.*

The Unrelenting Search For Etan Patz

By **SELWYN RAAB** | July 26, 1979

EVERY DAY DETECTIVE WILLIAM BUTLER retraces the route that 6-year-old Etan Patz should have taken on that morning two months ago when he disappeared.

Starting at 7:30 a.m., Detective Butler, a husky man who stands 6 feet, 2 inches tall, walks slowly back and forth for two hours on Prince Street: past a health-food store, a restaurant, several art galleries and a bakery. He is searching desperately for something—a witness or a clue— that might have been overlooked in the investigation of the boy's disappearance on May 25 in SoHo.

"Yes, it's a long shot," Detective Butler said, "but by now I feel like he's my own son, and you can't give up."

The possible kidnapping of Etan, a blond-haired first grader who is 3 foot, 4 inches tall and weighs 50 pounds, has led to the most extensive and longest search for a missing child in New York in decades,

according to the Missing Persons Squad. Etan was last seen walking from his home at 113 Prince Street to a schoolbus stop less than two blocks away. It was the first time his parents had let him go to the bus unescorted.

Detective Butler, who has six children of his own, was assigned to the investigation the day the boy was reported missing. He has interviewed more than 200 people, talked with psychics who maintain that they have had visions of the youngster, wandered through scores of vacant buildings and climbed a water tower in response to a report that a boy was seen on a roof.

Longtime detectives in the Missing Persons Squad say they cannot recall a similar case where a child as young as Etan has been missing for so long. "This is the toughest of crimes to solve," said Lieut. Earl J. Campazzi, commander of the squad. "There are virtually no clues." ∎

Why Hedda Nussbaum Fascinates: Most Can Identify

By **WILLIAM GLABERSON** | December 9, 1988

WHY IS NEW YORK SO FASCINATED BY HEDDA Nussbaum's story? Quite simply, people wonder what separates her from them. Her very ordinariness, experts in human behavior say, is the attraction, a reminder that even a life with all the trimmings of stability can slide into disarray.

Hedda Nussbaum is a daughter of the middle class—a former teacher and

children's book editor who was living with a lawyer and raising two children. That apparently heightens the attraction as a media event. Stories of family violence in poor neighborhoods rarely draw attention. But, the experts say, there is something in her tale of submission that fascinates people of all races and classes both in New York and across the country.

The interest in the Steinberg trial, said William B. Helmreich, a professor of sociology at the City College of New York, is much like the public focus on a string of other cases in recent years. Trials that provoke mass public interest are often vehicles for people to test themselves and the limits set by society, Mr. Helmreich said. The interest in the Steinberg trial, he

Bright Promise And Dark Decline

By **STEVEN ERLANGER** | November 6, 1987

ABOVE: *Hedda Nussbaum, 2002.*

IN ONLY EIGHT YEARS, HEDDA NUSSBAUM'S friends and former colleagues say that she was transformed from a skillful, articulate senior editor and author of children's books at Random House to an

said, is much like the public focus on a series of other trials in recent years. The trial last spring of Robert E. Chambers Jr. and the 1980 murder trial of Jean Harris both had similar elements, Mr. Helmreich said.

In many such cases, it is the common-ness of the anguish behind the misdeeds that captivates the public, said Burton M. Leiser, a professor of philosophy and law at Pace University. "People have become entangled in webs of their own making that result from ordinary human impulses," he said. "Every parent tries to help their child. In the Joel Steinberg case, every parent has felt moments when they could imagine being violent . . . These things are fascinat-ing and scary to all of us." ▪

increasingly ineffective and absent employee whom the publishing house had to dismiss, reluctantly, in August 1982.

The loss of that institutional affiliation seemed to accelerate Ms. Nussbaum's isolation, estrangement and deterioration, these friends say. She became even more dependent on her longtime lover, Joel B. Steinberg, a lawyer described by those who have met him as a Svengali with a mesmeric hold on a woman with little remaining self-respect, whom, they say, he frequently beat and belittled.

Mr. Steinberg and Ms. Nussbaum are now accused of murdering a child they had adopted in 1981. It had become so clear by then that she was regularly beaten—despite Ms. Nussbaum's regular denials—that at least one co-worker at Random House said she had tried to have the adoption stopped. She called the Society for the Prevention of Cruelty to Children. But when she was informed that any effort to interfere with an adoption would require a public complaint, she desisted.

Larry Weinberg, a lawyer turned writer, worked with Ms. Nussbaum at Random House and was represented, for a time, by Mr. Steinberg. Like most of those interviewed, he said he was convinced that Ms. Nussbaum would have never harmed her adopted children, but that she remained with Mr. Steinberg, in part, to protect them.

"Hedda is a victim," he said. "She is a woman who has undergone brutalization for many years, mental and physical.

After adopting Elizabeth, Ms. Nussbaum often took the child to the office. And there were increasing, unexplained absences from work, often followed by Ms. Nussbaum's appear-ing with bandages on her face and dark glasses.

"One day after Hedda wasn't in," a colleague said, "I saw her wheeling the baby down the hall. And the baby had a cut lip, and Hedda had on sunglasses and a bandage. I just said, 'Hello.' But everybody knew she was a lady with a lot of trouble." ▪

Youths Rape and Beat Central Park Jogger

By **CRAIG WOLFF** | April 21, 1989

A YOUNG WOMAN, JOGGING ON HER USUAL nighttime path in Central Park, was raped, severely beaten and left unconscious in an attack by as many as 12 youths, who roamed the park in a vicious rampage, the police said.

The woman, a 30-year-old investment banker, was found in the early morning wearing only a bra, her hands bound with her sweatshirt and her mouth gagged. Her body temperature, the police said, dropped to 80 degrees while she lay bleeding in a puddle for nearly four hours about 200 yards from where she had been set upon.

The woman, who was found by two passers-by at 1:30 yesterday morning, was listed in critical condition yesterday at Metropolitan Hospital with two skull fractures.

Five youths were arrested in connection with another attack the same night, and the police said that they were considered suspects in the assault on the jogger.

The teenagers began marauding shortly after 9 p.m., with the robbery of a 52-year-old man at 102nd Street on the East Drive. The youths got away with just a sandwich, and the police were unsure how the man, who was walking and carrying a shopping bag, was able to fend them off.

In the next hour, they threw rocks at a taxicab, chased a man and woman riding a tandem bicycle at 100th Street on the East Drive and attacked a 40-year-old jogger, hitting him on the head with a lead pipe, the police said. The jogger told the police that the group turned on him after he came upon them as they attacked a woman on the bridle path about 96th Street, just east of the jogging track around the Reservoir. The man was not seriously injured.

At 10 o'clock, the police said, the group came upon the female jogger as she was running on a desolate transverse. The police said that the youths numbered as many as 20 when the attacks began and that as many as 12 assaulted the jogger. ■

ABOVE: *Trisha Meili, who went public in 2003 with a memoir, "I Am the Central Park Jogger."*

Convictions Are Voided In Central Park Jogger Attack

By **SUSAN SAULNY** | December 20, 2002

THIRTEEN YEARS AFTER AN INVESTMENT banker jogging in Central Park was savagely beaten, raped and left for dead, a Manhattan judge threw out the convictions yesterday of the five young men who had confessed to attacking the woman on a night of violence that stunned the city and the nation.

In one final, extraordinary ruling that took about five minutes, Justice Charles J. Tejada of State Supreme Court in Manhattan relied on new evidence pointing to another man, Matias Reyes, a convicted murderer-rapist who stepped forward in January, as the probable sole attacker of the jogger. He was linked to the rape by DNA and other evidence that cast doubt on the earlier confessions.

Police Commissioner Raymond W. Kelly reacted to the judge's decision with a bluntly

In Central Park Slaying, The Darkness Beneath the Glitter

By **SAMUEL G. FREEDMAN** | August 28, 1986

FOR JENNIFER DAWN LEVIN AND ROBERT E. Chambers Jr., life was private schools, fancy apartments, foreign vacations and underage drinking at a preppy hangout called Dorrian's Red Hand, where they spent the hours before Miss Levin's murder. But for Mr. Chambers, life was also unemployment, academic futility and signs of cocaine abuse.

The two had known each other for about two months and dated several times, the police said, before they met early Tuesday morning at Dorrian's Red Hand, at 300 East 84th Street. The owner, Jack Dorrian, said he knew both as regulars.

Mr. Chambers and Miss Levin left together at 4:30 a.m., exchanging "boy-girl talk" as they walked toward Central Park, the police said. It was there, the police believe, that she was killed.

Less than two hours later, a passer-by found Miss Levin's body in the park, just behind the Metropolitan Museum of Art.

His lawyer, Jack Littman, entered a plea of not guilty at the arraignment in Manhattan Criminal Court before Judge Richard Lowe 3d.

At one point Judge Lowe asked, "Are you saying this was an accident?" "Yes, your honor," said Mr. Littman. "At the hands of the defendant?" asked the judge. "Yes, your honor, a tragic accident." Mr. Chambers wept.

After the arraignment, details of both Mr. Chambers's life and Miss Levin's began to emerge—details that contradicted Mr. Chambers's golden-boy image and revealed a naivete beneath Miss Levin's worldly exterior.

Mr. Chambers had a particular way with young women. Mr. Dorrian, the bar owner, said: "He didn't have to chase girls. They chased him." But he added that Mr. Chambers had "a drug problem" and had gone to treatment program in Michigan about three months ago.

Mr. Dorrian said Ms. Levin's regular boyfriend was vacationing in Europe this summer. Miss Levin had dated several different co-workers from Flutie's, the restaurant in the South Street Seaport where she had worked as a hostess, according to Eric Barger, the manager.

Miss Levin's father, Steven, said that his daughter was "always the straight kid of her crowd." Still, he acknowledged that his daughter "liked to go out at night." Mr. Dorrian said she came into his bar two or three times a week. And amid Miss Levin's belongings at the murder scene, the police found a learner's driving permit giving her age as 22. It had been her passport into Dorrian's Red Hand. ∎

worded statement that underscored the breach that had opened in recent weeks between the police department and the district attorney's office. Among other things, Mr. Kelly challenged the credibility of Mr. Reyes's claim that he had acted alone.

Technically, Justice Tejada's ruling made a new trial possible. But after he vacated the convictions, Peter Casolaro, an assistant district attorney, immediately responded with a motion dismissing the indictments and forgoing a new trial.

Justice Tejada replied, "The motion is granted. Have a very merry Christmas and a happy New Year."

The stuffy, crowded courtroom erupted in screams, cheers and applause by family and supporters of the five young men— Antron McCray, Kevin Richardson, Yusef Salaam, Kharey Wise and Raymond Santana. They are now 28 to 30 years old and have all completed prison terms of 7 to 13 years for the park offenses. None attended the hearing.

"I think I stopped breathing for a minute," said Angela Cuffee, Mr. Richardson's sister. "I can't even tell you—it doesn't feel real. I can't even speak." ∎

Malcolm X Assassinated At Rally of Followers

By **PETER KIHISS** | February 22, 1965

MALCOLM X, THE 39-YEAR-OLD LEADER OF A militant black nationalist movement, was shot to death yesterday afternoon at a rally of his followers in a ballroom in Washington Heights.

Shortly before midnight, a 22-year-old Negro, Thomas Hagan, was charged with the killing. The police rescued him from the ballroom crowd after he had been shot and beaten.

Malcolm, a bearded extremist, had said only a few words of greeting when a fusillade rang out. The bullets knocked him over backward.

Pandemonium broke out among the 400 Negroes in the Audubon Ballroom at 166th Street and Broadway. As men, women and children ducked under tables and flattened

> The police said seven bullets had struck Malcolm.

themselves on the floor, more shots were fired. Some witnesses said 30 shots had been fired.

The police said seven bullets had struck Malcolm. Three other Negroes were shot.

About two hours later the police said the shooting had apparently been a result of a feud between followers of Malcolm and members of the extremist group he broke with last year, the Black Muslims. However, the police declined to say whether Hagan is a Muslim.

One police theory was that as many as five conspirators might have been involved, two creating a diversionary disturbance. As Hagen fired at Malcolm, said Capt. Paul Glaser of the Police Department's Community Relations Bureau, Reuben Francis, a follower of Malcolm, drew a .45-caliber automatic pistol and shot Hagan in the leg. Francis, 33, of 871 East 179th Street, the Bronx, was charged with felonious assault and violation of the Sullivan Law.

James X, New York spokesman for the Black Muslims, denied that his organization had had anything to do with the killing. A week ago, Malcolm was bombed out of the small brick home in East Elmhurst, Queens, where he had been living. James X suggested that Malcolm had set off firebombs himself "to get publicity."

Assemblyman Percy Sutton, Malcolm's lawyer, said the murdered leader had planned to disclose at yesterday's rally "the names of those who were trying to kill him."

Mr. Sutton added that Malcolm had taken to carrying a pistol "because he feared for his life" and had notified the police by telephone that he was doing so even though he did not have a permit. Assistant Chief Inspector Taylor, however, said Malcolm was unarmed when he was shot. ∎

BELOW: *Malcolm X speaking at the Domestic Peace Corps Center in Harlem, 1964.*

John Lennon Killed; Suspect Held In Shooting at the Dakota

By **LES LEDBETTER** | December 9, 1980

JOHN LENNON, ONE OF THE FOUR BEATLES, was shot and killed last night while entering the apartment building where he lived, the Dakota, on Manhattan's Upper West Side. A suspect was seized at the scene.

The 40-year-old Mr. Lennon was shot in the back twice after getting out of a limousine and walking into an entrance way of the Dakota at 1 West 72nd Street, Sgt. Robert Barnes of the 20th Precinct said.

"Obviously the man was waiting for him," Sergeant Barnes said of the assailant. The suspect was identified as Mark David Chapman, 25, of Hawaii, who had been living in New York for about a week, according to James L. Sullivan, chief of detectives of the 20th Precinct.

Jeff Smith, a neighbor, said that he heard five shots shortly before 11 p.m. Other witnesses said they heard four when the shooting occurred at 10:45 p.m.

With the singer when he was shot was his wife, Yoko Ono, who was not hurt by the bullets that struck her husband as they entered an archway that led into the courtyard of the Dakota complex.

Witnesses said the suspect paced back and forth in the entrance way to the Dakota after shooting the musician, arguing with the door- man and holding the gun in his hand pointing downward. One witness, Ben Eruchson, a cab driver from Brooklyn, said, "He could have gotten away. He had plenty of time."

Lieut. John Schick of the 20th Precinct said the gunman let the Lennons pass him and enter the building's passageway before shooting the singer. Lieutenant Schick said the man called out "Mr. Lennon" and then pulled a gun from under a coat and started firing.

The police said the suspect stepped from an alcove and emptied several shots into Mr. Lennon who then struggled up six stairs and inside the alcove to a guard area where he collapsed.

Employees at the Dakota said someone resembling the alleged assailant had obtained an autograph from Mr. Lennon earlier in the day.

Chief Sullivan said the suspect had been seen in the neighborhood of the Dakota for several days.

An eyewitness, who only gave her first name, Nina, said that she had approached the suspect after the shooting. "I asked him what had happened and he said, 'I'd go away if I were you,'" she said. ∎

BELOW: *A silent vigil in memory of John Lennon was held in Central Park five days after he was shot.*

Mafia's Code in New York

May 16, 1893

ALIENS WHO PLACE BUT SLIGHT VALUE ON human life have hitherto found easy entrance through the port of New York, and many of them have carried with them the criminal habits and propensities acquired in the haunts of bandits and the home of the vendetta. It is for this reason that the newspapers have to record so many shooting and stabbing affrays among persons of Italian nativity.

While an Italian was wandering in the streets of Brooklyn yesterday morning with some of the contents of a Mafia carbine in his body, another Calabrian was hiding in ambush for an intended victim in Harlem, as he would have done in his native country to avenge a real or fancied slight.

John J. Brennan, a young mechanic who lived with his family, had been assaulted last month by Filipo Vetro, an Italian laborer residing in First Avenue, between 112th and 113th Streets, which region is part of the district known as "Little Italy." The assault grew out of his paying court to an Italian girl who was wooed by Vetro also.

Brennan's impulses are American, and he followed them by procuring a warrant for the arrest of Vetro.

Vetro's impulses are dominated by the traditions of the Mafia. His arrest was an insult that cried for retaliation, and, finding out what Brennan's habits were, he decided to "get even" with him in true Palermitan style.

Crouching in 115th Street, near First Avenue, the swarthy assassin was not disconcerted when he saw that his rival was accompanied by a friend, Frank Albert of 329 East 111th Street.

As Brennan was about to pass the doorway in which the Italian was concealed, the latter sprang out and shot him in the thigh. He could doubtless have put another bullet into a more vital part had not Albert grappled with him.

Here the razor came into play. One slash of it across Albert's head produced a deterrent effect. Vetro attempted to escape, but a policeman who had heard the shot intercepted him. Brennan's wound, although not serious, was severe enough to necessitate his removal to the Harlem Hospital. Albert went home after an ambulance surgeon had dressed a long cut on his head. ∎

Abe Reles Killed Trying to Escape

November 13, 1941

ABE RELES, SQUAT, BULGY-JAWED INFORMER against the Brooklyn murder ring, climbed out on a window ledge on the sixth floor of the Half Moon Hotel on Coney Island boardwalk, fully dressed but hatless. Strong wind from the gray sea tugged at his long, crisp black hair and tore at his gray suit.

Reles let two knotted bedsheets down the hotel's east wall. He let himself down to the fifth floor. One hand desperately clung to the sheet. With the other Reles tugged at the screen and at the windows of the vacant fifth-floor room.

The strain was too much for the amateur knot. Reles plunged to the hotel's concrete kitchen roof, a two-story extension, 42 feet below. He landed on his back, breaking his spine.

Detectives assigned to the hotel guard insisted Reles was asleep when they looked into his room at 6:45 a.m. and again at 7:10 a.m.

The detectives were not sorry to see Reles dead. He had been arrogant, surly, unclean in his habits. An internal condition accompanied by frequent hemorrhage, which

THE MOB

Anastasia Is Slain in Barber Shop

By **MEYER BERGER** | October 26, 1957

DEATH TOOK THE EXECUTIONER YESTERDAY. Umberto (Albert) Anastasia, master killer for Murder, Inc., a homicidal gangster troop that plagued the city from 1931 to 1940, was murdered by two gunmen. They approached him from behind at 10:20 a.m. as he sat for a haircut in the Park Sheraton Hotel barber shop at Seventh Avenue and 55th Street.

he took no trouble to conceal, heightened their distaste. He had boasted from the witness stand that in 10 years as an executive in the murder ring he had killed or helped to kill 10 men, yet he seemed delighted when his testimony sent five former companions-in-arms to the death house.

There were rumors that Charles (Buggsy) Siegel, West Coast head man for the combination, had persuaded Mrs. Reles that if her husband could get away from the police, the West Coast group would give her $50,000 and help Reles get out of the jurisdiction. But some of the detectives were inclined to shrug this theory off.

The men he sent to the death house grew up with him. These included Harry (Happy) Malone and Frank (The Dasher) Abbandano, the first two members of the murder ring brought to trial by District Attorney William O'Dwyer. They are still in the death house, pending appeal. The second pair sent to the death house, chiefly through Reles's testimony, were Harry (Pittsburgh Phil) Strauss and Martin (Buggsy) Goldstein, who had loafed on the same Brownsville corners with Reles. They died in the electric chair a few months ago.

The fifth man was Irving (The Plug) Nitzberg, like the others a friend of Reles's for many years. ∎

The trigger-men fired 10 shots. Five took effect. The first two caught Anastasia's left hand and left wrist. One tore into his right hip. The fourth got him in the back after he had come out of the chair and had stumbled into the mirror he had been facing as the barber worked. The fifth bullet caught him in the back of the head.

Both killers had scarves over the lower part of their faces. They got away. The pistols used in the killing were dropped right after they were used.

Eleven people besides Anastasia were in the shop when the gunmen entered—five barbers, two other customers, two shoeshine men, a valet and a manicurist. They fled screaming and shouting into the street, with the killers among them or right behind them.

The police issued a 13-state alarm for two men in the murder. Although 100 detectives were thrown into the case immediately, the police had no positive motive for the killing. There was talk that Anastasia was trying to reorganize the remnants of old racket groups in town, and that the younger hoodlums would have none of his leadership.

Anastasia strolled into the hotel barber shop at about 10:15 and called greetings to the help. He was dressed all in brown—brown shoes with rather an amateur polish, brown suit, a rather untidy brown tie.

"Haircut," he said, and he seemed to need one.

The room, 35 by 28 feet, was filled with a customary hum. Arthur Grasso, the shop owner, was at the cashier's stand near one of the doors leading from a hotel corridor.

A minute or two later, Joseph Bocchino, who holds down Chair 4, plied the clippers from Anastasia's left side. The door opened. The gunmen stepped in. Their weapons came out.

One spoke through his scarf. He told Mr. Grasso: "Keep your mouth shut if you don't want your head blown off." The trigger-men moved behind Anastasia's chair. Both men seemed to open fire at once. ∎

Joe Gallo is Shot to Death In Little Italy Restaurant

By **ERIC PACE** | April 8, 1972

JOESPH GALLO, THE MAFIA FIGURE KNOWN as Crazy Joe, was assassinated early yesterday as he celebrated his 43rd birthday in a restaurant on Mulberry Street. The police said they knew neither the identity nor the motive of the killer who also wounded Gallo's bodyguard in a gun battle that spilled into the narrow streets of the Little Italy section.

But Gallo's sister, Mrs. Carmella Fiorello, sobbing over her brother's body, reportedly said, "He changed his image—that's why this happened."

With Gallo was his bride of three weeks, the former Sina Essary, whom he had courted after being paroled last March from the Ossining State Correctional Facility, where he had served eight years for extortion. Since then he had been seen with Jerry Orbach, the actor, and other show-business figures and had let it be

known that he was writing his memoirs with Mrs. Orbach.

The Gallos spent the evening drinking champagne at the Copacabana. Then at 4 a.m. they drove to Little Italy and parked outside the restaurant, Umberto's Clam House, which Gallo had never visited before. The party sat at two butcher-block tables at the rear, near a side door, eating "Italian delicacies." Mr. Gallo had just ordered a second helping when the assassin strode silently in the side door.

Women screamed and customers hit the floor as he started shooting. Mortally wounded, Gallo staggered out the front door as the killer kept firing after him. The killer fled out the back door, chased by the unknown man, who also kept shooting.

Little Italy was in an uproar. Down Mulberry Street, Sal Lapolla, a liquor store owner, was philosophical about Gallo's death. "These people, it's their choice," he said. "It's their life they lead. It's not our kind of life." ◼

BELOW: *Passersby examine the area on East 46th Street where Paul Castellano was shot.*

Gangland Killing Lures Gawkers To 46th Street

By **WILLIAM E. GEIST** | December 18, 1985

"IS THIS THE SPOT?" JANET D'AMICO ASKED as she joined the crowd.

"This is the spot," said Akeem Reynolds, who seemed to be there for the day, "from now on."

There was no formal ceremony, but a patch of pavement in front of Sparks Steak House, on East 46th Street near Third

Shot by Shot, Ex-Aide to Gotti Describes Castellano's Killing

By **ARNOLD H. LUBASCH** | March 4, 1992

SALVATORE GRAVANO, AN ADMITTED MAFIA underboss, gave a detailed and chilling account yesterday of the murder of Paul Castellano and several other slayings that he said were ordered or authorized by John Gotti.

In his second day on the stand, Mr. Gravano, a crucial prosecution witness who turned informer four months ago, testified in a gruff, matter-of-fact voice. He said he and Mr. Gotti waited together in a nearby car while several of their associates gunned down Mr. Castellano, the boss of their crime family, and his close aide, Thomas Bilotti, on an East Side street on Dec. 16, 1985.

Mr. Gravano said he sat beside Mr. Gotti, who drove a Lincoln sedan with tinted windows to the northwest corner of Third Avenue and 46th Street. He described himself as "a back-up shooter."

A car drew up alongside them and stopped for a red light, Mr. Gravano recalled. He said it was Mr. Castellano in another Lincoln driven by Mr. Bilotti.

He said he used a walkie-talkie to notify the gunmen up ahead that "they were stopped at the light, the first car, and they were coming through."

When the light changed, the car with Mr. Castellano drove across Third Avenue and parked in front of Sparks Steak House, Mr. Gravano said. Waiting for the two men, he said, were four gunmen wearing "white trench coats and black Russian hats." Mr. Castellano was shot first, he said, and Mr. Bilotti was getting out of the car when "somebody came up behind him and shot him."

Then, he said, Mr. Gotti drove slowly up to the murder scene.

Mr. Gravano said he was told later that Thomas Gambino, a reputed Gambino captain who was Mr. Castellano's nephew, entered Sparks Steak House moments later and encountered a reputed Gambino leader, Frank DiCicco, who had been scheduled to meet Mr. Castellano.

"Frankie told him that your uncle just got shot, just go back to your car and leave," Mr. Gravano said. ▪

Avenue, took its place in the annals of New York Mafia folklore yesterday as the place where Paul Castellano was murdered.

That is outside the posh East Side eatery where "Big Paul" Castellano—reputed Mafia chieftain, kingpin, czar, *capo di tutti capi* and graduate of the infamous 1957 Apalachin, N.Y., crime caucus—was rubbed out in a hail of bullets as he stepped from a chrome-plated black limousine in his $200 loafers, elegant dark-blue mohair suit and fat, gold pinky ring.

There were cries of anguish from regular patrons who believed that all the publicity would make the restaurant so popular that they'd never get a table again.

A man who described himself as the owner of a restaurant in Manhattan remarked that he would have "dragged the body around the corner to my place" if he had realized the gangland killing would bring so much publicity. He looked upon the throngs and the television crews and said tour buses were sure to follow.

Mike Cetta, who owns Sparks with his brother, Pat, and who spent much of the day being interviewed in front of the restaurant, said he was thankful the shooting took place outside, rather than inside, the restaurant. "We do not want to capitalize on this in any way," he said. "Could you put down that we were named the best steak place in New York?" ▪

Trash-Hauling Industry Linked to the Mafia

By **JOSEPH P. FRIED** | April 20, 1993

THE MAN WHO PROSECUTORS SAY HAS LONG controlled New York City's private trash-hauling industry for the Mafia was indicted on federal racketeering charges. Federal officials described the indictment as the second blow in a week to the mob's stranglehold on the industry in the New York region.

The accused man, 74-year-old James Failla, has long been the head of the Association of Trade Waste Removers of Greater New York, the largest trash industry trade group in the city. The government contends that Mr. Failla is a captain in the Gambino crime family and has used force and threats of violence to divide up collection routes in a way that has given New York City the highest commercial trash-hauling rates in the nation.

Mr. Failla was also charged with conspiring with John Gotti and others to murder another reputed mobster who was cooperating with prosecutors investigating the Gambino family. Mr. Gotti, who is in prison, is the head of the Gambino group.

The private trash-collection industry in New York City reportedly takes in $1 billion a year in revenues, picking up garbage at office buildings, restaurants and other commercial sites in the five boroughs. The city's Sanitation Department picks up garbage from private homes and apartment buildings.

The indictment of Mr. Failla (pronounced fye-YAL-ah) follows last week's indictment of Salvatore Avellino Jr., a reputed mobster said to be the long-dominant figure in Long Island's private garbage-collection business. Mr. Avellino was indicted on charges of racketeering and murder in connection with racketeering. Law-enforcement officials say that Mr. Avellino is a captain in the Lucchese crime family.

Mr. Failla, a white-haired man who walks with the aid of two crutches, pleaded not guilty before Judge Charles P. Sifton in Federal Court in Brooklyn. He was released after posting $1 million in bail. Investigators say that Mr. Failla is known in the underworld as Jimmy Brown, because of a penchant for brown clothes, but in court yesterday he was dressed in a blue sports jacket and blue slacks. ▪

Secretive Genovese Clan Seemed Almost Immune From the Law

By **SELWYN RAAB** | August 29, 1996

UNTIL THIS SUMMER, THE MAFIA'S MIGHTiest faction had seemed immune from prosecution. Even in the ultrasecretive world of the mob, the hierarchy of the Genovese crime family took extreme measures to evade surveillance and electronic eavesdropping.

They used code names, such as uncle or the skinny guy, when referring to leaders. Rarely did they speak about criminal matters on the telephone or inside their clubhouse hangouts, preferring walk-and-talk sessions on busy streets. Genovese dons even distrusted their counterparts in the four other Mafia families in the New York area.

Their secretiveness paid off. Unlike the other New York families—the Gambino, Lucchese, Colombo and Bonanno groups— the Genovese family was never undermined by turncoats, people who violate the "omerta," the Mafia's code of silence.

Recently, however, the family has suffered three severe blows capped by a federal judge's ruling that the family's reputed boss, Vincent (Chin) Gigante, is

"Alarming Alliance" of Mafia And Street Gang Is Broken Up

By DAVID W. CHEN and DAVID KOCIENIEWSKI | December 19, 2007

NEW JERSEY AUTHORITIES ON TUESDAY broke up what Attorney General Anne Milgram said was an "alarming alliance" between the Lucchese crime family and the Bloods street gang to supply drugs and cellphones to gang members inside a New Jersey prison.

mentally and physically competent to stand trial in Brooklyn on murder and racketeering charges. The ruling against Mr. Gigante comes two months after federal prosecutors in Westchester County indicted 19 suspected Genovese members— including three men who were accused of being Mr. Gigante's underboss, street boss and consiglieri—on separate racketeering and murder charges.

Last week, New Jersey state authorities arrested 12 members of a powerful Genovese crew who were accused of infiltrating and defrauding the health-care industry in several states. And in June, Mr. Gigante's brother Mario was indicted on charges that he masterminded a scheme to dominate the garbage-disposal industry in several counties north of New York City.

Organized crime experts say that the Genovese family in recent years supplanted the Gambino family as the nation's largest and wealthiest Mafia group. Law enforcement officials say it reaps millions in loot every year from its gambling, loansharking and narcotics operations and from labor racketeering and extortion in Port Elizabeth and Port Newark in New Jersey.

"They may be in disarray but they are far from being out of business," said Lewis D. Schiliro, the head of the Federal Bureau of Investigation's criminal division in the New York region. ▪

Two members of the Lucchese family connected to the prison scheme, Ms. Milgram said, were also involved in a sports gambling ring. The gambling operation took in $2.2 billion in bets over 15 months, mainly through the Internet, law enforcement officials say, and relied on violence and extortion to collect debts.

New York's five organized crime families have long built alliances with nontraditional organized crime groups in the city. But in New Jersey, the prison scheme provided the first evidence of an organized crime family from New York working with the Bloods street gang, one of the state's largest.

"What we have here in this case is really the realization of what we feared: connecting old-school organized crime, the Mafia, with new-school organized crime, gangs," Ms. Milgram said.

According to law enforcement officials, the prison scheme revolved around a prisoner, Edwin B. Spears, 33, who has served time for a variety of offenses since 2002.

Officials said that Mr. Spears, who is reputed to be a "five-star general" in the Nine Trey Gangsters faction of the Bloods, cooperated with two Lucchese members— Joseph M. Perna and Michael A. Cetta—to smuggle heroin, cocaine, marijuana and prepaid cellphones into East Jersey State Prison in Woodbridge.

They enlisted the help of Michael T. Bruinton, a senior prison guard, by offering him $500 each time he allowed smuggled goods to pass through, Ms. Milgram said. Mr. Perna and Mr. Cetta are suspected of having given money to Mr. Spears's brother, Dwayne E. Spears, to buy drugs and phones. Dwayne Spears then passed the goods to Mr. Bruinton, officials said, and they were given to inmates who had placed orders with Edwin Spears.

As of Tuesday night, Mr. Bruinton was still at large. "He wasn't home or at work," said Peter Aseltine, a spokesman for Ms. Milgram. ▪

Crime Board Tells How Boy Gangs Rise in New York Slums

March 20, 1927

THE DEGRAW STREET GANG, THE SACKETT Street gang, "the Harrisons," "the Cat's Alleys," the Rush Street gang and 21 other gangs of the Red Hook section of Brooklyn are the subjects of study by the New York State Crime Commission's Subcommission on Causes, which made public its findings yesterday.

The Red Hook section was selected first for a painstaking social survey because the ratio of juvenile delinquency there is five times as great as in the rest of Brooklyn.

Most of the misdeeds of the children result from their search for play and amusement in an environment which affords very little normal, wholesome sport or entertainment for children. They steal largely to get the money for amusements or for materials for toys and games, according to the report. The ordinary checks on misbehavior are largely missing in the district, because of bad home life and bad environment, race conflicts, the confusion of many languages, bad housing and other factors.

Gang life still has its thrills. The initiation to one gang, for instance, is said to consist of "drinking 12 glasses of wine and

> Gang life still has its thrills.

having a revolver held over their heads while taking an oath. The members of Gang T are said to be pledged to avenge wrongs done to any of its members of their relatives. The pastimes of Gang S are reported to be "shooting pool, playing craps, playing cards and prizefighting," while its delinquencies are "robbery and getting revenge on enemies."

The report gives the following close-up of the Sackett Street gang:

"This gang meets on Beach Place, a vacant section on the water front. They are quite an old gang and fairly large, consisting of between 20 and 25 members between the ages of 9 and 14 years. The members are Italian and Porto Rican. Its leader is a boy of 14. One of the members of this gang showed the informant a large scar on the back of his head, received in gang warfare, and he was quite proud of this." ▪

Yankee Caps Pulled After Protesters See Gang Links in Symbols and Colors

By RICHARD SANDOMIR | August 25, 2007

MAJOR LEAGUE BASEBALL'S OFFICIAL CAP manufacturer said yesterday that it would remove headwear bearing the colors and symbols of three gangs—the Bloods, the Crips and the Latin Kings—after activists

protested the sale of the caps at retail stores in East Harlem.

Two white Yankee caps made by New Era Cap were wrapped with red and blue bandannas that appear to represent the Bloods and Crips, and a black Yankee cap was embroidered with a crown symbolic of the Latin Kings.

The Yankees said in a statement that they were unaware of the caps' gang symbolism and had no approval rights on their design. The team said it learned about the caps yesterday and contacted Major League Baseball, which had already

Brooklyn Youth Gangs Concentrating on Robbery

August 1, 1974

SIX "HARD-CORE, ANTISOCIAL" YOUTH gangs are responsible for more than half of the criminal gang activity in northern Brooklyn, a Police Department gang intelligence officer said yesterday.

Lieut. Henry Murphy, who has charted youth gang movements in Brooklyn for more than two years, told the State Select Committee on Crime that in the last year the pattern of youth-gang activity in Brooklyn had "changed completely" from intergang warfare to a concentration on robbery, burglary and larceny.

This year, he said, there were 191 arrests of gang members in northern Brooklyn for robbery. The robbery arrest figure for Bronx gang members through mid-July was 429, a sharp increase over previous years.

"They're committing the same type crimes that organized crime or adults commit," Lieutenant Murphy said at a hearing on juvenile crime.

Lieutenant Murphy said that the largest percentage of youth gang members arrested for robbery and burglary in Brooklyn were those aged 14. Both he and Sgt. H. Craig

Collins of the Bronx gang intelligence unit said that many gangs now used members under 16 to commit murders because such youths get more lenient treatment in the courts.

Sergeant Collins declared that "gang incidents are declining and gangs are declining" in the Bronx. But he also showed the committee an arsenal of .30-caliber carbine automatics, rifles, shotguns, pistols and clubs confiscated last April from one gang leader's girlfriend's apartment. Sergeant Collins said many Bronx gang members were Vietnam veterans well-versed in sophisticated weaponry. ■

> The robbery arrest figure for Bronx gang members through mid-July was 429, a sharp increase over previous years.

BELOW: *Some gang members use Yankee baseball caps to display gang colors and symbols.*

taken action with New Era to recall them.

"Our concern was that parents weren't aware of the caps and their kids could get cut," said Stan Koehler, the executive director of Peace on the Street, a martial arts academy and meditation center that works with gang members.

Johnny Rivera, who led the rally, said he spotted the caps while shopping with his 11-year-old son a week ago, then walked around the neighborhood asking children what they thought they denoted.

"From 8 years old and up, they knew they represented violent gangs," he said. ■

The Mob in New York—
A Day of Infamy and Disgrace

August 14, 1863

THE INITIATION OF THE DRAFT ON SATURDAY in the Ninth Congressional District was characterized by so much order and good feeling as to well-nigh dispel the forebodings of tumult and violence which many entertained in connection with the enforcement of the conscription in this city. Very few, then, were prepared for the riotous demonstrations which prevailed almost unchecked in our streets.

As early as 9 o'clock, some laborers employed by two or three railroad companies, and in the iron foundries on the eastern side of the city, formed in procession in the 22nd Ward, and visited the different workshops in the upper wards, where large numbers were employed, and compelled them, by threats in some instances, to cease their work. The mob founds its way to the building where draftees' names were being called, (corner of Third Avenue and 46th Street), attacking it with clubs, stones, brickbats and other missiles. The upper part of the building was occupied by families, who were terrified beyond measure at the smashing of the windows, doors and furniture. Following these missiles, the mob rushed furiously into the office on the first floor, where the draft was going on, seizing the books, papers, records, lists, etcc., all of which they destroyed, except those contained in a large iron safe. The drafting officers were set upon with stones and clubs, and, with the reporters for the press and others, had to make a hasty exit through the rear.

Among the most outwardly features of the riot was the causeless and inhuman treatment of the negroes of the city. It seemed to be an understood thing throughout the city that the negroes should be attacked wherever found, whether they offered any provocation or not.

The Orphan Asylum for Colored Children was visited by the mob at about 4 o'clock. When it became evident that the

> Very few were prepared for the riotous demonstrations.

crowd intended to destroy it, a flag of truce appeared on the walk opposite, and the principals of the establishment made an appeal to the excited populace but in vain.

Here is where the Chief Engineer Decker showed himself as one of the bravest among the brave. After the entire building had been ransacked, a fire was set on the first floor. Mr. Decker did all he could, but when he was overpowered, with his own hands he extinguished the flames. A second attempt was made, this time in the three different parts of the house. Again he succeeded in defeating the incendiaries, with the aid of half a dozen of his men. ▪

Riots in Harlem:
The Overview

March 24, 1935

LAST TUESDAY AFTERNOON A 16-YEAR-OLD Puerto Rican boy, wandering through a Harlem five-and-ten-cent store, stole a penknife, worth a dime, from a counter tray. He was caught. It was a minor case of shoplifting, but its results were major, for within a few hours the streets of Harlem were overrun by 3,000 angry Negroes, who smashed store windows, attacked whites, fought the police, looted and fired buildings. The theft of a ten-cent knife set off a race riot.

In that riot more than 100 men, black

Race Riots

Thousands Riot in Harlem Area; Scores Are Hurt

By **PAUL L. MONTGOMERY** and **FRANCIS X. CLINES** | July 19, 1964

THOUSANDS OF RIOTING NEGROES RACED through the center of Harlem last night and early today, shouting at policemen and white people, pulling fire alarms, breaking windows and looting stores. At least 30 people were arrested.

There was no estimate on the number injured. Scores of people with bloodied heads were seen throughout the eight-block area between Eighth and Lenox Avenues and 123rd and 127th Streets, where most of the rioting occurred.

The riot grew out of a demonstration in front of the West 123rd Street police station protesting the slaying of a Negro youth by a white police lieutenant last Thursday. The demonstration followed a rally at 125th Street and Seventh Avenue, where speakers decried the shooting of the boy, 15-year-old James Powell, by Lieut. Thomas Gilligan in Yorkville.

When the police sealed off the block in front of the station house, between Seventh and Eighth Avenues, the shouting, keyed-up crowd spread out in angry groups in the surrounding neighborhood.

Shots fired into the air by policemen to disperse the milling crowds echoed through streets littered with overturned garbage cans and broken glass. More than 500 policemen, including all members of the tactical patrol force on duty in Manhattan and Brooklyn, were called out to control the mobs. But the crowds continued to grow as rumors of the rioting spread through the community.

Fire apparatus was brought in at 1 a.m. in an effort to block off streets in the riot area. Police roamed the streets with revolvers drawn.

On Lenox Avenue, between 125th and 126th Streets, police fired at people who were throwing bottles and bricks down at them from roofs. Some people milling at the corner of 125th Street and Lenox Avenue ran as the policemen fired. Others stood their ground, laughing and applauding. ∎

and white, were injured by bullets, knives, clubs or stones. The fighting went on for almost 12 hours. It was something new for New York, which had prided itself for years on the fact that here the two races lived in harmony.

A series of trivial events led up to the street warfare. First, there was the theft of the knife. A Negro women saw store employees search the thief; she became hysterical and shouted that the prisoner was being beaten by his captors, although he was not harmed, and soon the word got about that a Negro boy had been killed.

By coincidence, a hearse appeared. By that time there were crowds in the streets and they were convinced that the body of the thief was to be taken away. Members of the Young Liberators, a radical organization, paraded in front of the store, passing out hastily mimeographed pamphlets telling of a "brutal beating."

Five hundred policemen were thrown into the area of disorder and high police officials went to the scene to direct them. By 4 a.m. Wednesday the streets were clear.

Mayor La Guardia expressed the belief that the riot was "instigated and artificially stimulated by a few irresponsible individuals," and he appointed a committee of 11 people, Negroes and whites, to get to the bottom of it.

District Attorney Dodge, who took the case before the grand jury, held that radicals were responsible. "From my information," he said, "Communists distributed literature and took an active part in the riot." ∎

Maximum Sentences
In Bensonhurst Case

By **WILLIAM GLABERSON** | June 12, 1990

A BROOKLYN JUDGE SENTENCED TWO WHITE men to maximum prison terms for their roles in the killing of a black teenager that inflamed racial passions and divided New York City.

One of the white men, Joseph Fama, who was convicted of murdering Yusuf K. Hawkins in the Bensonhurst section of Brooklyn on Aug. 23, 1989, was sentenced to a term of 32 years and 8 months to life in prison.

Keith Mondello, who once admitted being the leader of a group of about 40 whites who pursued Mr. Hawkins and three black friends in the mostly white neighborhood, was sentenced to a term of 5 years and 4 months to 16 years.

Mr. Mondello was acquitted of murder and manslaughter charges but convicted of riot and other lesser charges last month in the case that has been at the center of intense emotions.

In Justice Thaddeus E. Owens's fourth-floor courtroom, a solid line of court officers separated the two sides of the room where the relatives of the accused and the family of the victim sat yesterday, as they had through the trial in April and May. Except for a brief outburst by Mr. Fama's family, the separate sentencing sessions were low-key.

Yusuf Hawkins's father, Moses Stewart, emerged from State Supreme Court arm in arm with his adviser, the Rev. Al Sharpton, who led the demonstrations in Bensonhurst after the killing that many said inflamed racial passions on both sides.

As the two men came out, a crowd of supporters cheered and both men raised their fists in a salute to victory.

"It is a small joy for myself," Mr. Stewart said, "but it is a great victory for black people all over the city."

Mr. Sharpton said there had been much strife and battle since Mr. Hawkins's death. But he added: "It was all worth it to make history today. I think we have made it clear to racists that they will be dealt with in New York." ∎

Once Again,
Racism Proves Fatal

By **SAM ROBERTS** | September 3, 1989

EARLY THIS SUMMER, WHEN SPIKE LEE'S "DO the Right Thing" opened, some commentators, white ones, mostly, nervously predicted that the film's portrayal of racial divisions in Brooklyn might provoke riots by blacks. It didn't.

But, on Aug. 23, a black teenager who ventured into Bensonhurst, Yusuf K. Hawkins, was gunned down by a group of whites— perhaps as a result of mistaken identity, but targeted, nonetheless, solely because he was black.

New York was never a melting pot. Each immigrant group enforced its own geographical and cultural boundaries that, at least until the newcomers achieved economic and political power, bred an insularity that still pervades enclaves like the blocks of Bensonhurst dominated by Italian immigrant families. Some members of virtually every immigrant group sought to elevate their own self-image by denigrating somebody else.

Blacks will always be singled out by their skin color. They are identified in some neighborhoods as outsiders.

Hate Crimes

Clashes Persist in Crown Heights

By **JOHN KIFNER** | August 22, 1991

BLACK YOUTHS HURLING ROCKS AND BOTTLES scuffled with the police in the Crown Heights section of Brooklyn overnight, even as Mayor David N. Dinkins tried personally to calm the racially troubled neighborhood after two nights of violence.

Mayor Dinkins's efforts turned sour as he was booed and jeered by hundreds of blacks when he tried to speak, and then was trapped inside the apartment of the family whose child died, as a black crowd outside pelted the building with rocks and bottles and pounded on the cars in the mayor's entourage.

Wedges of police officers formed a human shield in the doorway of the brick apartment house at 1671 President Street around 7:45 p.m. as the crowd surged around them, shouting: "This is not Palestine! We want justice!"

Mr. Dinkins finally got out, surrounded by a phalanx of bodyguards, only when Colin Moore, a lawyer respected locally for his civil rights work and defending blacks in difficult cases, including that of the Central Park jogger, pleaded with the crowd through a bullhorn: "Let the mayor go. Let the mayor go back to City Hall."

A march by several hundred black youths had already veered off to the headquarters of the Lubavitcher Hasidic sect—where a homemade Israeli flag was burned—and there were running, bottle-throwing skirmishes along Eastern Parkway for almost an hour by the time the mayor arrived for a meeting with about 50 black youths at Public School 167 around 5:30 p.m.

The focus of the black protesters had shifted through the day from the Hasidic community itself to the police, who were accused of favoring the Hasidim. The mayor had already incensed the Hasidic community by failing to attend the funeral yesterday morning of Yankel Rosenbaum, the visiting Australian Hasidic scholar who was stabbed to death by a group of black youths. The attack on the 29-year-old Mr. Rosenbaum was in apparent retaliation for the death of 7-year-old Gavin Cato, who was struck by a car driven by a Hasid. ∎

That was true of Yusuf Hawkins, who ventured into Bensonhurst to answer an advertisement for a used car and was mistaken for a friend of a young white woman from the neighborhood, and of Michael Griffith, chased to his death in Howard Beach after the car in which he was riding had broken down.

Last week, after black demonstrators showing their discontent were taunted by some bystanders in Bensonhurst, Spike Lee talked to young residents of the white community where Yusuf Hawkins was killed.

"What you're talking about is the way people think," he said. "You cannot change that overnight."

ABOVE: *Marchers protesting the killing of Yusef H. Hawkins in 1989.*

Nor can talk of change be heard over shooting and shouting. ∎

Officer, Seeking Some Mercy, Admits to Louima's Torture

By **DAVID BARSTOW** | May 26, 1999

JUSTIN A. VOLPE ADMITTED YESTERDAY THAT he rammed a stick into Abner Louima's rectum and then thrust it in his face, an act, the police officer acknowledged, intended to humiliate and intimidate the handcuffed Haitian immigrant.

"If you tell anybody about this, I'll find you and kill you," Mr. Volpe said he told Mr. Louima moments after the Aug. 9, 1997, assault in the restroom of the 70th Precinct station house in Brooklyn.

> "If you tell anybody about this, I'll find you and kill you," Mr. Volpe said.

ABOVE : *Abner Louima's lawsuit against the city ended with in a settlement of $8.75 million, the largest police brutality settlement in New York City history.*

By admitting guilt, Mr. Volpe hoped to be spared a life sentence for an assault that cast a shadow on the entire New York Police Department. But while he offered grim details about acts he has long denied, Mr. Volpe did not implicate any other officers by name, even though four others are still on trial in the case. As he confessed to six federal crimes, Mr. Volpe at times struggled for words when pressed to explain the forces that compelled him to torture Mr. Louima.

"When you put the stick up towards his face, having shoved it into his rectum, was a part of your effort to humiliate him?" Judge Eugene H. Nickerson of Federal District Court asked, his tone quietly insistent.

Mr. Volpe paused, unsure of himself. "I was in shock at the time, Your Honor," he said.

The judge repeated the question.

"I couldn't believe what happened," Mr. Volpe said, again seeming to fumble. And then, "I was mad."

Still unsatisfied, Judge Nickerson tried once more. "You intended to humiliate him?"

"Yes," Mr. Volpe finally said, averting his eyes.

Mr. Volpe, 27, wept only once, at the end of the 45-minute hearing, when he said to Judge Nickerson, "Your Honor, if I could just let the record reflect I'm sorry for hurting my family."

The judge cut him off. "You'll get a chance to do that when you come to sentence," he said.

Mr. Volpe wiped the tears from his eyes, and then turned and looked into the audience for his most outspoken defender, his father, Robert Volpe, a retired police detective once renowned for solving art thefts. The son managed a weak smile as guards escorted him from the courtroom.

"There are all different kinds of hell," Robert Volpe said later. "It's not easy seeing your son taken away." ■

Cleared as Criminals, But Forever on Trial

By **CLYDE HABERMAN** | April 29, 2008

YOU HAD TO WONDER IF THE SETTING WAS somebody's misguided stab at irony.

Four hours after being absolved of criminal wrongdoing, the three police detectives put on trial in the shooting death of Sean Bell stood last Friday before a battery of cameras and notebooks. The three men stood side by side in a conference room at the headquarters of their union, the Detectives' Endowment Association. Painted on the wall behind them was the union's circular logo. "The Greatest Detectives in the World," it said.

Oh, really? The greatest detectives in the world.

Granted, those words were meant for the city's detectives as a unit. No matter what they think of the judge's not-guilty verdict few are likely to hail these three men as the greatest detectives in the city, let alone in the world.

Even the judge, Justice Arthur J. Cooperman of State Supreme Court, implied that he did not think much of their performance on that November night in 2006. Yes, he cleared them of criminal behavior. But he also referred not once but twice to "carelessness and incompetence."

It boils down to a question of whether the city can safely, or sanely, put a gun in a police officer's hand and send him into the streets after he displayed judgment so flawed as to reasonably meet Justice Cooperman's standard of "carelessness and incompetence."

The odds seem long against a finding that these are indeed the greatest detectives in the world. ▪

The Legacy of a 41-Bullet Barrage

By **DAN BARRY** | February 27, 2000

THE DEATH OF AMADOU DIALLO LAST YEAR became a defining event for the New York Police Department. The shooting of the unarmed West African immigrant by four white officers spurred protests, prompted various examinations of the department's admittedly aggressive tactics, and attracted so much attention that police officials blamed the news media for what they said was a sudden timidity among the rank-and-file.

On Friday, a jury capped a riveting and often tense trial by finding the four officers not guilty of murder and several lesser charges.

The Diallo family, dismayed by the verdict, is expected to file a multimillion-dollar lawsuit against the city. The state attorney general's office is critically examining the department's "stop-and-frisk" policy. The officers may still face internal misconduct charges. The United States attorney for the Southern District of New York will review the evidence to determine whether the shooting violated federal civil rights laws.

And the Street Crime Unit has gone from being a jewel in the Giuliani administration's law-enforcement efforts to serving as Exhibit A in critics' charges that aggressive stop-and-frisk tactics violate basic rights; today, the unit bears only a trace resemblance to what it was when four of its members killed Mr. Diallo. The days of an elite corps of plainclothes officers roaming the city to prevent crime and seize guns appear to be over. ▪

Knapp Panel Describes
Police Corruption as "Extensive"

By **DAVID BURNHAM** | December 28, 1972

THE KNAPP COMMISSION ASSERTS IN ITS final report that high New York police officials ignored federal information that some of their men were suspected murderers, extortionists and heroin dealers.

The commission said its investigators had discovered evidence of three separate instances in which police officials, including former First Deputy Police Commissioner John F. Walsh, had failed to investigate allegations of serious misconduct made by the Bureau of Narcotics and Dangerous Drugs.

The commission also concluded that as of October 1971, police corruption in New York City was "an extensive, department-wide phenomenon, indulged in to some degree by a sizable majority of those on the force."

The commission report said that City Council President Sanford D. Garelik, formerly the chief inspector, had told the commission "that as a field commander he had received gratuities from businessmen he came in contact with in the course of his duties."

"Instead of returning these gifts or asking that they not be sent," the commission report said, "he stated he attempted to respond by giving return gifts of equal value."

A spokesman for Mr. Garelik, who was in Florida on vacation, said the commission's "use of the word gratuity is unfair and misleading."

"There certainly was nothing morally or ethically wrong in his actions," he added.

In a separate case, the commission concluded that Jay Kriegel, one of Mayor Lindsay's closest associates; Arnold G. Fraiman, city commissioner of investigation from 1966 to 1968 and now a state supreme court justice; and Commissioner Walsh all failed to act when informed of widespread bribery among plainclothes policemen responsible for enforcing the gambling laws in the Bronx.

The commission did not offer a judgment about whether Mayor Lindsay was culpable for the inaction. But the commission did conclude that "it is clear that the mayor's office did not see to it that the specific charges of corruption" made by one policeman—Frank Serpico—"were investigated." ▪

For Mr. Fix-It, A New Scandal To Mop Up

By **AL BAKER** | January 26, 2008

IN THIS STREET MATRIX OF MANAGEMENT styles, Deputy Chief Joseph J. Reznick might well come under the heading "Dominant/ Aggressive," maybe even "Hostile."

Now, the arrest of four narcotics officers in Brooklyn has given the Police Department a black eye, and Chief Reznick, a veteran whose name pops up in all manner of big cases, has been brought in to clean up a scandal that has caused 80 drug prosecutions to collapse.

The chief would not discuss the drugs-for-informants scandal in Brooklyn South Narcotics, nor what his plans were in dealing with it. But he spoke at length about his career, and his outlook.

Chief Reznick joined the department in December 1973 after a stint in the Navy. More remarkable than his longevity is the number of times he has been in the middle of the latest hot issue at the department.

He was involved in the investigation of the torture and killing of Jonathan M. Levin, a

Charges of Police Misconduct Prompt Change in Department

By **ELISSA GOOTMAN** | September 23, 2002

MORE THAN FIVE YEARS HAVE PASSED SINCE Abner Louima became a household name in New York City, a chilling symbol of what could go wrong in a police department praised for making the city a safer, cleaner place.

Those years have been dotted with transformative events for the department. There was the case of Amadou Diallo, the unarmed black man shot on his doorstep by police officers who thought he was pulling out a gun. There were protests, as critics lumped the two cases together, and there were policy changes, as the department responded by setting up panels and committees that ensured input from black neighborhoods, and tried with modest success to recruit more black and Hispanic officers.

There was a change in leadership at City Hall, with Mayor Michael R. Bloomberg winning praise from many of his predecessor's critics. And then there was Sept. 11, which took the lives of officers and cast a glow of heroism on the survivors.

"It is not the same police department that it was five years ago," said Thomas A. Reppetto, president of the Citizens Crime Commission of New York City, a criminal justice research group.

And changes, in turn, have been made, some of them in direct response to the Louima case and others stemming from events that overtook it. Allegations of police misconduct to the Civilian Complaint Review Board have declined in recent years. Last year, 4,260 complaints were filed, a figure 11 percent lower than the number of complaints received in 1997: 4,768.

And there have been other changes, like the creation of a Board of Visitors, through which teachers, lawyers and other community members review the department's recruitment and training practices.

"It's a gradual change that's happened," said Richard E. Green, a community leader in Crown Heights, Brooklyn, and a member of the Board of Visitors. "They're taking a very proactive approach, putting checks and balances in place to ensure that it doesn't happen or when it does happen, there is a quick remedy." ▪

teacher, in his Manhattan apartment in 1997; the murder of Irene Silverman in her Upper East Side town house in 1998; and the murder of the girl they called "Baby Hope," a 5-year-old whose body was found packed into a picnic cooler off the Henry Hudson Parkway. He also led the chase for the suspects in the killing of Officer Russel Timoshenko, 23. They were captured off Interstate 80 in Pennsylvania.

It's been just a few days since he got the assignment to Brooklyn South Narcotics. Two narcotics officers, Detective Sean Johnstone and Officer Julio Alvarez, are accused of lying about the amount of cocaine they recovered from a suspect. Detective Johnstone was later recorded talking about withholding drugs and the practice of giving them to informants.

A subsequent inquiry led to the arrests last week of two other officers in the unit, Sgt. Michael Arenella and Officer Jerry Bowens. They are accused in court papers of taking drugs and cash they had recovered and of giving them to a confidential informant as payback.

As a result, four high-level police commanders have been transferred, and Chief Reznick has been brought in. He would say only that he'll use "my skills, my experience, as I've done in the past, to make good" in Brooklyn South Narcotics. ▪

The Line of Fire Is Again Part Of the Line of Duty

By **RANDY KENNEDY** | March 16, 2003

THEY DID NOT DIE FIGHTING A HORRIFIC ACT of international terrorism. They did not die trying to rescue thousands of people. The place where they died was not instantly recognizable around the world, nor will it ever be. It was a nondescript patch of road through a working-class Staten Island neighborhood, where last week a small tuft of paper roses sat near a chain-link fence, next to a laminated paper sign that said, "May God Bless Our Two Heroes."

As one police lieutenant said, the deaths of the two undercover detectives felt, in an unexpected way, like a return to normal— "a very sad normal." But as the first line-of-duty deaths in the city's uniformed services since Sept. 11, 2001, the slayings of Detectives James V. Nemorin, 36, and Rodney J.

BELOW: *Detective Rodney J. Andrews's fellow officers served as pallbearers at his funeral service at the Elim International Fellowship Church in Brooklyn.*

Andrews, 34, reminded the city of the way police officers have always died on the job and will continue to die as long as there is violence and random chance: doing the everyday, incremental, perilous work that keeps one more gun, one more criminal, off the streets.

For the public and even for officers themselves, the World Trade Center attack profoundly changed the context of line-of-duty deaths. In several interviews last week inside and outside the police department, those who talked about the detectives' deaths said that the shootings seemed like a reminder of an older kind of reality—no less tragic than Sept. 11, but different.

"It's a reminder of the daily terror on the streets, as opposed to the foreign terror, the daily terror that was rampant for years before 9/11," said Eli B. Silverman, a professor of police studies at the John Jay School of Criminal Justice. "The public knows that crime has gone down, but are they really aware of how that actually happens, every day, on the streets? I don't think they are, and this is a reminder that it's never easy."

Police officers have of course never forgotten how hard or dangerous the job is. But they said the killings on Staten Island— the first fatal shooting of a police officer on the job since 1998—brought back, even to them, a kind of feeling they have not had in a long time. The World Trade Center attack, because it was so extraordinary, did not bring the same sense of vulnerability to some officers that a shooting in the line of duty does.

"This hit home: You know the peril, that feeling in your heart when something is about to go wrong," said Marq Claxton, a detective in the 90th Precinct in Williamsburg, Brooklyn, who worked for five years in undercover narcotics operations and knew Detective Andrews. "If you did that kind of work, you know that undercover operations are just one itchy trigger finger, one turn of emotion or fit of anger away from tragedy." ∎

In High Crime Neighborhoods Community Policing Has Its Limits

By **LYNETTE HOLLOWAY** | July 18, 1993

OFFICER MICHAEL LOPEZ WAS WALKING HIS beat in East New York, Brooklyn, recently when the barrage began: rocks, bottles and debris hurtled toward him from the rooftop of a housing project.

Officer Lopez ducked, ran for cover and, getting the message, established a new policy: never to walk alone near high-rises again.

As a community police officer, he is supposed to build ties and cooperation within neighborhoods to help fight crime, but in the 75th Precinct, one of the city's most violent and a place where mistrust of the police runs high, that is no easy task.

Community policing is being phased in throughout the city, and some progress has been reported in more stable neighborhoods. But the toughest test for New York's new crime-fighting philosophy will come in high-crime neighborhoods like East New York, where officers work in an atmosphere of fear, hostility and alienation, the kind of tension that afflicts relations between the police and minority residents throughout the country. Residents say they sense the officers' fear, increasing the friction.

The idea behind community policing is to get officers out of squad cars and onto neighborhood streets. Many experts say the limits of this type of policing become apparent in areas like East New York, which often lack the civic cohesion that can help prevent crime.

In the 75th, 38 community police officers are divided into 26 beats throughout the six-square mile precinct. As they walk their beats, they are expected to create networks of cooperation and information-sharing among residents and solve persistent crime problems. Officers have started green thumb programs, growing cabbage and tomatoes in vacant lots where crack houses once flourished; coordinated street cleanups and, most significantly, reached out to the area's youth in the hopes of changing their attitudes about the police.

But such efforts go only so far in East New York, which often resembles a war zone with its many charred buildings, trash-filled vacant lots and barren streets. The 75th Precinct counted 90 murders within its borders last year, second only to the 34th in Washington Heights, and the number is up sharply this year, 71 through June. Overall crime fell 3.1 percent last year but that was far below the 7.8 percent drop for the entire city.

> The toughest test for New York's new crime-fighting philosophy will come in high-crime neighborhoods like East New York, where officers work in an atmosphere of fear, hostility and alienation.

The rules that govern residents' everyday existence prohibit them from developing close ties with the police, enveloping them in a code of silence almost as strong as that of the "blue wall" of silence that is said to exist among police officers. Tenant patrols or neighborhood watch groups are fragmented, if they exist at all.

"People don't want you to come to their houses because the criminals might think they're giving up information," said Officer Lopez, who works in an area west of Pennsylvania Avenue once labeled the "Dead Zone" because of the vacant lots and the frequency of killings there. "They could get hit. So I do a lot of work by phone." ∎

Seven Masked Thugs Get More Than $3 Million in JFK Holdup

By **PRANAY GUPTE** | December 12, 1978

SEVEN MASKED MEN, BRANDISHING SHOT-guns and automatic pistols, drove up to a Lufthansa cargo facility at Kennedy International Airport in the middle of the night, handcuffed nine employees and beat up another, disconnected an alarm and made off with a reported $3 million in cash and jewelry worth possibly $2 million.

If estimates of the loss are correct, the robbery would be the second largest cash theft in United States history, exceeded only by the $4.3 million loss in the robbery at Purolator Security in Chicago in October of 1974.

The police noted that the robbers at Kennedy were familiar with the layout of the cargo building and knew the exact location of a high-value storage room where the currency was kept.

"It went off like clockwork," said James Connolly, a spokesman for the police force of the Port Authority of New York and New Jersey, which runs the airport.

Officials said the trouble began at 3:15 in the morning. Kerry Whalen, an employee of the West German airline, was working in the ramp area of the huge building. Mr. Whalen heard a van approaching, but because vans and trucks come and go in the cargo area, he thought little of it.

It was a black 1978 Ford Econoline Series 150 van, and there were seven men in it. Six of them, all masked and waving shotguns or automatic handguns, jumped out. Mr. Whalen ran back toward the ramp, shouting: "Help!" He was overtaken by one of the intruders, hit on the head with a pistol and pummeled with fists as he fell to the ground. The gunmen moved up the delivery ramp toward a high-value storage room behind the ramp.

As they went there, Ralph Rebmann, a guard, arrived. He had heard, from a distance, Mr. Whalen's cry for help. Mr. Rebmann was spotted by the masked men, overpowered and dragged along to the storage room. The bandits knew where the alarm was, and as they approached the storage room, they accosted another employee, whom they forced to disconnect the alarm.

Four men then opened the storage-room door with a key that one produced from his pocket. Eventually nine employees were handcuffed and taken to a third-floor cafeteria.

It was laborious work carting off the currency; the money was in solid metal boxes. The jewelry, too, was in boxes—35 in all.

At 4:15 a.m. the masked men took one last look around, went back to their van and drove away. About 15 minutes later one of the handcuffed employees managed to stand up and stagger toward the stairs. He apparently saw an incoming worker, who quickly assessed the situation and called the police. ∎

Not Exactly Dillinger, But Prolific

By **MICHAEL WILSON** | September 12, 2003

FOR TWO YEARS, THE MAN SLIPPED AWAY from a remarkable 36 bank robberies in Queens and Manhattan. He came away from eight other attempts empty-handed. Nothing flashy: Mets cap, sunglasses and a long-sleeved shirt, passing the teller a short note demanding money, and rarely showing a gun. There was even the hint of opportunistic cleverness: on the day after Sept. 11, 2001, he robbed three banks.

So whomever the police expected to find when they came through an apartment door in Jamaica, Queens, it was probably not the 44-year-old man they said they found loafing on the couch: Raymond Masi, a homeless

ROBBERIES

Workers Foil Bank Robber; Passers-By Return His Loot

By **CHRISTINE HAUSER** | November 26, 2008

THREE A.T.M. TECHNICIANS HELPED FOIL A robbery at a garment district bank on Tuesday morning, the police said, and passers-by helped gather the bills that scattered when the robber fled, and returned them.

All the stolen money was accounted for, the police said.

The scene unfolded just before 10:45 a.m., when a man walked into the Sterling National Bank at 512 Seventh Avenue, near 38th Street, and handed a teller a note demanding money. The teller handed over $1,082 to the man, who did not have a weapon, said the chief police spokesman, Paul J. Browne.

"As the man was leaving the bank, the teller shouted: 'Stop him! He just robbed the bank!'" Mr. Browne said.

The technicians, who were repairing the bank's A.T.M.s, heard the cry and gave chase, Mr. Browne said. The bank robber ran onto 38th Street, where traffic was at a standstill. As he wove between cars, the technicians grabbed him, the police said, and pushed him onto the hood of a vehicle.

When officers arrived, Mr. Browne said, one of the posse was holding the robber, while the other two were nearby, with a large crowd around them. The cash had scattered, some of it in a small pile between two cars. Pedestrians walked up to police officers or bank employees and handed over bills they had picked up, a witness and the police said.

"Even in the bad economy, all $1,082 that had been scattered before the police arrived was recovered in full," Mr. Browne said.

The robbery suspect was identified as Thomas Slater, 43, Mr. Browne said. He faces a bank robbery charge and is being investigated in three other bank robberies, Mr. Browne said.

A short time later, the police commissioner, Raymond W. Kelly, said at a briefing, planned before the Seventh Avenue robbery, that bank robberies were on the rise this year, and that most were carried out by robbers who passed notes. As he has before, he attributed the increase to the opening of more branches and to the extended hours offered by more banks. He also some banks were not adopting practices recommended by the police department, like using bullet-resistant barriers as dividers between customers and tellers.

heroin addict for most of his adult life, a man with a long, low-level criminal history who sometimes lived in the woods.

Others have been arrested recently in serial bank robberies: 12 robberies here, 14 there. But nothing close to 36.

Asked if he could recall a more prolific bank robber, Capt. Michael Hines, commander of the major case squad, said, "Not in my memory, no."

The police did not release a dollar amount of the money Mr. Masi is accused of stealing, but said he had robbed banks 36 times and made 8 other attempts that were unsuccessful.

The police said the long gaps between some robberies—sometimes a month or more—correspond with Mr. Masi's jail time for smaller crimes, most recently in January, when he served 120 days for petty larceny, Captain Hines said. "He's basically claiming he learned about it"—robbing a string of banks—"in jail," Captain Hines said. ▪

The Sterling National branch, where tellers work behind partitions, was closed for several hours. Only bank employees were allowed in.

Cyrus Harrison, the owner of a small clothing and accessories store on Seventh Avenue near the bank, said he was standing in front of his shop when the robber fled. "He dropped the cash on the ground, then got apprehended," said Mr. Harrison. ▪

Victims and Heroes
DISASTERS

Ordinary police-blotter entries, these are not: snowstorms that break records dating to just after the Civil War; construction cranes that tumble from high above crowded sidewalks; gasoline-laden barges that explode with a rumble like an earthquake, rocking everything for miles.

In New York even the close calls are closer, the miracle escapes more miraculous. A window washer survives a 47-story plunge from an apartment building. A jetliner taking off from LaGuardia Airport crosses paths with high-flying Canada geese that knock out both of the plane's big engines, but the pilot steers the way to a smooth landing in the Hudson River. Everyone—all 150 passengers and 5 crew members—steps out onto the wings, safe.

Or what about the man who had a seizure while waiting for the subway, and fell to the tracks as

▼ PAGE 308

▲ PAGE 302

a train pulled into the station. A 50-year-old construction worker named Wesley Autrey dove from the platform and pushed the man into the shallow space between the rails. The worried crowd on the platform sighed with relief on hearing the hero's voice: "We're O.K. down here."

In New York, there are century-old steam pipes that split open once in a while, shooting geysers of steam like Old Faithful. There are needless tragedies: fires that engulf social clubs where the exits have been chained shut.

These are events the journalist and best-selling author Jon Meacham had in mind when he said that "the dramas particular to New York, a place of extremes, are more often of universal interest than, well, Kansas City's."

So the lights go out—all the lights, at once. In seconds, eight million people are totally disconnected. Imagine that.

In forty years that happened not once, not twice, but three times, and the three blackouts caught the city at three different moments. As noted in one of the articles excerpted here, the first big power failure, in 1965, was the good blackout, the one when the city could still grin and bear it. The social fabric did not fray that

night. But in some neighborhoods it disintegrated completely during the second blackout, twelve years later—the bad blackout, the one that is remembered as yet another chaotic night in a troubled summer when people were already jittery about the Son of Sam serial killings and financial crises that had left City Hall all but bankrupt. That night in 1977, it was as if there were suddenly two New Yorks. In the one that encompassed the lower two-thirds of Manhattan, people once again pulled together—pedestrians stepped in to direct traffic because the stop lights were out, and restaurants gave away food before it spoiled. In other parts of the city, looters smashed plate glass windows, emptied store shelves, even carted away major appliances like washing machines. The police arrested 3,700 people, 10 times as many as during race riots in Harlem and Brooklyn in 1964.

The 2003 blackout was different from either of the earlier ones. It was the first citywide catastrophe since the 9/11 attacks 20 months before. This time, the cause was nothing so deliberate—or ominous. Somewhere in the Midwest, a tree had knocked down a power cable. A cascade of overloaded circuits shut down about 100 power plants

in the Midwest and Northeast in about nine seconds.

In New York, people went home, relieved that their first suspicion had been wrong: this was not a terrorist attack on the nation's electrical grid. In some neighborhoods people partied in the streets until the wee hours. In midtown Manhattan, suburbanites who could not make it home or hotel guests who could not make it to their rooms simply slept on the sidewalks. Some 850 people were arrested overnight, noticeably fewer than the usual nightly average of 950. "New Yorkers showed that the city that burned in the 1970's when facing similar circumstances is now a very different place," the mayor said.

It was indeed a different place, because the 9/11 attacks had changed things in ways that other catastrophes could not. The scope remains almost unimaginable: the twin towers of the World Trade Center collapsed in less than two hours, leaving behind tons of debris smoldering at what came to be called "ground zero" and leaving rescue workers to sift through twisted metal and potentially toxic dust. They hoped that the next time their radios crackled with word of trouble, it would not be like this.

▼ PAGE 315

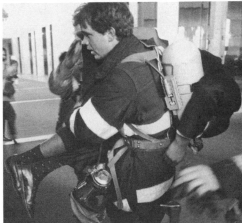

Power Failure Snarls Northeast; 800,000 Caught in Subways

By **PETER KIHSS** | November 10, 1965

THE LARGEST POWER FAILURE IN HISTORY blacked out nearly all of New York City, parts of nine Northeastern states and two provinces of southeastern Canada. Some 80,000 square miles, in which perhaps 25 million people live and work, were affected.

It was more than three hours before the first lights came back on in any part of the New York City area. When they came on in Nassau and Suffolk Counties at 9 p.m., overloads plunged the area into darkness again in 10 minutes.

Striking at the evening rush hour, the power failure trapped 800,000 riders on New York City's subways. Railroads halted. Traffic was jammed. Airplanes found themselves circling, unable to land.

Five thousand off-duty policemen were summoned to duty. Ten thousand National Guardsmen were called up in New York City alone.

The Fire Department, too, brought in off-duty firemen because their overloaded telephone and telegraphic communications made it difficult to keep contact with scattered fire apparatus in the field. The Fire Department radio was out of service from 5:30 p.m. to 8:30 p.m. and the dispatchers had to keep in touch with the firehouses and vehicles by telephone. They had the radio system back in operation at 8:30.

The lights and the power went out first at 5:17 p.m. somewhere along the Niagara frontier of New York State. Nobody could tell why for hours afterward.

At 5:27 p.m. the lights began sputtering in New York City, and within seconds the giant Consolidated Edison system blacked out in Manhattan, the Bronx, Queens and most of Brooklyn—but not in Staten Island and parts of Brooklyn that were interconnected with the Public Service Electric and Gas Company of New Jersey. ◼

Down These Mean Streets

By **FRANCIS X. CLINES** | July 15, 1977

THE LOOTERS SCATTERED, ROACHLIKE, IN the morning sunlight, then stopped to watch when the owner of Joe's candy store showed up and saw his store disemboweled on the Brownsville sidewalk. He let out a howl and went after one edge of the crowd that held his candy bars and cigarettes.

The looters skittered off a bit more, the children and women in screams and laughter, the teenaged boys swaggering, like toreadors.

The crowd was discovering after a night of looting that not only could the store-breaking be continued in daylight, but also

that the arrival of the owner only heightened the occasion to a mass tease, like the running of the bulls in Pamplona.

"Oh, those scum, those bastards, those rotten scum," said Frank Mason. All along Pitkin Avenue, the Brownsville shopping district where he grew up, the texture of the blackout this time was becoming visible. And on Pitkin Avenue the texture of the blackout this time eclipsed fond remembrances of 1965 and its sense of friendly survival.

The darkness this time was blood on the window shards of Kiddie Bargain Town on Pitkin Avenue, where the looters wadded themselves in and popped back out with baby carriages and strollers and infant parapher-nalia. The darkness this time was two little boys initiating themselves into theft, clambering through the charred remains of

When Looters Loot Looters

By **MARTIN GOTTLIEB** and **JAMES GLANZ** | August 15, 2003

THERE WERE, UNTIL NOW, THE GOOD BLACKout and the bad blackout: the 15-hour power loss in 1965 that was largely characterized by cooperation and overriding good cheer, and the 25-hour one in 1977 that was defined by widespread looting and arson in the city's poorer neighborhoods.

Until Sept. 11, 2001, they were the most wide-ranging catastrophic events in modern New York City, causing, in the case of the 1977 blackout alone, 3,800 arrests and more than $1 billion in damage that can still be seen in the Bushwick neighborhood of Brooklyn. The first blackout instantly became an emblem of civic spunk and resilience, the second of civic disarray and uncertainty at a time of overwhelming municipal budget woes, economic deterioration, and fear caused by a serial killer known as Son of Sam.

In 1965, the city underwent an epidemic of pluck. People voluntarily directed traffic, handed out candles and settled down at Grand Central Station for a night of sleep, without much of a worry about their wallets.

In 1977, many veterans of the 1965 blackout headed to the streets at the first sign of darkness. But they did not find the same spirit. The Fire Department counted 1,037 fires in the city that night, more than 50 of them serious. On streets like Brooklyn's Broadway the rumble of iron store gates being forced up and the shattering of glass preceded scenes of couches and televisions being paraded through the streets.

"The looters were looting other looters, and the fists and the knives were coming out," said Carl St. Martin, who was a third-year medical student and spent the night suturing a succession of angry wounds at Wyckoff Heights Hospital. Before the lights came back on, even Brooks Brothers on Madison Avenue had been looted. ∎

BELOW: *Looters in Bedford-Stuyvesant, Brooklyn began running after hearing police sirens in 1977.*

John's Bargain Store, coming out with school supplies and almost getting trampled by an old woman protecting an armful of pots.

"Hey, like everything's free," said Albert Figueroa, summarizing the crowd's mood even as he helped his neighbors at a looted jewelry store by keeping his leashed German shepherd, King, snarling at the doorway.

Mr. Mason took it all personally. "This is my roots, where I grew up," he said, moving toward his own auto repair shop, which had been spared. He stopped outside 1707 Pitkin, the Jewel Box, plundered apart. "That's where I got my wife's engagement ring—aw, man," Mr. Mason said. He looked sad standing next to a small boy who was showing off a fine gold chain he had picked up in the daylight. ∎

Power Surge Blacks Out Northeast Once Again

By **JAMES BARRON** | August 15, 2003

A SURGE OF ELECTRICITY TO WESTERN NEW York and Canada touched off a series of power failures and enforced blackouts that left parts of at least eight states in the Northeast and the Midwest without electricity. The problems forced the evacuation of office buildings, stranded thousands of commuters and flooded some hospitals with patients suffering in the stifling heat.

In an instant that one utility official called a "blink-of-the-eye" moment shortly after 4 p.m., the grid that distributes electricity to the eastern United States became overloaded. As circuit breakers tripped at generating stations from New York to Michigan and into Canada, millions of people were instantly caught up in the largest blackout in American history.

The power in New York City was shut off by officials struggling to head off a wider blackout. Cleveland and Detroit went dark, as did Toronto and sections of New Jersey, Pennsylvania, Connecticut and Massachusetts.

Officials worked into the night to put the grid back in operation and restore electric service. Mayor Michael R. Bloomberg said that that the power was back on in parts of Brooklyn, the Bronx and Queens by 11 p.m.—but not in Manhattan.

The blackout began just after the stock exchanges had closed for the day, a slow summer day of relatively light trading. Office workers who were still at their desks watched their computer monitors blink off without warning. Soon hospitals and government buildings were switching on backup generators to keep essential equipment operating, and the police were evacuating people trapped in elevators.

Thousands of subway passengers in New York City had to be evacuated from tunnels, and in a city still jittery from the Sept. 11 terror attacks, some people worried as they tried to find their way home. "All I could think was here we go again—it's just like Sept.

11," said Catherine Donnelly, who works at the New York Stock Exchange.

So there was no air conditioning, no television, no computers. There was Times Square without its neon glow and Broadway marquees without their incandescence—all the shows were canceled. And there was a skyline that had never looked quite the way it did last night: the long, long taut strings of the bridges were dark, the red eyes that usually blink at the very top not red, not blinking.

There was at least one pocket of trouble: On the Lower East Side, an upscale sneaker store was broken into and one of the owners beaten between 11 p.m. and midnight. ∎

A Powerless New York Endures

By **DAVID BARSTOW** | August 15, 2003

A TIMES SQUARE WITH NO WORKING TRAFFIC lights is not a pretty sight.

But there stood Debra Ramsur, a traffic officer with spotless white gloves and a gleaming silver whistle, who for a time yesterday afternoon single-handedly tamed the great tides of cars and people. "Back it up!" she barked to a taxicab. "Let's go!" she bellowed to a laggard pedestrian. And then, a bit more sweetly, "Watch out, folks."

On a day of colossal disruption, New York City was filled with similar scenes of stubborn resilience—and also with moments of overheated frustration, spontaneous generosity, instant profiteering, anger and humor.

It was also, as many residents were quick to note, a day with faint and unsettling echoes of the way the city felt and looked and acted on Sept. 11. Buses were packed, with

More Lights Go On in Queens, One Unhappy Block at a Time

By **ROBERT D. MCFADDEN** | July 24, 2006

CONSOLIDATED EDISON REPORTED MAJOR progress in the week-old struggle to restore power to western Queens, but thousands faced a new workweek without electricity and frustrations boiled over as some officials called for a declaration of emergency and the resignation of the utility's chief executive.

Kevin Burke, Con Ed's chairman and chief executive, said at a briefing that utility crews had restored power to nearly 16,000 of the approximately 25,000 customers affected by the blackout. In human terms, that meant that the lights, elevators, refrigerators and air-conditioners were

back on for an estimated 64,000 of the 100,000 people who had suffered through the ordeal.

Mr. Burke insisted that he could still provide no estimate of when full power might be restored to eight square miles of Astoria, Long Island City, Woodside, Sunnyside, Hunters Point and other sections. Underground cables had burned out in those areas, apparently overloaded by the utility's decision to keep the power flowing to most of the 400,000 residents of western Queens despite the loss of 10 major feeder cables that power the area.

That decision meant that all of the area's power was running through only 12 feeder cables, and through transformers and secondary cables that were not designed to take such a heavy load.

Mr. Burke said he had no explanation for why the 10 major cables went down while Con Edison's 56 other feeder cable networks continued to work. The root cause of the blackout, one of the city's most prolonged in decades, is under investigation by the utility itself and by the Queens district attorney's office, the City Council and the state's Public Service Commission. ▪

commuters pressed right up to the front windshields. Mini-communities instantly formed near every car radio and boom box. People walked along dialing again and again on cellphones that did not work, trying to reach their families.

But if there was palpable relief as word spread that this was not the work of terrorists, there were also real though isolated moments of terror, and even tragedy.

One middle-aged woman walked down many flights of stairs inside the darkened Met Life Building. Then she collapsed. A team of paramedics tried to resuscitate her. She stopped breathing. The paramedics tried desperately to call for an ambulance. There were none to be found quickly on this afternoon of sudden chaos.

And so she lay there for more than half an hour, her body growing cold, in a dimly lit corner of Café Centro. The paramedics never gave up. Yet by the time an ambulance could be flagged down, it was too late. The woman was pronounced dead at St. Clare's Hospital in Manhattan. ▪

BELOW: *Con Ed employees pulling cable in Astoria during the 2006 blackout, which affected 174,000 people and caused business losses of tens of millions of dollars.*

Blast Hits Trade Center; Car Bomb Is Suspected

By **ROBERT D. MCFADDEN** | February 27, 1993

AN EXPLOSION APPARENTLY CAUSED BY A car bomb in an underground garage shook the World Trade Center in lower Manhattan with the force of a small earthquake, collapsing walls and floors, igniting fires and plunging the city's largest building complex into a maelstrom of smoke, darkness and fearful chaos.

The police said the blast killed at least five people and left more than 650 others injured, mostly with smoke inhalation or minor burns, but dozens with cuts, bruises, broken bones or serious burns. The police said 476 were treated at hospitals and the rest by rescue and medical crews at the scene.

The explosion, which was felt throughout the Wall Street area and a mile away on Ellis and Liberty Islands in New York Harbor, also trapped hundreds of people in debris or in smoke-filled stairwells and elevators of the towers overhead and forced the evacuation of more than 50,000 workers from a trade center bereft of power for lights and elevators for seven hours.

The blast also knocked out the police command and operations centers for the towers, which officials said rendered the office complex's evacuation plans useless. There had been no warning of an impending explosion, Police Commissioner Raymond W. Kelly said.

The effects of the blast radiated outward, and on a day of high drama, tragedy and heroism, there were a thousand stories: rescuers digging frantically for victims in the collapsed PATH station under the towers, soot-streaked evacuees groping for hours in the city's tallest buildings, a woman in a wheelchair carried down 66 stories by two friends, a pregnant woman airlifted by helicopter from a tower roof, and the tales of many others stumbling out, gasping for air, terrified but glad to be alive.

And among the most poignant was that of a class of kindergartners from Public School 95 in Gravesend, Brooklyn. Caught on the 107th

Horse Truck Explodes On Wall Street

September 17, 1920

AN EXPLOSION, BELIEVED TO HAVE BEEN caused by a time bomb, killed 30 people and injured probably 300 others at Broad Street and Wall Streets yesterday at noon.

The blast shattered windows for blocks around, threw the financial district into a panic and strewed the street in its immediate vicinity with the bodies of its dead and injured victims. Investigating authorities are almost certain that the disaster was due to an infernal machine left on an uncovered one-horse truck in Wall Street directly in front of the new United States Assay Office next door to the Sub-Treasury, and directly across the street from the J.P. Morgan building.

While no arrest has been made up to last midnight, Federal, State, and city authorities were agreed that the devastating blast signaled long-threatened Red outrages.

Throughout the nation the same interpretation was placed upon the explosion, and public buildings and great storehouses of wealth as well as conspicuous men in several cities, were placed under vigilant guard.

A guard of thirty detectives was placed around the Morgan home in Madison Avenue last night. Pedestrians were not allowed to pass in front of the house. It was said the guard would be kept on duty all night.

floor observatory, they took all day to walk down, singing to keep up their spirits.

The blast, which erupted at 12:18 p.m. on the second level of a four-story underground parking garage beneath the trade center's 110-story twin towers and the complex's Vista Hotel, sent cars hurtling like toys, blew out a 100-foot wall and sent the

Police investigators are convinced that they face a piece of organized deviltry, executed with a terrible effectiveness that dwarfed such anarchist and other radical crimes of the past as the attempts on the lives of Russell Sage and Henry C. Frick, and the bombs in Union Square, and St. Peter's Cathedral.

If their interpretation is correct, the conspirators in large measure failed of whatever direct objects they had beyond sheer terrorization. They evidently timed their infernal machine for an hour when the streets of the financial district were crowded, but chose as well the hour when not the captains of the industry but their clerks and messengers were on the street. J.P. Morgan himself, who already had escaped one attempt of assassination, was in Europe. ▪

ABOVE: Six people were killed as a result of the 1993 WTC bombing and 1,042 people were injured.

floor collapsing down several stories, creating a crater 60 feet wide that reached deep into the parking complex.

It also collapsed the ceiling of a mezzanine in the adjacent Port Authority Trans Hudson train station, leaving dozens trapped under rubble on a concourse one floor above the platforms where hundreds awaited trains. Witnesses and rescue workers told of a blast of incredible force—of bodies hurtling through the air, of cars wrapped around pillars, of people burning and scores trapped.

"We crawled under pipes when we arrived and everything was on fire," said Edward Bergen, a 38-year-old firefighter who was one of the first to reach the scene of the blast. "Suddenly, a guy came walking out of the flames, like one of those zombies in the movie, 'The Night of the Living Dead.' His flesh was hanging off. He was a middle-aged man."

Nearby, Vito de Leo, 32, an airconditioning mechanic, was eating lunch at his desk with other basement trade center workers. Suddenly, the desk rose up, came down and landed on top of him; its well protected him from a rain of falling debris. "There was total blackness," he said. "I thought I was dead." ▪

U.S. Attacked; Hijacked Jets Destroy Twin Towers and Hit Pentagon

By **SERGE SCHMEMANN** | September 12, 2001

ABOVE: *United Airlines Flight 175, which should have been headed for Los Angeles, struck the World Trade Center shortly after 9 a.m. on Sept. 11, 2001.*

HIJACKERS RAMMED JETLINERS INTO EACH of New York's World Trade Center towers yesterday, toppling both in a hellish storm of ash, glass, smoke and leaping victims, while a third jetliner crashed into the Pentagon in Virginia. There was no official count, but President Bush said thousands had perished, and in the immediate aftermath the calamity was already being ranked the worst and most audacious terror attack in American history.

The attacks seemed carefully coordinated. The hijacked planes were all en route to California, and therefore gorged with fuel, and their departures were spaced within an hour and 40 minutes. The first, American Airlines Flight 11, a Boeing 767 out of Boston for Los Angeles, crashed into the north tower at 8:48 a.m. Eighteen minutes later, United Airlines Flight 175, also headed from Boston to Los Angeles, plowed into the south tower.

Then an American Airlines Boeing 757, Flight 77, left Washington's Dulles International Airport bound for Los Angeles, but instead hit the western part of the Pentagon, the military headquarters where 24,000 people work, at 9:40 a.m. Finally, United Airlines Flight 93, a Boeing 757 flying from Newark to San Francisco, crashed near Pittsburgh, raising the possibility that its hijackers had failed in whatever their mission was.

In all, 266 people perished in the four planes. Numerous firefighters, police officers and other rescue workers who responded to the initial disaster in Lower Manhattan were killed or injured when the buildings collapsed.

Within an hour, the United States was on a war footing. National Guard units were called out in Washington and New York, and two aircraft carriers were dispatched to New York harbor.

President Bush, who had been in Florida, remained aloft in Air Force One for hours, following a secretive route and making only brief stopovers at Air Force bases in Louisiana and Nebraska before finally setting down in Washington at 7 p.m. The White House, the Pentagon and the Capitol were evacuated, except for the Situation Room in the White House where Vice President Cheney remained in charge.

Nobody immediately claimed responsibility for the attacks. But the scale and sophistication of the operation, the extraordinary planning required for concerted hijackings by terrorists who had to be familiar with modern jetliners, and the history of major attacks on American targets in recent years led many officials and experts to point to Osama bin Laden, the Islamic militant believed to operate out of Afghanistan. Afghanistan's hard-line Taliban rulers rejected such suggestions, but officials took that as a defensive measure.

Back in Washington, President Bush vowed that the United States would hunt down and punish those responsible for the "evil, despicable acts of terror." He said the United States would make no distinction between those who carried out the hijackings and those who harbored and supported them. ■

9/11

A Day When Terror Hit Close to Home

By **N. R. KLEINFIELD** | September 12, 2001

THE HORROR ARRIVED IN EPISODIC BURSTS OF chilling disbelief, signified first by trembling floors, sharp eruptions, cracked windows. There was the actual unfathomable realization of a gaping, flaming hole in first one of the tall towers, and then the same thing all over again in its twin. There was the merciless sight of bodies helplessly tumbling out, some of them in flames.

Finally, the mighty towers themselves were reduced to nothing. Dense plumes of smoke raced through the downtown avenues, coursing between the buildings, shaped like tornadoes on their sides.

Then every sound was cause for alarm. A plane appeared overhead. Was another one coming? No, it was a fighter jet. But was it friend or enemy? People scrambled for their lives, but they didn't know where to go. Stay outside, go indoors? People hid beneath cars, beneath each other. "I don't know what the gates of hell look like, but it's got to be like this," said John Maloney, a security director for an Internet firm in the trade center.

> "I don't know what the gates of hell look like, but it's got to be like this."

It was the people outside, on the sidewalk, who saw and heard the beginning—the too-low roar of a jet engine. "He didn't try to maneuver," said Robert Pachino, a witness. "This plane was on a mission."

James Wang, 21, a photography student snapping pictures of people doing tai chi at a nearby park, looked up and saw people high in the north tower. They seemed like tiny figurines, and he didn't know if they were awaiting rescue or merely looking out. "They were standing up there," he said. "And they jumped. One woman, her dress was billowing out." ▪

When They Were Young and the Towers Were New

By **JIM RASENBERGER** | September 23, 2001

THEY WERE YOUNG MEN THEN, AND THE job was the sort that ironworkers crave when they are young. It was enormous, it was monumental, and nobody had ever put up anything like it. So the ironworkers who built the World Trade Center had a special bond to the towers that fell on Sept. 11. They erected the 192,000 tons of structural steel that went into the buildings' frames column by column, piece by piece. It was work they could admire and feel proud of for the rest of their lives. Or so they thought.

"I feel deprived," said Jack Doyle, 58. "Every building down there I worked on. That's six years' work, and now it's all gone."

Mr. Doyle was only 26 when he became the pusher, or foreman, of a raising gang on 1 World Trade Center, the north tower. Working with one of the eight tower cranes that rose with the buildings, he and his five-man gang lifted huge steel columns and girders off the backs of trucks, swung them into place and secured them with bolts. Mr. Doyle stayed on the job from foundation to summit. And when it came time to top out—a old tradition of ironwork—it was Mr. Doyle's gang that raised the American flag on the final piece of high steel. The year was 1970.

"It's still hard to believe it's gone," Mr. Doyle said. "It's like they ripped a big section out of my scrapbook. Of course, it's nothing compared to what some people are suffering. You can always build another building." ▪

New York Bends, But Doesn't Break

By **CLYDE HABERMAN** | September 16, 2001

USUALLY, YOU CAN'T GO WRONG TURNING TO E.B. White. His classic 1949 essay, "Here Is New York," remains the touchstone for anyone seeking explication of Gotham's mysteries.

"New York is peculiarly constructed to absorb almost anything that comes along," White wrote, and it does so "without inflicting the event on its inhabitants."

"So that every event is, in a sense, optional," he said, "and the inhabitant is in the happy position of being able to choose his spectacle and so conserve his soul."

Not this time.

This time, no New Yorker escaped the agony inflicted by the terrorists who hijacked passenger planes and turned them into missiles. Now, everyone knew the acrid smell of death. Now, they knew fear. There was no getting around the fact that New York's knees buckled. But it did not fold, not for a second.

ABOVE: *Witnesses react as they saw the first trade center tower fall.*

> No New Yorker escaped the
> agony inflicted by the terrorists.

Over time, New Yorkers have banded fiercely together during subway strikes and blackouts. A notable exception was the power failure in 1977, with widespread looting and thousands of arrests. But normally New Yorkers come through, channeling their bruising, often coarse nature into a positive force. Nothing has changed that, including the great wave of immigration that been reshaping the city for 20 years. The accents may be different now, but not the spirit.

No one embodied that spirit more than the mayor, Rudolph W. Giuliani, a complex man, capable of displaying extraordinary leadership one minute and breathtaking pettiness the next. His superb performance gave him one more claim to history.

During his eight years, he has enabled residents and visitors to think of the city as a safe place, but "safe" is relative. A decade ago, New York's perils grew out of its own flaws, its own criminals and drug addicts and street crazies. This week's came out of its greatness, because it is America's financial, cultural and communications capital, a worthy target.

Improbable though it may seem, New Yorkers viewed their city with a certain innocence, living with small-town familiarity in self-sufficient neighborhoods and filling their basic needs without needing to travel more than a few blocks. That has now been shattered by the worst catastrophe in their history, far eclipsing the previous top disaster, the wreck of the General Slocum, an excursion boat that caught fire and then could not navigate the treacherous waters of Hell Gate. At least 1,021 people perished that day, June 15, 1904. The historian Kenneth T. Jackson says that funerals for the victims lasted more than a week. One procession of 156 hearses stretched for almost a mile.

This time, the hearses could extend to the horizon. ■

Melody Belkin, Noah, And the Kindness of Strangers

By JIM DWYER | December 28, 2001

AS ONE AMBULANCE AFTER ANOTHER WAILED past, Melody Belkin switched on the car radio. Plane crashes into tower. At that moment, she was under New York Harbor in the Brooklyn-Battery Tunnel, driving directly toward the World Trade Center.

When Ms. Belkin reached the end of the tunnel, she abandoned the car, then grabbed her kids and the stroller. She put Noah, 4, under one arm. She put Ava, 22 months, into the yellow stroller, the one she had lobbied for last summer, when they shopped for a new stroller on Fifth Avenue in Brooklyn.

The day Noah was born, he underwent five hours of surgery. His esophagus did not connect to his stomach. He had a nonfunctioning kidney. By the time he was 4, he had gone through 13 operations. He takes nourishment through a feeding tube. He has had a tracheotomy to help him breathe. All this makes speech difficult for him, but not impossible. Noah, his family says, is a happy, peaceful child, who speaks English and uses sign, the language of the hearing or speech-impaired.

> "This total stranger overheard and handed me $100 in twenties."

Now, as they ran, a stranger—he looked college-age to Ms. Belkin, who is 35—ripped up his T-shirt and gave her pieces for protection from the filthy wind. At the Battery, a man passed out dust masks from the back of his truck. Through the cloud, he saw the bright yellow stroller.

"Throw the babies in the front of the truck," he yelled. They shared the cab with two young men and a woman. Ava sat on the woman's lap. Ms. Belkin worked on Noah's tracheotomy. He needed a fresh cover for the opening. One of the men, Drew, tore his

shirt. "A Ralph Lauren," Ms. Belkin said. "The piece he gave Noah had the logo on it."

The second tower collapsed. "Drew started saying that psalm," Ms. Belkin said, "the one with 'though I walk through the valley of death.'"

The truck driver ran to the door of the American Park restaurant, which quickly became a shelter.

The backpack with Noah's formula and vacuum had gone astray. On his second trip back to the truck, Drew found it.

A park ranger arrived. He escorted Ms. Belkin and her children onto the first ferry to New Jersey. There, while the emergency medical workers checked Noah, Ms. Belkin realized that she had left her purse on the stroller, back on some broken street across the river.

"I was telling the E.M.T.'s I don't have my insurance cards, I don't even have any money," Ms. Belkin said. "This total stranger overheard and handed me $100 in twenties. I kept $20 and gave the rest back. I tried to get his phone number to return it, but he wouldn't hear of it."

The bright yellow stroller, it turned out, had been rescued by the truck driver, who left it and Ms. Belkin's purse at the American Park restaurant. The restaurant returned a scrubbed-clean stroller to Noah's father, Peter Klein, delighting Noah, who had picked it out in the first place.

Since then, Noah has answered one question precisely the same way.

"Noah," Mr. Klein, said. "Did you see the buildings fall?"

"No," Noah said. "But I…"

Then he stopped speaking with his mouth, and turned to the language of sign.

The little boy lifted two fingers to the side of his head. He slammed them against his ear.

No.

But I

HEARD

"Them," Noah said. ■

Rescue Workers Rush In, Many Do Not Return

By **JANE FRITSCH** | September 12, 2001

NEW YORK FIREFIGHTERS, IMPELLED BY instinct and training, rushed to the World Trade Center to evacuate victims. Then the buildings fell down. The firefighters never came out.

More than 300 firefighters were unaccounted for when the day ended. There was no trace of three of the fire department's most elite units, Rescues 1, 2 and 4. Among those known to have died were Chief of Department Peter J. Ganci and First Deputy Fire Commissioner William M. Feehan. Also killed was one of the department's Roman Catholic chaplains, Mychal Judge, who had rushed to the scene to comfort victims.

With scores of firefighters and police suddenly missing, random groups of people took command. Building superintendents became lifesavers—guiding panicked residents to basements. Consolidated Edison workers guided people to safety. And small groups of people responding to calls from panicked friends—including one woman trapped with her twin children—descended on the neighborhood to help. In one spot, a jagged four-story section of the building jutted straight in the air. In another, a six-story section lay flat on its side. And all around them were 50-foot mounds of twisted metal, concrete chunks and shattered glass.

By the time the buildings collapsed, more than 400 firefighters were at the scene. Many were from six-person units that specialize in building collapses, and many are now missing, presumed to have died when the buildings went down.

"I managed to get out of the building just a few seconds before it collapsed," he said Robert Byrne, from a fire company on Houston Street. "I don't know what happened to the company. Just me and the lieutenant got out." ■

Report Says 9/11 Workers Not Getting Enough Care

By **ANTHONY DEPALMA** | July 25, 2007

NEARLY SIX YEARS AFTER THE 9/11 ATTACKS, the federal government still does not have an adequate array of health programs for ground zero workers—or a reliable estimate of how much treating their illnesses will cost—according to a federal report.

The report, produced by the Government Accountability Office, an arm of Congress, concluded that thousands of federal workers and responders who came to ground zero from other parts of the country do not have access to suitable health programs.

The report also said that an estimate of health care costs made late last year by the National Institute for Occupational Safety and Health was based on questionable assumptions, inconsistent data and instances of double billing. As a result, the report concluded, "It is unclear whether the overall estimate overstated or understated the costs of monitoring and treating responders."

The institute's revised estimate last week put this year's costs at $195 million. But it said the total figure for 2007 and 2008 could be between $428 million and $712 million if more workers register to participate in the programs and a greater percentage of them need medical or mental health treatment. Treatment money from the federal government became available only last year. ■

Just Regular Guys, Until the Bell Rings

By **MICHELLE O'DONNELL** | September 23, 2001

FIRE DEPARTMENTS, LIKE THE CITIES THAT foster them, have their own personalities. The New York Fire Department, like the dense, sprawling city itself, is both large and well ordered, turning on the same axis of planning and hope that moves New York forward each day.

Like the residents they would die to protect, New York firefighters are brash and funny, loud and sentimental, opinionated and thoughtful. They have New Yorkers' big-city edge, and they have their small-town sensibility and neighborly friendliness.

New York's firefighters live in houses named whimsically but proudly: Nuthouse, Pride of Midtown, Say No More and No Fear. They eat off mismatched plates, buy in bulk, sleep in dormitory-style rooms and eat in spare, industrial-size kitchens.

They are regular guys: chewing on cigars, cracking jokes, planning fishing trips and ribbing each other constantly. Until the bells ring, that is, and they race to the emergency call that could be a false alarm or an all-hands disaster, ready to save lives while risking their own. It is not their willingness to take such risks that sets them apart from their colleagues around the nation, but the scale on which this city forces them to do it.

They use humor like oxygen. They can be dead serious. They have take-charge attitudes. It is the shadow of terrible possibility that forces them to be so. One captain, who has seen scores of firefighters die on duty in his three-decade career, always says goodbye to special friends with, "I love you." One never knows.

It is the ordinary qualities of New York's firefighters—men and women with families and mortgages and aging parents and long commutes on the Long Island Expressway— that make their contribution so staggering. It elevates those who could rush toward, not from, exploding twin towers. They gain a stature in our minds; we can hardly begin to imagine what drives them. Is it a job? Is it a calling? Must it be both?

Last Monday night, almost one week after the World Trade Center attacks, it was back to work for Engine 33 of Greenwich Village. The engine company, which lost six men on Sept. 11, sped up Fifth Avenue against traffic, sirens screeching, and pulled up in front of a New York University apartment house. The officer hopped out of the rig and shined his flashlight high on the windows, looking for signs of smoke. Students milled in the entranceway, paying no attention to the firefighters.

Finding no smoke, the officer signaled "all clear" and climbed back into his seat. Passers-by walking dogs and holding hands watched. A woman approached the engine and said, "Thank you."

"Yeah, yeah, we're firemen," the officer replied. "It's what we do." ∎

BELOW: *343 firefighters and paramedics who responded to the attacks on Sept. 11 lost their lives, and many more were injured.*

Oct. 17, Once the Fire Department's Darkest Date

By **ROBERT F. WORTH** | October 12, 2003

ON OCT. 17, 1966, 12 FIREFIGHTERS DIED while responding to a catastrophic fire across Broadway from the Flatiron Building. For 35 years, the tragedy remained the New York Fire Department's single greatest loss of life.

Photographs from the '66 fire eerily foreshadow the images of Sept. 11. Thousands of haggard firefighters gathered at the scene as the dead were carried out of the blackened building. Thousands more lined Fifth Avenue during the funeral cortege four days later. The heroism of the dead men was proclaimed in headlines for weeks afterward.

"It really stopped New York City," said Daniel Andrews, who at the time followed Engine 18 as a teenage fire buff and now works in the Queens borough president's office. "You could hear a pin drop on Fifth Avenue during those funerals."

It all began on a cool evening at 9:30 p.m. Manuel Fernandez, a former professional boxer who had been with Engine 18 on West 10th Street for six years, said that smoke was rising from one of the buildings along Broadway. But no flames were visible, and the firefighters were confused about the source of the fire.

"I dropped them off on the 23rd Street side, and it was hazy in there, like a pool room," Mr. Fernandez said. As the "chauffeur," his duty was to man the motor pump on the engine. But he heard a dull roar and knew that something was wrong, so he went into the drugstore building where five of his fellow firefighters had gone. "You had about a foot of clear vision," he recalled.

He saw a burst of flame, and a tremendous wave of heat struck him in the face. He heard popping—the sound, he later realized, of drug or perfume bottles exploding—and turned to run out.

He did not know it at the time, but a fire raging in the cellar had caused a vast section of the building's first floor to collapse, taking 10 firefighters down with it and killing two

others who had not fallen in. The flames he had seen were rising straight up from the cellar.

A rescue party made heroic efforts to reach the doomed men, according to a history published in 1993 by the Uniformed Firefighters Association. One firefighter, stumbling forward in the darkness, reached the edge of the collapsed area and fell in. One hand clutched the nozzle of the hose as he fell, and for a few moments, he hung swaying over the abyss, flames licking at his body, before other firefighters pulled him to safety. ∎

The Living Search The Faces of the Dead

By **JAMES BARRON** | March 26, 1990

JEROME FORD STARED AT THE PHOTOGRAPHS spread on the table at Public School 67 in the Bronx yesterday. He recognized five faces: his wife's three brothers, a teenage niece and a cousin. He realized what the photographs meant: the five had been trapped when an illegal social club was transformed from an oasis of dancing and drinking into an inferno.

His eyes were red, his Sunday-morning stubble of a beard streaked with tears. Oblivious to the sirens and the police officers shouting into their bullhorns, keeping the crowd in line, he could think of nothing but the advice he wished his relatives had taken.

"I told them not to go," he said, "but kids are kids. I knew it was dangerous."

The awful ritual of identification was repeated time after time at P.S. 67. The corridors and classrooms, usually filled with the chatter of students, were filled with the sobs of relatives, friends, friends of friends, young and old.

87 Die in Blaze at Illegal Club

By **RALPH BLUMENTHAL** | March 26, 1990

EIGHTY-SEVEN PEOPLE, CRAMMED INTO AN illegal Bronx social club, were asphyxiated or burned to death within minutes in a flash fire early yesterday morning. The police later arrested a man who they said had set the blaze with gasoline after a quarrel there.

It was the worst loss of life in a fire in New York City since the Triangle Shirtwaist Company fire of 1911, exactly 79 years ago to the day.

The club—the Happy Land Social Club, at 1959 Southern Boulevard, off East Tremont Avenue—had no state liquor license. City officials said it was ordered closed for fire hazards and building-code infractions 16 months ago, but had continued to operate.

Police Commissioner Lee P. Brown identified the arrested suspect as Julio Gonzalez, 36 years old. Lieut. Raymond O'Donnell, a police spokesman, said Mr. Gonzalez had argued with a former girlfriend who worked at the club and had been ejected by a bouncer, but then returned with gasoline and set the fire.

His girlfriend and at least three others survived. But the flames cut off the only open door and filled the club with smoke. Some victims suffocated so rapidly that they were found with drinks in their hands.

Like Mr. Ford, they knew the faces in the photographs—the photographs of the dead, snapshots the authorities had taken before the 87 bodies were sent to the morgue in Manhattan. Some of the loved ones screamed at the sight. Some grieved wordlessly.

For many, the trip confirmed the terrible suspicions they had had since daybreak, when they realized that loved ones had never made it home. Over and over during the day, people who had seen the pictures would come out and tell others in line the sad truth: whoever they were looking for was dead. Kelly Mena found the photo of his 30-year-old brother, Rene. "He had on his black leather coat," he said, blinking back tears.

Some relatives brought photographs of their own. Alva Romero went to the school with snapshots of her 18-year-old daughter, Alva Escoto; her 32-year-old brother, Kerri Romero, and four cousins: Luis Manaiza, 22; Wendy Manaiza, 18; Norman Clarke, 17, and Isabel Christina Lopez, 17. The family had moved to the Bronx from Honduras over the last seven years, she said.

"We came looking for a better life," she said, tearfully. "We just found disappointment and disgrace." ▪

> It was the worst loss of life in a fire in New York City since the Triangle Shirtwaist Company fire of 1911, exactly 79 years ago to the day.

Detective Lieut. James Malvey of the 48th Precinct said last night that Mr. Gonzalez, in a videotaped statement for the District Attorney's office, told of picking up a plastic jug at the club after threatening, "I'll be back." Mr. Gonzalez, the detective said, filled the jug with $1 worth of gasoline at a nearby service station and returned.

"He threw the gasoline on the floor," Detective Malvey said. "He threw in a couple of matches." He said Mr. Gonzalez "didn't know how bad it was when he left, but he came back and watched the firemen fight the fire." ▪

A Thousand Lives Lost in Burning Of the General Slocum

June 16, 1904

AN ESTIMATED TOTAL OF A THOUSAND DEAD, besides several hundred injured, is the record of the fire disaster which yesterday destroyed the big excursion steamer General Slocum, which was burned to the water's edge before her captain succeeded in beaching her on North Brother Island. Nearly all the dead and mussing are women and children and were members of an excursion part taken out by St. Mark's German Lutheran Church of East 6th Street.

The disaster stands unparalleled among those of its kind. Whole families have been wiped out. In many instances a father is left to grieve alone for wife and children, and there was hardly a home in the parish, whence but a few hours before a laughing happy crowd went on its holiday, that was not in deep mourning last night.

The scenes attendant upon the disaster have seared themselves in the brains of the survivors never to be effaced. Women were roasted to death in sight of their husbands and children, and babes by the score perished in the waters of the East River, into which they had been thrown by frenzied mothers. With the death by fire behind them, hundred leaped to their doom in the river. Out of the awful record there stands forth bright and clear the heroic work of the watermen, the police, nurses, and the doctors, who saved hundreds at the risk of their own lives. Frenzied thousands, who had lost relatives thronged the Alexander Avenue station in the Bronx, the Morgue, the piers, and the vicinity of the church all night.

The General Slocum started from her prier at East 3rd Street shortly after 9 o'clock. Accounts differ as to just where the boat was when the fire started. Certain it is that it went through Hell Gate without evidences of panic being noticed, for the band was playing and people on the shore remarked that the Slocum had a big party on board that was apparently having a good time.

It is believed that the fire started from the explosion of a stove in the galley on the lower deck, where chowder was being cooked. Here a lot of odds and ends of rope, canvas, oily rags, and other truck were stored.

The dread cry of "Fire" sounded through the boat about an hour after she left her pier. Almost immediately there was a muffled explosion, and a sheet of flame enveloped the forward part of the boat. It was then that the trouble was first seen from the shore, the boat being opposite 135th Street.

Survivors say the life preservers were worthless and rotted away in the hands of those who attempted to use them.

ABOVE: *A view of the monument to Slocum victims in Lutheran All Faiths Cemetery in Queens.*

FIRES

65 Years Later, Recognition of a Seaman's Heroics

By **CLYDE HABERMAN** | November 11, 2008

ON VETERANS DAY, AMERICA PAYS TRIBUTE to those who served, including some whose achievements went unrecognized for far too long. Someone, for example, like Seymour Wittek.

During World War II, the Brooklyn-born Mr. Wittek, now 87, was Seaman Second Class Wittek of the United States Coast Guard, assigned to a munitions detail in Jersey City. He and his mates loaded bombs and ammunition destined for American troops fighting in Europe. One ship that they filled with explosives was El Estero, a freighter of Panamanian registry docked at a New Jersey pier.

On April 24, 1943, the Estero caught fire below deck. It is impossible to overstate how serious this was. Roughly 5,000 tons of bombs, depth charges and small-arms ammunition were stored on the Estero and nearby ships and railroad cars. If the Estero exploded—and that was a real possibility—a chain reaction could have engulfed all that ammunition and spread to fuel storage tanks in Bayonne, N.J., and on Staten Island. Later estimates of the potential death toll on both sides of the Hudson reached into the thousands, even the tens of thousands.

Beyond the carnage, "the course of history could have been changed," said James J. McGranachan, a civilian spokesman for the Coast Guard. "It would have shut down the port. When you think of all the supplies that were coming out of New York, it could have affected the landing at Normandy"—D-Day, June 6, 1944.

Without blinking, Seaman Wittek and dozens of his fellow seamen volunteered to board the burning ship and fight the out-of-control fire, which was later found to have been accidentally caused. On the deck, he recalled, the heat from below was so intense that he could feel it through his shoes.

Soon, an order came to scuttle the ship. In a race against time, it was towed to deep water in Upper New York Bay, where fireboats pumped water into the cargo holds. "Some flares and shells exploded," The New York World-Telegram reported in an article that did not appear until two years later, a delay that reflected wartime secrecy. But, nearly four hours after it caught fire, the freighter sank into the bay. Not a single death resulted from the operation.

Time passed, and memories of the Estero faded. But it always stuck in Mr. Wittek's craw that New York City never formally recognized the heroics of those seamen. Some had received medals in the 1940's from Bayonne, but not from New York or, for that matter, from the Coast Guard.

> Seaman Wittek and dozens of his fellow seamen volunteered to board the burning ship and fight the out-of-control fire. On the deck, the heat from below was so intense that he could feel it through his shoes.

On this Veterans Day, the oversight will finally be corrected. Mr. Wittek, long retired from the fur industry, will receive the Coast Guard Commendation Medal for "outstanding achievement."

The Coast Guard looked for others to honor, but "they couldn't find anybody else but me," Mr. Wittek said. His buddies will be there in spirit, though. "I'm going to say," he explained with a catch in his voice, "that I'm accepting this in the name of all my friends. It's for the rest of the guys." ∎

Air Tragedy Raises Big Questions

December 18, 1960

WITH THE ADVENT OF THE JET, AIR TRAVEL has expanded enormously. More and more planes fly faster and more often with ever-growing passenger loads. Traffic congestion—particularly around big cities where airlines converge—has become a problem that seems constantly to outgrow man's efforts to solve it.

That problem was driven home with stunning impact last week by the greatest airline disaster in United States history. Out of lowering skies over Brooklyn a jet plunged into a block of houses and turned them into a holocaust. At the same moment a prop-driven plane fell in pieces onto Staten Island; in the wreckage was one of the jet's engines—grim evidence that the two planes had collided. The toll, 137 people in the planes and on the ground, made 1960 the record year for air fatalities.

A mixture of rain and snow was falling as two big commercial airliners approached the New York area. One was a United Airlines four-engine DC-8 jet bound for Idlewild from Chicago with 84 people aboard. The other was a TWA four-engine Super Constellation bound for La Guardia from Dayton and Columbus, Ohio, with 44 people aboard. Visibility was poor.

> The toll, 137 people in the planes and on the ground, made 1960 the record year for air fatalities.

The DC-8 was ordered by the air traffic center to enter the rectangular stack over Preston, N.J., at 5,000 feet. The Constellation was directed to enter another stack over Linden, N.J., at 6,000 feet before getting clearance to come down to 5,000 feet and approach La Guardia. There should have been five miles of air space between the rectangular routes of the two planes in their respective stacks.

Instead, they apparently collided. One of the DC-8's jet engines was found on Staten Island. Investigators also recovered a sealed recording device from the DC-8, which contains a taped transcript of data about changes in course, speed or altitude. ◼

The Day the Boy Fell From the Sky

By **WENDELL JAMIESON** | March 24, 2002

BARBARA LEWNES WAS BARBARA STULL THEN, 22 years old and six months out of the nursing school at Methodist Hospital. She remembers it as a fine time: dates in Manhattan with young doctors, including the one she married a few years later. Broadway shows. Drinks at Trader Vic's. And being a nurse.

Her sweet but sometimes vague memories click into focus on Dec. 16, 1960. She heard the sirens at 10:30 a.m., when she was walking down the street, half a block from the hospital. Inside, she heard the words: plane crash.

There was talk of a survivor from the jet, a little boy found in a snowbank and taken to Methodist in a police car. A fireman told her that the boy had been flying without his parents and had lived because he'd been sitting on a stewardess's lap in a jump seat. When the jet hit, the fireman surmised, the back door had popped open and the child had been thrown out. She looked over the snowbank: the plane's door was still open.

Around 6 p.m., she stopped at the security office to tell the director of nursing, Edith Roberts, that she would be back for her shift at midnight. There was a pause. Miss Roberts said to wait, and she went to talk to someone.

A Wounded City Sheds New Tears

By **DAN BARRY** | November 13, 2001

WHEN THE WORD CAME IN THE MORNING, IT was almost too much.

There they were in Midtown, hundreds of mental-health workers attending a Red Cross seminar on how to help people cope with the terrorist attacks of Sept. 11. For purposes of comparison, they were watching a presentation on the airplane explosion in 1988 that devastated the Scottish town of Lockerbie, when, suddenly, the lights went up and an urgent message was delivered: a jetliner had just crashed in Queens.

Dr. Paul Ofman, who interrupted the program to deliver the news, is an expert in the aftereffects of disaster and chairman of emergency services for the Red Cross in New York. Even so, his initial reaction was visceral, and universal.

"This can't be real," he remembers thinking.

But it was. For a city and a region, the plane crash was the deadly car accident that derails the funeral procession. Just when a city and region was returning to what passes these days as normality, bang: hundreds more dead, the Rockaways ablaze, tons of debris falling from the heavens, and a community in panic.

All the while, the horrific words and images emanating from Queens carried the unsettling air of the familiar. The bridges and tunnels were being closed—again. Hundreds of soot-covered firefighters were battling a monstrous disaster—again. Mayor Rudolph W. Giuliani was urging residents to remain calm—again.

Just two months and a day from the morning when two jetliners crashed into the World Trade Center, the only hint of comfort lay in the reactions of law-enforcement officials who did not respond as if this jetliner crash had been caused by terrorism. "That this would be a source of relief, or confer a sense of safety, is a sign of how altered these times that we live in are," said Dr. Ofman.

Deriving good news from a plane crash that killed hundreds was an unsettling process for many. Fran Rushing, a California resident who was visiting her son in Long Island City, said that she was shocked at times by how she digested the morning's news. She said that she dreaded the thought that came next: "That we'd settle in and say, 'Oh thank goodness, it's just a normal old 300-person-dead plane crash.'"

"What have I come to?" she asked. ▪

A few minutes later, Miss Roberts said, "'Barbara, we'll use you. You'll special him tonight.'"

"Special." That terribly burned boy would be hers.

He had been placed in a glassed-in nursery and was surrounded by doctors, nurses, equipment. Shortly before midnight, the doctors updated her on Stephen's condition. Then, one by one, their orders given, they left. By 12:30 a.m., she realized that she was alone with two young nursing students and Stephen Baltz.

Silence, except for Stephen's halting breaths.

Stephen had been sleeping when she got there, but a little later, he suddenly chirped up with the bell-like voice of a healthy child. He felt fine. He wanted a television. "Maybe tomorrow," she said gently. "I'll see about finding one."

Around 7 a.m., a doctor reappeared. Soon, the room was crowded with doctors and administrators—and her day-shift replacement.

"He seemed more alert," she said. "I decided, you know, he's going to make it." She headed back to her apartment. It was going to be a beautiful, clear winter day.

Stephen Baltz died at 10 a.m.

The hospital never called her to tell her. She learned about it from the radio, when she woke up that afternoon. ▪

Flaming Horror on the 79th Floor

By **JAMES BARRON** | July 28, 1995

THE LAST THING THE AIR TRAFFIC CONTROL-ler at La Guardia Airport told the pilot that foggy Saturday morning 50 years ago today sounded almost like an afterthought: "At the present time, I can't see the top of the Empire State Building."

"Roger, tower, thank you," the pilot, Lieut. Col. William F. Smith Jr., muttered into his push-to-talk cockpit microphone, heading west toward Newark.

A minute or two later, disoriented and dodging the skyscrapers of Manhattan, the B-25 saw the top of the Empire State Building—through the windshield. Roaring along at 200 miles an hour, the plane slammed into the 78th and 79th floors,

gouging an 18-by-20-foot hole 913 feet above 34th Street. Fourteen people died in the crash and the fire that followed: Colonel Smith and the two others in the plane, and 11 in what was then the world's tallest building.

The fuel tanks exploded. An engine and part of the landing gear plummeted through an elevator shaft into the subbasement. The other engine plowed through the building, emerging on the 33rd Street side and crashing through the roof of a sculptor's studio. Windows shattered even on the tall building's lowest floors, hurling chunks of glass toward the street.

To New Yorkers who had watched their steel-frame skyline climb higher and higher in the 1920's and 1930's—and who had worried about enemy airplanes as World War II dragged on—it was one of those where-were-you-when moments, like the assassination of John F. Kennedy a generation later.

"I don't think any one of us had any idea of what had happened," said Therese Fortier Willig, a secretary in the Catholic War Relief office on the 79th floor. "Who'd have thought a plane?"

Mrs. Willig said she and those in her office who were not killed instantly crowded into a room with a door they could close to seal out the smoke. "I thought we were going to die," she said. In despair, she pulled her rings off her fingers—her high-school graduation ring and a friendship ring from her boyfriend—and lobbed them out the window, never expecting to see them again.

But a few days later, the Fire Department found them amid the debris on 34th Street, and returned them. A couple of years later, she married the man who had given her the friend- ship ring, and had a son who also had an affinity for high places—George Willig, who climbed the World Trade Center in the 1970's. ■

LEFT: *Photographer Ernie Sisto crawled out on a ledge while two newsmen held his legs as he took this photo in 1945.*

Old Hands Didn't Have To Be Told What to Do

By **JIM DWYER** | January 17, 2009

AROUND 3:30 ON THURSDAY AFTERNOON, Capt. Carl Lucas fired up the engines on the Athenia, a high-speed catamaran ferry docked at a pier in Weehawken, N.J., getting ready for the evening commuters on the Hudson River. The first wave would start in half an hour.

Then he spotted a plane in the water.

"We just threw off the lines and went out there," said Captain Lucas, 34.

At the same pier, Capt. John Winiarski, 52, and a deckhand, Frank Illuzzi, 62, were on board the catamaran the Admiral Richard E. Bennis. They noticed the Athenia speeding away.

"We seen them scurrying out into the river, so we turned around and saw the plane in the river," Captain Winiarski said. "We made a beeline."

And so it went: a flotilla of rescuers, created by people who caught glimpses of something going wrong and did not have to be told to help. The Athenia, the Admiral Bennis and 12 other boats — all operated or chartered by New York Waterway — picked 135 people out of the river. The crews stopped their work and changed the world.

One of the ferry captains, Manuel Liba, ticked off the strokes of fortune: the pilot brought the plane down smoothly, the Hudson was calm, it was daylight and it was 45 minutes before the evening rush on the river.

There was more than luck. On a bitter, frigid afternoon, the plane had come down minutes from people who regularly practice helping. The first ferry to reach it was the Thomas Jefferson, which pulled out of Pier 79 on the Hudson River at 39th Street in Manhattan. "As we turned around, we noticed the plane in the water," said Vincent Lombardi, captain of the Thomas Jefferson. "We thought it was an odd-looking vessel."

He radioed the Coast Guard, then headed for the plane.

"It was hard to stay next to it, but you practice that by throwing life rings in the water and trying to stay alongside them," said Brittany Catanzaro, 20, the captain of the Thomas Kean and a ferry pilot for five months. "One of the people got on board, turned around and hugged my deckhand. We're just working as if we're training and drilling."

The last person to leave a life raft was Chesley B. Sullenberger III, the captain of the US Airways flight. He climbed aboard the Athenia after everyone else had been lifted to safety. "Very calm," Captain Lucas reported. "He had a metal clipboard with the passenger manifest. He came up into the wheelhouse, and we tried to organize a count of who was recovered from the water. I asked him if he thought there was anyone left on the plane. He said no, that he had checked twice himself."

> "You train so much, you don't have to think about it."

Muscle memory had steadied people in the currents of a disaster and the strong tides of the Hudson: an airline pilot remembering his metal clipboard, and ferry pilots who never moved out of reach of the bobbing airplane.

"You train so much, you don't have to think about it," Captain Lucas said. "I didn't have to give any orders to the crew."

And by Friday, another kind of memory began to take hold.

"We were getting the boat ready, and we saw the plane going down," said Captain Liba, 52, who pilots the ferry Moira Smith. "We called management, we said, 'We got to go.' We just took off for the airplane. Right away, the doors flew out from the plane, and people came out.

"It's like a dream. I still can't believe it." ■

Crane Collapses on the East Side, Leaving Four Dead

By **ROBERT D. MCFADDEN** | March 16, 2008

A CRANE TOWERING OVER A HIGH-RISE construction site on the East Side of Manhattan collapsed in a roar of rending steel, raining death and destruction across a city block as it slashed down on an apartment building, broke into sections, crushed a town house and cut away a tenement facade.

At least four people were killed and more than a dozen others were injured, and damage was expected to run into the millions of dollars in what the authorities called one of the city's worst accidents—a calamity that turned a neighborhood near the United Nations into a zone of panic, pulverized buildings, wailing sirens, evacuations, searches in the rubble and covered bodies in the streets.

LEFT: *A crane toppled and collapsed onto a high-rise apartment building on March 15, 2008.*

Mayor Michael R. Bloomberg arrived at the scene surrounded by an army of police officers, firefighters, city officials and reporters. "It's a sad day," he said, as the lights of scores of emergency vehicles revolved and flashed.

As people were evacuated from a half-dozen buildings and rescue workers using dogs, listening devices and thermal imaging cameras searched the rubble for victims—taking care to cause no further collapses—the mayor said the four known dead were believed to be construction workers on or near the crane. The injured included at least three civilians taken to hospitals in critical condition.

The cause of the accident on a sunny, windless day was unclear and under investigation by city, state and federal agencies. But Stephen Kaplan, an owner of the Reliance Construction Group working at the site, told The Associated Press that a piece of steel had fallen and sheared off one of the girders holding the crane to the building.

A construction worker on the 15th floor, Ismael Garcia, said he saw something fall and strike one or more of the girder ties, weakening or breaking the connections. "Out of the corner of my eye, I saw a piece falling," he said, and then the crane pulled away.

Witnesses told of a rising, thundering roar and clouds of smoke and dust as the crane—a vertical latticed boom for its base, topped by a cab and jib, the swinging arm that lifts building materials—fell across 51st Street and onto a 19-story apartment building at No. 300, demolishing a penthouse and shaking the building with the force of an earthquake.

Mike Shatzkin, a resident of the 17th floor, said he was talking on the phone when it hit. "All of a sudden, I felt a very violent shake, and stuff fell off the walls, and my wife said a bomb went off." After discovering that their building had been struck by the crane from across the street, he said, "We worried about this crane every day." ■

New Miracles For Window Cleaner Who Fell 47 Floors

By **JAMES BARRON** | January 4, 2008

ALCIDES MORENO PLUNGED 47 STORIES THAT morning last month, clinging to his 3-foot-wide window washer's platform as it shot down the dark glass face of an Upper East Side apartment building. His brother Edgar, who had been working with him on the platform, was killed.

Somehow, Alcides Moreno survived.

He was given roughly 24 pints of blood and 19 pints of plasma and underwent an operation to open his abdomen in the emergency room because, his doctor said, they did not want to risk moving him to an operating room. As December went on, he endured nine orthopedic operations.

Yet somehow, Alcides Moreno, the man who fell from the sky, survived.

In his hospital room, amid all the machines that helped keep him alive, his wife, Rosario, lifted his hand again and again to stroke her face and her hair, hoping against hope that a simple tactile sensation would remind him, would help bring him back.

Then on Christmas Day, Alcides Moreno reached out—and stroked the wrong face.

"Apparently he tried to do it to one of the nurses," Rosario Moreno said, describing how she chided him, gently, when she was told what had happened. "I looked at him and said, 'You're not supposed to do that. I'm your wife, you touch your wife.'"

For the first time since the accident on Dec. 7, he spoke. "He turned around and, in English, said, 'What did I do?'" she said. "It stunned me because I didn't know he could speak."

Surrounded by doctors who had helped save her husband, Mrs. Moreno told her story at a press conference at which medical professionals with long years of experience in treating traumatic injuries used words like "miraculous" and "unprecedented" to describe something that seems remarkable: a man who fell nearly 500 feet into a Manhattan alleyway is now talking and, with a little more luck, a few more operations and some rehabilitation therapy, may well walk again.

"If you are a believer in miracles, this would be one," said Dr. Philip S. Barie, the chief of the division of critical care at New York-Presbyterian Hospital/Weill Cornell Medical Center in Manhattan, where Mr. Moreno, 37, is being treated.

"We are very pleased—dare I say astonished?—at the level of recovery that this patient has enjoyed so far," he added, "and although there is more work to be done, we are very optimistic for his prospects for survival."

> "This is right up there with those anecdotes of people falling out of airplanes and surviving, people whose parachutes don't open and somehow they manage to survive."

The doctors predicted that his recovery would be complete in about a year. Asked at the press conference whether Mr. Moreno would walk again, Dr. Barie said, "We believe so, yes." He noted that Mr. Moreno's pelvis had not been injured in the fall. Dr. Barie also said that all the injuries to Mr. Moreno's legs—some 10 fractures—had been "repaired" except one.

"This is right up there with those anecdotes of people falling out of airplanes and surviving, people whose parachutes don't open and somehow they manage to survive," Dr. Barie said in an interview after the press conference. "We're talking about tiny, tiny percentages, well under 1 percent, of people who fall that distance and survive." ∎

CONSTRUCTION

DISASTER 323

A Bite of the Big Apple

FOOD

◄ PAGE 328

In New York, there are people who don't just eat to live, they live to eat. Fortunately for them, the city probably deserves the title of world restaurant capital on the basis of numbers alone, although quality and variety have soared too. New York has more than 20,000 restaurants. You could dine out every day for 55 years and never order from the same menu twice.

That total takes in the handful of four-star restaurants presided over by the world-famous chefs, the checkered-tablecloth bistros where you can have a casual supper with friends, the stylish Manhattan sushi bars and the more authentic outer-borough ethnic places, the lunch-counter diners that serve eggs any style (and just about anything else) at any hour. Even the chain coffee shops count as restaurants—and are required by the city health department to post calorie counts showing how fattening that grande nonfat latte really is. And of course there are the places and people you read about in the gossip columns: the hotel dining room where V.I.P.'s have their see-and-be-seen power breakfasts, the Midtown restaurants where that former Secretary of State is at this table, that television personality is at that table and that best-selling author is across the room.

The tab? It's not always a budget-breaker. Back in 1992, the city's convention and visitors bureau organized a weeklong promotion that featured three-course meals for $19.92. Restaurant week has continued with a tiny allowance for inflation. That pushed the price to $19.93 the following year, then $19.94 and $19.95 and so on. By 2009, restaurant week stretched to nearly a month as desperate maitres d'hotel worried about filling tables

▲ PAGE 326

Soon, restaurants became a new kind of theater, with celebrity chefs who performed in glass-walled "open" kitchens where their every move was as closely watched as Baryshnikov's. Tableside audiences thrilled to the twist of this and the dash of that that made all the difference—and sometimes the temper tantrums that made the papers. The chefs found their inspiration in cross-cultural "fusion" recipes and other innovations that turned top chefs into best-selling authors and international entrepreneurs.

Restaurant reviews became as closely read as opening-night drama reviews. Excerpted here are a handful, including Ruth Reichl's famous description of her schizoid experience at Le Cirque, first as an ordinary customer relegated to a back table where the service was ho-hum, then as a restaurant critic welcomed with the truffles-and-flourishes treatment.

So the food's the thing, and New York foodies love those only-in-New-York specialties. A bagel anywhere else (or a piece of cheesecake or a slice of pizza or a pickle) is still a bagel (or a piece of cheesecake or—well, you get the idea). But it's just not the same.

▼ PAGE 334

suddenly emptied by a plunging economy—and not just on Wall Street. For once, Manhattan's infamously snooty reservations-takers dialed down the attitude.

Sheer numbers aren't the only reason to count New York as the restaurant capital, though: New York has had a front-row banquette for some of the greatest culinary developments of the last 30 years. The "food revolution" that began in the mid-1970's remade the way New Yorkers eat, the way they think about food and, when they go the do-it-yourself route, the way they cook. Now they hunt for fresh vegetables and herbs, not frozen or dried ones; for sea salt that explodes in your mouth, not the processed, iodized kind; for almost-fat-free hamburgers that taste like more like filet mignon than ground chuck.

They don't have to go far to find much better ingredients than were available a generation ago. More than 40 Greenmarkets like the one in Union Square bring produce to the city soon after it is harvested. Providing profitable places for local farmers to sell homegrown fruits and vegetables has a back-to-the-future ring: For much of the nineteenth century, Brooklyn was the nation's number one top-producing agricultural area. In the 1960's and 1970's,

when suburban supermarkets trucked in delicious-looking produce from the West Coast, New Yorkers complained that the produce in their markets was past its prime: brown lettuce, overripe avocadoes and rotten tomatoes. Good produce was not far away: the farms that supply the greenmarkets (and some of the corner vegetable-and-flower markets that also sprang up in Manhattan) are in upstate New York and rural New Jersey. As specialty markets caught on, the mantra among homemakers who worshipped fine food was that it was more important to know where to shop than it was how to cook. That changed, of course, with Julia Child on public television and her successors on cable.

But the food revolution also made dining out less of a special occasion. That turned the restaurant business into a growth industry that helped remake whole neighborhoods as they went through "gentrification." Restaurants led the way in making destinations of SoHo and TriBeCa and—ironically—the meatpacking district on Manhattan's far west side, where the chefs set up shop across the street or down the block from where real meat-packers still unload beef carcasses and trundle them into refrigerated cutting rooms.

Pizza Now Rivals the Hot Dog In Popularity

By **HERBERT MITGANG** | February 12, 1956

PIZZA MAY NEVER REPLACE HOT DOGS AS THE great American "bite," but their amazing acceptance in recent years prompts a question: Why pizza and not, say, Mexican enchiladas? The entertainment weekly Variety reported that the "extent to which the pizza pies are replacing hot dogs at drive-ins was demonstrated at the concession trade show at Allied States Ass'n convention which featured more pizza-making machines than frankfurter heaters."

But a Neapolitan *pizzaiuolo* might be startled by pizza in the United States. There is a dainty appetizer prefabricated in the food chains going under a name that sounds like little bo-pizza. At a "pizza bar" in a large Manhattan department store—where thousands are absorbed weekly by hungry shoppers—three kinds are for sale: plain pizza (a pie); pizzaret (a muffin); and a best-seller called the pizza-bagel, created, after some protest, by a turncoat *pizzaiuolo* from Florida.

The search for a down-to-hearth pizza is a constant game for cavaliers of authentic cooking. Gennaro Lombardi seemed to be the man to turn to. Nobody has disputed his claim to having the oldest pizzeria in the United States.

"I'll make you a pizza myself just like Dad used to make in the old days," said one of Lombardi's boys, George, 40. "Dad'll be here later—he takes it a little easier now. He broke me in."

Young Lombardi took a piece of dough from the refrigerator. "I made the dough myself this morning," he said. "A little flour, water, salt, yeast and the secret." (Every pizzeria worthy of the name has one top secret.) "Notice I don't have to toss it in the air," he continued, flattening the dough on a marble table. "The show doesn't make the pizza. I spread it evenly so that it comes out a quarter of an inch thick. Less than that burns the bottom; more, it doesn't get crisp.

"Then I spread these big chunks of Italian mozzarella cheese over the dough. Some places sprinkle little bitsy pieces or even use American cheese. The mozzarella before the tomatoes—it melts right that way. Then the real Italian olive oil." No Sicilian oregano? George frowned: "That's what they serve uptown." ∎

You Can Call It Ray's, but Expect A Lawsuit to Go

By **WILLIAM E. GEIST** | May 2, 1987

"HELLO, RAY'S PIZZA," SAID THE WOMAN answering the telephone.

"May I please speak to Ray?" she was asked.

"Ray?" she replied. "Oh, Ray. Ray cannot come to the phone.... You know, there is no Ray, really.... Nobody is Ray."

It had been hoped that talking to Ray himself might straighten out the Ray's pizza imbroglio.

Rosolino Mangano has decided to do something about it himself. Mr. Mangano, who opened his first Original Ray's Pizza at 1073 First Avenue—and went on to open nine additional Original Ray's—said that he has filed a lawsuit to enjoin all the other Ray's pizza parlors in Manhattan from using the good name of Ray.

This would apparently include, but would not be limited to: Ray's Pizza, Original Ray's, Ray's Original, Famous Ray's, Ray's Famous, Famous and Original Ray's, the One and Only Famous Ray's, Real Ray's and so on.

New York Pizza, the Real Thing, Makes a Comeback

By **ERIC ASIMOV** | June 10, 1998

NEW YORK PIZZA IS A PHRASE SYNONYMOUS with pizza greatness, yet for years New Yorkers could find the genuine article in only a few isolated spots. Now pizza lovers can rejoice: the true New York pizza is back in town.

As recently as 10 years ago, the classic pizza was on the endangered list, treasured as an artifact of old New York but bypassed by a culture that preferred its pizzas fast, cheap and delivered. Just a few pizza landmarks, most famously John's Pizzeria on Bleecker Street, Patsy's Pizza in East Harlem and Totonno's Pizzeria Napolitano in Coney Island—all presided over by rival clans—zealously preserved the traditions. Disciples were required to make pilgrimages to these hallowed halls for a taste.

Today, those three families, plus a newcomer, are almost entirely responsible for a pizza renaissance in New York. The landmarks have been joined by a new set of great names: Grimaldi's under the Brooklyn Bridge; Lombardi's on Spring Street; Nick's in Forest Hills, Queens, and Rockville Centre, on Long Island; Candido on the Upper East Side; Polistina's on the Upper West Side; Zito's in the East Village and, most recently, Angelo's on West 57th Street.

The legendary pizza makers—John Sasso of John's, Patsy Lancieri of Patsy's and Anthony (Totonno) Pero of Totonno's—are all said to have learned their craft at Gennaro Lombardi's brick-walled coal oven in Little Italy. Nearly a century later, their descendants, including Lombardi's grandson, are fueling the expansion. New York's pizza dynasties are now in their third and fourth generations, and counting.

Yet a lot of the energy has come from new blood, the Angelis-Tsoulos clan, which joined the pizza pantheon just a few years ago. In 1994, Nick Angelis, the son of a Greek pizza maker who learned the art in Naples, opened Nick's Pizza in Forest Hills. It is dedicated to preserving the tradition of New York's great pie men. Paradoxically, he uses a new kind of gas oven that can achieve the high heat necessary for the best pies. No matter. It's hard to imagine a better crust than Nick's: blackened and barely crisp, glistening and golden, with a faintly smoky flavor. The crust is matched by the other ingredients: pure, creamy mozzarella, delicious roasted peppers, terrific sausage. ■

"It is unbelievably confusing," said Nelson Birgene, having a pepperoni and mushroom slice yesterday at the Ray's on Seventh Avenue at 53d Street. "This one is called 'Famous' and 'Original Ray's,' so I figured I was covered."

Most of the Ray's—and those in the business say there are dozens—are unrelated, yet have certain characteristics in common. Virtually all claim to be the first Ray's. And none seems to have a real Ray.

Why Ray? Why not Guido's or Benito's or Giuseppe's famous and original pizza? "Ray is a nice name," said Mr. Bari. "If our restaurant was named Michelle's, the whole city would be full of Michelle's pizza." ■

All About Bagels

By **BEATRICE** and **IRA HENRY FREEMAN** | May 22, 1960

ABOVE: *Bagels at Le Bagel Delight in Park Slope, Brooklyn.*

RECENTLY A TIMES CORRESPONDENT IN Poland cabled the harrowing news that the militia was cracking down on bagel bootleggers in Ostrowiec Swietorkrzyski, an iron-mining town of 36,000. Nobody would pay the bagel taxes. The militia closed the underground bakeries.

It could never happen here. New York is the bagel center of the free world, where hundreds of thousands of people find that a bagel makes breakfast almost worth getting up for.

Philip Levine, counsel to the Bagel Bakers Council of Greater New York, says that some 250,000 are made every day, seven days a week, except on those Jewish holidays when leavened bread is banned from the table.

Mr. Levine thinks that, just as the pizza has found favor with non-Italians, so the bagel is winning friends among non-Jews here. "Last St. Patrick's Day we turned out green-dyed bagels for Irish bagelniks and their sympathizers," he said.

The peak bagel workload comes on Fridays and Saturdays, to provide an adequate supply of fresh bagels to be eaten with cream cheese and lox—smoked salmon—at Sunday brunch. In the New York area there are 30 bagel bakeries employing 450 men. The actual baking is done by 350 craftsmen of the Beigel (alternate spelling) Bakers Union, Local 338, American Bakery and Confectionary Workers.

Ben Greenspan, business agent for the union, says it takes three to six months to train a competent bagel baker. Bagel bakers are divided into two groups: bench men, who knead the dough and mold and boil the bagel; and oven men, who do the baking. The pay for the Teamsters who deliver them includes two dozen bagels per day per man.

The bagel bakers strictly enforce their rule that their product be made only by them, by hand, and never preserved in any way. The bagel bakers feel some responsibility to the public. During a strike last year, for example, they operated one bakery to produce just enough bagels to sustain human life. ■

Fix the Water? Let's Talk About Bagels

By **JAMES BARRON** | July 21, 2006

THAT WONDERFUL WATER, ACCORDING TO some. That muddy water, according to others.

Water purity was up for discussion among bakers who labor in bagel shops and make focaccia in four-star restaurants like Daniel Boulud's Daniel. Federal officials are concerned that city water now contains too much clay, stirred up in part by wild weather upstate, where the reservoirs are. The city

East and West Side Bagel Bakeries Lay Claim to a Name

By **BARBARA STEWART** | December 15, 1998

EVER SINCE JERRY SEINFELD BEGAN USING A stage-set version of the H & H at Broadway and 80th Street on his sitcom, its reputation as a New York institution has reached across the country.

But there are actually two competing H & H bagel companies, each with its own recipe. One is H & H Bagels, with the store at Broadway and 80th Street and a factory and store at 12th Avenue and 46th Street. The other is H & H Bagels East, on Second Avenue near 80th Street.

Now, in a dispute that would have fit right into a "Seinfeld" episode, the West Side H & H is suing the East Side company, claiming exclusive rights to the H & H name.

H & H East is countersuing. It contends that it has every right to be known by the valuable initials, maybe even more right. "We are just as old," said Richard Spehr, the lawyer for H & H East, "and have used the name as long as they have."

In the early 70's, when they were founded, they were one company, using one recipe. Mr. Toro, a baker from Puerto Rico, and Hector Hernandez, his sister's husband, bought the shop on Broadway and renamed the enterprise after themselves: Helmer and Hector, H & H. They soon opened the East Side store.

But in 1985, the partnership faced bankruptcy. The two stores were split up and sold. Mr. Toro bought back the store on Broadway on his own. Mr. Hernandez became a livery-cab driver until his death in a hit-and-run accident in 1996.

During the last 10 years or so, the demand for bagels has boomed. So Mr. Toro decided to make a run at exclusive ownership of the H & H name.

It is, said Diane Alexiou, whose father bought the East Side store after the bankruptcy, "a very painful case for us."

"We have the more upscale customer," Ms. Alexiou said, "and it is a source of shame and embarrassment to them. We have marble floors. We sell Italian cookies and muffins and gourmet coffee. They're just basically bagels." ▪

has been dumping tons of sediment-scrubbing chemicals in the water, but that may not be enough. It may have to build a filtration plant.

That could cost billions of dollars, a financial headache, perhaps. But a culinary one? Maybe, maybe not.

"I have another store in New Jersey in a town that filters the water," said Louis Thompson, who owns Terrace Bagels, on Prospect Park West in Windsor Terrace, Brooklyn. "My bagel comes out just as good in New Jersey as it does in New York."

The wrong water can ruin things, he said. "You can't use well water to make bagels," he said. "You could, but they won't come out right. What, exactly is in that water, I don't know. I'm not a chemist, I'm just a bagel maker."

"I think New York water is still the secret ingredient," said Debra Engelmayer, an owner. "I don't think filtering makes the difference."

Mr. Thompson, of Terrace Bagels, experimented before he opened his New Jersey shop and cafe. He hauled 150 gallons of filtered New Jersey water to Brooklyn and made a batch of bagels.

"The bagels came out just as good," he said. "In towns in New Jersey you can't find a decent bagel. I don't know if that's the water or the people that make them." ▪

Lindy's Long-Kept Secret?

By **CRAIG CLAIBORNE** | May 18, 1977

WHEN LINDY'S RESTAURANT IN MANHATTAN closed in 1969, it was the end of a legend in more ways than one. Most of all it was renowned for its cheesecakes, which were as integral a part of Gotham culture as Yankee Stadium, Coney Island or Grant's Tomb.

Approximately 20 years ago, shortly before his death, I approached Leo Lindemann, the owner, and pleaded with him to let me have the recipe for his cheesecake. I was rewarded with a rather tolerant smile, as though I had demanded the Kohinoor diamond.

But I now have what is purported to be that recipe. It was offered by Guy Pascal, the distinguished pastry chef at La Côte Basque. How Mr. Pascal came into possession of it is a story of intrigue in and around the flour barrels of a kitchen in Las Vegas that began when he opened a small pastry shop there 10 years ago.

"One day," Mr. Pascal said, "an old man came to ask for a job, and among his other credentials he told me that he had spent years in New York preparing the cheesecake at Lindy's. At that time I'd never heard of Lindy's cheesecake. Well, he started to make his dessert and my business started to boom: people were standing in line. I offered him money for the recipe. He refused and I offered him more. He still refused.

"For weeks I didn't mention the cake. But I kept a strict account of the number of cakes he produced balanced against the amount of cream cheese we purchased. As the weeks passed I figured out the quantity of orange peel he used, how much lemon peel, the number of eggs and so on. And after six months I had it perfected." ∎

A Quest for the Best

By **ED LEVINE** | March 17, 2004

ON THE LAST DAY OF A MONTHLONG HUNT for the best cheesecake in New York, I took a cab to Rao's, at the corner of 114th and Pleasant Avenue in East Harlem. Its cheesecake, I had heard, was ethereal, perfect stuff. Repeated calls to the restaurant's owner, Frankie Pellegrino, had not been returned. Nor was a written request for an interview. There may have been a reason for this. Mr. Pellegrino's nickname, known to many who have asked him for a table, is Frankie No.

I called his son, Frankie Pellegrino Jr., who owns Baldoria, on West 49th Street.

(There's cheesecake on his menu, too.) The younger Mr. Pellegrino chuckled when I asked him about his father's cheesecake source. "I don't even know her name myself," he said. "It is great cheesecake. I'll call my dad and get back to you." He did not.

I walked into Rao's and took a seat at the bar in front of Nicky the Vest, so known for the 142 vests he owns and wears to pour drinks. "I don't have a reservation," I said. "But could I have a piece of cheesecake here at the bar?"

Nicky the Vest shook his head, doing his best Frankie No.

"We don't have any cheesecake," he said. "The lady that makes it broke her arm bad. I don't know if she's ever going to be able to

A Restaurant Legend Undergoes A Little Retelling

By **JAMES BARRON** | May 9, 2006

IT IS, AT MOST, A FOOTNOTE TO WHAT THE world remembers about Junior's, one of New York's storied restaurants, a footnote to its famous recipe for one of the things that people think of when they think of New York. Jeffrey Horowitz acknowledges all that.

But when he heard a radio report recently that Junior's, the Brooklyn palace of cheesecake as well as corned beef, was building a 180-seat restaurant near Times Square, he decided it was time to tell a story that has been forgotten, except, it seems, by his family.

It is a story of three families—his and two others—and the restaurant business after World War II. That much seems certain. According to him, it is also the story of a $100-a-year licensing agreement, a corporate bankruptcy and the recipe for Junior's quintessential cheesecake.

The family that has run Junior's since it opened in 1950 flatly denies Mr. Horowitz's account of how the cheesecake originated, and disputes other parts of his story. But after so long, there is really no way to prove or disprove Mr. Horowitz's version of who did what to the cheesecake.

Mr. Horowitz, 60, maintains that he is one of the two people for whom Junior's restaurant was named. He also says that Brooklyn's most famous cheesecake originated not in Brooklyn but in Miami Beach, at another Juniors (though missing an apostrophe), opened by his father. And he says that it was his father, working with the baker at the Miami Beach Juniors, who came up with the cheesecake recipe, a denser, slightly less sweet variation on a staple of old-time New York restaurants like Lindy's.

That is not the way the Rosens, who run Junior's of Brooklyn, tell things. "None of this operation came from there," Walter Rosen said. The Rosens say Harry Rosen worked with a baker at Junior's, Eigel Peterson, to get the ingredients just right.

In Mr. Horowitz's telling, the Rosens met his father through a lawyer he remembered as Louis Shapiro, who knew both families. "Shapiro says to my father, 'I have a client, a restaurateur on Flatbush Avenue, going bust. Let him license the name Juniors and copy everything for $100 a year.'" The 20-year deal "wasn't just for the name, it was the look, the menus," Mr. Horowitz said.

In 1990, the Rosens registered the name Junior's as a trademark. That was shortly before Arthur Horowitz, by then in his late 70's, started selling takeout food under the name Juniors in Florida. Jeffrey Horowitz says Junior's of Brooklyn demanded a $10,000 payment in exchange for using the name.

Jeffrey Horowitz has a sheaf of letters from lawyers about that dispute. Walter Rosen said, "Doesn't mean a thing to me—and the 90's, I'd remember."

make it again, but you could try back in a couple of months."

That's something to live for. In the meantime, here's my list of the city's best: Eileen's Special Cheesecake, 17 Cleveland Place at Kenmare Street in SoHo; Helen's Fabulous Cheesecake, 126 Union Street, between Columbia and Hicks Streets; Mona Lisa Pastry Shoppe, 1476 86th Street, at 15th Avenue, in Bay Ridge, Brooklyn; Monteleone's, 355 Court Street at President Street in Carroll Gardens, Brooklyn; Monte's Venetian Room, 451 Carroll Street, between Nevins Street and Third Avenue in Carroll Gardens, Brooklyn; Two Little Red Hens, 1652 Second Avenue, between 85th and 86th Streets; Yura & Company at 1659 Third Avenue at 93rd Street. ▪

A Man, a Plan, a Hot Dog

By **WILLIAM GRIMES** | January 25, 1998

IT'S ONE OF LIFE'S LITTLE IRONIES THAT IN New York, a gastronomic paradise, the classic of classics is the lowly hot dog, served from a street cart. Nestled in a bun, topped with mustard, onions and sauerkraut, the $1.50 dog exudes the city's essence as no other food can.

> There is no doubt where [the hot dog] rose to fame: the boardwalk on Coney Island.

Like many stars, the hot dog has mysterious origins. No one agrees who invented it or who named it. But there is no doubt where it rose to fame: the boardwalk on Coney Island. There, in the late 1860's or early 70's, a German immigrant named

BELOW: *The 15-bite hot dog at Brooklyn Diner USA, on West 57th Street, is $13.50 with onion rings and sauerkraut.*

Charles Feltman added a heating unit to his meat-pie wagon and began selling hot sausages wrapped in a roll as he worked his way up and down the beach.

Feltman parlayed his profits into a restaurant on West 10th Street that extended from Surf Avenue to the beach, where seven grills cooked thousands of hot dogs that were sold for 10 cents apiece. One grill worker, Nathan Handwerker, stared long and hard at the sausage on a roll and saw his future. In 1916, he began selling his own hot dogs from a building on Surf Avenue. He charged a nickel, the newly constructed subway line brought a stream of customers, and a New York legend, Nathan's Famous Frankfurters, was born.

In 1939, Coney Island honored its most famous symbol by organizing National Hot Dog Day. "It is difficult to measure the contribution the hot dog has made to the fame and popularity of this great resort," one official said. "Why, Coney Island is even shaped like a frankfurter!" Catching the spirit of the occasion, Milton Berle stepped onto the podium and announced, "Let our slogan be 'E Pluribus Hot Dog.'" ∎

It's All in How the Dog Is Served

By **ED LEVINE** | May 25, 2005

YOU KNOW THOSE HOT DOGS THAT YOU KNOW and love, and can't wait to eat this time of year? The ones served at Katz's Delicatessen, Gray's Papaya, Papaya King, the legendary Dominick's truck in Queens and the best "dirty water dog" carts?

They're all the same dog, manufactured by Marathon Enterprises, of East Rutherford,

Expanding a Kingdom of Franks and Fruit Juice

By **GLENN COLLINS** | August 29, 1999

IT WAS 1:30 P.M. ON 125TH STREET IN Harlem, only 20 minutes after the stealth opening of the newest Papaya King hot-dog emporium. The debut was unheralded by necessity, because it had taken three days just to get Consolidated Edison to connect the gas to the frankfurter grills.

Even so, a line of 17 eager frankophiles snaked out the door. Jermel Vanderhorst, 27, a manager of the Blockbuster Video store next door, was eager to order. "I've been waiting for this place to open since July," he said.

The store where Mr. Vanderhorst could finally get his two chili cheese dogs and a grape juice is the prototype of a planned new global Papaya King empire.

"Papaya King has a great brand," said Daniel Horan, chief executive of PK Operations Inc., an entrepreneurial subsidiary of the Manhattan venture capital firm Founders Equity that plans to hazard millions of dollars over the next few years to populate New York, and then the world, with Papaya Kings.

Mr. Horan and his investors hope that the very Noo Yawk pairing of hot dogs with papaya and other tropical fruit drinks is as nationally marketable as other mysteriously successful culinary relationships, like pastrami and rye or peanut butter and jelly. And Papaya King has "a national reputation," according to Mr. Horan, 32, who holds an M.B.A. from Yale and worked as a manager at Gourmet Garage, the high-end Manhattan grocer.

Through the years, "we've been approached by countless people who wanted to take us national," said Peter Poulos, the chief executive of the original Papaya King store.

Mr. Poulos, 61, who joined the family business in 1958, received an undisclosed fee from Founders Equity for the rights to use the Papaya King name and has been given a 12 percent stake in PK Operations. As part of the deal he and several experienced workers and managers came over from the 86th Street operation to help get the new store going.

The 1,200-square-foot prototype, which cost more than $300,000 to build, showcases its stand-up fare with green and orange neon and a galaxy of homely signs that, as in the original store, extol the store's "Tastier Than Filet Mignon Frankfurters" for which "NO ONE, and we mean NO ONE, has our formula!" ∎

N.J., the parent company of Sabrett. They may vary in size, preparation and condiment selection (and Papaya King has Marathon add a secret spice to its mixture), but they're the same ol' dog. In fact, until a few years ago, Marathon made Nathan's hot dogs.

So, you might think you would have to work to find a truly special hot dog, one that stands out because of the frank itself, its trimmings, the bun or the surroundings. New York has hot dogs that approach the $20 barrier. The Old Homestead serves an 11-ounce footlong made from American-raised Kobe beef for $19. I found it mushy and bland, and not redeemed by the white truffle mustard, the Kobe beef chili, the Vidalia onions, the Dutch bell peppers and the Cheshire Cheddar sauce that accompanied it. For the same price you can have a Gray's Papaya special of two stupendous hot dogs and a papaya drink ($2.45) for a week and still have change in your pocket.

If you insist on a haute dog, share the 15-bite hot dog ($13.50) at the Brooklyn Diner USA. It is an excellent, snappy all-beef hot dog from a secret source (not Marathon, I'm told), weighs almost a pound, and comes with excellent onion rings and sauerkraut studded with juniper berries. ∎

Let There Be Pickles

By **TARA BAHRAMPOUR** | August 26, 2001

LONG, LONG AGO, BEFORE TRENDY RESTAUR- ants, realty agencies and kitsch shops occupied its storefronts, Orchard Street on the Lower East Side was known for something else. It was, as Irving Howe wrote in "World of Our Fathers," his classic study of Jewish immigrant life, "pushcart territory," a narrow lane teeming with vendors of "shawls, bananas, oilcloth, garlic, trousers, ill-favored fish, ready-to-wear spectacles."

Arguably the best known of these pushcarts wares was the pickle. And it is still a fixture in New York delis, where a half-sour spear is often wrapped up with each sandwich. But the briny, rough-skinned pickle that was once such an integral part of the city's landscape is in danger of becoming a memory.

A century ago, New York was home to 200 family-run pickle shops, half of them on the Lower East Side, where wholesale cucumbers were sold. Over the years, however, they dwindled.

"When I came, there were five here," said Alan Kaufman, who has worked at Guss's Pickels on Essex Street since 1981. "This place is the last of the last."

> Pickling has helped bring some people closer to their roots.

Part of the problem is escalating rents. Another problem, Mr. Kaufman said, is that "kids today would rather be a doctor or a lawyer than a pickle man."

Enter the Pickle Savior. In a cramped office at New York University, Lucy Norris pored over a pile of recipes, handwritten books and family histories from around the world. She is working on a master's degree in food studies. She comes from a pickling family.

She says that pickling has helped bring some people closer to their roots. Ms. Norris mentioned a young woman she had met in an N.Y.U. preserving class.

"She was this fast-paced New York chick—blond, long hair, dressed in black, never talked to her parents," Ms. Norris recalled. But the class sparked hidden memories, and the next time the woman visited her family in New Jersey, she dug up an old five-gallon ceramic crock in which her grandfather used to pickle tomatoes.

As Ms. Norris remembered it, the woman said, "All of a sudden everything that I had forgotten about my childhood all kind of flew back to me, and it just kind of slowed my life down completely." ■

Go, Eat, You Never Know

By **FRANK BRUNI** | May 30, 2007

THEY COME AROUND EVERY FEW YEARS, these rumors that Katz's Delicatessen is about to close or move or somehow betray itself and those of us who care about it, and our response is always the same.

We gasp. Then we listen for—and let ourselves be consoled by—the denials. And then our attention wanders, because there's a part of us that doesn't really believe Katz's could ever crumble.

It's been around, after all, since 1888. That's longer than Cindy Adams. It's a strand of the city's DNA, a bridge between past and present that's no less a landmark than some bona fide architectural treasure. It's immutable, isn't it?

Isn't it?

Of course not, and let's come back to that—to a conversation, by turns reassuring and slightly worrisome, with one of the restaurant's owners—in short order.

Putting an Ageless Pleasure Between the Rye

By **ED LEVINE** | April 30, 2003

PASTRAMI IS DELI FOOD, AND DELI FOOD IS something New Yorkers have argued about —and loved—for as long as there have been delis in New York. It is a comfort to both Jew and non-Jew, male and female, black and white, Asian and Latino—to all New Yorkers, at least all those who relish the luscious, fatty pleasures of cured, smoked and steamed beef navel on rye. (We'll start that diet on Monday.)

But where did pastrami come from? And what constitutes real pastrami?

Joan Nathan, author of "Jewish Cooking in America" (Knopf, 1998), says the word pastrami comes from a Turkish word, basturma. It describes a meat that is sliced, wind-dried, pickled with dried spices and then pressed.

The technique was adopted by itinerant Jewish peddlers, Ms. Nathan said, who began to cure kosher meat in the same manner. Anyone looking for a taste of basturma should head to the Midwood section of Brooklyn, where the Mansoura family makes a fine version at the bakery of the same name at 515 Kings Highway.

The development of pastrami as we know it today happened in America, Ms. Nathan said, when kosher beef became more widely available in the 19th century. These preserved meats were not easy to make in the home. Delicatessens, or stores selling prepared meats, rose up to help fill the need. By the 1930's, said Joel Denker, author of "The World on a Plate: A Tour Through the History of America's Ethnic Cuisine" (Westview Press), there were 5,000 of them in New York City, most serving home-cured pastrami.

But first let's do something we don't do often enough. Let's take the occasion of the most recent rumors to pause and appreciate Katz's. To take its measure in a format that grants it the kind of recognition typically reserved for restaurants more proper but no more deserving.

To revel in its pastrami sandwich, one of the best in the land, with an eye-popping stack of brined beef that's juicy, smoky, rapturous. To glory in the intricate ritual of the place: the taking of a ticket at the door; the lining-up in front of one of the servers who carves that beef by hand; the tasting of the thick, ridged slices the server gives us as the sandwich is being built; the nodding when we're asked if we want pickles, because of course we want pickles.

At Katz's I prefer the pastrami, though I'm crazy, too, about the tongue, which is less commonly available these days than it should be, given the tenderness of the meat. Katz's sells about 1,000 pastrami sandwiches a day, and there's about a pound of meat, pre-trimming, per sandwich. ∎

Most pastrami in New York is now made by large meat sellers, often as eager as the busy home cook or overworked deli owner to save time and money. One of them is Ira Rosner, a third-generation pastrami maker and the owner of Nation's Best Wholesale Meat and Deli, a purveyor in the Hunts Point meat market in the Bronx.

"Pastrami making has come a long way," he said. "When my grandfather started out, he was coating his navels with salt and other stuff and hanging it to cure. Then he moved to wet-curing in wooden barrels. Then my dad started to hand-pump the navel with syringes containing the brining solution. Now look."

Mr. Rosner pointed to a conveyor belt, on which navels were passing beneath a contraption that plunged needles into each one and filled them with a seasoned brine. From the belt and after a night's rest, he told me, they go into an oven and are smoked with hickory and apple wood, 3,000 pounds at a time. Mr. Rosner makes 100,000 pounds of pastrami a week, and it's quite good. ∎

Braving a Growl
For a Thick Cup of Soup

By **SUZANNE HAMLIN** | March 6, 1996

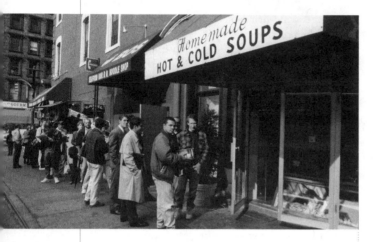

ABOVE: *People lined up for a taste of soup from the infamous 'Soup Nazi,' on November 7, 1996.*

AL YEGANEH, THE SOUP MAN OF WEST 55TH Street, makes a mean pot of soup, which may explain why customers are willing to run a gantlet to get it.

Mr. Yeganeh, whom television viewers know, sort of, from the sitcom "Seinfeld," unquestionably makes great soup. But is it worth a 40-minute wait in a biting wind? It was for several hundred people standing in line the day after a rerun of the "Seinfeld" episode that made him famous. The line snaked around the corner from Mr. Yeganeh's Soup Kitchen International, a tiny storefront near Eighth Avenue.

"This is a New York thing to do now, like going to the Empire State Building," said Rick Wheaton, 23, a tourist from Orlando, Fla.

On "Seinfeld," an actor with an uncanny resemblance to Mr. Yeganeh portrays the stern soup-shop owner, who is referred to as "the Soup Nazi," a name Mr. Yeganeh said is "a horrible term, which should never be used, ever."

Mr. Yeganeh's takeout-only menu changes daily but always includes 8 to 11 thick, hot soups and 4 or 5 cold ones. The rich seafood bisque changes every day, depending on the availability of fresh ingredients.

"This is art, not soup," said Steve Melnick, a Wall Street analyst who had taken the subway uptown to the shop.

Seemingly, none of the soup supplicants objected to the posted rules: know what you want when you reach the counter, speak quickly and ask no questions, have your money ready and move to the extreme left after ordering.

"No bread and no fruit!" the Soup Man yelled to his three helpers when a hapless fur-clad woman tried to change her order from mushroom barley to chicken chili.

Bread and fruit are sometimes added at no charge. Why some are blessed and others are not may seem a mystery to most customers but is obvious to Mr. Yeganeh. The fruit and bread people have not interrupted the flow of the transaction, which he believes should be seven seconds a customer, tops.

> Know what you want when you reach the counter, speak quickly and ask no questions, have your money ready and move to the extreme left after ordering.

Mr. Yeganeh himself is not always so quick to respond. Both HarperCollins and Crown publishers offered him a $150,000 advance, a substantial amount for a first cookbook, but have withdrawn their offers.

The hitch is in the details, Mr. Yeganeh said. "They want me to go around the country to publicize the book," he explained. "But I ask you, how could I leave my soup?" ■

CHARACTERS

His Way, Or No Way

By **CHRISTINE MUHLKE** | October 9, 2008

THE LEGENDARY BON VIVANT LUDWIG Bemelmans once observed, "The most strenuous customer-versus-proprietor battles occur in the smart restaurants of Paris and New York. This kind of restaurant, as a rule, is small. It is benefited by a certain type of guest and injured by another, and the latter must be discouraged from coming. In a man confronted daily with the task of separating the wanted from the unwanted, a degree of arrogance is indispensable."

Confronted daily with the task of deciding who gets to eat at Shopsin's General Store, his 20-seat restaurant in the Essex Street Market, the cook and owner Kenny Shopsin separates the wanted from the unwanted with a degree of foulmouthed eloquence that makes Lenny Bruce look like Sirio Maccioni. "We have a really wonderful relationship with our customers for the most part," he said. "We kick [expletive] out. Regularly."

Order off the menu? Out. Cell phone call? Forget it. Or maybe Shopsin simply doesn't like you. Let's just say that years ago, when I took Alain Ducasse to dinner at Shopsin's—I ate there weekly for eight years, until I lost it in the divorce—I knew better than to introduce him to the cook whose food he was praising. I waited weeks to tell Shopsin, who softened and got borderline misty for a second before bellowing that he would have kicked him out.

It's not the most Danny Meyer-like approach to cultivating clientele, but after 28 years behind the stove, Shopsin wants to cook only for people he likes. "I'm not a very mature person," he says after a lunch shift, his white hair kept at bay by an appropriately McEnroesque headband. "Sometimes my mind works a bit too fast, and I come to the conclusion of a relationship with customers faster than they get there. The abruptness of my understanding the essence of what's happening is really upsetting to them and makes them vindictive and angry." (One man, refused service at the original Bedford Street grocery-turned-restaurant, ripped a toilet out of the floor.)

> "We have a really wonderful relationship with our customers for the most part," he said. "We kick [expletive] out. Regularly."

Unlike other restaurateurs, Shopsin has refused publicity. Whenever I tried to write about him, he would tell the fact-checkers that Shopsin's was a shoe store or out of business or insist that they do something uncheckable to themselves. But two regulars, a Knopf editor and a literary agent, persuaded him to write a cookbook. "Eat Me: The Food and Philosophy of Kenny Shopsin" blends recipes with uncensored thoughts on cooking ("The only explanation I can give for . . . how I came to this method of cooking is that it's a product of a lot of psychotherapy, drugs and making chicken potpies").

Shopsin is dreading the attention "Eat Me" will attract, claiming it will draw the wrong people for the wrong reasons. "The brilliance of my restaurant is that the customer base is soooo special," he says. They know that the real reason Shopsin's has been successful for so long is that it has such a huge heart.

"I was thinking I could learn to be insincere," he says in book mode. "But the first day I really go off, I'll probably just close for a month." ∎

On Spring Street, Revival

By FRANCIS X. CLINES | March 28, 1978

AFTER ALL THE MEN HAD DIED—GENNARO the founder; his son, Giovanni; and Uncle Patsy, the maitre d'—Grandmother Filomena kept the Lombardi family's restaurant open until she got too old and it finally faded like the rest of Spring Street. In her mid-70's she kept offering her rich sauce-and-pasta dishes when many neighbors had run out after that man Robert Moses said his expressway would be coming right through this part of Little Italy.

"Grandma was a tough old lady," says her 34-year-old grandson, Gerry—the latest Lombardi to carry the name Gennaro. "She'd always say in Italian, 'They'll have to carry me out.' That's what happened—she died in the back of the restaurant, in the middle dining room."

By then, three years ago, Spring Street between Mulberry and Lafayette—a single block that had once served well as a lively substitute for Naples—was a grave-yard. The old butcher had gone, along with a grocer, a barber, a drugstore, a leather-worker's shop, an ice-cream parlor, a clothing store and the Spring Lounge, a bar on the corner of Mulberry Street where the young customers used to keep a secure eye on the neighborhood.

Filomena thought so much of the building that she instructed the family in her will that if one of the grandchildren wanted to revive the restaurant, the heirs should cooperate before putting the building on the market. Gerry took the chance and got a half-price bargain from the family on the building. He got a small-business loan and renovated the restaurant, uncovering its old terrazzo floors and porcelain kitchen ceiling. He hired Giovanni Calderon as chef to add a lighter northern cream touch to the menu.

Then Mr. Guidetti, a local undertaker, rented one of the abandoned stores on the Mulberry corner and opened an espresso café, Primavera. Across the way, one of Gerry's boyhood friends, Rocco Morelli, opened Rocky's pizza and sandwich shop. They talked Danny the newsdealer from across Lafayette into moving to their block. The Spring Lounge reopened after two years.

The merchants themselves cleaned up DeSalvio Park. They also bought a long fire hose, and every night after 12 they take turns hooking it up to a hydrant and hosing down the sidewalks and gutters of Spring Street, making it so fresh, Gerry says, that Filomena would have been proud. ■

A Big Bite of Italy And Old New York

By REGINA SCHRAMBLING | August 28, 2002

ARTHUR AVENUE IN THE BRONX CULTIVATES the image of "Cucina Paradiso," complete with a booming soundtrack by Dean Martin at his sappiest. It would be easy to write the neighborhood off as a culinary theme park, a Neapolitan Epcot Center staffed by stock characters. There's enough sweet abbondanza to choke a hardened Manhattanite.

But merchants in this gritty Little Italy say it is thriving while the better-known one downtown has been hurting since the 9/11 attacks. And that's because Arthur Avenue has never catered to fickle tourists, but to passion-ately loyal shoppers looking for mozzarella so fresh it oozes, for the supplest veal, for fettuccine cut to order, for sausages in a dozen variations.

It's Citarella on steroids, Zabar's on Xanax—it has everything, but the mood is amazingly mellow. Ritual is the real nourish-ment. Every transaction is personalized. Ask for mozzarella at the Casa Della Mozzarella

338   THE NEW YORK TIMES BOOK OF NEW YORK

A Family, a Feud And a Six-Foot Sandwich

By **GLENN COLLINS** | December 8, 2001

SINCE THE 9/11 ATTACKS, THERE HAS BEEN no shortage of heartwarming stories about long-feuding families setting aside their differences in an inspirational repudiation of strife-mongering in a war-torn world. This is not one of them.

Salvatore Dell'Orto and his youngest brother, James—each the proprietors of New York culinary landmarks bearing the name Manganaro—are still not speaking. After 25 years.

Indeed, the five daughters of Sal (as everyone calls him) do not speak to the three sons and three daughters of Jimmy (as everyone calls him). This, despite the reality that both families spend all their days, and not a few nights, working on either side of a common wall that is two bricks thick. The wall separates Manganaro's Hero-Boy—a 40-year-old sandwich shop at 492-494 Ninth Avenue, near 37th Street—from the Manganaro Grosseria Italiana (formally known as Manganaro Foods), a century-old specialty grocery and restaurant at 488 Ninth Avenue.

Even in the annals of New York's most appalling food fights, the Manganaro battle is an envelope pusher. It has been in court for 14 years. At issue is which store has the right to take telephone orders for party-size sandwiches— the famous Hero-Boy— under the Manganaro name. So far, Hero-Boy has prevailed.

In July, Manhattan Supreme Court Justice Barbara R. Kapnick agreed to a special referee's finding that Sal owes his brother Jimmy $422,240 in damages. This followed a 1999 ruling by Justice Kapnick that Salvatore was in contempt for violating—bear with us here—another judge's 1989 ruling in the case.

Sal, standing in the modest old-world Grosseria, with its 100-year-old tin ceilings and ancient marble countertops, says his yearly revenues are $500,000 to $600,000 now, down from double that in the early 1990's. He estimates his brother's revenues at $3 million a year; Jimmy, who is 65, will not confirm that, but recently spent $2 million remodeling his 180-seat restaurant.

The Grosseria has made two offers to settle, one of which prompted a counteroffer that "would not be consistent with my client staying in business," said Clyde Eisman, Sal's latest lawyer.

Although the Sept. 11 tragedy has brought many families together, "to have any reconciliation, one of the parties has to say 'I'm sorry,'" said Jimmy. "I don't feel the need to apologize to him for anything, and I don't think he's going to apologize to me." ∎

and the quiz begins: Fresh or smoked? Small, medium or large? Salted or unsalted?

But no shop compares with Borgatti's, where a curtain separates the kitchen from the showroom and ancient signs advise "this corner for ravioli." When I asked what kind of fresh pasta was available, the grandmotherly clerk pulled out a tattered chunk of cardboard painted with yellow stripes in increasing widths.

I pointed to No. 2. She went to a pile of sheets of fresh pasta, weighed out a pound, then carried it across the room and ran it through a hand-cranked cutter to produce fettuccine-size strands. Next she mounded them onto a sheet of white paper, dusted them with a scoop of cornmeal from a barrel on the counter, tossed them until they were coated and finally folded them into a tidy little package before taking my $1.60.

When I cooked the noodles the next day, they were still pliable, not at all like the crackling strands of indeterminate age sold in every other food shop in this city. And they tasted like the essence of Italy, with that firm texture and eggy flavor that makes sauce almost superfluous. ∎

Let the Meals Begin: Finding Beijing in Flushing

By **JULIA MOSKIN** | July 30, 2008

ABOVE: *A young woman eats sweet beans and shaved ice at the Flushing Mall in Queens.*

SEATED AT A RICKETY TABLE, SALTSHAKER poised above a bowl of delicate chicken-and-ginseng soup, the young Taiwanese woman considered a question: why not use soy sauce?

"Soy sauce is so American," she said finally. "It makes everything taste the same."

Everything tastes different in Flushing, Queens, the best neighborhood in New York for tasting the true and dazzling flavors of China. The dumplings are juicier, the noodles springier, the butter cookies flavored with a bit of salty green seaweed, as a cookie at a French bakery might be sprinkled with fleur de sel. The perfume of roasted Sichuan peppercorns and the sound of dough slapping against countertops lures visitors down to the neighborhood's subterranean food malls, where each stall consists of little more than a stove and a specialty: slow-cooked Cantonese healing soups; fragrant, meaty Sichuanese dan dan noodles; or Fujianese wontons, no bigger than a nickel, that spread their fronds in clear broth.

The food of Flushing now includes dishes that don't fit many American notions of Chinese food: griddle-baked sesame bread from China's large Muslim minority, potato-eggplant salad from Harbin in the northeast, Beijing-style candied fruit, and grilled lamb skewers, from China's long-unreachable western frontier near Kazakhstan. There is now a mind-bending variety of noodles and dumplings: the flour foods (mian shi in Chinese), those wheat-based staples that feed China's north and west, as rice traditionally feeds the southeast. (The Yangtze River is the divider.) These places often feel a thousand miles away from Midtown, especially when you try to order or ask questions in English. Practicing the following terms might help: jiao zi (jee-OW tsuh) is the generic word for "dumplings," and mian tiao (MYAHN tee-ow) for "noodles."

One of the best cooks in the food court of the Golden Mall—a grand-sounding name for a basement warren of folding tables —is a man who goes by the name Shi Liangpi, based on his signature dish. He is originally from Xi'an in central China, the beginning of the ancient Silk Road. "Xi'an was one of the world's first great cities," he said. And Mr. Shi's cooking does seem to represent a sophisticated civilization. For liangpi, a dish of cold noodles in a sauce that hits every possible flavor category (sweet, tangy, savory, herbal, nutty and dozens of others), he prepares both translucent wheat noodles and springy wheat gluten from scratch, in addition to four different sauces, and mountains of bean sprouts, slivered cucumbers and sprigs of cilantro. His lamb stew is infused with fresh green chilies and cumin: stuffed into hot, griddled bread rolls, it makes the best sandwich in Flushing. ■

asian

Solving a Riddle Wrapped In a Mystery Inside a Cookie

By **JENNIFER 8. LEE** | January 16, 2008

SOME 3 BILLION FORTUNE COOKIES ARE MADE each year, almost all in the United States. But the crisp cookies wrapped around enigmatic sayings have spread around the world. They are served in Chinese restaurants in Britain, Mexico, Italy, France and elsewhere. In India, they taste more like butter cookies. A surprisingly high number of winning tickets in Brazil's national lottery in 2004 were traced to lucky numbers from fortune cookies distributed by a Chinese restaurant chain called Chinatown.

But there is one place where fortune cookies are conspicuously absent: China.

Now a researcher believes she can explain the disconnect, which has long perplexed American tourists in China. Fortune cookies, Yasuko Nakamachi says, are almost certainly originally from Japan—an idea that is counterintuitive, to say the least.

"I am surprised," said Derrick Wong, the vice president of the largest fortune cookie manufacturer in the world, Wonton Food, based in Brooklyn. But, he conceded, "The weakest part of the Chinese menu is dessert."

Ms. Nakamachi, a folklore and history graduate student at Kanagawa University outside Tokyo, saw her first fortune cookie in the 1980's in a New York City Chinese restaurant. At that time she was merely impressed with Chinese ingenuity, finding the cookies an amusing and clever idea. It was only in the late 1990's, outside Kyoto near one of the most popular Shinto shrines in Japan, that she saw that familiar shape at a family bakery called Sohonke Hogyokudo.

"They were shaped exactly the same," she said, "and there were fortunes."

A visit to the Hogyokudo shop revealed that the Japanese fortune cookies Ms. Nakamachi found there and at a handful of nearby bakers differ in some ways from the ones that Americans receive at the end of a meal with the check and a handful of orange wedges. They are bigger and browner, as their batter contains sesame and miso rather than vanilla and butter. The fortunes are not stuffed inside, but are pinched in the cookie's fold. (Think of the cookie as a Pac-Man: the paper is tucked into Pac-Man's mouth rather than inside his body.)

"People don't realize this is the real thing because American fortune cookies are popular right now," said Takeshi Matsuhisa as he folded the hot wafers into the familiar shape.

His family has owned the bakery for three generations, and it has used the same 23 fortunes for decades. (In contrast, Wonton Food has a database of well over 10,000 fortunes.) Hogyokudo's fortunes are more poetic than prophetic, although some nearby bakeries use newer fortunes that give advice or make predictions. One from Inariya, a shop across from the Shinto shrine, contains the advice, "To ward off lower back pain or joint problems, undertake some at-home measures like yoga." ∎

BELOW: *There are approximately 2,500 Chinese restaurants in New York City and most of them serve fortune cookies.*

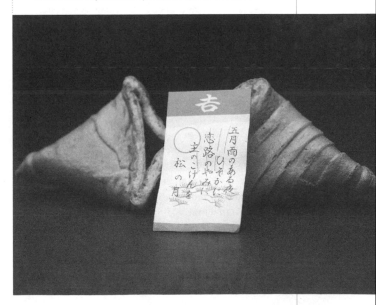

Brooklyn's "Little Odessa"

By **BRYAN MILLER** | July 20, 1983

THERE AREN'T MANY BEACHES THIS SIDE OF the Baltic Sea where sunbathers can cool off at a boardwalk food stand with a chilled bowl of beet-red borscht and sour cream. In the Brighton Beach section of Brooklyn, not only can bathers do that, at a takeout lunch stand called Gastronom Moscow, but they can also walk a block away to restaurants that serve such Russian specialties as Caucasian lamb casserole, grilled chicken with walnut sauce, Ukrainian dumplings, mutton soup, piroshki and, of course, caviar and iced vodka.

Brighton Beach is one of the newest patches in New York City's colorful ethnic quilt, a home for an estimated 25,000 Russian immigrants, most of whom are Jewish and have arrived in the past five years. They have brought to this once-fading seaside neighborhood their exotic alphabet, uplifting music and megacaloric foods.

Once referred to as the Nice of New York because of its broad urban beach, the area's new nickname, "Little Odessa," is now more appropriate. Many of the immigrants come from that Ukrainian city on the Black Sea, which they say in some ways resembles this seaside neighborhood. The feel of this corner of the city can best be experienced on a stroll along Brighton Beach Avenue, where most of the Russian-owned stores can be found.

One of the more bustling spots is M & I International Food on Brighton Beach Avenue, sort of the Ukrainian version of Zabar's. It is a two-level store that stocks a wide variety of Russian- and American-style smoked fish, sausages, cold cuts, canned goods, breads, pastries and candies.

On a recent afternoon the downstairs meat counter was thick with animated Russian women calling orders to a half-dozen employees behind the counter. Except for the bountifully stocked display counters and some boxes of American breakfast cereal, the shop could be a scene in Odessa or Kiev. Virtually all the food signs are in Russian without English subtitles, and not a word of English could be heard. The store was doing a brisk business in Russian-style rolled shoulder of veal seasoned with garlic and black pepper as well as spicy homemade kielbasa and black bread.

Upstairs at the International is devoted to pastries and candies. An American's attempt to elicit an explanation for one intriguing-looking dessert—stubby chocolate fingers with little candy decorations—illustrates the frustration non-Russian-speaking customers can face.

"Patata, patata," replied the saleswoman matter-of-factly when asked what they were. "You mean they are made from potatoes?" "Patata, yes, patata." It turned out that they were marzipan potatoes, a popular pastry named for their potato shape. ∎

Indian Food For Indian Diners

By **ANDREA KANNAPELL** | January 19, 1997

CHINESE PACK THE RESTAURANTS OF CHINA-town and Japanese fill good sushi bars, but in the Indian restaurants on Sixth Street, a South Asian face is rare at the table.

A trip to Jackson Heights, Queens, helps solve this urban mystery. Centered on 74th Street and 37th Avenue is a bigger Little India. And here, among the sari and grocery stores, the diners and import music outlets, immigrants from Delhi to Bombay to the Punjab uniformly greeted questions about Sixth Street with a polite, but complete, lack of interest.

Food is, of course, the main issue. Jacob Bino, the 28-year-old manager of the

A Random Tasting Tour: The Flavor Is Ethnic

By **MICHAEL T. KAUFMAN** | October 6, 1993

As everybody knows, any fool with money can eat scrumptiously in this city, there being no lack of good or fancy restaurants and no shortage of guidebooks. But where can you get really good pofpof, moinmoin and iddlies? Where is there palm wine? In other words, where can you taste delicious things you have never even heard of for the price of a movie or less?

Robert Sietsema knows. He is a Midwesterner who more than 15 years ago abandoned his doctoral dissertation on Robert Louis Stevenson to pursue a woman, now his wife, to New York City. He worked in book publishing and became the bass player for a well regarded but now extinct Alphabet City noise band. For the last several years he has been processing words in a job he does not love.

Delhi Palace restaurant, spoke for many when he said he had never even been to a restaurant on Sixth Street. "Sixth Street is known for cooking for Americans," he said. "Also, I think the price is very cheap. Real Indian cooking is very expensive. The spices—cardamom, cinnamons. Very expensive. Saffron. Even the clay oven for tandoori, that costs $7,000 or $8,000."

A few doors down 74th Street, at the counter of Sargam Audio Video, the manager, Raju Bains, 29, said there are other obstacles. "There are so many parking problems in Manhattan," he pointed out. "I went one time, to Gandhi, three years ago," he said. "It was good. But here, I'm right near the Jackson Diner and Delhi Palace. That's good food also. The restaurants here, they have parking." ■

What he does love is the great variety of foods in ethnic eateries. Most of his lunch hours are spent checking out leads like a pushcart in Astoria that reportedly has the best souvlaki. So great is his enthusiasm for his subject that he spent a recent day off on what turned out to be a 46-mile scarfing expedition.

"This I believe is the best jerk in the city," said Mr. Sietsema at the first stop, Harry's Jerk Center, a five-table establishment on East Gun Hill Road in the Bronx. "Other Jamaican places grill the chicken or the pork before they coat it with allspice," Mr. Sietsema said over the music. "Here they barbecue, which provides the smoke you need for first-rate jerk."

My mind was filled with thoughts of Indian food as we headed to Queens. Specifically I was imagining a plate of chole puri, a simple enough Punjabi dish that I grew to love during the four years I lived in India. There it was on the menu of the Jackson Diner, a place that was all the more unusual in that it offered both the well-known dishes of north India and the vegetarian patties of south India, the iddlies dosai and uthappam.

We worked off that meal by driving into Brooklyn, to the Valle of Mexico Aztec Grocery in Williamsburg. "Every day at 4 o'clock the woman who owns the shop comes out on the sidewalk and makes really delicious tacos over a camping stove." She was there as he said she would be, and the tacos were indeed delicious.

We needed to sit somewhere and wash it all down. Mr. Sietsema led the way to the Demu Nigerian Cafe on Fulton Street. That's where breakfast includes pofpof and moinmoin, but it was too late in the day for that. Instead we shared a large cold bottle of palm wine. Palm wine, it turns out, is a little tart and goes very well with doing nothing.

"You want to try a spleen sandwich at Vasteddi's on First Avenue and Seventh Street in Manhattan?" Mr. Sietsema asked.

Next time. ■

Curb Food Markets Boom; Summer Brings Brisk Trade to the Pushcarts

By **CATHERINE MACKENZIE** | August 18, 1935

ALL THE YEAR ROUND NEW YORK BUYS foodstuffs in the streets, but summer is the peak season for trading at the curbs. At fixed pushcart stands, or from itinerant peddlers, housewives shop for bargains in melons and peaches, in cucumbers and carrots and new green corn.

This month has seen the first big move to change the old order of the pushcarts, and all the official assurances of the Department of Markets have not banished the peddlers' uneasiness.

Up on Park Avenue, under the New York Central Bridge, from 116th to 121st Street, New York's biggest pushcart market is still trying to settle down at its temporary stand, while the city decides about building the new stalls long projected for the old market area from 111th to 116th Street. The vendors moved in August.

BELOW: *Food vendors continue to clash with authorities. Piedad Cano turns her famous arepas from 10:00 p.m. to 5:00 a.m. on Fridays and Saturdays to avoid the police.*

The discussion concerns the glass fronts that will protect the new stalls, instead of the old tarpaulins; the steam heat that will warm them in winter instead of scattered little fires of broken crates and barrel staves. But will there be room for them all? Will the fees be too high? "They" say it will be all right, but anyway you take it, things will never be quite the same without the pushcarts.

> Upward of 6,500 permits
> are held by
> pushcart peddlers.

There are 55 active retail public markets in Greater New York. Of these the largest of those enclosed are the downtown Washington Market, the municipal market at First Avenue under the Queensboro Bridge, and the Bronx Market. None of these attracts the poor or the thrifty housewife in such numbers as the pushcart markets do; upward of 6,500 permits are held by pushcart peddlers. The majority are stationary in pushcart markets.

Each of the larger pushcart markets has its special reputation for produce and values. The biggest of all the pushcart markets is the one on Harlem's Park Avenue, where there are 700 licensed pushcarts. The new stalls may make for a more efficient market, but never one so picturesque. The shoppers are shrewd about values and wary of short weight and short change. They look out for counterfeit money, too. Suspiciously the dealer crumples the proffered dollar, warily the purchaser inspects the quarters and half dollars offered in change. It is something for the sightseer, but the market patrons are here to get their money's worth. ∎

When the "Alphas" Come, Street Vendors Run

By **JAMES BARRON** | April 24, 1994

IT WAS NOT QUITE NOON WHEN GOPAL SAHA, Mobile Food Vendor No. 18575, made his first sale of the day: a $2 Haagen-Dazs Cookie Dough Dynamo sandwich. "Looking good," he said, stuffing the two already-crinkled bills deep in a blue jeans pocket. In another 20 or 30 minutes, the crowd swirling past his pushcart on West 49th Street in Rockefeller Center would swell to three or maybe even four abreast on the sidewalk. Potential customers all.

Suddenly, Mr. Saha's worst nightmare began to come true. "The alphas are coming," yelled the hot-dog vendor down the block. That is street-seller talk for the police, who have begun a crackdown on food carts in congested Midtown neighborhoods the city has declared off limits.

A blue-and-white police van whizzed down the block, stopping next to Mr. Saha's stand. Officer Henry Dopwell of the Peddler Task Force's summons enforcement unit hopped out and told Mr. Saha to hand his license to Officer Jose DeJesus, behind the wheel.

"Hard day," said Mr. Saha, 28, who was a rice- and vegetable-wholesaler in Bangladesh before he immigrated four years ago. "Hard job. Too many problems. I pay taxes. I pay for a vendor's license. And then they close me down."

Not quite. All the two officers did was to hand Mr. Saha a summons and tell him to move outside the no-vendor zone. But it was Mr. Saha's third summons of the week, meaning a fine of at least $100, up from the first-ticket minimum of $25. Officer Dopwell warned that if Mr. Saha did not get going, the police would confiscate his cart, presumably without letting him remove his merchandise, which would soon melt.

The Giuliani administration says the crackdown on food carts is part of a campaign on "quality of life" issues. Mr. Saha sees it the opposite way: food carts improve the quality of life in New York, he says.

Still, he moved on, pushing his cart, dodging potholes and talking about his wife, Shipah. They were married four months ago, but she is still in Bangladesh. Mr. Saha said her emigration papers had been filed, but knowing that is small compensation for so great a separation. "Every other month, I call her on the telephone," he said. "One dollar per minute, maybe $1.20. Ten minutes, 15 minutes go very fast. A lot of income to talk."

And on this day, at least, not much income was coming in. He sold two more Haagen-Dazs sandwiches after he got the summons, for a total of three by lunch hour. On a good day, he takes in about $200 and nets $60 to $70, about a third. Not today. "Six dollars," he said at lunchtime. "A profit of $1.50, maybe."

He sold off a bit more of his inventory in the afternoon, after moving to 47th Street and the Avenue of the Americas, a crowded corner where he was the latecomer among four carts.

The inventory would keep for one more day. "After that," he said, "it's no good." ■

BELOW: *There are over 3,000 food carts in the city today.*

A Last Whiff of Fulton's Fish

By **DAN BARRY** | July 10, 2005

IT SMELLS OF TRUCK EXHAUST AND FISH GUTS. Of glistening skipjacks and smoldering cigarettes; fluke, salmon and Joe Tuna's cigar. Of Canada, Florida, and the squid-ink East River. Of funny fish-talk riffs that end with profanities spat onto the mucky pavement, there to mix with coffee spills, beer blessings, and the flowing melt of sea-scented ice.

This fragrance of fish and man pinpoints one place in the New York vastness: a small stretch of South Street where peddlers have sung the song of the catch since at least 1831, while all around them, change. They were hawking fish here when a presidential aspirant named Lincoln spoke at Cooper Union and when the building of a bridge to Brooklyn ruined their upriver view.

Soon the rains will rinse this distinct aroma from the city air. Some Friday soon, the fish sellers will spill their ice and shutter their stalls, pack their grappling hooks and raise a final toast beneath the ba-rump and hum of the Franklin D. Roosevelt Drive.

And on the Monday, they will begin peddling their dead-eyed wares inside a custom-made building in the Hunts Point section of the Bronx, to be named the New Fulton Fish Market Cooperative. The old Fulton Fish Market, that raucous stage of open-air overnight commerce, will be no more.

Before it leaves us, then, one last look at a part of the city taken for granted, save by fish people, nighthawks and urban anthropologists. One long, last inhalation of the Fulton Fish Market bouquet as forklifts clatter over rutted pavement, unloaded trucks sigh in escape, and workers pierce wax-coated cases with grappling hooks—whup! whup!—to move fish from here to there.

> That raucous stage of open-air overnight commerce will be no more.

In one stall stands Vincent Tatick, of the Joseph H. Carter Fish Company. His father ran Frank Tatick Fillet under the old Sweet's Restaurant. Both are gone now, and here is the son, twirling a grappling hook as though it were a child's toy. He sports five pencils and a pack of Parliaments in his breast pocket, and keeps a Marine Corps knife on his hip. Rambo among fish.

Mr. Tatick has no opinion about the market's move, he says, other than: what is, is. But he wonders about leaving behind the nuns at St. Rose's Home, on the Lower East Side, who nursed his father in his final two years. During that time, the Taticks agreed that it would be nice to give the nuns some fish, 25 pounds worth, every Friday.

When his father died, Mr. Tatick says, "I didn't know how to say, 'Sorry, the deal is off.' So I never said anything."

That was more than 40 years ago, he says. "I still give them fish." ∎

BELOW: *During much of its 183-year tenure at the original site, the Fulton Fish Market was the most important wholesale East Coast fish market in the U.S.*

From Oreos and Mallomars To a Market

By **CHRISTOPHER GRAY** | August 7, 2005

THE OVENS AT THE NATIONAL BISCUIT COMpany complex in what is now west Chelsea once baked everything from Saltines to Oreos. Those ovens went cold a half century ago, when the company moved out, but newer ovens have been working over the last decade in a part of that old complex—at Chelsea Market, on Ninth Avenue between 15th and 16th Streets.

In 1890, eight large eastern bakeries amalgamated to form the New York Biscuit Company and soon absorbed a dozen more firms. It was competing against another consortium, the American Biscuit and Manufacturing Company of Chicago, and it began building a Romanesque-style complex of bakeries on the east side of 10th Avenue, running from 15th to 16th Street, designed by Romeyn & Stever.

The two cookie consortiums joined forces in 1898 as the National Biscuit Company, which soon provided half the biscuit production in the United States, and the New York complex grew as the new company brought out such new products as the Uneeda Biscuit, Premium Saltines, Fig Newtons and, in 1913, both the Oreo (originally Oreo Biscuit) and the Mallomar.

Within a few years of the merger, the New York bakery complex covered most of the block back to Ninth Avenue. In 1913, the architect Albert Zimmerman designed the most prominent building in the complex, the 11-story structure from 10th to 11th Avenue and 15th to 16th Street. It was built on landfill: the timbers, chain and anchor of a two-masted schooner were found during excavation.

In 1932, the architect Louis Wirsching Jr. replaced some of the 1890 bakeries on the east side of 10th Avenue with an unusual structure, which accommodates an elevated freight railroad viaduct. Its great open porch on the second and third floors was taken by the railroad as an easement for the rail tracks that still run through it.

By then, a new generation of long, continuous "band ovens" were remaking the baking industry. According to William Cahn's company history, "Out of the Cracker Barrel: The Nabisco Story from Animal Crackers to Zuzus" (Simon & Schuster, 1969) National Biscuit installed some band ovens in the New York complex, but long horizontal industrial processes adapted better to the low single-story buildings that were going up in outlying areas.

By 1958, National Biscuit was producing its line from a plant in Fair Lawn, N.J., and in 1959 it sold the New York complex. The neighborhood was sliding into a sort of Rust Belt-like graveyard.

In the 1990's, the complex was reinvented as the Chelsea Market, with technology companies upstairs and a long interior arcade of food stores on the ground floor.

To walk through the Chelsea Market is to stroll through a sort of postindustrial theme park, carefully festooned with the detritus of a lost industrial culture. Fragments of the National Biscuit heritage are sprinkled all over the complex, like the trim, elegant "NBC" monograms in the mosaics in the little entryways along 15th Street. But the entrance to the 1913 building at 85 10th Avenue is among the most haunting sights in New York. ∎

ABOVE : *Former National Biscuit Company building (in a 1930's photo). The building is now home to Chelsea Market.*

Behind Zabar's Counters, Three Feuding Partners

By **GLENN COLLINS** | March 16, 1985

THE THREE PARTNERS WHO OWN ZABAR'S are in complete agreement on a number of things. They are feuding, but they are not feuding. They will sell Zabar's, but they will not sell Zabar's. A cookie mogul has the inside track to buy Zabar's, but he may not be able to buy Zabar's.

The uncertainty over Zabar's, a magnet for food lovers all over the country, began with reports that David Liederman, the Goliath of the David's Cookies chain, had offered to buy the store with the intention of bringing it to the wider world, something he had previously done for the pecan chocolate chunk cookie.

This financial story has been overshadowed by the unraveling of the family partnership that has spanned three generations.

Murray Klein, the 62-year-old operational manager of Zabar's, says he wants to retire, and from his point of view he is forcing his partners to buy him out, to decide whether to sell the firm or to keep it in the Zabar family. As for the other partners, Saul Zabar, 56, said that he and his brother Stanley, 52, are tired of the stresses of the partnership and want to disengage themselves from the business.

At stake in the partners' complex, emotionally trying predicament are not just millions of dollars and some choice Manhattan real estate, but also the future of a pacesetter in the world of food whose committed customers are deeply anxious.

"The entire West Side is having a nervous breakdown over this," said Nora Ephron, the writer, who lives a block from the store.

Saul Zabar said that "the normal irritations in a partnership" become "more abrasive" over time. "That's the main reason for this," he said of the possible sale. "The personality conflicts that existed throughout the years—well, as you get older you don't want to tolerate them anymore."

Many credit Mr. Klein with the store's pioneering innovations and praise his obsessive focus on the customer and his passion for underselling the competition. "Macy's and Bloomingdale's—that was Klein," said Saul Zabar, referring to Zabar's price war with department stores that culminated in the 1983 Battle of Beluga, a caviar competition with Macy's. "He just did not want to be undersold."

Many have expected the Zabars to pass the business to their heirs, and such an outcome is still a possibility. "David is the only one of the children who has taken an interest in the business," Mr. Zabar said, speaking of Stanley's 29-year-old son, David Zabar, who has been working as a fish buyer. Mr. Klein "made sure" his children were not in the business, he said of his son and daughter. "I would not want for them to work these terrible hours." ▪

BELOW: *Zabar's, located at 2245 Broadway (and 80th Street), turned 75 in 2009.*

At Balducci's, a House Divided Stands in Name Only

By **MARIAN BURROS** | June 28, 2000

THE OPENING OF A NEW BALDUCCI'S ON THE Upper West Side struck many in the neighborhood as a marvelous gift from one of the city's finest food shops.

But to some the West Side store represents a new chapter in a rancorous family fight that has gone on for years. The estrangement is now so complete that at both Balducci's the only thing left of the family is the name. And that was sold to an outside company last year.

For years the food world has buzzed about the hostility among the three Balducci siblings, two of whom ran the famous Greenwich Village store with their parents and some of their children until 1985, when Grace Balducci Doria and her husband, Joe, left to open Grace's Marketplace on the Upper East Side. Balducci's itself is now owned by Sutton Place Gourmet, a Maryland-based company whose products have never been on the level Balducci's were in its best days.

Why did the stores end up out of the family?

The answer is a byzantine story of family jealousies and court fights. Sibling rivalry between Andy, 74, and Charles, 76, dates back more than 70 years, when it became clear that Charles was his father's favorite son, even before he became "my son the doctor."

Andy married Nina D'Amelio in 1952 and left Balducci's in 1953 to work for his father-in-law's marble and granite business. Andy returned to Balducci's 15 years later, four years before they signed a lease to move to Avenue of the Americas and Ninth Street. That's where the humble but successful fruit and vegetable market became something more.

Before they signed the lease, they formed a new corporation, with four partners: Andy and Nina owned 51 percent; Grace and Joe 49 percent.

Grace said that she didn't understand that whoever owns 51 percent is the boss.

Dr. Charles Balducci, her brother, has another take on the situation. He says his father's will called for giving each of his three children a third of the business. The new corporation, Dr. Balducci said, was "strictly done to get me out of the will."

Grace says there was friction, that Andy humiliated her and her husband every day. She says her brother offered them $500,000 for their share before they left. They sued him. Their father sued him at the same time, for his share.

> The estrangement is now so complete that at both Balducci's the only thing left of the family is the name.

The case was settled out of court. Joe Doria says Louis Balducci received $2.5 million, the Dorias another $2.5 million. (Andy disputes the figures: "They got a hell of a lot more than $2.5 million. I'm not going to divulge any number.")

In 1999, when Andy sold Balducci's to Sutton Place for $26.5 million, a number of longtime employees left, including Andy's cousin Charlie Balducci, who said he did not want to work for a corporation. So important is it for Sutton Place to create the impression that there are still Balduccis at Balducci's that this month's company newsletter suggests that Alan Butzbach, the vice president of operations, is married to a Balducci daughter.

In fact, Mr. Butzbach has been divorced from the Balduccis' youngest daughter for years; she died after they separated. ∎

Keeping the Greenmarket In the Pink

By **BARBARA STEWART** | August 3, 1997

YOU THINK THE UNION SQUARE GREEN-market just manages itself? The farmers drive in, unload the beets and tomatoes and Ruby Crescent potatoes and just relax until customers show up? And the park simply turns itself into a lush, odorous cornucopia of vegetables, still dripping dirt, and at night turns itself back into a park? All by itself?

Don't say that to Joel Patraker, the manager of the city's two dozen markets, who is all too familiar with the constant tending required.

Looking at Union Square today, it's hard to remember how downtrodden it used to be before the market opened 21 years ago. "It was ruled by drug dealers, the original needle park," said Rob Walsh, the former president of the 14th Street-Union Square Business Improvement District. "The buildings were derelict. A lot of people threw up their hands."

When Barry Benepe, a planning consultant, created the first Greenmarkets, many people thought nobody sane would shop at Union Square. With $15,000 in

> The Greenmarkets let the 200 farmers sell most of their harvest directly to consumers

private grants, Mr. Benepe persuaded a few farmers to drive to New York City to sell directly to city shoppers.

The farmers were leery. "They thought that there would be gangsters," Mr. Benepe recalled. But they needed what the city people had. "Money." (The administrators' salaries are paid from farmers' rents, $65 for the biggest space. The city government has never donated nor received money from the markets.)

The Greenmarkets let the 200 farmers sell most of their harvest directly to consumers at retail prices, bypassing wholesalers. But the Greenmarkets are more than buying and selling. The markets that thrive become town centers, where people speak easily with strangers. Urban residents discovered that farmers are frequently highly educated. Farmers found that city people could be friendly and reasonably honest.

"It's like theater," said the chef David Bouley, a buyer of Greenmarket produce. "It exudes energy. At the Greenmarkets you can feel the purity. There is no commercial marketing. It's all from the gut. There's no promotion, no marketing. You walk through the stands and the farmers are proud of what they're selling. They live with it, they teach people how to enjoy it. "

The same could be said for the interaction between urban and rural people. A few, like the Greenmarket managers, feel at home with both.

"Sometimes I feel like I'm hiding in the middle of New York City with my brother and my wife and my friend, Tony," Joel Patraker said. "We all get to live in a little rural village and be in the city, too." ■

BELOW: *The Union Square Greenmarket began in 1976 and is currently held every Monday, Wednesday, Friday and Saturday.*

Lucy in the Greenmarket With Fava Beans

By **JENNIFER BLEYER** | July 1, 2007

LUCY WOLLIN, AN ARDENT FAN OF THE CITY'S greenmarkets, arrived at the Union Square Greenmarket with a burlap sack over her shoulder, ready to appraise the day's offerings.

"Look at these interesting lettuces," Ms. Wollin said, examining tufts of speckled romaine, red oak leaf and butterhead lettuce with a gem dealer's eye. A farm manager pointed toward a bushel basket near the back of his booth.

"Fava beans!" she said happily. "Can I have one so I can remember?"

Ms. Wollin plucked a single arched fava bean pod from the basket and stuck it in her bag, to be mentioned later that morning on her blog, Lucy's Greenmarket Report. She continued wandering among the booths, commenting on the tail-end-of-the-season asparagus and expertly evaluating the strawberries.

Ms. Wollin, a retired school librarian who is 64 and lives nearby on East 15th Street, has followed the Union Square market since it opened in 1976. She started her report (at www.echonyc.com/lwollin/greenmarket.html) with the simple desire to help "the Greenmarket be as terrific as it is."

Her blog entries, read by both professional and amateur chefs, are typically a few succinct, often exuberant lines noting what she discovered that morning: "You can still get strawberries from some farmers and Phillips has blueberries! Yuno has gorgeous salad."

Many of the sellers know Ms. Wollin. They also know how to entice her with their wares.

"Do you have my treasure?" Ms. Wollin said to a seller from Mountain Sweet Berry Farm in Roscoe, N.Y. A small bundle of chervil, a licorice-tinged herb, was handed over.

She also surveyed edible flowers, checked on sugar snap peas, swooned over the lavender and commended the young garlic. Then she paused to review what she would say on her blog.

"I'll talk about the chervil, two new kinds of strawberries, the black peppermint, the speckled romaine, the last gasp of peonies and the fava beans," she said. "Tomato season will be when I get hysterical." ∎

Delmonico's Succumbs To Prohibition and High Rent

May 20, 1923

DELMONICO'S, LONG ONE OF NEW YORK'S most famous restaurants, will follow the lead taken by Shanley's, Murray's and other well-known dining places, and close its doors at Fifth Avenue and 44th Street tomorrow at midnight. This was announced at Delmonico's last night and formal notice was forwarded to all regular patrons.

It was explained, however, that it is not the purpose of E. L. C. Robins, who with Miss Josephine Delmonico controls the establishment, to go out of business entirely. But it was admitted that with Prohibition and high rent the restaurant had failed to make both ends meet.

"The closing is due to the unwillingness of the landlords to permit alterations to the building," a statement said. "Litigation in respect to these alterations has been in progress for some time." The alterations he wanted would have enabled the restaurant company to derive revenue from several stores on the Fifth Avenue side of the building, but the Delco Realty Company would not permit them.

Delmonico's has been located at Fifth Avenue and 44th Street since November 15, 1897, having moved uptown from 26th Street and Fifth Avenue. The building consists of a Fifth Avenue restaurant, Palm Room and grill room on the first floor, six private dining rooms and a hall accommodating 200 on the second floor, a ballroom accommodating 600 and a small ballroom for 200 people on the third floor. ∎

BELOW: *Some claim that Chicken à la King and Eggs Benedict originated at Delmonico's, shown here in 1907.*

C'est la Fin! Lutèce Closing After 43 Years

By **ERIC ASIMOV** | February 11, 2004

AFTER SERVING ONE LAST VALENTINE'S DAY dinner, Lutèce, the renowned landmark French restaurant on the East Side, will close, ending a 43-year run as a pillar of French dining in the United States.

"Since 9/11 we have not had enough business to meet expenses," said Michael Weinstein, president of Ark Restaurants, which has owned Lutèce since 1994. "This is probably a decision that should have been made a year ago."

Mr. Weinstein said that Lutèce had lost much of the expense-account business that

Lutèce Both Elegant and Expensive

By **CRAIG CLAIBORNE** | March 28, 1961

LUTÈCE WAS THE ORIGINAL NAME OF PARIS. It also is the name of a recently opened restaurant in Manhattan that is at once impressively elegant and conspicuously expensive. There is much that is visually appealing about this establishment, including the candlelight, napery and walls, which boast a modest wealth of tapestries, paintings and a mural by Jean Pagès in colors as gay as a carousel.

The menus at Lutèce are opulently styled. On the cover is a print of a famous 19th-century painting of French roses by Redoute. It is a point of interest that there are, in fact, two menus at Lutèce. One is for the host at each table, the other for the guests, and there is this difference in the menus: The one presented to the host lists the cost of the various dishes; the menus presented to the guests list only the dishes.

There are approximately 30 items on each menu. There are three soups, seven first courses, nine main dishes, six vegetables, a platter of cheeses and seven desserts.

Lutèce has been opened for scarcely more than a month and perhaps it is this youth that causes an unevenness in the quality of the cuisine.

A few of the dishes, a foie gras en brioche or a roast veal with kidney, for example, could qualify as superb; others, such as a poussin rôti aux girolles (squab chicken with wild mushrooms) are routine. A few of the dishes, such as a fillet of sole sampled recently, are disappointing in the extreme. It is this reviewer's opinion that the food at Lutèce could not be called great cuisine. ∎

had sustained it for years, especially at lunch. He also suggested that an attempt to modernize the classic French cuisine that customers had long worshiped at the Lutèce temple had been misguided.

"We probably made a wrong turn a couple of years ago when we decided to make this menu edgy and more modern," he said.

Though it has been more than a decade since Lutèce was in its glory days, the restaurant played a crucial role in the culinary development of the United States almost from the moment it opened its doors in 1961. André Soltner, who was the chef for 34 years and the owner for most of that time, was one of the first chefs in America to emphasize the freshest possible ingredients. While his nightly specials often included rustic dishes from his native Alsace, like a puffy onion tart, Mr. Soltner's cuisine evoked the classic elegance of the Old World.

The closing of Lutèce, along with the announcement that La Côte Basque, another old-line Manhattan French restaurant, will close in March—and the opening of the glossy new high-end restaurants in the Time Warner Center at Columbus Circle—cements the changing of the guard in New York restaurants. Long gone are the days when the city's best restaurants were indisputably French, some tracing their lineage back to the restaurant at the French Pavilion at the 1939 World's Fair.

Now the big excitement is reserved for chefs at the Time Warner Center like Thomas Keller and Gray Kunz, who, though they are masters of French methods and techniques, offer thoroughly personal styles of cooking. ∎

Spectacular in Décor and Menu

By **CRAIG CLAIBORNE** | October 2, 1959

THERE HAS NEVER BEEN A RESTAURANT better keyed to the tempo of Manhattan than the Four Seasons, which opened recently at 99 East 52nd Street.

Both in décor and in menu, it is spectacular, modern and audacious. It is expensive and opulent and it is perhaps the most exciting restaurant in New York within the last two decades. On the whole, the cuisine is not exquisite in the sense that la grande cuisine Francaise at its superlative best is exquisite.

Both the luncheon and dinner menus at the Four Seasons are extensive and, to a degree, bewildering. For example, the evening card lists more than a score of cold appetizers and nearly as many hot hors d'oeuvre. Typical in the cold selection is an "herbed lobster parfait." If memory serves, this contains large chunks of lobster enrobed in a devastatingly rich blend of whipped cream and hollandaise sauce.

Flaming dishes are among the most popular items. One of the best of these is the traditional beef Stroganoff, which is prepared at tableside in a somewhat unconventional

> Flaming dishes are among the most popular items.

but thoroughly tempting fashion. It is made of quarter-inch slices of prime tenderloin seasoned with sweet paprika. The meat is then sautéed in butter, flamed with Cognac and bathed in a sauce containing meat glaze and sour cream.

Like most facets of the Four Seasons, the décor is a conversation piece. The walls are hung with a fortune in art and tapestries by such modern geniuses as Picasso, Joan Miro and Jackson Pollock. There are massive plants that reflect seasonal changes; from the ceiling in the bar area are hung thousands of brass rods to produce what is called a "sculptured chandelier" effect.

It is estimated that the average luncheon check for two with wines and without cocktails totals about $25. Dinner on the same basis is about $40. ∎

Still Going Strong

By **MIMI SHERATON** | January 12, 1979

FEW THINGS CAN MAKE US FEEL OLDER THAN the realization that this year the Four Seasons is celebrating its 20th birthday. July 20 will mark that date for a restaurant that was spectacularly innovative when it opened and has weathered so well that it is still the handsomest and grandest modern restaurant anywhere.

The high-flown palatial interior, with its swagged, rippling, coppery-chain curtains, the marbled splendor of its reflecting pool, the garden of greenery and the gleaming, dark, French-rosewood-paneled walls and black upholstery of the barroom, brightened by Richard Lippold's hanging brass-rod sculptures, all came from the drawing board of Philip Johnson, himself now virtually a fixture in the barroom at lunch almost every day. The late Albert Stockli, then executive chef of Restaurant Associates, tested and retested many of the dishes, which are still prepared under the expert hand of the chef, Seppi Renggli.

Five and a half years ago, Restaurant Associates sold the Four Seasons to Tom Margittai, then a vice president in charge of operations for that company, and Paul Kovi,

Restaurants

Herbert Woods, Consort of a Soul Food Queen, Dies at 76

By DOUGLAS MARTIN | June 15, 2001

HERBERT WOODS, WHO STAYED MODESTLY in the shadows as his wife, Sylvia, played center stage as Harlem's "Queen of Soul Food" at their famous restaurant, died on Wednesday at 76.

Mr. Woods played a far greater role than many of the patrons greeted by his vivacious wife realized. He handled purchasing and real estate decisions and was known to put in the occasional shift as chef. His income as a long-distance truck driver was a critical ingredient in the early success of Sylvia's Restaurant, which is on Lenox Avenue near 127th Street.

Busloads of foreign tourists, delivery boys, chorus girls and celebrities from Roberta Flack to Robert F. Kennedy have flocked to Sylvia's for feathery, moist cornbread, tangy ribs, perfectly seasoned collard greens and crisp fried chicken.

Mrs. Woods many times insisted that one spice made it all possible: love. Her own love story, she never failed to add, was her life's inspiration.

Sylvia Pressley was 11 when she met Herbert Deward Woods, 12, who had been born in their hometown, Hemingway, S.C., on May 25, 1925. They were picking beans in the hot sun. "We kept our eyes on each other," Mr. Woods once said in an interview with The New York Daily News.

They became inseparable, until Sylvia moved to New York with her mother in 1939. Mr. Woods joined the Navy and worked as cook on light cruisers and destroyers in the Pacific. "When I was in the Navy, that's all you could be," he said of the era's segregated armed forces.

He married Sylvia as soon as he was discharged, and they moved to Harlem. He drove a cab, and she found a factory job on Long Island. When she wearied of the commute, she jumped at the chance to work as a waitress at Johnson's Luncheonette in Harlem. In 1962, when the owner offered to sell it to her, she first thought it was a joke, but was able to buy it when her mother mortgaged the family farm.

On Aug. 1, 1962, the restaurant opened as Sylvia's, featuring Southern fare. It had 15 stools and six booths. It has since grown into an empire, selling prepared foods in supermarkets, operating a restaurant in Atlanta and holding Sunday gospel brunches in Sag Harbor.

Moreover, Mr. Woods gradually assembled real estate, including all the other stores on the restaurant's Lenox Avenue block and several nearby brownstones.

In addition to his wife, he is survived by their sons, Van and Kenneth; their daughters, Bedelia and Crizette; 17 grandchildren; and three great-grandchildren. Almost everybody in the family works at the restaurant. ■

who was director of the Four Seasons. Starting shakily at first, they turned out food that was, to be generous, uneven. But now they seem well on their way to success with a kitchen that rates a solid two stars and may be on its way to three.

Prices are astronomical, especially in the pool dining room (unless you have the $19 pre-theater dinner or late supper). Main courses, mostly ungarnished, range from $13.50 to $20 a person, and most are between $16.50 and $18.50. Everything else is proportionately as high, and there is a zapping and inexcusable cover charge ($2 for lunch, $2.75 for dinner). ■

> Mrs. Woods insisted that one spice made it all possible: love.

Restaurants

By **RUTH REICHL** | October 29, 1993

BEING A NEW RESTAURANT CRITIC IN TOWN has its drawbacks: there are a lot of restaurants I haven't yet eaten in. But it also has its advantages: there are a lot of restaurants where I am still not recognized. In most places I am just another person who has reserved weeks in advance, and I still have to wait as more important people are waltzed into the dining room. I watch longingly as they are presented with the chef's special dishes, and then I turn and order from the menu just like everybody else.

One of my first interests was to review the cooking of Sylvain Portay, who became chef at Le Cirque late last year. Over the course of five months I ate five meals at the restaurant; it was not until the fourth that the owner, Sirio Maccioni, figured out who I was. When I was discovered, the change was startling. Everything improved: the seating, the service, the size of the portions. We had already reached dessert, but our little plate of petit fours was whisked away to be replaced by a larger, more ostentatious one. An avalanche of sweets descended upon the table, and I was fascinated to note that the raspberries on the new desserts were three times the size of those on the old ones.

Food is important, and Mr. Portay is exceptionally talented. But nobody goes to Le Cirque just to eat. People go for the experience of being in a great restaurant. Sometimes they get it; sometimes they don't. It all depends on who they are.

DINNER AS THE UNKNOWN DINER

"Do you have a reservation?"

This is said so challengingly I instantly feel as if I am an intruder who has wandered into the wrong restaurant. But I nod meekly and give my guest's name. And I am sent to wait in the bar.

There we sit for half an hour, two women drinking glasses of expensive water. Finally we are led to a table in the smoking section,

where we had specifically requested not to be seated. Asked if there is, perhaps, another table, the captain merely gestures at the occupied tables and produces a little shrug.

There is no need to ask for the wine list; there it is, perched right next to me on the banquette where the waiters shove the menus. Every few minutes another waiter comes to fling his used menus in my direction. I don't mind, because I am busy with the wine list, but I have only reached page 3 before the captain reappears.

"I need that wine list," he says peremptorily, holding out his hand. I surrender, and it is 20 minutes before it returns. Still, persistence is rewarded. The list is large and good, and has many rewards for the patient reader. Given a little time, I unearth a delicious 1985 Chambolle-Musigny for $46.

Our first course, sauteed foie gras with white peaches, is so good that the memory of it carries us through most of the meal. The sweet, soft fruit is a brilliant pairing with the rich meat.

I like the next course, too, curried tuna tartar. Encircling the silky chopped fish, which has just the perfect touch of spice, is a lovely mosaic of radish slices. But would a really great restaurant send out these pale and flabby pieces of "toast"?

We are considering this when the captain appears and informs us that a table has opened up and we will be permitted to leave the smoke zone. The move should make me happy, but when the busboy trails us to our new table, shoves our crumpled old napkins into our hands and dumps our used glasses onto the table, I can't help feeling disgruntled. Later, as I pay the bill I find myself wishing that when the maitre d' asked if I had a reservation, I had just said no and left.

DINNER AS A MOST FAVORED PATRON

"The King of Spain is waiting in the bar, but your table is ready," says Mr. Maccioni,

sweeping us majestically past the waiting masses. Behind us a bejeweled older woman whines, "We've been waiting a half-hour," but nobody pays her any mind. Mr. Maccioni smiles down at us. "Let me get you some Champagne," he says as one of his assistants rushes up with a sparkling pair of flutes.

Who wouldn't be charmed? He has not even checked the book to see if we have reserved (in fact we have, but we are 20 minutes early). My date and I suddenly feel chic, suave and important. And that's before we see that there is a luxurious table for four, a little sea of space in this crowded room, waiting for the two of us.

The first course comes; it is a luxurious layering of scallops and truffles nestled inside a little dome of pastry. It is followed by more truffles, white ones this time, shaved over an absolutely extraordinary risotto. Next there is lobster, intertwined with chanterelles, artichokes and tiny pearl onions. This dish is so tremblingly delicate, so filled with flavor, I feel as if I have never really tasted lobster

before. It is followed by turbot, a fine, firm white fish, simply surrounded with zucchini, turnips and red peppers.

Now the captain is coming to the table with tiny glasses of golden sauternes. Is there foie gras in our future? Yes, here comes a slim slice, simply sauteed. Combined with the sweet satiny wine, each bite is an essay on richness.

But there is still dessert. They bring six if you don't count the plate of pastries with its gorgeous ribbon of pulled sugar.

We order espresso. Tiny cups filled with intense little puddles of coffee appear. Each sip takes your breath away; it is the perfect ending to the perfect autumn meal.

I walk reluctantly out into the cool evening air, sorry to leave this fabulous circus. Life in the real world has never been this good. ▪

Four-Star Reviews

JEAN GEORGES: The Steady Center of an Expanding Universe

By **FRANK BRUNI** | April 19, 2006

I WENT TO JEAN GEORGES WITH SOME TREP-idation, instilled by disappointing experiences at Jo Jo, Vong and other restaurants in Mr. Vongerichten's sprawling empire. It began to vanish as soon as the amuse-bouches appeared.

A crab beignet was a cascade of sensations. First came the coolness and gentle sweetness of strands of peekytoe crab, bound with béchamel, coated with panko, and fried. Then came a sliver of pineapple's more pointed sweetness and slight acidity. And then, fast on their heels, the heat of pink peppercorn, but only for an instant.

Mr. Vongerichten loves this sort of dance, in which one effect often defers so quickly to another that it seems like a memory almost as soon as it's experienced. He isn't seeking a seamless blend; he wants each sensation to have its say without overstating its case—to frame, tame and joust with the other players.

There was brilliant choreography behind a dish of Japanese snapper sashimi. The lusciousness of the fish was brightened by the sweetness of sliced muscat grapes, which was in turn offset by a buttermilk vinaigrette's faintly sour notes. Mixed into the dressing or sprinkled onto the fish was a bevy of herbs and spices, including mint, tarragon, basil and Thai chili, each of which registered a fleeting, teasing impression. The proportions were precise. The results were dazzling.

LE BERNARDIN: Only the Four Stars Remain Constant

By **FRANK BRUNI** | March 16, 2005

LE BERNARDIN GRABBED HOLD OF FOUR STARS from Bryan Miller in The New York Times less than three months after it opened in early 1986 and has never let them slip from its grasp, maintaining its superior rating more than twice as long as any of the other New York restaurants in its elite company. (The runner-up, Jean Georges, earned four stars in mid-1997.)

Le Bernardin has aged with astonishing grace, more Deneuve than Dunaway, doing what it must to remain youthful without ever making an elastic fool of itself, staying true to its identity while adapting to changing times. Now as before, it is a high church of reverently prepared fish. But more than ever global currents inform and influence what emerges from a kitchen that can no longer be succinctly described as French.

* * * * *

SUSHI AT MASA: It's a Zen Thing

By **FRANK BRUNI** | December 29, 2004

I COULD REACH DEEP INTO A HEADY BROTH OF adjectives to describe the magic of the sushi at Masa. I could pull up every workable synonym for delicious. Or I could do this: tell you about watching a friend bite into one of Masa's toro-stuffed maki rolls.

His eyes grew instantly bigger as his lips twitched into a coyly restrained grin. Then the full taste of the toro, which is the buttery belly of a bluefin tuna, took visible hold. Forget restraint: he was suddenly smiling as widely as a person with a mouthful of food and a modicum of manners can. His eyes even rolled slightly backward.

This play of emotion mirrored my own toro-induced bliss. It also explains why Masa, despite its chosen peculiarities and pitiless expense, belongs in the thinly populated pantheon of New York's most stellar restaurants. Simply put, Masa engineers discrete moments of pure elation that few if any other restaurants can match. If you appreciate sushi, Masa will take you to the frontier of how expansively good a single (and singular) bite of it can make you feel.

· · · · ·

PER SE:
The Magic of
Napa in New York

By **FRANK BRUNI** | September 8, 2004

IT IS NOT WONDROUS 100 PERCENT OF THE time, and it can be maddening: at moments too intent on culinary adventure or too highfalutin in its presentation and descriptions of dishes, one of which came with a choice of four salts from three continents. To get a reservation may well require a degree of planning and effort that verge on masochistic, and a multicourse, mini-portion extravaganza may well require four hours, which is more time than many diners have or want to spend.

But here is the thing: the return on that patience and that investment is more than a few mouthfuls of food that instantaneously bring a crazy smile to your face and lodge in your memory for days and even weeks to come.

DANIEL:
Promise Fulfilled

By **WILLIAM GRIMES** | March 14, 2001

THERE'S A DEFINITE TONE AT DANIEL, a warmth usually associated with small neighborhood restaurants, and it emanates from the kitchen. Mr. Boulud has both feet planted in the rich gastronomic soil of the Lyonnais region, an area renowned for its robust, no-holds-barred cuisine. His personality, as a proprietor, has been shaped by the little restaurant that his parents once ran, and if he does not actually stand outside on the sidewalk greeting guests, there is an unmistakable spirit of generosity hovering over the dining room that makes Daniel unique. The name says it all.

If Daniel has a fault, it is that Mr. Boulud offers too much. His menu is overwhelming, with a dozen appetizers and 10 main courses supplemented by a daily list of specials and assorted tasting menus. The dessert menu is two menus, with a second page devoted entirely to chocolate. The wine list comes in two bound volumes.

This all adds up to a lot of reading, and painful choices. The diner who orders the sublime velouté of mussels, sweetened with carrot and spiced precisely with a few specks of cumin, must forgo the sea scallop ceviche in a clean, bracing oyster-water nage touched with horseradish, lime and sea urchin. Rarely have I experienced so much distress in ordering dinner, or witnessed so much around-the-table envy once the food arrived. Mr. Boulud's go-for-broke menu inspires greed. You want it all. ▪

Dress Code: The Last Gasp

By **WILLIAM GRIMES** | January 28, 1998

ADAM DOLLE WAS LOOKING FORWARD TO A big night out. The date was December 16, his 47th birthday, and Mr. Dolle, an interior decorator, had a dinner reservation at Le Cirque 2000 with his roommate. It would be an exaggeration to say he was dressed like a million bucks. He was dressed, to be precise, like 4,050 bucks, attired in a $700 Ralph Lauren pearl-gray-and-beige sport coat, a $30 Barneys T-shirt, a $300 gray cashmere polo shirt buttoned to the neck, a $200 pair of gray gabardine trousers from New Republic, a $20 pair of heathered McLaughlin socks, a $300 pair of suede Gucci loafers and a $2,500 Bulgari watch. It was a look that Mr. Dolle characterizes as "urbanely chic" and "discreetly in the know."

> In a small experiment, The Times enlisted the cooperation of an ordinary citizen to test the dress code at several restaurants.

He and his similarly dressed roommate, Joe Brown, did not eat at Le Cirque that night. Or any other night. As bad luck would have it, they had selected one of the few remaining restaurants in New York that require gentlemen to wear a necktie.

Mr. Dolle pleaded. He joked. He cajoled. He appealed to reason, justice and mercy. He did not prevail. Nothing could alter the policy emblazoned on the sign that guards the stairway to Le Cirque's doors: "Jacket and tie are required to enter Le Cirque."

Le Cirque belongs to a dwindling breed: even the swankiest restaurants no longer insist on jacket and tie. The trend line is clear. Before too much longer, neckties in restaurants could become as rare as fedoras in Yankee Stadium. For the moment, a lonely handful continue to hold the line against casualness.

But are they really?

In a small experiment, The Times enlisted the cooperation of an ordinary citizen to test the dress code at several restaurants. Patrick Webb, 42, an artist, showed up for his assignment last weekend dressed in expensive black slacks, handmade British shoes and a bottle-green mock turtleneck.

First stop, Le Cirque 2000.

At 7 p.m. on Saturday, Mr. Webb walked past the forbidding dress-code stanchion, approached the reception area and announced his intention to have a drink at the bar, which is governed by the same jacket-and-tie policy. As he unpeeled his overcoat, the receptionist's head snapped back, his eyebrows shot upward and he executed a full-body wince. "A jacket and tie are required," he said, sharply.

Mr. Webb came clean. "I only have a turtleneck," he said. The shade of Mr. Dolle, hurled from the gates of paradise a month earlier, seemed to hover nearby. Suddenly, and inexplicably, resistance evaporated. "She has a jacket for you," the receptionist said quietly, gesturing toward the coat-room attendant.

Mr. Webb slipped into his borrowed jacket. Versace V2. Not bad, although a couple of sizes too big. His sense of good fortune ebbed a bit on entering the bar, however. Two other customers with turtlenecks under jackets had also penetrated the inner sanctum. The vaunted dress code seemed to be flexible.

Refreshed by a glass of Perrier-Jouet, Mr. Webb proceeded uptown to the Carlyle.

The receptionist appraised this new specimen and inhaled slowly, emitting a soft, disapproving hiss. "I'll have to get you a jacket," he said, and dashed off to the coatroom, where he flapped both arms quickly, funky-chicken style, to indicate that a jacket was needed. Mr. Webb slipped into a navy-blue blazer with gold buttons, a tad conservative perhaps, and lacking a label, but a perfect fit.

Twenty-four hours later, Mr. Webb invaded La Cote Basque, where his tieless attire brought him a stereophonic rebuke from the receptionist ("You'll have to have a jacket") and the coatroom attendant ("A jacket is required for the gentleman"), who was vigilant despite her tiny television set tuned to the Super Bowl.

Navy blue again. Double-breasted. Pierre Cardin.

But things are changing at other restaurants, and even Le Cirque seems to be softening. When asked to explain the Le Cirque dress policy, Sirio Maccioni, the restaurant's owner, simply overruled his own sign. "You know, we prefer a tie, but if someone comes in a nice turtleneck, we try to be pleasant," he said. "We say O.K."

Give it another try, Mr. Dolle. Just tell them Sirio sent you. ▪

BELOW: *At Le Cirque, Patrick Webb was given a Versace V2 jacket that was a few sizes too big.*

Damn Yankees

SPORTS

▼ PAGE 364

New York is, without question, a sports town. It has high-profile teams, highly demanding fans and high-flying stars, from Joe DiMaggio to Bill Bradley to Joe Namath to Alex Rodriguez to Pedro Martinez to next year's draft picks. And it's hard to imagine Babe Ruth's off-the-field carousing, Yogi Berra's malapropisms, Billy Martin's temper or George Steinbrenner's management anywhere else.

But really, it's a fan town. There are fans who mourn the Brooklyn Dodgers' move to Los Angeles more than fifty years ago. There are fans who still mourn the loss of the baseball Giants, who decamped to San Francisco about the same time. There are Jets fans who say they were raised to hate the football Giants. Week after week, they cheer for two teams: the Jets, and whoever the Giants are playing. Basketball fans suffer as the Knicks and

▲ PAGE 385

the Nets stagger onward, "knees buckling, shoulders sagging, propelled by the sheer tropism of will and desperation," the Times sports columnist George Vecsey wrote. The players hope against hope that they can make the playoffs, sign LeBron James and, in the case of the Nets, move to Brooklyn.

As the author Peter Handrinos has noted, sports are at the center of New York's turbulent identity. Sports complement the city's "No. 1" self-image, its obsession with winning and losing, its preoccu-pation with who's hot and who's in a slump. Sports are, after all, about competing. And New York is about competing—even snatching a taxi away from the guy on the opposite corner when you're really in a hurry. Handrinos maintains that New York would be different without the daily dramas that sports provide: "We'd be a Metropolis without Superman, a Gotham without Bruce Wayne."

Season in and season out, sports provides something that everyone can talk about— doormen, investment bankers, teachers, doctors. Consider Brett Favre's Cinderella year with the New York Jets in 2008. He had retired from the Green Bay Packers at the end of the previous season. Then he decided that retirement wasn't for him and he wanted to play one more year. The Packers traded him to the Jets. But was Favre, who turned 39 while playing for the Jets, too old? Long before he threw his first pass in a Jets' uniform, the opinions were flying.

The teams have changed as the city has changed. The Brooklyn Dodgers integrated baseball by signing Jackie Robinson in 1947. He endured epithets from players on other teams and road trips where the rest of his team stayed in whites-only hotels. Players on some teams talked of boycotting games against the Dodgers if Robinson was in the lineup. Ford Frick, the president of the National League, put a stop to the talk by declaring, "This is the United States of America, and one citizen has as much right to play as another." (The Yankees were slow to integrate. They did not have a black player on their roster until Elston Howard arrived in 1955.)

Half a century later, the New York Mets hired the first Hispanic general manager in baseball history, Omar Minaya. He built a lineup, and a marketing strategy for the underdog Mets, around ethnic identity, signing Pedro Martínez, Carlos Beltran and Carlos Delgado.

Both baseball teams opened new stadiums with the 2009 season—"houses of baseball worship," The Times columnist Harvey Araton called them. The Mets' new Citi Field is smaller and more elegant than Shea Stadium was (and has more bathrooms). "Citi Field is the cozy cousin," Araton wrote. "Yankee Stadium is shock and awe. Ticket prices may stretch the limits of affordability and perhaps fan loyalty in both, but there is something to be said for the Mets' having built their ballpark to a nearly 42,000-seat scale that isn't a monument to a generation of American excess." But the Mets are the Mets, too often a study in haplessness and, for fans, frustration. The first home run at the new stadium was hit by Jody Gerut of the the San Diego Padres, a team that had lost 99 games the previous season. That first game did not go well for the Mets: they lost to the Padres, 6-5.

The Yankees' $1.5 billion stadium replaced the one where, on opening day in 1923, Babe Ruth looked around and said, "Some ballyard! I'd give a year of my life if I could hit a home run." He blasted the stadium's first homer, in the third inning of a 4-1 win over the Boston Red Sox. The Times called it a "savage home run that was the real baptism of Yankee Stadium." In the new stadium, Mark Texeira smashed two home runs in an exhibition game a couple of days before the baseball season opened. "I think this is going to be a pretty good hitter's park," Texeira said. Not a word about shortening his life. But Texeira's teammate Derek Jeter joked that he had to caution Teixeira to hold the homers until the games counted.

▼ PAGE 394

Giants Capture Pennant, Beating Dodgers 5-4 in 9th

By JOHN DREBINGER | October 4, 1951

IN AN ELECTRIFYING FINISH TO WHAT LONG will be remembered as the most thrilling pennant campaign in history, Leo Durocher and his astounding never-say-die Giants wrenched victory from the jaws of defeat at the Polo Grounds, vanquishing the Dodgers, 5 to 4, with a four-run splurge in the last half of the ninth.

A three-run homer by Bobby Thomson that accounted for the final three tallies blasted the Dodgers right out of the World Series picture. This afternoon at the Stadium it will be the Giants against Casey Stengel's American League champion Yankees in the opening clash of the World Series.

Seemingly hopelessly beaten, 4 to 1, as the third and deciding game of the epic National League playoff moved into the last inning, the Giants lashed back with a fury that would not be denied. They routed big Don Newcombe while scoring one run.

Then, with Ralph Branca on the mound and two runners aboard the bases, came the blow of blows. Thomson crashed the ball into the left field stand. Forgotten on the instant was the cluster of three with which the Brooks had crushed Sal Maglie in the eighth.

For a moment the crowd of 34,320, as well as all the Dodgers, appeared too stunned to realize what had happened. But as the long and lean Scot from Staten Island loped around the bases behind his two teammates, a deafening roar went up.

The Brooks club had blown a 13½-game lead. But that would have been forgotten and forgiven had Branca held that margin in the last of the ninth.

But with one out and runners on second and third Chuck Dressen, the Brooks' pilot and as daring a gamester as Durocher, chose to follow the "book." He refused to walk Thomson because that would have represented the winning run. Yet behind Bobby was Willie Mays, a dismal failure throughout the series and behind that the Giants had even less to offer. It's something the second-guessers will hash over through many a winter evening. ■

Ball Park Well Built And "Could Have Lasted Forever"

By ROBERT LIPSYTE | May 31, 1964

THE SCOREBOARD CLOCK IS FROZEN AT 10:24, and nobody seems to know whether it was day or night when the electrician pulled the plug on the Polo Grounds for the last time.

It hardly seems to matter now. From Coogan's Bluff the ballpark looks like a wood and concrete corpse rotting into a steel skeleton. A great crane reaches down and picks up pieces of nostalgia, a section where many men spent their boyhood, an aisle where some hero's mighty home-run ball landed among scrambling fans. A torch sputters and sparkles, and a piece of steel falls—so slowly— from a light tower, end over end until it plunges into tractor-scarred earth that once was left field.

"One thing I'll say for this place, no collapse action here, very well built," said Harry Avirom, the vice president of the Wrecking Corporation of America, the firm that is demolishing the park.

"Very well built," he said. "It could have lasted forever."

By August it should be a vacant lot, and soon after that apartment houses will rise on the site.

"Wrecking is some business, let me tell you," he said. "Gotta make the right moves. Gotta take calculated risks. Yeah, yeah, something like baseball, you could say." ■

Giants Defeat Indians 5-2
In World Series Opener

By **JOHN DREBINGER** | September 30, 1954

AT PRECISELY 4:12 O'CLOCK BY THE HUGE clock atop the center-field clubhouse at the Polo Grounds, Leo Durocher decided it was time to play his trump card.

It was the last half of the 10th inning in the opening game of the 1954 World Series. The tense and dramatic struggle had a gathering of 52,751, a record series crowd for the arena, hanging breathlessly on every pitch.

The score was deadlocked at 2-all. Two Giants were on the base paths and on the mound was Bob Lemon, 23-game winner of the American League, who had gone all the way and was making a heroic bid to continue the struggle a little further. Then Leo made his move.

He called on his pinch-hitter extraordinary, James (Dusty) Rhodes, to bat for Monte Irvin. Lemon served one pitch. Rhodes, a left-hander, swung down the right-field foul line.

The ball had just enough carry to clear the wall barely 270 feet away. But it was enough to produce an electrifying three-run homer that enabled the Giants to bring down Al Lopez' Indians, 5 to 2.

Then, in the eighth, Wertz connected for another tremendous drive that went down the center of the field 459 feet, only to have Willie Mays make one of his most amazing catches.

Traveling on the wings of the wind, Willie caught the ball in front of the right-center bleachers with his back to the diamond.

And in the 10th it was Willie the Wonder who set the stage for Rhodes's game-winning homer. With one out, Mays drew his second walk of the day.

Then, with Lemon pitching carefully to Henry Thompson, Willie stole second. Up went Dusty. An instant later he leaned into the first pitch and produced a shot that doubtless was heard around the world, though for distance it likely could go as one of the shortest homers in World Series history. ▪

BELOW: *The Polo Grounds was demolished 1964 and a public housing project was erected on the site.*

SPORTS   **365**

Opening Day at Ebbets Field: Dodgers Triumph Over Reds, 6-1

By **ROSCOE MCGOWEN** | August 27, 1939

PENNANT FEVER HIT FLATBUSH WHEN 33,535 of the most hopeful fans in any major league city swarmed into Ebbets Field to see the double-header with the league-leading Reds. Their temperatures dropped a bit when Bill McKechnie's men took the opener, 5-2, but rose again with a 6-1 Dodger triumph in the nightcap.

Bucky Walters, Dodger nemesis, allowed only two hits in annexing his 21st victory and his sixth straight over Brooklyn. Luke (Hot Potato) Hamlin, trying for No. 16, blew a 3-0 lead over Walters in the eighth and was knocked out, charged with his tenth loss.

In the nightcap Hugh Casey breezed through to his ninth triumph, aided by Dolf Camilli's 22nd homer of the year off John Niggeling with Cookie Lavagetto aboard in the second frame. Dolf also contributed a scorching double in the third that knocked the veteran knuckleball hurler out.

The Dodgers scored four times in that frame, Lavagetto's double driving in one run, Camilli's another and Ernie Koy's single off Whitey Moore bringing the other pair home. The one run off Casey, in the eighth, was unearned, Ival Goodman having been put on base by Camilli's low throw to Casey. Singles by Frank McCormick and Nino Bongiovanni got Goodman across.

Walters's pitching performance was one of his best, Babe Phelps getting the only clean hit off him, a line single off the right-field wall in the second, when the Dodgers scored both their runs. The other blow was a grounder by Dixie Walker in the first that hit Lavagetto on the baseline between first and second, thus becoming an automatic hit for Walker and an automatic out for Cookie. ∎

A Second Plaque, A Larger Triumph

By **DAVE ANDERSON** | June 26, 2008

WHEN JACKIE ROBINSON WAS ON THE HALL of Fame ballot in 1962, he requested that the voters among the Baseball Writers Association of America judge him only as a player. He didn't want his social significance as the modern major leagues' first black player to be considered. Vote for him—or don't vote for him—on his merits as a player, as all the other Hall of Famers from Babe Ruth and Cy Young had been measured.

When he was elected, the words on his bronze plaque at Cooperstown reflected his wishes.

Those words began, "Leading N.L. Batter in 1949," and followed with his fielding and stolen base statistics, and then "Most Valuable Player in 1949. Lifetime Batting Average .311" before concluding with more fielding statistics.

Nice numbers. But over his 10 seasons with the Brooklyn Dodgers, Jackie Robinson was more than numbers to baseball and to America. Now a new plaque has been unveiled, reflecting that. It concludes with these words: "Displayed Tremendous Courage and Poise in

BELOW: *In May of 1952, with the bases loaded, Jackie Robinson stole home against the Chicago Cubs.*

Jackie Robinson Signs with Dodgers, First Black Player in the Majors

By **LOUIS EFFRAT** | April 11, 1947

JACKIE ROBINSON, 28-YEAR-OLD INFIELDER, yesterday became the first Negro to achieve major-league baseball status in modern times. His contract was purchased from the Montreal Royals of the International League by the Dodgers and he will be in a Brooklyn uniform at Ebbets Field when the Brooks oppose the Yankees in the first of three exhibition games over the weekend.

1947 When He Integrated the Modern Major Leagues in the Face of Intense Adversity."

In a very real sense, Jackie Robinson also integrated America.

More than a decade before the Rev. Dr. Martin Luther King Jr. put the phrase civil rights into the nation's vocabulary, Jackie Robinson taught millions of baseball's white fans that black was beautiful. That if they could root for Jackie and Roy Campanella, Don Newcombe, Willie Mays, Hank Aaron and Elston Howard, they could accept a black family in their neighborhood and black students in their schools.

As black players followed him into the majors, Robinson always checked them out. In 1954, before a spring training exhibition game in Mobile, Ala., with the Milwaukee Braves, he had his first look at a skinny 20-year-old rookie.

"See that kid," I remember him telling me that day. "You're going to be watching him for a long time."

That kid was Hank Aaron, who would hit 755 home runs. Jackie Robinson knew a hitter when he saw one. But more than anyone else, he knew what it was like to have integrated the big leagues, if not America. And whether he likes it or not, what he did "in the face of intense adversity" is finally on his Hall of Fame plaque. ∎

A native of Georgia, Robinson won fame in baseball, football, basketball and track at the University of California at Los Angeles before entering the armed service as a private. He emerged a lieutenant in 1945 and in October of that year was signed to a Montreal contract. Robinson's performance in the International League, which he led in batting last season with an average of .349, prompted President Branch Rickey of the Dodgers to promote Jackie.

The decision was made while Robinson was playing first base for Montreal against the Dodgers at Ebbets Field. Jackie was blanked at the plate and contributed little to his team's 4-8 victory before 14,282 fans, but it was nevertheless a history-making day for the well-proportioned lad.

Jackie had just popped into a double-play, attempting to bunt in the fifth inning, when Arthur Mann, assistant to Rickey, appeared in the press box. He handed out a brief, typed announcement: "The Brooklyn Dodgers today purchased the contract of Jackie Roosevelt Robinson from the Montreal Royals." Robinson will appear at the Brooklyn offices this morning to sign a contract.

According to the records, the last Negro to play in the majors was Moses Fleetwood Walker, who caught for Toledo of the American Association when that circuit enjoyed major-league classification in 1884.

The call for Robinson was no surprise. His path in the immediate future may not be too smooth, however. He may run into antipathy from Southerners who form about 60 per cent of the league's playing strength. In fact, it is rumored that a number of Dodgers expressed themselves unhappy at the possibility of having to play with Jackie.

Jackie, himself, expects no trouble. He said he was "thrilled and it's what I've been waiting for." When his Montreal mates congratulated him and wished him luck, Robinson answered: "Thanks, I'll need it." ∎

Dodgers Capture Their First World Series

By **JOHN DREBINGER** | October 5, 1955

BROOKLYN'S LONG CHERISHED DREAM finally has come true. The Dodgers have won their first World Series championship.

Smokey Alston's Brooks, with Johnny Podres tossing a brilliant shutout, turned back Casey Stengel's Yankees, 2 to 0, in the seventh and deciding game of the 1955 baseball classic.

This gave the National League champions the series, 4 games to 3. As the jubilant victors almost smothered their 28-year-old left-handed pitcher from Witherbee, N.Y., a roaring crowd of 62,465 joined in sounding off a thunderous ovation. Not even the stanchest American League die-hard could begrudge Brooklyn its finest hour.

Seven times in the past had the Dodgers been thwarted in their efforts to capture baseball's most sought prize—the last five times by these same Bombers. When the goal finally was achieved the lid blew off in Brooklyn, while experts, poring into the records, agreed nothing quite so spectacular had been accomplished before. For this was the first time a team had won a seven-game world series after losing the first two games.

Podres, who had vanquished the Yankees in the third game as the series moved to Ebbets Field last Friday, became the first Brooklyn pitcher to win two games in one series.

Tommy Byrne, a seasoned campaigner who was the Yanks' "comeback hero of the year," carried the Bombers' hopes in this dramatic struggle in which victory would have given them their 17th series title. But Byrne, whose southpaw slants had turned back the Dodgers in the second encounter, could not quite cope with the youngster pitted against him.

In the fourth inning a two-bagger by Roy Campanella and a single by Gil Hodges gave the Brooks their first run.

In the sixth a costly Yankee error helped fill the bases. It forced the withdrawal of Byrne, though in all he had given only three hits.

Stengel called on his right-handed relief hurler, Bob Grim.

Bob did well enough. But he couldn't prevent Hodges from lifting a long sacrifice fly to center that drove in Pee Wee Reese with the Brooks' second run of the day.

Fortified with this additional tally, Podres then blazed the way through a succession of thrills while a grim band of Dodgers fought with the tenacity of inspired men to hold the advantage to the end.

Fittingly, the final out was a grounder by Elston Howard to Reese, the 36-year-old shortstop and captain of the Flock. Ever since 1941 had the Little Colonel from Kentucky been fighting these Yankees. Five times had he been forced to accept the loser's share.

Many a heart in the vast arena doubtless skipped a beat as Pee Wee scooped up the ball and fired it to first. It was a bit low and wide. But Hodges, the first sacker, reached out and grabbed it inches off the ground. Gil would have stretched halfway across the Bronx for that one. ■

ABOVE: *The Dodgers celebrate after winning the 1955 World Series.*

Dodgers and Giants Can Move to California

By **JOSEPH M. SHEEHAN** | May 29, 1957

THE BROOKLYN DODGERS AND THE NEW YORK Giants received permission from the National League to switch their respective bases of operation to Los Angeles and San Francisco.

The permission, granted unanimously by the other club owners at the league's mid-season meeting here, was conditional on two items that continued to leave room for conjecture that there might be a shift as soon as next season.

The approval in advance of the transfers was predicated on these points:

That the Giants and Dodgers request the shifts before October 1, 1957.

That they make the moves together.

If these conditions are met, Warren C. Giles, the president of the National League, is empowered by the action taken today to approve the transfer applications. If one club wants to move and one wants to stay, the league would have to reconsider, Giles said.

Walter F. O'Malley, the president of the Dodgers, and Horace C. Stoneham, the president of the Giants, both emphasized that it still was far from definite that they would move their clubs. While listening with an attentive ear to the blandishments of Los Angeles, the Dodger president still is on record as hoping that the long-stalled campaign to build a new, downtown Brooklyn stadium for the Dodgers will get off the ground. ▪

BELOW: *Fans rally outside the clubhouse after the final game played by the New York Giants at the Polo Grounds on September 29, 1957.*

Brooklyn Is Trying to Forget Dodgers and Baseball

By **GAY TALESE** | May 18, 1958

BROOKLYN, ONCE DESCRIBED AS THE WORLD'S largest city with no railroad, no daily newspaper and no left fielder, now is the nation's leading producer of an unpatented item called The Bitter Baseball Fan—an individual dedicated to blaming the Dodgers for every stolen wallet, every head cold and every parking ticket in Flatbush.

The Dodgers' once-faithful multitude in Brooklyn is still frustrated and seething over the team's shift to Los Angeles. Boris Karloff has more fan clubs in Brooklyn now than Walter O'Malley, the Dodgers' president.

A Los Angeles Dodger business executive who still works in Ebbets Field these days says he sees Brooklyn fans walking by slowly and sadly. Sometimes, he says, they look up at his open window and yell. "Hey, when you going to burn this place down?"

As quickly as possible, Brooklyn seems to want to forget all about the Dodgers. On Friday night at the Ball Field Tavern on Bedford Avenue, where Dodger fans used to abound, the drinkers watched Jerry Lewis on Channel 4 rather than the Dodgers-Cardinals game on Channel 13.

Although the Dodgers will be as close as Philadelphia next Sunday, Brooklyn fans generally are disinterested.

"We'll be lucky to get 100 Brooklyn people into Connie Mack Stadium that day," said the Phillies' ticket manager. An organization attempting to lure Brooklyn into Philadelphia by bus (at $9.99 round trip, including ticket) yesterday had reservations for barely one busload.

Hilda Chester, once the loudest of Brooklyn barkers, said she wouldn't be caught dead in Philadelphia next Sunday.

The Dodger Sym-Phoney Band will be there to boo the Dodgers and play a funeral march.

"They're in last place and we're going to bury them," said Lou Soriano, the snare drummer. "We're tickled pink they're last." ∎

ABOVE: *The Ebbets Field Houses now stand on the site of the old stadium.*

Another Year Without The Dodgers

By **LEONARD KOPPETT** | April 2, 1972

THERE WAS A TIME WHEN THE WORDS "Opening Day" needed no elaboration, least of all in Brooklyn. They meant the first official game of a new major league baseball season would be played that day, one year in Ebbets Field, the next somewhere else.

Another National League baseball season is about to start, although the New York area representative, the Mets, will not return to Shea Stadium in Queens until a few days later. And the phrase "Opening Day" is likely to elicit the response "of what?"

Contemplate, for a moment, opening day in Brooklyn 25 years ago: April 15, 1947.

It's a clear, brisk day. About 26,000 people have come to the 32,000-seat park to see the Dodgers play the Boston Braves.

It's a historic occasion. The Dodger first baseman is Jackie Robinson, about to play his first major league game. He will be the first Negro (it was considered insulting

DODGERS

The Game Is Back in Brooklyn, But on a Smaller Scale

By **ANDY NEWMAN** | June 23, 2001

THE SLAVIN BROTHERS, IRISH BOYS FROM THE neighborhood, were discussing the topic of the day at Farrell's tavern in Windsor Terrace.

"It's the best thing that ever happened to Brooklyn," said John, 49. "Now we have something to call our own. It's not hard to get to, the seats are cheap."

Mike Slavin, 38, was not convinced. "Single-A, though," he reminded his older brother. "It's like high school baseball."

"Come on, Mikey," John Slavin said. "Lee Mazzilli played around here and came

then to call him a "black") to play in the majors since the 1880's.

But this is not, actually, the main topic of conversation. The big issue is Leo Durocher. Only a week before, the always controversial, abrasive, fast-talking Dodger manager had been suspended for the year by Commissioner Happy Chandler. The Dodgers still have no regular manager—Clyde Sukeforth is in charge. Joe McCarthy has rejected an offer and Branch Rickey, the boss, won't settle on Burt Sutton until later in the week.

The Dodgers win that day, 5-3, and there is joy in Flatbush. With Robinson and Eddie Stanky on base, Pistol Pete Reiser hit a double just inside the right-field foul pole, the ball hitting the screen. Reiser scored later in the inning on Gene Hermanski's long fly ball, and Johnny Sain found himself the losing pitcher.

Hal Gregg, who had been the losing pitcher on opening day against the Braves the year before, was the winning pitcher in relief in this game, which got the Dodgers off to a fast start in quest of the National League pennant.

They won the pennant, all right, but they lost the World Series in seven games to the Yankees of the contemptible Bronx. ■

up through the minors. John Candelaria used to pitch at the Parade Grounds. Maybe we have a chance that some kid from the neighborhood, from Brooklyn, is going to make it through the system."

Let the economists grumble that $39 million—the amount Rudolph W. Giuliani, in the soft twilight of his mayoralty, lavished on a minor-league stadium in Coney Island—would have been better spent on an industrial park. Let Brooklyn's own borough president fume that the city would have been far better served by playing fields for high school and college teams.

All of that, for the moment, is beside the point. People are talking baseball in Brooklyn again.

Maybe not Willie, Mickey and the Duke. But a professional baseball pitcher is about to dig his spikes into Brooklyn soil for the first time since 1957.

The team is called the Cyclones. Brooklyn Dodger fans may need to ratchet down their expectations a notch. "These guys are not a championship major-league team," said Jeffrey S. Wilpon, the chief operating officer of the team. "We hope to fill a little bit of that void for people who just want to hear the sound of the bat on the ball and see kids hustling."

It is little wonder, then, that the Brooklyn Dodger generation harbors mixed feelings about the second coming of baseball. On a recent evening, a lone man in a baseball cap stood outside the new stadium, peering through the fence. He was Eli Miller, one of the city's last surviving seltzer deliverymen, and he was torn.

With one breath, Mr. Miller, 63, said of the Cyclones, "As a Dodger fan, I feel it's a bad substitute for a team. Brooklyn deserves a major-league team." With the next, he acknowledged that he had been coming to the site for months to check on its progress. "Just out of curiosity, I might go to a few games." ■

Yanks Buy Babe Ruth For $125,000

January 6, 1920

BABE RUTH OF THE BOSTON RED SOX, base-ball's super-slugger, was purchased by the Yankees for the largest cash sum ever paid for a player. The New York club paid Harry Frazen of Boston $123,030 for the sensational batsman who last season caused such a furor in the national game by hitting 29 home runs, a new record in long-distance clouting.

Colonel Ruppert, president of the Yanks, said that he had taken over Ruth's Boston contract, which has two years more to run. This contract calls for a salary of $10,000 a year. Ruth recently announced that he would refuse to play for $10,000 next season, although the Boston Club has received no request for a raise in salary.

Manager Miller Huggins is now in Los Angeles negotiating with Ruth. It is believed that the Yankee manager will offer him a new contract which will be satisfactory to the Colossus of the bat.

President Ruppert said yesterday that Ruth would probably play right field for the Yankees. He played to left field for the Red Sox last season, and had the highest fielding average among the outfielders, making only two errors during the season. While he is on the Pacific Coast Manager Huggins will also endeavor to sign Duffy Lewis, who will be one of Ruth's companions in the outfield at the Polo Grounds next season.

Ruth was such a sensation last season that he supplanted the great Ty Cobb as baseball's greatest attraction. He scored the greatest number of runs in the American League last season, crossing the plate 103 times. Cobb scored only 97 runs last year. Ruth was so dangerous that the American League pitchers were generous with their passes and the superlative hitter walked 101 times, many of these passes being intentional. Ruth also struck out more than any other batsman in the league, fanning 59 times. He also made three sacrifice hits and he stole seven bases. ∎

Yanks Sweep Series, Wild Pitch Beating Pirates in Ninth

By **JAMES R. HARRISON** | October 9, 1927

THERE WERE THREE ON AND TWO WERE OUT, the score was tied and it was the ninth inning of the big game. Now, in such a setting Ralph Henry Barbour would have had the modest hero step up and slam one over the fence while 60,000 roared their acclaim of the great man.

But reality is not always as glamorous as fiction and sometimes falls short. No resounding slap over the fence and far away. Just a wild pitch and a rolling ball—and curtains for the Pittsburgh Pirates.

The Yankees won by 4 to 2—the fourth team in 24 world's series to take the championship with four straight victories. Let it be recorded, to the eternal credit of the Pirates, that they went down fighting like men.

It would have made a prettier story if the home run that George Herman Ruth hit into the right-field stand in the fifth had won the game. It would have been nicer if Gehrig or

61,808 Fans Roar Tribute to Gehrig

By **JOHN DREBINGER** | July 5, 1939

IN PERHAPS AS COLORFUL AND DRAMATIC A pageant as ever was enacted on a baseball field, 61,808 fans thundered a hail and farewell to Henry Lou Gehrig at the Yankee Stadium.

To be sure, it was a holiday and there would have been a big crowd and plenty of roaring in any event. For the Yankees, after getting nosed out, 3 to 2, in the opening game of the double-header, despite a ninth-inning home run by George Selkirk, came right back in typical fashion to crush the Senators, 11 to 1, in the nightcap. Twinkletoes Selkirk embellished this contest with another home run.

Meusel or Lazzeri could have produced a ringing blow with the bases full and nobody out in the throbbing ninth.

Here was the big moment of the series, with G. Herman Ruth at bat, two on base and the world's championship hanging in the balance. Would the Pirates pitch to Ruth or not? If they did, would he bunt or swing?

They walked him and took a chance on an infield grounder and a play at the plate. But with the bases full and nobody out the Pirates' hopes looked as bleak as the October sky above.

Gehrig was at bat—the great Gehrig, who drove more runs across the plate this season than any other batter in baseball history. He had sent 179 runs whizzing over the white disk, and at this moment he would have gladly exchanged any 10 of them for even a long sacrifice fly.

Miljus's first delivery was a curve inside, which Red Ormsby called a strike. Ball one was low: strike two, a half-slow ball, ball two, outside the plate. And then Miljus wound up again in his slow, deliberate way and broke a resplendent curve across the inside edge. Gehrig's bludgeon swished through the air—and "mighty Casey had struck out." ∎

But it was the spectacle staged between the games which doubtless never will be forgotten by those who saw it. For more than 40 minutes there paraded in review two mighty championship hosts—the Yankees of 1927 and the current edition of Yanks who definitely are winging their way to a fourth straight pennant and a chance for another world title.

From far and wide the 1927 stalwarts came to reassemble for Lou Gehrig Appreciation Day and to pay their own tribute to their former comrade-in-arms who had carried on beyond all of them only to have his own brilliant career come to a tragic close when it was revealed that he had fallen victim to a form of infantile paralysis.

In conclusion, the vast gathering, sitting in absolute silence for a longer period than perhaps any baseball crowd in history, heard Gehrig himself deliver as amazing a valedictory as ever came from a ball player.

So shaken with emotion that at first it appeared he would not be able to talk at all, the mighty Iron Horse, with a rare display of that indomitable will power that had carried him through 2,130 consecutive games, moved to the microphone at home plate to express his own appreciation. ∎

Why They Cheer Joe DiMaggio

By **GILBERT MILLSTEIN** | July 9, 1950

JOSEPH PAUL DIMAGGIO, A MAN WHO HAS, without visible strain, acquired the rich patina of an institution, is currently afflicted with the most spectacular batting slump of his 12 years in the major leagues. He has become the object of a sort of kindly evasion on the part of sportswriters, who like to point out that anyway he has hit more home runs and batted in more runs so far this season than any other Yankee.

Earlier in the season, in the course of a double-header against the Cleveland Indians at Yankee Stadium, he came to bat eight times but was unable, as the trade says, to buy a hit. Despite this painful consistency, the center fielder for the New York Yankees was applauded with more vigor and greater warmth the last time he took his turn than he had been the first.

The public faith in his ultimate productivity was rewarded. Toward the end of last month, DiMaggio achieved another intimation of immortality: he became the 88th major-league baseball player since 1876 to make 2,000 hits. Next Tuesday, at Chicago, he will appear in his 11th All-Star game.

There is little question in the minds of most people that DiMaggio is the finest player of his era. Casey Stengel, the manager of the Yankees, watched DiMaggio working out in the batting cage one morning recently, and then said: "He makes big-league baseball look simple. It isn't that simple. He would make any manager look good. That's about the best thing you can say about any ball player."

Some years ago a veteran player, intent on driving home the implications of DiMaggio's greatness, took a rookie aside in the dressing room and pointed to DiMaggio. "See that?" the veteran said. "That's class." He paused for emphasis. "That guy," he said, "changes his shirt every day." ∎

ABOVE: *Joe DiMaggio in 1937.*

The Boy Grew Older

By **ARTHUR DALEY** | April 22, 1952

MASTER MICKEY MANTLE SPRAWLED IN A corner of the Yankee Stadium dugout just before the home opening, the picture of lazy contentment. His hat was tilted over his eyes and he chewed his gum with methodical unconcern. This was just another ball game, and he was a full-fledged big leaguer.

He knew he'd be a little nervous in his first time at bat because he always was. But he also knew that a great calm would immediately settle over him and he'd be at ease.

One year later, Mantle is an old pro. Last season Gil McDougald and Mickey were two kids trying to make good. At spring training, they practiced fielding and hitting at every chance they got and were despondent if not used in intrasquad games. At St. Pete this spring, however, neither acted as if he had a care in the world.

The Homer Epidemic

By **ARTHUR DALEY** | October 3, 1961

THIS WILL BE KNOWN AS THE YEAR OF THE Home Run. Never before has one phase of the game so dominated the sport or so captured public interest. The man who provided the high drama was Roger Maris, of course. He kept ducking under deadlines and brushing against disaster like Pearl White in that ancient serial, "The Perils of Pauline."

On the final day of the 154-game segment of the season, he wrenched away from the grip of Jimmy Foxx and Hank Greenberg, both clouters of 58 homers, and slammed his 59th. Only the mighty Babe Ruth had done better over such a span. Then on the final day of the expanded 162-game season, he tagged his 61st. That was one more than even the Babe had hit.

The first thing Mickey did upon arriving at the Stadium this year was to go prowling about the outfield in right center, searching for the spot where he had come to grief in the World Series, injuring his knee. He thinks he tripped over the cover to a water pipe outlet.

"All I can remember is racing after Willie Mays' shot and hearing Joe DiMaggio call, 'I got it,' " he said. "So I pulled up short and—boom!—I could feel my leg snap. I lay there, too scared to move. I really thought my leg had fallen off at the knee." It was apparent that he had envisioned the end of a career which hardly had begun.

But the world didn't end after all. He's back in business, a far more poised and confident ball player, and there was talk that Stengel would let him gain experience in right field before shifting him to center. Did he have any preferences?

"Nope," he said. "As long as I play every day, I don't care where I play." ∎

Maris wasn't the only homer-hitter in the big league last season—although it may have seemed that way at the end. He was just part of an epidemic, a contagion that reached its most virulent form in the American League, which produced a record of 1,534 homers to go fantastically beyond the previous high of 1,091. Expansion had a lot to do with it. Now ball parks in Los Angeles and Minnesota were homer-havens. But the Yankees alone slashed out 240 homers.

Some fans deeply resent the commissioner's ruling that only the first 154 games be considered for the legitimization of the Maris record as a replacement for the Ruthian mark. They say: Why not the last 154 games? (Roger went without a homer in his first nine.) They say a lot of things.

The Ruth idolators scorn Maris—which is grossly unfair. Roger is strictly top-drawer as an outfielder. They say he's a Johnny-come-lately, which is true. Ruth was different, and he will not have a challenger until someone else approaches his lifetime total of 714 homers. At the moment Maris trails him by 556. ∎

BELOW: *Mickey Mantle slams a homer into the bleachers on July 1, 1961, gaining the 1,000th RBI of his career.*

Yankees Take Series As Jackson Hits Three Homers

By **JOSEPH DURSO** | October 19, 1977

WITH REGGIE JACKSON HITTING THREE home runs in his last three times at bat, the New York Yankees swept all those family feuds under the rug and overpowered the Los Angeles Dodgers, 8-4, to win their first World Series in 15 years.

They won it in the sixth game of a match that rocked Yankee Stadium last night as hundreds of fans poured through a reinforced army of 350 security guards and stormed onto the field after the final out. And it marked a dramatic comeback from the four-game sweep the Yankees suffered last October at the hands of the Cincinnati Reds.

For Jackson, who led the team in money, power hitting and power rhetoric, this was a game that had perhaps no equal since the World Series was inaugurated in 1903. He hit his three home runs on the first pitches off three pitchers, and became the only player to hit three in a Series game since Babe Ruth did it for the Yankees twice, in 1926 and again in 1928. But nobody had ever before hit five in a World Series, a feat that Jackson accomplished during the last three games in California and New York.

> He also knocked in
> five runs, and later suggested:
> "Babe Ruth was great.
> I'm just lucky."

"This is very rewarding," Manager Billy Martin said. "I'm proud of our players and what they accomplished this year. Reggie? He was sensational."

The Dodgers knew full well that only three teams in baseball history had lost three of the first four games in a World Series and then won three straight for the title. Inside one inning they rattled Torrez for two runs as they fought to force this Series into a winner-take-all finale.

But inside of two innings, the Yankees retaliated on a home run by Chris Chambliss. Then, after Reggie Smith hit one for the Dodgers in the third inning, Reginald Martinez Jackson took charge on three swings of the bat: a home run off Hooton in the fourth inning, another off Elias Sosa in the fifth and another off Charlie Hough in the eighth.

He also knocked in five runs, and later suggested: "Babe Ruth was great. I'm just lucky." ■

Murcer Drives in 5 As Yanks Win, 5-4

By **MURRAY CHASS** | August 7, 1979

COMPLETING A GRUELING, EMOTION-RACKED four days, the Yankees returned somberly from Thurman Munson's funeral in Ohio and rallied for a 5-4 victory over the Baltimore Orioles. Bobby Murcer, one of two Yankee players who eulogized Munson, drove in all five runs.

Murcer lashed a three-run home run off Dennis Martinez in the seventh inning and rapped a two-run single off Tippy Martinez in the ninth, enabling the Yankees to overcome a 4-0 lead the Orioles had built against Ron Guidry.

The players felt the way they did on Friday night in their first game after Munson was killed in a plane crash: no one really wanted to play this game.

When Murcer stepped to the plate in the seventh inning with runners at second and third and two out, the Orioles already had

He's Back, and He's Still the Boss

By **DOUGLAS MARTIN** | October 25, 1992

GEORGE MICHAEL STEINBRENNER 3D learned early on that there are no free lunches, even for the scion of a shipbuilding empire. His father refused to give him an allowance, and presented him instead with a flock of chickens and a few turkeys so he could start his own egg and poultry company.

Thus it was at the age of 9 he found himself chopping the heads off birds in the exurbs of Cleveland. "That chicken would run around with no head," he said as if visualizing the whole grisly scene. "Suddenly he'd flop down and you had to pick the feathers."

scored four runs on Lee May's homer and double and Ken Singleton's two-run homer. Murcer lashed a fastball from Dennis Martinez into the right-field stands for his first Yankee home run since Sept. 22, 1974. Prior to that blow, the 33-year-old left-hander had batted only .214 and knocked in five runs in 31 games since the Yankees re-acquired him June 26 from the Chicago Cubs.

When Murcer came to bat in the ninth, the same runners were in the same positions, second and third, but there were no outs. Bucky Dent had led off with a walk and raced to third when Tippy Martinez fielded Willie Rendolph's bunt and fired it past first base into right field.

Martinez got two strikes on Murcer but then threw a fastball closer to the plate than he wanted, and Murcer punched it to left field for a single that brought home both runners. An ecstatic Murcer was not too tired to leap into the air after he reached first base.

"I think we were playing on the spirit of Thurman," he said. "I think that's what carried us through the game. I know it did me." ∎

This was one of the nascent Boss's first business lessons: work hard and chop true. That came in handy when he fired— he prefers the word removed—18 New York Yankees managers in 19 years.

Mr. Steinbrenner, now 62 years old, comes across as larger than life, or maybe that's just what one expects. Rock-hard handshake. Diamond-studded 1978 World Series ring. Blue eyes sparkling at one of the memories. A hearty laugh perhaps issuing forth just a second too soon.

Baseball's most outspoken owner—the only one who has ever hosted "Saturday Night Live"—is returning to his field of screams. Sometime before spring training the Boss will be allowed to take the helm of the Yankees, of which he is 55 percent owner.

If you're less than charmed by this cheery news, well, pay your money and boo the Boss at the park. This activity once seemed as common as hot dogs at Yankee Stadium.

He suggests that distance from daily controversies may have heightened his previously uncelebrated sensitivity. He mentions a favorite painting by Monet, in which the gobs of paint gain resolution as the viewer steps back. "Perhaps I've had a chance to step back," he said, sipping a glass of skim milk.

But in an ensuing sentence, he would sound emphatically like the Steinbrenner of old.

"Winning is everything," he said. "I don't care what they tell you." ∎

A Team You Almost Had to Like

By **FRANK BRUNI** | October 29, 1996

FOR A WHILE, ALAN LEIDNER'S ROMANCE with the Yankees turned stormy.

Although wedded to the team by geography and history, Leidner could not summon the same affection for the club that he had felt as a boy, when the players seemed genuinely heroic and his first trip to Yankee Stadium was rewarded with a home run by Mickey Mantle.

Part of the problem, he said, was George Steinbrenner, who could be unbearably brash. Part of it was the team's players, who could be impossibly temperamental.

> "As this season went on,
> I got the disorienting feeling that
> I didn't hate them anymore."

Then, this season, everything changed. Suddenly, the team had a warmth to offset its cold corporate determination. It had underdogs like Dwight Gooden and Darryl Strawberry, returning from exile for a shot at redemption. It had Joe Torre, a hometown boy with a wizened exterior but the hint of a tear forever in his eye.

"There was just so much about this team that was so poignant," said Leidner, 48. Like Leidner, the fans who rallied around the Yankees during their pilgrimage to the World Series were attracted not merely by the hoopla that inevitably attends an organization on a hot streak or the thrill of associating with champions. The Yankees became a sort of municipal soap opera and, in the end, a symbol of strength through diversity and triumph through tenacity for a city that likes to believe in both.

"There is a fundamental difference between the way this team did it and the way the Chicago Bulls did it or the way Babe Ruth-era Yankees did it or the way mega-corporations do it," former Gov. Mario Cuomo said yesterday. "They do it through sheer power and dominance and muscle. The Yankees this year went beyond body and muscle to soul."

Indeed, their victory was celebrated not only by people who knew exactly how good the moment would feel, but also by those who never anticipated they would care.

"As this season went on, I got the disorienting feeling that I didn't hate them anymore," said Danny Greenberg, 51, who grew up loving the Brooklyn Dodgers, which meant hating the Yankees, "and I wondered if I was actually rooting for them." ∎

Yankees Use Their Home Advantage

By **GEORGE VECSEY** | October 1, 1998

THE 114 VICTORIES DON'T COUNT ANYMORE, but they did one thing for the Yankees—they guaranteed that the extra game in the league playoffs, if needed, would take place in front of the most demonstrative fans in baseball. In typical New York self-involvement, the fans like to believe how important they are. They like to think they cause outfielders to stumble and umpires' arms to jerk into a called-strike punch-out.

"Those fans in right field are crazy," said Shane Spencer, the instant idol, who whacked yet another home run in the Yankees' 3-1 victory over the Texas Rangers in Game 2 last night. "Thank God I'm doing good."

Spencer was starting against a right-hander, Rick Helling, a task that Darryl

Sun Sets on the Old Stadium

By **MANNY FERNANDEZ** | September 22, 2008

THE NEW $1.3 BILLION YANKEE STADIUM SAT like a jewel of the South Bronx, its fresh concrete and gold lettering gleaming in the late September sunshine. But it was the old stadium across the street—85 years and 5 months old—that people swarmed around and snapped pictures of and stared at one last time.

Matt Aquino, 48, who saw his first game there in 1964, told the story about the day he and his father watched Mickey Mantle hit a home run. His father set down his favorite Zippo lighter to pick him up so that he could see. The lighter was lost for good when they sat back down, and his father never let him forget it. He said he thinks about his father, who died 10 years ago, every time he returns to Yankee Stadium.

Strawberry might have had except that Strawberry is undergoing tests for worrisome intestinal problems that have the Yankees concerned. ("Sure, cancer always comes to mind," admitted Joe Torre, the manager.)

In the meantime there are the fans, and there is Spencer. He also singled and scored a run, after taking a curtain call to please the crowd, which has been treating him like a reincarnation of Mickey Mantle. If they demand a curtain call, you'd better pop out of the dugout, arms waving.

"I could hear them yelling, and I said, 'Oh, here we go,'" Spencer said. "But Joe told me to go out there. If he says so, I will."

Scott Brosius, the third baseman, who hit a two-run homer last night, compared it to playing in the Metrodome, the Minnesota Twins' dismal fabric bubble that holds the noise quite well. He said, "The dome is loud, but you just don't see fans in other places standing up with two strikes on every batter." ■

Other stories poured forth from people outside the stadium who remembered some small, touching moment in the life of the hulking stadium. The Yankees played their last game there on Sunday night, and tens of thousands of people — fathers and sons, women wearing T-shirts proclaiming, "I was there," children in Yankee pinstripes — converged to mourn the passing of what many of them considered sacred ground.

It was perhaps a testament to the stadium's pull that some fans did not even have tickets to the game. "I just wanted to say my proper goodbye," said Robert Liebowitz, 48, a post office manager from Brooklyn. He sat outside, next to a placard he had made that listed his first game (June 11, 1967), last game (June 22, 2008) and hot dogs eaten (many).

One man said they should have called the new stadium something different, anything but Yankee Stadium.

"The new Yankee Stadium will never be like this one," said another fan, Al Fekety, 46, of Staten Island. "It's kind of like when you fall in love. You fall in love once, and you fall in love with one stadium." ■

BELOW: *The final out of the last game at the old Yankee Stadium on September 21, 2008.*

Another Record: Mets Lose *116th

By ROBERT M. LIPSYTE | September 23, 1962

EVEN IN THE AUTUMN OF THEIR PATHETIC despair, the New York Mets cannot escape history. Each step and misstep seem destined to remain forever in the dusty recesses of major league archives.

Yesterday, at the Polo Grounds, there were at least four such footnotes. They obscured the Mets' 116th defeat, a dreary 9-2 drubbing by the Chicago Cubs.

The saddest of the four is what Met officials disregard as a "negative statistic." Al Jackson, one of the two best pitchers on the club, was clobbered for five runs on seven hits during the two and a third innings he pitched.

The slim left-hander was charged with his 20th loss of the season in 28 decisions. This is the first time since 1936 that a National League club has had two 20-game losers.

The second footnote, also negative, was predictable: The Mets have now lost more than any other National League club in this century. They are within one of tying the modern major league record of 117, set by the 1916 Philadelphia Athletics.

The third footnote is the happiest: Ed Kranepool, a 17-year-old husky recently graduated from James Monroe High School in the Bronx, made his major league debut, relieving Gil Hodges, at 38 the oldest Met, in the seventh inning. Kranepool batted only once, in the eighth, and grounded out.

Footnote No. 4 was certainly the most memorable for the 3,744 fans. Richie Ashburn, who at 35 has played 14 seasons of distinction in various outfields around the National League, played an inning of glorious second base.

It was his first time at any other position besides the outfield. It almost showed.

Nelson Mathews, the first batter in the ninth, was struck by one of Craig Anderson's pitches. He immediately stole second. Ashburn dropped Choo Choo Coleman's throw, but he fell on Mathews, making further advance impossible.

The next batter lined back to Anderson, the fourth Met pitcher of the afternoon. Anderson threw to Richie to double up Mathews, but Richie dropped the ball.

Mathews went on to steal third and scored on Alex Grammas's single for the ninth and last Cub run. Grammas, thinking Ashburn a pushover, lit out for second, but a fine throw from Coleman and a splendid tag by Ashburn erased his hopes.

In the ninth, Ashburn doubled to right, proving his worth at any position. ∎

*In 162-game season.

The Mets Trade "Tom Terrific"

By JOSEPH DURSO | June 16, 1977

IN AN ERA OF SUPERSTARDOM IN PROFESsional sports, when a basketball franchise totters if Julius Erving is traded, when a football franchise makes Page One if Joe Namath departs from Broadway—the baseball franchise of the New York Mets finally shook the firmament, too.

Trade Tom Seaver? No Santa Claus? Yes, Virginia, the Mets went to the very brink and beyond in the "war" between their celebrated pitcher and the chairman of the board of directors, M. Donald Grant. It was one thing to trade away stars like Nolan Ryan, Amos Otis and Rusty Staub; to dismiss Yogi Berra, to get into a public quarrel with Willie Mays. But it was unthinkable to trade Tom Terrific, who had arrived in 1967 when the Mets were always finishing in last place and who led their climb to respectability and to the "impossible dream."

Mets Win the World Series, 5-3, And a Grateful City Goes Wild

By **JOSEPH DURSO** | October 17, 1969

THE METS ENTERED THE PROMISED LAND yesterday after seven years of wandering through the wilderness of baseball.

They defeated the Baltimore Orioles, 5-3, for their fourth straight victory of the 66th World Series and captured the championship of a sport that had long ranked them as comical losers.

They did it with a full and final dose of the magic that had spiced their unthinkable climb from ninth place in the National League—100-to-1 shots who scrounged their way to the pinnacle as the waifs of the major leagues.

At 3:17 o'clock on a cool and often sunny afternoon, their impossible dream came true when Cleon Jones caught a fly ball hit by Dave Johnson to left field. And they immediately touched off one of the great, riotous scenes in sports history, as thousands of persons swarmed from their seats and tore up the patch of ground where the Mets had made history.

The deciding run was batted home in the eighth by Ron Swoboda, who joined the Met mystique in 1965 when the team was losing 112 games and was finishing last for the fourth straight time.

But, like most of the Mets' victories in their year to remember, the decision was a collective achievement by the youngest team in baseball, under Manager Gil Hodges—who had suffered a heart attack a year ago after the Mets "surged" into ninth place.

The wild, final chapter in the story was written against the desperate efforts of the Orioles, who had swept to the American League pennant by 19 games as one of the most powerful teams in modern times. ■

They ran dead last in five of their first six summers while they fixed themselves i n the public's affections as warmly comical ragamuffins. Then, without warning in 1969, the year men walked on the moon, the Mets marched to the world championship—and George Thomas Seaver led the march, winning 16 games and becoming the first man on a last-place club to be voted rookie of the year.

Three times he was voted the Cy Young Award as the best pitcher in the National League. Four times he pitched more than 20 victories in one season, including 25 in the year of the "miracle." Five times he pitched one-hitters. He also could hit and field, and for a decade he reigned—proudly, even a bit pompously to some observers—as "The Franchise."

Even before the free-agent "revolution" last year, he became one of the leaders in the recurring labor wars between the players and club owners. He finally took the offensive against Grant by declaring that his first obligation was to his family and that he would play out his option unless the Mets paid more. Grant replied that Seaver was an "ingrate," and Seaver's private war was on. ■

BELOW: *Fans storm the field after the Mets capture their first World Series title in 1969.*

The '86 World Series: Mets Win It, City Loves It

By PETER ALFANO | October 28, 1986

MOOKIE WILSON STOOD IN A CORNER OF THE Mets' clubhouse, just enjoying the view. He has seen World Series celebrations before, the champagne being sprayed like a tugboat fire hose on the Fourth of July, joyous teammates hugging in a moment all baseball players dream about but few ever experience.

"I know what it's like to be in the cellar, to be at home during this time of year watching the World Series with a pizza and beer," Wilson said of his early years with the Mets. "You have to give credit to the young guys on this club. They showed the world you don't need 10 years' experience and three in the playoffs to win."

The Mets celebrated as a team. But to each player, the World Series championship had a special meaning. The Mets won 116 games this season, but the final eight victories in the National League championship series and World Series were excruciating.

So Tim Teufel breathed a sigh of relief, thankful that the error that cost the Mets the first game of the World Series against the Red Sox, 1-0, would be a footnote overshadowed by the sixth and seventh games.

Their comeback in Game 6 claimed a number of victims, even on the winning team. Darryl Strawberry was removed from the game in a lineup switch with the score tied because Dave Johnson, the Mets' manager, could not afford to use another pitcher. Strawberry was angry in victory and said he did not think he could communicate with Johnson ever again.

Strawberry said he still was hurt by the manager's decision but will try to understand the reasoning. "Davey is a fine man and we just disagreed on some things," he said. "I know I'm a clutch player, and after three and a half years here, I didn't think that kind of thing could happen to me anymore. I'm just happy I could contribute that home run tonight. To hit one in a World Series is a great thrill." ∎

Gooden Fans 16 And Sets Record

By JOSEPH DURSO | September 13, 1984

IN A DAZZLING DISPLAY OF VIRTUOSO PITCH-ing by a 19-year-old rookie, Dwight Gooden fired the Mets to a 2-0 victory over the Pittsburgh Pirates, striking out 16 batters and hurtling past strikeout records set by Tom Seaver, Nolan Ryan and Herb Score.

The tall and taciturn right-hander from Tampa, Fla., overpowered the Pirates on five hits, gave no walks, pitched his second straight shutout and seventh straight victory and ended the evening with more strikeouts than any other rookie in history.

He passed that milestone in the sixth inning when he struck out Marvell Wynne. It was his 11th strikeout of the night and the 246th of his brief career in the big leagues, and it broke the record set by Score for the Cleveland Indians 29 years ago.

But there was more. By the time he had finished, Gooden had a total of 251 strikeouts in 202 innings in 29 games. He also had broken Ryan's club record of 14 strikeouts by a rookie in a game, set in 1968, and Seaver's one-season record of 13 games with 10 or more strikeouts, set in 1971. And he struck out more batters in a game than any Met pitcher in 10 years.

"Sometimes, you think about it," Gooden said later, in a rare touch of personal reaction. "You think about it going home, or lying in bed before falling asleep. You think, 'Am I dreaming?' It's a great, great feeling."

Gooden pitched his classic to a rookie catcher, Mike Fitzgerald, who rushed out to the mound when Score's record fell as the crowd of 12,876 gave Gooden a standing ovation. "Congratulations," Fitzgerald said. "Let's not stop here." ∎

mets

Yanks and Mets Ready For a Wild Ride

By **BUSTER OLNEY** | October 21, 2000

IT HAS BEEN 16,083 DAYS SINCE THE END OF the last Subway Series, when the Yankees shut out the Dodgers in the final game of the 1956 World Series, and a city is on edge. It has been five days since the Mets, who have lived in the shadows of their Bronx big brothers for most of the last decade, clinched the National League pennant. It's been four days since the Yankees, the nearest thing to a dynasty that baseball has seen in a quarter-century, wrapped up the American League.

> "There is a lot of buildup," Yankees pitcher David Cone said, "almost like a Super Bowl atmosphere."

"There is a lot of buildup," Yankees pitcher David Cone said, "almost like a Super Bowl atmosphere."

Al Leiter, who started the last World Series game not won by the Yankees—as a member of the Florida Marlins, in 1997—will face Pettitte. The Mets' Mike Piazza, the starting catcher for 124 games in the regular season, will be the designated hitter in Game 1, and Todd Pratt—who has had one at-bat in this postseason—will start at catcher.

Pettitte is left-handed, and in explaining his decision, Mets Manager Bobby Valentine said Pratt was the best right-handed hitter among his reserves. Pratt is generally considered a better defensive catcher than Piazza, who said, "I know I'll get my action behind the plate before the series is over."

Finding ways to beat Leiter and Mike Hampton, the Mets' other left-handed starter, is what the Yankees must do if they are to become the first team since the Oakland Athletics of 1972, '73 and '74 to win three consecutive titles. The Yankees' starting lineup will include three veteran left-handed hitters who can all hit left-handers, but Leiter held lefties to a .118 batting average in the regular season, the second-lowest figure in the last 25 years, according to the Elias Sports Bureau.

As the Yankees finished batting practice yesterday, some of the Mets filtered from their dugout and onto the field for their workout. Some coaches from the two teams chatted, and there were a few waves across the field by the players, but mostly, there was little contact. Second baseman Edgardo Alfonzo stood behind the cage, stoic, a blank expression.

Why so quiet? "What do you think I'm feeling inside?" Alfonzo asked, his face splitting into a grin. "I'm about to play in my first World Series. I'm just trying to keep my emotions inside." ■

BELOW: *Special "Subway Series" subway trains ran in October of 2000. The Yankees went onto to win the series, 4 games to 1.*

National Pro Football Title Is Won by Giants, 30-13

By **ROBERT F. KELLEY** | December 10, 1934

IN ONE OF THE MOST WILDLY EXCITING periods that any football game has ever seen, the New York Giants scored 27 points in the final session of play at the Polo Grounds to come from behind and defeat the Chicago Bears, 30 to 13.

Trailing on the short end of a 13-to-3 score when the last quarter opened, the Giants roared through to an amazing victory while 37,000 fans went wild with excitement. Four times the Giants crossed the Bears' goal line for touchdowns in that final period as they captured the national professional championship and toppled the Bears from the throne they have occupied since 1932.

During most of the first half, after the Bears had overcome a first-period lead that Ken Strong gave the Giants with a 38-yard placement goal, the Westerners, undefeated in 13 National Football League games this year, seemed the certain winners. Then when Jack Manders, the great kicker, shot across a 23-yard field goal late in the third period it was apparently all over but the shouting.

The Bears had come back in the second period with a touchdown when Bronko Nagurski bulled his way across from the one-yard mark. A pass paved the way to this score. Then Manders had made his first field goal, a rifle shot from the 17-yard mark. The third-period goal was apparently the final touch.

But with Lou Little, Columbia's coach, sitting up in the stands and phoning to the bench, Steve Owen directing down there and Strong playing one of the greatest games any back has ever turned in, the Giants came back to win. They returned to the field in the second half with basketball shoes replacing the cleated football shoes. The solidly frozen ground made cleats useless, and the basketball shoes made all the difference.

The final touchdown was quarterback Ed Danowski's. The stage had been set by Molenda's interceptions of a Ronzani pass,

> Four times the Giants crossed the Bears' goal line for touchdowns in that final period

followed by a lateral to Burnett. The interception came on the Bears' 34-yard line and the play ended on the 22.

Danowski, the ex-Fordham ace, punched out a first down just over the 10. He went off right and on the next play and cut back behind fine blocking to cross the line standing up. Molenda added the extra point. ∎

Giants Win Super Bowl With Nail-Biting Finish

By **ROBERT MCG. THOMAS JR.** | January 28, 1991

HOW 'BOUT THEM GIANTS?

That, more or less, was the rhetorical question of the moment among the New York fans last night as the team they call Big Blue came from behind in the fourth quarter and then held off a last-minute surge to defeat the Buffalo Bills, 20-19, in Super Bowl XXV.

It was the second Super Bowl victory for the Giants in five seasons, but unlike their 39-20 romp over the Denver Broncos in 1987, this one was a clinical heart-stopper. The lead changed four times and the outcome was not decided until the last four seconds.

The game was watched by 73,813 flag-waving fans in Tampa Stadium, by tens of millions on television across the United

Giants Stun Patriots In Super Bowl XLII

By **JUDY BATTISTA** | February 4, 2008

THE GIANTS WERE NOT EVEN SUPPOSED TO BE here, taking an unlikely playoff path through the behemoths of their conference and regarded, once they alighted on Super Bowl XLII, as little more than charming foils for the New England Patriots' assault on immortality.

But with their defense battering this season's National Football League's most valuable player, Tom Brady, and Giants quarterback Eli Manning playing more like Brady than Brady himself, the Giants produced one of the greatest upsets in Super Bowl history Sunday night, beating the previously undefeated Patriots, 17-14.

The Patriots' coach, Bill Belichick—who was the Giants' defensive coordinator the last time the Giants won the Super Bowl, in 1991—led his team to the brink of a historic 19-0 perfect season and had survived a spying scandal that cost him money and the Patriots a first-round draft pick. But he could only watch as it all collapsed under the weight of the Giants' ferocious pass rush. For another year, the 1972 Miami Dolphins will stand alone with the only perfect season in N.F.L. history.

"It's the greatest victory in the history of this franchise, without question," the Giants co-owner John Mara said, his voice hoarse. "I just want to say to all you Giants fans who have supported us for more than 30 years at Giants Stadium, for all those years in Yankee Stadium and some of you even back to the Polo Grounds, this is for you."

Manning connected with Plaxico Burress for the winning touchdown, a 13-yard pass with 35 seconds remaining in the game. Manning drove the Giants 83 yards in just over two minutes after the Patriots had marched down the field to take a 14-10 lead. ∎

States and via satellite relay by tens of thousands of the nation's military men and women on war duty in the Persian Gulf.

After more than a week of news dominated by missile attacks and aerial bombardments, a contest in which the most potent weapon was the forward pass seemed a decided relief.

There were stark reminders, however, that a nation of football fans is also a nation at war: the most extensive security ever mounted for a sporting event and a pregame flyover by four F-15 jets.

For the Giants, who trailed 12-10 at the half, took the lead on a third-quarter touchdown, lost it when the Bills scored a touchdown in the fourth and then went up a point on a field goal by Matt Bahr. The ending was a mirror image of their last-second defeat of the San Francisco 49ers the week before.

This time it was the Giants' opponents who needed a last-minute field goal to win, and this time the kick, by Scott Norwood, was wide. ∎

BELOW: David Tyree wrestles the ball away from Patriot Rodney Harrison in the fourth quarter of Super Bowl XLII.

Jet Propulsion

By **ARTHUR DALEY** | January 14, 1969

JOE NAMATH TALKS BIG. HE ALSO ACTS BIG. It was the wizardry of this quarterbacking marvel that lighted the afterburners of the New York Jets and sent them rocketing to unexpected heights in a Super Bowl upset of historic proportions. The Jets beat the supposedly invincible Baltimore Colts, 16-7, and thereby became the first American Football League team to humble the proud and condescending National League in world championship action.

The Colts had been favored by something like 17 to 20 points. That's what made the result so difficult for the Establishment to take, and that's why the red faces of the assembled experts were not entirely caused by the Florida sunshine. In the final analysis, though, the thing that confounded them most was that it was no fluke.

The Jets won on their merits. On this day, at least, they were the better football team. They showed no respect to a club whose awesome efficiency on both offense and defense all season had set almost matchless standards of excellence. Like the disdainful Namath, they treated the Colts with the utmost impoliteness and savaged them outrageously. The Jets were pretty much in control of the situation all the way.

"Namath psyched two teams," said George Blanda of the Oakland Raiders, pro football's oldest inhabitant. "He psyched the Jets into believing they could win and he psyched the Colts into doubting that they could win."

It's a reasonable observation, although the doubts that crept into the Colts may have been planted there not so much by the Jet quarterback as by their own, Earl Morrall, a gypsy who has played for four teams in a dozen years. Reading men's minds is a rather arcane art, but I seem to sense the Baltimore confidence oozing out like air escaping from a captive balloon. ∎

For Many Jets Fans, It's Super Sunday In Name Only

By **VINCENT M. MALLOZZI** | February 3, 2008

NOT SINCE JOE NAMATH MADE GOOD ON HIS guarantee to beat the Baltimore Colts in 1969 have the Jets been back to the Super Bowl. The players continually change, so the wait may be harder on longtime Jets fans who have endured two victories in three Super Bowl appearances by the rival Giants.

So what will some of those green-with-envy, rabid Jets fans be doing Sunday during Super Bowl XLII, in which the Giants will play the New England Patriots in Glendale, Ariz.?

"I'll be playing video games with my two sons," said Joey Fiordalisi, 38, a printer who lives in Hamilton, N.J. "I can't watch because it kind of makes me sick to my stomach, and if I sound like a jealous Jets fan, well, I am."

Fiordalisi has a theory about why the Jets have been to only one Super Bowl.

"I think Joe Namath made a deal with the devil," he said. "The devil said, 'O.K., Joe, I'll give you this one, but your Jets will never win another.'"

Caryl Cohen of Secaucus, N.J., who is retired as the director of teacher recruitment for the New York City Department of Education, said that despite her loyalty to the Jets, she would root for the Giants.

"When it comes down to it, I have to root for the New York team," she said. "I hate the Pats, so I would have been rooting for whoever played them, anyway."

Cohen said she would watch the game with fellow Jets fans.

"Misery loves company," she said. "We want to commiserate." ∎

To the Crowds, He's Everybody's Joe

By **JOSEPH DURSO** | January 23, 1969

ABOVE: *Joe Namath at Giants Stadium in October 2000.*

BROADWAY JOE CAME BACK TO BROADWAY and touched off waves of hero worship from City Hall to Times Square.

Like conquering heroes, Joe Willie Namath and his teammates on the New York Jets were lionized throughout a tumultuous day as they officially brought home the championship of professional football.

Most of the public passion was lavished on Namath, the 25-year-old quarterback with the Rhett Butler sideburns and the most celebrated passing arm in the land. He upstaged Mayor Lindsay, he turned on thousands of teenagers, he calmed the multitudes with a wave of his hand, he led a police caravan through the midtown streets, he made two graceful speeches, he accepted a sports car as the outstanding performer in the Super Bowl—and then he required a wedge of 12 policemen to cross a sidewalk thronged with female admirers.

Broadway Joe's triumphal return started on the steps of City Hall at noon. It was 12 days since the Jets had upset the odds and the Baltimore Colts, 16-7, in the Super Bowl game.

The door of City Hall opened and Mayor Lindsay stepped down through a double line of policemen toward the platform facing City Hall Park. Solid booing broke out, as though the mayor was a Baltimore Colt.

A stride behind him marched Namath. The booing dissolved into roaring cheers.

Then the mayor stepped to the microphone to pay tribute to "our conquering team, the greatest football team in the world." This time he was drowned out by a rising chant of "Namath for Mayor, Namath for Mayor."

"I noticed some Giants' fans out there," Namath said, and his public hooted and hollered. Then, turning more serious, he nodded toward his teammates and said:

"You see here Matt Snell—who was our most valuable player in the Super Bowl game."

More cheering erupted, and it continued as each of the dozen Jets on hand came forward to receive a gift from the city fathers—a tie clasp and cuff links engraved with the municipal seal. In return, the Jets gave the mayor a gift—a framed LeRoy Neiman painting of Joe Namath in action.

Then the Jets got into half a dozen limousines and one team bus and headed uptown for the second half. The frenzy shifted to West 48th Street between Times Square and Eighth Avenue because Namath & Co. roosted at Mamma Leone's restaurant. En route uptown along the Avenue of the Americas, the police gave the Jets the full hero treatment—sirens, flashing red lights and all. The midday crowds waved and clapped.

Namath was there primarily to accept Sport magazine's 11th annual pro football award, and as teenage girls packed the sidewalk outside and peered through windows of the restaurant, Namath was given the keys to his prize car by Al Silverman, the editor of Sport.

When Namath went outside to inspect the car, Jet pennants were being hawked for 75 cents and the police were fighting a long battle against the young crowd. It was like a combined appearance by Frank Sinatra, the Beatles and Tiny Tim.

"If you had lost the big game," somebody told Namath, "you would've avoided all this." ∎

Three City College Aces and a Gambler Held In Basketball "Fix"

By **ALEXANDER FEINBERG** | February 17, 1976

THREE CITY COLLEGE BASKETBALL PLAYERS, members of the team that won two national championships last season, were arrested yesterday on bribery charges.

District Attorney Frank S. Hogan said they had admitted receiving sums up to $1,500 each for "fixing" three Madison Square Garden contests in the current season. In each case they were supposed to lose or to keep the margin of victory below the point-spread that City College was favored by in advance betting. City lost all three games.

Taken into custody when they returned with Coach Nat Holman and the remainder of the squad from a record-setting victory over Temple University at Philadelphia on Saturday night, the three— co-captains Ed Roman and Ed Warner, and Al Roth—were questioned all night. Confronted with incriminating testimony, they shamefacedly acknowledged a gambler's payoffs, Mr. Hogan said.

> They had admitted receiving sums up to $1,500 each for "fixing" three Madison Square Garden contests in the current season.

Arrested with them were Salvatore Tarto Sollazzo, a 45-year-old jewelry manufacturer and ex-convict described as a "sure-thing" gambler; Eddie Gard, a Long Island University senior named by Mr. Hogan as Sollazzo's intermediary; and Harvey (Connie) Schaff, a basketball player at New York University. Mr. Hogan said Schaff had attempted to line up a teammate at N.Y.U. for the gambler, but had been rebuffed.

The case explained at least in part why a City College team that had won both the National Invitation Tournament at Madison Square Garden and the National Collegiate Athletic Association Tournament in the 1949-50 season could amass a record of only 11-7 in 1950-51.

Three games were "fixed," Mr. Hogan said. In each City College was an 8-to-12 point favorite. The "fix" was for the City stars to keep their margin of victory down to no more than six points, Mr. Hogan said. They did better than that; they saw to it that their team was beaten in all three games. ∎

Short Shots In All Directions

By **ARTHUR DALEY** | November 1, 1946

THERE IS SOMETHING FASCINATING ABOUT any new endeavor in sports, particularly when success is virtually ordained from the start. Such a newcomer is the Basketball Association of America, a professional group whose franchises are held by the arena owners and who therefore are more than halfway around third base in the race for home plate. This is an important distinction because lack of adequate facilities has been the main stumbling block for all previous circuits.

The B.A.A. formally opens its schedule tonight when the New York Knickerbockers, sponsored by Madison Square Garden, journey to Toronto's Maple Leaf Gardens for the first joust of a 60-game list. Then they swing over to the Chicago Stadium and the St. Louis Arena before they return for their home inaugural at the Garden a week from Monday.

Knicks Take First Title, Beating Lakers, 113–99

By **LEONARD KOPPETT** | May 9, 1970

THE NEW YORK KNICKERBOCKERS, DISPLAY-ing their finest qualities with the limited physical but important spiritual aid of a limping Willis Reed, won the championship of the National Basketball Association last night by routing the Los Angeles Lakers, 113-99, at Madison Square Garden.

Walt Frazier, with 36 points and 19 assists, was the most brilliant individual, but this, like most Knick successes, was basically a team enterprise as the Knicks finally claimed the first title in their 24-year history. They gave New York's happy sports fans their third professional world championship in 16 months. The football Jets won the Super Bowl game in January 1969, and the baseball Mets took the World Series last fall.

Reed, as always, was indispensable, but this time in an unusual fashion. He had injured a muscle in his right leg in the fifth game of the series. His injury seemed to doom the Knicks to defeat, because it left them with no counterweapon to Wilt Chamberlain, the 7-foot-2-inch Laker center and the greatest scorer in basketball history.

As it turned out, after some pain-killing injections and a few minutes of shooting practice, Reed was able to start. He took the first shot at the basket, with the game 18 seconds old, and made it.

A minute later, he hit another, making the score 5-2, and the effect on his teammates was electric. The Knicks shot better, defended better, hustled more, ran faster, jumped higher, passed more accurately and stole the ball more often.

Dave DeBusschere, the rugged forward whose arrival from Detroit more than a year ago transformed the Knicks into a great team (by allowing Reed to move to center as well as by DeBusschere's own contributions) had another superb game. He had to do the heavy rebounding, taking down 17, and scoring 18 points.

Bill Bradley, not at his best in much of the series, was in top form this time, with 17 points and five assists. And the much-appreciated Knick bench—Nate Bowman as Reed's relief, Dave Stallworth, Cazzie Russell and Mike Riordan—did its share, although only Bowman played as much as usual (and more). ◾

Father Knickerbocker's Knicks are under the watchful eye of Edward Simmons Irish, who rarely makes mistakes. He signed the shrewd Neil Cohalan as his coach and liberally larded his squad with top-flight local boys. But the more important factor is that Ned is interested in it. Other sections of the country might scream denials, but there is no escaping the fact that Irish, through his Garden productions, is the man who had made college basketball the game that it is today.

He'll do the same with pro ball. Backing the new league are the controlling interests at the Boston Garden, the Cleveland Arena, the Detroit Olympia, Pittsburgh's Duquesne Gardens, Washington's Uline Arena, the Philadelphia Arena and assorted other indoor pavilions. Unfortunately, Ned put the squeeze on himself by getting into the play-for-play phase of the dribble diversion after most of the Garden dates were taken. His Knicks will stage only 4 of their 34 home games in the Eighth Avenue sports palace, with the rest of them listed for the 69th Regiment Armory. ◾

> This was a team enterprise as the Knicks finally claimed the first title in their 24-year history.

Knicks Legends Welcome Ewing To Their Ranks

By **LIZ ROBBINS** | March 1, 2003

THE QUESTION WAS RAISED BEFORE THE jersey was, a cocktail-hour debate before the party.

On a night of tributes for Patrick Ewing, a number of Knicks players, coaches, opponents, friends and fans from across the years came to celebrate his legacy last night and put his place in the Madison Square Garden rafters into perspective.

Is No. 33 the greatest Knick ever? The answers in the unofficial poll were split. No one scored more points, grabbed more rebounds, blocked more shots or played more minutes. No Knick had more All-Star appearances (11) than Ewing. But he does not have what all but one other in his company of retired numbers have, a championship ring.

Ewing was overwhelmed by the Hall of Famers around him, and he deferred to them. "I don't think I'm the greatest Knick when I see all these guys sitting here," Ewing said during the halftime ceremony in which his number was retired.

Walt Frazier, who led the Knicks to two championships, had agreed with Ewing before the game. "Patrick, I always say he's second to Willis and I put myself third," Frazier said. "I always say Willis Reed first because mostly what I learned about the game, I learned from him."

Dave DeBusschere saw all sides of the debate. "It's all eras—in 1950, someone was the greatest, in 1960, in the 70's, 80's, there's always going to be somebody," he said.

That was Jeff Van Gundy's point when he defended Ewing as the greatest player to wear a Knick uniform.

"If you look in those jerseys up there, they had each other," Van Gundy, Ewing's cherished coach, said. "He had some great teammates, but he was never surrounded by that one other Hall-of-Fame-type player. He really carried a team for a long time just with his will to win." ∎

The Knicks' Crying Game: Disappointment Reigns

By **CLIFTON BROWN** | June 24, 1994

THE PAIN RUNS DEEP FOR THE KNICKS, THE kind of pain that will not subside quickly.

Fewer teams seemed to work harder this season to win a championship. Fewer teams seemed to want it more. No team is more disappointed.

The Houston Rockets earned their first championship the hard way, beating the Knicks, 90-84, in Game 7 of the National Basketball Association finals. While the Rockets spent yesterday celebrating their triumph in a city that rejoiced in its first professional sports championship, the Knicks somberly boarded a plane and went home, unable to find comfort or satisfaction in their effort or their achievements.

As the Knicks Wilt, New York Feels Yet Another Loss

By **CHARLIE LEDUFF** | March 14, 2002

ALLAN HOUSTON PROBABLY DID NOT SEE HIM sitting up there in Section 413, Row B, Seat 9.

There, Paul Kincaid, the little big man, dreams of the shooting guard's job. Paul is 11 years old and a sixth grader at P.S. 33 in Chelsea and considers himself something of an expert on, among other things, King Tut and the Knicks. He came to Madison Square Garden Tuesday night with his Y.M.C.A. team. Despite the Knicks' miserable play this season, Paul is sure they will make the playoffs.

"I was born a Knicks fan and I always have to hope," he said as he fiddled with his sneakers.

The Knicks had a special season, winning the Eastern Conference, winning the Atlantic Division and surviving two seven-game playoff series against the Chicago Bulls and the Indiana Pacers.

But the Knicks have been building toward winning a championship ever since Pat Riley became their coach three seasons ago. They felt it would happen this season. Guard Hubert Davis wept openly in the Knicks' locker room when Game 7 ended. Other players hurt too much to cry.

It was a particularly dreadful ending for center Patrick Ewing, whose nine-year quest for a championship in New York remained unfulfilled, and for guard John Starks, whose terrible Game 7 performance featured 2-for-18 shooting and just 8 points.

Ewing had vowed that this would be the Knicks' season to win their first N.B.A. championship since 1972-73. Ewing kept his emotions in check during the post-game interviews, but a look of remorse was etched on his face.

"I thought we gave it 110 percent," he said, "and unfortunately it wasn't enough." ▪

To some, the Knickerbockers are more than a team and basketball is more than a game. They can be the tether and the language between father and son. Paul and his pop used to watch a lot of Knicks together.

Dad moved out not long ago, and Paul is left to watch the games by himself on the weekdays. On this night, he was alone with his team as the Knicks were booed off the court, having blown a 20-point lead to the Philadelphia 76ers, one more low-water mark in a truly awful season.

Every home game starts the same. Latrell Sprewell leads the Knicks out of the locker room and bounces a soft pass to Spike Lee, who is standing in front of his $1,600 courtside seat with his hands out and his No. 8 Sprewell jersey hanging limply on his narrow shoulders.

Some people associate Spike Lee with the Knicks as much as they do Patrick Ewing or Clyde Frazier. And now, in this season of losing, people out on the streets feel free to take their shots.

"What happened to your Knicks, Spike?" a cabdriver yells. "Where'd your boys go, Spike? You paid too much."

"Every day it happens," he says. "People come to me like I know what's going on, like I'm in the room when the decisions are being made. I'm just a fan with a good seat."

And so Spike Lee goes to home games, sits in his outrageously priced seat, eats outrageously priced food and by halftime against Philadelphia, the Knicks were up 15 points and he was bouncing around the court feeling good.

But, true to form, the Knicks folded like a cheap card table, and near the end of the game, with another loss certain, Spike Lee was slumped in his chair, picking his beard, curling his lip and dreaming about the Knicks' draft pick this summer. ▪

Rangers Take Stanley Cup Title

By **SEABURY LAWRENCE** | April 15, 1928

THE NEW YORK RANGERS WON THE STANLEY Cup and the world's championship in hockey by defeating the Montreal Maroons by a 2-1 score before 14,000 frenzied fans at the Forum.

It was a savage and bitter battle all the way, with the Maroons going down fighting, but conquered by a team whose spirit and pluck in desperate circumstances finally won over all obstacles in the fifth and final game of this hard-fought series.

> It was a savage and bitter battle all the way . . . conquered by a team whose spirit and pluck in desperate circumstances finally won over all obstacles.

All of the Rangers played the most courageous and spirited kind of hockey, but three figures stood out in this battle of heroes: Frank Boucher, who scored both Ranger goals on thrilling individual plays; Joe Miller, who gave a wonderful exhibition of goal tending with his right eye badly injured; and Ching Johnson, who, with leg, eye and nose injuries, kept on body checking the heavy Maroons to a standstill.

The game had hardly started when a flying disk from Hooley Smith struck Miller in the right eye and he fell to the ice. Miller returned to the fray after 10 minutes with the eye almost closed but saved scores time and again by cool, deft plays.

After the injury the odds turned heavily against the Rangers. But the Maroon fans had not figured on Frank Boucher as a situation saver, scoring a second Ranger goal at 15:15 after another brilliant individual play.

Phillips scored the only Maroon goal at 17:50 on a pass from Siebert. Bill Cook got a major penalty for stick-ending Stewart. The Rangers were down to five men as the game ended, but the Maroons could not crash through for another one.

It was a rough as well as a swift game, with 21 penalties handed out by the referees. Ching Johnson went off four times for penalties and three times for injuries and came back smiling every time.

Miller made several good stops before the game was two minutes old. Boucher kept poke-checking the disk away from the Maroon forwards as they skated down and twice got through with Bill Cook, only to have Benedict turn the shots aside. ▪

Champs Again After 54 years

By **ROBERT MCG. THOMAS JR.** | June 15, 1994

THE STANLEY CUP JINX IS DEAD, AND THE New York Rangers are the champions of the National Hockey League.

The Rangers won their fourth championship last night at Madison Square Garden, and the fact that it had been 54 years since the last one made the 3-2 victory over the Vancouver Canucks that much sweeter.

And when Brian Leetch became the first American-born player to be named the playoffs' most valuable player, it was just icing on the cup.

When time ran out on Game 7 of the seven-game series, a city that had lived through several wars and social revolutions since its previous Stanley Cup

Rangers Top Leafs in Overtime, 3-2, Winning Stanley Cup

By **JOSEPH C. NICHOLS** | April 14, 1940

THE RANGERS WON THE STANLEY CUP AND the hockey championship of the world by subduing the stubborn Maple Leafs tonight, 3-2. Two goals behind with only 12 minutes left, the Blue Shirts squared matters and sent the battle into overtime. After 2 minutes 7 seconds of extra play, Bryan Hextall, New York right wing, fired the puck past Turk Broda for the score that decided the series, 4 games to 2.

Hextall's climactic drive brought disappointment to the crowd of 14,894, mostly home-team sympathizers. They had been led to expect a decisive triumph by the ease with which the Toronto skaters flashed into the lead by two goals before the game was half over. They almost refused to believe their eyes when the winning goal flew home.

The Rangers finally broke Broda down at 8:08 in the third period when Neil Colville beat him and then scored a second time in 10:01, when Alfie Pike drilled a shot into the cords.

These fast goals, important in giving the Ranger skaters new life, also earned for them a psychological advantage. When the game went into overtime the Rangers, helped by a rest of 20 minutes, massed themselv es about the Leaf goal and, though the home skaters sent two fast "breakaway" rushes into New York ice, the Blue Shirts maintained the edge.

In all, the Rangers were able to put 23 shots on Broda's stick, while the Leafs reached Kerr 24 times. ∎

---

victory in 1940 erupted into a celebration half a century in the making.

> The jinx that had seemed to dog the Rangers through three previous Stanley Cup finals didn't die easily.

The jinx that had seemed to dog the Rangers through three previous Stanley Cup finals didn't die easily. After jumping to a 2-0 lead in the first period and holding on at 3-1 through the second, the Rangers sa w their lead cut to 1 at the beginning of the third, and suddenly old fears surged to the surface.

But this is 1994, not 1940. ∎

BELOW: *The 1994 Championship Rangers raise the Stanley Cup along the ticker-tape parade route.*

Billie Jean King Defeats Miss Evert

By **NEIL AMDUR** | September 11, 1971

THE ENDLESS SUMMER CAME TO A HALT FOR Chris Evert yesterday, before the brilliance of Billie Jean King.

Reaffirming her status as one of the sport's most versatile players, the top-seeded Mrs. King rushed past the unseeded 16-year-old Cinderella girl of the United States Open tennis championships, 6-3, 6-2.

Mrs. King, who needs less than $25,000 to become the first women professional to top $100,000 in a single year, will play a familiar face, Rosemary Casals, tomorrow for the $5,000 first prize.

The second-seeded Miss Casals played her best match of the tournament, beating Kerry Melville, 6-4, 6-3, in the first of the women's semifinal matches. But she will have to play even better in the final to handle an inspired, eager Mrs. King, who has lost only one of their 10 meetings this year.

Miss Evert, a high school student from Fort Lauderdale, Fla., had not lost a singles match since last February—a string of 46 consecutive victories—and one of her victims had been Mrs. King, who was forced to default a match in St. Petersburg because of cramps.

Mrs. King, who watched last year's tournament as a frustrated spectator after knee surgery, lost the opportunity for the opening-game break. Miss Evert scored five straight points, but the Californian squandered few other chances, twice scrambling back from love-30 on service and never allowed Miss Evert a break-point on her serve.

"I didn't hit out as much as I wanted," Mrs. King said. "But I wanted to hit the ball short on my approach instead of deep so the ball would bounce lower and make it more difficult for her to return." ∎

McEnroe Captures Tumultuous Match

By **NEIL AMDUR** | August 31, 1979

IT BEGAN AS A TENNIS MATCH AND ENDED as a tragic soap opera. In the middle, John McEnroe and Ilie Nastase exchanged roles as heroes and villains. There were cheers, boos, point penalties, game penalties, police on the court, a switch in umpires and even some brilliant shot making.

When it was over, the third-seeded McEnroe had defeated the 33-year-old Nastase, 6-4, 4-6, 6-3, 6-2, in a tumultuous three-hour match that was almost as trying for the 10,549 spectators at the National Tennis Center as it was for the players, officials and Frank Hammond, the umpire.

The third day of the United States Open championships began with the hottest weather of the week and wound up at 12:36 a.m. after Mike Blanchard, the tournament referee, had replaced Hammond in the umpire's chair and restored order to a match that had been forecast as stormy and was delayed 17 minutes at one point.

The chaos erupted in the fourth set after Hammond had capped a series of warnings and penalized Nastase a full game for stalling with McEnroe serving at 2-1, 15-0. Earlier in the match, with McEnroe serving at 2-2, 40-0, Hammond had awarded a point penalty and the game to the left-hander.

The game penalty produced loud booing. When Hammond was unable to silence the crowd or induce Nastase to serve the next game, he finally said, "Game, set, match, McEnroe," over the public-address system

A Message To All, A Duel for the Ages

By **HARVEY ARATON** | September 6, 2001

THE STADIUM WAS FULL AND THE STARS WERE out but the new kids with the blustery serves and the windmill forehands who grew up watching Pete Sampras and Andre Agassi were awake late in their hotel rooms, watching the masters at work. On a cool and vintage United States Open night in New York, Sampras versus Agassi in the quarterfinals would become that rarest of tennis events, turning phenoms to fans.

"I'm probably going to get a late hit in," Andy Roddick had said before Sampras defeated Agassi 6-7 (7), 7-6 (2), 7-6 (2), 7-6 (5) last night, staging a show for the ages. "I doubt I'll hang out there. But I'll definitely watch it. My two biggest influences—I'm still a huge fan." Still, and after last night, undoubtedly bigger than ever.

Eleven years ago, when Sampras announced himself here as a legend-in-the-

making, Roddick was an 8-year-old struggling to return his older brother's serve. Lleyton Hewitt, Roddick's opponent tonight in a kid stuff quarterfinal, was a 9-year-old kid in Australia. Marat Safin, next up for Sampras in Saturday's semis, was on an American tennis tour with a bunch of Russian prodigies.

They all watched Sampras win the Open that summer, thumping Agassi in a straight-sets final, riveted by the emergence of new blood. "These are the two guys I idolized growing up," Hewitt said after beating Tommy Haas yesterday. "Love watching those guys play, Grand Slam finals and stuff like that over so many years."

"Classical," said Safin, anticipating the event, without knowing how right he'd be.

Agassi had tortured himself running Las Vegas hills and whipped himself into the best shape of his life. Agassi would admit he was no beacon of dedication for a bunch of those years and nobody's role model either. His long road to the Arthur Ashe Stadium was as different from Sampras's as their respective playing styles—the aggressive baseliner against the hammer of serve-and-volley—which they would cling to so brilliantly all night.

In their private over-30 division, the oldest men of the Open had to inspire the young ones. ■

after a final 30-second warning to the Romanian. This disqualification set off an even louder disturbance from the spectators, some of whom ran onto the court.

With the match now totally out of control, Blanchard asked Hammond to leave the chair for the first time in his 32-year umpiring career, a decision that Hammond later called "ludicrous."

The tumult began after McEnroe broke for 2-all in the third set with a running forehand pass down the line. Nastase lingered in the backcourt, and Hammond began his warnings. After the point penalty, Nastase kicked over a cup of water and got into a heated argument with Hammond.

"I protected you as much as I can," Hammond said to Nastase, audible from the microphone in the umpire's chair. "You play tennis like everyone else." ■

BELOW: *Pete Sampras hugs Andre Agassi after winning the U.S. Open Men's Singles championship in 2001.*

Louis Defeats Schmeling with First Round Knockout

By **JAMES P. DAWSON** | June 23, 1938

THE EXPLODING FISTS OF JOE LOUIS CRUSHED Max Schmeling in the ring at the Yankee Stadium and kept sacred that time-worn legend of boxing that no former heavyweight champion has ever regained the title.

The Brown Bomber from Detroit, with the most furious early assault he has ever exhibited here, knocked out Schmeling in the first round of what was to have been a 15-round battle to retain the title he won last year from James J. Braddock. He has now defended it successfully four times.

In exactly two minutes and four seconds of fighting Louis polished off the Black Uhlan from the Rhine, but though the battle was short, it was furious and savage while it lasted, packed with thrills that held three knockdowns of the ambitious

ex-champion, every moment tense for a crowd of about 80,000, one of the largest in boxing's history.

They paid receipts estimated at between $900,000 and $1,000,000 to see whether Schmeling could repeat the knockout he administered to Louis just two years ago, or whether the Bomber could avenge this defeat as he promised.

Thrilling to the spectacle of this short, savage victory which held so much significance were a member of President Roosevelt's Cabinet, Postmaster General James A Farley; several governors, mayors, Representatives and Senators; judges and lawyers; doctors; stars of the stage and screen; and ring champions of the past and present—all assembled eagerly.

The Bell Tolls 10 Times for the Ring At Madison Square Garden

By **FRANK LITSKY** | September 20, 2007

FIGHTERS RETIRE. TRAINERS AND MANAGERS retire. But a boxing ring?

In a ceremony in Madison Square Garden's lobby, the Garden retired its 82-year-old ring. It is headed for the International Boxing Hall of Fame in Canastota in

> "The ring is dead.
> Long live the ring."

upstate New York, and a new and slightly larger ring will replace it.

The ring made its debut in 1925 for a light-heavyweight title fight in which Paul Berlenbach outpointed Jack Delaney, a French-Canadian born Ovila Chapdelaine, whose last name, to American ears, sounded like Jack Delaney.

It was used for title fights at Yankee Stadium and the Polo Grounds. In promotional stunts, it was set up for exhibition bouts in Times Square, on 125th Street and in front of the Nathan's hot dog stand in Coney Island. Joe Frazier—who defeated Muhammad Ali in the so-called Fight of the Century at the Garden in 1971—said he also boxed (but not hard) with his son Marvis in that ring once when it was set up on a street in Little Italy.

As far as the length of the battle was concerned, the investment in seats, which ran to $30 each, was a poor one. But for excitement, for drama, for pulse-throbs, those who came from near and far felt themselves well repaid because they saw a fight that was surpassed by few for thrills.

On the third knockdown Schmeling's trainer and closest friend, Max Machon, hurled a towel into the ring, admitting defeat for his man.

The signal is ignored in American boxing, and Referee Arthur Donovan, before he had a chance to pick up the count in unison with knockdown timekeeper Eddie Josephs, who was outside the ring, gathered the white emblem in a ball and hurled it through the ropes.

Returning to Schmeling's crumpled figure, Donovan took one look and signaled an end of the battle. Donovan could have counted off a century and Max could not have regained his feet.

Louis, in the records, will be deprived of a clean-cut knockout. It will appear as a technical knockout because Referee Donovan didn't complete the full 10-second count over Schmeling. But this is merely a technicality. No fighter ever was more thoroughly knocked out than was Max. ∎

"It was the best ring ever built," said Bobby Goodman, who promoted Garden fights for almost 10 years, "and we took care of it. We shined the posts, which were solid brass, and the television people yelled because there was too much glare."

The ceremony attracted a Who's Who of boxing greats and world champions: Joe Frazier, Emile Griffith, Bernard Hopkins, Buddy McGirt, Carlos Ortiz, and a score of others.

McGirt, 43, fought 25 times at the Garden (Tony Canzoneri holds the record of 29).

"That ring was the foundation of my career," McGirt said. "Most of my fights were here. The first time you're coming through that tunnel, knowing you're here in this arena with its history, you can't describe it. And I had to love it because I never got knocked out in it."

The only part of the old ring that will remain is the brass bell. Everything else will be gone. As the promoter Don King said: "The ring is dead. Long live the ring." ∎

LEFT: *Louis, right, and Schmeling, left, became very good friends outside the ring.*

Fireman Wins First Marathon

By **AL HARVIN** | September 14, 1970

GARY MUHRCKE, A 30-YEAR-OLD FIREMAN running for the Millrose Athletic Association, finished nearly a half-mile ahead of his nearest competition as he won the first New York City Marathon in 2 hours 31 minutes 38.2 seconds.

Finishing second over the 26-mile, 385-yard course laid out on the roadway of the park, which is closed to auto traffic but open to cyclists on Sunday, was Tom Fleming, a student at Paterson State College in New Jersey. His time was 2:35:34.

Of 126 runners who started in front of the Tavern on the Green at 11 a.m., 55 finished. The first 10 received wristwatches, the next 35 clocks and everybody who competed got commemorative trophies.

In addition Muhrcke, from Freeport, L.I., who finished 10th in the Boston Marathon three years ago, received a big trophy with a Miss Liberty atop holding a torch.

The lone woman in the race—unofficially—was Mrs. Nina Kuscsik. She went home empty-handed, having dropped out after the third circuit, covering 14.2 miles in 1:39. Her husband, Richard, did not finish either.

"I wanted to finish very badly," said Mrs. Kuscsik, who completed the Boston Marathon in 3:11 unofficially earlier this year. "But I had a virus earlier this week and I just couldn't. I can't accept any awards and, by dropping out, I avoided any problems with the A.A.U. [Amateur Athletic Union]."

Moses Mayfield of Philadelphia, running unattached, led on every lap, but started to feel dizzy on the last. He fell behind and finished eighth in 2:49:50.

"This is a nice, easy course," said Mayfield, who finished 23rd in the Boston Marathon. "I don't know why I got dizzy. I'm in very good shape. I'm going to a doctor to check it out."

"I knew Moses was going to fade," said Muhrcke. "He always starts fast. I passed him around 90th Street with about three miles to go." ∎

A Marathon Turns Into a Sprint; Kenyan Wins It By Just a Step

By **JERÉ LONGMAN** | November 7, 2005

AFTER RUNNING 26 MILES WITHOUT DECIDING yesterday's New York City Marathon, Paul Tergat of Kenya and Hendrick Ramaala of South Africa began a grimly beautiful sprint to the finish.

With grand desperation, the two men ran shoulder to shoulder for the final 385 yards in Central Park. Tergat, the elegant world-record holder, clenched his teeth in frantic determination, while Ramaala, the defending champion, opened his mouth wide as if to shout or to gulp for oxygen to fuel his tired legs.

Tergat drew ahead, then Ramaala, two exhausted men running at top speed, or whatever speed they could summon after more than two hours in the heat and humidity on a course made rugged by hills and bridges. Even with 25 yards left, there was no clear winner, only a great struggle between two men who would deliver the closest race in this marathon's 36-year history.

"It's not nice," Ramaala, 33, said later of the pained stretch run. "You don't enjoy it."

Race Becomes More Than An Annual Event

By **GLORIA RODRIGUEZ** | November 3, 2003

THOSE WHO LIVE BY BEDFORD AVENUE AND South Fourth Street in Brooklyn had their 11th-mile welcoming all set for the New York City Marathon runners yesterday. Salsa music blasting from a top-floor window filled the street, volunteers lined up to hand out water and spectators held up signs for the runners.

"Victoria, the runners," Maria Molina told her 5-year-old daughter, who sat in a small lawn chair, as the first female runners passed.

For Molina and others who live nearby, the marathon is more than an annual event. It has become a neighborhood tradition. Several of her family members gather every year to hand out water and cheer on the runners. Molina's mother makes chicken soup and hot chocolate for the neighbors, and they play the salsa music from Molina's home.

"It is something we grew up with," Molina said. "It is something we do every year. It is part of our neighborhood."

Melissa Gonzalez, 20, has been volunteering at the water stations on Bedford Avenue

> "It is something we do every year.
> It is part of our neighborhood."

since she was 7. Gonzalez's grandmother, who died two years ago, first signed her up as a volunteer. Gonzalez said the marathon played a big role in the neighborhood.

"You see more and more people coming out to help," she said.

Mayra Laro tried to give the runners strength with oranges. For the third year, Laro offered the runners sections of oranges from the sidewalk. She stood with her 2-year-old daughter and her 5- and 11-year-old sons by South Sixth Street. She woke up early yesterday to cut 75 oranges.

"I like to help them and I want my children to continue the tradition," she said in Spanish. "Maybe in the future they can run in it, too." ∎

On and on they ran, one man unable to separate himself from the other. In the final yards, Ramaala gave a hopeful lunge, leaning for the tape more like a sprinter than a marathoner, but he had begun to stagger, and in that last moment, after all those miles, Tergat crossed the line first in 2 hours 9 minutes 30 seconds. A stride behind, Ramaala reached the finish officially one second later and collapsed to the pavement in heartbreakingly narrow defeat.

"I know the feeling," Tergat, 36, said, having lost the 10,000 meters at the 2000 Summer Olympics in Sydney, Australia, by nine-hundredths of a second, caught at the tape by Haile Gebrselassie of Ethiopia. Afterward Tergat consoled

Ramaala against despondency, telling him: "Take it easy. This is sport."

The victory would prove as redemptive as it was exhilarating for Tergat. Although he holds the marathon world record of 2:04:55, set in Berlin in 2003, he has known a career of aching defeat. Twice he finished second on the track to Gebrselassie at the Olympics and three times he had to settle for the runner-up spot at marathons in London and Chicago.

Tergat's exact clocking was 2:09:29.90; Ramaala's exact time was 2:09:30.22. Meb Keflezighi of the United States took third in 2:09:56. Another naturalized American, Abdihakim Abdirahman, took fifth in 2:11:24. It was the first time since 1993 that two Americans finished among the top five men in New York. ∎

All Around the Town

neIGHBORHOODS

Enough generalizing about how New York is big, which it is. Or crowded. It's that too. Or noisy. Or impersonal, which it can be. New York's identity really comes from its neighborhoods, each a city-within-the-city, each distinctly different from the one a few blocks away, each with its own particularly character, tempo and history.

You'd never mistake Manhattan's Upper East Side, with its arrow-straight avenues and expensive apartment houses, for, say, Brooklyn's Ditmas Park, a low-rise world of Victorian homes and small storefronts. You'd know you were in Astoria, Queens, and not Brighton Beach, Brooklyn, because you'd hear Greek on the

▲ PAGE 429

streets of one and Russian on the streets of the other.

Over time, some neighborhoods disappeared: the parts and repair shops of Manhattan's Electronics Row were demolished in the 1960s to make way for the World Trade Center. Some neighborhoods were redefined by highways that sliced through after the houses in their path had been condemned and torn down. Some neighborhoods emerged and took on a new personality when they were suddenly exposed: the removal of Manhattan's elevated railways in the 1940s and 1950s let the sun shine in on Third Avenue, on Sixth Avenue (later renamed the Avenue of the Americas but still called Sixth Avenue by nearly everyone) and on Ninth Avenue.

Some neighborhoods were made to order: Battery Park City in Lower Manhattan was laid out according to a 1960s blueprint for a "comprehensive community." So was Riverside South, the development in the West 60s and West 70s that replaced an abandoned railroad yard. You may not like the tallish, boxy buildings that Donald J. Trump and his partners built there, but they define a neighborhood—even if it remains emotionally distinct from the rest of the Upper West Side.

Most neighborhoods are not like that: they are a hodgepodge of the old and new. In the 1990s, Woody Allen and his neighbors on the Upper East Side fought plans for an apartment tower, claiming that a structure so tall and modern should not be squeezed between their low-rise townhouses and 1920s apartment buildings. The city agencies eventually approved a compromise plan for a somewhat shorter tower—but even now, some cannot walk along Madison Avenue without complaining that it blocks the sky.

All this is evidence of one constant in the life of every neighborhood: the internal change that is a sign of a large, living city that often seems to be at war with itself. That has been a characteristic of New York since the days when most of Manhattan was farmland. Rundown neighborhoods get gentrified—that's one way of putting it. Another way is to say that dilapidated buildings get renovated, but only after longtime tenants have been thrown out. And they cannot afford the post-makeover prices. So the old residential neighborhoods become peopled by other people. Go away for a couple of years, and stores that once had mainly Jewish or Italian customers now cater to Muslims.

Old boundaries blur: Chinatown spilled into Little Italy and has now all but taken it over. What was Williamsbridge in the

Bronx has become Wakefield. And don't confuse Williamsbridge with Williamsburg, the Brooklyn neighborhood where former factories became lofts for artists. The hipsters call it Billburg.

People now live, shop and dine expensively in Manhattan's meatpacking district, once a no-man's-land of grimy ware-

houses and butcher shops. Converted factories in Queens and Brooklyn have been remade as apartment houses—a sign of the economic tide that swept inland from the Hudson River and the East River, eliminating more than 16,000 longshoremen's jobs in the mid-1950s.

New neighborhoods have invented new names for themselves, funny-sounding acronyms: SoHo, NoHo, Nolita and Dumbo— for South of Houston and, obviously, North of Houston; North of Little Italy; and, in Brooklyn, Down Under the Manhattan Bridge Overpass. Those and other

neighborhoods become fashionable after being ignored for years—Chelsea, for example. It went from rundown to chic in the 1980s and, starting in the 1990s, added "high culture" to the upscale mix with art galleries. So did the Flatiron District, in the wedge-shaped shadow of the Flatiron Building.

▲ PAGE 412

That neighborhood's identity has become so much a part of the city's consciousness that real estate agents no longer bother to advertise apartments there as "near Gramercy Park." And nowadays prices on the Upper West Side are higher than the Upper East side which used to be the most fashionable, most expensive slice of New York. Thanks to long tradition and fairly tight zoning restrictions, there are still no big stores on Park Avenue between 59th and 96th Streets (and only a handful of small ones). But maybe it's only a matter of time.

Greater New York, Now the Second Largest City in the World

May 9, 1897

THERE IS ALREADY A PUBLIC PARK AREA OF nearly 7,000 acres in the five boroughs, with elaborate plans of park extension under consideration in Brooklyn and Queens.

No consolidation with sister communities was needed to make New York an imperial city. With her unsurpassed location, a constantly decreasing death rate, a population that nearly touches the two million mark and $4 billion of wealth, she already wears royal honors. So great is she, indeed, that she is obliged to submit to a division under the new scheme and go piecemeal into greater New York as the two boroughs of Manhattan and of the Bronx.

Here is a city containing already 6 square miles of territory, 102,000 buildings, 1,560,000 inhabitants, 750 miles of streets, 575 miles of sewers, 5,000 acres of parks, and a water supply of 300,000,000 gallons per day; a city illuminated nightly by 40,000 lamps (gas and electric) and protected by 5,000 policemen; and a city in which the street railways carry 1,370,000 passengers each day.

> But the new municipality
> is more even than that.
> It is about 32 miles long and
> from 12 to 18 miles in width,
> containing about
> 360 square miles of territory;

But the new municipality is more even than that. It is about 32 miles long and from 12 to 18 miles in width, containing about 360 square miles of territory; a municipality including the five boroughs of Manhattan, the Bronx, Brooklyn, Queens, and Richmond; a municipality containing a population of 3,312,000. In this great new city there are 54 jurisdictions of sufficient importance to have a federal postmaster. There is an aggregate tangible wealth of real and personal property amounting to $4,560,000,000. There is a waterfront of nearly 300 miles—this is in reality a city on the ocean. No such exposure to outside attack has ever before been made by a great and rich city. ■

ABOVE: *The Brooklyn Eagle Almanac celebrates the consolidation in 1898.*

Celebrating a Century Of Uneasy Unity

By **DOUGLAS MARTIN** | May 4, 1997

THE MAYORS OF BROOKLYN AND NEW YORK vetoed the idea, only to be overridden by the State Legislature. Preachers in Brooklyn railed against it. The State Senate defeated it, then changed its mind.

Clearly, the welding of the modern New York City from more than 40 local governments a century ago was not easy. But as the city begins a yearlong 100th birthday party for itself, there is a strong view that it was historically inevitable. Ruth Abram, president of the Lower East Side Tenement Museum, sees the creation of the new city as a direct reaction to social, political and economic strife that had torn America since the Civil War.

"This deep-seated yearning for union may explain why the opponents of the consolidation of New York simply could not prevail," she said.

To be sure, there are other views, not the least being that consolidation represented a last-ditch effort by the ruling elite to cement its power in the face of waves of immigrants. But the importance of Gov. Frank S. Black's signature on what is known as "Chapter 378 of the Laws of 1897," a three-inch thick document dated May 4, 1897, is incontrovertible. It redefined New York from being just Manhattan and the Bronx, both then part of New York County, to include the other three boroughs—Brooklyn, Queens and Staten Island—which had been separate.

The effect was an unprecedentedly large city of 359 square miles, one whose population had instantly rocketed to 3.4 million from 2 million. Only London, of all the world's cities, was larger. Chicago, proudly resurgent after its 1871 fire, no longer threatened to become the nation's first city.

"Consolidation is a tame word for such a magnificent moment," Robert A. Caro, the historian, said. "What we're celebrating is the moment the city received critical mass."

To celebrate that moment, there will be museum exhibitions, lectures, seminars and an official tourism campaign. The Convention and Visitors Bureau has created a logo and plans a national ad campaign for "New York History Year," and Mayor Rudolph W. Giuliani boasts that the celebration comes at a time when New York has bounced back, citing lower crime and increased tourism. "This is a very wonderful time for the city," he said.

But plans for a performance of the "Jubilee March of the Greater New-York" by W. C. Parker, believed to have been performed only once, have been reluctantly postponed until Jan. 1, 1998, the centennial of the date on which consolidation became effective.

"Put it this way," explained Schuyler G. Chapin, commissioner of cultural affairs and former general manager of the Metropolitan Opera. "The piece cannot be learned overnight." ∎

BELOW: *The completion of the Brooklyn Bridge opened the way for the 1898 consolidation.*

Living Where So Many Do Business

February 3, 1929

FEW OF THE SOME 500,000 PEOPLE WHO pass daily through the business area of furthest downtown New York realize that aside from its 9 to 5 o'clock dwellers it has approximately 12,500 permanent residents. The tip of Manhattan was and is a community settlement. Its borders still embrace the nation's first port of entry, the city's seat of government. Now as then, printeries, taverns, fish markets, warehouses, law offices, hospitals, shops, recreation centers, mingle oddly together, combining their varied interests into a composite whole. The old village today is as truly an integral unit of community life and purpose as it was in its yesterdays—that yesterday in 1661, for example, when the first ferry piled the North River to Jersey City.

As world problems became intense and complex, even so did life and conditions in far downtown. In 1915 the Bowling Green Neighborhood Association was formed. It was pledged to attend to the "social and health problems of the district." The association outgrew its quarters at 45 West Street and in 1926 moved into its new home at 107 Washington Street, whence it reaches out to serve not only the 12,500 permanent residents, but some of the 500,000 business "dwellers."

Clinics have been established, and Public Health nurses literally "feel the pulse" of the neighborhood. Through them the association learns the needs and wins the confidence of the population. Daily they come into intimate contact with the families of the district, acting as the messengers of science and guiding the busy mothers in the application of its principles. Last year nurses made 4,500 visits to the homes in the district. ▪

BELOW: *Downtown Manhattan today.*

Near Ground Zero, A Mixed-Use Revival

By **PATRICK MCGEEHAN** | September 9, 2007

SIX YEARS AGO, IN THE AFTERSHOCK OF THE terrorist attack that reduced the World Trade Center to a smoldering pile, local officials wondered whether people would want to live or work around the financial district again.

Today, as new residents fill converted office buildings and jam the raucous block party that erupts nightly on Stone Street, the more likely curiosity about Lower Manhattan is: Where did all these people come from, and how can they afford to live here?

Despite the slow pace of reconstruction at ground zero, the area below Chambers Street is humming with activity, much of it designed to appeal to the well-heeled professionals who are transforming the neighborhood. Already, it has added hundreds of condominium units and hotel rooms, a thriving restaurant row, a private school charging $27,000 a year, a free wireless Internet service, a BMW dealership and an Hermès boutique.

Downtown: Not Just Wall Street

By **MURRAY SCHUMACH** | April 29, 1971

EVERY WEEKDAY, FROM EARLY MORNING until mid-afternoon, a minibus leaves Beekman Downtown Hospital to pick up the elderly and infirm for treatment from Chinatown, Little Italy and the Spanish and Jewish areas of the Lower East Side.

And any time there is a serious emergency south of Canal Street—fire in a skyscraper, accident in a subway, clashes at City Hall—patients wind up in the emergency ward of Beekman.

To millions who live in and around the city, or come as tourists, the downtown area is a place to work or gawk. But to Beekman, the only hospital between Canal Street and the Battery, this area is a neighborhood.

For sheer contrast there are few sections in the world like lower Manhattan. It has Wall Street and street vendors; the sailing vessels of the past at the South Street Seaport Museum and batteries of the latest computers; the world's greatest complex of banks and a sprawl of low-cost housing. It has colleges, hot-dog carts, historic churches and stores that sell anything from electronic parts to exotic fish.

Since 1960, the area's resident population has jumped from about 20,000 to more than 30,000. Ambitious plans by the state and city provide for low-, middle- and luxury-income housing in Battery Park City that will raise the resident population to 100,000 during the 1980's.

The working population is already about 460,000, according to the Downtown-Lower Manhattan Association, with the World Trade Center still incomplete.

"It has been estimated," said a man at the City Planning Commission, "that if everyone working or living in the area came out on the street at the same time, they would be standing two-and-a-half persons on top of one another all over the place."

But residents find the area has its advantages. Those with city, state or federal jobs in the vicinity of Foley Square, or with private jobs in the financial district, can walk to work. And security measures in the South Bridge Mitchell-Lama cooperative are extraordinary. Every tenant has an identification card as well as keys. A security guard is at every door and the doors are locked from 6 p.m. to 6 a.m.

"I was living in the Village," said Zelva Rogers, who was moving in the other day. "It was a tiny studio apartment. Here I'll have three rooms and a terrace. And this is a fascinating area." ▪

"There were very few who would have predicted that Lower Manhattan would have rebounded as quickly as it has, despite all of the false starts and delays and emotional overlays," said Carl Weisbrod, president of Trinity Real Estate and former president of the Alliance for Downtown New York.

But the rebound has left some downtown merchants with mixed feelings. Karena Nigale has found the new financial district to be more attractive as a place to run a business, but less affordable as a place to live. Since 9/11, she has opened two hair salons within a few blocks of the New York Stock Exchange.

Ms. Nigale lived above her first salon until the din from carousers on the street below, along with a rent increase of more than 30 percent, drove her out. "I need two bedrooms, and there's nothing for less than $4,000 a month around here," said Ms. Nigale, who moved to Jersey City with her 11-year-old daughter.

Her business, though, is thriving. Her customers all have "big watches, expensive handbags," and no qualms about the cost of her services, she said. ▪

Reporter Tours Through the District Where Conditions Are the Worst

June 13, 1908

MRS. MEYER FRANKEL, WIFE OF DR. FRANKEL of 248 East Broadway, both of whom are members of the Children's Relief Committee, which is providing a free meal each day to any child at the lunchroom at 106 Canal Street, took a reporter from The Times on a tour of the Lower East Side yesterday. A Jewish family occupying two rooms at 21 Forsyth Street was the first visited.

They were the Sluzkins, the mother a widow, with three children and an old grandmother. The mother, the only breadwinner, is a firemen's nurse when she is well, but she was lying ill in a bed by the window in the living room yesterday. The children were playing.

A respectable looking neighbor came in to help in explaining their situation. "What have they to eat?" she said, repeating a question. "Nothing at all. I believe that is half the cause of the mother's illness, and they are not able to pay their rent, and I suppose they will have to go."

The children have gone to the lunch-room for one meal a day since it was started on Tuesday.

Louis Adler is a tailor at 53 Orchard Street who has been out of work for months. "It is $7 a month that I pay for my rent, and my landlord is a good man," he said. "He takes $2 or $3 when I can give it to him. But now it is two months and a half that it is not paid. He says that there are many who do not pay, and he can wait no longer."

Mrs. Frankel said that lack of work caused by hard times was responsible for much of the destitution.

"I know a number of traveling men," she said, "who bring in orders that give this part of the city much of its work. They went out this spring, but came back with practically no orders, and that meant no work. I know factories where 700 persons are usually employed, but where they are laying off 20 and 40 at a time now." ▪

BELOW: *Orchard Street on the Lower East Side in the early 1900's.*

Trendiness Among The Tenements

By **JOSEPH BERGER** | September 2, 2004

H. ECKSTEIN & SONS WAS NOT QUITE AS much a fixture of the Lower East Side as Guss's Pickles or Yonah Schimmel Knish Bakery. Still, Brenda Zimmer spent much of her life there, haggling with customers in the cramped and hectic cloth-ing store on Orchard Street that her family owned, hanging on until it finally shut its doors in 1998.

When she told friends a few years ago that her daughter, Amy, a 28-year-old Yale graduate and freelance writer, was moving into one of the neighborhood's storied tenements, "they looked a little shocked," she said.

"Everybody spent their lives trying to get out of there, and my daughter is trying to come back," Mrs. Zimmer said.

Ethnic Groups Disputing Plans For Lower East Side

March 12, 1980

THE SWEET SMELL OF EARLY MORNING baking drifted through Edna's Delicatessen on the Lower East Side as Edna Leib, who was a refugee from postwar Europe, put down a tray of hot noodle pudding.

"If they build more low-income housing it will kill the Jewish community here," she said, looking out at four blocks of decrepit houses and vacant lots.

A short distance to the north, Juan Otero waited for customers behind stacks of yucca and plátanos at La Borinqueña Meat and Vegetable Market. "Without more low-income housing," he said, "the Spanish people here can't survive."

The rapid changes in a neighborhood famous as the squalid foothold for immigrants just off the boat have produced more than a few such expressions of astonishment. There are still many people around who were glad to escape the neighborhood when the old life seemed to be seeping out of it more than a half-century ago. Some of them are now wonderstruck as their adventurous children and grandchildren return.

Mrs. Zimmer seemed tickled that her daughter had actually settled a few blocks from where Amy's grandfather was born and where Mrs. Zimmer worked full time for 15 years. Sure, only a handful of the wholesale and retail stores were still around. But the neighborhood had once again quickened to life, something closer to the bustle of the days when the walk-up tenements were teeming and the dowdy stores drew shoppers from all over for their Sunday bargains.

"Now it's exciting," Mrs. Zimmer said. "It's prestigious to live there." ∎

The land between Mrs. Leib and Mr. Otero is the focus of an emotional dispute, soon to be heard by the Board of Estimate, over housing, jobs, ethnic origins and the future of a neighborhood that has long been known as a first home for immigrants in America. Through the years, as community groups fought over whose project would be built, the site has been dormant.

A group of mainly Hispanic organizations wants low-income housing built on the site. A coalition of Jewish organizations wants a shopping mall, to create jobs. And a Chinese-American social service agency wants a project to house some of the thousands of elderly Chinese workers living in tenements a few blocks away.

All three are preparing for a battle at the Board of Estimate over a proposal by City Hall to give each group at least part of what it wants: 100 units of low-income housing, a 150-unit project for Chinatown's elderly and space for new businesses on a strip of land along Delancey Street between Essex Street and the approach to the Williamsburg Bridge. The Koch administration says the plan offers the best hope for resolving a 15-year-old issue that has grown out of decades of ethnic change in a once predominantly Jewish neighborhood.

The United Jewish Council of the Lower East Side, its offices on a block where 13 brownstone synagogues stand shoulder to shoulder, opposes the compromise plan. It wants to see built an enclosed three-block shopping mall, which it says would earn the city more than $1 million a year in tax revenue and create hundreds of jobs.

"You have to build something to keep the young people and the middle-income people here," said Mrs. Leib, whose delicatessen on Grand Street faces the site. "If you build more low-income housing, the young people leave and the neighborhood is gone." ∎

The Artists' District of Last Resort

By **GRACE GLUECK** | May 11, 1970

HUNDREDS OF PEOPLE HEARD A JAZZ CONCERT on Wooster Street over the weekend, watched Eddie Johnson build a cardboard sculpture in Greene Street, and visited 20 artists' lofts on West Broadway. The more adventurous walked through a water fountain hitched to a fire hydrant and basked in a "fog-light-sound" environment by Bill Birch.

These, and nearly 100 other loft and performance events, were part of a three-day festival that flowered in the dingy blocks of SoHo, the burgeoning artists' community in downtown Manhattan.

SoHo's name does not derive from the Soho section of London, but instead from South Houston Industrial District, the City Planning Commission's one-time designation for what was originally the nation's leading red-light district.

Today, although its 50-odd blocks are sadly dilapidated, it is a virtual outdoor museum of cast-iron architecture, extensively used here in the 1860's for elegant commercial buildings. But Many SoHo residents object to the name, suggestive as it is of the grubby Bohemian district in London that the area here does not resemble.

"It's just another example of the American inferiority complex about European names," grumbled Ivan Karp, a former uptown art dealer who recently opened a gallery on West Broadway. As a name for the neighborhood, Mr. Karp prefers Hell's Hundred Acres, a sobriquet that the area apparently once bore because there were so many fires there.

Whatever its designation, SoHo is a kind of last resort for artists, the only area left in Manhattan where the loft space they need is still available at reasonable rates. But because the City Planning Commission has zoned it for light manufacturing only, they live there illegally. They do not get such city services as garbage collection, and they are constantly in conflict with building and fire regulations.

And the artists have cause to worry about their future in the neighborhood. Some real estate developers would jump at the chance to replace the buildings with profitable high-rises. And some would like to see the entire area razed for middle-income housing.

"Right now, the best thing we can do is to leave SoHo the way it is," said Mike Levine, the young planner in charge of Greenwich Village for the Planning Commission. "The artists are an extremely vital cultural industry." ∎

SoHo Grows Up Rich and Chic

By **FRED FERRETTI** | October 12, 1975

ONLY A FEW YEARS AGO, SOHO WAS A PLACE where artists wandered, uninvited, into Larry Poons's loft for his weekly anybody-drop-in party. Nowadays, the social scene there is a great deal less casual. More characteristic, perhaps, is Robert Rauschenberg, wearing suits made entirely of sewn-together neckties, giving a chic by-invitation-only party for Princess Christina of Sweden—with salmon flown in fresh from the fjords—to the delight of such guests as Henry Geldzahler, August Heckscher, Robert Scull and other uptown culture mavens.

This change in party style is expressive of SoHo's transformation from a low-rent district for artists to a playground of uptown chic. Ten years ago, for $100 a month, artists could live and work in 2,500 square feet of high-ceilinged lofts in this area south of Houston Street. Today, SoHo is no longer cheap. Lofts are co-op apartments which sell for as much as $150,000 to doctors and psychoanalysts.

Still Surviving After All These Years

By JENNIFER BLEYER | February 18, 2007

SOHO SHED ITS PERSONALITY AS A GRITTY industrial neighborhood inhabited primarily by artists years ago, but a few redoubts of the old SoHo remain. A handful of artists who settled the neighborhood back in the 1970's are still here: in the spacious, sunny lofts they bought for a song, or the rent-stabilized apartments they have managed to hang onto. Though not necessarily famous by the art world's standards, they continue to live and work in the same neighborhood in which they came of age creatively.

Some artists have stayed and accommodated themselves to the changes in their district—in fact, some say they like the diversity of the "new" SoHo—but others have fled, believing that SoHo is on its way to becoming another Greenwich Village, possessing a tradition of art but producing little worthwhile art, becoming a stage on which other aspects of culture ape the visual arts that inspired them.

Says artist Paul Harbut, "SoHo can't be isolated just for artists. It's sad. You just can't preserve it as an artists' neighborhood . . . the artists have become cynically promoted. They've become technocrats, and the galleries lean to those painters who produce work done with a saleable technique."

Roy Lichtenstein's Guggenheim Museum poster sells for $15 in Poster Originals— another uptowner now downtown—but it's $500 signed. And dealer Ivan Karp, in his O.K. Harris Gallery across the street, offers a set of four photo-offset reproductions of artists in his stable for $275, framed, to the tourists awed by his Warhol Campbell Soup wall hanging. ∎

One is Sal Lindsay, a 4-foot-11-inch-tall, 69-year-old, talkative firecracker, who moved to SoHo in 1971. Her loft, which occupies the entire 12th floor of a building on lower Broadway, is carved into a maze delineated by old bookshelves, antique bureaus and slabs of stained glass that she salvaged from a church in Turtle Creek, Pa. To the left as you enter is her studio, with tubes of oil paint lined up on a table and bright, gauzy portraits on the walls.

She still has a sense of ownership of the streets. "Those of us who've been here since the beginning still think of it as our neighborhood, our lofts," she said the other day as she sipped English tea at her kitchen table.

Though most of her friends don't live in SoHo anymore, a few do. She belongs to a painting group that includes two other longtime SoHo artists, and they gather monthly at one or another's studio to drink wine and assess work. Sometimes they talk about the neighborhood and its old bohemianism.

> "Those of us who've been here since the beginning still think of it as our neighborhood."

"When Bloomingdale's opened up across the street," Ms. Lindsay said with a laugh, "I said the neighborhood is going to the dogs."

Another SoHo pioneer is Dominick Di Meo, a self-acknowledged recluse who makes complicated, silvery mixed-media reliefs and sculptures, often imprinted with a repeated image of a face with its mouth agape. He came to SoHo in 1974, but he did not immediately love the neighborhood.

"It's nicer now that most of the artists have left," he said. "Artists are prima donnas, you know." ∎

TriBeCa Follows SoHo, Gingerly

By **LAURIE JOHNSTON** | August 25, 1977

"TRIBECA ISN'T SOHO, BUT YOU'LL NOTICE there are fixture fees for even those 'loftments,'" said the apartment-hunting young artist, who was really not speaking in tongues. "From what I've seen, though, a lot of places down here will never get a C. of O. to qualify for a J-51 from the city."

That's the way they talk these days in TriBeCa—the unofficial name for the Triangle Below Canal Street (pronounced Try-beeka by logic, Try-becka by custom, and as rarely as possible by many residents, who call it "a real-estate word" and prefer to say that they live "downtown").

The Manhattan race for space, which opened up the SoHo loft area south of Houston Street for artists' living—and soon overpriced it for most of them—is now transforming TriBeCa, the 40-square-block area that begins somewhat south of Greenwich Village and extends nearly to the World Trade Center. Unlike SoHo, TriBeCa's newly legalized conversion for living is not limited to artists.

Philippe Petit, the mime, lives in a building that is dominated by the World Trade Center towers that Mr. Petit high wire-walked between in 1974. David Forman, a rock singer-songwriter, is another tenant there. TriBeCa's "loft people" also include Twyla Tharp and Kel Takei, dancer-choreographers; Betsey Johnson and Rosanna Polizzotto, fashion designers; and James DeWoody, painter, and his wife, Beth Rudin DeWoody, a filmmaker and daughter of Lewis Rudin, the real estate executive.

The area was New York's Les Halles for more than a century. It was a commodity market and a cornucopia of fresh food and exotic delicacies. Now, however, the rush is on to convert TriBeCa's sound-but-seedy commercial buildings into residential-priced rental lofts or cooperative apartments.

"It still feels like Little Old New York but not for long," said Jim Moore, a partner in the mime studio where Mr. Petit rents part of the living space. The 10-story building has been sold to a real estate broker who wants the occupants, now paying $325 to $400 in commercial rent, to buy their 2,100-square-foot as a cooperative at $45,000 each. He and Mr. Petit and the others are looking, not very optimistically, for a building they could still get for a down payment of $10,000 each.

"A lot of new tenants are pretty naïve," said Amalie Rothschild, a filmmaker and member of Community Board 1. "They don't even know they're being exploited until it's pointed out to them." Barry Chusid, partner and co-loftholder with Rosanna Polizzotto in a business called Garbo Garbs, put it more bluntly.

"These people," he said, "come down here looking for living lofts and wearing a sign that says, 'Hi! I'm your newest sucker. Take me for a ride.'"

Residential Real Estate—TriBeCa Is the Priciest Neighborhood

By **DENNIS HEVESI** | May 17, 2002

A ZIP-CODE BY ZIP-CODE ANALYSIS OF THE New York real estate market shows that TriBeCa, with its apartments converted from expansive lofts, was the highest priced residential neighborhood in Manhattan last year. Apartments there were on average about 50 percent more expensive than those in the neighborhood that might have seemed like the obvious choice, the Upper East Side.

What a Difference 38 Years Makes

By **DAN SHAW** | October 14, 2007

IN 1969, WHEN VINCENT INCONIGLIOS MOVED to a loft on Gansevoort Street in the meatpacking district, it was a no man's land. "People did not believe you when you told them where you lived," he said.

Now, 38 years later, he cannot believe that his once-obscure neighborhood is a destination. He is dumbstruck by charter buses that deposit tourists to shop at the designer boutiques and dine at the trendy restaurants. Like other artists of his generation, Mr. Inconiglios, 61, had ventured into the grimy meatpacking district in search of cheap studio space. "Originally, there were five of us who shared a floor," he recalled. "We paid $50 apiece."

Mr. Inconiglios now has two floors, each about 2,000 square feet. He won't say how much rent he pays now, but he considers it something of a miracle that he has managed to hold on to his lease for all these years.

The lofts were raw, and the upgrades were often improvisational, like a dropped ceiling made from old canvases a former tenant left behind. The utilitarian metal shower stall in Mr. Inconiglios's bathroom is a reminder that the term "luxury loft" used to be an oxymoron. Two or three decades ago, the neighborhood was defined by something quite different.

"You could smell this neighborhood," he said. "You could feel the air. You'd walk down the street and smell pickles. That Italian restaurant down the block was a pickle factory. An importer of Spanish melons was downstairs, and he would leave the spotted ones they couldn't sell out on the street, and I'd take them home. And there were big barrels of bones on the street because there was meat everywhere and men in bloody white coats." He knew how to spot potential trouble: "If you saw a group of guys in white coats and sneakers, you knew they were not butchers but thieves because the butchers always wore heavy boots." ∎

While apartments in TriBeCa were the most expensive, the highest average price per square foot remained on the Upper East Side, in the 10021 ZIP code, where it was $856.

The survey, conducted by Jonathan Miller, president of the Miller Samuel appraisal company, looked at the co-op and condominium market in 35 of Manhattan's 43 ZIP codes through a total of 7,787 closed transactions, based primarily on public records and reports from managing agents. For the entire borough, the study found, the average sales price was $785,753.

In TriBeCa, the average price was $1,638,811, 53 percent higher than the $1,070,897 average price on the Upper East Side. ∎

BELOW: *The Meatpacking District has become a popular nightlife destination.*

Greenwich Village Attracts Investors

By **LEE E. COOPER** | October 31, 1940

GREENWICH VILLAGE, A RATHER INACTIVE neighborhood during the worst years of the Depression, is again attracting investors. Two sales in that colorful old residential section of Manhattan emphasized the attention being paid to buying opportunities there.

Both of the transactions involved corner apartment groups on West Tenth Street in the Village. An investing client of Charles R. Faruolo bought through the Duross Company the five five-story tenements at the northwest corner of Hudson and West Tenth Streets, in the first change of ownership of the property since 1889.

The buildings accommodate 82 families and 8 retail firms, and are reported fully rented, bringing in about $20,000 annually. The assessed valuation is $156,000, of which $98,000 is on the land. The sale was made subject to a first mortgage of $60,000 held by the Bank for Savings. The seller was the estate of Frank E. Schaeffer, who was a well-known builder in his day and who erected the houses there 51 years ago.

The two six-story apartment houses at 211-15 West Tenth Street, at the corner of Bleecker Street, were purchased by the Georgecrest Estates Corporation from the Exposition Realty Company. The buildings contain 44 apartments and 7 stores. The location is one block from Sheridan Square, in the heart of the Village, and within a stone's throw of the former Schaeffer property. The buyers paid cash above a first mortgage of $150,000. ■

BELOW: *Pedestrians pass outdoor diners at a corner restaurant at West Fourth and Perry Streets, in the West Village in 2007.*

"Village" Named A Landmark

By **MAURICE CARROLL** | April 30, 1969

WITH A QUOTATION FROM HENRY JAMES ON the charm of the neighborhood, the Landmarks Preservation Commission designated Greenwich Village as a historic district yesterday.

"It has," Mr. James wrote in "Washington Square," "a kind of established repose . . . a riper, richer, more honorable look . . . the look of having had something of a history."

To help maintain that comfortable look, the commission will have to approve building owners' exterior alteration plans in an area north and west of Washington Square. "The Landmarks Preservation Commission," said Harmon H. Goldstone, chairman, "will now be responsible for guiding the hand of hundreds of property owners. Each exterior alteration or addition—no matter how trivial in itself—can just as easily be made an asset to the community instead of a detriment." ■

Next Stop, the West Village

By **GERRY SHANAHAN** | September 23, 2007

LIKE ANY OTHER REAL NEW YORKER, I HATE to leave the apartment. But I must, of course, to go to the job, restock the cupboards and walk the dogs.

Once I'm out, though, it's not that bad, because I step out onto Perry Street in the West Village, on the block between Bleecker and West Fourth Streets, which the city's Landmarks Preservation Commission described as "a delightful and interesting street" when it designated the Greenwich Village Historic District in 1969 and protected more than 2,000 historically significant buildings. This clean, tree-lined stretch of Perry is still delightful and interesting and, thanks to the commission, still residential, intimate and human in scale.

Over at No. 66, a stately Italianate brownstone from 1866, another busload of tourists is taking turns posing for pictures as they sit on the high stoop. They're on the daily "Sex and the City" Tour ($37 each), and these are the very steps that Carrie Bradshaw ran up and down at her apartment, which on the show was supposed to be in the East 70's.

I mention this not because Villagers like to show off, which we do, or because our geography is a fetish, which it is, but to illustrate why we Villagers are the hardest working tribe in New York.

"Yo," I say as I pass them, "You know this house is from the 1800's, and so are most of the others on the street. If you like No. 66, check out the brownstone at No. 70, the best on the block, French Second Empire. Look over there —there's a Beaux-Arts, and over there, a bit of Romanesque Revival."

They appear unimpressed, but I've just performed one of the labors that come with being a Villager: imparting Village lore to everyone and anyone.

A friend walking with me on, say, Bedford Street, will hear, "That's the oldest house in the Village that's still standing, from 1799" (No. 77). On Grove Street, it's "They say John Wilkes Booth plotted Lincoln's assassination here" (No. 45). On Bank Street, it's "Here's where Lauren Bacall lived when she was crowned Miss Greenwich Village 1942" (No. 75).

Small-town chauvinism? Fact, or myth and exaggeration? In the Village, we mix it all together and call it history. If you want to be here, be prepared to take on the unpaid job of learning it, repeating it, and along with the buildings, preserving it. It falls to us Old Villagers to keep the neighborhood's reputation alive, handing down the oral history so the Village will forever be remembered as the one true American artistic and intellectual bohemia, the place from which every American enlightenment sprung: Beatniks, sexual freedom, Abstract Expressionism, gay lib, women's lib, folk music, counterculturalism and so on.

Picketing one another is also a job that regularly falls to the guardians of ZIP code 10014. The Greenwich Village Society for Historic Preservation led the protests at Julian Schnabel's old home at 360 West 11th, which is just past where the 1969 landmark district ends. Mr. Schnabel had decided to cash in on this decade's real estate market by adding an 11-story condo tower. It is Pepto-Bismol pink. The historic society moved quickly to extend the landmark district and put the kibosh on a Miami-on-Hudson, which I support, of course.

The impetus for residential towers here was the pair of 16-story green-glass ones on Perry at West Street designed by Richard Meier. If you live in the towers, you can get room service. After a hard day of picketing and preserving, there is no more delightful and interesting place around to have a drink than at Perry Street.

Quite a few times, I've secretly wished that I lived in that tower. Please, please don't tell the historic society I said that. ∎

Chinatown Leaps Into Little Italy

By **FRED FERRETTI** | July 13, 1980

WHEN FORMAL FUNERALS WIND SLOWLY through the narrow streets of Little Italy these days, with the trumpets and drums of the Bacigalupo Funeral Home on Mulberry Street mournfully playing "Rock of Ages," more likely than not the cars in procession are filled with Chinese. Perhaps nothing else is quite so symbolic of what that patch of Lower Manhattan called Little Italy has become.

It may be Little Italy to city planners and to the few Italian-Americans for whom it is still home, and the unbroken ranks of restaurants along Mulberry may present a facade that is solidly Italian, but Little Italy is in fact rapidly disappearing as New York's historic Italian enclave. Many of the Italians have now moved to the suburbs or to Bensonhurst, Brooklyn. And the Chinese are rapidly buying in.

> One realtor estimated recently that within the 37 square blocks of Little Italy, Chinese own 70 percent of the buildings.

The newcomers are not from Canton, the origin of the early Chinese arrivals, but from the north, from Shanghai mostly, and from Taiwan. It is these newcomers, with fresh money, who have made the Chinatown-Little Italy area an investment boomtown.

One realtor, John Zaccaro, estimated recently that within the 37 square blocks of Little Italy, Chinese own 70 percent of the buildings.

They are buying those buildings for enormous prices with money that has lately come from Taiwan and Macao. The relatively new Golden Pacific National Bank on Canal Street is a reportedly a haven for Taiwan funds. At least one building in Chinatown, the glass-faced square at Mott and Chatham Square, reportedly was built with gambling proceeds from Macao's casinos and dog tracks.

Says Mr. Bastiano, "The attitude here was, the buyers would say, 'I'll buy anything'; the seller would say, 'Whatever you offer, I'll take.' And it usually was a lot more than the market value." ∎

Plans to Rebuild Chinatown And Two Other Slums Started

By **MILTON M. LEVENSON** | May 25, 1950

THE FIRST ACTUAL STEPS TOWARD REBUILDING three major slum areas in the city are being taken. Within five years Chinatown is to be changed from a quaint city landmark of 25,000 cramped residents into a sunlit, park-filled area retaining aspects of Chinese life such as "pagoda-touched" architecture, according to proposals made by State Housing Commissioner Herman T. Stichman. Three projected housing projects are expected to cost $20 million.

At a meeting in the Chinese Public School at 64 Mott Street, Mr. Stichman told representatives of Chinatown that its "living conditions are a reproach to the city." He cited the lack of private baths in 1,784 apartments out of 2,502.

He promised every aid in keeping Chinese characteristics in the new "village." But he declared also that others than Chinese would live in the new houses because discrimination would not be permitted. ∎

Where All Sojourners Can Feel Hua

By **JENNIFER 8. LEE** | January 27, 2006

THERE IS NO CONSISTENT NAME FOR "CHINA-town" in Chinese. Newspapers use one name, popular speech uses others. At the Canal Street subway station on Broadway the chosen translation is delicately pixeled together from colorful tiles: "huabu." Hua means "Chinese," but with a sense that transcends geography and has nothing to do with the nation of China. Bu means "place" or "town."

For all the trips my family took to Chinatown when I was growing up, I never knew that Chinatown was known as huabu until I saw the characters after the station renovation. Hua is the distilled essence of being Chinese, free of fissures caused by wars and colonization. You can be hua even if you hold a passport from Singapore, the United States or Peru. You can be hua even if you have never set foot in China and don't speak a word of Chinese.

Like many Asian professionals who came after the 1965 immigration reforms, my parents were liberated from the confines of working-class, Cantonese-speaking Chinatown by education and English. My family, like other Chinese who live abroad, are often called huaqiao, Chinese sojourners, as though one day we all might return, pulled back by the tentacles of Chineseness. In the meantime, huaqiaos seek and create Chinatowns. And New York has three—one each for Manhattan, Brooklyn and Queens, though only the original can claim the name. Since the 1980's, Flushing has flourished as the Chinatown for Mandarin speakers from Taiwan, Shanghai and northern China. More recently, Manhattan's working-class Chinese population has been squeezed down the N subway line to Sunset Park, Brooklyn, and other satellite clusters farther out.

Today Chinatown is large enough to have two main arteries: Canal Street, the tourist-friendly thoroughfare that is still predominantly Cantonese, and East Broadway, which has become Main Street for

BELOW: *Shops along Broadway in Chinatown.*

Fujianese immigrants. My Chinese friend Charlene (who went by the English name "Beryl," assigned by a middle-school teacher, until I pointed out that "Beryl" was out of date, and renamed her) agreed that East Broadway looks like China. Charlene, origi-nally from Xian, now a graduate student at Syracuse University, was in the city for a visit.

Charlene, raised in the north, didn't want the southern Chinese food all around us. She wanted hotpot, a festive Chinese dining ritual where food is tossed into a pot of boiling water.

So off we went to Flushing. First we bought Xinjiang-styled lamb kabobs on Main Street for $1. "Do you like America?" we asked the vendor, who had come from the western Chinese city of Urumqi on the Silk Road. "I like American money," he said. But he would never raise his kids here—he doesn't like the values.

We trudged to Minni's Shabu Shabu, a hotpot restaurant off Main Street. Charlene ordered the thin slices of lamb, which she flash-cooked in the hot water; I ordered fish balls. It was definitely hotpot as an American experience, she observed. In China, everyone would use one big boiling pot, mixing their food together. Not here: "Each person has their own hotpot." She had been lectured on American individualism in college and smiled at this simple example. ■

A Block of Gardens Is Refuge From the Busy City

By **PHYLLIS EHRLICH** | October 23, 1959

BENEATH THE HARD SURFACE OF MANHATtan's sophisticated life exists another kind—family life in small, closely-knit neighborhoods. These areas are becoming scarcer because of the push for space by huge apartment houses and office skyscrapers.

Among such neighborhood cases still in existence is one of brownstones on the Upper East Side. In this "family block," residents center their interests on parental duties, the children's well-being and informal social activities— despite their own busy, sometimes glamorous lives.

"One of the enchantments of our neighborhood is the reassuring sight of the children playing happily together," says Mrs. Al Hirschfeld, wife of the artist. The Hirschfelds, who are the parents of a 14-year-old daughter, Nina, have lived in the area for 11 years. Mrs. Hirschfeld is Dolly Haas, the actress.

Several families have converted their gardens into practical playgrounds, with swings, slides, seesaws and similar equipment. Sometimes a mother, such as Mrs. Vincent Sardi Jr., wife of the restaurateur, finds herself in the family playground with her own four children and six or eight others.

One mother, originally a Californian, is a firm believer in the outdoors. In fair weather, she and her husband pitch a sleeping tent in the yard for their sons. Because friends sometimes spend the night with her children, this mother also has some sleeping bags to accommodate the overflow of young "campers."

And Mrs. William Riva (Maria Riva, the actress) has an unusual way of calling her youngsters for meals when they are playing in other yards. "I find a blast or two on an old ship's whistle brings them home quickly," she says. ∎

Prewar Housing Aplenty

By **MICHAEL STERNE** | November 18, 1984

OTHER NEW YORKERS' REASONS FOR NOT living on the Upper East Side say something about what it is and is not. Some prefer the less buttoned-up atmosphere of Greenwich Village. Others like the melange of ethnicities to be found on the West Side, or the opportunity to live an alternate life style afforded by SoHo, or the sense of the city's ongoing history to be had in such older parts of town as Murray Hill and Brooklyn Heights.

The primary advantage of the Upper East Side is this: Along Park and Fifth Avenues and on the cross streets is clustered the city's largest stock of luxury-class prewar apartment houses. Prewar is the essential characteristic. Almost nothing built since the 1930's affords the same amenities—large rooms, high ceilings, windowed kitchens and baths, redundant closets, working fireplaces.

Single-family town houses still exist, with prices in excess of $1 million, but they have a major drawback. They cannot be left alone for a weekend without risking a burglary. The Upper East Side is a prime target.

A stroll on Madison is a window shopper's delight, and you can drop in at the Whitney, the Metropolitan, the Asia Society, the Frick Collection and the New York Society Library.

It may not be apparent to outsiders, but the Upper East Side is a church- and synagogue-going community. These institutions, surprisingly, find themselves increasingly dealing with the problems of the poor, and recently established the Neighborhood Coalition for Shelter. It serves homeless women who have been drawn to the neighborhood by its relatively safer streets, which is one of the reasons the rich people live there. ∎

UPPER east SIDE

Reluctantly Embracing The Upper East Side

By **LYNN ERMANN** | November 11, 2007

FOR YEARS, I LIED ABOUT WHERE I LIVED. At parties in neighborhoods like Williamsburg or the East Village, I would pretend that the apartment I occupied on East 74th Street actually belonged to my grandmother, not to me. New acquaintances would nod sympathetically at my sad predicament, at my being forced to live on the Upper East Side.

The truth, too shameful to admit, was that in 1995, at age 24, I bought an apartment in a neighborhood that I and everyone I knew considered bland, conformist and kind of a bore. My friends came up here only to be hospitalized or to visit their parents or grandmothers.

I grew up on the Upper East Side. By the time I returned to the neighborhood after college, big-box stores had taken over 86th Street and everyone I knew, all my artist and writer friends, lived below 14th Street. I did, too—for a while—until my parents' requirement that I live in a doorman building made it cost-prohibitive. So I relented and rented a tiny studio in a boxy postwar building near Second Avenue on 79th Street. I felt isolated.

Just as I was planning my escape, I came into a small inheritance from Grandma Eva, enough to buy an apartment. My eagle-eyed parents saw a real estate listing for an apartment in a doorman building on a street that Sue, my real estate savvy stepmom, knew well.

"You can sell it in a few years and buy a bigger place in another neighborhood," she said reassuringly.

I agreed, reluctantly, to what I considered to be a minor detour on the way to my dream apartment. When I moved in, J. G. Melon was still there, in a tenement painted forest green, with its trademark two-story-high neon sign anchoring the block. It was full to capacity every night.

Six years after my arrival, I realized that my apartment was between two disparate Upper East Sides: the one my parents had lived in—the one offering services and affordable restaurants—and the one around Fifth Avenue that my Grandma Bea had inhabited, which is the one I associated with snobbism.

Now I also saw the beauty and surprising quirkiness of the Park Avenue side.

It is the mix of town houses and prewar and postwar buildings that makes the Upper East Side so singular. I was surprised by how varied the town houses were, that one with a Greek Revival facade might be right next to a stately brownstone. A Federal-style clunker is smack up against a lighter-than-air Italian villa.

In early 2005, the man I had been dating and I decided to get married. It was time to find that bigger place in another neighborhood. We scouted around near his apartment in Harlem and in prewar apartment buildings east of Third where the prices were lower and the ceilings higher.

We hit an unexpected hurdle: Board approval anywhere would be near impossible since we're both freelancers. So Jonathan and I stood in the foyer of the 74th Street apartment and asked: Can we make this work?

On a wall in the living room, adjacent to the window, we installed a long, narrow mirror to reflect the view of water towers and rooftop gardens, of town houses and tenements, of pre- and postwar brick apartment buildings, the singular skyline of our Upper East Side. ∎

BELOW: *Townhouses on East 82nd Street between Madison and Park Avenues.*

Rising Fear
On Upper West Side

By **LAYHMOND ROBINSON** | June 25, 1964

FOR THOUSANDS OF NEW YORKERS, MAN-hattan's Upper West Side has become a "fortress of fear," a survey reveals.

Apprehension over frequent muggings, thefts, robberies and other forms of violence cause many residents to "seal themselves in at night" and not venture outdoors after dark.

"It's like a combat zone," reported Joseph Lyford, who has been conducting a two-part survey of the West Side for two years for the Fund for the Republic. He said that "more than half of the people polled were tremendously worried about muggings, theft and other types of violent crime."

The part of the survey conducted by the John F. Kraft public opinion organization, which involved extensive interviews of 200 whites, 157 Puerto Ricans and 44 Negroes in a 40-block area, showed that more residents felt the police were doing a good job than not.

"Their chief complaints," Mr. Lyford said, "were that there were not enough policemen, that they were not around when you needed them. But there was very little mention of police brutality."

He and Jefferson Berryman, vice president of the Kraft organization, said the survey also showed the following:

• That Puerto Ricans, who make up 39 percent of the 60,000 inhabitants of the 40-block area, were establishing a "stable, healthy community and were moving toward a middle-class economy."

• That Negroes, who make up 11 percent of the area's population, had no roots in the community and were largely "drifters or transients" on their way to other communities.

• That the Puerto Ricans, most of whom had moved into the survey area from nearby neighborhoods, were less satisfied with such city services as streetlighting and garbage collections than were the Negroes, who had generally come from Harlem, or the whites, who had been there for many years. ▪

On the Job On
"Nannies Row"

By **WILLIAM E. GEIST** | October 17, 1984

IT WAS "WESTWARD HO!" THE STROLLERS ON A warm, sunny October morning. The babies were out in force on the Upper West Side, rolling along the sidewalks on nearly every block and converging at 83rd Street and Riverside Drive.

Most of the strollers were propelled by hired help down the hill and into the playground in Riverside Park known locally as "Nannies Row." There lurked Susan Pierce. She does not consider herself a nanny-napper, but she was prepared to kidnap a nanny if need be.

With something of a baby boom in the neighborhood, and with mothers scurrying back to their careers, nannies are in great demand. Miss Pierce, a 32-year-old mother, was there to ask if they knew of anyone to watch her 4-month-old daughter, Sarah, when Miss Pierce returns to work. Implicit in her generous offer was the suggestion that they might want to leave their employers.

Marjorie, a nanny who was watching Jordan, 22 months old, toddle about, said there were more nannies than ever on Nannies Row, with new ones showing up every week. She said that nanny-nappers generally tried to lure them away with more money, better hours and less work.

Some of the nannies said the job had never been more demanding, what with a new generation of parents who have them taking children as young as three months to exercise, music appreciation, dance and art classes—as well as demanding plenty of "social interaction," which means setting up "play dates" with other children. "With a few of them," said Bea Newell, another nanny, "you really wonder why they bothered having children at all." ▪

Downtown's Uptown Suburb

By **AMANDA HESSER** | March 21, 1999

SANDWICHED BETWEEN FRIENDS IN A BOOTH at Lot 61 on West 21st Street, dressed in leather pants and Manolo Blahnik heels, Tait Chatmon took a moment to appreciate the view. "In one glance you have dreads, then you have lawyer types, then you have city kids, then you have bridge and tunnel," she said, dragging her finger across the room as if swiping icing off a cake. "I love it!"

That's what you get on a Monday night downtown, and that's why Ms. Chatmon and half a dozen of her friends make the trip down here. They come by car.

But they're not bridge and tunnel. They're from a part of Manhattan where strollers are more menacing than cab drivers, where the Gap is never more than a short walk from one's doorstep and an exciting cultural moment is the opening of a new branch of Gracious Home. The Upper West Side.

Ms. Chatmon and her friends—like many, many Upper West Siders in need of a style fix—shop everywhere but their neighborhood and do almost all their socializing downtown. The Upper West Side is their bedroom community, bridged to the city by the Nos. 1 and 9 local subway lines.

The Upper West Side has gone through phases. Once a literary and artistic haven of creative eccentrics and liberals, it became a swinging singles scene in the 1980's. But now its trendsetting appeal has eroded. Nearly everything that once gave the Upper West Side its quirky charm—from Shakespeare & Company books to Charivari, the clothing store—has been wiped out.

The triangle of real estate roughly defined by Zabar's, Lincoln Center and the Museum of Natural History is a style-free zone. In between the Nine Wests and the Eddie Bauers are countless restaurants, clubs and shops. Yet many who live there insist that there's nowhere to eat or go out to. At Rain, a Vietnamese restaurant, the droopy fernlike plants seem left over from the 80's. People who live on the Upper West Side get their hopes up with every new flurry of openings, often only to be disappointed. Recently, a dozen or so boutiques and restaurants designed to make the area more of a style destination have opened. The most sophisticated newcomer, Calle Ocho, serves Latin American fare, the cuisine of the moment, but in an oversize room teeming with Banana Republic émigrés. Balthazar it isn't.

Which is why many residents feel shame when confronted by someone who lives south of the border at Central Park South. When a young woman was recently at dinner with Adam Rapoport, an editor at Time Out New York magazine, who lives in the West Village, and mentioned that she lives on the Upper West Side, his response was typical. "I've heard of that," he said. ∎

BELOW: *Susan Lally walks her son Teddy to school in their Upper West Side neighborhood.*

How Harlem Became Big Time

By **MARY ROSS** | March 1, 1925

BLACK FINGERS WHIPPING FURIOUSLY OVER the white keys, beating out cascades of jazz; black bodies swaying rhythmically as their owners blow or beat or pluck the grotesque instruments of the band; on the dancing floor throngs, black and white, gliding, halting, swinging back madly in time to the music— this is the Harlem of the cabarets, jazz capital of the world.

Downtown specialists who have wearied of the tricks of Broadway come northward to this new center of pleasure. In some of its 15 cabarets black and white eat together, dance together in the rich abandon of the race which evolved that first jazz classic, the Memphis Blues; which refined the cakewalk into the fantastic fling of the "Charleston."

Fifteen years ago Harlem looked much as it does today on the surface—a prosperous district north of Central Park, with brownstone houses bordering the broad streets, with "new-law" tenements, costly churches, magnificent avenues. Originally a Dutch village, it had become in turn predominantly Irish, then Jewish and Italian. About 1904 a few negroes began to trickle in east of Lenox Avenue. The district had been overbuilt, and a negro real estate operator, Philip A. Payton, offered to fill the vacant houses with self-respecting negro tenants. There was first organized opposition by the whites, then a panic which left rows of houses vacant. If one negro family moved into a block, every one else moved out.

With the war a black tide of laborers rolled in from the South and the West Indies to the metropolitan district, where work was waiting at wages beyond their rosiest dreams. The white resistance in Harlem broke.

And then those negroes, who were earning big money for the first time in their lives, bought the real estate of Harlem, which in the war slump could be had at prices far below their actual value. During the height of that fever it was no unusual thing to see a negro cook or washerwoman or workman go into a real estate office and plunk down $1,000, or $2,000, or $5,000 on the price of a house. Fifteen years ago there were only a few negroes in all Manhattan who owned real estate. Now it is estimated conservatively by John E. Nail, a negro real estate operator in Harlem, that the property owned and controlled by negroes in that district alone exceeds $60 million . ▪

The Harlem Renaissance

By **ISHMAEL REED** | August 29, 1976

IT WAS CALLED THE HARLEM RENAISSANCE because Harlem was where the action was. Some of the writers belonging to the movement didn't even live in Harlem. That didn't matter. Harlem became the symbol for the international black city. It was home of "The New Negro" (Uncle Tom and Sambo have passed on . . .) from the title of a book, compiled by Alain Locke, the brilliant Harlem Renaissance philosopher.

I still remember Langston Hughes, witty, such enormous sophistication behind that cigarette holder, inviting me for a drink at Max's Kansas City. He encouraged young writers even though, shortly before his death, he told Arlene Francis, on a radio show, that we were all downtown writing poems even we didn't understand. That was Langston Hughes, who wrote all day, breaking only for cocktails and dinner. The walls of his Harlem town house were covered with Afro-American cultural memorabilia, particularly from the Harlem Renaissance.

Recently, the Harlem Renaissance has come under fire. Some say the writers weren't

Mixed Feelings on 125th Street

By **TIMOTHY WILLIAMS** | June 13, 2008

IT ISN'T NEWS THAT UNTIL A COUPLE OF YEARS ago, Harlem had a paucity of bank branches and grocery stores, or that now that more affluent people have started to move there, upscale shops and restaurants have followed.

But change can have surprising results. Longtime residents have found themselves juggling conflicting emotions. And those who enjoyed a measure of stability in the old

militant enough. That they were writing for white people. Wallace Thurman was a novelist, playwright, screenwriter, editor, and publisher of a magazine called Fire, but some contemporary critics seem only interested in the quantity of gin he drank. There was that extraordinary statement printed in Black World, a literary magazine that recently ceased publication, the organ of Black Aesthetic criticism, which said that the Harlem Renaissance was part of a conspiracy to divert attention from the more militant figures of the time.

In other words, every time Cullen, McKay and Hughes wrote a poem they thought, "How can I make this poem divert attention from the more militant spokesman of these times?"

Hughes, Cullen, McKay, Thurman and the others aren't here to defend themselves, but I'm sure that they would agree: That just as with airline pilots, teachers, students, advertising men, actors, carpenters, editors, publishers and cat burglars, you judge workers by the quality of their work, not by how much gin they drink, or how many men or women they kiss, or who their friends are, or which parties they attend, or whether they've successfully created a plan to end the world's evils, or have prevented the universe from collapsing. ∎

Harlem now long for the past—not necessarily because it was better but because it was what they knew.

"The majority of the stores, the 99-cent stores, they're gone," said Gwen Walker, 55, a longtime resident of West Harlem. "The bodegas are gone. There's large delis now. What had been two for $1 is now one for $3. My neighbor is a beer drinker, and he drinks inexpensive beer, Old English or Colt 45 or Coors—you can't even buy that in the stores. The stores have imported beers from Germany. The foods being sold—feta cheese instead of sharp Cheddar cheese. That's a whole other world."

Gentrification, it turns out, can have an odd psychological effect on those it occurs around. Almost no one is wishing for a return of row upon row of boarded-up buildings, the mornings when lifeless bodies turned up in vestibules or the evenings when every block seemed to have its own band of drug dealers and subordinate crackheads.

The neighborhood's devolution was so complete that between about 1960 and 1990, Harlem had lost a third of its population and half of its housing stock. In 1990, during the height of the crack epidemic, 261 people were murdered in the police precincts that cover Harlem. Last year, there were about 500 murders in the entire city.

Last month, the City Council approved another significant change: the rezoning of 125th Street to allow for high-rise office towers and 2,100 new market-rate condominiums. Earlier this year, the average price for new condos in Harlem hit $900,000, although average household income remains less than $25,000.

The Rev. Dr. Charles A. Curtis, senior pastor of Mount Olivet Baptist Church, one of Harlem's oldest black churches, said that people feel powerless when they see change that they believe is not intended to benefit them.

"There are great developments going on," said Pastor Curtis. "You can see things in your sight, but they're just out of reach." ∎

Puerto Ricans Remember When El Barrio Was Theirs Alone

By **ED MORALES** | February 23, 2003

EL BARRIO. IN MY CHILDHOOD ITS MERE mention conjured all kinds of feelings, from a kind of reverence for proud beginnings to my parents' wariness of its slow descent into hard times. It was a reference to a place that curiously seemed to belong to us. As more of us moved to various corners of the Bronx, El Barrio increasingly became the source of authenticity, like the bacalaltos (codfish fritters) on 116th Street that were the closest thing to what you could get on the island.

Today, although Puerto Ricans are still the city's most populous Spanish-speaking group—of the 2.2 million Latinos, 830,000 are Puerto Ricans—we can sometimes feel like an afterthought in the Latin New York we all but created.

And the Spanish Harlem of the mind, dotted with the world's greatest cuchifrito stands (fried Caribbean snacks) and old-school pirague ros (men who sell flavored ices from pushcarts) is threatened with extinction. The changing face of East Harlem is due not only to the real estate charge from south of 96th Street, but also to a surge of Latino immigrants. That new presence is personified by Valente Leal, a 14-year-old immigrant from Mexico who has lived in East Harlem for the past eight years.

Valente has a bushy spiked punk haircut, likes hard rock bands like Korn and Slipknot, is an occasional painter and wants to be a doctor. And Valente's got a theory about why so many people from south of 96th Street are moving in. "Ever since 9/11 there's all these people from downtown around here," he said, wide-eyed. "I think they got scared or something."

So, as the strip on Lexington between 104th Street and 96th morphs from Barrio to boho periphery, a loose confederation of mostly Puerto Rican politicians, activists and residents is trying to make a stand to preserve the area's Latino identity. Rafael Merino, a graphic designer who grew up on the Lower East Side and recently moved from Williamsburg, thinks what's happening uptown is bigger than mere nostalgia.

"It's not about Latinos losing El Barrio, it's about New York City losing El Barrio," said Mr. Merino, who lives on 116th Street. "This is one of those diverse gems that makes the city what it is." ∎

Harlem Altered By Public Housing

By **THOMAS W. ENNIS** | June 23, 1957

IN A MASS ATTACK ON ONE OF THE WORST slum areas in the metropolitan area, the New York City Housing Authority is leveling 137 acres of slums in East Harlem. Blocks of old, dark buildings have been ripped out. Structures worth saving have been left standing, as an invitation to rehabilitation by private enterprise.

Twelve projects, providing new homes for 13,500 families—some 53,000 people—are taking the place of decayed and overcrowded buildings. Most of them take in and consolidate two to six or seven adjacent city blocks, forming a superblock.

The housing authority finds that super-block projects make planning, construction and management more economical and efficient. In addition, the buildings can be widely spaced, exposing them to sunshine and air on all sides; and much of the open space between can be landscaped and part of it used for playgrounds and off-street parking.

Four of the 12 housing projects are forming a strip of superblocks between 112th and 115th Streets, extending from Lenox Avenue to Thomas Jefferson Park on the East River. ∎

Spanish Harlem

As East Harlem Develops, Its Accent Starts to Change

By **TIMOTHY WILLIAMS** and **TANZINA VEGA** | January 21, 2007

INSIDE A WOODEN SHACK IN A GARDEN ON East 117th Street, a group of Puerto Rican men, many of them in their 70s and 80s, is playing a spirited game of dominoes on a rainy afternoon.

Outside their little retreat, a thick dust, the pounding of hammers and the shouts of construction workers inundate the block, signaling the transformation of East Harlem, also known as Spanish Harlem or El Barrio (the neighborhood). Many see it changing from the Puerto Rican enclave it has been for decades to a more heterogeneous neighborhood with a significant middle-class presence, luxury condominiums and a Home Depot.

It is a familiar story of gentrification in New York City, but this one comes with a twist: the many newcomers who are middle-class professionals from other parts of the city are joining a growing number of working-class Mexicans and Dominicans.

The result is a high degree of angst among many Puerto Ricans, who worry they will be unable to prevent their displacement from a neighborhood that is far more than a place to live and work. "You have a choice, try to pay that rent, or move out," said Tony Ramirez, a plumber who has lived in East Harlem for 43 of his 47 years. "Puerto Ricans in El Barrio is like being extinct. None of the people I grew up with are around. People feel like strangers in their own town."

An illustration of his lament can be seen on several blocks of 116th Street, long Puerto Rican East Harlem's main shopping strip, which are now filled with shops selling Mexican food, flags and pastries.

In 1980, there were 856,440 people of Puerto Rican descent living in New York City, compared with 787,046 in 2005, according to census data. In East Harlem, the number of Puerto Ricans has also been declining, to 37,878 in 2005, from 40,542 in 1990, according to the census. They now make up

ABOVE: *One the big new developments going up above 96th Street in East Harlem.*

about 35.3 percent of the neighborhood's population, down from 39.4 percent in 1990.

The changes are unmistakable.

For decades, there had been no doubt about where the Upper East Side ended and East Harlem began: 96th Street, the last major east-west street before the start of East Harlem's clusters of high-rise public housing projects.

That demarcation line is softer now. Peter Lorusso, 25, who works for a shipping company, has lived for about a year in a 234-unit luxury apartment complex at 101st Street and First Avenue, where half of the units rent at market rates. He said the building is "an extension of the Upper East Side," where he and his friends go to "do the pub crawl."

"People are bringing more money north, which is a good thing," he said. "You just got to be street smart." ■

There'll Always Be a Brooklyn

By **ANNA QUINDLEN** | May 25, 1983

ABOVE: *Sunday at the Brooklyn promenade in 2002.*

IN FRONT OF A HOUSE ON LAFAYETTE AVE-nue in Bedford-Stuyvesant stands a magnolia tree as big as a brownstone. It is a magnolia grandiflora, and it usually grows nowhere north of the Mason-Dixon line.

Somehow, improbably, this tree has grown in Brooklyn for 100 years. It is no more likely that it will wither and die than that Cohen's Pharmacy, on a corner in the shadow of the Franklin Avenue Shuttle, will close down, or that Irwin Lefkowitz, whose grandfather drove a livery horse and carriage, will move his taxicab company from Bergen Street and Fourth Avenue, or that the red brick house in which the Patterson family now lives in Brooklyn Heights, built in 1832, will crumble to red dust on the quiet corner of Sidney Place and State Street.

There are a good many things like this in Brooklyn, things that last. Not all of them are bridges.

This is not to say that Brooklyn is just what it was. Mr. Lefkowitz works in Brooklyn, but like so many others he moved to what he calls "greener pastures" on Long Island. The Dodgers play in Los Angeles, despite the proprietary way people in Brooklyn still talk about them.

Changes have come to this borough of 80 square miles, which has either 2.25 million people if you believe the census, or 2.5 million if you believe the borough president, who in typical Brooklyn fashion says Brooklyn was robbed. But life in Brooklyn is the same song with new lyrics. The city of churches now has many mosques. There are immigrants living in three rooms with four children and two jobs—they are just different immigrants, from Poland in Greenpoint, from Russia in Brighton Beach, from the Caribbean countries in Bedford-Stuyvesant.

Bergen Street west of Mr. Lefkowitz's garage is a pastiche, part faded row houses, part handsome restorations, part sheets hung at windows, part lace curtains and antique brass doorknobs and knockers.

> "It'd take a guy a lifetime to know Brooklyn t'roo an' t'roo. An' even den, yuh wouldn't know it all."

"They want us to leave," said a grimy man drinking from a paper bag with some friends on the steps of one of the down-at-the-heels houses, "but we ain't leaving." It's the same old song, but with new lyrics. Thomas Wolfe once wrote: "It'd take a guy a lifetime to know Brooklyn t'roo an' t'roo. An' even den, yuh wouldn't know it all." ∎

The Great Awakening

By **SUKETU MEHTA** | June 19, 2005

AT A PARTY ON THE UPPER WEST SIDE IN 2000, a distinguished American author, a longtime Manhattanite, asked where I lived.

"Brooklyn," I told him.

He snorted. "Poor people live in Brooklyn." Then he turned away to get some meat.

Borough of Fear

By **EMANUEL PERLMUTTER** | December 7, 1966

AT A FIVE-HOUR CONFERENCE ON LOCAL crime, Brooklyn was depicted as a crime-ridden borough where women were afraid to visit their doctors at night, church services were not held after dark and merchants closed their stores early.

"To put it simply, our people no longer feel safe in the streets, at their places of business or even in their homes," said Borough President Abe Stark. "Our people feel they are going through a nightmare of violence and terror."

Mr. Stark and most of the 55 speakers urged the assignment of more foot patrolmen to Brooklyn as a way of curbing crime.

Police Commissioner Howard R. Leary said that the police were trying to do their best to cope with the problem. He said he hoped to release more policemen for foot patrol and that the scooter patrols would be increased from the present total of 150 to 500 vehicles.

"There are many things that the police can't help," he said. "These are the problems of poverty, lack of opportunity and poor education that lead to crime." Mr. Leary also asserted that recent judicial decisions that limit interrogations and confessions "make it difficult for the Police Department to be as effective as in the past." ■

Shortly after the party, to see if I could move from my rented apartment in Boerum Hill, I went looking to see what I could buy in a part of Fort Greene where cars parked on the street were still regularly stolen. I told the broker that it would be nice for my kids to have a house by a park. "We just sold a house by the park: $510,000," the broker said. But there was a catch. "It had no walls or ceilings."

What happened, I wondered, to the distinguished author's "poor people"?

It has become a cliché to say that Brooklyn is booming. Brooklyn now buzzes with a momentum that would have stunned residents of its sleepy streets not long ago. With 2.5 million people, it is bigger than San Francisco, Boston, Atlanta and St. Louis combined. The population is approaching the historic high of 1950, when Brooklyn was home to 2.74 million. Turn around, and you will see the renaissance.

The two boroughs with the most housing starts of late are Queens and Brooklyn. Why so many homes? Brooklyn's prime appeal is relatively low cost.

For me, Brooklyn became a neighborhood one steamy August night in 2003. It was the night of the great Northeastern Blackout. The streetlamps were out, and people strolled about with flashlights and lanterns. There was a bright white moon high above the city competing with the red glory of Mars, the warrior planet, which hadn't been so close to Earth in 60,000 years.

At midnight, the bars were still dispensing ice for our whiskies. We took our drinks out on the sidewalk; we'd make our own laws tonight. Everyone's face was illuminated in flickering, flattering light, and everybody looked beautiful, desirable. In the glow Brooklyn was revealed to be what we had forgotten it really is: an impossibly romantic, a 19th-century city. ■

BROOKLYN

Guarding the Charm of Long Ago

By **JOHN P. CALLAHAN** | December 2, 1956

"Outsiders" often speak with disparagement of Brooklyn as a hinterland—the home of raucous Dodger rooters, the place where comedians find inspiration for their characterizations of grammatical offenders. The 25,000 residents of the Heights are happy about this, and hope that nobody will try to change that opinion.

Much of the credit for not trying goes to a quiet but determined group of 1,200 citizens who are members of the Brooklyn Heights Association. It has been able to resist the commercial building and public housing pressures that threaten to break through the 100-square-block borders of the Heights.

A few of the former have succeeded, but only after they met architectural demands. An example was a chain grocery store that had to redesign its coldly utilitarian plans and construct a two-story colonial building.

> That pride of ownership
> should be reflected not only
> in one's own home,
> but in one's neighborhood.

The atmosphere of yesteryear lingers in the luxurious Georgian drawing rooms seen through windows with long lace curtains. It appears in the trim front-yard lawns behind low iron fences and gates that swing open to basement entrances. It is found, too, in the spacious red-block approaches to former stables where haylofts have been made over into rooms with a suggestion of French Provincial design.

When a Georgian Colonial on Columbia Heights was put up for sale a few years ago its owner found a buyer down the street who held it until recently, when the right kind of bid came in. Price was secondary, she said.

The important point was to find a buyer who felt as she and her neighbors feel about the Heights—that pride of ownership should be reflected not only in one's own home, but in one's neighborhood. ▪

Co-ops Lead the Latest Renaissance In Brooklyn

By **LAURIE JOHNSTON** | October 16, 1979

Two young lawyers, one from a Park Avenue firm and the other from Wall Street, talked jauntily as they headed home up Henry Street from the steamy subway station under the St. George Hotel in Brooklyn Heights. They had both bought floor-through, two-bedroom apartments in the same brownstone a year ago for $60,000 each, and had also paid part of the cost of conversion and renovation, but their maintenance was under $400 a month. "And already I could make a profit," one said.

They had found Brooklyn Heights rentals and co-op fees lower than comparable ones in Manhattan ("I'd say 20 percent lower," one said). But the young lawyers—both married and one with a small child—also knew that rental apartments on the Heights had been dwindling and, as a general rule, nonexistent for less than $600 or $700 for two bedrooms.

"With a big income, especially with two people in the family working," one said, "you'd better buy."

• • •

Brooklyn Heights is in the middle of another dramatic shift in economics and living arrangements, and the single-family-owned

From Afterthought to Sought-After

By JEFF VANDAM | October 22, 2006

IT IS UNCLEAR WHO FIRST STRUNG TOGETHER the words "Down Under the Manhattan Bridge Overpass" to form the acronym representing a tiny warehouse enclave on the Brooklyn waterfront—or whether there is

house may soon be about as rare as among the Canarsies who once lived there. The brownstone pioneers of the 1950's and 1960's, waving goodbye to their baby-boom offspring (and faced with inflated costs), are converting their houses into cooperative apartments for a "new class" of upscale, two-income, often childless couples.

"I feel sad to do it because it's making a different kind of neighborhood out of Brooklyn Heights—I'd like to see a family occupy our brownstone as we did," said Margaret Kenny, who with her husband, Jack, an airline pilot, moved into their former rooming house in 1959 with four young children.

Also being turned into co-ops for the affluent are a dozen once-chic or genteel residential hotels that gradually have slid into grimly seedy single-room occupancy. These conversions range from the beautiful, 10-story former Hotel Margaret, just above the harborside Esplanade, to the Queen Anne-style Montague on the Brooklyn Heights "main street" of the same name.

Some of the conversions will have fair-sized apartments but, as a well-known Heights resident put it, citing a once-private 51-room mansion that had been converted to 26 apartments, "the co-op studio apartment is becoming the luxury S.R.O. of the Heights."

"Owners of the old hotels, and often the brownstone-buyers, don't want to face the rising costs and regulations as landlords," the resident said, "so they dump it all on the tenants as a cooperative." ■

really even a Manhattan Bridge overpass. But such questions are passé in today's Dumbo, one of the most expensive and sought-after loft districts in New York, now buoyed further by a building miniboom bringing several hundred more apartments to its tiny market.

Starting in 1998 with the opening of 1 Main Street, known in the neighborhood as the Clocktower, a series of luxury conversions of Dumbo's iconic prewar commercial buildings has created a new neighborhood, one with million-dollar views and multimillion-dollar floor plans. Streets that ended at the East River with the Manhattan or Brooklyn Bridge looming above were barren five years ago. Now there is life on nearly every corner, with strollers and bicycles bumping along the Belgian-block streets, and aromas of eggs Florentine and shiitake mushroom ravioli spilling onto the sidewalks.

"You've got a massive influx of people coming in," said Arturo Torres, 32, a lawyer and mortgage company owner who moved to Dumbo with his wife, Jacqueline, in 2002. "There's a need for all these retail shops and restaurants. Four years ago, walking to the subway late at night, you weren't feeling too safe."

With Dumbo's old buildings already having made the transition to residential from bottle-cap or corrugated-cardboard manufacturing, it only remained for developers to pursue new construction in the area—which they are, in a big way.

Echoing the builders of 40 Wall Street and the Chrysler Building, who in 1929 engaged in a "race to the top," the developers of two Dumbo condo skyscrapers, J Condominium and the Beacon Tower, are neck and neck. Each tower is almost complete, and sales have already begun, with most unit prices beginning just under $1 million and edging upward. ■

Park Slope, Reshaped by Money

By **JIM YARDLEY** | March 14, 1998

BELOW: *A Park Slope stoop on Sixth Avenue.*

IN FITS AND STARTS OVER SEVERAL DECADES, Park Slope has become a laboratory for assimilation and gentrification. The Irish and the Italians once brawled on Fifth Avenue, followed by the Puerto Ricans, who elbowed into the mix. There were Jamaicans, and by the 1970's, the hippies had arrived, enticed by the lure of stately but inexpensive brownstones in need of repair.

With each successive layer, Park Slope's identity deepened as well: a self-consciously funky village-within-a-metropolis that embraced tolerance and diversity. But now, the Brooklyn neighborhood is enduring another wave of immigrants, a group that is regarded with more concern than any that came before: well-to-do people, many of them refugees from Manhattan.

"The death of a small neighborhood," complained Thomas Spennato, 47, a Park Slope native who owns Soundtrack, a compact-disc store. "Oh, yes, it is. It'll never be the Park Slope people grew up in. It's changing more like other neighborhoods."

This sort of angst is hardly new for either Park Slope or Brooklyn, where nostalgia is a cottage industry. But the latest real estate boom is unquestionably reshaping Park Slope. Brownstones are selling for seven-figure prices. The neighborhood's main commercial hub, Seventh Avenue, once known for its quaint, small shops, now boasts a Barnes & Noble, a Rite Aid and a Radio Shack. Rent increases in recent years have forced several small-shop owners to close or move out of the neighborhood.

Of equal concern to many Park Slope residents is a sense that the neighborhood's character, its granola-crusted soul, is under assault. Once, people in Park Slope scoffed at the commercialization of another bastion of liberalism, the Upper West Side. Now, a favorite pastime of weekend strollers along Seventh Avenue is examining the latest listings in the windows of real estate agencies.

The newest of the newcomers sometimes feel as though they're on a sort of neighborhood probation. Phil Battaglia, a lawyer who moved three months ago from Chelsea into an $825,000 Park Slope brownstone, said he noticed an initial wariness among some of his new neighbors, many of whom had spent decades restoring their homes. "They don't want a bunch of rich people coming in who just have the place and go away every weekend," he said.

Having moved to Park Slope in 1970, Rita Knox can compare her own evolution to that of her neighborhood. When she arrived, she drove a white Gremlin with a red racing stripe and taught English. Now, after first graduating to a Karmann Ghia, Ms. Knox drives a gold Mercedes-Benz and owns her own real estate agency. She has brokered many of the deals that have changed the face of Park Slope.

Ms. Knox is white and her husband is black, and she does not believe Park Slope is less tolerant or diverse than in the past. The changes, she said, are simply signs of maturity. "That's the evolution of a neighborhood," she said. "I would love to be 21 again, but we all get older. I'd like to have my Karmann Ghia again, but I don't think my back could take it." ∎

Has Billburg Lost Its Cool?

By **DENNY LEE** | July 27, 2003

HE LISTENS TO ELECTROCLASH MUSIC, HAS 40-plus pals on Friendster and creates art with discarded household paint under the moniker Scooter. So when James Edward LaForge made the big move to New York from San Francisco two years ago, there seemed to be only one choice.

"Williamsburg," said Mr. LaForge, a goateed 35-year-old whose arms are plastered with tattoos. "I wanted to check out the art scene and live in a large loft."

Through a lamppost flier, he found just that, a 2,000-square-foot apartment on North 11th and Berry Streets, in a grimy warehouse.

Mr. LaForge explored the cafe society of Bedford Avenue he had heard so much about. By day, he shared war stories with other hardscrabble artists over chai and iBooks. By night, he frequented the local bars, and groaned about Manhattanites who were crossing the East River and crowding his watering holes. Then the edginess started to dull. "It's a cool spot," Mr. LaForge said. "But you know what? It started to get too cool and too hip."

So Mr. LaForge turned his back on Williamsburg, swam against the current and landed on Avenue C, in the heart of the East Village. "As an artist, I feel more inspired here," he said. Another thought dawned on him as he unpacked that first night. "I felt like I had finally arrived in the city."

A smattering of recent statistics, combined with an increasing amount of anecdotal evidence, suggest that Mr. LaForge is among a growing number of hipsters who are making the reverse migration from Williamsburg, back to the granddaddy of counterculture and underground chic: downtown Manhattan.

Williamsburg is hardly over. Since the mid-90's, a growing number of fledgling galleries and fashionable boutiques have taken root where working-class ethnic communities once intersected. They offered something fresh and charmingly proletariat at the time when Manhattan seemed to fall under the spell of dot-com millionaires.

Robert Lanham, the author of "The Hipster Handbook," and the founder of a Webzine called Free Williamsburg, would seem like the last person to knock the neighborhood. But when Mr. Lanham, who has lived in Williamsburg since 1996, looks outside his window, he sees what he called the "paradox of hipster culture" slowly coming to an end.

"Williamsburg is having an identity crisis," Mr. Lanham said. "It's kind of absurd that these kids who went to fancy schools are dressing like they're construction workers. The struggling artist is a myth. Williamsburg is a pseudo bohemia."

Rather than stick around, Mr. Lanham has started an apartment hunt himself.

"I even looked at a couple of places in Manhattan," he said. "If I can find a nicer place with cheaper rent, I'll take it. I'll go wherever the best rents take me." ▪

BELOW: *Despite gentrification, South Williamsburg still has a large Yiddish-speaking Hasidic population.*

Growing Pains Come And Go in Bed-Stuy

By **MANNY FERNANDEZ** | July 27, 2008

DAKOTA BLAIR ACKNOWLEDGES THAT BOTH he and the apartment building where he lives are somewhat out of place.

Mr. Blair, 23, a software engineer from East Texas, pays $1,700 a month for a studio in what he calls the Yuppie Spaceship: a new luxury apartment building on an unluxurious corner in Bedford-Stuyvesant, Brooklyn. After nine months in the neighborhood, which New York magazine labeled the city's "next hipster enclave," Mr. Blair is considering moving out.

Even for hipsters, life in one of New York City's frontier neighborhoods—long-troubled places at the fringes of gentrification—can be anything but smooth, particularly in uncertain economic times. New residents like Mr. Blair have grown frustrated waiting for change to come to Bed-Stuy, with its high rates of crime and foreclosures, trash-strewn streets and limited nightlife. And the owners of businesses that have recently opened to cater to this new population wait, in turn, for a surge that has not yet arrived.

ABOVE: *Stuyvesant Heights is one of the four neighborhoods within Bedford-Stuyvesant.*

There used to be a 12-foot-wide, blue-colored mural at Myrtle and Nostrand Avenues, diagonal from Mr. Blair's building. The painting listed the names of neighborhood murder victims inside the chalk outline of a body.

Mr. Blair took a picture of the mural in January. The snapshot is already an antique: Someone covered it up with a thin layer of concrete, and now only one side of it remains, a tribute to lives cut short itself cut short. The half-covered mural is an apt symbol of Bed-Stuy: a changing neighborhood not quite changed, transforming not in broad strokes but in half-steps.

Mr. Blair is white. He said his decision to consider leaving had nothing to do with living in a largely black neighborhood. But he and other recent arrivals described being the targets of hostile racial remarks, isolated incidents that they said detracted from the positive reaction they received from others in the neighborhood.

Henry L. Butler, 41, a longtime Bed-Stuy resident and the chairman of Community Board 3, said the race of newcomers was not the issue. "It's about income," said Mr. Butler, who wants to see more housing that is affordable to working-class tenants. "I'm not looking to Harlemize Bedford-Stuyvesant." ∎

Brooklyn

Well, the Ices Are Still Italian

By **JOSEPH BERGER** | September 17, 2002

WHAT SAL CALABRESE HAS ALWAYS LOVED about Bensonhurst, Brooklyn, the city's largest Italian neighborhood, is that it provides the intimacies of a village.

"If I walk out," he said, "I will say hello to 15 or 20 people and they to me. 'Hi, Sal. How are you? How's your father?' Like the old days."

But Mr. Calabrese worries that Bensonhurst may soon lose the congenial feeling that comes from a place of common habits and pleasures. Bensonhurst is losing its Italians. According to the 2000 census, the number of residents of Italian descent is down to 59,112, little more than half that of two decades ago, and the departed Italians have been replaced by Chinese and Russian families.

Mr. Calabrese is part of that movement. His parents still live in the neighborhood and he runs a thriving real estate agency there, but three years ago he moved to Bedminster, N.J., to a 34-acre farm where he breeds Arabian horses.

Despite the reputation of immigrant groups for die-hard allegiance to old neighborhoods, what is happening, sociologists say, is the continuation of a trend that has been going on for several decades now: the children who grew up in the working-class and middle-class homes of immigrant neighborhoods are, like Mr. Calabrese, now professionals, managers and business people who want suburban homes with backyards of grass, not concrete.

In Bensonhurst, the Italian-American residents, who once passed houses on to their own relatives or those of their neighbors, are selling them to the highest bidders: Chinese moving up from nearby Sunset Park and Russians moving up from Brighton Beach.

And so they are adapting. Salvatore Alba, whose bakery has drawn long lines for its cannoli and cheesecake since his Sicilian parents opened it in 1932, has hired a Chinese-American woman to sell Italian ices.

"I figure if they can't speak English, we'll get someone to speak to them in Chinese," Mr. Alba said of his newer customers. ◾

BELOW: *Russian and Ukrainian men play dominos at Milestone Park in Bensonhurst, another sign that the neighborhood is now a multi-ethnic neighborhood.*

Growth of Queens Borough

By **WALTER I. WILLIS**, Secretary, Chamber of Commerce of the Borough of Queens | May 7, 1916

QUEENS WILL SEE DURING THE COMING year the start of the greatest real estate and building development that has taken place in that borough since it became a part of Greater New York, for trains will be running in less than six months on all the elevated extensions in Queens that are part of the Dual Subway System.

With a five-cent fare to Long Island City, Astoria, Woodside, Elmhurst, Corona, Woodhaven, Richmond Hill, Morris Park, Jamaica and other sections, Queens Borough at last will become a real integral part of New York City.

In addition to the development that will come from rapid transit operation, the greatest industrial development that possibly has ever taken place in any community has already started in Queens. New factories are locating on an average of at least one a week in all parts of the borough, bringing thousands of new employees who must be housed.

For the first four months of 1916, 20 new factories have located in Queens that will have more than 5,000 employees and require the erection of new factory buildings costing over $1 million. Not only are one- and two-family houses being constructed in great numbers, especially in the vicinity of the new Liberty Avenue and Jamaica Avenue elevated extensions to Morris Park, Richmond Hill and Jamaica, but the records of the Tenement House Department show that for the first quarter of 1916, there has been a great increase in the construction of tenements.

Is there another section in New York City, or, for that matter, any similar area, in the United States, with such a bright future ahead of it? Queens may well be called "the Borough of Magnificent Opportunities." Queens was never more prosperous, never more attractive for business development than it is today. Every indication points to a wonderful new era. ▪

If It Really Takes All Kinds, Queens Has What It Takes

By **MURRAY SCHUMACH** | March 2, 1977

QUEENS HAS SUPPLANTED MANHATTAN, Brooklyn and the Bronx as the city's most bubbly melting pot. And there is strong evidence that despite the decline of some neighborhoods in Queens and the tensions and hostilities inherent in shifting populations in other parts of the borough, the human melting pot is working better in Queens than in most other parts of the city.

"People think of Queens as Archie Bunker country because they watch 'All in the Family' on television," said Richard Gambino, professor of educational philosophy at Queens College and an authority on Italian-Americans. "But the truth is that almost all ethnic groups in Queens set along better than anywhere else in the city."

Borough President Donald R. Manes points out that all major ethnic groups are represented on community planning boards in the borough. "In that sense," he said, "they are working together. In general, they are living side by side in relative harmony."

More objective evidence is the following:

• In Astoria, probably the largest Greek community in the Western Hemisphere, about 15 percent of the Greeks are marrying Roman Catholics, Protestants and Jews.

One Borough, Many Flags

By **SETH KUGEL** | December 9, 2007

A LOT OF FOREIGN TOURISTS—AND THAT includes Europeans, Californians and Manhattanites—have had occasion to stick their toe into the borough of Queens. Perhaps it was a trip to the Museum of Modern Art, during its temporary relocation to Long Island City. Maybe a sari and samosa shopping trip to 74th Street in Jackson Heights. Or a pilgrimage to Sripraphai, the Thai restaurant in Woodside with legendary status among crowds that speak in phrases like "best fried watercress salad in the city."

But few put it all together and make Queens a destination. Part of the problem: Queens doesn't necessarily consider itself one destination, either. It was cobbled together in 1898 from different towns—Newtown, Flushing and Jamaica, for instance—and those towns still exist in postal addresses or residents' minds. And, though the diversity of its 2.2 million people (Uzbeks! Indonesians! Serbs!) is exhilarating, it can make the borough feel Balkanized, even in parts where nobody is from the Balkans.

It's getting there, though. As more Manhattanites snap up the relatively low-end real estate just across the East River, Queens is drawing visitors from Manhattan and out of town who suddenly realize that it is as close to Midtown as Brooklyn is to downtown.

The Modern went back to Manhattan three years ago, but Long Island City still maintains its identity as Queens's arts center. There's P.S. 1, the contemporary art museum affiliated with the Modern, two subway stops from the Modern, and included with your Modern ticket. Also in Long Island City, the peaceful Noguchi Museum and the Socrates Sculpture Park (fully outdoors, with views of Manhattan).

Another center of cultural gravity is near the end of the 7 line, in soccer-crazy Flushing Meadows Park. There, on what were the grounds of two World's Fairs, you'll find the Queens Museum of Art, whose signature exhibition is the Panorama of the City of New York, a scale model of the entire city. But the museum also includes the Neustadt Collection of Tiffany Glass, as well as exhibitions that reflect the international vibe of the borough. Those tugging along kids might opt for the New York Hall of Science instead; it's more hands on. ■

- In Laurelton, a federation of 180 block associations is making progress in building amity between blacks and whites.
- In Parker Towers, a high-rise complex in Forest Hills, one hears Hebrew, Japanese, Hindi, Chinese, Spanish, Russian, French, Hungarian and Turkish.
- In Flushing, the First Baptist Church conducts Sunday services in Chinese and Spanish, as well as in English, and a small supermarket is booming because it specializes in Chinese, Japanese and Korean foods.
- And in Elmhurst, where some portions have become shabby, newly arrived Hispanic people pouring into the area are forming political clubs and becoming increasingly active in the economic life of the community. ■

BELOW: *Roosevelt Avenue in the heart of another multi-ethnic neighborhood, Elmhurst, Queens.*

A Slice of Europe Near The East River

By **DEBORAH BALDWIN** | June 22, 2008

ABOVE : *A cluster of row houses on Ditmars Boulevard in Astoria, Queens.*

JUDITH KLEIN CAME FOR THE FOOD AND stayed for the kitchen.

A blogger by moonlight under the name Foodista, Ms. Klein was born in Slovakia and says that living in the culturally diverse Ditmars-Steinway area—near the Bohemian Hall and Beer Garden—makes her feel "very at home." Also nice: being able to gather provisions in this food-obsessed swath of Astoria and cook in a kitchen bigger than a bread box. "My friends who live in Manhattan are surprised it's so large," she said.

Matt Mahoney, another young commuter, described the area as "cheaper than Park Slope—and closer." After boarding the elevated N line—which starts on 31st Street, above Rosario's Italian deli and Choo-Choo's Chicken 'n Crepes—he gets to his office on West 57th Street in 20 minutes.

"Best food in the entire world, and every ethnicity is within a two-block radius," said Peter Vallone Jr., a councilman and third-generation resident.

Ditmars-Steinway is about 60 percent white, 20 percent Hispanic, 9.8 percent Asian and 1.4 percent black—and 45 percent foreign-born, according to a Queens College compilation of 2000 census data. Greeks colonized the area from the 1920's to the '60s, joining Italian, Irish and German immigrants. Today, "the schools record 118 nationalities," said George Delis, a former district manager for Community Board 1.

Despite an influx of "yuppies by the bushel," as the Greek-born Mr. Delis put it, the neighborhood is largely working class.

Despite its small size—just under two square miles—Ditmars-Steinway packs in five power plants, generating about 75 percent of the city's electricity. Add the planes at La Guardia and the traffic as prison employees drive on and off Rikers Island, and no wonder some call the neighborhood Asthma Alley. "It's not fair for one community to bear that burden," Mr. Vallone said, "and it's only going to get worse." Still, he says he wouldn't raise his own children anywhere else.

If Manhattan has high-rises and Brooklyn has brownstones, Ditmars-Steinway has one- and two-family red-brick row houses in a style that "I would characterize as nondescript," said Gerald Caliendo, an architect who works in the area. They have small yards and often contain rental units.

But the Victorian-era row houses on 41st Street are remnants of a village—complete with a school, church and post office—that William Steinway built in the 1870's for his piano makers (Steinway & Sons has had a factory in the neighborhood since 1870). At the top of 41st Street, overlooking Bowery Bay, is a 27-room mid-19th-century fixer-upper that was once the Steinways' country house. The current owner, Michael Halberian, puts it on the market periodically. He says he might part with it for $5 million. ∎

queens

Newcomers Help Push Up Prices

By **JEFF VANDAM** | August 21, 2005

THE EXHAUST-RIDDEN ARTERY THAT IS Queens Boulevard slices through the neighborhood of Forest Hills. But to step into its grand homes and apartment buildings is to forget the traffic and leave behind the ideas of what city living is like.

"You've got dense, populated areas if you're into apartment houses," said Kathleen Histon, district manager for Community Board 6 in Forest Hills. "Then you can walk a block or two and you have these lovely streets filled with beautiful Tudors."

And with a new luxury condominium tower rising above the neighborhood, the influx into Forest Hills from pricier parts of the city is beginning. Melanie Fox and her husband, Glenn France, married for three years, were renting in Clinton Hill, Brooklyn, when they wanted their own brownstone.

They began looking at up-and-coming areas of that borough like Bedford-Stuyvesant and Prospect-Lefferts Gardens, but found the competition too fierce. For one house, they were trumped by buyers bidding $200,000 over the asking price.

So when she and Mr. France, a specialist on the American Stock Exchange, accompanied some friends to explore real estate in Forest Hills, they were surprised at how nice everything seemed. They returned later for an open house at a three-bedroom town house on Fleet Street for $740,000, and soon after, they grabbed it.

Forest Hills is essentially split into three parts, each with its own distinct feel. The centerpiece is Forest Hills Gardens, a private community south of Queens Boulevard with security patrols, wide curving streets and stately houses, which are protected by alteration guidelines and an approval process similar to those in historic districts.

The grand entrance to "the Gardens," as everyone calls them, is Station Square, adjacent to the Long Island Rail Road station, which greets visitors with cobblestone streets, quaint shops and graceful archways. Continuing into the neighborhood, the confusing Queens street grid ends and is replaced by a web of shaded, pleasant roads with names like Slocum Crescent and Summer Street.

"It's serene," said Anna Pinto, who is raising her two children in the Gardens and works with Mr. Ambron at Madeleine Realty. "Most people who live in the Gardens don't want to leave the Gardens."

To the immediate west, the streets straighten out and take on an alphabetical order (Austin to Olcott). Row houses and stand-alone houses prevail, though on streets closer to Queens Boulevard some houses take on the grandeur of the Gardens.

North of Queens Boulevard, large apartment buildings dominate, the most desirable units located in prewar complexes named for George Washington, Grover Cleveland and other presidents. Between 108th Street and the Grand Central Parkway, the theme changes to single-family homes in an area some refer to as Cord Meyer, after the developer who built most of them and is also building the new Windsor tower. ∎

BELOW: *A house in Forest Hill Gardens, Queens.*

Prosperity of the "North Side"

December 17, 1899

FROM A REAL ESTATE POINT OF VIEW THE past year has been a remarkable one in the borough of the Bronx. Values have taken fabulous jumps. Single lots have been sold for $20,000, a figure that a couple of years ago would have been considered a ridiculous valuation even by the most audacious boomer. During the early part of the year there was a great hue and cry raised against high taxes, but this had little or no effect upon the transactions and throughout the length and breadth of the borough real estate men report excellent business for the year, while fortunes have been made by builders, speculators and investors.

Mr. Charles M. Kaeppel, one of Bronx Borough's prominent real estate dealers, in reviewing the business of the year, said to The New York Times yesterday:

"It is not so many years ago that this section of the city was dubbed 'The Annexed District.' The name alone was enough to keep

> Single lots have sold for $20,000.

investors away and give them an idea that the section north of the Harlem River was an insignificant chunk of wilderness tacked on to the City of New York in order to please the population of farmers and backswoodsmen who inhabited it. If we attempted to assert our rights as citizens of the metropolis we were good-naturedly laughed at, and if you gave your address, the question would be, 'How far are you from Jerome Avenue?' And later on, 'Are you anywhere near Third Avenue?'

Today the borough is popularly alluded to as the north side, a name given to it before the Greater New York consolidation act became a law, and it is beginning to assume its proper place in the city." ■

Borough is More Than South Bronx

By **FRANCIS X. CLINES** | July 6, 1978

AS GOOD AS THE LAST WORLD SERIES SHOULD have been for the Bronx, it is remembered by the borough president for the night Howard Cosell kept showing a burning building on television.

In a Roone Arledge age, in which news and diversion are blurring together, the burning building viewed by America from a blimp offered sociological graphics that didn't eat up a lot of costly air time. The orange flame over a ways from the stadium's bright dish of light was a neat segue for the attention span that nicely set up more

popular events in which Reggie finally hit those home runs and established that winning is an egocentric fact, not a boroughwide one.

"Howard Cosell," Robert Abrams, the Bronx borough president, fairly sighs. "I can't tell you what that picture did. It reinforced the image people have of the Bronx. It is devastating in the boardrooms of banks. And the TV kept showing it."

We should hasten to point out, however, that it might have been just that kind of thing that got President Carter to visit the South Bronx, for whatever that gesture may turn out to mean, and to stand there moodily as if he were Lincoln at Gettysburg.

America is like that: One quick picture is worth a thousand documentaries. And Mr. Abrams wearily acknowledges that there is nothing like the South Bronx for a quick

As Maps and Memories Fade, So Do Some Boundary Lines

By **MANNY FERNANDEZ** | September 16, 2006

LLOYD ULTAN WENT LOOKING FOR A BRONX neighborhood the other day called Williamsbridge.

He was overqualified for this seemingly simple task. Mr. Ultan, the borough historian, teaches a course at Lehman College on the history of the Bronx and has written or co-written eight books about the borough. He even wrote the 182-word entry on Williamsbridge in the Encyclopedia of New York City.

Williamsbridge is a section of the Bronx near Woodlawn Cemetery that has a clearly defined border separating it from Wakefield, another neighborhood to the north, according to city maps and Mr. Ultan's entry in the encyclopedia: East 233rd Street. But as Mr. Ultan stood on White Plains Road at East 228th Street in theoretical Williamsbridge, merchants and residents, asked to identify the neighborhood, called it White Plains Road or Wakefield instead.

picture, for your standard empty building, as death's head, for a few lines of urban thanatopsis.

The worst effect of the South Bronx image, Mr. Abrams says, is on the people still living in the rest of the borough. "They run into old friends and keep hearing, 'Oh my God—the Bronx? You're still in the Bronx?' Perception and imagery are very important in life and have a great influence on whether a person keeps a commitment to a neighborhood."

Yet the borough is bigger than the South Bronx or Co-op City or any of its parts, and the record should note that you can wander quietly through middle-class mile upon mile, so commonplace these real parts of the Bronx that they would look boring through a zoom lens from a blimp. ▪

"I never hear it called anything but White Plains Road," said Juliet Adler, 43, who works in a hair salon and has lived nearby on East 224th Street for six years.

In the Bronx, as Mr. Ultan has long suspected, it's easy to find an address, but hard to find a neighborhood.

People in parts of Williamsbridge say they live in Wakefield. Some people in Edenwald say they live in Wakefield, too, and some people in Eastchester say they live in Baychester. There are those in Longwood who say it's Hunts Point, and those in Allerton who say it's Pelham Parkway.

"Borders have bled all over the Bronx," said Mr. Ultan, 68, who, when asked where he lives, gives people a helpful yet vague sense of place rather than the name of a specific neighborhood ("south of Van Cortlandt Park," he says).

Perhaps the biggest area with debatable borders is the South Bronx. The Encyclopedia of New York City calls it "an imprecise term used after 1950 to designate an area of shifting boundaries in the southwestern Bronx."

As arson and abandonment laid waste to entire neighborhoods in the 1970's and 1980's, the northern border of the South Bronx kept expanding, first to the Cross Bronx Expressway, then as far north as Fordham Road.

Today, no one is quite sure just where the South Bronx begins. You could be at the counter of an Italian deli on Arthur Avenue ordering a veal parmigiana hero—four miles from the heart of Mott Haven—and by some definitions be standing in the South Bronx.

The label has stuck nevertheless, though now it has come to signify a syndrome of social ills, an era even, but not exactly a place. Dan Donovan, topographic engineer and urban planner in the borough president's office, is often asked by residents and researchers to pin down the northern edge of the South Bronx. "Personally, I refrain from that completely," he said. ▪

Carter Takes "Sobering" Trip To the South Bronx

By **LEE DEMBART** | October 6, 1977

IN AN EFFORT TO DEMONSTRATE A COMMITMENT to cities, President Carter, in New York on United Nations affairs, made a sudden and dramatic trip to the South Bronx, where he viewed some of the country's worst urban blight.

> "Gee whiz," said someone on the stoop, "this is really something, talking to the president of the United States on our own doorstep."

The presidential motorcade passed block after block of burned-out and abandoned buildings, rubble-strewn lots and open fire hydrants, and people shouting "Give us money!" and "We want jobs!"

Twice Mr. Carter got out of his limousine, walked around and talked to people. He said the federal government should do something to help, but he made no specific commitment.

"It was a very sobering trip for me to see the devastation that has taken place in the South Bronx in the last five years," he said after the tour, when he returned to the United Nations Plaza Hotel. "But I'm encouraged in some ways by the strong effort of tenant groups to rebuild. I'm impressed by the spirit of hope and determination by the people to save what they have. I think they still have to know we care."

The two stops that the president made were designed to show him one of the few hopeful projects and the much more common hopeless areas of the Bronx.

The first stop was at 1186 Washington Avenue, between 167th and 168th Streets, where Mr. Carter visited a housing renovation project. There 40 people have converted a six-story tenement into a building boasting freshly painted hallways, 28 oak-floored apartments and solar heat collectors on the roof.

"Gee whiz," said someone on the stoop, "this is really something, talking to the president of the United States on our own doorstep."

"I feel ecstatic," Ramon Rueda, the executive director of the People's Development Corporation, which undertook the renovation, said later. "He seemed completely sincere, and if he was putting on a show he was certainly making a good impression. I hope he will come back when we finish the next phase of our project."

The next phase includes a rehabilitation of five buildings in the area backed by a $3 million federally-financed loan and funds from the Comprehensive Employment and Training Act to train the workers. ▪

Rising Property Values and Suburban Living

By **BARBARA STEWART** | November 2, 1997

SUNDAY AFTERNOON. A MIDDLE-AGED COUPLE slowly cruise up and down rows of nearly identical ranch houses on streets lined with trees. The wife looks intently at the homes on the right; the husband, at the wheel, scans the left.

Friends had told him about a house for sale on Louis Nine Boulevard. Just what they wanted: three bedrooms on a quarter-acre lot

Bronx

A Neighborhood in Waiting

By **JAKE MOONEY** | August 12, 2007

ELVIA NUÑEZ FIRST ARRIVED IN THE BRONX at age 11, when her family moved to the Fordham neighborhood from Mexico. They settled on Lorillard Place, just below Fordham Road. There, they found an ethnically diverse neighborhood with a growing Latin American population.

Ms. Nuñez, now 30 and a math teacher in a local middle school, says she sees signs that the familiar Fordham neighborhood she grew up in is showing new energy. There is construction all around, she said, including a row of new houses by Jerome Avenue where there used to be a parking lot.

Ms. Nuñez and her husband, Juan, who moved to New York from the Dominican Republic when he was a teenager, hoped to take advantage of that new liveliness when they began looking for more space. They focused on Fordham, mainly because her in-laws are nearby and can help with baby-sitting for their three young children.

She had also come to appreciate the area's casual friendliness. "You see people sitting outside their houses, and they say hi to you," Ms. Nuñez said. "You see the kids playing street basketball, sitting outside in the neighborhood."

Fordham has long been a place for working-class people who want to live within a short train ride of Manhattan, and near the busy Fordham Road commercial strip. The area avoided the urban blight that struck the southern parts of the Bronx in the 1970's and 80's, but there were doldrums, local officials said. Now, with Upper Manhattan an established spot for real estate investment, they hope more people will make the jump across the Harlem River.

Of course, the absence of gentrification has its advantages, said Obi Ugbomah, a musician and real estate agent who moved from Brooklyn to buy a three-story house near Lorillard Place and Third Avenue in 2005. "When I first came here, I discovered that I could have a bottle of beer and a plate of food for under $10," he said. "I was like, 'What?' Now you know Park Slope is not like that." ▪

BELOW: *Arthur Avenue, probably the most famous dining street in the Bronx, is located in the Fordham neighborhood.*

in the right neighborhood. But when he got there, the owner said it had already been sold, for $185,000.

The winning bidders were Diana and Steven Gonzalez, who paid $185,000 to have everything they have been deprived of in their South Bronx apartments: their own roomy home on a safe, quiet street. Living in Charlotte Gardens, they said, they can raise their three daughters comfortably and be close to relatives.

"It's a whole new community," Diana Gonzalez said. "I won't be worried about my girls. They'll be protected there, definitely. They're not going to be South Bronx kids— they're going to be Charlotte Gardens kids." ▪

Staten Island's Worst Problem? New Jersey

By **ALAN RICHMAN** | March 9, 1979

CORNELIUS VANDERBILT WAS BORN ON Staten Island. His first home appears to have been a Stapleton farmhouse later torn down to make way for the Paramount Theater. Now boarded up, the theater is showing only graffiti from the street artists of the projects nearby.

Matthew Brady, the photographer, lived on Staten Island. While there, he is not known to have taken any pictures.

Col. Ichabod Crane, immortalized by Washington Irving, is buried in Asbury Memorial Cemetery. His grave has been desecrated.

Many Staten Islanders care little for what has gone before them, unless it's the 8:30 ferry that pulled out as they were sprinting to the terminal gate. Their own ancestors are forgotten, even if they care a great deal about the ancestry of the family that moves in next door.

Each borough of New York, except Manhattan, occasionally proclaims itself the forgotten one, and none has been more deserving of the title than Staten Island.

Lacking accessibility, industry and voters, Staten Island was always the one borough every politician could live without. If it is not yet the boom borough, the predicted onslaught of post-Verrazano-Narrows Bridge humanity having been slowed by inadequate transportation and city services, it is still a potential promised land. Staten Island has the look of paradise to New Yorkers dreaming of a single-family detached life.

Across the Arthur Kill is the natural wonder of New Jersey, stretching in panorama to the west and, in some places, less than half a mile away. On a clear day, from New Brighton to Tottenville, you can see New Jersey. On a polluted day, you can smell it. Fumes from Garden State industries, which almost always waft over Staten Island, are blamed for the respiratory-cancer death rate, the highest in the city.

State Senator John J. Marchi, a Republican who represents Staten Island, predicts that the 1980 census will show it has a larger population than Buffalo. In fact, the borough president, Anthony R. Gaeta, stands proudly in his fading reception room and says there is only one real obstacle impeding the future.

"New Jersey," he says, his tone that of a Balkan prince censuring a neighboring state, "New Jersey is the worst problem we have." ▪

Where Isolation Is Both Curse and Charm

By **SARAH LYALL** | July 24, 1989

STATEN ISLANDERS HAVE BEEN TALKING about breaking away from the city and governing themselves for a long time. When the United States Supreme Court ruled this spring that the city's system of government was unconstitutional, a decision that would weaken the borough presidents' power, Staten Islanders began to fear that their voice in city affairs would be all but silenced. Talk of secession and self-determination began in earnest.

The State Legislature passed a bill that would allow residents of Staten Island to vote on whether to secede. While many of the island's residents say they want to look more closely at the question before they take such a dramatic step, the issue is causing them to examine what makes them Staten Islanders and what, if anything, makes them New Yorkers.

About an Island That's Worth Remembering

By **CLAIRE WILSON** | August 17, 2001

WHENEVER I TELL ANYONE I WAS BORN AND raised in the city's so-called forgotten borough, the reaction is always the same: disbelief, sometimes disdain. "Staten Island? You must be kidding." As if the only thing out there was the Fresh Kills Landfill and now that it has closed, the borough has nothing left to redeem it.

Which couldn't be more wrong. Staten Island, a terrific place to grow up, is a wonderful place to explore—and to some of us, it's so "out" it's "in." There are great little museums, three centuries of American architecture, extensive gardens, 7,500 acres of lush protected parkland, miles of uncrowded beaches, and wetlands that are ripe for canoeing and communing with herons and cormorants.

The borough's newest landmark, the Richmond County Bank Ballpark, is headquarters of the Staten Island Yankees minor league baseball team. The Baby Bombers draw huge crowds as much for the sport—and the rivalry with the Brooklyn Cyclones, the Mets' minor league team—as for the stadium's sweeping views of New York Harbor.

Another new landmark for St. George is the National Lighthouse Museum. Housed in what was most recently a Coast Guard base adjacent to the ferry terminal, it will explore the science and lore of lighthouses. In the late 19th century, when shipping was a vital local industry, it was the United States Lighthouse Depot, the country's main center for technological development and the manufacture of lighthouses.

"To tell you the truth, I don't like the city that much," said Anthony DiStefano, a 23-year-old part-time plumber, as he strolled down his road in Tottenville. "There's too much traffic and too many people," he said. "Here, you go to the beach, take a walk, play football in the streets, go swimming in your pool. I feel like Staten Island is its own little place."

Its own little isolated place. Janet Barker said she spends an hour and 45 minutes commuting to work at a bank in Manhattan's financial district. "It takes so long to get home, I feel like it's altogether a different state," she said. "Any farther, and you might as well be in Pennsylvania."

But while many Staten Islanders say they moved there seeking a quiet suburban life away from the city, they complain endlessly about the lack of services, like transportation and road repair, and about the Fresh Kills Landfill, the world's largest garbage dump. Staten Islanders grimly refer to it as Mount Trashmore, and as much as anything, it has united them against the rest of the city— and added to the feeling that they might do better on their own. ▪

The borough's best known art and performance site, the 83-acre Snug Harbor Cultural Center, is about 15 minutes away. It was opened 200 years ago as a haven "for aged, decrepit and worn-out sailors"—or Snugs, as the retired seamen were called. Its 28 buildings include a music hall that is one year younger than Carnegie Hall.

On Lighthouse Hill, the Crimson Beech, a 1950's prefab house designed by Frank Lloyd Wright, is regarded as a piece of important mid-20th century culture.

The same can be said for Mandolin Brothers, a bustling little shop-cum-museum close to the zoo. The shop has been responsible for bringing some unlikely tourists to Staten Island: Joni Mitchell, for one, who immortalized the shop in a song, and George Harrison, who popped in one day unannounced and went on a 40-minute shopping spree. The owner, Stan Jay, doesn't mind visitors' picking up the priceless Fender Stratocasters and giving themselves an Eric Clapton moment. ▪

Index

Page numbers in *italics* indicate illustrations.

Photo Credits

All photographs are © The New York Times except for pg 68 & 402, courtesy of Merlis Archive/ Brooklynpix.com; pg 133, Irving Underhill © Library of Congerss; pg 210 © Library of Congress; pg 352 © New York Public Library.

Special thanks to the following photographers:

Michelle V. Agins, 115, 300
Monica Almeida, 160
Michael Appleton, 203
Allyn Baum, 24
Keith Bedford, 196, 357
Nicole Bengiveno, 81, 100, 234, 350, 415, 428
Neal Boenzi, 176, 245
G. Paul Burnett, 28, 73, 120
Kitra Cahana, 212
Robert Caplin, 411
Tony Cenicola, 324, 330, 332
Don Hogan Charles, 15 top, 122, 246, 278, 287
Alan Chin, 186
Hillary Clark, 435
Cary Conover, 221, 325 top and bottom
Fred R. Conrad, 44, 57, 64, 90, 249, 273, 279, 366
Rebecca Cooney, 344, 423
Bill Cunningham, 183
Suzanne DeChillo, 6, 39, 125, 127, 151
Joyce Dopkeen, 114 top
Jim Estrin, 65, 276, 291
Michael Falco, 417
Tina Fineberg, 377, 401, 413
Aaron Lee Fineman, 430
Joe Fornabaio, 327
Angel Franco, 97, 346, 370, 404
Ruth Fremson, 109, 118, 132,
Shiho Fukada, 184
Kate Glicksberg, 434

Kelly Guenther, 308
George M. Gutierrez, 27
Josh Haner, 403
Todd Heisler, 79, 128
Maxine Hicks, 30
Tyler Hicks, 7, 142, 431
Oscar Hidalgo, 351
Chester Higgins Jr., 15 bottom, 32, 40, 51, 108, 229, 231 bottom, 264
Paul Hosefros, 207
Erik Jacobs, 170
Edward Keating, 18
Casey Kelbaugh, 53 bottom right
Lars Klove, 154
Sara Krulwich, 14, 42, 43, 50, 93, 94, 155, 161, 162, 165, 255, 282
Kate Lacey, 209
Vincent Laforet, 9, 103 top, 111, 387, 464
Chang W. Lee 116, 322, 379
Chris Lee, 175
Richard Lee, 129
Meyer Liebowitz, 172
Julie Lemberger, 139
Norman Y. Lono, 187, 361
Jack Manning, 24, 114 bottom, 336
John Marshall Mantel, 71
Hiroko Masuike, 199, 340
Chris Maynard, 75, 275, 310
Keith Meyers, 102, 258, 261
RJ Mickelson, 23

Doug Mills, 363 top
Andrea Mohin, 38, 147, 225, 316
Ozier Muhammad, 107, 171, 292, 305, 345, 383
Peter Muhly, 250
Michael Nagle, 231 top right
Krista Niles, 313
Katie Orlinsky, 328
Steve Payne, 31
Richard Perry, 2, 188 bottom, 247
Frances Roberts, 134, 226, 419
Librado Romero, 6
Jeffery A. Salter, 153
Ko Sasaki, 341
Fred J. Sass, 366
Rahav Segev, 178
Kelly Shimoda, 223
Nancy Siesel, 166, 393
Jacob Silberberg, 87, 265
Barton Silverman, 138, 174, 182, 385, 395
Ernie Sisto, 320, 362
John Sotomayor, 66
Ruby Washington, 48, 85, 267
Earl Wilson, 424
Jim Wilson, 266
Damon Winter, 29, 34, 74
Marilyn K. Yee, 103 bottom, 104, 140, 141, 211, 228, 296, 348, 363 bottom, 400, 429, 433
Alan Zale, 101